NATIONAL *Sciences*
ACADEMIES *Engineeri*
Medicine

A New Vision for High-Quality Preschool Curriculum

Sue Bredekamp, Linda Espinosa, Rebekah Hutton, and Amy Stephens,
Editors

Committee on a New Vision for High Quality Pre-K Curriculum

Board on Children, Youth, and Families

Division of Behavioral and Social Sciences and Education

Consensus Study Report

NATIONAL ACADEMIES PRESS 500 Fifth Street, NW Washington, DC 20001

This activity was supported by a contract between the National Academy of Sciences and the Bill & Melinda Gates Foundation (INV-034971) and the National Academy of Sciences W. K. Kellogg Foundation Fund. Support for the work of the Board on Children, Youth, and Families is provided by the Robert Wood Johnson Foundation (79846). Any opinions, findings, conclusions, or recommendations expressed in this publication do not necessarily reflect the views of any organization or agency that provided support for the project.

International Standard Book Number-13: 978-0-309-71401-3
International Standard Book Number-10: 0-309-71401-X
Digital Object Identifier: https://doi.org/10.17226/27429
Library of Congress Control Number: 2024943316

This publication is available from the National Academies Press, 500 Fifth Street, NW, Keck 360, Washington, DC 20001; (800) 624-6242; http://www.nap.edu.

Copyright 2024 by the National Academy of Sciences. National Academies of Sciences, Engineering, and Medicine and National Academies Press and the graphical logos for each are all trademarks of the National Academy of Sciences. All rights reserved.

Printed in the United States of America.

Suggested citation: National Academies of Sciences, Engineering, and Medicine. 2024. *A New Vision for High-Quality Preschool Curriculum*. Washington, DC: National Academies Press. https://doi.org/10.17226/27429.

The **National Academy of Sciences** was established in 1863 by an Act of Congress, signed by President Lincoln, as a private, nongovernmental institution to advise the nation on issues related to science and technology. Members are elected by their peers for outstanding contributions to research. Marcia McNutt is president.

The **National Academy of Engineering** was established in 1964 under the charter of the National Academy of Sciences to bring the practices of engineering to advising the nation. Members are elected by their peers for extraordinary contributions to engineering. John L. Anderson is president.

The **National Academy of Medicine** (formerly the Institute of Medicine) was established in 1970 under the charter of the National Academy of Sciences to advise the nation on medical and health issues. Members are elected by their peers for distinguished contributions to medicine and health. Victor J. Dzau is president.

The three Academies work together as the **National Academies of Sciences, Engineering, and Medicine** to provide independent, objective analysis and advice to the nation and conduct other activities to solve complex problems and inform public policy decisions. The National Academies also encourage education and research, recognize outstanding contributions to knowledge, and increase public understanding in matters of science, engineering, and medicine.

Learn more about the National Academies of Sciences, Engineering, and Medicine at **www.nationalacademies.org**.

Consensus Study Reports published by the National Academies of Sciences, Engineering, and Medicine document the evidence-based consensus on the study's statement of task by an authoring committee of experts. Reports typically include findings, conclusions, and recommendations based on information gathered by the committee and the committee's deliberations. Each report has been subjected to a rigorous and independent peer-review process and it represents the position of the National Academies on the statement of task.

Proceedings published by the National Academies of Sciences, Engineering, and Medicine chronicle the presentations and discussions at a workshop, symposium, or other event convened by the National Academies. The statements and opinions contained in proceedings are those of the participants and are not endorsed by other participants, the planning committee, or the National Academies.

Rapid Expert Consultations published by the National Academies of Sciences, Engineering, and Medicine are authored by subject-matter experts on narrowly focused topics that can be supported by a body of evidence. The discussions contained in rapid expert consultations are considered those of the authors and do not contain policy recommendations. Rapid expert consultations are reviewed by the institution before release.

For information about other products and activities of the National Academies, please visit www.nationalacademies.org/about/whatwedo.

COMMITTEE ON A NEW VISION FOR HIGH QUALITY PRE-K CURRICULUM

SUE BREDEKAMP (*Co-Chair*), Early Childhood Education Specialist and former Director of Professional Development, National Association for the Education of Young Children
LINDA ESPINOSA (*Co-Chair*), Professor, College of Education, University of Missouri
DEANA AROUND HIM, Research Scholar, Child Trends, Johns Hopkins School of Nursing
GARNETT BOOKER III, Early Childhood Practitioner, District of Columbia Public Schools
DOUGLAS CLEMENTS, Distinguished University Professor, Kennedy Endowed Chair in Early Childhood Learning, Morgridge College of Education, Marsico Institute for Early Learning, University of Denver
LILLIAN DURÁN, Professor, College of Education, University of Oregon
IHEOMA U. IRUKA, Research Professor, Department of Public Policy, The University of North Carolina at Chapel Hill
SUSAN LEVINE, Rebecca Anne Boylan Distinguished Service Professor of Education and Society, Department of Psychology, The University of Chicago
JOAN LUBY, Samuel and Mae S. Ludwig Professor of Child Psychiatry, Washington University
CAMILLE MABEN, Former Executive Director, First 5 California (Retired)
DEBORAH PHILLIPS, Professor Emerita of Psychology and Affiliated Faculty, McCourt School of Public Policy, Georgetown University
CHRISTINA WEILAND, Associate Professor, Marsal Family School of Education, University of Michigan
VIVIAN WONG, Associate Professor, Curry School of Education, University of Virginia

Study Staff

REBEKAH HUTTON, Study Director
NATACHA BLAIN, Senior Board Director
EMILY P. BACKES, Deputy Board Director
AMY STEPHENS, Associate Board Director, Board on Science Education
TARA NAZARI, Senior Program Assistant (*as of January 2024*)
LIBBY TILTON, Research Associate
MEREDITH YOUNG, Program Officer

NOTE: See Appendix C, Disclosure of Unavoidable Conflict of Interest.

BOARD ON CHILDREN, YOUTH, AND FAMILIES

JONATHAN TODRES (*Chair*), Georgia State University College of Law
RICHARD F. CATALANO, JR., University of Washington School of Social Work
TAMMY CHANG, University of Michigan
DIMITRI A. CHRISTAKIS, Seattle Children's Research Institute, University of Washington
ANDREA GONZALEZ, McMaster University
NANCY E. HILL, Harvard University
CHARLES HOMER, Economic Mobility Pathways
MARGARET KUKLINSKI, University of Washington
MICHAEL C. LU, School of Public Health, University of California, Berkeley
STEPHANIE J. MONROE, Wrenwood Group
STEPHEN RUSSELL, The University of Texas at Austin
NISHA SACHDEV, Premnas Partners, Washington, DC
JANE WALDFOGEL, Columbia University School of Social Work
JOANNA L. WILLIAMS, Rutgers University

Staff

NATACHA BLAIN, Senior Board Director
EMILY P. BACKES, Deputy Board Director

Reviewers

This Consensus Study Report was reviewed in draft form by individuals chosen for their diverse perspectives and technical expertise. The purpose of this independent review is to provide candid and critical comments that will assist the National Academies of Sciences, Engineering, and Medicine in making each published report as sound as possible and to ensure that it meets the institutional standards for quality, objectivity, evidence, and responsiveness to the study charge. The review comments and draft manuscript remain confidential to protect the integrity of the deliberative process.

We thank the following individuals for their review of this report:

AJAY CHAUDRY, New York University
ADAM HOLLAND, University of North Carolina, Chapel Hill
LAURA JUSTICE, Ohio State University
DORE LAFORETT, Child Trends
LISA LOPEZ, University of Southern Florida
MICHÈLE M.M. MAZZOCCO, University of Minnesota
SHANTEL E. MEEK, Arizona State University
JESSICA WHITTAKER, University of Virginia
BRIAN L. WRIGHT, University of Memphis

Although the reviewers listed above provided many constructive comments and suggestions, they were not asked to endorse the conclusions or recommendations of this report nor did they see the final draft before its release. The review of this report was overseen by **ROBERT C. PIANTA**, School of Education and Human Development, University of Virginia, and

JEANNE BROOKS-GUNN, Columbia University, Teachers College. They were responsible for making certain that an independent examination of this report was carried out in accordance with the standards of the National Academies and that all review comments were carefully considered. Responsibility for the final content rests entirely with the authoring committee and the National Academies.

Acknowledgments

This report would not have been possible without the contributions of many people. First, we thank the sponsors of this study—the Bill & Melinda Gates Foundation and the National Academy of Sciences W. K. Kellogg Foundation Fund.

The committee and project staff would also like to express gratitude to the numerous experts and consultants who contributed to the development of the report. We extend our deep gratitude to the authors of the committee's literature review from School Readiness Consulting and Center on the Ecology of Early Development at Boston University: Angélica Montoya Ávila, Laura Hawkinson, Stephanie Curenton, Emily K. Miller, Mariam Dahbi, Sherrell House, Faith Tabifor, and Maya Manning. We thank Allison Friedman-Krauss for her work on a commissioned paper for the committee on state- and program-level selection. We thank Nathan James, Kimberly Hefling, and Catherine Ahmad for their insights and assistance with communications and dissemination of the report. Thanks are also due to the numerous experts who volunteered significant time and effort to address the committee during our public information-gathering and listening sessions: Doris Baker, Janet Bock-Hager, Catherine Goins, "Kate" Kezia Goodwin, Jennifer Grisham, Choquette Hamilton, Christopher Jones, Jennifer Keys Adair, Patricia Lozano, Lisa Lopez, Lisa Luceno, Scott Moore, Kim Nall, Sarah Neville-Morgan, Susan Sandall, Megan Vinh, Amanda Willford, and Osnat Zur. We thank Heather Kreidler for fact checking the report. Finally, we thank Rona Briere, Allison Boman, and John Hawkins for editing the report.

We would also like to thank the many staff members of the National Academies of Sciences, Engineering, and Medicine who provided invaluable support throughout this process: Natacha Blain for her oversight as director of the Board on Children, Youth, and Families; Faye Hillman and Javed Khan for their financial management assistance; Doug Sprunger and Jennifer Olsen for their assistance with communications and dissemination of the report; Emily Backes, Alexandra Beatty, and Patricia Morison for their insights on early drafts of the report; Bea Porter and Kirsten Sampson Snyder for their guidance throughout the report review process; and Clair Woolley for her assistance with the final production of the report. We would like to extend gratitude to the members of the project staff who worked directly with the committee over the course of the project—Rebekah Hutton, Amy Stephens, Tara Nazari, Libby Tilton, and Meredith Young—for their significant contributions to supporting the committee's work.

Finally, the committee wishes to thank its co-chairs, Sue Bredekamp and Linda Espinosa, for their dedication to this work and the exceptional leadership and guidance that they have provided throughout this process.

Contents

Preface	xvii
Acronyms and Abbreviations	xxi
Summary	1

1   Introduction   15
    ABOUT THIS STUDY, 20
    STUDY APPROACH, 20
    KEY TERMS USED IN THIS REPORT, 27
    HISTORICAL BACKGROUND AND CONTEXT, 27
    EARLY CHILDHOOD CURRICULA:
        CURRENT STATE OF THE FIELD, 33
    REPORT ORGANIZATION, 40
    REFERENCES, 41

2   Evidence on the Effectiveness of Preschool Curricula   49
    CURRICULUM TYPE, 51
    OUTCOMES USED FOR ASSESSING EFFECTIVENESS, 53
    STUDENT CHARACTERISTICS, 54
    TEACHER CHARACTERISTICS, 56
    PRESCHOOL SETTING, 57
    MACRO CONDITIONS, 58
    CONCLUSION, 59
    REFERENCES, 60

3 The Science of Early Learning and Brain Development 65
   NEUROBIOLOGICAL AND SOCIAL-EMOTIONAL
      DEVELOPMENT, 66
   HOW CHILDREN LEARN: THE SCIENCE OF
      EARLY LEARNING, 70
   IMPLICATIONS FOR PRESCHOOL CURRICULUM:
      CULTURAL VARIATIONS IN LEARNING OPPORTUNITIES
      AND LEARNING, 94
   CONCLUSION, 95
   REFERENCES, 97

4 Developing High-Quality, Equitable Preschool Curricula 113
   MOVING BEYOND FALSE DICHOTOMIES, 114
   CHARACTERISTICS OF HIGH-QUALITY, EQUITABLE
      PRESCHOOL CURRICULUM, 117
   WHO DEVELOPS VARIOUS CURRICULUM TYPES AND
      APPROACHES, 129
   CURRICULUM FOR SOCIAL-EMOTIONAL LEARNING, 132
   CURRICULUM IN THE CONTENT DOMAINS, 141
   CURRICULUM TYPES AND APPROACHES, 159
   EDUCATIVE CURRICULA: TEACHING BOTH CHILDREN
      AND THEIR TEACHERS, 173
   DEVELOPING RESEARCH-BASED AND EMPIRICALLY
      VALIDATED CURRICULA: A FRAMEWORK, 174
   CURRICULA BEYOND PRESCHOOL, 178
   CONCLUSION, 180
   REFERENCES, 181

5 Optimizing the Learning Environment for Effective and
   Equitable Curriculum Delivery 215
   OVERALL QUALITY OF EARLY CHILDHOOD SETTINGS
      AND EFFECTIVENESS AND EQUITY
      OF CURRICULUM, 216
   THE EDUCATOR–CHILD RELATIONSHIP AS
      FOUNDATIONAL TO LEARNING, 218
   ADDRESSING PEER-RELATED ADVERSITY WITHIN
      THE CLASSROOM, 221
   EDUCATORS' APPROACHES TO CLASSROOM
      MANAGEMENT, 223
   THE ESSENTIAL ROLE OF TEACHER WELL-BEING, 225
   PROFESSIONAL DEVELOPMENT OF THE EARLY
      EDUCATION WORKFORCE, 227

FOSTERING INCLUSIVE AND EQUITABLE EARLY
    CHILDHOOD LEARNING ENVIRONMENTS, 231
CONCLUSION, 238
REFERENCES, 240

6   Specialized and Targeted Curricula and Practices for
    Supporting Children with Disabilities   253
    THE NEEDS OF CHILDREN WITH DISABILITIES, 254
    SOCIAL AND EMOTIONAL DEVELOPMENT, 261
    CURRICULA DESIGNED FOR CHILDREN WITH
        DISABILITIES, 264
    MULTILINGUAL LEARNERS WITH DISABILITIES, 271
    CONCLUSION, 275
    REFERENCES, 276

7   High-Quality Early Childhood Curriculum for
    Multilingual Learners   287
    SHIFTING FROM DEFICIT-BASED TO ASSET-BASED
        APPROACHES, 289
    CURRENT RESEARCH ON EARLY BILINGUAL
        DEVELOPMENT, 293
    RESEARCH-BASED PRINCIPLES FOR EARLY
        CHILDHOOD EDUCATION CURRICULUM FOR
        MULTILINGUAL LEARNERS, 301
    RESEARCH-SUPPORTED CURRICULUM, STRATEGIES,
        AND PRACTICES FOR MULTILINGUAL
        LEARNERS, 304
    ASSESSMENT PRACTICES FOR MULTILINGUAL
        LEARNERS, 313
    TEACHER COMPETENCIES FOR MULTILINGUAL
        LEARNERS, 315
    CONCLUSION, 317
    REFERENCES, 318

8   State- and Program-Level Curriculum Decision Making
    and Selection   327
    HOW ARE CURRICULUM DECISIONS MADE?, 328
    CRITERIA FOR SELECTION AND ADOPTION, 337
    EARLY LEARNING STANDARDS, 338
    WHAT CURRICULA DO STATES APPROVE AND SUPPORT?, 341
    IMPACT OF THE COVID-19 PANDEMIC ON SUPPORTS
        FOR CURRICULUM IMPLEMENTATION, 345

FIDELITY OF CURRICULUM IMPLEMENTATION, 345
WHO ATTENDS PRESCHOOL PROGRAMS WITH
     CURRICULUM SUPPORTS?, 347
IMPLICATIONS FOR ASSESSMENT, 348
CONCLUSION, 353
REFERENCES, 354

9 Examining Variation in Curriculum Effects   361
   IDENTIFYING SOURCES OF EFFECT VARIATION, 362
   WITHIN- AND BETWEEN-STUDY APPROACHES FOR
        EXAMINING SOURCES OF EFFECT VARIATION, 368
   REPRESENTING SOURCES OF EFFECT HETEROGENEITY
        FOR GENERALIZED FINDINGS, 372
   CONCLUSION, 373
   REFERENCES, 374

10 Conclusions, Recommendations, and Research Needs   377
   KEY CONCLUSIONS AND RECOMMENDATIONS, 378
   RESEARCH AGENDA, 395
   CLOSING THOUGHTS, 403
   REFERENCE, 404

Appendix A   Existing Curricula Identified by the
             Committee's Commissioned Literature Review   405
Appendix B   Committee Member and Staff Biosketches   415
Appendix C   Disclosure of Unavoidable Conflict of Interest   423

Boxes, Figures, and Tables

BOXES

S-1 Vision for High-Quality Preschool Curricula, 4

1-1 Statement of Task, 21
1-2 Definitions of Key Terms, 28

4-1 Indigenous Curricula and Pedagogy, 162
4-2 Children Discovering Their World, 164

5-1 Key Features of Effective Professional Learning for Instructional Practices, 230
5-2 African-Centered Curricula and Pedagogy, 233

7-1 Dual Language/Multilingual Curricula and Pedagogy, 292
7-2 Summary of Research Findings for Multilingual Learners from Birth to Age 5, 295
7-3 African American English (AAE): An Example of Variation in the English Language, 302
7-4 Heritage Language Revitalization Programs, 309

8-1 State-Developed Curricula: *STREAMin³*, 341
8-2 Multitiered Systems of Support, 350

10-1 Vision for High-Quality Preschool Curricula, 379
10-2 Themes for Additional Research, 396

xv

FIGURES

1-1   A conceptual framework for understanding factors that influence and define high-quality preschool curriculum, 24
3-1   Playful experiences differ along a continuum in terms of initiation and direction of the experience and whether there is a learning goal, 73
3-2   Learning by observing and pitching in, 79
3-3   Assembly-line instruction, 80
5-1   Factors that contribute to the quality of professional practice and ultimately to improving child outcomes, 229
8-1   Percent of state-funded preschool programs meeting the Curriculum Supports benchmark each year, 330
8-2   Multitiered system of supports inclusive of all students, 350
10-1 A continuous improvement model for advancing implementation of the committee's recommendations, 380

TABLES

4-1   Characteristics of High-Quality, Equity-Driven Preschool Curriculum, 127
4-2   Preschool Curriculum Types and the Teacher's Role in Implementation, 131
4-3   Goals of Curriculum Research, 177
4-4   Categories and Phases of the Curriculum Research Framework, 179
8-1   Supports for Curriculum Selection and Implementation Used by State-Funded Preschool Programs in 2021–2022, 332
8-2   Percentage of State-Funded Preschool Programs Using Each Comprehensive Curriculum, 342
8-3   Subject-Specific Curricula Used in State-Funded Preschool, 344

Preface

More than 50 years of research demonstrates the lasting positive effects of high-quality early childhood programs for success in school and later life. This report is a clarion call to preschool educators, researchers, policy makers, and families to reconsider what we mean by "high-quality" for all children, and specifically what is meant by high-quality, effective, equity-driven preschool curriculum, particularly for Black, Latine, and Indigenous children; multilingual learners; children with disabilities; and those living in poverty. While we know high-quality preschool programs have many documented benefits for all young children, there is compelling evidence that access to high-quality, effective early learning experiences may be limited, inadequate, and in some cases inappropriate based on factors such as a child's race, location, gender, home language, identified disability, and socioeconomic background. As a result, there are far too many missed opportunities for every child to reach their full potential.

The charge to this committee was to help redress these inequities by developing a new vision for high-quality preschool curriculum. All the committee members have been personally committed to more equitable early childhood education through their educational experiences, practical and professional values, and research and policy work. Guided by their professional knowledge, personal experiences, and aspirations for a more just and equitable early education system, the committee set out to review the research, weigh the evidence, and integrate multiple perspectives to offer a vision of preschool curriculum that would enhance education and improve outcomes for all preschoolers.

The research presented in this report clearly shows that, historically, early childhood curricula have not been centered on equity. In practice, equity does not mean equal or the same treatment of every child. We believe equity means that all children have a fair opportunity to thrive; this requires valuing all individuals, languages, cultures, and populations equally, fully recognizing systemic racism and oppression, rectifying historical and contemporary structural biases and injustices, and providing resources and supports accordingly.

Although every 3- and 4-year-old child deserves joyful, engaging, safe, enriching, and affirming preschool experiences, many are denied the power and promise of preschool experiences that foster holistic and healthy development and learning for all children, regardless of place or socioeconomic background; affirm children's full identities, including race, culture, home language, gender, and ability; and recognize and build on their strengths while providing the supports they need to develop and learn optimally. Indeed, it is not possible to achieve equitable child outcomes by the end of preschool by teaching all children in the same way at the same time or offering them the same experiences. Rather, achieving equity may require adapting experiences depending on children's prior learning, abilities, strengths, and needs to enable them to achieve desired learning and developmental goals. Appropriate, engaging content and effective learning experiences may not be the same for every child. For example, to achieve the goal of early literacy, Black, Latine, and Indigenous children will need books that reflect their identity and their cultural and linguistic knowledge. Similarly, emergent bilingualism is an equitable goal for children who speak a language other than English or in addition to English in the home. Children with disabilities need individualized, tailored goals and may require specialized adaptations and supports, unique resources, specific teacher competencies, and increased levels of intensity.

Curriculum—what and how children learn in a program—is a critical determinant of the quality and effectiveness of a preschool program. While considerable evidence exists on the lasting positive effects of high-quality preschool programs in general, we now have a growing body of research focused on the key role and efficacy of specific curricula. However, curriculum implementation often varies considerably, depending on teacher qualifications, levels of support, and relationships with children; the quality of the learning environment; the individual strengths and backgrounds of the children; and their social, cultural, and linguistic contexts. Although this report is highly evidence based, the committee confronted the reality of the difficulty of finding research conducted on specific components of curriculum essential to achieving equity, such as cultural and linguistic relevance. For some crucial constructs, including child agency, racial identity and pride, and attitudes toward school and learning, the research methods and tools needed to reliably capture their contributions to children's learning have not yet been fully developed. Similarly, more study is urgently needed for highly valued goals, including anti-bias/anti-racist, inclusive curriculum and pedagogy. There is also limited research on curricula that meaningfully address the developmental needs of children with disabilities to support inclusion.

A well-planned, research-based, and preferably validated curriculum provides an essential scaffold that can guide early childhood educators on what to teach and when; how to engage children; and how to support adaptation for individual, cultural, and linguistic diversity. This scaffolding is particularly important if educators have had minimal teacher preparation; lack deep content knowledge; have little classroom support; or teach in classrooms in which the children have a wide range of abilities, cultures, and languages.

This report calls on early childhood educators, program leaders, and decision makers at every level to reject long-held deficit perspectives of young children, particularly Black, Latine, and Indigenous children, multilingual learners, children with disabilities, and children living in poverty. Only by embracing children's individual, cultural, and linguistic strengths and assets can we achieve a new vision of high-quality, equity-driven preschool curriculum for every 3- and 4-year-old child.

We want to express our sincere thanks to the committee members for their deep commitment and sustained and expert contributions to this report. The conduct of this study was a highly collaborative process that required each member to listen, reflect, and compromise at times to achieve consensus on the vision set forth in this report and its application. The challenge of fairly including multiple areas of expertise and perspectives into one coherent report was heightened by the post-COVID-19 logistics of conducting the committee's work virtually. Particularly at this moment in history, the urgency of the issues being addressed continually inspired the committee to move forward with the hope of a better future for children and families, especially those from marginalized communities who are frequently not embraced and supported.

Having been colleagues and friends for almost 40 years, it was our pleasure and privilege to co-chair this committee and guide its work on one of the most important challenges facing the nation and early childhood education programs today.

Sue Bredekamp, *Co-Chair*
Linda Espinosa, *Co-Chair*
Committee on a New Vision
for High Quality Pre-K Curriculum

Acronyms and Abbreviations

AAE	African American English
ABA	applied behavior analysis
ACSES	Assessing Classroom Sociocultural Equity Scale
AEPS	Assessment, Evaluation, and Programing System
AMS	American Montessori Society
ASI	Assembly Line Instruction
C4L	*Connect4Learning*
CBO	community-based organization
CCPSN	*Carolina Curriculum for Preschoolers with Special Needs*
CLASS	Classroom Assessment Scoring System
COI	Cycle of Inquiry
CRF	Curriculum Research Framework
DEC	Division for Early Childhood
DLL	dual language learner
DTT	discrete trial training
ECE	early childhood education
ECERS	Early Childhood Environmental Rating Scale
ECSE	early childhood special education
EHA	Education for All Handicapped Children Act
ELLS	Enhanced Language and Literacy Success
GAE	General American English

HELP	Hawaii Early Learning Profile
HSELOF	Head Start Early Learning Outcomes Framework
ICPS	*I Can Problem Solve*
IDEA	Individuals with Disabilities Education Act
IEP	Individual Education Program
IES	Institute of Education Sciences
IFSP	Individualized Family Service Plan
KEEP	Kamehameha Early Education Program
LOPI	Learning by Observing and Pitching In
MTSS	multitiered systems of support
MTSS-R	MTSS-Reading in Early Elementary School
NAECS	National Association of Early Childhood Specialists in State Departments of Education
NAEYC	National Association for the Education of Young Children
NIEER	National Institute for Early Education Research
NRC	National Research Council
OWL	*Opening the World of Learning*
PATHS	Promoting Alternative Thinking Strategies
PCER	Preschool Curriculum Evaluation Research
pre-K	prekindergarten
PRT	pivotal response treatment
REDI	*Head Start Research-Based Developmentally Informed*
RCT	randomized controlled trial
SEER	Standards for Excellence in Education Research
SEL	social-emotional learning
STAR	Strategies for Teaching based on Autism Research
STEM	science, technology, engineering, and mathematics
STSA	story telling and story action
VOLAR	*Vocabulary, Oral Language, and Academic Readiness*

Summary[1]

Access to high-quality preschool experiences can be valuable for young children. Indeed, a large body of research—including a landmark study by the National Academies of Sciences, Engineering, and Medicine, *From Neurons to Neighborhoods* (2000)—has yielded robust evidence on the crucial role the early years play in brain development and shows the potential of early educational experiences to influence children's long-term trajectories and life outcomes. However, it also reveals a concerning reality: historically, not all children have had equal access to high-quality preschool experiences as the result of several factors (e.g., lack of funding, lack of availability), and definitions and measures of "quality" have often excluded considerations of factors (e.g., supporting home language development; recognizing children's diverse lived experiences) that significantly affect the experiences of children from populations that have been historically marginalized. Despite the well-documented benefits of high-quality early educational experiences, access remains unevenly distributed, with children from historically marginalized communities facing greater barriers in access to preschool and uneven access to high-quality experiences within programs. In addition, they are more likely to be enrolled in programs that are underfunded, have less-qualified teachers, and do not support their home language and culture. As a result, these children are less likely to benefit from the same opportunities as their more privileged peers.

---

[1] This chapter does not include references. Citations to support the text and conclusions herein are provided in following chapters of the report.

The Committee on a New Vision for High Quality Pre-K Curriculum was formed to conduct a study of the quality of pre-K curriculum in the United States for children aged 3–5, with particular attention to the needs of specific subpopulations, including Black and Latine children, multilingual learners, children with disabilities, and children experiencing poverty. In order to develop recommendations regarding the development of equitable pre-K curriculum, state- and center-level curriculum selection, and local curriculum implementation, the committee was asked to: (1) explore the fundamental assumptions, principles, and definitions that should guide the content, development, and use of high-quality, equity-driven curriculum for pre-K children; (2) identify the components, criteria, and/or features of a high-quality pre-K curriculum that supports equity and learning and development for all children; (3) describe how the components, criteria, and/or features of high-quality, equitable curriculum should be used by state and local preschool program directors to make curricular decisions for diverse populations of learners, as well as the guidance needed to facilitate such selection; (4) describe the curricular supports and professional development opportunities needed by early childhood educators across diverse pre-K settings to enable the effective and equitable implementation of high-quality pre-K curricula; (5) describe funding mechanisms, state and federal policies, and new innovations that can support the selection and use of effective pre-K curricula; and (6) identify research needed to address current gaps in understanding of the components, criteria, and/or features of high-quality pre-K curricula (see Chapter 1 for the committee's full statement of task). The expertise represented by the committee's membership (early childhood education, child development, preschool program development, curriculum development, curriculum evaluation, implementation science, public policy, children with disabilities, multilingual learners, child health, mental health, and neuroscience) reflects the scope of the committee's statement of task.

Decades of research in early education in the United States have shown significant effects of curricula on teaching and learning. Accordingly, there is a need for high-quality curricula to be grounded in strong evidence. High-quality preschool programs are the context within which high-quality curricula are implemented, yet many children do not have equitable access to either. In this report, the committee defines equity as the goal and process of ensuring that everyone has a fair opportunity to thrive, which requires valuing all individuals and populations equally; fully recognizing systemic racism and oppression; rectifying historical and contemporary structural injustices, systemic biases, and oppression; and providing resources and supports accordingly.

SUMMARY

There is a clear need for equitable access for all children to preschool experiences that foster holistic and healthy development and learning regardless of place or socioeconomic status; affirm children's full identities, including race, culture, home language, gender, and ability; and recognize and build on their strengths while providing the supports they need to reach their full potential. Thus, in addition to providing high-quality preschool programs, it is important to address the systemic inequities that prevent children from marginalized communities from accessing these programs and for the curricula used in these programs to support all children's learning and development. To this end, there is a need for increased funding for preschool, expanded availability of high-quality programs, and curricula that allow all children to reach their full potential and that affirm children's full identities, in order to ensure that all children receive appropriate services and have the opportunity to benefit from the positive effects of high-quality preschool experiences.

As a part of conceptualizing a new approach to high-quality and equitable experiences for all children, it is crucial to reimagine the preschool curriculum. Many public programs are using curricula that do not meet the needs of all children. There is compelling evidence that access to high-quality early learning experiences may be limited and inadequate based on factors such as a child's race, location, gender, home language, disability status, and socioeconomic status. It is crucial to recognize that these characteristics themselves are not the cause of differences in experiences. Rather, differences in experiences stem from broader structural factors (e.g., resource inequity, discriminatory policies, biased interactions) that perpetuate disparate outcomes.

In working to define a vision for high-quality curriculum that can support equity, the committee recognizes that this is a highly creative, complex endeavor that takes into account multiple demands and requires multiple resources—factors representing the rich tapestry that undergirds curriculum effectiveness. These factors include the written content of the curriculum itself, including the learning environments in which the curriculum will be delivered; the supports for teachers and their own needs, such as professional learning experiences (including preservice education and ongoing professional development), the culture of the workplace environment, how teacher wellness is supported, and the resources to which they have access; and the systems and policies in place, including those who make decisions about the policies and the drivers that influence their decisions. Most important, however, and central to these varied factors and the vision, is the child: the vision must incorporate the learning experiences to which each child has access, children's varied opportunities to experience engaging content that can spark their curiosity and desire to learn, and the ways in which learning can be adapted to support the whole child and the child's individual needs. Considering all these many factors, the committee developed the vision for high-quality preschool curricula described in Box S-1.

Importantly, the committee recognizes that attention is also needed for issues of implementation and continuous quality improvement within a broader system. Curriculum in and of itself will not solve the deep, intractable challenges faced in early education from inadequate funding, inadequate wages, uneven workforce preparation and supports, and growing issues with staff recruitment and retention, to larger social and economic inequities. However, curricula can play a critical role in ensuring that, regardless of these systemic challenges, children, through their interactions with teachers, other adults, and peers in the learning environment, will experience safe, healthy, affirming, and enriching learning opportunities that promote lifelong success.

Box S-1
Vision for High-Quality Preschool Curricula

The committee's vision for high-quality preschool curricula aims to fulfill the promise of an education that fosters holistic and healthy development and learning for every child, regardless of place or socioeconomic status, and affirms children's full identities, including race, culture, home language, gender, and ability. It is grounded in an equity and justice-oriented perspective from inception to implementation and evaluation, and therefore is designed with an understanding of the diverse contexts of children's development, including adverse and traumatic conditions. Curricula aligned with the committee's vision would:

- incorporate the perspectives, experiences, cultures, languages, strengths, and needs of a diverse range of children, families, and workforce settings;
- include rich and meaningful content that centers child engagement and agency;
- include well-designed learning experiences, intentional responsive teaching strategies, well-defined objectives and outcomes, embedded formative assessments, and differentiation based on understanding children's ability levels, cultural and linguistic backgrounds, interests, and dispositions;
- have a scope and sequence that follow children's ways of thinking and learning with research-validated learning trajectories, are culturally and linguistically affirming, and include effective supports for children with disabilities; and
- demonstrate effectiveness in yielding positive school and life outcomes for the children and families they are intended to reach.

KEY CONCLUSIONS AND RECOMMENDATIONS

The committee's statement of task did not include evaluation or rating of existing curricula against the criteria outlined in the committee's vision. The committee's key conclusions and recommendations are directly aligned with specific questions outlined in the study's charge and fall across four categories: (1) guidance for the content design, development, selection, implementation, and formative and summative evaluation of high-quality, equity-driven curriculum; (2) supports and professional development needed for equitable and effective curriculum implementation; (3) funding mechanisms, state and federal policies, and innovations to support the selection and use of effective and equitable preschool curricula; and (4) creation of an evidence base to advance curriculum development and implementation. Chapter 10 of this report provides additional discussion of the findings that support the committee's conclusions and recommendations.

Equity-Driven Preschool Curricula: Guidance for Content Design, Development, Selection, and Implementation

Conclusion 1: To create psychologically safe spaces that promote positive learning outcomes and success in school and life, it is vital to support holistic, healthy development and enable children to realize their potential by leveraging their assets and building on their prior knowledge—which is a product of their cultural and linguistic experiences at home and in their communities.

Conclusion 2: Learning is shaped by the interaction between the biological processes involved in brain development and early life experiences, including those with adults, other children, and the broader environment. Such interactions are embedded within social, cultural, and linguistic contexts. Children learn in a multiplicity of ways, including child-initiated and teacher-guided play, exploration, observation, social engagement, intentional teaching in small and large groups, individual hands-on experiences, and other pedagogy that is responsive to their strengths and interests.

Conclusion 3: In the development and evaluation of preschool curricula, it is important to include efforts to identify and reject long-held biases, deficit framings, and/or stereotyped assumptions about children from racially, culturally, and linguistically minoritized communities, as well as children with disabilities and children experiencing poverty.

Conclusion 4: Evidence-based preschool curriculum that is well implemented has been shown to help promote equitable outcomes in mathematics, language, literacy, and social-emotional skills seen at kindergarten entry, particularly for children living in poverty and Black and Latine children. However, studies have generally not assessed curriculum effects on home language development for multilingual learners.

Conclusion 5: A preschool curriculum that provides guidance for content-specific teaching, rich and varied learning experiences, and supports for all aspects of children's development (including linguistic and cultural adaptations) will likely be most effective in improving child outcomes. Some localities have created such curricula with promising impacts, largely by systematically combining different evidence-based, domain-specific curricula or integrating domain-specific curricula into a comprehensive curriculum to support all domains of children's learning.

Conclusion 6: Early childhood leaders and practitioners typically use comprehensive preschool curricula that are intended to address all domains of children's learning and development and are required by their funding agencies. When compared with domain-specific curricula, the most widely used comprehensive curricula have shown significantly smaller gains in domain-targeted outcomes, such as mathematics, science, literacy, and social-emotional development at kindergarten entry. There has been little evidence of differential effectiveness for nontargeted domains. Much of this research has been conducted in Head Start and other public programs serving children from marginalized groups, including children from families with low-income, multilingual learners, and Black and Latine children.

Conclusion 7: Nearly one-third of young children growing up in the United States are growing up with exposure to more than one language in the home and could be considered multilingual. Research has shown that the most effective language model for multilingual learners teaches them English systematically while actively supporting their home language development. Full proficiency in more than one language is associated with cognitive, cultural, social, and economic benefits. However, most states, school districts, and local programs have yet to develop a procedure for accurately identifying preschool multilingual learners, rarely provide dual language instruction, and have few bilingual early childhood educators qualified to support home language development or provide dual language instruction. Additional research, materials, professional development, and multilingual educators can support the realization of the new vision.

Conclusion 8: Although family child care settings enroll a small proportion of children overall, they enroll a larger proportion of children from racially and linguistically marginalized populations, children from rural communities, and children from families experiencing poverty. Mixed-age programs are also common in family child care settings. However, few commercially available preschool curricula are designed for family child care settings, and few offer guidance in adapting curriculum or sequencing content for mixed-age groups.

Based on these conclusions, the committee makes the following recommendations:

Recommendation 1: In the next 5 years, federal agencies, state and school district policy makers, foundations and funders, publishers, and teacher educators should support the revision of existing curricula and development of new curricula to align with the committee's vision. These curricula should be developed or revised by collaborative teams of researchers, curriculum developers, teacher educators, and practitioners—informed by the needs of children, families, and communities—following equity-based and rigorous, empirically driven, iterative design and evaluation processes as described in this report.

Recommendation 2: In the next 5 years, program leaders should transition to adopting and implementing evidence-validated curricula that, when integrated coherently, support the learning and development of the whole child. Essential features of evidence-based curricula include developmentally appropriate learning goals, a scope and sequence, coherent alignment with specific domains, and rich content.

Recommendation 3: In the next 5 years, researchers and curriculum developers should (1) develop and evaluate appropriate criteria and metrics for assessing racial, cultural, linguistic, and ability bias in curricula; (2) continually review curricula for these potential racial, cultural, linguistic, and ability biases; and (3) develop and provide adaptations and revisions so that the curricula are culturally and linguistically responsive and foster an anti-bias, anti-racist, multilingual, and inclusive approach in early childhood education.

Recommendation 4: From the outset, curriculum developers, in partnership with researchers and teacher educators, should develop curricula and supporting materials in Spanish, English, and other languages commonly spoken by children with a home language other than English. Whenever possible, curriculum developers should include adaptations for other language groups and those who speak dialects of English, such as African American Vernacular English; they should also consider the unique approach warranted in Indigenous communities that are invested in language revitalization and maintenance.

Recommendation 5: In the next 5 years, funders should support the development of new, or revision of existing, child assessment measures aligned with the committee's vision. These assessment measures should be both formative and summative, should consider the role of bias (e.g., race, language, culture, disability status) in assessment, and should capture the full range of meaningful child outcomes and experiences (i.e., including positive social-emotional development, positive racial identity for children of color, and bilingualism/biliteracy for multilingual learners).

Empowering Educators: Supports and Professional Development for Equitable and Effective Curriculum Implementation

Conclusion 9: Providing educators of young children with psychosocial, economic, and professional development supports is critical; however, the availability of such supports varies greatly based on funding streams and governing systems.

Conclusion 10: Educators of young children are not only intentional teachers but also sources of nurturance and security for children. The effective realization of these roles depends greatly on teachers' attention to fostering reciprocal and responsive relationships, examining and checking their biases, and cultivating a positive emotional environment, all of which affect the quality of the broader learning environment on which the provision of effective and equitable curricula depends.

Conclusion 11: Preschool programs generally offer children warm and emotionally supportive environments; however, some populations of young children, such as Black children and children who are multilingual learners, may experience various individual and systemic inequities (e.g., biased perceptions of behavior, assumptions about the value of languages other than English, conflictual teacher–child relationships). On average, preschool programs fall short in offering children rich content and in advancing children's thinking. This is especially true in mathematics, early language, literacy, science, and support for emerging multilingualism.

Conclusion 12: Strong connections between families and preschool staff are essential for understanding when and how to adapt preschool curricula to address the strengths and needs of children, in order to create a meaningful link between home and school experiences. Unfortunately, research continues to show that minoritized families, especially Black families and to some extent families that speak a language other than English, are less likely to report close relationships with teachers; likewise, teachers report less close and trusting relationships with them. Thus, it is important that curricula include guidance for educators focused on effective approaches and strategies to foster inclusive and culturally responsive home–school partnerships in support of children's learning.

Based on these conclusions, the committee makes the following recommendations:

Recommendation 6: Curriculum developers should incorporate resources and structures that help teachers gain knowledge about effective teaching strategies and practices, including bolstering content knowledge and understanding how children's thinking and learning can be best supported.

Recommendation 7: Early childhood educators should collaborate with families to co-construct curricular components that are meaningful and relevant for all children in the classroom; authentically elevate the role of families in supporting their children's development; recognize the diversity in and value of family practices and integrate these practices when possible; honor their languages, cultures, beliefs, traditions, and talents; and invite these assets into the classroom.

Recommendation 8: Program leaders and policy makers should ensure that educators receive professional development, regular in-classroom coaching, and access to materials tied to the implementation of evidence-based curricula, including supports for delivering curricula in children's home language alongside English, or for monolingual English-speaking teachers, supporting multilingual learners through cross-linguistic connections and other research-informed practices that bridge languages.

Recommendation 9: Curriculum developers should provide scaffolded supports,[2] developed in partnership with researchers and teacher educators, that increase opportunities for effectively integrating children with disabilities in general education early childhood settings while effectively meeting their unique developmental needs and fostering healthy peer relationships.

Investing in Equity: Funding Mechanisms, Policy Strategies, and Innovations to Support Selection and Implementation of Effective Preschool Curricula

Conclusion 13: To expand access to high-quality early educational experiences, there is a significant need for infrastructure to support the development, implementation, and evaluation of curricula and to encourage adoption of new or revised curricula that align with the committee's vision. This includes collaboration between researchers and practitioners, data collection that captures characteristics of the populations being served and the curricula being used in the programs children attend, quality measures that capture the strengths and lived experiences of all children, and professional development and supports for practitioners.

Conclusion 14: High turnover rates are prevalent in the field of early education. Providing educators with the financial security and benefits that promote their physical and mental health is necessary for supporting the implementation of high-quality, equitable curriculum and maintaining a diverse, well-qualified workforce that is large enough to meet the demand of families for high-quality educational experiences for young children. Ongoing data collection is critical to assessing and addressing the needs of educators, programs, and the families and communities they serve.

---

[2]Scaffolding is the process through which instructional supports are added to facilitate mastery of tasks by building on existing knowledge. As tasks are mastered, these supports can be adjusted and eventually removed.

Based on these conclusions, the committee makes the following recommendations:

Recommendation 10: The U.S. Department of Education, in partnership with the U.S. Department of Health and Human Services and state early childhood education agencies, should

- create a research-practice-partnership network of diverse researchers and early childhood programs that are willing to engage in research to study curricula and practices aligned with the committee's vision;
- create a data system for capturing details on curricula being used in programs, along with characteristics of the children being served, the quality of programs, and a comprehensive set of outcomes;
- align quality metrics, measures, and rating systems with the new vision of curricula and associated practices;
- incentivize the adoption and use of high-quality curricula that align with the new vision; and
- provide quality improvement supports and resources for addressing equity and inclusion gaps.

Recommendation 11: As curricula aligned with the committee's vision are adopted and implemented, state and local early care and education agencies and public education institutions should develop policies, provide technical assistance, and target funding to support ongoing professional development for educators that aligns with the vision, as well as strong curriculum implementation, with strategies and resources for addressing the high staffing turnover rates experienced across the country in early childhood programs.

Recommendation 12: As curricula aligned with the committee's vision are adopted and implemented, state and local early care and education agencies and public education institutions should identify opportunities to expand children's access to schools, communities, and programs that implement these curricula and associated practices.

Bridging the Knowledge Gap: Creating an Evidence Base to Advance Curriculum Development and Implementation

Conclusion 15: Additional research could help determine the contextual factors and child characteristics that affect the differential effectiveness of curriculum approaches and their implementation.

Conclusion 16: To date, most evaluation studies of curricula have not assessed important outcomes such as development of children's creativity, positive identity, curiosity, and emergent multilingualism. Moreover, limited evidence is available on the effects of curricula on child outcomes such as sense of belonging, agency, and group pride; evidence is also limited on how teachers' implicit and explicit biases affect curriculum implementation. Such evidence is needed to ensure that curricula meet the needs of the whole child.

Conclusion 17: Currently, preschool curricula give little attention to the inequitable impact of racism, English language learning status, and disability status. More research is needed to understand the role of preschool curricula in supporting children's intersectional identities, in order to promote justice through healthy child development, equitable outcomes, and school success.

Conclusion 18: Culturally relevant and sustaining curricula and teaching have been identified as supports for important aspects of development, such as positive identity and racial pride. Additional research is needed to guide the development and implementation of culturally and linguistically affirming, anti-bias curricula for preschool programs, as well as to evaluate existing curricula on these dimensions. This includes much-needed research on defining what specifically is included in culturally and linguistically affirming and anti-bias curricula, what is effective, and what should be measured as outcomes.

Conclusion 19: Curricula with scaffolded supports, targeted adaptations, and accommodation for children with disabilities are crucial for authentically, meaningfully, and effectively supporting the full inclusion of children with disabilities. Future research could inform the development and testing of curricula that are designed for inclusive settings to address identified instructional needs and support equitable access, experiences, and supports for young children identified with disabilities or developmental delays.

Based on these conclusions, the committee makes the following recommendations:

Recommendation 13: In the next 5 years, publishers should collect and provide rigorous and meaningful evidence of improved short- and long-term academic and developmental outcomes for all children, with particular attention to Black, Latine, Indigenous, Asian, and Pacific Islander children; multilingual learners; children with disabilities; and children living in poverty. They should also document the experiences of children in grades K–2 and determine whether there is coherence in the curricular vision across the transition from preschool to these early grades.

Recommendation 14: Researchers should continue to conduct rigorous evaluations of curriculum approaches, along with implementation research, to assess the extent to which curricula promote children's holistic and healthy development and learning, regardless of place or socioeconomic status, and affirm children's full identities, including race, culture, home language, gender, and ability.

Recommendation 15: To build the necessary evidence base over the next 5–10 years, relevant federal agencies, states, and philanthropies should invest in ongoing research aimed at developing implementation systems to support the transition to evidence-based curricula that are practical and accessible. These investments should

- ensure the representation of Black, Indigenous, Latine, Asian, and Pacific Islander children, multilingual learners, children with disabilities, and children living in poverty in study samples with explicit attention to their unique experiences;
- support implementation research that describes and identifies effective practices used by individual educators and programs for delivering and adapting curricula in ways that are culturally and linguistically responsive and relevant for children and families in their programs;
- support studies that compare different domain-specific combinations and outcomes beyond those traditionally used, in order to capture new understanding of what the term "whole child" encompasses in a diverse society (i.e., to capture culturally and linguistically affirming and anti-bias practices);
- expand measured child outcomes of interest to include multilingual development, sense of belonging, agency, group pride, curiosity, creativity, and problem solving, and expand teacher outcomes to include the reduction of implicit and explicit bias, effective teaching, and cultural and linguistic responsiveness; and
- launch a federal technical assistance center that is grounded in implementation science, is dedicated to supporting the development of new curricula and the adoption and implementation of evidence-based curricula, and includes supports for assessing fidelity.

The committee also presents a research agenda that identifies areas of inquiry and considerations for additional research: equity in study samples; multilingual learners; locally specific versus widely disseminated curricula; curriculum standards; systemic exclusion and bias; supports for successful curriculum implementation; investigator collaboration; family involvement in assessment dialogue among teachers, students, and peers; and expansion of outcome measures. The committee highlights the need for a comprehensive research agenda to gather evidence on this new vision for preschool curriculum. This includes: (1) creating resources to better understand and document study conditions of curriculum effectiveness; (2) standardizing approaches for examining, reporting, and interpreting potential sources of curriculum effect heterogeneity; and (3) organizing large-scale studies that coordinate multiple teams of researchers to address questions of critical scientific and policy relevance.

The evidence that the committee reviewed underscores the myriad ways in which high-quality early childhood education can promote children's learning and development. However, many children do not have access to preschool experiences that recognize their unique strengths and the strengths of their families and communities. Equity in early childhood education calls for curricula that adapt to individual children's strengths and needs, cultural backgrounds, and linguistic contexts and empower every child to reach their full potential.

Meeting this challenge will require continued commitment to refining research methodologies, confronting the complexities of evaluating curriculum efficacy, and expanding the knowledge base. Only through continuous inquiry and adaptation can society fully realize the promise of equitable and transformative early childhood education for all children.

1

Introduction

Preschool provides young children with the promise of meaningful early learning experiences, and *high-quality* preschool experiences offer an opportunity to support young children and their families while reducing educational inequities. Curriculum is an important factor that interacts with other factors to shape the quality of a child's learning experience in the classroom. Curriculum has been shown in research to be a key ingredient in the quality of preschool programs (Burchinal et al., 2016; Institute of Medicine & National Research Council [NRC], 2015; NRC, 2009; Yoshikawa et al., 2013), and it is also an important building block in realizing the promise of preschool to improve developmental outcomes equitably, for all children (Engle et al., 2011; Magnuson et al., 2007; Melhuish et al., 2015; National Association for the Education of Young Children [NAEYC], 2019; Phillips et al., 2017; Yoshikawa et al., 2013).

Preschool offers a chance to combat educational disparities experienced by historically underserved groups, such as children from racially and ethnically marginalized communities, multilingual children, children living in poverty, and children with disabilities. When equitable opportunities and practices are in place, educational disparities can be reduced (National Academies of Sciences, Engineering, and Medicine, 2023a,b). However, preschool is not universally available to children in the United States, and many children from populations that have been historically marginalized lack access to high-quality early learning opportunities (Bassok & Galdo, 2016; Dobbins et al., 2016; Nores & Barnett, 2014). Improving access to high-quality preschool for these children is a clear need, and meeting this need requires a rich understanding of program features that can support effective learning and social experiences (National Academies, 2023b).

Decades of research have shown that high-quality preschool is linked to positive social and academic outcomes (Phillips et al., 2017; Yoshikawa et al., 2013). The National Association for the Education of Young Children, the nation's largest professional organization of early childhood educators, administers a national accreditation system for high-quality early childhood programs and promulgates guidelines for developmentally appropriate practices in these programs (NAEYC, 2020, 2022). These guidelines state that high-quality preschool programs are learning environments in which teachers create a caring community of learners, intentionally support children's learning and development, foster reciprocal partnerships with families, observe and assess children's development and learning, and use curriculum as a planning tool for promoting children's learning (NAEYC, 2020). A substantial body of research spanning decades, encompassing longitudinal randomized controlled trials, program evaluations, meta-analyses, and nonexperimental studies, has established the multifaceted advantages of high-quality early childhood education programs for children (Institute of Medicine & National Research Council, 2015; National Academies, 2023a).[1] These benefits can not only manifest in the short term but persist through adolescence and into adulthood, shaping children's long-term developmental trajectories. For example, children who participate in high-quality preschool programs compared with those who do not tend to have higher educational attainment, earnings, and health outcomes, as well as less involvement with the criminal justice system as adults (Belfield et al., 2006; National Academies, 2023a; Reynolds et al., 2018; Schweinhart et al., 2005; Yoshikawa et al., 2013). Society at large also benefits from high-quality preschool programs because they support the development of healthy adults and communities while reducing the need for more expensive interventions later in a child's life (Heckman & Karapakula, 2019a,b). However, this research base also illuminates the stark disparities in access to and quality of early education programs, highlighting how these differential experiences can affect later developmental and academic outcomes. Children from marginalized communities consistently face greater barriers to accessing such programs. Furthermore, even within programs, children from these communities often experience markedly lower-quality education compared with their White, higher-income, and native English-speaking peers—which perpetuates inequities (National Academies, 2023a).

The complexity of the current early childhood education system and the diversity of program options leads to great variability in children's

---

[1] For a broader discussion of research related to early education program quality and outcomes, see Chapter 2 of *Closing the Opportunity Gap for Young Children* (National Academies, 2023a).

preschool experiences. The United States has a mixed delivery system for early childhood programs, with a variety of program types, including center-based programs, home-based programs, and multiple care arrangements. In addition, programs are funded through a variety of sources, including private tuition, foundation grants, public funding, and other streams. Demographic data for 2019 reveal that 74% of children aged 3–5 who were not yet in kindergarten were in at least one weekly nonparental care arrangement, and 26% had no such arrangement. Among the former children, 83% were in center-based care (i.e., child care centers, Head Start programs, preschools, pre-Ks, and other early childhood programs), 26% were in relative care, and 14% were in nonrelative care. Some children were also in a combination of settings (Cui & Natzke, 2021).

Unfortunately, racially and linguistically marginalized children do not have the same level of access to preschool programs as do White children. In addition, program cost is a barrier for many families, and this is especially true for those children whose families have low income (National Academies, 2023a). Because privately funded preschool is expensive, access to preschool is unaffordable for many families without government financial support (National Academies, 2018). Examples of government-funded support for preschool include child care subsidies, Head Start, state and locally funded public pre-K, and pre-K programs for children with disabilities. Children in low-income families can also gain access to free pre-K through local school districts (National Academies, 2018). However, for all children, program slots are limited and unevenly distributed because of a number of factors related to geography, income, race and ethnicity, and age (National Academies, 2023a). For example, families in rural areas face particular challenges in finding licensed child care[2] that is both affordable and conveniently located, and Indigenous and Latine families are more likely than any other subpopulation to live in a child care desert (Malik et al., 2018).

Preschool enrollment varies based on children's racial and ethnic background. In 2021, for instance, among 3- to 5-year-olds, the enrollment rate was higher for White children (56.1%) than for children who were Black (52.6%), of two or more races (55.2%), or Asian (51.3%), and these rates were all higher than the enrollment rates for children who were

---

[2]Child care licensing is a process in which state and local governments set minimum health and safety requirements (e.g., criminal background checks for staff, ongoing safety training for staff, sanitation, building safety, child and caregiver health) that child care programs must meet. These requirements do not guarantee quality, but rather are minimum health and safety requirements. Compliance with these requirements is monitored as part of licensing (Childcare.gov, n.d.). Accreditation is a voluntary process that requires early childhood education programs to meet standards beyond those required by regulatory requirements. These standards have been developed by a number of organizations (National Center on Child Care Quality Improvement, 2018).

Indigenous (49%), Latine (48.6%), or Pacific Islander (41.2%; National Center for Education Statistics, 2022). The COVID-19 pandemic exacerbated these inequities; the greatest enrollment declines due to COVID-19 occurred among non-White children from low-income households (Barnett & Jung, 2021). Even before the pandemic, however, children who were non-White, multilingual, and/or from families with low income were less likely to attend universal public pre-K programs (Friedman-Krauss et al., 2022; Shapiro et al., 2019).

Even when low-income and racially and ethnically marginalized children do have access to preschool, they are more likely than their White, higher-income peers to be enrolled in programs of lower quality (National Academies, 2023a). For instance, state-funded preschool programs offered in low-income and racially and ethnically marginalized communities tend to have lower quality scores compared with programs in predominantly White and affluent neighborhoods (Bassok & Galdo, 2016; Valentino, 2018). For example, a 2019 report from the Education Trust reported that only 1% of Latine and 4% of Black children were enrolled in public pre-K programs that meet the National Institute for Early Education Research's (NIEER's) pre-K benchmarks, which include elements such as early learning and development standards, curriculum supports, teacher education, specialized training in pre-K, professional development and coaching for staff, class size, staff–child ratio, health screenings and referrals, and presence of continuous quality improvement systems, among others (Gillespie, 2019; National Academies, 2023a; National Institute for Early Education Research, 2019). Highlighting how much work there is to be done, NIEER has long emphasized these benchmarks are a *floor* on quality; they do not cover whether programs use evidence-based curricula or compensate pre-K teachers with parity with K–12, for example. These inequities can have detrimental effects on marginalized and low-income children, families, and communities because they lose the potential benefits of access to high-quality preschool. On the other hand, if programs incorporate children's heritage cultures and languages or dialects in meaningful ways while also providing developmentally appropriate and rigorous content, children are likely to engage in classroom activities, develop both social-emotional and academic skills, and improve their self-concept (Craig & Washington, 2006; Gort & Sembiante, 2015; Hancock, 2017). Additionally, culturally and linguistically responsive programs can help foster teacher–family relationships and parent involvement (National Academies, 2023a).

Research conducted over several decades has established numerous consistent indicators of program quality associated with positive child experiences and outcomes; however, there is significant variation in the definitions of quality, which often overlook dimensions that are vital to children from historically marginalized communities—in particular, children who have a home language other than English, children of color, and children with disabilities (National Academies, 2023a). Quality is typically conceptualized as encompassing aspects of structural quality, such as physical infrastructure; teacher–child ratios; evidence-based curricula; language of instruction; discipline policies; a highly skilled and supported workforce; and process quality, such as quantity of and access to engaging learning experiences, richness of teacher–child interactions, emotional responsiveness, and family engagement (National Academies, 2023a). These dimensions of quality are interconnected and influenced by systemic factors such as funding and policy. Crucially, specific dimensions of quality, both structural and process-based, significantly impact the experiences of children of color and those from historically marginalized communities in particular. These dimensions include cultural responsivity, access to bilingual staff, differential teacher expectations, and strong relationships with families whose home language is not English. These factors shape children's experiences demonstrably, particularly for children who are immigrants, Latine and Asian American children, and multilingual learners (Adair, 2015; Limlingan et al., 2020; National Academies, 2017, 2023a; Suárez-Orozco et al., 2010).

Preschool curriculum—the focus of this report—is a key dimension of overall structural and process-based quality, and it differs across multiple dimensions, such as theoretical underpinnings, content, developmental domains covered, format, expectations for teachers and children, and assessment strategies (Jenkins & Duncan, 2017; Jenkins et al., 2018). And although curriculum quality is important in determining a child's learning experience, the quality of its implementation matters as well. There is vast diversity in the contexts and circumstances in which curricula are implemented.

The quality of young children's learning experiences and interactions with curriculum depends on teachers' qualifications and professional development and the fidelity of implementation, as well as the extent to which teachers differentiate instruction, make curricula culturally and linguistically responsive to children, engage families, and use data and assessment to drive instruction. School district, state, and federal contextual factors and policies are also linked to the effectiveness and equity of curriculum. However, this educational landscape is fragmented and, in some instances, lacks sufficient coordination (National Academies, 2023a).

Overall, the quality and implementation of curriculum are recognized as important elements of high-quality preschool. Existing evidence can provide insights into components of effective curricula and the supports needed for implementation, but it rarely focuses explicitly on the needs of children from marginalized populations (Bredekamp & Joseph, 2024; NAEYC & National Association of Early Childhood Specialists in State Departments of Education, 2003). Clear information and consensus are needed on what constitutes high-quality preschool curriculum, taking into account the landscape of the preschool years, including the wide array of programs that are responsible for meeting the various program standards and requirements, as well as the diversity of contexts children come from. A better understanding of the historical contexts in which programs were developed, who was included in the development, and implications for the research that exists to date is also critical. In relation to these questions, the committee's task includes proposing recommendations that integrate evidence about what works best for target populations—what has been missing and how to identify strengths to realize potential of all children.

ABOUT THIS STUDY

Sponsored by the Bill & Melinda Gates Foundation, the Board on Children, Youth, and Families of the National Academies of Sciences, Engineering, and Medicine convened an ad hoc committee of relevant experts to gather information on and explore the range of issues associated with the need to build a consensus definition of high-quality preschool curriculum. The committee was tasked with building a vision of what constitutes an effective, high-quality preschool curriculum that can serve to reduce inequities in children's learning experiences during the preschool years (see Box 1-1 for the committee's statement of task). It should be noted that the committee was not asked to evaluate individual curricula, isolated strategies or approaches, or training programs as part of this study. The 13-member committee included experts in early childhood education, early childhood development, equity, curriculum development, implementation science, public policy, children with disabilities, multilingual learners, child health, mental health, and neuroscience.

STUDY APPROACH

The committee met six times over a one-year period in 2021–2022. During this time, it reviewed the published literature pertaining to its charge, including peer-reviewed materials, book chapters, reports, working papers, government documents, white papers and evaluations, editorials, and previous reports of the National Academies. In addition, the committee conducted three public information-gathering sessions and two public listening sessions. These sessions included expert presentations on high-quality pre-K curriculum for dual language and multilingual learners, communities of learning and the role of language and culture in curriculum development, future considerations for designing and adapting curriculum for children with disabilities, state policies and decision making related to early care and education, and curriculum adaptation and enactment.

> **BOX 1-1**
> **Statement of Task**
>
> The National Academies will convene an ad hoc committee to conduct a study on pre-K curriculum quality for children ages three through five, with special attention to the needs of Black and Latinx children, dual language learners, children with special needs, and children experiencing poverty. The study will support equitable curriculum development, state and center-level pre-K curriculum selection, and local curriculum implementation. The committee will review research on early childhood development, including research on access to contemporary early learning opportunities, and consider the lived experience of diverse young children, their families, and early childhood educators.
>
> The committee will make recommendations aimed at creating a new vision for high-quality pre-K curriculum, including:
>
> - the fundamental assumptions, principles, and definitions that should guide the content, development, and use of high-quality, equity-driven curriculum for prekindergarten children.
> - the components, criteria, and/or features of high-quality pre-K curriculum that support equity and learning and development of all children. Special considerations that may be needed for Black and Latinx children, culturally and linguistically diverse learners, children with special needs, and children experiencing poverty.
> - how the components, criteria, and/or features of high-quality, equitable curriculum should be used by state and local preschool program directors to make curricular decisions for diverse learners and guidance needed to facilitate selection of curricula.
> - curricular supports and professional development opportunities needed by diverse early childhood educators in diverse pre-K settings to enable the effective and equitable implementation of high-quality pre-K curriculum.
> - funding mechanisms, state and federal policies, and new innovations that can support the selection and use of effective and equitable pre-K curriculum.
> - research that is needed to address current gaps in understanding of components, criteria, and/or features of high-quality pre-K curricula.

The committee also commissioned two papers to help address questions in the statement of task. It commissioned School Readiness Consulting and Boston University's Center on the Ecology of Early Development to conduct a comprehensive literature review and synthesize research findings related to high-quality pre-K curriculum. The aim of this literature review was to inform the committee in its effort to build a consensus definition of high-quality preschool curriculum, with special attention to the needs of Black and Latine children, multilingual children, children with disabilities, and children experiencing poverty. The committee commissioned a second paper to provide an analysis of state- and program-level selection of curriculum. This analysis was focused on reviewing criteria for selecting curricula, including considerations related to state-level funding, state standards, and the state and local decision-making entities involved in the process.

The findings from the committee's review of these evidence sources informed the committee's deliberations and served as the basis for its key conclusions and recommendations, which are presented in Chapter 10.

Evidence Standards

The committee's commissioned literature review helped to inform its effort to build consensus around a vision for high-quality preschool curriculum by providing a foundational understanding of what is currently known about curriculum quality for preschool programs for children aged 3–5 years in the United States. This review drew on empirical, peer-reviewed research on preschool curriculum, as well as complementary sources highlighting the lived experiences of children, families, and educators who engage with this curriculum. The review included both quantitative and qualitative literature across multiple disciplines.

Building on the findings of the commissioned literature review, the committee took an expansive view of evidence in developing this report and drew on and privileged a diversity of methods and evidence types. The committee reviewed many types of studies, including meta-analyses and syntheses; experimental and quasi-experimental evaluations of curriculum; qualitative case studies; ethnographic and field studies; and interviews, focus groups, and surveys. Consistent with previous National Academies reports, the committee adopted recommendations from the foundational NRC (2002) report *Scientific Research in Education*, which support "a wide variety of legitimate scientific designs available for education research" (p. 6).

The committee remained mindful that a study's results and conclusions may be influenced by the assumptions of the researchers who conducted it. In reviewing the evidence, then, the committee considered the theoretical perspectives, positionality, and methodologies involved in how study results were collected, analyzed, and interpreted. In particular, the committee discussed and evaluated the extent to which study findings and their interpretation may have been limited by perspectives not compatible with the committee's new vision for high-quality, equitable preschool curriculum. For example, some early evaluation studies of preschool programs were conceptualized and designed from a deficit-oriented perspective that did not recognizing the knowledge and strengths of children and families from marginalized communities (National Academies, 2023a); this perspective may have affected researchers' interpretation of what it means for curriculum to be high quality and effective in promoting desired outcomes. The specific outcomes included in studies may also have been narrowly restricted to mathematics and literacy in English without consideration of additional languages children and families may speak and additional competencies not addressed, such as initiative, positive identity, and curiosity. In considering the evidence, the committee also evaluated whether the methodologies and tools used for determining curriculum effectiveness are appropriate for assessing the knowledge, skills, and assets of diverse young children and their families, especially those from marginalized communities.

The development of a new vision for high-quality preschool curriculum considers the multiple and complex ways in which cultural and linguistic, individual, and contextual factors interact with curriculum choice in ways that will affect children's developmental outcomes. As in previous studies of the National Academies, the committee relied significantly on studies that had undergone the peer review process to help ensure the quality of design, methods, and conclusions. While the committee's conclusions rely primarily on peer-reviewed journals and books, the committee reviewed the literature in the context of systemic biases that may have affected the availability of published findings. The committee also reviewed practitioner journals, technical reports, and policies, and invited testimony from members of the early childhood education community with differing perspectives. Additionally, the committee considered the perspectives of educators, program directors, and state policy makers who implement and administer preschool programs.

Building an evidence base for a new vision of high-quality preschool curriculum takes time, resources, and coordinated effort from multidisciplinary researchers. It also requires confronting a central tension: that research in this field tends to lag behind the state of the art in emerging theories, perspectives, and approaches.

Conceptual Framework

The committee's conceptual framework for understanding factors that influence and define high-quality preschool curriculum (Figure 1-1) draws on a number of sources, and guides the organization of this report (García Coll et al., 1996; Iruka, 2020; Iruka et al., 2022; Spencer et al., 1997). This framework is based on the realities that characterize how children from populations that have been racially and ethnically minoritized, children who are multilingual learners, children with disabilities, and children living in poverty grow up in the United States. Racism, bias, and discrimination permeate all the systems and direct experiences that are part of the lives of racially, ethnically, and linguistically minoritized children, and thus impact their development immeasurably (García Coll et al., 1996; Iruka et al., 2022). An unrelenting and

24

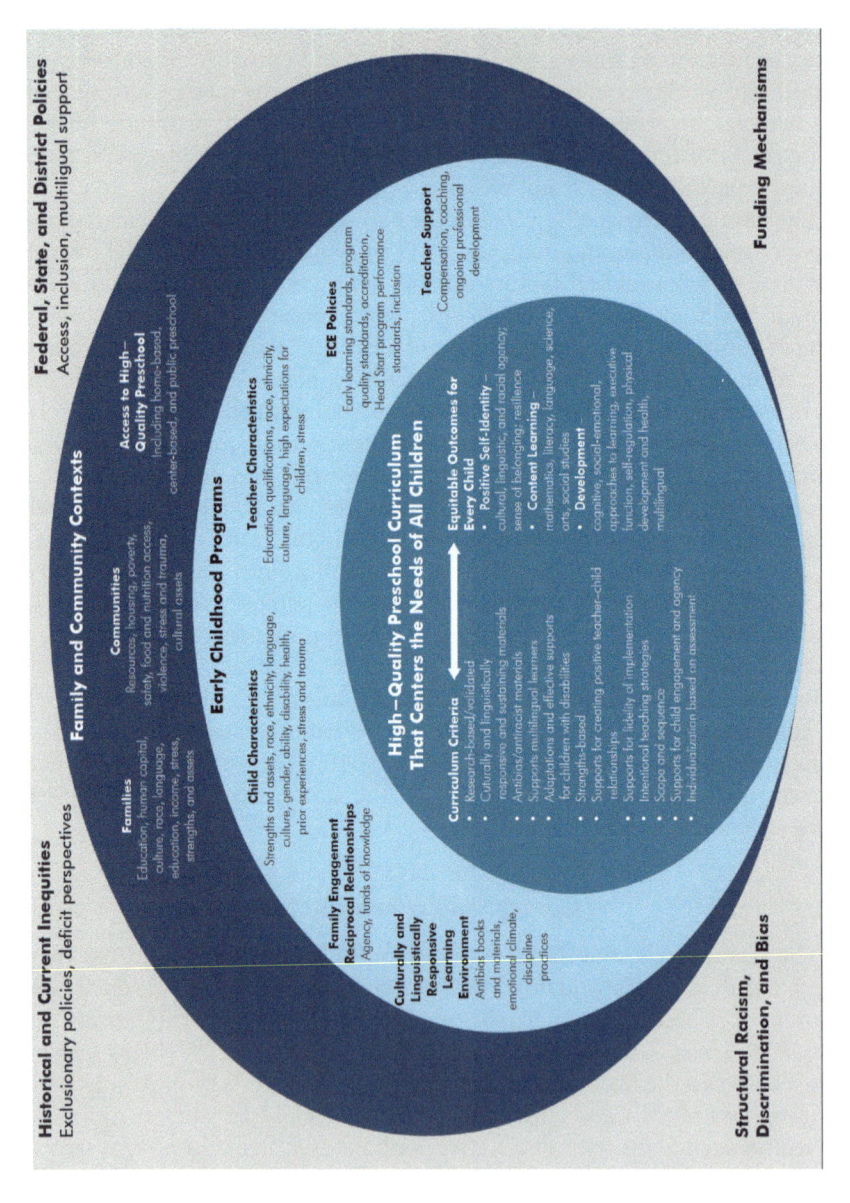

FIGURE 1-1 A conceptual framework for understanding factors that influence and define high-quality preschool curriculum.
SOURCE: Committee generated.

accumulating source of toxic stress for minoritized children is daily exposure to negative stereotypes, microaggressions, and discrimination (Center on the Developing Child, 2020). Such high levels of unrelenting stress can impact children's mental and physical health negatively (Center on the Developing Child, 2020). The continuing impact of historical bias and discrimination is evident in these children's unequal quality of educational opportunity, disproportionately harsh discipline, preschool suspension and expulsion rates, and much more (Meek et al., 2020). Persistent biases also negatively affect the development of children with disabilities, who have historically been excluded from educational settings and continue to be, despite federal laws requiring their inclusion (Meek et al., 2020). Similarly, policies that do not support the development of children's home language in addition to English promote a deficit model for teaching multilingual learners rather than capitalizing on their linguistic knowledge and potential for bilingualism.

These are the realities of the lives of minoritized children, children with disabilities, and children who are multilingual learners, as well as children experiencing poverty. However, negative outcomes are not inevitable for these children (García Coll et al., 1996). Awareness of these historical and current inequities is vital to transforming preschool curriculum to ensure the health, well-being, and school achievement of every child. Most important, the committee's framework emphasizes that high-quality, equity-driven curriculum rejects a deficit perspective on children; rather, the committee's new vision for preschool curriculum focuses on children's strengths, assets, and resilience. Thus, the framework incorporates the lived experiences of children, families, and educators while pointing to evidence-based curriculum and teaching practices that can ensure equitable, positive outcomes for each child.

The outermost section of Figure 1-1 describes the larger systems and structures that impact the everyday experiences of marginalized and minoritized groups of people in the United States. Unquestionably, these forces impact children and must inform the development, content, and use of high-quality, equity-driven curriculum for diverse learners; they include historical and current inequities; structural racism, discrimination, and bias; federal, state, and district policies; and a variety of funding mechanisms. The influence of these macro variables has the potential to be operationalized in a child's life, as well as in the development of curriculum and of high-quality early education (Bronfenbrenner & Crouter, 1983). As noted by García Coll et al. (1996), children from marginalized and minoritized groups face unique developmental conditions based on "three major derivatives of social stratification (social position, racism, and segregation)," and it is these nonshared experiences that promote or inhibit warm and inclusive learning environments, cultural and linguistic adaptations of curriculum, and the attainment of developmental competencies (García Coll et al., 1996, p. 1896).

Within this broader macrosystem exist the family and community contexts that influence a child's cultural identity; spoken language or languages; socialization; physical health and well-being; and access to resources, including high-quality preschool, among many other factors. Developmental outcomes for diverse groups of children and contributors to both their risk and resiliency can be influenced by poverty, race, school quality, and neighborhood factors, as well as intermediate experiences of stress, including the safety of their physical environment and exposure to violence (National Academies, 2023a; Reading et al., 2005). Similarly, their strengths and assets, including their sense of agency, are influenced by the family and community contexts, which then impact the system at the level of early childhood programs, including family engagement and reciprocal relationships, culturally and linguistically responsive learning environments, child characteristics, teacher characteristics and support, and program quality (NAEYC, 2019). Finally, in the center of the framework is high-quality preschool curriculum itself and its vital connection to ensuring equitable outcomes for every child. The two-way arrow indicates that "children change from experiencing the curriculum, and the curriculum changes in response to the learners' interests, strengths, experiences, abilities, and progress" (Bredekamp & Joseph, 2024, p. 380).

The quality of early childhood programs is typically defined as having two dimensions: structure and process (Burchinal & Farran, 2021). As noted earlier in this chapter, structural quality includes readily evaluated features such as maximum group sizes, teacher–child ratios, and teacher qualifications. Process quality, on the other hand, refers to the quality of teacher–child relationships, and the appropriateness and effectiveness of the learning experiences and teaching strategies for individual children. Process quality consists of human factors that are more difficult to evaluate but are the most important determinants of the quality of children's experiences and their learning outcomes (Center on the Developing Child, 2016). Process quality describes daily life for children, how they should be treated, and how teachers implement an engaging curriculum and teach effectively (Bredekamp & Joseph, 2024). Structural and process-based variables are integrally connected. Positive relationships between teachers and children are more likely if group sizes and teacher–child ratios are relatively small (Burchinal & Farran, 2021). A developmentally appropriate, well-equipped, culturally responsive environment is also essential to protect children's health and safety and promote optimal learning.

High-quality preschool curriculum is a structural and process-based determinant of the quality of children's experiences and their outcomes. That is, a program may adopt a validated curriculum, whether domain-specific or comprehensive; but if it is to be effective, teachers need to implement it with fidelity and to individualize and adapt their instruction in culturally and linguistically responsive ways based on regular assessment of children's progress. These elements are all interrelated. For example, teacher qualifications, preparation, and compensation affect the process variables that influence child outcomes, such as positive self-identity, content learning, and physical and cognitive development. State and local policies and program standards vary, and these also may affect curriculum availability and selection, as well as the additional qualified staff and curriculum supports needed to provide equitable early education for children of color, multilingual learners, and children with disabilities. This consensus report and the committee's conceptual framework build on pioneering work in the field, such as Bronfenbrenner's ecological systems theory (Bronfenbrenner, 2004; Bronfenbrenner & Morris, 2006). However, the committee's framework differs from previous work in that it pays special attention to the strengths and needs of Black and Latine children, multilingual learners, children with disabilities, and children experiencing poverty. Children from diverse backgrounds benefit from culturally and linguistically responsive education in a variety of ways. This report highlights the fallacy that merely supplementing mainstream early childhood programs with culturally relevant material is adequate for all learners (Nāone & Au, 2010). A new vision of preschool curriculum can seek to expand the epistemology of curriculum, including the goal, purpose, and outcomes of learning, and create transformative, social justice–oriented curricula that ensure equity and, more important, humanity for all.

KEY TERMS USED IN THIS REPORT

This section provides definitions for key terms used throughout this report (Box 1-2). Terms not defined here are used less frequently in the report and are explained and/or defined in the chapters in which they appear.

HISTORICAL BACKGROUND AND CONTEXT

As noted earlier in this chapter, a key component of understanding what features and criteria constitute high-quality pre-K curriculum is understanding the diversity of the landscape of preschool programs, as well as the historical contexts in which existing programs were developed and who was involved in their development. A cursory examination of early childhood curricula suggests that they are tacitly or explicitly based on theories of learning and teaching that, for the most part, originated in and reflect White Western European cultural perspectives. As a foundation for this report, this section examines the underlying theoretical foundations of these curricula, including the epistemology from which the most widely used curricula and associated approaches emanated. Importantly, the committee

BOX 1-2
Definitions of Key Terms

The term **Black** includes all people of African descent, as well as their cultures. The report uses "Black" instead of "African American" to be inclusive of all children from across the global diaspora, which encompasses diversity in terms of language, national heritage, and immigrant experience. The term is intended to represent psychosocial and social-political status within the United States, not to denote any genetic or epidemiological significance (Agyemang et al., 2005).

Children with disabilities describes children who, because of an identified disability or other special educational, developmental, physical, emotional, behavioral, or medical condition, require additional care and effective supports, or whose activities are restricted by a certain condition.

Comprehensive curricula (also called global or whole-child curricula) address all or most developmental domains.

Curriculum is a cohesive set of principles, learning goals, intentional teaching strategies, activities, experiences, and materials designed to help children learn and thrive. (This definition is adapted from that of the Institute for Education Sciences and the National Center for Education Evaluation [School Readiness Consulting, 2022]).

A **deficit model/perspective** attributes outcomes such as lack of achievement or learning to a personal lack of effort or deficiency in the individual, rather than to failures or limitations of systems grounded in racism, classism, ableism, sexism, xenophobia, and other forms of oppression.

Domain- or content-specific curricula address one or a limited number of developmental domains or content areas.

Equity is the goal and process of ensuring that everyone has a fair opportunity to thrive, which requires valuing all individuals and populations equally; fully recognizing systemic racism and oppression; rectifying historical and contemporary structural injustices, systemic biases, and oppression; and providing resources and supports accordingly (Curenton et al., 2017; Jones, 2014; Muhammad, 2023).

Indigenous, an overarching term, describes Native populations in colonized places; it includes American Indians, Alaska Natives, Native Americans, and Pacific Islanders. The term "American Indian" or "Native American" is used in the U.S. Census and in many research studies; however, the committee's preference is to use the term "Indigenous" unless the population in a research study being cited uses another term.

The term **Latine** denotes people in the United States who are immigrants from Latin America or descendants thereof. The committee chose to use this term to reflect its solidarity with and understanding of the current language trends. "Latine" is gaining popularity among young activists and scholars, and it appears to align with current global efforts to degenderize the Spanish language (see, e.g., Melzi et al., 2021; Miranda et al., 2023).

Marginalized populations are those relegated to a marginal position within a society or a group on the basis of factors such as race, gender, age, physical ability, or language (Merriam-Webster, n.d.a; Pratt & Fowler, 2022).

Minoritized populations are those that are marginalized or persecuted as a result of systemic oppression. This term is used instead of "minority people" or similar terms (National Institutes of Health, 2024).

A **mixed-delivery system** combines different program types (center-based programs, which may be located in schools or community programs, and home-based programs) and different funding mechanisms (including tuition paid privately by families; private funding, such as foundation grants or university sponsorship; and publicly funded prekindergarten, Head Start, child care subsidies, and other public funding streams) together in order to maximize access to programs or to enhance their quality (Morris & Smith, 2021).

Multilingual learners are those children who are developing proficiency in multiple languages and who are using one or more languages other than or in addition to English in the home, in early care and education settings, and in their communities. The committee may sometimes use the term "dual language learners" when a research study being cited uses this term.

Prekindergarten (pre-K) programs typically serve children between the ages of 3 and 5 years and focus on kindergarten preparation. Many of these programs are open only during the school year and are offered by states at free or low cost to qualifying families. This term is often associated only with publicly funded programs (Childcare.gov, n.d.).

Preschool is used broadly to refer to early care and education programs offered to children aged 3–5 years, including those in family child care settings. Although the committee discusses both privately and publicly funded programs (e.g., Head Start and state-funded programs), this report predominantly uses the term "preschool" rather than "pre-K" or "prekindergarten."

Racialization is the act of giving a racial character to someone or something or the process of categorizing, marginalizing, or regarding according to race (Merriam-Webster, n.d.b).

also examines the sociocultural and historical origins of these curricula and the underlying theories—and the theorists—which have influenced the predominant early childhood education curricula in the United States.

One approach to addressing these matters is informed by Brazilian educator and scholar Paulo Freire (1973), who discussed adopting a "critical consciousness lens" to dismantle systems of oppression and inequity by understanding: (1) the historical, political, and social implications of a situation (i.e., the context); (2) one's own social location in the context; (3) the intersectionality of one's multiple identities (e.g., race, socioeconomic class, gender); and (4) the inherent tensions between a vision of social justice and current societal conditions for all people. This lens can be used to examine how history and ideology can significantly influence which curricula are widely used in early education programs; to identify how existing curricula may exclude or perpetuate harmful narratives about marginalized communities; and to elevate excluded, ignored, or erased perspectives.

Many preschool curricula purport to be rooted in sociocultural or constructivist theories of development, which posit that people develop and learn by interacting with others, exploring their environments, and building on their prior experiences (Branscombe et al., 2013; DeVries et al., 2002; Zigler & Bishop-Josef, 2006). The committee found that the most frequently cited underpinnings of curricula are "inquiry-based," "project-based," and "play-based." In carrying out its charge to identify the fundamental assumptions, principles, and definitions that should guide the content, development, and use of high-quality, equity-driven curriculum, the committee also had to examine the assumptions, principles, and definitions related to existing curricula—for example, why these are the pedagogical underpinnings of the most widely used curricula in early childhood, as well as which approaches may be missing and why.

In reviewing the historical roots of early childhood curricula in the United States, several theorists from as early as the 1600s are often highlighted as key influencers (e.g., John Amos Comenius, Johann Heinrich Pestalozzi, John Locke; Lascarides & Hinitz, 2000). The philosophies of these influencers emphasized concepts such as the societal benefits of literacy and the benefits of sensory exploration and critical thinking as essential components of learning. Another major early education influencer was Friedrich Fröebel (1782–1852), a German educator who developed the first kindergarten, or "children's garden," based on his belief that child development unfolds naturally. The kindergarten movement was widely adopted in the United States and highly influential in the history of early childhood education. Fröebel believed that children learn through play and that education should be based on children's interests and active involvement. He developed concrete materials and planned experiences designed to teach skills (called "gifts and occupations"). Fröebel focused on teachers' observing children and developing activities that supported children's skill levels. Another major influencer in the field was Maria Montessori (1870–1952), an Italian physician and educator. She emphasized children as the source of knowledge and educators as the facilitators who prepare the classroom environment and experiences to engage children in learning content and social skills. She viewed the teacher's role as observing and facilitating but not interfering with children's natural exploration. Montessori founded *Casa dei Bambini* for children living in the impoverished neighborhoods of Rome who were considered to have cognitive disabilities. Her program demonstrated that giving children from impoverished communities enriching experiences could greatly enhance their development. Montessori also developed sensorimotor materials to be used in specific practical ways. Montessori stressed the value of engaging children in independent hands-on, real-life activities as opposed to pretend play (Lillard, 2013) (see chapter 4 for a discussion of Montessori education today).

Jean Piaget (1896–1980) described children's development as a series of fixed stages—sensorimotor, preoperational, and concrete operational. His stage theory has since been criticized for assuming universality and ignoring cultural determinants of development and learning (Matusov & Hayes, 2000). However, the most lasting and influential aspect of Piaget's theory is constructivism—the idea that children construct their own knowledge and understanding through direct and active interaction with the environment and other people. Also highly influential, Russian theorist Lev Vygotsky (1896–1934) believed that interaction, especially adult–child interaction, is critical in supporting children's linguistic, social, and cognitive development. In particular, he introduced the concept of a zone of proximal development that requires teachers (and parents and other adults or capable peers) to scaffold children's learning with tasks that are just beyond or just within their capability. Vygotsky also believed that grouping children of mixed ages in a learning environment supports their acquisition of skills and knowledge. Vygotsky was a strong believer in the power of sociodramatic play to promote the development of self-regulation.

John Dewey (1859–1952), professor at the University of Chicago, believed in the idea of democratically run and socially conscious schools where learning emanates from children's interests and firsthand experiences, leading to project-based learning. Dewey is considered the founder of the progressive education reform movement, focused on making U.S. schools more democratic and responsive to children's needs. In his view, teachers' roles are to promote children's curiosity and inquiry. Dewey believed that children should engage with subject matter content in ways they could understand, so he introduced the idea of integrated and child-centered curriculum. Erik Erikson (1902–1994) stressed the importance of social-emotional support and positive development, as a key component of children's experiences and early childhood curriculum. Italian educator Loris Malaguzzi (1920–1994), in collaboration with teachers, parents, and children, founded the Reggio Emilia approach, which has had widespread impact in the United States and around the world. The approach is based on the "image of the child as rich in potential, strong, powerful, competent and, most of all, connected to adults and children" (Cagliari et al., 2016; Penn, 1997, p. 117). A key principle is "the hundred languages of children," referring to how children's understanding is transformed by representing and re-representing their learning using diverse media, such as drawing, painting, sculpting, writing, photography, and video. In this view, children and teachers co-construct knowledge through long-term projects, and teachers use systematic documentation to display and revisit children's work and thinking processes.

These theorists and their approaches focus attention on providing what current early childhood curricula (and approaches) seek to do: create an environment that is enriching and engaging for children (i.e., child-centered) and facilitates their cognitive development and social competence through interactions with one another, adults, and the physical environment. Thus, it is not surprising that the most commonly used curricula (and approaches) in early childhood draw on these theorists. *The Creative Curriculum* is said to draw on Piaget and Vygotsky, emphasizing inquiry, exploration, and discovery. *HighScope*, created by David Weikart (1931–2003), is said to draw on the theories of Piaget, Dewey, and Vygotsky, focusing on broadening children's social and intellectual skills through active learning experiences. Through the *HighScope* "plan–do–review" process, children discuss each day how they will plan their experiences during the child-choice time of day, typically 45–55 minutes (Epstein, 2014); children then follow their plan, and finally review and reflect on what they did and learned with their teacher and how to follow up the next day. The often-referenced Perry Preschool studies documenting long-term positive outcomes and financial benefits to society were based on children in classrooms that were implementing an early version of the *HighScope Preschool Curriculum* (Heckman & Karapakula, 2019a,b; Schweinhart et al., 2005).

Although some historical documents note that Indigenous cultures on the African continent (Hilliard, 1985, 1986) and in the Americas likely influenced the European theorists who are often cited as pillars of early childhood curricular approaches, these influences are often not elevated. For example, many Indigenous populations in the United States, such as the Lakota and Anishinaabe, have values and character principles rooted in creation stories that highlight wisdom, courage, and honesty; yet the preservation of knowledge through oral traditions, coupled with genocide, has resulted in Indigenous North American philosophies being largely obscured (Administration for Children and Families, 2022; Reyhner & Eder, 2017).

EARLY CHILDHOOD CURRICULA: CURRENT STATE OF THE FIELD

This section describes the prevalence of preschool curricula, the underlying theories and approaches among existing curricula, the topical domains that are covered, curricula intended for various early childhood settings, and the availability of existing curricula.

A wide array of curricula have been developed and studied. The committee's commissioned literature review identified 172 existing preschool curricula[3] (see Appendix A). The curricula identified include only those that are discussed or referenced in publications or other publicly available resources; preschool curricula that are proprietary, locally developed, or not included in published sources may not be represented in this count. Although many curricula exist, only a few are used widely by preschool programs. Nationally representative surveys show that the top two commercially available curricula used in publicly funded pre-K programs are *The Creative Curriculum* and *HighScope*—both of which are multidomain (Doran et al., 2022; National Survey of Early Care and Education Project Team, 2015). *The Creative Curriculum* is the most common primary curriculum in both Head Start programs and preschool programs funded by state or local agencies. Locally developed curricula and no use of curriculum are less common in Head Start programs than in other publicly funded preschool programs (Doran et al., 2022); this difference in use is most likely based on program requirements (e.g., Head Start Program Performance Standards require a curriculum).

Preschool Curricula by Domain

Preschool curricula vary in the topic areas and domains of learning they include, with some curricula covering multiple domains and others focusing on a specific subject area or domain of learning. Comprehensive curricula (also referred to as whole-child or global curricula) are aimed at supporting children's physical, cognitive, and social-emotional development, and include content across the multiple academic and social domains of early childhood education (Jenkins & Duncan, 2017; Odom et al., 2019; Zigler & Bishop-Josef, 2006). Implicit in the concept of comprehensive curricula is inclusion of all domains that are important or relevant for young children's development and achievement. In addition, Head Start and many state-funded pre-K programs require the implementation of comprehensive curricula (Fantuzzo

---

[3] The curricula identified as a part of the committee's commissioned literature review were not evaluated for their effectiveness or for their alignment with the committee's definitions of quality or equity.

et al., 2011). The commissioned literature search revealed that comprehensive curricula are often advertised as complete sets of instructional materials and strategies that cover most or all domains. In this report, the committee uses the term "comprehensive curricula" to indicate when more than one domain is included but does not assess the extent to which these domains include all important content. National organizations (e.g., NAEYC, 2018; NAEYC & NAECS-SDE, 2003) recommend using these wide-scope, comprehensive curricula to promote whole-child development.

In contrast with comprehensive curricula, domain-specific curricula (also known as developmentally focused, content-specific, or targeted curricula) center on a particular subject area or developmental domain, such as mathematics, literacy, or social-emotional development (Jenkins & Duncan, 2017). Supporters of domain-specific curricula have pointed to the strong evidence base for these curricula as an effective approach for improving children's outcomes in competencies with a focused scope (Jenkins et al., 2018; Phillips et al., 2017; Yoshikawa et al., 2013).

There are differing perspectives on the advantages of using multidomain versus domain-specific curricula in classrooms. A key advantage of comprehensive curricula is that all instructional content is theoretically coherent and aligned within the single set of curriculum materials, without requiring early childhood educators individually to determine the pacing and integration of multiple curricula. On the other hand, a key advantage of domain-specific curricula is that the instructional materials may provide more depth and focus on that one domain, with the possibility of better supporting child learning in that topic area. In practice, educators use a variety of approaches to curriculum content, including using just one comprehensive curriculum, using a domain-specific curriculum to supplement a comprehensive curriculum (e.g., *HighScope* supplemented by *Numbers Plus* math [Wakabayashi et al., 2020]), and combining several domain-specific curricula. For example, Boston's public preschool program combined two domain-specific curricula with strong evidence of effectiveness—a math curriculum called *Building Blocks* (Clements & Sarama, 2007) and a language- and literacy-focused curriculum called *Opening the World of Learning* (Schickedanz & Dickinson, 2005)—to support children's learning in those two domains (Weiland & Yoshikawa, 2013). More recently, Boston developed its own comprehensive curriculum—*Focus on PreK*—based on *Opening the World of Learning* and *Building Blocks*; it includes separate programs for children ages 3 and 4 years. The content of the curriculum addresses Massachusetts state pre-K standards, including approaches to learning, literacy, language, social-emotional learning, social studies, science and engineering, and the arts. In addition, the 2023 revision includes a focus on equitable literacy and projects (Boston Public Schools Department of Early Childhood, 2023).

About half (n = 88) of the preschool curricula identified in the literature search address multiple developmental domains—usually from four to eight domains. Most comprehensive preschool curricula address the domains of literacy/language, mathematics, science, social-emotional learning, and the arts. Comprehensive curricula are especially popular in Head Start programs because the Head Start Program Performance Standards require that curricula be aligned with the Head Start Early Learning Outcomes Framework and state early learning standards, which vary from state to state. In addition, curricula must educate the "whole child," offering developmentally appropriate learning experiences in the domains of language, literacy, social-emotional development, mathematics, science, social studies, creative arts, and physical development (U.S. Department of Health and Human Services, 2016).

Of the curricula identified in the literature review, about half are domain specific, with nearly half of those focused on literacy and language. The second most common domain-specific curricula target social-emotional development. Few domain-specific curricula center on mathematics, science, social studies, or the arts. These findings are consistent with prior research on teachers' and families' beliefs about language and literacy, which tend to view language/literacy development as more important than math development (see NRC, 2009, for a review). These results also echo the core findings from a recent National Academies (2022) report on science and engineering in preschool through the elementary grades—that science is seldom attended to in the early grades and that language and literacy is prioritized over other domains.

Family Child Care Settings

Preschool education can be offered in various settings, including public schools, Head Start agencies, private schools, private child care centers, and home-based or family child care. These settings vary in characteristics, funding sources, and requirements (Jenkins et al., 2019). Although most published preschool curricula are designed to be implemented in any educational setting or program, the curricula do not always meet the needs of family child care providers. These settings stand apart from the other types in that they serve small, mixed-age groups of children (typically, ages 0–5 years), so they need curricula that can be used not only with preschoolers but also with younger children (Bromer et al., 2021). In reviewing the evidence, the committee found limited information on family child care and few commercial preschool curricula (with the exception of *The Creative Curriculum for Family Child Care* and *Redleaf Family Child Care Curriculum*) that target family child care or offer guidance in adapting the curriculum to mixed-age groups. In addition, family child care providers have shared in prior studies (e.g., School Readiness Consulting [SRC], 2019, 2021) that most curricula cater to center- or school-based providers that serve single-age or narrow age-range groups and have more staff and children.

Preschool Curricula by Availability

The landscape of preschool curricula includes those that can be purchased as commercial off-the-shelf packages; those that have been developed for public use but are not widely available (and may or may not be included in the research literature); those that are proprietary and were developed for use in specific private preschool programs, which are not available for purchase; and those that were developed locally and were designed by local educators or districts for use in their own classrooms, but are not intended for public distribution (Jenkins et al., 2018).

Most preschool curricula are commercially available, and publishing companies have a significant influence on curriculum uptake by preschool programs (Jenkins et al., 2018; SRC, 2022). Preschool curricula are often created by educational researchers and practitioners and then sold to programs by publishers (Jenkins et al., 2018). The committee found that over the past 20 years, McGraw-Hill has published the largest number of preschool curricula—14 of the 172 identified in the literature search. During this same period, most other large curriculum publishers (e.g., Kaplan Early Learning, Brookes Publishing, Pearson) produced 3–6 curricula. In total, 17% of the identified curricula (30 of 172) were sold by medium to large publishing companies. A small proportion of the identified curricula were commercialized by universities or by small publishing companies. These curricula are typically less well known and have a smaller market share than curricula published by large companies. Importantly, the committee's literature review found, based on the reviewed publications and publishers' websites, that none of the commercially available curricula are described as grounded in equity principles, anti-bias approaches, or cultural responsiveness (SRC, 2022)—although, as discussed below, some curricula offer suggestions for incorporating children's and families' cultures.

Proprietary and locally developed curricula are unavailable to the public. The literature review revealed that 17 (10%) of the existing curricula were developed by private child care organizations and are not publicly available. For example, KinderCare Learning Centers—a for-profit operator of more than 1,300 child care facilities across 39 states and the District of Columbia—developed a comprehensive preschool curriculum that is not commercially available (*Early Foundations Curriculum for Prekindergarten*) and is used solely in its facilities.[4]

---

[4] See https://www.kindercare.com/our-centers#AL for more information on KinderCare.

Additionally, preschool curricula developed by local educators are often unavailable to the public (Jenkins et al., 2018). Locally developed curricula may incorporate components of various commercial curricula and/or activities that local teachers have created (Jenkins et al., 2018). Nationally representative surveys indicate that locally developed curricula are especially common in family child care settings and private child care centers, where teachers/providers generally have more flexibility to design their own lesson plans and assessment tools (Doran et al., 2022; Jenkins et al., 2019; National Survey of Early Care and Education Project Team, 2015).

In essence, very few preschool curricula are freely available. Two comprehensive curricula (*CIRCLE Pre-K Curriculum* and *Focus on Pre-K*) and two domain-specific curricula (*Problem Solvers*, a math curriculum, and *Read It Again–PreK*, a literacy curriculum) are offered for free in their digital format. These curricula were developed through collaborative partnerships involving academics, teachers, administrators, and district- or state-level leaders (see Justice & McGinty, 2013; McCormick et al., 2024). While research on *CIRCLE Pre-K* and *Problem Solvers* is scant, there is growing empirical evidence of the positive effects on children's outcomes of *Read It Again* (see Durán et al., 2016; Hilbert & Eis, 2014; Justice et al., 2008; Mashburn et al., 2016) and *Focus on Pre-K*[5] (McCormick et al., 2024; Weiland, 2016; Weiland & Yoshikawa, 2013). The free curricula are not as well known or widely used as commercially available curricula, and the limited number of free or low-cost curricula, as well as the lack of public awareness and low uptake of those that exist, may be a factor contributing to differences in curriculum use.

Culturally and Linguistically Responsive Program Approaches and Curricula

A number of notable small-scale longitudinal studies from the 1960s and 1970s demonstrated that high-quality early childhood educational experiences have the potential to convey long-term benefits for children, including improved school performance, higher future earnings, health, and well-being (Campbell et al., 2002, 2012; National Academies, 2023a; Schweinhart et al., 2005). Yet while these rigorously reviewed programs (e.g., Abecedarian Project, HighScope Perry Preschool study, Chicago Child–Parent Center study) have resulted in long-term positive outcomes for children, some scholars have criticized the approaches used in these older studies (e.g., terminology, deficit perspective), how quality was defined, and lack of attention to the lived experiences of young children from diverse backgrounds and contexts (Allen et al.,

---

[5] https://www.bpsearlylearning.org/focus-on-prek

2021; Bruno & Iruka, 2022; Derman-Sparks & Moore, 2016; National Academies, 2023a).

The philosophies underpinning existing early childhood programs often were historically grounded in one of two perspectives: the first held that "lower income families were incapable of properly socializing their children"; the second emphasized the "potential benefits that would accrue to young children from a program attuned to their developmental needs—one that also prepared them for elementary school," noting that "as far back as the 1820s and 1830s, infant education was promoted as a kind of 'head start' for children's educational careers" (Cahan, 1989, pp. 10–11). However, programs that focused on enrichment were available only for middle- and upper-income White families, creating a two-tier system.

The goal of programs serving children from poor families, such as the early programs in Boston and the federal and religious boarding schools targeting Native American children, was to provide them with moral training, assimilate them into the larger society, and suppress their languages and cultural identity (Newland, 2022). Thus, while the underlying philosophical premise of early childhood curriculum is ostensibly focused on child-initiated experiences, inquiry, discovery, and the development of social competence, without consideration of their cultural and linguistic strengths, the implementation of these curricula for Black, Indigenous, and other children of color; multilingual children; children with disabilities; and children living in poverty may have unintentionally focused on "fixing" them to remedy their "cultural deprivation" under the assumption that "other" cultural groups (apart from White European, middle-class families) are unable to support children's holistic development.

In contrast, contemporary scholars advocate for revisiting these early models with strengths-based program approaches that consider the relevance and sensitivity of program outcomes, processes, and practices to children's sociocultural heritage, language, cultural values, and healthy racial identity development (National Academies, 2023a). Strengths-based approaches also incorporate children's sociocultural context into the program design (Allen et al., 2021; Bruno & Iruka, 2022). Such strengths-based approaches are "rooted in respect and appreciation for the role of culture in children's learning and development" (National Center on Early Childhood Development, Teaching, and Learning, 2020, p. 10).

As noted earlier, however, although contemporary approaches (e.g., culturally responsive teaching [Gay, 2018], culturally relevant pedagogy [Ladson-Billings, 1995]) view curricula that acknowledge and respect difference and diversity as a goal, early childhood curricula firmly rooted in the theoretical values and worldviews of the diversity of cultures and languages of Black, Indigenous, and other children of color are lacking. Few curricula today are considered to show full evidence of cultural responsiveness—that is, the curriculum offers specific guidance and teaching strategies related to cultural responsiveness embedded throughout the materials (National Center on Early Childhood Development, Teaching, and Learning, 2020). The commissioned literature review found that among the 17 mainstream preschool curricula identified, only 5—*The Creative Curriculum for Preschool, Galileo Pre-K Online Curriculum, HighScope Preschool Curriculum, Frog Street Pre-K*, and *World of Wonders*—showed moderate evidence of cultural responsiveness (i.e., the curricula provide general guidance on effective practices, but do not provide specific, embedded teaching strategies throughout the materials). Moreover, while these curricula provide some guidance for teachers on how to adapt lessons and materials to children's diverse home culture and languages, no specific strategies are included to help teachers interact with children and their families, create culturally responsive learning experiences, and use relevant instructional resources, although home-based curricula are more effective in this regard (SRC, 2022). Such curriculum adaptations may be especially helpful for teachers who are unfamiliar with culturally responsive, anti-bias curriculum and teaching practices, and teachers who are new to such approaches often need guidance on putting them into practice and incorporating their students' identities and languages into daily classroom activities (Derman-Sparks & A.B.C. Task Force, 1989; Derman-Sparks & Edwards, 2020; Kimura et al., 2022; Nganga, 2015). Thus, curriculum can serve as a scaffold for teachers to move from theoretical to practical understanding of cultural and linguistic responsiveness and anti-bias education (Nganga, 2015).

Some preschool curricula not yet considered mainstream warrant recognition for their cultural responsiveness. For example, the publicly available *Focus on K0/K1* curricula used by Boston Public Schools are guided by an asset-based approach to classroom cultural diversity. In professional development materials focused on teachers' cultural competency, it is emphasized that "cultural responsiveness is not just celebrating holidays, different customs, traditions, etc. but also actively challenging bias, stereotypes, and building children's ability to do the same" (Ramsey, 2020). Cultural responsiveness is made visible in the classroom through classroom materials (e.g., images and resources representative of the children in the classroom and the wider world, nursery rhymes and music from around the world), processes (i.e., providing children with background information so they can interact meaningfully with instructional content), and products (i.e., making children's learning visible to highlight diverse cultural understandings and experiences). Recently, researchers at New York University developed a Culturally Responsive Curriculum Scorecard (Bryan-Gooden et al., 2019), which consists of checklists intended to help place specific practices, instructional materials, and interactions on a continuum from culturally responsive to culturally destructive.

While some curricula are designed to promote culturally responsive instruction, recent literature highlights the need to go beyond responsiveness and actively practice anti-bias pedagogy. Anti-bias instruction goes beyond celebrating diversity, infusing everything that happens in a program—including interactions among teachers, children, families, and administrators—and shaping how the curriculum is implemented every day (Derman-Sparks & Edwards, 2020). Anti-bias instruction fulfills four distinct goals: "support children's development of a confident sense of identity without needing to feel superior to others; an ease with human diversity; a sense of fairness and justice; the skills of empowerment and the ability to stand up for themselves or for others" (Derman-Sparks & Edwards, 2020). However, there is no evidence that any present curriculum is explicitly grounded in anti-bias/anti-racist principles, although scholars (e.g., Husband & Escayg, 2022) have laid out theoretical models for such curricula.

There is a need to address the ecosystem of early childhood curricula, from publishers to developers, as well as to interrogate the theoretical frameworks that guide curriculum development and implementation. Also needed is explicit attention to how curriculum and pedagogy (along with other processes, such as assessment) converge to create culturally incongruent and inequitable learning opportunities. Curricula that fail to take the lived experiences of the plurality of minoritized children, families, and communities into account merely maintain the status quo.

REPORT ORGANIZATION

The committee was charged with developing a new vision for high-quality preschool curriculum that would support equitable curriculum development, state- and program-level preschool curriculum decisions and selection, and local curriculum implementation. The remaining chapters of this report present the committee's findings, conclusions, recommendations, as well as areas for future research. As a foundation for the committee's vision, Chapter 2 describes the current evidence base for the effectiveness and implementation of high-quality preschool curriculum. This is followed in Chapter 3 by an overview of findings from neuroscience and other research on how children develop and learn optimally. Building on this evidence base, Chapter 4 articulates the committee's new vision for high-quality, equity-driven curricula and provides guidance for curriculum developers and decision makers. Chapter 5 then describes conditions for learning environments needed to effectively implement curriculum and early education for all children. Chapter 6 looks at specialized and targeted curricula for children with disabilities, while Chapter 7 focuses on high-quality curricula and practices that support multilingual learners. Chapter 8 reviews state- and program-level policies that impact and guide the selection and implementation of high-quality curricula. Chapter 9 examines variations in curricular effects. Finally, Chapter 10 presents the committee's key conclusions and recommendations regarding support for high-quality, equitable curriculum development, state- and program-level preschool curriculum selection, and local curriculum implementation. This chapter also outlines key areas for future research based on gaps identified by the committee during its review of the literature, as well as resources needed to support research that can produce valid and reliable estimates of variations in curriculum effects and identify sources of variation.

REFERENCES

Adair, J. K. (2015). *The impact of discrimination on the early schooling experiences of children from immigrant families*. Migration Policy Institute. https://www.migrationpolicy.org/research/impact-discrimination-early-schooling-experiences-children-immigrant-families

Administration for Children and Families. (2022). *Innovations in tribal early childhood programs: Findings from a webinar series with practitioners, researchers, and policymakers*. U.S. Department of Health and Human Services. https://www.acf.hhs.gov/sites/default/files/documents/ecd/Innovations-in-Tribal-Early-Childhood-Programs-Report-on-a-Webinar-Series.pdf

Agyemang, C., Bhopal, R., & Bruijnzeels, M. (2005). Negro, Black, Black African, African Caribbean, African American or what? Labelling African origin populations in the health arena in the 21st century. *Journal of Epidemiology & Community Health, 59*(12), 1014–1018. https://doi.org/10.1136%2Fjech.2005.035964

Allen, R., Shapland, D. L., Neitzel, J., & Iruka, I. U. (2021). Creating anti-racist early childhood spaces. *Young Children, 76*(2), 49–54. https://fpg.unc.edu/publications/viewpoint-creating-anti-racist-early-childhood-spaces

Barnett, W. S., & Jung, K. (2021). *Seven impacts of the pandemic on young children and their parents: Initial findings from NIEER's December 2020 Preschool Learning Activities Survey*. National Institute for Early Education Research. https://nieer.org/research-library/seven-impacts-pandemic-young-children-their-parents

Bassok, D., & Galdo, E. (2016). Inequality in preschool quality? Community-level disparities in access to high-quality learning environments. *Early Education and Development, 27*(1), 128–144. https://doi.org/10.1080/10409289.2015.1057463

Belfield, C. R., Nores, M., Barnett, S., & Schweinhart, L. (2006). The High/Scope Perry preschool program cost-benefit analysis using data from the age-40 followup. *Journal of Human Resources, 41*(1), 162–190. http://www.jstor.org/stable/40057261

Boston Public Schools Department of Early Childhood. (2023). *Focus on Pre-K: Orientation to the revised curriculum*. www.bpsearlylearning.org

Branscombe, N. A., Burcham, J. G., Castle, K., & Surbeck, E. (2013). *Early childhood curriculum: A constructivist perspective* (2nd ed.). Routledge.

Bredekamp, S., & Joseph, G. E. (2024). *Effective practices in early childhood education: Building a foundation* (5th ed.). Pearson Education.

Bromer, J., Porter, T., Jones, C., Ragonese-Barnes, M., & Orland, J. (2021). *Quality in home-based child care: A review of selected literature* (OPRE Report No. 2021-136). Office of Planning, Research, and Evaluation, Administration for Children and Families, U.S. Department of Health and Human Services. https://www.acf.hhs.gov/opre/report/quality-home-based-child-care-review-selected-literature

Bronfenbrenner, U. (Ed.). (2004). *Making human beings human: Bioecological perspectives on human development*. Sage Publications, Inc.

Bronfenbrenner, U., & Crouter, A. C. (1983). The evolution of environmental models in developmental research. In W. Kessen (Series Ed.) & P. H. Mussen (Vol. Ed.), *Handbook of child psychology: Vol. 1. History, theory, and methods* (4th ed., pp. 357–414). Wiley.

Bronfenbrenner, U., & Morris, P. A. (2006). The bioecological model of human development. In R. M. Lerner & W. Damon (Eds.), *Handbook of child psychology* (6th ed.), *Vol. 1, Theoretical models of human development* (pp. 793–828). John Wiley & Sons, Inc.

Bruno, E. P., & Iruka, I. U. (2022). Reexamining the Carolina Abecedarian project using an anti-racist perspective: Implications for early care and education research. *Early Childhood Research Quarterly, 58*, 165–176. https://doi.org/10.1016/j.ecresq.2021.09.001

Bryan-Gooden, J., Hester, M., & Peoples, L. (2019). *Culturally responsive curriculum scorecard.* Metropolitan Center for Research on Equity and the Transformation of Schools. New York University. https://steinhardt.nyu.edu/metrocenter/ejroc/services/culturally-responsive-curriculum-scorecards

Burchinal, M. R., & Farran, D. C. (2021). What does research tell us about ECE programs? In *Foundation for Child Development, Getting it right: The conversation guide for preparing the next generation of implementation researchers* (pp. 19–27).

Burchinal, M., Soliday Hong, S. L., Sabol, T. J., Forestieri, N., Peisner-Feinberg, E., Tarullo, L., & Zaslow, M. (2016). *Quality rating and improvement systems: Secondary data analyses of psychometric properties of scale development* (OPRE Report No. 2016-26). Office of Planning, Research and Evaluation, Administration for Children and Families, U.S. Department of Health and Human Services. https://www.acf.hhs.gov/sites/default/files/documents/opre/qris_secondary_analysis_report_for_publication_b508.pdf

Cagliari, P., Castagnetti, M., Giudici, C., Rinaldi, C., Vecchi, V., & Moss, P. (Eds.). (2016). *Loris Malaguzzi and the schools of Reggio Emilia: A selection of his writings and speeches, 1945–1993.* Routledge.

Cahan, E. D. (1989). *Past caring: A history of U.S. preschool care and education for the poor, 1820–1965.* National Center for Children in Poverty. https://researchconnections.org/sites/default/files/pdf/rc2088.pdf

Campbell, F. A., Pungello, E. P., Burchinal, M., Kainz, K., Pan, Y., Wasik, B. A., Barbarin, O. A., Sparling, J., & Ramey, C. T. (2012). Adult outcomes as a function of an early childhood educational program: An Abecedarian Project follow-up. *Developmental Psychology, 48*(4), 1033–1043. https://doi.org/10.1037/a0026644

Campbell, F. A., Ramey, C. T., Pungello, E., Sparling, J., & Miller-Johnson, S. (2002). Early childhood education: Young adult outcomes from the Abecedarian Project. *Applied Developmental Science, 6*(1), 42–57. https://doi.org/10.1207/S1532480XADS0601_05

Center on the Developing Child. (2016). *From best practices to breakthrough impacts: A science-based approach to building a more promising future for young children and families.* Harvard University. https://developingchild.harvard.edu/wp-content/uploads/2016/05/From_Best_Practices_to_Breakthrough_Impacts-3.pdf

———. (2020). *How racism can affect child development.* Harvard University. https://developingchild.harvard.edu/resources/racism-and-ecd

Childcare.gov. (n.d.). *Prekindergarten programs.* Administration for Children & Families, Office of Child Care. https://childcare.gov/consumer-education/prekindergarten-programs

Clements, D. H., & Sarama, J. (2007). Effects of a preschool mathematics curriculum: Summative research on the Building Blocks project. *Journal for Research in Mathematics Education, 38*(2), 136–163. http://www.jstor.org/stable/30034954

Craig, H. K., & Washington, J. A. (2006). *Malik goes to school: Examining the language skills of African American students from preschool–5th grade.* Lawrence Erlbaum Associates, Inc.

Cui, J., & Natzke, L. (2021). *Early childhood program participation: 2019* (NCES Report No. 2020-075REV). National Household Education Surveys Program. National Center for Education Statistics, Institute of Education Sciences, U.S. Department of Education. https://nces.ed.gov/pubs2020/2020075REV.pdf

Curenton, S. M., Iruka, I., & Durden, T. (2017). Introduction. In S. M. Curenton, I. Iruka, & T. Durden (Eds.), *African American children in early childhood education: Making the case for policy investments in families, schools, and communities advances in race and ethnicity in education* (Vol. 5, pp. 3–13). Emerald Group Publishing Limited. https://doi.org/10.1108/S2051-231720170000005001

Derman-Sparks, L., & A.B.C. Task Force. (1989). *Anti-bias curriculum: Tools for empowering young children*. National Association for the Education of Young Children.

Derman-Sparks, L., & Edwards, J. O. (2020). *Anti-bias education for young children and ourselves* (2nd ed.). National Association for the Education of Young Children.

Derman-Sparks, L., & Moore, E. K. (2016). Our proud heritage: Two teachers look back—The Ypsilanti Perry Preschool, part I. *Young Children, 71*(4). https://www.naeyc.org/resources/pubs/yc/sep2016/ypsilanti-perry-part-1

DeVries, R., Zan, B., Hildebrandt, C., Edmiaston, R., & Sales, C. (2002). *Developing constructivist early childhood curriculum: Practical principles and activities*. Teachers College Press.

Dobbins, D., McCready, M., & Rackas, L. (2016). *Unequal access: Barriers to early childhood education for boys of color*. Robert Wood Johnson Foundation. https://www.childcareaware.org/boysofcolor

Doran, E., Reid, N., Bernstein, S., Nguyen, T., Dang, M., Li, A., Kopack Klein, A., Rakibullah, S., Scott, M., Cannon, J., Harrington, J., Larson, A., Tarullo, L., & Malone, L. (2022). *A portrait of Head Start classrooms and programs in spring 2020: FACES 2019 Descriptive data tables and study design* (OPRE Report No. 2022-15). Office of Planning, Research, and Evaluation, Administration for Children and Families, U.S. Department of Health and Human Services. https://www.acf.hhs.gov/opre/report/portrait-head-start-classrooms-and-programs-spring-2020-faces-2019-descriptive-data

Durán, L. K., Gorman, B. K., Kohlmeier, T., & Callard, C. (2016). The feasibility and usability of the Read It Again Dual Language and literacy curriculum. *Early Childhood Education Journal, 44*(5), 453–461. https://doi.org/10.1007/s10643-015-0729-y

Engle, P. L., Fernald, L. C. H., Alderman, H., Behrman, J., O'Gara, C., Yousafzai, A., De Mello, M. C., Hidrobo, M., Ulkuer, N., Ertem, I., & Iltus, S. (2011). Strategies for reducing inequalities and improving developmental outcomes for young children in low-income and middle-income countries. *Lancet, 378*(9799), 1339–1353. https://doi.org/10.1016/S0140-6736(11)60889-1

Epstein, A. S. (2014). *Essentials of active learning in preschool: Getting to know the HighScope curriculum*. HighScope Press.

Fantuzzo, J. W., Gadsden, V. L., & McDermott, P. A. (2011). An integrated curriculum to improve mathematics, language, and literacy for Head Start children. *American Educational Research Journal, 48*(3), 763–793. https://psycnet.apa.org/doi/10.3102/0002831210385446

Freire, P. (1973). *Education for critical consciousness*. Seabury Press.

Friedman-Krauss, A. H., Barnett, W. S., Garver, K. A., Hodges, K. S., Weisenfeld, G., Gardiner, B. A., & Jost, T. M. (2022). *The state of preschool 2021: State preschool yearbook*. National Institute for Early Education Research. https://nieer.org/state-preschool-yearbooks-yearbook2021

García Coll, C., Lamberty, G., Jenkins, R., McAdoo, H. P., Crnic, K., Wasik, B. H., & Vázquez García, H. (1996). An integrative model for the study of developmental competencies in minority children. *Child Development, 67*(5), 1891–1914. https://doi.org/10.1111/j.1467-8624.1996.tb01834.x

Gay, G. (2018). *Culturally responsive teaching: Theory, research, and practice*. Teachers College Press.

Gillispie, C. (2019). *Young learners, missed opportunities: Ensuring that Black and Latino children have access to high-quality state-funded preschool*. Education Trust. https://edtrust.org/wp-content/uploads/2014/09/Young-Learners-Missed-Opportunities.pdf

Gort, M., & Sembiante, S. F. (2015). Navigating hybridized language learning spaces through translanguaging pedagogy: Dual language preschool teachers' languaging practices in support of emergent bilingual children's performance of academic discourse. *International Multilingual Research Journal, 9*(1), 7–25. https://doi.org/10.1080/19313152.2014.981775

Hancock, R. E. (2017). Global citizenship education: Emancipatory practice in a New York preschool. *Journal of Research in Childhood Education, 31*(4), 571–580. https://doi.org/10.1080/02568543.2017.1346731

Heckman, J. J., & Karapakula, G. (2019a). *Intergenerational and intragenerational externalities of the Perry Preschool Project* (NBER Working Paper No. 25889). National Bureau of Economic Research. https://doi.org/10.3386/w25889

———. (2019b). *The Perry Preschoolers at late midlife: A study in design-specific inference* (NBER Working Paper No. 25888). National Bureau of Economic Research. https://doi.org/10.3386/w25888

Hilbert, D. D., & Eis, S. D. (2014). Early intervention for emergent literacy development in a collaborative community pre-kindergarten. *Early Childhood Education Journal, 42*(2), 105–113. https://doi.org/10.1007/s10643-013-0588-3

Hilliard, A. G. (1985). Kemetic concepts in education. *Journal of African Civilizations, 6*(2), 133–153.

———. (1986). Pedagogy in ancient Kemet. In M. Karenga & J. H. Carruthers (Eds.), *Kemet and the African world view: Research, rescue and restoration* (pp. 131–148). University of Sankore Press.

Husband, T., & Escayg, K. A. (2022). "Safe and sound": Anti-racist curriculum models for the early years classroom. *Mid-Western Educational Researcher, 34*(2), 168. https://scholarworks.bgsu.edu/mwer/vol34/iss2/5

Institute of Medicine & National Research Council. (2015). *Transforming the workforce for children birth through age 8: A unifying foundation.* National Academies Press. https://doi.org/10.17226/19401

Iruka, I. U. (2020). Using a social determinants of early learning framework to eliminate educational disparities and opportunity gaps. In *Getting it right: Using implementation research to improve outcomes in early care and education* (pp. 63–86). Foundation for Child Development. https://www.fcdus.org/assets/2020/06/GettingitRight_UsingImplementationResearchtoImproveOutcomesinECE_ 2020.pdf

Iruka, I. U., Gardner-Neblett, N., Telfer, N. A., Ibekwe-Okafor, N., Curenton, S. M., Sims, J., Sansbury, A. B., & Neblett, E. W. (2022). Effects of racism on child development: Advancing anti-racist developmental science. *Annual Review of Developmental Psychology, 4,* 109–132. https://doi.org/10.1146/annurev-devpsych-121020-031339

Jenkins, J., & Duncan, G. (2017). Do prekindergarten curricula matter? In D. Phillips and K. Dodge (Eds.), *The current state of scientific knowledge on pre-kindergarten effects* (pp. 37–44). Brookings Institution and Duke University.

Jenkins, J., Whitaker, A., Nguyen, T., & Yu, W. (2019). Distinctions without a difference? Preschool curricula and children's development. *Journal of Research on Educational Effectiveness, 12,* 514–549. https://doi.org/10.1080%2F19345747.2019.1631420

Jenkins, J. M., Duncan, G. J., Auger, A., Bitler, M., Domina, T., & Burchinal, M. (2018). Boosting school readiness: Should preschool teachers target skills or the whole child? *Economics of Education Review, 65,* 107–125. https://doi.org/10.1016%2Fj.econedurev.2018.05.001

Jones, C. P. (2014). Systems of power, axes of inequity: Parallels, intersections, braiding the strands. *Medical Care, 52*(10), S71–S75. http://www.jstor.org/stable/24465890

Justice, L. M., & McGinty, A. S. (2013). *Read It Again–PreK!: A preschool curriculum supplement to promote language and literacy foundations.* Crane Center for Early Childhood Research and Policy, College of Education and Human Ecology, The Ohio State University. https://readitagain.osu.edu

Justice, L. M., Mashburn, A., Pence, K. L., & Wiggins, A. (2008). Experimental evaluation of a preschool language curriculum: Influence on children's expressive language skills. *Journal of Speech, Language and Hearing Research, 51*(4), 983–1001. https://doi.org/10.1044/1092-4388(2008/072)

Kimura, A. M., Antón-Oldenburg, M., & Pinderhughes, E. E. (2022). Developing and teaching an anti-bias curriculum in a public elementary school: Leadership, K–1 teachers', and young children's experiences. *Journal of Research in Childhood Education, 36*(2), 183–202. https://doi.org/10.1080/02568543.2021.1912222

Ladson-Billings, G. (1995). Toward a theory of culturally relevant pedagogy. *American Educational Research Journal, 32*(3), 465–491. https://lmcreadinglist.pbworks.com/f/Ladson-Billings%20%281995%29.pdf

Lascarides, V. C., & Hinitz, B. F. (2000). *History of early childhood education*. Routledge.

Lillard, A. S. (2013). Playful learning and Montessori education. *Namta Journal, 38*(2), 137–174. https://files.eric.ed.gov/fulltext/EJ1077161.pdf

Limlingan, M. C., McWayne, C. M., Sanders, E. A., & López, M. L. (2020). Classroom language contexts as predictors of Latinx preschool dual language learners' school readiness. *American Educational Research Journal, 57*(1), 339–70. https://doi.org/10.3102/0002831219855694

Magnuson, K. A., Ruhm, C., & Waldfogel, J. (2007). Does prekindergarten improve school preparation and performance? *Economics of Education Review, 26*(1), 33–51. https://doi.org/10.1016/j.econedurev.2005.09.008

Malik, R., Hamm, K., Schochet, L., Novoa, C., Workman, S., & Jessen-Howard, S. (2018). *America's child care deserts in 2018*. Center for American Progress. https://www.americanprogress.org/article/americas-child-care-deserts-2018

Mashburn, A., Justice, L. M., McGinty, A., & Slocum, L. (2016). The impacts of a scalable intervention on the language and literacy development of rural pre-kindergartners. *Applied Developmental Science, 20*(1), 61–78. https://doi.org/10.1080/10888691.2015.1051622

Matusov, E., & Hayes, R. (2000). Sociocultural critique of Piaget and Vygotsky. *New Ideas in Psychology, 18*(2–3), 215–239. http://dx.doi.org/10.1016/S0732-118X(00)00009-X

McCormick, M. P., MacDowell, C., Weiland, C., Hsueh, J., Maier, M., Pralica, M., Maves, S., Snow, C., & Sachs, J. (2024). Instructional alignment is associated with PreK persistence: Evidence from the Boston Public Schools. *Early Childhood Research Quarterly, 67*, 89–100. https://doi.org/10.1016/j.ecresq.2023.11.008

Meek, S., Iruka, I. U., Allen, R., Yazzie, D., Fernandez, V., Catherine, E., McIntosh, K., Gordon, L., Gilliam, W., Hemmeter, M. L., Blevins, D., & Powell, T. (2020). *Start with equity: Fourteen priorities to dismantle systemic racism in early care and education*. Children's Equity Project. https://childandfamilysuccess.asu.edu/cep

Melhuish, E., Ereky-Stevens, K., Petrogiannis, K., Ariescu, A., Penderi, E., Rentzou, K., Tawell, A., Slot, P., Broekhuizen, M., & Leseman, P. (2015). *A review of research on the effects of Early Childhood Education and Care (ECEC) upon child development: Curriculum Quality Analysis and Impact Review of European Early Childhood Education and Care*. CARE. https://dspace.library.uu.nl/bitstream/handle/1874/326604/new_version_CARE_WP4_D4_1_Review_on_the_effe cts_of_ECEC.pdf?sequence=1

Melzi, G., Curenton, S., Harris, K., & Jarquin, C. (2021, May 26). CEED is embracing Latine. *CEED blog*. https://www.bu-ceed.org/community-blog/ceed-is-embracing-latine

Merriam Webster. (n.d.a). Marginalized. In *Merriam-Webster dictionary*. https://www.merriam-webster.com/dictionary/marginalized

———. (n.d.b). Racialization. In *Merriam-Webster dictionary*. https://www.merriam-webster.com/dictionary/racialization

Miranda, A. R., Perez-Brumer, A., & Charlton, B. M. (2023). Latino? Latinx? Latine? A call for inclusive categories in epidemiologic research. *American Journal of Epidemiology, 192*(12), 1929–1932. https://pubmed.ncbi.nlm.nih.gov/37392097/

Morris, S., & Smith, L. (2021, June 17). Examples of mixed-delivery early care and education systems. *Bipartisan Policy Center Blog.* https://bipartisanpolicy.org/blog/examples-of-mixed-delivery-early-care-and-education-systems

Muhammad, G. (2023). *Unearthing joy: A guide to culturally and Historically responsive teaching and learning.* Scholastic.

Nāone, C. K., & Au, K. (2010). Culture as a framework versus ingredient in early childhood education: A native Hawaiian perspective. In O. Saracho & B. Spodek (Eds.), *Contemporary perspectives on language and cultural diversity in early childhood education* (pp. 147–165). Information Age.

National Academies of Sciences, Engineering, and Medicine (National Academies). (2017). *Communities in action: Pathways to health equity.* National Academies Press.

———. (2018). *Transforming the financing of early care and education.* National Academies Press. https://doi.org/10.17226/24984

———. (2022). *Science and engineering in preschool through elementary grades: The brilliance of children and the strengths of educators.* National Academies Press. https://doi.org/10.17226/26215

———. (2023a). *Closing the opportunity gap for young children.* National Academies Press. https://doi.org/10.17226/26743

———. (2023b). *Reducing intergenerational poverty.* National Academies Press. https://doi.org/10.17226/27058

National Association for the Education of Young Children (NAEYC). (2018). *NAEYC early learning program standards.* https://www.naeyc.org/sites/default/files/globally-shared/downloads/PDFs/accreditation/early-learning/overview_of_the_standards.pdf

———. (2019). *Advancing equity in early childhood education* (Position statement). https://www.naeyc.org/sites/default/files/globally-shared/downloads/PDFs/resources/position-statements/advancingequitypositionstatement.pdf

———. (2020). *Developmentally appropriate practice* (Position statement). https://www.naeyc.org/sites/default/files/globally-shared/downloads/PDFs/resources/position-statements/dap-statement_0.pdf

———. (2022). *Developmentally appropriate practice in early childhood programs serving children from birth through age 8* (4th ed.).

National Association for the Education of Young Children & National Association of Early Childhood Specialists in State Departments of Education. (2003). *Early childhood curriculum, assessment, and program evaluation: Building an effective, accountable system in programs for children birth through age 8* (Position statement). https://www.naeyc.org/sites/default/files/globally-shared/downloads/PDFs/resources/position-statements/pscape.pdf

National Center for Education Statistics. (2022). *Table 202.25. Percentage of 3- to 5-year-old children enrolled in school, by race/ethnicity and state: 2021* [Table]. U.S. Department of Commerce, Census Bureau, American Community Survey; U.S. Department of Education. https://nces.ed.gov/programs/digest/d22/tables/dt22_202.25.asp

National Center on Child Care Quality Improvement. (2018). *National accreditation organizations for early childhood programs.* https://www.regent.edu/app/uploads/sites/5/2018/12/National-Accreditation-Organizations-for-Early-Childhood-Programs.pdf

National Center on Early Childhood Development, Teaching, and Learning. (2020). *Preschool curriculum consumer report.* Office of Head Start, U.S. Department of Health and Human Services. https://eclkc.ohs.acf.hhs.gov/sites/default/files/featured_file/preschool-curriculum-consumer-report-032519.pdf

National Institute for Early Education Research. (2019). *Benchmarks for high-quality pre K: Checklist* [Infographic]. Rutgers Graduate School of Education. https://nieer.org/sites/default/files/2023-08/benchmarks-check-list-png-410x1024.png

National Institutes of Health (2024). *Minoritized populations*. https://www.nih.gov/nih-style-guide/race-national-origin#minoritized-populations

National Research Council (NRC). (2002). *Scientific research in education*. National Academies Press. https://doi.org/10.17226/10236

———. (2009). *Mathematics learning in early childhood: Paths toward excellence and equity*. National Academies Press. https://doi.org/10.17226/12519

National Survey of Early Care and Education Project Team. (2015). *Measuring predictors of quality in early care and education settings in the National Survey of Early Care and Education* (OPRE Report No. 2015-93). Office of Planning, Research and Evaluation, Administration for Children and Families, U.S. Department of Health and Human Services. https://www.acf.hhs.gov/sites/default/files/documents/opre/measuring_predictors_of_quality_mpoq_in_the_nsece_final_092315_b508.pdf

Newland, B. (2022). *Federal Indian boarding school initiative investigative report*. Bureau of Indian Affairs. https://www.bia.gov/sites/default/files/dup/inline-files/bsi_investigative_report_may_2022_508.pdf

Nganga, L. (2015). Culturally responsive and anti-biased teaching benefits early childhood preservice teachers. *Journal of Curriculum and Teaching, 4*(2), 1–16. https://doi.org/10.5430/jct.v4n2p1

Nores, M., & Barnett, W. S. (2014). *Access to high quality early care and education: Readiness and opportunity gaps in America* (Center on Enhancing Early Learning and National Institute for Early Education Policy Report). Center on Enhancing Early Learning Outcomes. https://nieer.org/wp-content/uploads/2014/05/ceelo_policy_report_access_quality_ece.pdf

Odom, S. L., Butera, G., Diamond, K. E., Hanson, M. J., Horn, E., Lieber, J., Palmer, S., Fleming, K., & Marquis, J. (2019). Efficacy of a comprehensive early childhood curriculum to enhance children's success. *Topics in Early Childhood Special Education, 39*(1), 19–31. https://doi.org/10.1177/0271121419827654

Penn, H. (1997). *Comparing nurseries: Staff and children in Italy, Spain and the UK*. Sage.

Phillips, D. A., Lipsey, M. W., Dodge, K. A., Haskins, R., Bassok, D., Burchinal, M. R., Duncan, G. J, Dynarski, M., Magnuson, K. A, & Weiland, C. (2017). Puzzling it out: The current state of scientific knowledge on pre-kindergarten effects: A consensus statement. In K. Dodge (Ed.), *The current state of scientific knowledge on pre-kindergarten effects* (pp. 19–30). Brookings Institution.

Pratt, A., & Fowler, T. (2022). *Deconstructing bias: Marginalization*. Eunice Kennedy Shriver National Institute of Child Health and Human Development. https://science.nichd.nih.gov/confluence/pages/viewpage.action?pageId=242975243

Ramsey, D. (2020, February 24). *Cultural competency* [Video]. YouTube. https://www.youtube.com/watch?v=6uMIwECHxDA

Reading, R., Haynes, R., & Shenassa, E. D. (2005). Neighborhood influences on child injury risk. *Children, Youth and Environments, 15*(1), 165–185. https://www.jstor.org/stable/10.7721/chilyoutenvi.15.1.0165

Reyhner, J., & Eder, J. (2017). *American Indian education: A history*. University of Oklahoma Press.

Reynolds, A. J., Ou, S., & Temple, J. A. (2018). A multicomponent, preschool to third grade preventive intervention and educational attainment at 35 years of age. *JAMA Pediatrics, 172*(3), 247–256. https://doi.org/10.1001/jamapediatrics.2017.4673

Schickedanz, J. A., & Dickinson, D. K. (2005). *Opening the world of learning*. Pearson Early Learning.

School Readiness Consulting (SRC). (2019). *Seattle Preschool Program process evaluation: Final cross-site report*. https://www.seattle.gov/documents/Departments/DEEL/FundingOpportunities/RFPs/2021/SPP_ProcessEvaluationReport_SchoolReadinessConsulting_2019.pdf

———. (2021). *Next steps for Michigan's Great Start to Quality: Findings from stakeholder engagement.* https://www.michigan.gov/-/media/Project/Websites/mde/ogs/cdc-2/landing_page_docs/michigan_findings_report_final.pdf?rev=e13641aa71294f0f9b347c03db3e0f5b

———. (2022). *Side by side: A playbook on centering and promoting equity in early education.* https://sidebysideplaybook.com/read/

Schweinhart, L. J., Montie, J., Xiang, Z., Barnett, W. S., Belfield, C. R., & Nores, M. (2005). *Lifetime effects: The High/Scope Perry Preschool study through age 40* (Monographs of the High/Scope Educational Research Foundation, No. 14). High/Scope Press. https://highscope.org/wp-content/uploads/2018/11/perry-preschool-summary-40.pdf

Shapiro, A., Martin, E., Weiland, C., & Unterman, R. (2019). If you offer it, will they come? Patterns of application and enrollment behavior in a universal prekindergarten context. *AERA Open, 5*(2). https://doi.org/10.1177/2332858419848442

Spencer, M. B., Dupree. D., & Hartmann, T. (1997). A phenomenological variant of ecological systems theory (PVEST): A self-organization perspective in context. *Development and Psychopathology, 9*(4), 817–833. https://doi.org/10.1017/s0954579497001454

Suárez-Orozco, C., Gaytán, F. X., Bang, H. J., Pakes, J., O'Connor, E., & Rhodes, J. (2010). Academic trajectories of newcomer immigrant youth. *Developmental Psychology, 46*(3), 602.

U.S. Department of Health and Human Services. (2016). *Head Start program performance standards.* https://eclkc.ohs.acf.hhs.gov/sites/default/files/pdf/hspps-appendix.pdf

Valentino, R. (2018). Will public pre-K really close achievement gaps? Gaps in prekindergarten quality between students and across states. *American Educational Research Journal, 55*(1), 79–116. https://doi.org/10.3102/0002831217732000

Wakabayashi, T., Andrade-Adaniya, F., Schweinhart, L. J., Xiang, Z., Marshall, B. A., & Markley, C. A. (2020). The impact of a supplementary preschool mathematics curriculum on children's early mathematics learning. *Early Childhood Research Quarterly, 53*, 329–342. https://doi.org/10.1016/j.ecresq.2020.04.002

Weiland, C. (2016). Impacts of the Boston prekindergarten program on the school readiness of young children with special needs. *Developmental Psychology, 52*(11), 1763–1776. https://doi.org/10.1037/dev0000168

Weiland, C., & Yoshikawa, H. (2013). Impacts of a prekindergarten program on children's mathematics, language, literacy, executive function, and emotional skills. *Child Development, 84*, 2112–2130. https://doi.org/10.1111/cdev.12099

Yoshikawa, H., Weiland, C., Brooks-Gunn, J., Burchinal, M. R., Espinosa, L. M., Gormley, W. T., Ludwig, J., Magnuson, K. A., Phillips, D.A., & Zaslow, M. J. (2013). *Investing in our future: The evidence base on preschool education.* Foundation for Child Development and Ann Arbor, MIL Society for Research in Child Development. https://www.fcd-us.org/assets/2016/04/Evidence-Base-on-Preschool-Education-FINAL.pdf

Zigler, E. F., & Bishop-Josef, S. J. (2006). The cognitive child versus the whole child: Lessons from 40 years of Head Start. In D. G. Singer, R. M. Golinkoff, & K. Hirsch-Pasek (Eds.), *Play = learning: How play motivates and enhances children's cognitive and social-emotional growth* (pp. 15–35). Oxford University Press.

2

Evidence on the Effectiveness of Preschool Curricula

Decades of research show that attending preschool (versus staying home with a family member) better prepares young children for kindergarten, with effects sometimes lasting into adulthood on important outcomes such as educational attainment and health (Heckman & Karapakula, 2019a,b; Phillips et al., 2017b; Reynolds et al., 2018; Yoshikawa et al., 2013). However, preschool programs are not equally effective; some children appear to learn more in some programs than others (Phillips et al., 2017b). Recently, research has examined the specific components that drive children's early learning gains in preschool programs (Weiland, 2018). One motivating factor for this shift has been extensive evidence that most public preschool programs are on average mediocre in their instructional quality, although they tend to score in the "good" range on organization, emotional climate, and structural factors (Burchinal, 2017; Weiland & Guerrero Rosada, 2022). Furthermore, and troubling with regard to equity, the programs attended by children from marginalized groups score lower on a range of quality metrics compared with those attended by their non-marginalized peers, and they rarely include languages other than English (Latham et al., 2021; Valentino, 2018; Weiland et al., 2022). Curriculum has emerged as one particularly potent component with the potential to move the needle on the stubbornly mediocre instructional quality of most public preschool programs, particularly those that disproportionately serve children from minoritized backgrounds (Chaudry et al., 2021).

Overall, research on the effects of preschool curricula on classroom processes and young children's learning is deep and broad. In curriculum evaluation studies, "curriculum effectiveness" is determined by comparing the outcomes for children who participate in a particular curriculum with the outcomes for similar children who did not participate in that curriculum (i.e., the control condition). The difference in outcomes between the two groups is described as the "average effect" of the curriculum. Multiple recent reviews and meta-analytic studies have summarized average effects of preschool curricula (e.g., Chambers et al., 2016; Jenkins et al., 2018; Phillips et al., 2017b; Yoshikawa et al., 2013); research in this area remains active, with studies of newer curricula and follow-up longitudinal studies into elementary school and beyond currently under way (e.g., Maier et al., 2022a; Sarama et al., 2017).

Important questions, however, remain unanswered. Given the diversity of early education settings, educators, and children, it is important to look not only at "average effects" of curriculum but also at the specific contexts and conditions under which curricula can succeed, and for which students (Weiss et al., 2014). Variation in curriculum effects is important if the size of the average difference between children who did and did not experience the curriculum differs systematically across groups of students, settings, delivery approaches, and outcomes. For example, a curriculum may be found to have a small average effect in improving students' early literacy skills, but the magnitude of the effect may vary substantially by preschool setting (e.g., Head Start versus child care center), by the experience of the educator delivering the curriculum, or by students' home language experiences and the outcomes measured.

From a policy perspective, understanding variation in curriculum effects is important because decision makers are often asked to make choices about the curriculum approaches that will best serve their communities and narrow early opportunity gaps for historically marginalized children. If the effects of curricula vary, there may not be a "one-size-fits-all" approach for choosing a preschool curriculum. Decision makers therefore need evidence about the extent to which curriculum effects vary, and the types of curricula that would be most effective for their specific settings, teachers, and students. Ideally, the curricula chosen will promote the learning of all students and will build on the strengths of children from diverse backgrounds.

This chapter reviews what is known about the effects of preschool curriculum, with a focus on how effects vary across several important dimensions, including curriculum type, outcomes used for assessing efficacy, student characteristics, teacher characteristics, preschool settings, and broader macro conditions. The chapter concludes with a discussion of gaps in the current evidence base and key conclusions that support the committee's recommendations for moving the field forward.

CURRICULUM TYPE

Curriculum is defined in this report as a cohesive set of principles, learning goals, intentional teaching strategies, activities, experiences, and materials designed to help children learn and thrive. The effects of preschool curricula may depend on the content included in a specific curriculum, as well as how it is delivered in different preschool settings. For example, effects may vary with the content or foci of the curriculum; on the pedagogical approaches used for teaching content or lessons; on the types of support materials available for implementing the curriculum, including professional development for teachers; and on the levels or intensity at which the curriculum is delivered. The effect of a curriculum will also depend on what the curriculum is being compared against (the control condition) and on what is defined as an outcome and how it is measured.

One important dimension on which preschool curricula vary is whether they purport to cover all developmental domains or a subset only (see Chapter 1). The most widely used curricula in publicly funded preschool programs tend to do the former, spanning language, literacy, mathematics, social-emotional skills, executive function, and motor skills, and sometimes science and social studies (Jenkins & Duncan, 2017). These curricula are commonly referred to in the field as comprehensive, whole-child, or global curricula. In contrast, preschool curricula that cover a subset of developmental domains tend to be referred to as domain-specific or supplemental curricula. They are meant to be implemented for a portion of the child's day, with other curricula covering the rest of the day (and other domains). The most successful of these curricula tend to have been developed by experts in the particular domains (Weiland et al., 2018; Yoshikawa et al., 2013). An example is a curriculum focused specifically on math or social-emotional skills.

Another important feature of curriculum and a key distinction between some comprehensive and domain-specific curricula is *scope and sequence*, that is, whether the curriculum includes activities to be carried out in a particular order, to match children's developmental trajectories, or whether the teacher is meant to choose the order. Domain-specific curricula with the strongest track record have a specific scope and sequence intended to accord with the science of children's development and learning in the target area—comprehensive curricula may also have a scope and sequence[1] (Sarama et al., 2017; Weiland et al., 2018; Yoshikawa et al., 2013).

Rigorous studies conducted over the last 15 years have provided evidence on the effectiveness of these various curricular approaches (Phillips et al., 2017b). In some of these studies, classrooms or schools were randomized

---

[1] This text was changed after release of the prepublication version of the report to clarify the statement regarding the comprehensive curricula having scope and sequence.

to implement a specific comprehensive curriculum versus business as usual (often teacher-created curricula), while in others, classrooms or schools were randomized to implement a domain-specific curriculum versus business as usual (a comprehensive curriculum lacking a specific scope and sequence and/or a teacher-created curriculum). Analyses of these studies have found some evidence that comprehensive curricula sometimes have positive effects on the quality of classroom interactions and in some outcome domains (e.g., Fantuzzo et al., 2011; Jenkins et al., 2018). In comparisons of domain-specific and comprehensive curricula, the evidence tends to show no difference in general interactions in the classroom but marked differences in instruction related to the skill area targeted by the domain-specific curriculum and positive impacts on child learning in that area. For example, multiple studies have found that math-specific curricula lead to increased time on and quality of math-specific learning in preschool classrooms and improve children's math learning (Clements et al., 2023; Jenkins et al., 2018; Mattera et al., 2018; Wakabayashi et al., 2020). Interestingly, a study using five different large-scale datasets found that classroom scores on literacy, mathematics, and quality of interactions varied just as widely for classrooms using the two most widely used comprehensive curricula in public preschool programs—*HighScope* and *The Creative Curriculum*—as for classrooms using no published curriculum (Jenkins et al., 2019).

The evidence is also clear that domain-specific curricula following a specific scope and sequence have generally been more successful in improving targeted child outcomes relative to comprehensive or teacher-created curricula (Clements et al., 2023; Jenkins et al., 2018; Mattera et al., 2018; Phillips et al., 2017b; Wakabayashi et al., 2020; Yoshikawa et al., 2013). Less evidence is available from settings outside the United States, but similar patterns in child outcomes have been shown (e.g., Arbour et al., 2023, in Chile; Rege et al., 2021, in Norway).

Of course, a practical challenge for programs is they are not charged with promoting children's learning and development in just one area or domain, nor do domain-specific curricula cover a full school day. Accordingly, some localities have combined domain-specific curricula. For example, Boston's public pre-K program combined a language and literacy–focused curriculum with a math curriculum (Weiland & Yoshikawa, 2013), and rural Head Start centers in Pennsylvania had success combining a social-emotional curriculum with a literacy curriculum (Bierman et al., 2008). Notably, too, some domain-specific curricula have produced effects on outcomes other than those directly targeted. For example, the *Building Blocks* math curriculum has shown positive effects on both executive function and language (Clements et al., 2023; Sarama et al., 2012; Weiland & Yoshikawa, 2013).

The literature in this area has several limitations, however. To the committee's knowledge, none of the curricula that have been rigorously studied to date have been evaluated for whether they were designed and implemented to be culturally and linguistically responsive to the children in the study sample. Nor is there much research on the effects of curricula when implemented in family child care homes. Further, it is standard practice in the field to use common measures to enhance cross-study comparability (Schneider, 2020; Slavin, 2019). But this is one of the many reasons why research in this area has neglected effects on important outcomes such as the development of children's home language among multilingual learners and skills that are more difficult to measure, such as creativity, positive identity, curiosity, and problem solving. The committee also found a troubling lack of information on the effects of curricula on such outcomes as children's explicit bias, sense of belonging, agency, and group pride, as well as teacher outcomes such as bias, expectations for children from different backgrounds, and differential discipline based on children's demographic characteristics. This is in part because there are very few measures of these outcomes and those that do exist lack the psychometric evidence for validity that tends to characterize frequently used measures of children's academic and social-emotional skills. These limitations (and others) are discussed further at the end of this chapter and throughout this report.

OUTCOMES USED FOR ASSESSING EFFECTIVENESS

As described throughout this report, curricula vary in the classroom and child outcomes they target. Further, studies of even the same curricula vary as to which outcomes and measures were used to assess curricular effects on classroom processes and child learning. Also critical in understanding variation by outcome is the nature of the construct or skill at hand. For example, preschoolers tend to master narrower skills, such as letter knowledge and print awareness, more quickly than broader skills or more domain-general skills that support development in multiple areas, such as vocabulary and productive language (McCormick et al., 2021). Even within the same domain, effects can vary depending on how narrow the skill addressed by a particular assessment is. For example, preschoolers are likely to show much larger effects on a vocabulary assessment of 15 words taught specifically in a curriculum than on overall vocabulary assessment of all the words the child knows.

Indeed, the empirical literature commonly shows much larger effects of preschool programs and specific curricula on narrower, domain-specific versus broader, domain-general child skills (Goodrich et al., 2017; Gormley et al., 2005; Weiland & Yoshikawa, 2013; Wong et al., 2008). This is not to suggest a hierarchy of skill types, in which some are more important than others. Both narrower and broader skills are foundational for children's learning and later school success (McCormick et al., 2021). Furthermore, learning is cumulative; skills in one area can support the development of skills in other areas (Blair & Razza, 2007; Clements et al., 2016; Phillips et al., 2017b). Nonetheless, in assessing variation in the effects of curricula, it is critical to differentiate which skills are more malleable than others in the short term.

Regarding the effects of curricula on classroom processes, the literature shows less variation in curriculum effects based on which outcome measure is chosen, in part because preschool curriculum studies tend to use fewer common classroom-level process measures than child-level measures, making findings more difficult to compare across studies. Measures in these studies include observational measures of curriculum fidelity, measures of the global quality of teacher–child interactions at the classroom level, domain-specific quality of instructional practices measures, time-use measures, and a combination of these (Nesbitt & Farran, 2021; Watts et al., 2018; Weiland & Guerrero Rosada, 2022). Furthermore, it is not uncommon to see relatively large impacts on classroom process outcomes and null effects on children's learning (Howard et al., 2021; Jenkins et al., 2018; Yoshikawa et al., 2015).

STUDENT CHARACTERISTICS

Even if an intervention is implemented with the same intensity and quality, it may be more effective for some groups and in some contexts than others (Steiner et al., 2019; Weiss et al., 2014). Subgroup effects for preschool curricula have been less well studied than average effects, in part because of sample size requirements. Often, limited resources or other practical constraints make it difficult to have enough sites, teachers, and children for a well-powered test of the average effect of a curriculum, let alone to examine variation in effects by subgroups.

This limitation is important in the context of this study because a curriculum that promotes equity for marginalized groups will ideally benefit all children's learning, but especially that of children from marginalized groups. Preschool attendance, for example, appears to have greater benefits for multilingual learners and children from families with low incomes than for their peers compared with other care options in the year before kindergarten (Phillips et al., 2017b; Yoshikawa et al., 2013). In reviewing sources of moderation (i.e., whether effects differ by child characteristics), the committee drew on studies that examined the question of moderators through formal testing where possible, but also on studies conducted primarily with a marginalized group. The committee's rationale for doing so was the assumption that if a curriculum study was conducted in Head Start, it could presumably inform discussion of effects for children from families with low incomes, even if the research team could not test whether these effects were greater than those for children from families with higher incomes because they were not enrolled in Head Start. Many preschool curriculum studies have been conducted in income-targeted publicly funded programs and for this reason, with disproportionate samples of minoritized children.

Overall, evidence is mixed for studies that have tested whether curriculum effects differ by child characteristics. For example, some studies found no differences by family income (Clements & Sarama, 2011), gender identity (Clements & Sarama, 2008; Dumas et al., 2019; Nesbitt & Farran, 2021; Weiland & Yoshikawa, 2013), child race or ethnicity (Sarama et al., 2008), disability (Clements et al., 2013; Nesbitt & Farran, 2021), or language status (McCarthy et al., 2015; Nesbitt & Farran, 2021). In other words, these groups appear to have experienced the same curriculum effects as their peers.

Other studies, however, did find differences in curriculum effects by these demographic characteristics. For example, effects of the *Building Blocks* math curriculum were greater for Black and Latino children than for their White peers in multiple trials (Clements et al., 2011, 2013; Dumas et al., 2019; Weiland & Yoshikawa, 2013). Multiple studies have found greater effects for multilingual learners than for their monolingual peers on English oral language outcomes, typically in studies with language- and literacy-focused curriculum compared with business-as-usual comprehensive curriculum approaches (Kaiser et al., 2011; Wilson et al., 2013). Some curricula also show greater effects for children who begin the preschool year with lower skills than their peers. For example, two studies of the *Building Blocks* math curriculum found that children with lower baseline math skills gained more in their math skills in the preschool year (Mattera et al., 2021; Watts et al., 2018). Studies of social-emotional curriculum have found greater gains in students with lower baseline skills (Finlon et al., 2015; Flook et al., 2015), but also greater gains in students with higher baseline skills (Shea & Jenkins, 2021).

Overall, drawing firm conclusions for particular groups or within specific contexts across preschool curriculum studies is challenging for three reasons: (1) most studies were underpowered for detecting subgroup differences; (2) some of the detected differences may have been due to chance (i.e., the multiple comparisons problem [Schochet, 2009]); and (3) standardized reporting is lacking, hindering interpretation of these findings. Nonetheless, taken together, these studies point to the potential for curricula, particularly some domain-specific curricula, to have greater effects for marginalized groups than for nonmarginalized groups, although more research in this area is needed, a point we return to at the end of this chapter and in Chapter 10.

TEACHER CHARACTERISTICS

The early care and education workforce is highly diverse with respect to professional training and development because of the fragmented early learning landscape and chronic underinvestment in the United States (Chaudry et al., 2021). Some of these teachers complete the kinds of preparatory programs common among teachers in grades K–12, which include a bachelor's degree (or higher), student teaching, and formal certification. Others, however, have more minimal preparation when they begin and gain their training largely on the job. Research is mixed on the degree to which teacher qualifications promote children's learning (Early et al., 2007; Institute of Medicine & National Research Council, 2015; Lin & Magnuson, 2018). For in-service teachers, training and in-classroom coaching can promote children's learning but generally has been found to do so only when tied to the implementation of a domain-specific curriculum and not general best teaching practices (Pianta et al., 2017; Piasta et al., 2017; Weiland et al., 2018; Yoshikawa et al., 2013, 2015). To move the needle on classroom processes and child learning, a preschool curriculum must be implementable at a high level of quality by teachers with a wide range of preparation and skills. Alternatively, the curriculum should be targeted only to teachers for whom it is well matched in terms of preparation.

Very few studies have explicitly tested whether curriculum effects on classroom processes and child learning vary by teacher characteristics, such as training and education or language proficiency. This is the case in part because teacher characteristics in a given setting may not vary much. For example, if a curriculum is being tested in a public preschool system that requires at least a bachelor's degree, researchers cannot test whether effects are different for teachers with less educational attainment. Issues of statistical power are at play here, too, just as they are for child characteristics.

Accordingly, some of the best evidence comes from comparisons across different studies rather than from within-study comparisons. Domain-specific curricula, when supported by training and coaching, for example, have shown positive effects on classroom processes and child learning in settings where teachers have lower educational levels (Bierman et al., 2008; Morris et al., 2014) or relatively higher educational levels (Weiland & Yoshikawa, 2013). At least one comprehensive curriculum, in contrast, showed some benefits for classroom processes but none for child learning gains, in a context in which most teachers had a bachelor's degree (Howard et al., 2021).

Other literature examines whether curricula are more readily implemented by teachers with different background characteristics and professional preparation. For example, a study of 74 mostly White (92%) and female (96%) teachers in Head Start and public pre-K in rural Appalachian communities found high rates of implementation fidelity for a domain-specific language and literacy curriculum, regardless of teacher education

(34% had an associate's degree or lower; 39% a bachelor's degree; and 23% a master's degree [Piasta et al., 2015]). Similar results were found in a study of a vocabulary and language curriculum in which teachers' preparedness and classroom management predicted their implementation fidelity but their education levels did not (Phillips et al., 2017a). Underscoring the importance of fidelity, some studies have found that fidelity of implementation predicted children's gains using preschool math curriculum (Sarama et al., 2008), language and literacy curriculum (Hamre et al., 2010), and curriculum focused on multiple domains (Maier et al., 2022b).

Taken together, early educators with a broad range of characteristics appear to be capable of implementing different preschool curricula. Teacher degrees, for example, do not appear to affect quality or fidelity of implementation decisively. However, this finding is difficult to test given the fragmented nature of the U.S. education landscape and the fact that rigorous evidence in this area is limited.

PRESCHOOL SETTING

Preschool is delivered in a range of settings, including family child care homes, community-based preschool classrooms, for-profit preschools, faith-based schools, charter schools, and traditional public schools (Chaudry et al., 2021). Much of the time, curriculum trials are conducted within one of these settings. For example, trials might be carried out entirely within Head Start sites (e.g., Morris et al., 2014) or within public preschool classrooms in traditional public schools (e.g., Clements et al., 2011). When trials are limited to one setting, curriculum effectiveness can be examined across settings only with cross-study comparisons. Some studies of curriculum, however, included a mix of setting types—for example, in Head Start, public schools, and other community-based organizations (CBOs), as in a recent trial of the *HighScope* curriculum (Howard et al., 2021), or in CBOs and public schools, as in a recent trial of the *Building Blocks* math curriculum (Mattera et al., 2018).

Here, overall, the evidence base is similar to that for teachers with different characteristics, given the often substantial sorting of teachers into settings by their qualifications (Weiland et al., 2022). For example, the evidence shows that teachers in CBO, Head Start, and public preschool settings can implement curricula at least moderately well (Yoshikawa et al., 2013). When a study covers multiple settings, researchers sometimes examine moderation of effects on classroom processes and child learning outcomes by setting. However, this practice is uncommon because of issues of statistical power. The available research shows some evidence of differential preintervention processes and differential effects of curriculum on both classroom processes and child learning by setting. As one example, a recent study found that, preintervention, CBO classrooms spent less time on math instruction and had lower-quality math instruction at baseline compared with public schools. A math-specific curriculum increased the amount of time children spent in mathematics in both settings; math skills improved for children in public preschools, and vocabulary and executive functioning skills improved for children in CBO settings (McCormick et al., 2022).

Setting characteristics are another important source of potential variation in effects that is underexplored in the literature. For example, some preschools are full day, while others are half day. Interestingly, a previous study of Tulsa's pre-K program found greater effects of the half-day program than for the full-day program, although children's characteristics were confounded by program type in that study (Gormley et al., 2005). A recent randomized trial of half- versus full-day programs in a context that implemented a domain-specific literacy curriculum found greater effects of full-day instruction on children's learning (Atteberry et al., 2019).

Critically, there has been almost no rigorous research on preschool curriculum in family child care homes, for-profit preschools, faith-based schools, or charter schools—another gap to which we return at the conclusion of this chapter and throughout the report.

MACRO CONDITIONS

Changes in the macro context may affect the size of curriculum effects; such changes include, for example, broader economic conditions, workforce policies, and shifts in parenting practices and children's skills over time that can influence child development. Broader economic changes such as economic growth and downturns have been shown to affect community- and family-level factors that in turn influence child development (Weiland & Yoshikawa, 2012).

Regarding the workforce, preschool teachers are frequently paid far less than their K–12 peers, which fuels teacher turnover (Chaudry et al., 2021). Accordingly, curricula may be less effective in settings in which teachers are trained and then leave, compared with settings with more workforce stability.

Regarding shifts in parenting practices, there is evidence that between the late 1990s and 2010, parents exposed young children to more books and educational games in the home and engaged more with their children, with the largest increases among parents with low incomes (Bassok et al., 2016). Over this same period, young children, particularly Black children, were entering kindergarten with stronger teacher-reported math and literacy skills (Bassok & Latham, 2017). Other evidence shows that the type of parent–child home learning activities affects children's gains in the preschool year (McCormick et al., 2020). Home learning activities also vary by family background; for example, Latine families in the United States are more likely to emphasize animals in science conversations with their children and to use mealtimes for rich family conversations (Leyva et al., 2022).

Taken together, these shifts mean curricula are supporting children whose experiences differ from those of their counterparts a generation ago. To our knowledge, there is no direct evidence on how macro shifts may have affected the findings of research on preschool curriculum. Nonetheless, this potential source of evidence is important as a lens for interpreting those findings, particularly when comparing trials from the early 2000s with today's evidence.

CONCLUSION

As summarized in this chapter, the available research shows that preschool curriculum can be a potent means of moving the needle on instructional quality, classroom processes, and children's early learning, particularly for children from marginalized groups. Effects of preschool curricula can vary by curriculum type, outcomes used to assess effects, and student characteristics; to a lesser degree, effects can vary by teacher characteristics, preschool setting, and broader macro conditions. However, important, unanswered questions remain about the effects of culturally responsive curricula; effects of curricula in family child care, for-profit, charter school, or faith-based school contexts; effects on less commonly measured child outcomes, such as creativity, problem solving, healthy racial identity, multilingual learners' growth in home language as well as English language development, and bias; and effects of widely adopted instructional approaches to preschool, such as Montessori, project-based learning, and Reggio Emilia (see Chapter 4 for a more detailed discussion of these approaches).

Realizing a new vision for preschool curriculum will require prioritizing and answering these questions. It will also require new approaches to translating evidence on curriculum into policy and practice. Thus far, the large evidence base on preschool curricula appears to have had little influence on the curriculum choices of public preschool programs. For example, these programs overwhelmingly use comprehensive curricula that, compared with domain-specific curricula, have been found to have smaller gains in domain-targeted academic skills (Jenkins & Duncan, 2017). A key challenge in moving the field forward on a new vision for curriculum that reflects the developmental strengths of children and families and is more inclusive of cultural and linguistic variations—particularly for the children with the least access to opportunity—is developing policy levers for curriculum choice and use that are more closely tied to the evidence base. These policy levers could include allocating additional public funding to incentivize programs to use evidence-based curricula; providing quality improvement supports and resources to address equity and inclusion gaps; and providing technical assistance and targeted funding to support ongoing professional development related to incorporating evidence-based curricula.

REFERENCES

Arbour, M., Soto, C., Alée, Y., Atwood, S., Muñoz, P., & Marzolo, M. (2023). Absenteeism prevention in preschools in Chile: Impact from a quasi-experimental evaluation of 2011–2017 Ministry of Education data. In *Frontiers in Education*, 7. https://doi.org/10.3389/feduc.2022.975092

Atteberry, A., Bassok, D., & Wong, V. C. (2019). The effects of full-day prekindergarten: Experimental evidence of impacts on children's school readiness. *Educational Evaluation and Policy Analysis*, 41(4), 537–562. https://doi.org/10.3102/0162373719872197

Bassok, D., & Latham, S. (2017). Kids today: The rise in children's academic skills at kindergarten entry. *Educational Researcher*, 46(1), 7–20. https://doi.org/10.3102/0013189X17694161

Bassok, D., Finch, J. E., Lee, R., Reardon, S. F., & Waldfogel, J. (2016). Socioeconomic gaps in early childhood experiences: 1998 to 2010. *AERA Open*, 2(3). https://doi.org/10.1177/2332858416653924

Bierman, K. L., Domitrovich, C. E., Nix, R. L., Gest, S. D., Welsh, J. A., Greenberg, M. T., Blair, C., Nelson, K., & Gill, S. (2008). Promoting academic and social-emotional school readiness: The Head Start REDI program. *Child Development*, 79(6), 1802–1817. https://doi.org/10.1111/j.1467-8624.2008.01227.x

Blair, C., & Razza, R. P. (2007). Relating effortful control, executive function, and false belief understanding to emerging math and literacy ability in kindergarten. *Child Development*, 78(2), 647–663. https://doi.org/10.1111/j.1467-8624.2007.01019.x

Burchinal, M. (2017). Measuring early care and education quality. *Child Development Perspectives*, 12, 3–9. https://doi.org/10.1111/cdep.12260

Chambers, B., Cheung, A. C., & Slavin, R. E. (2016). Literacy and language outcomes of comprehensive and developmental-constructivist approaches to early childhood education: A systematic review. *Educational Research Review*, 18, 88–111. https://doi.org/10.1016/j.edurev.2016.03.003

Chaudry, A., Morrissey, T., Weiland, C., & Yoshikawa, H. (2021). *Cradle to kindergarten: A new plan to combat inequality* (2nd ed.). Russell Sage.

Clements, D. H., & Sarama, J. (2008). Experimental evaluation of the effects of a research-based preschool mathematics curriculum. *American Educational Research Journal*, 45, 443–494. https://doi.org/10.3102/0002831207312908

———. (2011). Early childhood mathematics intervention. *Science*, 333(6045), 968–970. https://doi.org/10.1126/science.1204537

Clements, D. H., Sarama, J., & Germeroth, C. (2016). Learning executive function and early mathematics: Directions of causal relations. *Early Childhood Research Quarterly*, 36, 79–90. https://doi.org/10.1016/j.ecresq.2015.12.009

Clements, D. H., Sarama, J., Spitler, M. E., Lange, A. A., & Wolfe, C. B. (2011). Mathematics learned by young children in an intervention based on learning trajectories: A large-scale cluster randomized trial. *Journal for Research in Mathematics Education*, 42(2), 127–166. https://doi.org/10.5951/jresematheduc.42.2.0127

Clements, D. H., Sarama, J., Layzer, C., & Unlu, F. (2023). Implementation of a scale-up model in early childhood: Long-term impacts on mathematics achievement. *Journal for Research in Mathematics Education*, 54(1), 64–88. https://doi.org/10.5951/jresematheduc-2020-0245

Clements, D. H., Sarama, J., Wolfe, C. B., & Spitler, M. E. (2013). Longitudinal evaluation of a scale-up model for teaching mathematics with trajectories and technologies: Persistence of effects in the third year. *American Educational Research Journal*, 50(4), 812–850. https://doi.org/10.3102/0002831212469270

Dumas, D., McNeish, D., Sarama, J., & Clements, D. (2019). Preschool mathematics intervention can significantly improve student learning trajectories through elementary school. *AERA Open*, 5. https://doi.org/10.1177/2332858419879446

Early, D. M., Maxwell, K. L., Burchinal, M., Alva, S., Bender, R. H., Bryant, D., Cai, K., Clifford, R. M., Ebanks, C., Griffin, J. A., Henry, G. T., Howes, C., Iriondo-Perez, J., Jeon, H.-J., Mashburn, A. J., Peisner-Feinberg, E., Pianta, R. C., Vandergrift, N., & Zill, N. (2007). Teachers' education, classroom quality, and young children's academic skills: Results from seven studies of preschool programs. *Child Development, 78*(2), 558–580. https://www.jstor.org/stable/4139245

Fantuzzo, J. W., Gadsden, V. L., & McDermott, P. A. (2011). An integrated curriculum to improve mathematics, language, and literacy for Head Start children. *American Educational Research Journal, 48*(3), 763–793.

Finlon, K. J., Izard, C. E., Seidenfeld, A., Johnson, S. R., Cavadel, E. W., Ewing, E. S. K., & Morgan, J. K. (2015). Emotion-based preventive intervention: Effectively promoting emotion knowledge and adaptive behavior among at-risk preschoolers. *Development and Psychopathology, 27*(4-1), 1353–1365. https://doi.org/10.1017/S0954579414001461

Flook, L., Goldberg, S. B., Pinger, L., & Davidson, R. J. (2015). Promoting prosocial behavior and self-regulatory skills in preschool children through a mindfulness-based Kindness Curriculum. *Developmental Psychology, 51*, 44–51. https://doi.org/10.1037/a0038256

Goodrich, J. M., Lonigan, C. J., & Farver, J. A. M. (2017). Impacts of a literacy-focused preschool curriculum on the early literacy skills of language-minority children. *Early Childhood Research Quarterly, 40*, 13–24. https://doi.org/10.1016/j.ecresq.2017.02.001

Gormley, W. T., Jr., Phillips, D., & Dawson, B. (2005). The effects of universal pre-K on cognitive development. *Developmental Psychology, 41*, 872. https://doi.org/10.1037/0012-1649.41.6.872

Hamre, B. K., Justice, L. M., Pianta, R. C., Kilday, C., Sweeney, B., Downer, J. T., & Leach, A. (2010). Implementation fidelity of MyTeachingPartner literacy and language activities: Association with preschoolers' language and literacy growth. *Early Childhood Research Quarterly, 25*(3), 329–347. https://doi.org/10.1016/j.ecresq.2009.07.002

Heckman, J. J., & Karapakula, G. (2019a). *Intergenerational and intragenerational externalities of the Perry Preschool Project* (NBER Working Paper No. 25889). National Bureau of Economic Research. https://doi.org/10.3386/w25889

———. (2019b). *The Perry Preschoolers at late midlife: A study in design-specific inference* (NBER Working Paper No. 25888). National Bureau of Economic Research. https://doi.org/10.3386/w25888

Howard, E., Weinberg, E., Yee, D., Ogut, B., & Lee, D. (2021). *HighScope preschool curriculum and professional development efficacy study: Results in brief.* American Institutes for Research. https://www.air.org/sites/default/files/HighScope-Results-in-Brief-Jan-2021.pdf

Institute of Medicine & National Research Council. 2015. *Transforming the workforce for children birth through age 8: A unifying foundation.* National Academies Press.

Jenkins, J. M., & Duncan, G. J. (2017). Do prekindergarten curricula matter? In D. Phillips and K. Dodge (eds.), *The current state of scientific knowledge on pre-kindergarten effects* (pp. 37–44). Brookings Institute. https://www.researchgate.net/profile/Jade-Jenkins-6/publication/317904908_Do_pre-kindergarten_curricula_matter/links/595e50a9a6fdccc9b17fd2f2/Do-pre-kindergarten-curricula-matter.pdf

Jenkins, J. M., Duncan, G. J., Auger, A., Bitler, M., Domina, T., & Burchinal, M. (2018). Boosting school readiness: Should preschool teachers target skills or the whole child? *Economics of Education Review, 65*, 107–125. https://doi.org/10.1016/j.econedurev.2018.05.001

Jenkins, J. M., Whitaker, A. A., Nguyen, T., & Yu, W. (2019). Distinctions without a difference? Preschool curricula and children's development. *Journal of Research on Educational Effectiveness, 12*(3), 514–549. https://doi.org/10.1080/19345747.2019.1631420

Kaiser, A., Dickinson, D., Roberts, M., Darrow, C., Freiberg, J., & Hofer, K. (2011). *The effects of two language-focused preschool curricula on children's achievement through first grade.* Society for Research on Educational Effectiveness.

Latham, S., Corcoran, S. P., Sattin-Bajaj, C., & Jennings, J. L. (2021). Racial disparities in pre-K quality: Evidence from New York City's universal pre-K program. *Educational Researcher, 50*(9), 607–617. https://doi.org/10.3102/0013189X211028214

Leyva, D., Weiland, C., Shapiro, A., & Yeomans-Maldonado, G. (2022). A strengths-based, culturally responsive family intervention improves Latino kindergarteners' vocabulary and approaches to learning. *Child Development, 93,* 451–467. https://doi.org/10.1111/cdev.13698

Lin, Y. C., & Magnuson, K. A. (2018). Classroom quality and children's academic skills in child care centers: Understanding the role of teacher qualifications. *Early Childhood Research Quarterly, 42,* 215–227. https://doi.org/10.1016/j.ecresq.2017.10.003

Maier, M., Hsueh, J., Somers, M., & Burchinal, M. (2022a). *Does classroom quality promote preschoolers' learning? A conceptual framework for evaluating the impact of classroom quality on child outcomes* (OPRE Report No. 2022-159). Office of Planning, Research, and Evaluation, Administration for Children and Families, U.S. Department of Health and Human Services. https://www.acf.hhs.gov/opre/report/does-classroom-quality-promote-preschoolers-learning-conceptual-framework-evaluating

Maier, M. F., McCormick, M. P., Xia, S., Hsueh, J., Weiland, C., Morales, A., Boni, M., Tonachel, M., Sachs, J., & Snow, C. (2022b). Content-rich instruction and cognitive demand in preK: Using systematic observations to predict child gains. *Early Childhood Research Quarterly, 60,* 96–109. https://doi.org/10.1016/j.ecresq.2021.12.010

Mattera, S., Jacob, R., & Morris, P. (2018). *Strengthening children's math skills with enhanced instruction: The impacts of Making Pre-K Count and High 5s on kindergarten outcomes.* MDRC. https://www.mdrc.org/publication/strengthening-children-s-math-skills-enhanced-instruction

Mattera, S. K., Jacob, R., MacDowell, C., & Morris, P. A. (2021). *Long-term effects of enhanced early childhood math instruction: The impacts of Making Pre-K Count and High 5s on third-grade outcomes.* MDRC. https://www.mdrc.org/publication/long-term-effects-enhanced-early-childhood-math-instruction

McCarthy, B., Li, L., Tiu, M., Atienza, S., & Sexton, U. (2015). *Learning with PBS KIDS: A study of family engagement and early mathematics achievement.* WestEd. https://www.wested.org/resources/learning-with-pbs-kids

McCormick, M., Weiland, C., Hsueh, J., Pralica, M., Weissman, A., Moffett, L., Snow, C., & Sachs, J. (2021). Is skill type the key to the PreK fadeout puzzle? Differential associations between enrollment in PreK and constrained and unconstrained skills across kindergarten. *Child Development, 92,* 599–620. https://doi.org/10.1111/cdev.13520

McCormick, M. P., Mattera, S. K., Maier, M. F., Xia, S., Jacob, R., & Morris, P. A. (2022). Different settings, different patterns of impacts: Effects of a pre-K math intervention in a mixed-delivery system. *Early Childhood Research Quarterly, 58,* 136–154. https://doi.org/10.1016/j.ecresq.2021.08.005

McCormick, M. P., Weissman, A. K., Weiland, C., Hsueh, J., Sachs, J., & Snow, C. (2020). Time well spent: Home learning activities and gains in children's academic skills in the prekindergarten year. *Developmental Psychology, 56*(4), 710. https://doi.org/10.1037/dev0000891

Morris, P., Mattera, S. K., Castells, N., Bangser, M., Bierman, K., & Raver, C. (2014). *Impact findings from the Head Start CARES Demonstration: National evaluation of three approaches to improving preschoolers' social and emotional competence. Executive summary* (OPRE Report No. 2014-44). Office of Planning, Research and Evaluation. https://www.acf.hhs.gov/opre/report/impact-findings-head-start-cares-demonstration-national-evaluation-three-approaches

National Center on Early Childhood Development, Teaching, and Learning. (2020). *Preschool curriculum consumer report.* Office of Head Start, U.S. Department of Health and Human Services. https://eclkc.ohs.acf.hhs.gov/sites/default/files/featured_file/preschool-curriculum-consumer-report-032519.pdf

Nesbitt, K. T., & Farran, D. C. (2021). Effects of prekindergarten curricula: Tools of the Mind as a case study. *Monographs of the Society for Research in Child Development, 86*(1), 7–119. https://doi.org/10.1111/mono.12425

Pianta, R., Hamre, B., Downer, J., Burchinal, M., Williford, A., Locasale-Crouch, J., Howes, C., La Paro, K., & Scott-Little, C. (2017). Early childhood professional development: Coaching and coursework effects on indicators of children's school readiness. *Early Education and Development, 28*, 956–975. https://doi.org/10.1080/10409289.2017.1319783

Piasta, S. B., Justice, L. M., McGinty, A., Mashburn, A., & Slocum, L. (2015). A comprehensive examination of preschool teachers' implementation fidelity when using a supplemental language and literacy curriculum. *Child & Youth Care Forum, 44*, 731–755. https://doi.org/10.1007/s10566-015-9305-2

Piasta, S. B., Justice, L. M., O'Connell, A. A., Mauck, S. A., Weber-Mayrer, M., Schachter, R. E., Farley, K., & Spear, C. F. (2017). Effectiveness of large-scale, state-sponsored language and literacy professional development on early childhood educator outcomes. *Journal of Research on Educational Effectiveness, 10*(2), 354–378. https://doi.org/10.1080/19345747.2016.1270378

Phillips, B. M., Ingrole, S. A., Burris, P. W., & Tabulda, G. (2017a). Investigating predictors of fidelity of implementation for a preschool vocabulary and language curriculum. *Early Child Development and Care, 187*(3–4), 542–553. https://doi.org/10.1080/03004430.2016.1251428

Phillips, D. A., Lipsey, M. W., Dodge, K. A., Haskins, R., Bassok, D., Burchinal, M. R., Duncan, G. J., Dynarski, M., Magnuson, K. A., & Weiland, C. (2017b). Puzzling it out: The current state of scientific knowledge on pre-kindergarten effects: A consensus statement. In *The current state of scientific knowledge on pre-kindergarten effects* (pp. 19–30). Brookings Institution. https://www.brookings.edu/wp-content/uploads/2017/04/consensus-statement_final.pdf

Rege, M., Størksen, I., Solli, I. F., Kalil, A., McClelland, M. M., ten Braak, D., Lenes, R., Lunde, S., Breive, S., Carlsen, M., Erfjord, I., & Hundeland, P. S. (2021). The effects of a structured curriculum on preschool effectiveness: A field experiment. *Journal of Human Resources, 58*(4). https://doi.org/10.3368/jhr.0220-10749R3

Reynolds, A. J., Ou, S. R., & Temple, J. A. (2018). A multicomponent, preschool to third grade preventive intervention and educational attainment at 35 years of age. *JAMA Pediatrics, 172*(3), 247–256. https://doi.org/10.1001/jamapediatrics.2017.4673

Sarama, J., Brenneman, K., Clements, D. H., Duke, N. K., & Hemmeter, M. L. (2017). Interdisciplinary teaching across multiple domains: The C4L (Connect4Learning) curriculum. In *Implementing a standards-based curriculum in the early childhood classroom* (pp. 1–53). Routledge.

Sarama, J., Clements, D. H., Starkey, P., Klein, A., & Wakeley, A. (2008). Scaling up the implementation of a pre-kindergarten mathematics curriculum: Teaching for understanding with trajectories and technologies. *Journal of Research on Educational Effectiveness, 1*(2), 89–119. https://doi.org/10.1080/19345740801941332

Sarama, J., Lange, A. A., Clements, D. H., & Wolfe, C. B. (2012). The impacts of an early mathematics curriculum on oral language and literacy. *Early Childhood Research Quarterly, 27*(3), 489–502. https://doi.org/10.1016/j.ecresq.2011.12.002

Schneider, M. (2020). *Making common measures more common*. Institute of Education Sciences. https://ies.ed.gov/director/remarks/5-05-2020.asp

Schochet, P. Z. (2009). An approach for addressing the multiple testing problem in social policy impact evaluations. *Evaluation Review, 33*(6), 539–567. https://doi.org/10.1177/0193841X09350590

Shea, Z. M., & Jenkins, J. M. (2021). Examining heterogeneity in the impacts of social-emotional curricula in preschool: A quantile treatment effect approach. *Frontiers in Psychology, 12*, 1–16. https://doi.org/10.3389/fpsyg.2021.624320

Slavin, R. (2019, October 24). Developer- and researcher-made measures. *Robert Slavin's Blog*. https://robertslavinsblog.wordpress.com/2019/10/24/developer-and-researcher-made-measures

Steiner, P. M., Wong, V. C., & Anglin, K. (2019). A causal replication framework for designing and assessing replication efforts. *Zeitschrift für Psychologie, 227*(4), 280–292. https://doi.org/10.1027/2151-2604/a000385

Valentino, R. (2018). Will public pre-K really close achievement gaps? Gaps in prekindergarten quality between students and across states. *American Educational Research Journal, 55*(1), 79–116. https://doi.org/10.3102/0002831217732000

Wakabayashi, T., Andrade-Adaniya, F., Schweinhart, L. J., Xiang, Z., Marshall, B. A., & Markley, C. A. (2020). The impact of a supplementary preschool mathematics curriculum on children's early mathematics learning. *Early Childhood Research Quarterly, 53*, 329–342. https://doi.org/10.1016/j.ecresq.2020.04.002

Watts, T. W., Duncan, G. J., Clements, D. H., & Sarama, J. (2018). What is the long-run impact of learning mathematics during preschool? *Child Development, 89*, 539–555. https://doi.org/10.1111/cdev.12713

Weiland, C. (2018). Pivoting to the "how": Moving preschool policy, practice, and research forward. *Early Childhood Research Quarterly, 45*, 188–192. https://doi.org/10.1016/j.ecresq.2018.02.017

Weiland, C., & Guerrero-Rosada, P. (2022). *Widely used measures of pre-K classroom quality: What we know, gaps in the field, and promising new directions: Measures for early success*. MDRC. https://www.mdrc.org/publication/widely-used-measures-pre-k-classroom-quality

Weiland, C., & Yoshikawa, H. (2012). The effects of large-scale economic change and policies on children's developmental contexts and developmental outcomes. *Child Development Perspectives, 6*, 342–350. https://doi.org/10.1111/j.1750-8606.2011.00222.x

Weiland, C., & Yoshikawa, H. (2013). Impacts of a prekindergarten program on children's mathematics, language, literacy, executive function, and emotional skills. *Child Development, 84*, 2112–2130. https://doi.org/10.1111/cdev.12099

Weiland, C., McCormick, M., Duer, J., Friedman-Krauss, A., Pralica, M., Xia, S., Nores, M., & Mattera, S. (2022). *Mixed-delivery public prekindergarten: Differences in demographics, quality, and children's gains in community-based versus public school programs across five large-scale systems*. (EdWorkingPaper No. 22-651). Annenberg Institute at Brown University. https://doi.org/10.26300/pncz-2233

Weiland, C., McCormick, M., Mattera, M., Maier, M., & Morris, P. (2018). Preschool curricula and professional development features for getting to high-quality implementation at scale: A comparative review across five trials. *AERA Open, 4(1)*. https://doi.org/10.1177/2332858418757735

Weiss, M. J., Bloom, H. S., & Brock, T. (2014). A conceptual framework for studying the sources of variation in program effects. *Journal of Policy Analysis and Management, 33*(3), 778–808. https://doi.org/10.1002/pam.21760

Wilson, S. J., Dickinson, D. K., & Rowe, D. W. (2013). Impact of an Early Reading First program on the language and literacy achievement of children from diverse language backgrounds. *Early Childhood Research Quarterly, 28*(2), 578–592. https://doi.org/10.1016/j.ecresq.2013.03.006

Wong, V. C., Cook, T. D., Barnett, W. S., & Jung, K. (2008). An effectiveness-based evaluation of five state pre-kindergarten programs. *Journal of Policy Analysis and Management, 27*(1), 122–154. https://doi.org/10.1002/pam.20310

Yoshikawa, H., Leyva, D., Snow, C. E., Treviño, E., Rolla, A., Barata, M. C., Weiland, C., & Arbour, M. C. (2015). Experimental impacts on classroom quality of an initiative to improve the quality of preschool education in Chile: A cluster-randomized trial. *Developmental Psychology, 51*(3), 309–322. https://doi.org/10.1037/a0038785

Yoshikawa, H., Weiland, C., Brooks-Gunn, J., Burchinal, M. R., Espinosa, L. M., Gormley, W. T., Ludwig, J. O., Magnuson, K. A., Phillips, D. A., & Zaslow, M. J. (2013). *Investing in our future: The evidence base on preschool education*. Foundation for Child Development and Society for Research in Child Development. https://www.fcd-us.org/the-evidence-base-on-preschool

3

The Science of Early Learning and Brain Development

The neurobiology of learning and the powerful influences of the early environment on brain development are central considerations in planning effective preschool curriculum. The principle that there are sensitive periods during early childhood when the capacity for learning is enhanced has been well established in specific domains (language, visual) and is the focus of ongoing investigation in cognitive, social, and emotional domains (Werker & Hensch, 2015; Woodard & Pollack, 2020). Broadly, the existence of sensitive periods and related high neuroplasticity during the early years of life represent a window of opportunity for enhancing early learning, as specific skills and abilities are known to be absorbed or learned more readily during these periods. In turn, because learning is a cumulative process, enhanced early learning can lead to long-term learning benefits. In contrast, when opportunities for environmental stimulation and expected experiential inputs are missed, the early years can be a period of unique vulnerability and can lead to learning challenges at later developmental periods.

Moreover, children's early learning depends on strong starting points as well as the experiences children have in their environments. Across cultures, infant studies show evidence of strong initial states—termed "core knowledge." Studies indicate that core knowledge is universal across disparate cultures (e.g., Spelke, 2022; Spelke & Kinzler, 2007). Core knowledge domains are evolutionarily ancient, are shared with other species, and have continuity across the human lifespan. They include knowledge about objects and their physical actions, such as their continuity and contact constraints (Aguiar & Baillargeon, 1999; Leslie & Keeble, 1987; Spelke, 1990);

knowledge about agents and their goal-directed actions and intentions (Spelke et al., 1995; Stavans & Csibra, 2023; Woodward, 2009); knowledge about what number is approximate for all but the smallest sets (Carey, 2004; Carey & Barner, 2019; Dehaene, 1997); knowledge about geometry, which allows infants and young children to navigate based on the geometry of spaces and to represent shapes based on angle and side length (Cheng & Newcombe, 2005; Dehaene et al., 2006; Izard & Spelke, 2009; Newcombe & Huttenlocher, 2003); and core social cognition, which enables babies to represent others with whom they interact and their social group (Kinzler & Spelke, 2011; Kinzler et al., 2007; Spelke, 2022). Importantly, core knowledge systems are malleable, and children's initial states change depending on their experiences. For example, as early as 3 months of age, infants show an own-race preference for faces, but this is based on their exposures and is not seen in infants who grow up in environments where they are exposed to other races (Bar-Haim et al., 2006; Kinzler & Spelke, 2011). Somewhat later, at 11 months, infants growing up in Latine or White families exhibit a bias to looking at minority group faces (Singarajah et al., 2017), which may reflect the preference for novelty outweighing the preference for familiarity (Aslin, 2007). In this way, children build on their core knowledge through their lived experiences, which occur within their sociocultural contexts (Gutiérrez & Rogoff, 2003; Gutiérrez et al., 2017).

This chapter briefly reviews the neurobiological and sociobehavioral research that shows the influence of early life experiences on early childhood development, including brain development, that can impact outcomes later in life. It then describes the science of early learning, detailing the multiplicity of ways children learn, from active exploration and observation of others to adults' explicitly sharing knowledge with them. Content and skills typically shared by adults with children include domain-general skills—social-emotional learning and executive function—as well as domain-specific skills—language, literacy, and math learning. The chapter concludes with a discussion of the implications of the science of early childhood development and early learning for preschool curriculum development, including cultural and linguistic variations in learning opportunities and learning.

NEUROBIOLOGICAL AND SOCIAL-EMOTIONAL DEVELOPMENT

The early developmental period is recognized as the most important developmental phase of the lifespan, during which the young child's experiences and exposures sculpt the brain to ready it for learning and positive adaptation. Building on these principles of neuroplasticity, the preschool period and preschool experiences may have a particularly important impact on developmental trajectories and provide opportunities to build strong foundational skills more efficiently than is the case later in development. Thus, the preschool period is a window of opportunity for enhanced learning, and the neuroscience of sensitive periods can be used to inform the content, timing, and pedagogical focus of early educational curricula. In other words, the neuroscience of sensitive periods provides a roadmap for the "what," "when," and "how" of early curricula.

Experiences across environmental contexts play a significant role in early development. As summarized in a recent report by the National Academies of Sciences, Engineering, and Medicine, *Vibrant and Healthy Kids*:

> A large body of recent research provides insights into the mechanisms by which early adversity in the lives of young children and their families can change the timing of sensitive periods of brain and other organ system development and impact the "plasticity" of developmental processes [. . .] a wave of neurobiological studies in model systems and humans found that responses to pre- and postnatal early life stress are rooted in genetic and environmental interactions that can result in altered molecular and cellular development that impacts the assembly of circuits during sensitive periods of development. The demonstration that certain systems involved in cognitive and emotional development are more sensitive to early disturbances that activate stress response networks, such as the frontal cortex, hippocampus, amygdala, and the hypothalamic-pituitary-adrenal axis, provided a basis for both short- and long-term functional consequences of early life stress. New research has clarified that altered nutrition, exposure to environmental chemicals, and chronic stress during specific times of development can lead to functional biological changes that predispose individuals to manifest diseases and/or experience altered physical, social-emotional, and cognitive functions later in life. (2019, p. 7)

This section reviews key features of early development with particular relevance for fostering positive outcomes for preschool-aged children, including the caregiving environment, the presence of stress, and access to resources.

Caregiving Environment

The early caregiving environment—including familial relationships; safe, stable, nurturing relationships and environments; healthy living conditions; economic security; nutrition and food security; neighborhood and community conditions; housing; and environmental exposures—is crucial for long-term development (National Academies, 2019). Importantly, children learn optimally when they feel safe and secure in their home and neighborhood environment before arriving at preschool. Critical for this sense of basic security and readiness to learn and thrive is the presence of at least one nurturing and reliable primary caregiver upon whom a child can rely for protection and necessary physical and emotional support and assistance (Brown et al., 2020). This is necessary under all circumstances but particularly critical in environments with high rates of early adversity, where buffering factors are of paramount importance to ensuring positive developmental trajectories (Brown et al., 2020).

Certain supports within the caregiving environment are also necessary to enable young children to benefit optimally from learning experiences. Along this line, one key prerequisite is regular daily rhythms, central to which is the opportunity for restful sleep, which has been shown to be a necessary precondition for optimizing learning and memory in early childhood, as well as throughout life (Spencer et al., 2017). A related finding is that unpredictable parenting signals (e.g., parents behaving erratically) are associated with poorer executive function in middle childhood (Davis et al., 2022; Granger et al., 2021), a phenomenon also seen in animal models, where alterations in the development of subserving brain circuitry have been demonstrated (Davis et al., 2022). The basic forms of adversity in early childhood that have been shown to impact brain development and learning negatively are deprivation, threat, and unpredictability; therefore, these key domains need to be addressed prior to school entry if learning is to be optimized (McLaughlin & Sheridan, 2016). Importantly, when children live in chaotic households and/or neighborhoods that are impoverished and have high rates of violent crime, their basic sense of security and regularity is undermined. More obvious is the need for adequate nutrition to maintain energy, focus, and alertness. These prerequisites within the caregiving environment—sleep, predictability, and nutrition—are often either overlooked or assumed to be available to all children. In fact, many children do not have these foundational biological supports, a social reality highly relevant, and representing a major impediment, to many developing children's ability to learn.

Early Exposure to Stress

Related to these prerequisites of security, safety, adequate protection, and necessary resources, studies have demonstrated that children exposed to trauma and chronic stress have physiological responses that impact brain development and functioning in ways that interfere with the learning process. High levels of chronic stress impact both brain and behavior in ways that put the child on "high alert" for ongoing and expected threats, which of necessity diverts their attention from the learning process and alters cognitive processes that allow consolidation of memory, executive function, and other elements essential to learning (Gunnar, 2020). These conditions elevate circulating stress hormones, notably cortisol, with receptors in brain regions key to learning and memory. Chronic exposure to elevated stress hormones without external buffers, such as supportive caregivers, has been shown to alter brain development and related cognitive capacities negatively over time (Lupien et al., 2007). Accordingly, children with these exposures may require additional supports before and in concert with their entry into preschool environments to facilitate their development of the basic prerequisites for their ability to learn.

In addition to psychosocial stressors, children living in low-resource environments also have greater exposure to environmental toxins (National Academies, 2023). It has become clear over the past several decades that exposures to low levels of a growing list of environmental toxins found in air and water contribute to poor outcomes including low birth weight, shorter gestation, and intellectual disability, as well as increased risk for psychopathology (Lanphear, 2015; National Academies, 2023). The detrimental effects of these exposures in utero and in early childhood is underscored by the fact that the blood–brain barrier is more permeable during this period and that growing organs are more susceptible to the negative effects of toxins. Based on these facts, these exposures, which are ubiquitous but more common in underresourced neighborhoods, pose a major threat to the young child's ability to learn (Kumar et al., 2023).

Minoritized children and families face structural inequities, unequal treatment, and acts of discrimination and racism that add to the cumulative burden of stress and require focused attention (Shonkoff et al., 2021). Researchers have recently turned their attention to the unique impacts of racism on the foundations of physical and mental health. Studies of residential segregation by race as they affect risk exposures and health have, for example, linked poorer pregnancy outcomes among women of color to disproportionate exposures to environmental toxins (Miranda et al., 2009). At the family level, parents' self-reported experiences of discrimination have been associated with their children's social and emotional problems, as well as with increased levels of cortisol and proinflammatory cytokines—indicators of disrupted stress-response systems (Bécares et al., 2015; Condon et al., 2019; Gassman-Pines, 2015, as cited in Shonkoff et al., 2021, p. 123). And Black children are three times more likely than their White counterparts to lose their mother by age 10 (Umberson et al., 2017). These are among the experiences of adversity arising from racism, and their impacts, that minoritized children bring with them into their early childhood settings. To facilitate learning for these children, then, early educators need to be sensitized to and prepared to buffer these experiences. Toward this end, knowledge of trauma-informed approaches is a critical component of the professional preparation of early educators (de la Osa et al., 2024).

Access to Resources

Related to these basic prerequisites for early learning, neurodevelopmental research has shown that family socioeconomic status, particularly poverty, is negatively associated with differences in brain structure and function in multiple domains, including language, cognition, executive function, memory, and social-emotional processes (e.g., Brooks-Gunn & Duncan, 1997; Hackman et al., 2015; Noble et al., 2007; Stevens et al., 2009). Moreover, experiences that include those discussed above, as well as differences in opportunities to learn, have been found to account for a significant portion of the relationship between socioeconomic status and learning and development (Brooks-Gunn & Duncan, 1997; Capron & Duyme, 1989; Duncan et al., 1994; Jimerson et al., 2000; Noble et al., 2007; Schiff et al., 1982). Recent data from the Child Opportunity Index, which ranks neighborhoods on multiple dimensions of opportunity, such as access to early childhood centers and healthy food outlets, reveal that a majority of Black, Latine, and Native American children reside in low- or very low–opportunity communities, compared with one in five White and Asian children (Acevedo-Garcia et al., 2020). In addition, there is increasing evidence that exposure to "green space" and outdoor spaces are important for multiple developmental domains, including emotional well-being (McCormick, 2017).

HOW CHILDREN LEARN: THE SCIENCE OF EARLY LEARNING

Children learn in a multiplicity of ways—through active exploration and play; through observation of others, notably older children and adults; and through adults' explicitly sharing knowledge with them. This section reviews each of these types of learning in turn.

While these three types of learning occur across all cultures, their prevalence differs depending on cultural context. For example, children from U.S.–Mexican heritage families in which mothers had experience with Indigenous ways were found to be much more likely to learn from observing a toy construction activity directed to another child than were Mexican heritage children whose mothers had extensive experience going to Western schools (Silva et al., 2010). Further, as discussed later in this chapter in the section on language learning, children learn through child-directed speech, as well as through listening to adult conversations, with the prevalence of these learning opportunities differing depending on cultural context (e.g., Casillas et al., 2020; Shneidman & Goldin-Meadow, 2012).

Exploration and Play

Exploration and play have long been recognized as universal aspects of childhood, and they are found in every culture that has been studied (e.g., Hughes, 1999; see Vandermaas-Peeler, 2002, for review). At the same time, play varies across cultural contexts in multiple ways, including the nature of play activities children engage in, reflecting the diversity of children's experiences and the materials that are available, the degree to which adults and older children are involved in the play, and the nature of their involvement (e.g., Haight et al., 1999; Roopnarine et al., 1998; Vandermaas-Peeler, 2002, for review). There is also cultural variation in the degree to which play is viewed as being tied to learning or as differing from learning, which is viewed as linked to work more directly (Metaferia et al., 2021).

Environmental factors can also affect the extent to which children have access to safe environments for play. As noted in the 2023 National Academies report *Closing the Opportunity Gap for Young Children*, children from families with lower incomes and children from minoritized populations are more likely to live in environments where there is a risk of exposure to environmental contaminants than are children from other backgrounds. In addition, children in disadvantaged neighborhoods are more likely to live in environments where there is poor urban planning, increased risk of injury from roadways and traffic, and higher rates of neighborhood violence (National Academies, 2023).

Various constructivist theorists have highlighted the importance of play and exploration in the development of children's thinking, language, and social skills (e.g., Bruner, 1983; Piaget, 1962; Vygotsky, 1967, 1978). These theorists posit that the information children gain through play and exploration is not just received passively but rather is integrated actively with their prior concepts and ideas (see Narayan et al., 2013, for review). They also characterize play as a joyful activity with an important role in development and learning. For example, Bruner (1983) characterized play as a joyful way of solving problems and as a testbed for trying out and combining ideas and skills without worrying about consequences of failing to achieve a goal. Dewey (1910) emphasized the importance of a playful attitude toward the process of learning, coupled with the serious attitude of work toward goals of learning. These theories differ in the emphasis they place on adults and older children as promoting children's learning through explorations and play. Piaget (1970), for example, focused on the role of the child's own explorations of the world, characterizing the child as a little scientist who actively gathers information by exploring the world. In contrast, Vygotsky, Dewey, and Bruner considered the role of adults and older children in supporting children's development during play and other activities via the provision of materials and through language interactions (e.g., Bruner, 1983; Dewey, 1910; Vygotsky, 1967, 1978). Notably, Vygotsky (1978) highlighted the role of adults in extending children's learning by providing scaffolding that allows them to extend their learning into their zone of proximal development.

Contemporary researchers have built on and extended the work of these theorists. A growing body of research shows that children engage in and learn from active exploration as early as infancy. For example, as early as 11 months of age, babies learned more and engaged in more relevant exploratory behaviors when objects violated their expectations than from nearly identical experiences that were consistent with their expectations (Stahl & Feigenson, 2015). Follow-up studies replicated these findings and showed that infants explored more after an event that violated their expectations (e.g., an object that appeared to float) because they sought an explanation for why objects behaved in this manner (Perez & Feigenson, 2022).

Studies involving preschool children provide compelling evidence that children learn from exploration and explore more than adults even when they know that exploration carries risks (e.g., Gopnik, 2012, 2020; Liquin & Gopnik, 2022; Schulz, 2012; Xu & Kushnir, 2013). For example, in a task that involved discovering how stimuli were classified differently, Liquin & Gopnik (2022) found that preschool children were more likely to explore than adults, and children's propensity to explore enhanced their success on this task. Another study showed that 4- to 6-years-olds learned more when active exploration was encouraged and when adults did not fill in all the gaps in children's knowledge. In one study, Bonawitz et al. (2011) gave preschool children (48–72 months; mean age 58 months) a novel toy with four different functions. Children were randomized into one of four conditions that varied in terms of the pedagogical support the adult provided. Two critical conditions were the pedagogical condition, where an adult showed them one function of the toy (that it squeaked) and a baseline condition in which the adult merely gave them the toy without demonstrating any of its functions. Strikingly, the children discovered significantly more of the functions of the toy in the nonpedagogical baseline condition (M = 4.0) than in the pedagogical condition (M = 5.3). Moreover, children played with the toy significantly longer in the nonpedagogical condition.

In another study, 4- to 5- year-old children were presented with finding out the "secret of shapes" (e.g., triangles), and were randomly assigned to one of three conditions. In the didactic, pedagogical condition the adult taught the attributes of triangles directly; in the guided play condition the child was encouraged to do the discovering with teacher scaffolding; and in the free play condition, children were simply given the shapes to play with. Strikingly, children learned more about the defining features of shapes when they were in the guided play condition compared with both the direct instruction and the free play conditions; this was true both immediately after the training and 1 week later.

Considered together, these findings highlight the benefits of guided play in supporting children's learning and persistence. Guided play provides the child with agency to test their nascent theories about the world. It also provides them with adult-guided situations and language that support their learning (Hirsh-Pasek et al., 2020). Contemporary researchers, aligned with the Vygotskian view, emphasize the role of guided play in supporting the child's active exploration of their environment and their learning. Research findings indicate that guided play supports not only the growth of content knowledge (the "what" of learning) but also the learning process (the "how" of learning), which together enable them to pursue their questions, problem solve, and collaborate. With the exponential growth of information in contemporary society, it is important that children's experiences help them gain content knowledge, confidence, curiosity, creativity, communication, and collaborative skills—known as the 6 Cs; each is valued in the 21st century (Hirsh-Pasek et al., 2020).

Aligned with research and theory highlighting the connection of play to children's learning, preschool teachers rate children who display curiosity as having higher learning ability/skills; and teachers' ratings of children's curiosity in preschool are associated with children's achievement levels at kindergarten entry (Shah et al., 2018). However, despite these documented benefits of exploration and play, preschool environments vary in terms of whether exploration and question asking are encouraged or discouraged in favor of more structured activities that emphasize correct answers and adults providing children with information (Reid & Kagan, 2022). This may be linked to the belief that play and learning are separate, a false dichotomy discussed in Chapter 4. As pointed out by Zosh et al. (2018), there are many different kinds of play, and failure to recognize the nuanced spectrum of types of play can lead to confusion about how play relates to and supports learning. Play ranges from adult-directed play activities, in which the adult has a learning goal in mind; to guided play, in which the adult gives the child agency but provides scaffolding and guidance with a learning goal in mind; to free play, in which the child both initiates and constructs play without a specific learning goal (Zosh et al., 2018). Zosh et al. (2018) point out that play can be characterized by three attributes: the level of adult involvement, the extent to which the child creates the play, and whether a learning goal is present (Figure 3-1).

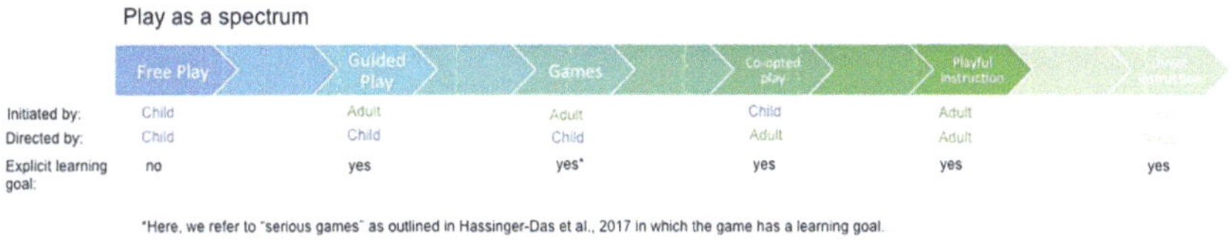

FIGURE 3-1 Playful experiences differ along a continuum in terms of initiation and direction of the experience and whether there is a learning goal.
SOURCE: Zosh et al., 2018.

Hirsh-Pasek et al. propose that guided play provides a sweet spot for supporting children's learning, as well as their curiosity, creativity, and collaborative skills (e.g., Hirsh-Pasek et al., 2008, 2020, 2022; Zosh et al., 2018). In guided play, the teacher plays the role of facilitator, which allows for intentional learning goals that can be tuned to the child's current skill levels. At the same time, the light-touch hand of the teacher in guided play activities provides the child with agency, which is positively associated with academic outcomes and interests (e.g., Bruner, 1983; Hirsh-Pasek et al., 2020, 2022). For example, one study examined parents' use of spatial language when playing with their 4-year-old children in three conditions—(1) free play with blocks, (2) guided play with blocks with a goal of building a particular structure, and (3) play with a preassembled structure (Ferrara et al., 2011). Parents in the guided play condition produced more spatial language than those in the free play or preassembled conditions. This finding is important because spatial language supports children's spatial thinking, which in turn predicts success in the disciplines of science, technology, engineering, and mathematics (e.g., Casasola et al., 2020; Hawes & Ansari, 2020; Mix et al., 2016, 2021; Pruden et al., 2011; Wai et al., 2009).

Related to these findings, pretend play and guided play are associated with oral language and literacy outcomes, likely because the language in which children engage during play is complex and contains rich vocabulary, including many mental-state verbs (e.g., Bruner, 1982; Dickinson & Tabors, 2001; Pellegrini & Galda, 1990; Roskos & Christie, 2001; Toub et al., 2018). Further, play activities support knowledge of mathematical language and thinking. Notably, play with a variety of materials provides opportunities to think about spatial relationships and patterns, either imagined or built; to compare magnitudes and shapes; and to enumerate sets (Eason et al., 2021, 2022; Fisher et al., 2013; Ramani & Siegler, 2008; Seo & Ginsburg, 2004; Siegler & Ramani, 2008).

While play-based learning is increasingly emphasized in research and practice in Western Euro-American contexts, a rich literature documents differences in the nature of play, the involvement of parents in play, and the amount of play children engage in depending on culture (see Vandermaas-Peeler, 2002, for review). Using three contrasting examples, Gaskins et al. (2007) highlight the fact that play is socially constructive and that adults' roles in children's play depend on culture. Whereas urban, educated American and Taiwanese adults cultivate children's pretend play, in Liberia, the Kpelle, who are subsistence horticulturists, accept but do not participate in children's play, as they need to conserve their time and energy to provide food and maintain their own strength. Instead, other children, including older children, are the playmates of younger children. Finally, in the Yucatec-Mayan culture, where people live in subsistence farming communities, development is seen as the unfolding of one's inner abilities and character. Consistent with this view, play is viewed as a distraction for children when they cannot help. Play still occurs, with older children taking the lead in pretend play, which typically involves pretending to do the work of adults rather than fantasy play. Additionally, the peak of pretend play in Yucatec-Mayan children is between ages 6 and 8, much later than the 3- to 6-year-old peak in Euro-American families. Rather than encouraging play, in the Yucatec-Mayan culture, children are encouraged to observe and work alongside adults in their community, as their work can eventually contribute to the overall productivity of the society. These cultural differences serve to illustrate the sociocultural nature of play.

Despite these cultural differences, the preschool landscape around the globe is currently undergoing rapid change, with many countries embracing play-based early education curricula. These changes are not without challenges, and they often mismatch with teacher and parent beliefs and lead to inequities; furthermore, professional development for teachers and large student–teacher ratios make these changes challenging to implement (Gupta, 2011; Yee et al., 2022). For example, in India, play-based private schools are equated with developmentally appropriate practices. Importantly, Gupta questions the appropriateness of Western, play-based approaches within a culture that prioritizes examination scores for access to higher education and advocates for approaches to early childhood education that emerge from Indian cultural values. Gupta (2011) records a teacher's statement that "it rains so children can play in the water," which connects a child-centered approach to the scarcity of water and the spirituality of the Monsoon season. In Korea, the revised Nuri curriculum (2019) put a heavy emphasis on free play, which has led to confusion among teachers about their role in supporting children's learning (Lee et al., 2023). The lack of professional development around play is a factor in this confusion, and the emphasis on free play is at odds with research findings showing that guided play is more conducive to supporting many learning goals.

The studies discussed above highlight the importance of considering play in a culturally responsive manner, not as something in which all children engage in a uniform manner. Viewed in this way, children's play has the potential to contribute to the cultural relevance of early education, as child-initiated play reflects children's cultural experiences and how they see themselves within the larger society, providing teachers with an important lens into children's lived experiences (Adair & Doucet, 2014). Moreover, children's play provides teachers with a way to engage in guided play, enabling the teacher to build on children's interests and skills, which, as we have discussed, may be one of the most effective ways to support learning.

A 2022 study involving interviews with 31 early childhood experts from different fields provides some relevant information with respect to play in early childhood education contexts that serve children from different demographic backgrounds (Reid & Kagan, 2022). The experts were broadly supportive of the importance of play in early childhood curricula and, relatedly, were supportive of autonomy-granting approaches that give young children a voice in how they learn. Their support for this kind of approach recognizes the importance of children's interests, curiosity, and explorations in the learning process and aligns with the research base. Nonetheless, the experts disagreed about the amount and nature of play that best supports children's learning. Roughly half called for more play in curricula, whereas others noted that play-based approaches have gone too far in some schools. A potential explanation for disagreements about the role of play in early childhood curricula may be the cultural differences in how play is valued and practiced, as discussed previously.

Many of the experts interviewed by Reid & Kagan (2022) also expressed the belief that the amount of play children experience varies by the socioeconomic status of the children in the classroom, such that children from a background of lower socioeconomic status experience less play. Consistent with this belief, Adair & Colegrove (2021) provide evidence that there is "segregation by experience" in educational settings, such that young children in classrooms characterized by higher socioeconomic status have more opportunities to be agents in their learning and are provided with more opportunities to carry out explorations of their world compared with children in classrooms characterized by lower socioeconomic status, who are disproportionately children of color. Instead, young children of color are more often required to sit with their legs folded and hands placed together in silence, not because they need to attend to pedagogical content but for the purpose of practicing valued behaviors (Adair & Colegrove, 2021).

Similarly, an influential paper utilizing two waves of the Early Childhood Longitudinal Study, Kindergarten Class data (1998 and 2011) reports evidence that, of the two, kindergarten was more like first grade (more structured with less play) in the 2011 cohort, influenced by the No Child Left Behind Act and increased accountability and testing. Bassok et al. (2016) found that this was more starkly the case in settings serving children eligible for free or reduced-price lunch or children who were non-White (Bassok et al., 2016). For example, kindergarten teachers serving a larger percentage of children eligible for free or reduced-price lunch (in the highest quartile of representation of this group) were significantly more likely to endorse the importance of children's knowing the alphabet at the time of kindergarten entry than was the case for kindergarten teachers serving students from backgrounds of higher socioeconomic status (51% versus 34%, respectively). These beliefs, whether implicit or explicit, are likely to have downstream consequences in terms of the nature of the pedagogy and curricula adopted in different early childhood settings, resulting in inequities in early learning opportunities.

The focus on more direct pedagogy and basic skills in classrooms serving children of lower socioeconomic status, racially minoritized, and immigrant backgrounds stems from deficit models, which incorporate the belief that minoritized children need direct instruction to build basic academic skills (e.g., vocabulary, letter recognition, counting) in order to narrow achievement gaps. Moreover, inequities in agentic learning stem from views about what children from different groups can handle, based, for example, on ideas about a "word gap" in children of Latine immigrants (Adair et al., 2017). When shown videos of Latine children engaging in agentic learning, teachers and school administrators said these practices are valuable but would not work in their classrooms because their students lacked vocabulary knowledge necessary for these practices to work. Moreover, children who viewed the videos were consistent in their evaluations of the children in the videos as being bad, not learning, being too noisy, and not listening to their teachers. While well meaning, limiting children's agency in early education contexts based on perceived shortcomings denies children the kinds of experiences they need to build advanced language and thinking skills, as well as skills necessary for pursuing learning in which they are interested and collaborating and conversing with other children. Differential access to autonomy-granting, play-based pedagogy in early education is potentially harmful and is typically rooted in stereotypes about weaknesses of children and their families instead of being attributed to systemic factors that contribute to group differences (Adair, 2015; Adair & Colegrove, 2021; Adair et al., 2017; National Academies, 2023).

Young children need to gain both basic skills and higher-order thinking skills and be afforded the opportunities to acquire these skills in early education settings. Focusing on basic skills through direct instruction to the exclusion of agentic play-based activities may have unintended negative consequences because such gains have been found to fade over time (Bailey et al., 2016, 2017, 2020). In contrast, instruction that includes more play-based activities designed to foster exploration, curiosity, complex language skills, and higher-order thinking (e.g., acting out child-created narratives; exploring the conditions that lead plants to grow at different rates) are associated with positive long-term effects on children's learning, as well as on their learning dispositions (e.g., Frausel et al., 2020, 2021). Thus, differences in pedagogical approaches that are related to biased perceptions about children's sociocultural and linguistic backgrounds may be harmful, as they are likely to contribute to the very disparities in achievement they are intended to close.

A shortcoming of the current research base examining the prevalence and benefits of play and exploration is that play-based curricula and learning have not been examined systematically in early education settings of different types, and in settings that serve children from differing cultural and socioeconomic backgrounds. While existing research suggests that there is a lack of equity in play-based approaches to learning in early education settings, more research is needed to confirm that this is the case and if so, to understand why this is happening. Further, research is needed to examine the benefits of play-based learning for children from different backgrounds. An essential step in addressing these gaps is conducting systematic research on children's experience with agentic learning in early education settings serving children from diverse backgrounds, and studying the benefits of this approach for children's learning as well as for culturally affirming practices that foster the belonging of children and families. In view of evidence from the science of learning, it is important that all children are provided with engaging, agentic learning experiences. With content knowledge exploding exponentially, educational approaches that support not only the "what" but the "how" of learning are of increasing importance. Children need to learn how to gain new knowledge, how to find answers to their questions, how to problem solve, how to communicate their ideas, and how to collaborate. These active, agentic, and playful approaches to learning, when implemented well, can serve to nurture children's excitement about learning.

Observation of Others

Beginning with Bandura's (1977) pioneering work on social learning, observational learning and imitation have been important for development and learning. Bandura posited that children observe and imitate role models and that this kind of learning requires attention, memory, reproduction, and motivation. More recent research has shown that humans, beginning in infancy, are astute observational learners. As early as 14 months of age, children engage in "overimitation," highlighting their sensitivity to the culture they experience. For example, when they see an adult turn a light on by bending forward from the waist and touching a panel with their head, they imitate this behavior (Meltzoff, 1988). Although it would have been easier and less awkward to turn on the light with their hands, the infants turned on the light with their heads, imitating not only the goal but the means by which the adult turned the light on. Additionally, findings show that infants do not imitate what they perceive to be accidental behaviors or actions carried out by inanimate devices, but rather imitate intentional behaviors, even when those behaviors fail to achieve the intended goal (Carpenter et al., 1998; Meltzoff, 1995). In other words, children imitate the intention of the agent as well as the means by which they achieved their goal. Moreover, as early as the second year of life, children are more likely to imitate the actions of a linguistic ingroup-member than an to imitate an agent who speaks a foreign language (Buttelmann et al., 2013; Howard et al., 2015). Preschool children are also less likely to imitate an onscreen robot than an onscreen human agent (Sommer et al., 2021). The proclivity of humans to imitate other humans, particularly members of their ingroup, represents a powerful way in which culture is shared intergenerationally. Thus, observation and imitation contribute to the accumulation and growth of knowledge across generations (e.g., Tomasello, 2020; Tomasello et al., 1993).

Building on findings showing that young children are astute cultural learners, Rogoff et al. (2015) studied the learning behaviors of children in Indigenous American communities, documenting differences in the learning behaviors and experiences of children growing up in different cultural contexts. Their Learning by Observing and Pitching In (LOPI) model characterizes a kind of learning that is common in, but not exclusive to, Indigenous American communities (Rogoff et al., 2015; Figure 3-2). LOPI consists of seven related facets, with the central facet being that the learner is incorporated in, and contributing to, meaningful family and community endeavors. LOPI involves wide-lens observing and listening-in on mature, purposive adult activities and conversations, being guided by members of the community to contribute meaningfully to communal goals and cultural activities, which increases their sense of belonging. Building on the LOPI model, Bang et al. (2015) highlight the more-than-human ecological interactions of Menominee Indian communities in Wisconsin, extending the

Learning by Observing and Pitching-In

3. Social organization of endeavors:
Collaborative, flexible ensemble,
fluidly coordinating and blending
ideas, agendas and pace.
All engage,
anyone may take the initiative.

2. Motive:
Learner is eager
to **contribute** and **belong.**
Others' motive is
to **accomplish** endeavor
(and maybe to guide).

4. Goal of learning:
To **transform** participation,
learn **consideration & responsibility**
along with information & skills,
to **contribute**
and belong in the community.

1. Community
organization of learning:
Learner is **incorporated**
and **contributing** to
family/community endeavors

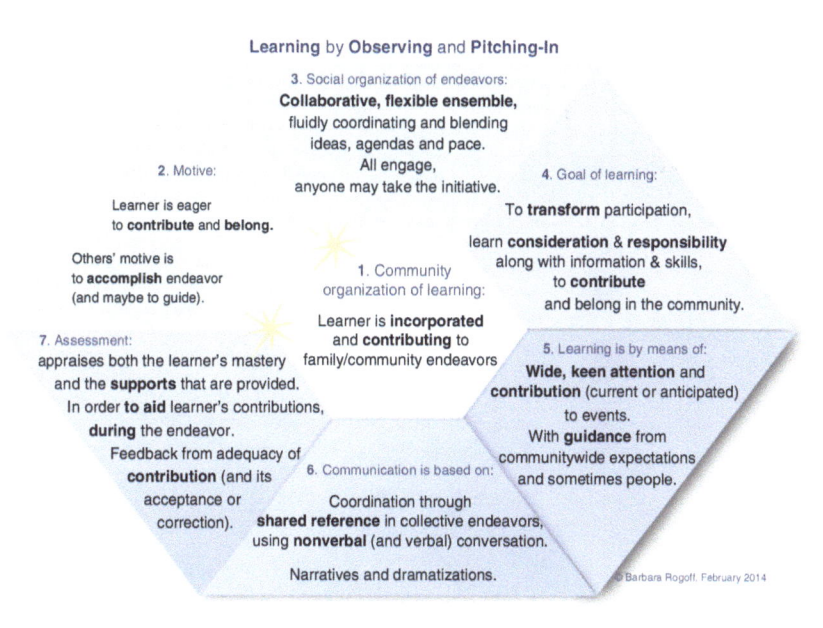

7. Assessment:
appraises both the learner's mastery
and the **supports** that are provided.
In order **to aid** learner's contributions,
during the endeavor.
Feedback from adequacy of
contribution (and its
acceptance or
correction).

5. Learning is by means of:
Wide, keen attention and
contribution (current or anticipated)
to events.
With **guidance** from
communitywide expectations
and sometimes people.

6. Communication is based on:
Coordination through
shared reference in collective endeavors,
using **nonverbal** (and verbal) conversation.
Narratives and dramatizations.

© Barbara Rogoff, February 2014

FIGURE 3-2 Learning by observing and pitching in.
SOURCE: Rogoff et al., 2015.

LOPI model to include human–nature as well as human–human interactions (e.g., extending component 5 of the LOPI model [see Figure 3-2] to include wide-lens attention to human interactions with animals, plants, and nonanimate natural kinds, such as water).

The LOPI model is concordant with basic research findings highlighting the early sensitivity of children to the purposeful behaviors of adults around them and their selective imitation of their behaviors. Importantly, as pointed out by Rogoff et al. (2015), LOPI is deeply embedded in the cultures of Indigenous American communities and is consistent with many other practices and values of these communities.

Rogoff et al. (2015) contrast LOPI learning to Assembly Line Instruction (ASI; Figure 3-3). ASI typically involves providing instruction outside of the context of adult activities, often at school (Rogoff et al., 2015). As pointed out by Pellegrini (2009), the type of instruction detailed in the ASI model is relatively recent and is associated with industrialized societies.

The careful work of these researchers shows that the ways children learn, as well as what they learn, are deeply connected to their cultural contexts. These findings hold important implications for early childhood education, as the kinds of learning that children experience may be very different from what they experience in their homes and communities.

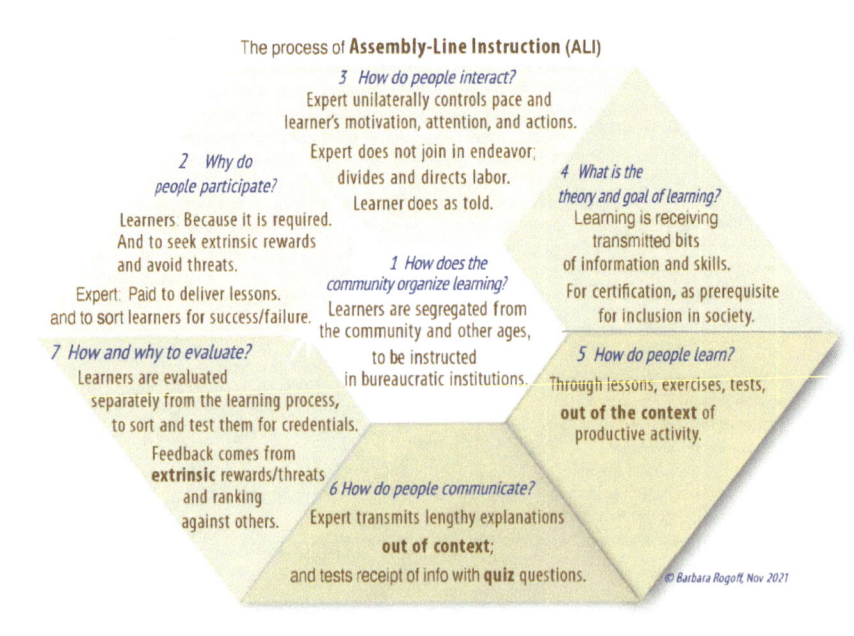

FIGURE 3-3 Assembly-line instruction.
SOURCE: Rogoff & Mejía-Arauz, 2022.

Sharing Knowledge Through Verbal Exchanges

Much of what children know and learn is influenced by the transmission of knowledge across generations. Indeed, the uniqueness of human cognition, including the human ability to innovate, depends on this intergenerational sharing, referred to as the "ratchet effect" (e.g., Tennie et al., 2009). Sharing knowledge with children occurs in a variety of ways, including via language, or "learning from testimony" (see Harris et al., 2018). This sharing occurs for multiple kinds of information but is particularly important for types of knowledge that are not accessible to children through their own explorations or firsthand observations. These include, for example, information about distant countries, historical events, microscopic entities, and the solar system (e.g., Harris, 2012; Harris et al., 2018).

Aligned with the views of constructivist theorists, young children are active participants in this sharing. That is, they do not just passively accept information that others share with them. Instead, they evaluate new information with respect to their preexisting knowledge and curate information based on whether the informant is credible (see Harris et al., 2018, for review). Koenig & Echols (2003) found that as early as 16 months of age, children are sensitive to the credibility of an informant—for example, looking longer at an informant that labeled a dog as a "cup." Similarly, 3- and 4-year-olds who were able to identify accurate and inaccurate labelers of objects showed trust in novel information provided by the accurate labeler (Koenig et al., 2004). In three meta-analyses, Tong et al. (2020) found that 3- to 6-year-old children trust the testimony of credible informants as well as the testimony of informants with more positive social characteristics (e.g., information provided by characters they perceive as nicer). In addition, they identified an important developmental change between ages 3 and 4 years: 4-years-olds weigh informants' knowledge more heavily than their social characteristics, while 3-year-olds do not, possibly because of increases in theory of mind at age 4 (Tong et al., 2020).

Children's Learning During the Preschool Years

This section briefly considers the kinds of skills children begin to acquire in the early years of life, including skills considered to be domain general and those considered to be domain specific. "Domain-general skills" include social-emotional learning and executive functioning skills. They also include language skills, which of course support communication and literacy, but provide tools for understanding relational concepts, (e.g., de Villiers & de Villiers, 2014; Gentner, 2016). "Domain-specific skills," such as numerical thinking and understanding the physical world, begin with core sensitivities that are present from birth onward, but require acquisition of knowledge (e.g., the count system) to transcend these starting points (e.g., Carey & Barner, 2019; Spelke & Kinzler, 2007). Importantly, learning in all of these domains predicts academic learning as well as important life outcomes, including health, income, and life satisfaction (e.g., Diamond, 2016; Moffitt et al., 2011; Ritchie & Bates, 2013; Watts et al., 2014).

As reviewed in Chapters 2 and 4, early childhood curricula can be broadly separated into comprehensive or whole-child curricula or focused, domain-specific curricula. Most multidomain preschool curricula address the domains of literacy/language, mathematics, science, social-emotional learning, and the arts. Importantly, during the preschool years, instructional activities often support multiple domains of learning. To take just one example, experiencing a book about sharing may support children's social-emotional learning, math learning, and language and literacy development. In the sections that follow, we provide a brief overview of research on young children's learning in key domains that are included in early education curricula, including social-emotional learning, executive function, language/literacy learning, and math learning.

Social-Emotional Development as Foundational for Learning

Decades of research have made clear that early emotional development—evidenced by the ability to identify and express one's own emotional states, accurately recognize emotions expressed by others, and adaptively regulate intense emotions—is key to adaptive success in childhood and later life (National Research Council [NRC] & Institute of Medicine [IOM], 2000). Evidence also shows that these skills can be fostered and enhanced in early childhood learning environments (Denham, 2019). These features of emotional competence—emotion knowledge; understanding of the causes, consequences, and display rules of an emotion (Izard et al., 2011); and the ability to regulate emotion—then foster the development of social skills. Together, social-emotional skills facilitate meaningful interpersonal relationships and interactions characterized by prosocial behavior, empathy, and interpersonal connectedness with peers. It also has become clear that these social-emotional competencies set the stage for enhanced learning trajectories, a finding validated by a meta-analysis showing that interventions focused on social-emotional learning increased academic performance by 11 percentile points (Durlak et al., 2011). Those children with better social-emotional skills also showed reduced conduct problems and emotional distress, more prosocial behaviors, and more positive social attitudes toward self and others. In keeping with this finding, greater social-emotional competence has been associated with less psychopathology and more adaptive and academic success broadly within early childhood and beyond (Finlon et al., 2015).

At preschool age or earlier, children are able to infer basic emotions from expressions and situations (Bell et al., 2019; Denham, 2019). Increased early exposure to language has been shown to support emotional development (Lindquist et al., 2015). More broadly, a supportive relationship with a primary caregiver has been established as foundational for social-emotional development (National Academies, 2023). The supportive primary caregiver may provide emotion language to aid in emotion knowledge. Perhaps more important, the caregiver serves as the child's external emotion regulator and emotion coach (also referred to as coregulation in infancy), and models and validates the appropriate expression of emotion in context. Further, evidence indicates that greater language skills support the young child's ability to regulate emotion autonomously instead of relying on caregiver-supported regulation (Eisenberg et al., 2005; NRC & IOM, 2000). Accordingly, many early childhood interventions designed for the prevention of later psychopathology target this element of the child–caregiver relationship and facilitate the child's emotion knowledge and competence (Bohlmann et al., 2015; Salmon et al., 2016; Shonkoff & Fisher, 2013). Furthermore, the importance of this focus on social-emotional development for early education is underscored by how predictive these skills are of later academic achievement. Thus, the preschool teacher (through curriculum and teacher–child relationship dynamics) can also play an important role in facilitating social-emotional development and should be an important focus of curriculum development and prioritization.

In summary, early social-emotional development represents foundational skills that are necessary for healthy learning trajectories. Furthermore, these skills are important beyond their role as foundational for cognitive development, having interactive effects across developmental domains: cognition and emotion are dynamic developmental processes, with the maturation of one serving as a catalyst for enhancement of higher-level skills in the other (Bell & Wolfe, 2004; Bell et al., 2019; Davidson et al., 2014).

Executive Function as Foundational for Learning

Executive functioning skills include working memory, inhibitory control, attention shifting, and cognitive flexibility (Miyake et al., 2000). These skills develop rapidly during the preschool years, with their development being related to the maturation of the prefrontal cortex (Diamond, 2020). Prior to about 4.5 years of age, the various components of executive functioning load on one factor and are less differentiated than at older ages (e.g., Wiebe et al., 2011). Early executive functioning and self-regulation skills are related to concurrent and future academic achievement (e.g., Alloway & Alloway, 2010; Blair, 2016; Bull et al., 2008; Schmidt et al., 2022; Zelazo et al., 1997).

Executive functioning skills are related to children's socioeconomic background by 54 months of age, and this relation is stable across development (Hackman et al., 2015; Lawson et al., 2018). Moreover, executive functioning skills partially mediate the relation of socioeconomic status to academic achievement in young children (Lawson & Farah, 2017; Waters et al., 2021). Additionally, family stress and family investment are related—that is, the emotional support (e.g., warmth) and cognitive stimulation families provide are positively related to children's executive functioning skills, whereas their intrusiveness and control are negatively related to children's executive functioning skills (see Koşkulu-Sancar et al., 2023, for review). Importantly, executive functioning skills are malleable; they improve when family economic circumstances improve, consistent with neurobiological evidence from animal models (Hackman et al., 2015; McEwen & Morrison, 2014).

A large body of research has examined the effects of various kinds of training on executive functioning skills (e.g., curricular/educational approaches, activities targeting particular executive functioning skills, multilingual exposure in the first years of life, computer games, physical activities; see Clements & Sarama, 2019; Diamond & Ling, 2016; and National Academies, 2017, for review). These efforts show mixed results and many questions remain about the kinds and intensity of training that are required to yield positive results, and particularly what determines generalizability and durability of training effects that are found. Diamond & Ling (2016) review existing evidence and conclude that many kinds of training enhance the trained skill in the same and similar contexts, but that generalization of trained executive functioning skills is narrow. That is, training does not extend beyond contexts that are highly similar to those used in training. Moreover, positive effects of training fade over time as is true for other cognitive skills (Diamond & Ling, 2016). There is also evidence that interventions may be more effective for children with low executive functioning skills, including children growing up in poverty and those diagnosed with attention deficit hyperactivity disorder (e.g., Diamond & Ling, 2016; Klingberg et al., 2005; Tominey & McClelland, 2011).

As mentioned above, preschool children's executive functioning skills relate to their academic achievement, including later literacy (e.g., Bierman et al., 2008) and math skills (e.g., Clark et al., 2010). The relation of early executive function to mathematics is stronger than its relation to literacy, perhaps because of greater executive functioning demands of early mathematics (e.g., Blair et al., 2011; Fuhs et al., 2015; McClelland et al., 2014; Monette et al., 2011; see Clements et al., 2016, for review). Of course, correlational evidence leaves the directionality of the executive function–academic achievement relation ambiguous, and experimental evidence is needed to determine the causal direction of these relations (e.g., Van der Ven et al., 2012; see Clements et al., 2016, for review). One study used this approach to examine the effects of different preschool curricula on children's kindergarten executive functioning skills. Findings of this randomized experiment showed that children who received the *Building Blocks* math curriculum in preschool had stronger executive functioning skills in kindergarten compared with both children in the *Building Blocks* plus Scaffolding Executive Functioning condition and the Business-as-Usual condition (Clements et al., 2020). These findings suggest that curricula that engage children in mathematical thinking have spillover effects that are beneficial to executive function, and in fact work better than a curriculum that focuses on both mathematics and executive functioning skills.

There is also some evidence that early education programs that directly support children's executive functioning skills are beneficial. For example, Montessori and *Tools of the Mind* curricula, where teachers are trained to exercise children's executive functioning skills, improve these skills more effectively than did curricula in control classrooms (Diamond et al., 2019; Lillard & Else-Quest, 2006).

Relatedly, research is needed to develop curricula and pedagogical approaches that support the learning of preschool children who display a wide range of executive functioning skills. This is particularly important as executive functioning skills develop rapidly during this period. Moreover, these settings often include children of different ages, further contributing to the variability in the executive functioning skills of children in the same classroom.

Language Learning

Young children are prodigious language learners from birth; this is true across cultural contexts (see Chapter 7 for a detailed discussion of multilingual learning). Of course, language learning depends on having access to language experiences, which vary both quantitatively and qualitatively within and across cultural contexts. A key takeaway from research on language learning is that it is resilient: across cultural contexts, children have capacity to learn their native language and multiple other languages (National Academies, 2017).

Language learning begins during the first year of life. An important early aspect of language learning is a perceptual narrowing of phonemic discrimination, which is characterized by an increase in native phoneme perception and a decrease in nonnative phoneme perception in the second half of the first year of life, as a result of language experience (Kuhl et al., 1992, 2006; Werker & Tees, 1984). Moreover, this narrowing is associated with more advanced language development at later ages during the preschool period, providing evidence that it is an important step in the commitment of the brain to a child's native period, and may represent a sensitive or critical period in language development (Kuhl et al., 2005).

As noted, the rate at which young children learn language is related to the quantity and quality of their language experiences. For example, preschool children who hear more words and a more diverse set of words show higher levels of vocabulary knowledge (e.g., Huttenlocher et al., 1991). Similarly, Huttenlocher et al. (2002) found that when teachers used more complex sentences in school (defined as sentences including more than one clause), children had better comprehension of complex sentences at the end of the school year, after controlling for the overall quality of the classroom environment and children's comprehension of complex sentences at the beginning of the year.

Other studies have focused on qualitative aspects of children's language interactions, including parents' responsiveness to children's vocalization, turn taking, and question asking, and how these interactions relate to language learning. Findings show that parents' responsiveness to children's early vocalizations (at 9 and 13 months of age) predicts children's vocabulary growth over and above their earlier milestones (Tamis-LeMonda et al., 2001). Parents' responsiveness is hypothesized to increase young children's pragmatic understanding that language is a tool for sharing intentions, which propels their language learning (Tamis-LeMonda et al., 2014).

Sociopragmatic approaches to language development emphasize the role of both members of the parent–child dyad and their joint attention in language interactions and in children's language learning (e.g., Bruner, 1983; Nelson, 2007; Tomasello, 2003). Research within this framework has examined how turn taking between an adult and child influences the child's language development. As shown in a meta-analysis, turn taking and adult word counts predict children's language proficiency independently (Wang et al., 2020). In addition, turn taking is related not only to the language skills of 4- to 6-year-olds, but also to neural activation in the left inferior frontal gyrus (Broca's area), which is implicated in language processes (Romeo et al., 2018). Taken together, these findings support the role of language interaction and active child involvement in the growth of language skills.

Tomasello (2020) theorizes that understanding a communicative partner as an intentional agent with whom one can share attention and collaborate is fundamental to symbolic communication and hence to the acquisition of language, which requires that the child understand that words are used to communicate with others intentionally. The importance of understanding and relating to others for language acquisition is supported by the difficulty that some children with autism spectrum disorder have with language learning (Hobson, 1993; Tomasello, 2000).

Relatedly, asking children open-ended questions supports their language development as well as their autobiographical memory skills; this is the case in the context of both play and book reading (Boland et al., 2003; Fivush et al., 2006; Rowe et al., 2016). Open-ended questions actively engage children in conversations, with positive effects on their language development and on their learning more generally. Further, open-ended questions provide adults with a window into children's language skills and thinking, which can guide the scaffolding of language development.

Research on shared book reading provides additional evidence supporting the importance of children's taking an active role in language learning. Dialogic reading, characterized by questions and prompts that evoke participation by children, has been shown to benefit children's language skills, including their vocabulary and narrative skills, both immediately after interventions and after delays. Positive effects of interventions involving dialogic reading have been found in studies involving parent–child dyads as well as those involving early childhood educators and their students (Beals et al., 1994; Whitehurst et al., 1988; Zevenbergen et al., 2003). These beneficial effects have been found for both native English speakers and children who are English language learners (Brannon & Dauksas, 2014). There is also evidence that this approach benefits the language development of preschool children with language learning disabilities (Crain-Thoreson & Dale, 1999; Dale et al., 1996). Moreover, even though shared book reading represents a relatively small percentage (9%) of young children's overall language input, evidence shows that it supports the language development of children between 1 and 2.5 years of age, after controlling for the language children hear in non–book reading contexts (Demir-Lira et al., 2019). This may be the case because books contain more diverse vocabulary and more complex syntactical structures than language shared outside of the book reading context (Demir-Lira et al., 2019; Montag et al., 2015).

Another aspect of shared book reading that is important in supporting children's identity development and sense of belongingness is seeing themselves depicted in the books (discussed in more detail in Chapter 4). However, racially minoritized (Adukia et al., 2021) and female characters are underrepresented in children's books (Casey et al., 2021). These findings are important, as depictions in books provide children with cues as to what is possible for them, and the underrepresentation of certain groups serves to limit possibilities for children in those groups.

Cultural context is another important dimension of language learning. Although children in all cultures hear both child- and adult-directed speech (also referred to as overheard speech), the relative amounts of these kinds of input vary markedly across cultural contexts. On average, for example, 65% of the language heard by young North American children aged 3–20 months is child directed (range 17–100%), with this percentage increasing with increasing maternal education (Bergelson et al., 2019). Moreover, research found no significant change in the amount of child-directed speech over this age range, but a decrease in adult-directed speech. In contrast, children in certain cultural contexts (e.g., Mayan cultures in Mexico) hear much less child-directed speech than do children in the United States. A longitudinal study compared the amount of child- and adult-directed speech heard by Yucatec Mayan children growing up in rural villages in southern Mexico and urban American children during the second and third years of life. At 13 months of age, only 21% of utterances heard by the Mayan children were child-directed, compared with 69% for 14-month U.S. children. By 35 months of age, however, 60% of the speech heard by the Mayan children was child directed, compared with 62% for the U.S. children at 30 months (Shneidman & Goldin-Meadow, 2012). This convergence in the amount of child-directed speech by 3 years of age may reflect that by this time, adults in both cultures consider children to be conversational partners.

Despite these differences in exposure to child-directed speech in different cultural contexts, there is evidence that children who hear less child-directed speech achieve language milestones, including first words and first word combinations, at the same age as U.S. children who hear more child-directed speech, supporting the resilience of language development (Casillas et al., 2020). This may be the case because children hearing low amounts of child-directed speech increase their attention to adult-directed speech, or because child-directed speech occurs in routine contexts with repetition—in other words, in bursts—which makes it more interpretable by young children. Hypotheses for how children in environments with little child-directed speech achieve language milestones at about the same ages as children who hear large amounts of child-directed speech include its burstiness and children's increased attentiveness to others-directed speech (Casillas et al., 2020; Schwab & Lew-Williams, 2016).

Although early language milestones are resilient, and children in diverse cultural contexts become fluent speakers of the language(s) to which they are exposed, there is also evidence that child-directed speech is more closely related to vocabulary size than is overheard speech in and across disparate cultural contexts. This is likely the case because child-directed speech focuses on aspects of the world to which children are attending, and that they therefore are more likely to understand (Shneidman et al., 2013). Nonetheless, and importantly, it is possible that learning language in contexts in which overheard speech predominates may build important strengths in deploying attentional capacities (e.g., Casillas et al., 2020).

Math Learning

Building on core knowledge about number and space, children's mathematical thinking and skills grow rapidly during the preschool years. Moreover, children's mathematical knowledge at kindergarten entry is related to long-term learning trajectories in mathematics, as well as academic achievement more broadly (Claessens et al., 2009; Duncan et al., 2007;

Watts et al., 2014, 2018). These relations hold after controlling for other likely predictors of mathematics achievement, including socioeconomic status, which underscores the importance of gaining greater understanding of young children's math learning and how to support it.

Broadly, early math skills include numerical skills, spatial skills, understanding of patterns, and understanding of data and measurement (NRC, 2009). Within the numerical domain, children typically learn the count list and how to use it to enumerate the number of objects in a set. Notably, during the preschool years, children gain an understanding of key counting principles, including (1) the one-one principle (each item should be tagged by a count word once and only once), (2) the stable-order principle (count words must be ordered in the same sequence each time a count is carried out, (3) the cardinal principle (the number word used to tag the last item is the summary symbol for the set size, (4) the abstraction principle (any set can be counted), and (5) the order-irrelevance principle (the items in a set can be tagged in any order; Gelman & Galistel, 1978). They also gain the ability to order sets, to compare the magnitude of sets, to compose and decompose sets, and to carry out simple calculations (e.g., Clements & Sarama, 2014; Feigenson et al., 2004; Fuson, 1988; Le Corre & Carey, 2007; Litkowski et al., 2020; Sarama & Clements, 2009; Wynn, 1992).

Although the attainment of early math skills is often viewed as synonymous with learning numerical skills and perhaps the names of shapes, these important aspects of mathematics do not represent the entirety of children's foundational math concepts. Notably, early math skills include two core areas: numerical thinking, which includes understanding whole numbers, operations, and relations; and geometry, spatial thinking, and measurement. Additionally, young children learn to notice relations and patterns, to reason about these relations, and to communicate their mathematical ideas (see NRC, 2009, for review). During the preschool years, for example, children gain foundational spatial skills, including the ability to categorize shapes based on their defining features; to compose and decompose shapes; to mentally manipulate shapes; and to represent relations among environmental entities, as well as the self and environmental entities (e.g., Casasola et al., 2020; Fisher et al., 2013; Hawes et al., 2015; Levine et al., 1999; Newcombe & Huttenlocher, 2003; Pruden et al., 2011). Moreover, children's numerical and spatial skills are highly related, and some researchers argue that mathematics is inherently spatial (e.g., Clements & Sarama, 2011; Dehaene, 1997; Verdine et al., 2017). Teaching young children spatial skills—either mental transformation skills or visuospatial working memory skills—also leads to improvements in performance on numerical tasks (Cheng & Mix, 2014; Mix et al., 2021).

Mathematical activities, both formal and informal, and "math talk" (talk about number and spatial relations) in the early home environment vary widely and are related to children's mathematical knowledge at preschool entry and beyond (Baroody & Ginsburg, 1990; Blevins-Knabe & Musan-Miller, 1996; Casey et al., 2018; Gunderson & Levine, 2011; LeFevre et al., 2009; Levine et al., 2010; Pruden et al., 2011; Ramani et al., 2015; Susperreguy & Davis-Kean, 2016). Opportunities to learn mathematics in early education settings also vary widely and are correlated to both math learning over the preschool year and achievement in mathematics through at least eighth grade (e.g., Claessens & Engel, 2013; Claessens et al., 2009; Duncan et al., 2007; Klibanoff et al., 2006).

Beyond studies reporting correlations between math learning opportunities and outcomes, several experimental studies have found that math learning opportunities are causally related to preschool children's early mathematics skills (e.g., Gibson et al., 2020; Ramani & Siegler, 2008; Siegler & Ramani, 2008). Consistent with these findings, preschool math interventions have been found to lead to gains in mathematics over the school year and to higher math skills as late as fifth grade (e.g., Raudenbush et al., 2020; Watts et al., 2018). Thus, children's math learning opportunities play an important role in their early mathematical development.

Qualitative aspects of the math learning opportunities young children experience are also related to their math learning. For example, Gunderson & Levine (2011) found that parents' number talk, when focused on actions such as counting or labeling visible sets, predicted children's understanding of cardinal numbers; but number talk referring to more abstract sets or concepts (e.g., being 3 years old) did not. Additionally, in a parent-delivered number book intervention study, books focused on small set sizes (1–3) resulted in gains in cardinal number understanding for children who understood the meanings of only the first two number words, whereas number books focused on larger set sizes (4–6) did not (Gibson et al., 2020). This finding is consistent with research showing the power of scaffolding in the child's zone of proximal development (Vygotsky & Cole, 1978). In an experimental study, Mix et al. (2012) found that children's understanding of the cardinal meanings of number words was enhanced when children were provided with the cardinal label of a set and the set was then counted, but not when the set was just labeled or just counted.

Another study found that when parents used a number word accompanied by a number gesture during naturalistic interactions with 14- to 58-month-old children, the children were more likely to respond with a number word, and with the correct number word, than when parents said a number word without an accompanying number gesture (Oswald et al., 2023). Further, parents' talk about more advanced math concepts for preschoolers attending Head Start—including the cardinal value of numbers, the ordinal relations of numbers, and arithmetic—predicted children's understanding of these more advanced concepts better than did simpler math talk consisting of counting and number identification. In addition, as for language development, actively engaging children in mathematical thinking through prompting and question asking has been found to be an effective way to support children's math learning (Eason et al., 2021). These studies suggest that beyond the quantity of math learning experiences, quality also matters.

Given the heterogeneity of young children's mathematical knowledge, connected to variations in their opportunities to learn math concepts and skills in the early home environment, teachers face an instructional challenge in supporting children's math development in early education settings. Formative assessments can help teachers provide instruction that is tuned to children's skill levels. To assess whether such assessment would result in positive learning results, Raudenbush et al. (2020) randomly assigned 49 classrooms serving children mainly from low-income backgrounds to a treatment or a business-as-usual control group. Teachers in the treatment classrooms implemented an assessment–instruction system, consisting of three cycles of formative assessments linked to instructional strategies. The researchers found positive effects of the intervention on children's foundational numerical skills, as well as their verbal comprehension skills. These findings are consistent with the positive effects found for the *Building Blocks* system, which encourages formative assessment, on mathematics outcomes, as well as on language and literacy (Clements & Sarama, 2008; Sarama & Clements, 2003; Sarama et al., 2012). They also mirror findings with elementary school children showing positive effects of this kind of approach (Connor et al., 2018; Hassrick et al., 2017). Taken together, these findings suggest that young children's math learning benefits when input is tuned to their knowledge levels, and that such a focus on math learning does not take away from but benefits their learning of language and literacy skills.

The above findings from naturalistic observations and experimental studies in laboratory, home, and school environments provide important information on effective ways to support children's number knowledge. However, this research has focused mainly on middle-income families from Western cultures and countries and needs to be extended to more diverse samples. Emerging evidence, mainly from studies of older students, indicates that math learning is strengthened with a culturally responsive, strengths-based approach. Such an approach attends to the meaningfulness of math learning activities, which increases interest in learning mathematics. This is the case both in classrooms and in engaging families in their children's math learning (e.g., Civil et al., 2008; Hunter et al., 2022). More research is needed to examine culturally responsive, strengths-based math instruction with young children, although existing evidence indicates that this instructional approach is likely to be beneficial.

Science and Engineering Learning

Related to the way they strive to understand their world, infants and young children are frequently characterized as "little scientists" who form intuitive theories about how physical and social aspects of their world operate. Supporting this view, by preschool age children can make inferences and predictions and carry out explorations that allow them to infer causal structures (Gopnik & Wellman, 2012; Kuhn, 2012; Lapidow & Walker, 2020; Shtulman & Walker, 2020; Sobel & Legare, 2014). They do this by exploring the world independently (Cook et al., 2011; Lapidow & Walker, 2020), by asking discriminating questions (Chouinard et al., 2007; Ruggeri et al., 2019), and by observing others (Mills, 2013; see Shtulman & Walker, 2020, for a comprehensive review). Beyond this behavioral evidence that children's acquisition of knowledge resembles that of scientists (Carey, 2013; Gopnik, 2012), computational models and Bayesian inferencing have provided evidence that young children's theory building and change are based on their prior understandings and the statistics of the new evidence they gather, much like the activities involved in scientific theory building (Gopnik, 2012; Gopnik & Tenenenbaum, 2007; Griffiths et al., 2011; Xu, 2019).

Of course, the intuitive theories (also referred to as folk theories) that young children construct are not identical in content or process to evidence-based scientific theories. Notably, the theories young children form are based largely on information that is perceptually available rather than on data that cannot be perceived by the senses (e.g., that matter consists of particles; that the earth is round; that animals and plants are both living things; for example, Shtulman & Walker, 2020). In addition, in contrast with the process of science, young children's theories are largely intuitive rather than explicit. As Shtulman & Walker (2020) explained, young children tend to think *with* a theory rather than *about* a theory, the latter involving meta-cognitive skills and practices such as controlling variables other than the variable of interest (Klahr & Nigam, 2004). Thus, while young children's intuitive theories provide them with starting points for science learning, these nascent theories may even impede the learning of actual scientific theories unless knowledgeable adults provide the child with guidance (Shtulman & Walker, 2020). Of note, engagement in science and engineering learning shares many features with play-based learning—notably, the involvement of agency, exploration, collaboration, and creativity. The power of guided play is also important, as well-designed curricular activities can help children explore and build on their intuitive theories more explicitly (e.g., Shtulman & Walker, 2020). A recent National Academies (2022) report provides four big ideas about early engineering and science learning in preschool through fifth grade; these are broadly applicable to learning in all domains: "(1) learning is a social and cultural process, (2) learning is a process of identity development, (3) children move through a range of cultural contexts where they learn science and engineering and variations in these contexts shape what and how children learn, and (4) learning in these disciplines is not neutral because the disciplines themselves are not neutral" (p. 53).

Taking a strengths-based, culturally responsive approach to science and engineering learning in preschool environments not only helps children learn science but also helps them build identities, among which are self-concepts that include their capability to engage in science and engineering. With respect to building positive science identities, recent research shows that describing science learning actively in terms of "doing science" rather than "being a scientist" supports the interest in science of preschool girls, a group that is often negatively stereotyped in this regard (Rhodes et al., 2019). The importance of providing science learning opportunities in preschool curricula is highlighted by recent theories suggesting that engaging in science and engineering learning benefits not only learning and interest in these domains but also learning in the language arts, social-emotional learning, and mathematics, as well as the acquisition of critical domain-general skills, including executive function and approaches to learning (Bustamante et al., 2018).

According to the above-referenced National Academies report (2022), however, despite the strong potential of science and engineering instructional activities to broadly support children's early learning, a paucity of science and engineering instruction in preschool and early elementary school represents a missed opportunity to support young children's curiosity about and interest in the world; to build foundational skills that are important for later learning; and to support their full participation as citizens in a democratic society, which requires problem solving, critical thinking, collaboration, and an ability to interpret data. The report adopts an equity approach to science learning and provides evidence that the lack of science learning opportunities is exacerbated in underresourced settings, impacting primarily underrepresented minorities and children of color (National Academies, 2022). While this finding highlights a problem, it also presents an opportunity to address inequities.

Another important conclusion of the National Academies (2022) report is that science learning is not neutral, but influenced by culture and community practices. Indeed, problems that are highly salient to young children are influenced by their lived experiences (e.g., the issue of clean drinking water). In addition, what constitutes evidence is influenced by children's lived experiences. Developing science and engineering instruction that relates to children's interests and lived experiences enhances learning (National Academies, 2022).

Pressing areas for research on early science and engineering education include effective ways to engage children in science and engineering learning and how to do so in culturally responsive ways. Two more specific areas highlighted in the National Academies (2022) report are particularly relevant: First, little is known about science and engineering learning among children with disabilities. Moreover, when children with disabilities are removed from mainstream classrooms, they may miss learning opportunities that other children experience. This is particularly the case for science and engineering instructional activities because they occur rarely compared with learning opportunities in other domains. Second, little is known about how best to engage children with particular disabilities in science learning.

IMPLICATIONS FOR PRESCHOOL CURRICULUM: CULTURAL VARIATIONS IN LEARNING OPPORTUNITIES AND LEARNING

As described in this chapter, a large body of evidence demonstrates that what and how young children learn are shaped by experiences and environments and therefore vary with cultural context. This phenomenon is often described in the literature as cultural learning, which is considered a unique feature of human learning even though it is observed to a limited extent in other species (see Tomasello et al., 1993, for review). A well-known example is the greater focus of Western cultures on independence and the greater focus of Eastern cultures on interdependence (e.g., Markus & Kitayama, 1991; Masuda & Nisbett, 2001; Nisbett et al., 2001). Consistent with these cultural differences, by 4 years of age Asian children are often more relational and American children are more objects focused (Kuwabara & Smith, 2012; Richland et al., 2010).

Importantly, different cultural contexts do not lead to better overall performance (Kuwabara & Smith, 2012). Rather, performance depends on the overlap of task demands and the lived experiences of children growing up in different contexts. For example, Kuwabara and Smith (2012) found that Japanese children outperformed American children when the task involved matching relations, whereas American children outperformed Japanese children when the task involved object search.

These findings support a strengths-based approach to understanding and valuing cultures and the experiences they afford for learning. This approach represents an important step forward compared with the deficit view of cultures that differ from "mainstream" American cultures, which reflect Euro-centric, largely White cultural values and practices. Accumulating research shows that strengths-based approaches, such as culturally and linguistically relevant pedagogy, have positive effects on children's learning (Gay, 2000; Ladson-Billings, 2014). Thus, there is an urgent need for culturally responsive, anti-bias pedagogy based on the increasing cultural and linguistic diversity of the children being taught in the United States, including in early childhood education settings (see Chapter 5). Culturally and linguistically responsive teaching increases learning, belongingness, and the meaningfulness of the learning process for all children. Additionally, it increases family engagement in children's learning, which is associated with children's higher achievement (Gay, 2000; Ladson-Billings, 2014).

Theorists also warn, however, that characterizing individuals, including young children, based on their membership in particular cultural, racial, or ethnic groups poses its own dangers. It is important to recognize that the lived experiences of individuals within and across cultural groups vary, and it is these variations that influence what children know and how they learn (Gutiérrez & Rogoff, 2003; Rogoff, 2016). Further, cultures shift dynamically over time. Notably, immigrant families in the United States are exposed to cultural and linguistic practices that are prevalent in this country and are likely to change their lived experiences across generations (Gutiérrez & Rogoff, 2023). Rogoff et al. (2018) call for a paradigm shift in studying children's developmental learning, based on the fact that all children learn through their everyday experiences embedded within cultural contexts. In the United States, moreover, many children experience a variety of cultural contexts, which they navigate and integrate. Thus, it is essential to recognize and understand young children's lived experiences and not limit their learning experiences in early education settings based on stereotypes about their cultural or linguistic groups. Doing so entails celebrating, discussing, and incorporating the diversity of experiences, languages, and cultures that children bring to the early education setting and to the implementation of curricula.

CONCLUSION

The early childhood period represents a window of opportunity for development and learning. Because neuroplasticity is heightened, specific skills and abilities are more readily absorbed and learned during the preschool period. Pre-K experiences may therefore have a particularly important impact on developmental trajectories and provide opportunities to build strong foundational skills more efficiently than is the case later in development. Conversely, when opportunities for environmental stimulation and expected experiential inputs are missed, the early years can be a period of unique vulnerability and developmental trajectories can be altered in a way that may lead to learning challenges throughout the life course.

Drawing on the science of early childhood development and learning, the committee summarizes the following core concepts that are critical for informing the development of preschool curricula:

- The interaction of the brain, biology, and environments shapes early childhood development and learning.
- The early caregiving environment, exposure to trauma and stress, and access to resources affect long-term development.
- Children learn in multiple ways—through active exploration; through observation of others, notably older children and adults; and through adults' explicitly sharing knowledge with them.
- Children learn from play, exploration, and pedagogy that are responsive to their interests. Children's play has the potential to contribute to the cultural relevance of early education, as child-initiated play reflects children's cultural experiences and how they see themselves within the larger society, providing teachers with an important lens into their lived experiences.
- Young children play an important role in their interactions and development and are active participants in sharing knowledge. Autonomy-granting, play-based pedagogy in early education builds advanced language and thinking skills as well as skills that involve pursuing learning in which young children are interested and collaborating and conversing with other children. Limiting children's agency in early education contexts is typically rooted in stereotypes about weaknesses of children and their families, rather than being attributed to systemic factors that contribute to group differences, such as differences in vocabulary size.

These core concepts from the literature point to the need for a strengths-based approach to understanding and valuing cultures and the experiences they afford for learning. Variations in the lived experiences of children influence what children know and how they learn, as all children learn through their environments and experiences, which are embedded within cultural contexts. Accordingly, celebrating, discussing, and incorporating this diversity of experiences and cultures within early education settings is critical to promoting positive early development and learning and setting young children on a positive trajectory for lifelong learning.

REFERENCES

Acevedo-Garcia, D., Noelke, C., McArdle, N., Sofer, N., Huntington, N., Hardy, E., Huber, R., Baek, M., & Reece, J. (2020). *The geography of child opportunity: Why neighborhoods matter for equity.* Brandeis University Heller School for Social Policy and Management, diversitydatakids.org. https://www.diversitydatakids.org/sites/default/files/file/ddk_the-geography-of-child-opportunity_2020v2_0.pdf

Adair, J. K. (2015). *The impact of discrimination on the early schooling experiences of children from immigrant families.* Migration Policy Institute. https://www.migrationpolicy.org/sites/default/files/publications/FCD-Adair.pdf

Adair, J. K., & Colegrove, K. S.-S. (2021). *Segregation by experience: Agency, racism, and learning in the early grades.* University of Chicago Press.

Adair, J. K., & Doucet, F. (2014). The impact of race and culture on play in early childhood classrooms. In L. Brooker, M. Blaise, & S. Edwards (Eds.), *The SAGE handbook of play and learning in early childhood* (pp. 354–365). SAGE Publications Inc. https://doi.org/10.4135/9781473907850.n30

Adair, J. K., Colegrove, K. S.-S., & McManus, M. E. (2017). How the word gap argument negatively impacts young children of Latinx immigrants' conceptualizations of learning. *Harvard Educational Review, 87*(3), 309–334. https://eric.ed.gov/?id=EJ1164890

Adukia, A., Eble, A., Harrison, E., Runesha, H., & Szasz, T. (2021). What we teach about race and gender: Representation in images and text of children's books. *SSRN.* https://doi.org/10.2139/ssrn.3901587

Aguiar, A., & Baillargeon, R. (1999). 2.5-month-old infants' reasoning about when objects should and should not be occluded. *Cognitive Psychology, 39*(2), 116–157. https://doi.org/10.1006/cogp.1999.0717

Alloway, T. P., & Alloway, R. G. (2010). Investigating the predictor roles of working memory and academic achievement. *Journal of Experimental Child Psychology, 106*(1), 20–29. https://doi.org/10.1016/j.jecp.2009.11.003

Aslin, R. N. (2007). What's in a look? *Developmental Science, 10*(1), 48–53. https://doi.org/10.1111/j.1467-7687.2007.00563.x

Bailey, D., Duncan, G. J., Odgers, C. L., & Yu, W. (2017). Persistence and fadeout in the impacts of child and adolescent interventions. *Journal of Research on Educational Effectiveness, 10*(1), 7–39. https://doi.org/10.1080/19345747.2016.1232459

Bailey, D. H., Duncan, G. J., Cunha, F., Foorman, B. R., & Yeager, D. S. (2020). Persistence and fade-out of educational-intervention effects: Mechanisms and potential solutions. *Psychological Science in the Public Interest, 21*(2), 55–97. https://doi.org/10.1177/1529100620915848

Bailey, D. H., Nguyen, T., Jenkins, J. M., Domina, T., Clements, D. H., & Sarama, J. S. (2016). Fadeout in an early mathematics intervention: Constraining content or preexisting differences? *Developmental Psychology, 52*(9), 1457.

Bandura, A. (1977). *Social learning theory* (Vol. 1). Prentice Hall.

Bang, M., Marin, A., Medin, D., & Washinawatok, K. (2015). Learning by observing, pitching in, and being in relations in the natural world. *Advances in Child Development and Behavior, 49,* 303–313. https://doi.org/10.1016/bs.acdb.2015.10.004

Bar-Haim, Y., Ziv, T., Lamy, D., & Hodes, R. M. (2006). Nature and nurture in own-race face processing. *Psychological Science, 17*(2), 159–163. http://www.jstor.org/stable/40064387

Baroody, A. J., & Ginsburg, H. P. (1990). Chapter 4: Children's mathematical learning: A cognitive view. *Journal for Research in Mathematics Education, 4,* 51–210. https://doi.org/10.2307/749912

Bassok, D., Latham, S., & Rorem, A. (2016). Is kindergarten the new first grade? *AERA Open, 2*(1). https://doi.org/10.1177/2332858415616358

Beals, D. E., De Temple, J. M., & Dickinson, D. K. (1994). Talking and listening that support early literacy development of children from low-income families. In D. K. Dickinson (Ed.), *Bridges to literacy: Children, families, and schools* (pp. 19–40). Blackwell Publishing.

Bécares, L., Nazroo, J., & Kelly, Y. (2015). A longitudinal examination of maternal, family, and area-level experiences of racism on children's socioemotional development: Patterns and possible explanations. *Social Science & Medicine, 142*, 128–135. https://doi.org/10.1016/j.socscimed.2015.08.025

Bell, M. A., & Wolfe, C. D. (2004). Emotion and cognition: An intricately bound developmental process. *Child Development, 75*(2), 366–370. https://doi.org/10.1111/j.1467-8624.2004.00679.x

Bell, M. A., Wolfe, C. D., Diaz, A., & Liu, R. (2019). Cognition and emotion in development. In V. LoBue, K. Pérez-Edgar, & K. A. Buss (Eds.), *Handbook of emotional development* (pp. 375–403). Springer Nature. https://doi.org/10.1007/978-3-030-17332-6_15

Bergelson, E., Casillas, M., Soderstrom, M., Seidl, A., Warlaumont, A. S., & Amatuni, A. (2019). What do North American babies hear? A large-scale cross-corpus analysis. *Developmental Science, 22*(1), e12724. https://doi.org/10.1111/desc.12724

Bierman, K. L., Nix, R. L., Greenberg, M. T., Blair, C., & Domitrovich, C. E. (2008). Executive functions and school readiness intervention: Impact, moderation, and mediation in the Head Start REDI program. *Development and Psychopathology, 20*(3), 821–843. https://doi.org/10.1017/s0954579408000394

Blair, C. (2016). Executive function and early childhood education. *Current Opinion in Behavioral Sciences, 10*, 102–107. https://doi.org/10.1016/j.cobeha.2016.05.009

Blair, C., Protzko, J., & Ursache, A. (2011). Self-regulation and early literacy. In S. B. Neuman & D. K. Dickinson (Eds.), *Handbook of early literacy research* (Vol. 3, pp. 20–35). Guilford Press.

Blevins-Knabe, B., & Musun-Miller, L. (1996). Number use at home by children and their parents and its relationship to early mathematical performance. *Early Development and Parenting, 5*(1), 35–45. https://doi.org/10.1002/(SICI)1099-0917(199603)5:1<35::AID-EDP113>3.0.CO;2-0

Bohlmann, N. L., Maier, M. F., & Palacios, N. (2015). Bidirectionality in self-regulation and expressive vocabulary: Comparisons between monolingual and dual language learners in preschool. *Child Development, 86*(4), 1094–1111. https://doi.org/10.1111/cdev.12375

Boland, A., Haden, C., & Ornstein, P. (2003). Boosting children's memory by training mothers in the use of an elaborative conversational style as an event unfolds. *Journal of Cognition and Development, 4*(1), 39–65. https://doi.ord/10.1207/S15327647JCD4,1-02

Bonawitz, E., Shafto, P., Gweon, H., Goodman, N. D., Spelke, E., & Schulz, L. (2011). The double-edged sword of pedagogy: Instruction limits spontaneous exploration and discovery. *Cognition, 120*(3), 322–330. https://doi.org/10.1016/j.cognition.2010.10.001

Brannon, D., & Dauksas, L. (2014). The effectiveness of dialogic reading in increasing English Language Learning preschool children's expressive language. *International Research in Early Childhood Education, 5*(1), 1–10. https://files.eric.ed.gov/fulltext/EJ1150938.pdf

Brooks-Gunn, J., & Duncan, G. J. (1997). The effects of poverty on children. *The Future of Children, 7*(2), 55–71. https://pubmed.ncbi.nlm.nih.gov/9299837/

Brown, S. M., Schlueter, L. J., Hurwich-Reiss, E., Dmitrieva, J., Miles, E., & Watamura, S. E. (2020). Parental buffering in the context of poverty: Positive parenting behaviors differentiate young children's stress reactivity profiles. *Development and Psychopathology, 32*(5), 1778–1787. https://doi.org/10.1017/S0954579420001224

Bruner, J. (1982). The formats of language acquisition. *American Journal of Semiotics, 1*(3), 1–16. https://www.proquest.com/scholarly-journals/formats-language-acquisition/docview/213746394/se-2

———. (1983). Play, thought, and language. *Peabody Journal of Education, 60*(3), 60–69. https://doi.org/10.1080/01619568309538407

Bull, R., Espy, K. A., & Wiebe, S. A. (2008). Short-term memory, working memory, and executive functioning in preschoolers: longitudinal predictors of mathematical achievement at age 7 years. *Developmental Neuropsychology, 33*(3), 205–228. https://doi.org/10.1080/87565640801982312

Bustamante, A. S., Greenfield, D. B., & Nayfeld, I. (2018). Early childhood science and engineering: Engaging platforms for fostering domain-general learning skills. *Education Sciences, 8*(3), 144. https://doi.org/10.3390/educsci8030144

Buttelmann, D., Zmyj, N., Daum, M., & Carpenter, M. (2013). Selective imitation of in-group over out-group members in 14-month-old infants. *Child Development, 84*(2), 422–428. https://doi.org/10.1111/j.1467-8624.2012.01860.x

Capron, C., & Duyme, M. (1989). Assessment of effects of socio-economic status on IQ in a full cross-fostering study. *Nature, 340*(6234), 552–554. https://doi.org/10.1038/340552a0

Carey, S. (2004). Bootstrapping & the origin of concepts. *Daedalus, 133*(1), 59–68. http://dx.doi.org/10.1162/001152604772746701

———. (2013). Are children fundamentally different kinds of thinkers and learners than adults? In S. F. Chipman, J. W. Segal, & R. Glaser (Eds.), *Thinking and learning skills* (pp. 485–518). Routledge.

Carey, S., & Barner, D. (2019). Ontogenetic origins of human integer representations. *Trends in Cognitive Sciences, 23*(10), 823–835. https://psycnet.apa.org/doi/10.1016/j.tics.2019.07.004

Carpenter, M., Akhtar, N., & Tomasello, M. (1998). Fourteen- through 18-month-old infants differentially imitate intentional and accidental actions. *Infant Behavior and Development, 21*(2), 315–330. https://doi.org/10.1016/S0163-6383(98)90009-1

Casasola, M., Wei, W. S., Suh, D. D., Donskoy, P., & Ransom, A. (2020). Children's exposure to spatial language promotes their spatial thinking. *Journal of Experimental Psychology: General, 149*(6), 1116–1136. https://doi.org/10.1037/xge0000699

Casey, B. M., Lombardi, C. M., Thomson, D., Nguyen, H. N., Paz, M., Theriault, C. A., & Dearing, E. (2018). Maternal support of children's early numerical concept learning predicts preschool and first-grade math achievement. *Child Development, 89*(1), 156–173. https://doi.org/10.1111/cdev.12676

Casey, K., Novick, K., & Lourenco, S. F. (2021). Sixty years of gender representation in children's books: Conditions associated with overrepresentation of male versus female protagonists. *PLoS One, 16*(12), e0260566. https://doi.org/10.1371/journal.pone.0260566

Casillas, M., Brown, P., & Levinson, S. C. (2020). Early language experience in a Tseltal Mayan village. *Child Development, 91*(5), 1819–1835. https://doi.org/10.1111/cdev.13349

Cheng, K., & Newcombe, N. S. (2005). Is there a geometric module for spatial orientation? Squaring theory and evidence. *Psychonomic Bulletin & Review, 12*(1), 1–23. https://doi.org/10.3758/BF03196346

Cheng, Y. L., & Mix, K. S. (2014). Spatial training improves children's mathematics ability. *Journal of Cognition and Development, 15*, 11–12. https://files.eric.ed.gov/fulltext/ED580905.pdf

Chouinard, M. M., Harris, P. L., & Maratsos, M. P. (2007). Children's questions: A mechanism for cognitive development. *Monographs of the Society for Research in Child Development, 72*(1). https://doi.org/10.1111/j.1540-5834.2007.00412.x

Civil, M., Díez-Palomar, J., Menéndez, J. M., & Acosta-Iriqui, J. (2008). Parents' interactions with their children when doing mathematics. *Adults Learning Mathematics, 3*(n2a), 41–58. https://files.eric.ed.gov/fulltext/EJ1068257.pdf

Claessens, A., & Engel, M. (2013). How important is where you start? Early mathematics knowledge and later school success. *Teachers College Record, 115*, 1–29. https://doi.org/10.1177/016146811311500603

Claessens, A., Duncan G., & Engel, M. (2009). Kindergarten skills and fifth-grade achievement: Evidence from the ECLS-K. *Economics of Education Review, 28*, 415–427. http://dx.doi.org/10.1016/j.econedurev.2008.09.003

Clark, C. A., Pritchard, V. E., & Woodward, L. J. (2010). Preschool executive functioning abilities predict early mathematics achievement. *Developmental Psychology, 46*(5), 1176. https://doi.org/10.1037/a0019672

Clements, D. H., & Sarama, J. (2008). Experimental evaluation of the effects of a research-based preschool mathematics curriculum. *American Educational Research Journal, 45*, 443–494. http://dx.doi.org/10.3102/0002831207312908

———. (2011). Early childhood mathematics intervention. *Science (New York), 333*(6045), 968–970. https://doi.org/10.1126/science.1204537

———. (2014). Learning trajectories: Foundations for effective, research-based education. In A. P. Maloney, J. Confrey, & K. H. Nguyen (Eds.), *Learning over time: Learning trajectories in mathematics education* (pp. 1–30). Information Age.

———. (2019). Executive function and early mathematical learning difficulties. In A. Fritz, V. G. Haase, & P. Räsänen (Eds.), *International handbook of mathematical learning difficulties: From the laboratory to the classroom* (pp. 755–771). Cham: Springer International Publishing.

Clements, D. H., Sarama, J., & Germeroth, C. (2016). Learning executive function and early mathematics: Directions of causal relations. *Early Childhood Research Quarterly, 36*, 79–90. https://psycnet.apa.org/doi/10.1016/j.ecresq.2015.12.009

Clements, D. H., Sarama, J., Layzer, C., Unlu, F., & Fesler, L. (2020). Effects on mathematics and executive function of a mathematics and play intervention versus mathematics alone. *Journal for Research in Mathematics Education, 51*, 301–333. https://doi.org/10.5951/jresematheduc-2019-0069

Condon, E. M., Holland, M. L., Slade, A., Redeker, N. S., Mayes, L. C., & Sadler, L. S. (2019). Associations between maternal experiences of discrimination and biomarkers of toxic stress in school-aged children. *Maternal and Child Health Journal, 23*(9), 1147–1151. https://doi.org/10.1007/s10995-019-02779-4

Connor, C. M., Mazzocco, M. M., Kurz, T., Crowe, E. C., Tighe, E. L., Wood, T. S., & Morrison, F. J. (2018). Using assessment to individualize early mathematics instruction. *Journal of School Psychology, 66*, 97–113. https://doi.org/10.1016/j.jsp.2017.04.005

Cook, C., Goodman, N. D., & Schulz, L. E. (2011). Where science starts: Spontaneous experiments in preschoolers' exploratory play. *Cognition, 120*(3), 341–349. https://doi.org/10.1016/j.cognition.2011.03.003

Crain-Thoreson, C., & Dale, P. S. (1999). Enhancing linguistic performance: Parents and teachers as book reading partners for children with language delays. *Topics in Early Childhood Special Education, 19*(1), 28–39. https://doi.org/10.1177/027112149901900103

Dale, P. S., Crain-Thoreson, C., Notari-Syverson, A., & Cole, K. (1996). Parent-child book reading as an intervention technique for young children with language delays. *Topics in Early Childhood Special Education, 16*(2), 213–235. https://doi.org/10.1177/027112149601600206

Davidson, D., Vanegas, S. B., & Hilvert, E. (2014). A cognitive-developmental approach to emotion processing in children. In R. Chen (Ed.), *Cognitive development: Theories, stages and processes and challenges* (pp. 33–58). Nova Science Publishers.

Davis, E. P., McCormack, K., Arora, H., Sharpe, D., Short, A. K., Bachevalier, J., Glynn, L. M., Sandman, C. A., Stern, H. S., Sanchez, M., & Baram, T. Z. (2022). Early life exposure to unpredictable parental sensory signals shapes cognitive development across three species. *Frontiers in Behavioral Neuroscience, 16*. https://doi.org/10.3389/fnbeh.2022.960262

de la Osa, N., Navarro, J.-B., Penelo, E., Valentí, A., Ezpeleta, L., & Dadvand, P. (2024). Long-term exposure to greenspace and anxiety from preschool and primary school children. *Journal of Environmental Psychology, 93*, 102207. https://doi.org/10.1016/j.jenvp.2023.102207

de Villiers, J. G., & de Villiers, P. A. (2014). The role of language in theory of mind development. *Topics in Language Disorders, 34*(4), 313–328. https://psycnet.apa.org/doi/10.1097/TLD.0000000000000037

Dehaene, S. (1997). *The number sense: How the mind creates mathematics.* Oxford University Press.

Dehaene, S., Izard, V., Pica, P., & Spelke, E. (2006). Core knowledge of geometry in an Amazonian Indigene group. *Science (New York), 311,* 381–384. https://doi.org/10.1126/science.1121739

Demir-Lira, Ö., Applebaum, L. R., Goldin-Meadow, S., & Levine, S. C. (2019). Parents' early book reading to children: Relation to children's later language and literacy outcomes controlling for other parent language input. *Developmental Science, 22*(3), e12764. https://doi.org/10.1111/desc.12764

Denham, S. A. (2019). Emotional competence during childhood and adolescence. In *Handbook of emotional development* (pp. 493–541). Springer Nature. https://doi.org/10.1007/978-3-030-17332-6_20

Dewey, J. (1910). *How we think.* D C Heath. https://doi.org/10.1037/10903-0000

Diamond, A. (2016). Why improving and assessing executive functions early in life is critical. In J. A. Griffin, P. McCardle, & L. Freund (Eds.), *Executive function in preschool-age children: Integrating measurement, neurodevelopment, and translational research.* APA Books.

Diamond, A. (2020). Executive functions. In J. L. Michaud, C. Bulteau, D. Cohen, & A. Gallagher (Eds.), *Handbook of clinical neurology* (Vol. 173, pp. 225–240). Elsevier.

Diamond, A., & Ling, D. S. (2016). Conclusions about interventions, programs, and approaches for improving executive functions that appear justified and those that, despite much hype, do not. *Developmental Cognitive Neuroscience, 18,* 34–48, https://doi.org/10.1016/j.dcn.2015.11.005

Diamond, A., Lee, C., Senften, P., Lam, A., & Abbott, D. (2019). Randomized control trial of Tools of the Mind: Marked benefits to kindergarten children and their teachers. *PLoS One, 14*(9), e0222447. https://doi.org/10.1371%2Fjournal.pone.0222447

Dickinson, D. K., & Tabors, P. O. (Eds.) (2001). *Beginning literacy with language: Young children learning at home and school.* Brookes Publishing.

Duncan, G. J., Brooks-Gunn, J., & Klebanov, P. K. (1994). Economic deprivation and early childhood development. *Child Development, 65*(2), 296–318. https://doi.org/10.2307/1131385

Duncan, G. J., Dowsett, C. J., Claessens, A., Magnuson, K., Huston, A. C., Klebanov, P., Pagani, L. S., Feinstein, L., Engel, M., Brooks-Gunn, J., Sexton, H., Duckworth, K., & Japel, C. (2007). School readiness and later achievement. *Developmental Psychology, 43*(6), 1428–1446. https://doi.org/10.1037/0012-1649.43.6.1428

Durlak, J. A., Weissberg, R. P., Dymnicki, A. B., Taylor, R. D., & Schellinger, K. B. (2011). The impact of enhancing students' social and emotional learning: A meta-analysis of school-based universal interventions. *Child Development, 82*(1), 405–432. https://doi.org/10.1111/j.1467-8624.2010.01564.x

Eason, S. H., Hurst, M. A., Kerr, K., Claessens, A., & Levine, S. C. (2022). Enhancing parent and child shape talk during puzzle play. *Cognitive Development, 64,* 101250. https://doi.org/10.1016/j.cogdev.2022.101250

Eason, S. H., Nelson, A. E., Dearing, E., & Levine, S. C. (2021). Facilitating young children's numeracy talk in play: The role of parent prompts. *Journal of Experimental Child Psychology, 207,* 105124. https://doi.org/10.1016/j.jecp.2021.105124

Eisenberg, N., Sadovsky, A., & Spinrad, T. L. (2005). Associations of emotion-related regulation with language skills, emotion knowledge, and academic outcomes. *New Directions for Child and Adolescent Development, 2005*(109), 109–118. https://doi.org/10.1002%2Fcd.143

Feigenson, L., Dehaene, S., & Spelke, E. (2004). Core systems of number. *Trends in Cognitive Sciences, 8*(7), 307–314. https://doi.org/10.1016/j.tics.2004.05.002

Ferrara, K., Hirsh-Pasek, K., Newcombe, N. S., Golinkoff, R. M., & Lam, W. S. (2011). Block talk: Spatial language during block play. *Mind, Brain, and Education, 5*(3), 143–151. https://doi.org/10.1111/j.1751-228X.2011.01122.x

Finlon, K. J., Izard, C. E., Seidenfeld, A., Johnson, S. R., Cavadel, E. W., Krauthamer Ewing, E. S., & Morgan, J. K. (2015). Emotion-based preventive intervention: Effectively promoting emotion knowledge and adaptive behavior among at-risk preschoolers. *Development and Psychopathology, 27*(4-1), 1353–1365. https://doi.org/10.1017/S0954579414001461

Fisher, K. R., Hirsh-Pasek, K., Newcombe, N. S., & Golinkoff, R. M. (2013). Taking shape: Supporting preschoolers' acquisition of geometric knowledge through guided play. *Child Development, 84*, 1872–1878. https://doi.org/10.1111/cdev.12091

Fivush, R., Haden, C. A., & Reese, E. (2006). Elaborating on elaborations: Role of maternal reminiscing style in cognitive and socioemotional development. *Child Development, 77*(6), 1568–1588. https://doi.org/10.1111/j.1467-8624.2006.00960.x

Frausel, R. R., Richland, L. E., Levine, S. C., & Goldin-Meadow, S. (2021). Personal narrative as a "breeding ground" for higher-order thinking talk in early parent-child interactions. *Developmental Psychology, 57*(4), 519–534. https://doi.org/10.1037/dev0001166

Frausel, R. R., Silvey, C., Freeman, C., Dowling, N., Richland, L. E., Levine, S. C., Raudenbush, S., & Goldin-Meadow, S. (2020). The origins of higher-order thinking lie in children's spontaneous talk across the pre-school years. *Cognition, 200*, 104274. https://doi.org/10.1016/j.cognition.2020.104274

Fuhs, M. W., Farran, D. C., & Nesbitt, K. T. (2015). Prekindergarten children's executive functioning skills and achievement gains: The utility of direct assessments and teacher ratings. *Journal of Educational Psychology, 107*(1), 207.

Fuson, K. (1988). *Children's counting and concepts of number*. Springer-Verlag. https://doi.org/10.1007/978-1-4612-3754-9

Gaskins, S., Haight, W., & Lancy, D. F. (2007). The cultural construction of play. In A. Göncü, & S. Gaskins (Eds.), *Play and development: Evolutionary, sociocultural, and functional perspectives* (pp. 179–202). Erlbaum.

Gassman-Pines, A. (2015). Effects of Mexican immigrant parents' daily workplace discrimination on child behavior and family functioning. *Child Development, 86*(4), 1175–1190. https://doi.org/10.1111/cdev.12378

Gay, G. (2000). *Culturally responsive teaching: Theory, research, and practice*. Teachers College Press.

Gelman, R., & Gallistel, C. R. (1978). *The child's understanding of number*. Harvard University Press.

Gentner, D. (2016). Language as cognitive tool kit: How language supports relational thought. *American Psychologist, 71*(8), 650. https://groups.psych.northwestern.edu/gentner/papers/Gentner_2016-Toolkit.pdf

Gibson, D. J., Gunderson, E. A., & Levine, S. C. (2020). Causal effects of parent number talk on preschoolers' number knowledge. *Child Development, 91*(6), e1162–e1177. https://doi.org/10.1111/cdev.13423

Gopnik, A. (2012). Scientific thinking in young children: Theoretical advances, empirical research, and policy implications. *Science, 337*, 1623–1627. https://doi.org/10.1126/science.1223416

———. (2020). Childhood as a solution to explore–exploit tensions. *Philosophical Transactions of the Royal Society B: Biological Sciences, 375*, 20190502. https://doi.org/10.1098/rstb.2019.0502.

Gopnik, A., & Tenenbaum, J. B. (2007). Bayesian networks, Bayesian learning and cognitive development. *Developmental Science, 10*(3), 281–287. https://psycnet.apa.org/doi/10.1111/j.1467-7687.2007.00584.x

Gopnik, A., & Wellman, H. M. (2012). Reconstructing constructivism: Causal models, Bayesian learning mechanisms, and the theory theory. *Psychological Bulletin, 138*(6), 1085. https://psycnet.apa.org/doi/10.1037/a0028044

Granger, S. J., Glynn, L. M., Sandman, C. A., Small, S. L., Obenaus, A., Keator, D. B., Baram, T. Z., Stern, H., Yassa, M. A., & Davis, E. P. (2021). Aberrant maturation of the uncinate fasciculus follows exposure to unpredictable patterns of maternal signals. *Journal of Neuroscience, 41*(6), 1242–1250. https://doi.org/10.1523%2FJNEUROSCI.0374-20.2020

Griffiths, T. L., Sobel, D. M., Tenenbaum, J. B., & Gopnik, A. (2011). Bayes and blickets: Effects of knowledge on causal induction in children and adults. *Cognitive Science, 35*(8), 1407–1455. https://doi.org/10.1111%2Fj.1551-6709.2011.01203.x

Gunderson, E. A., & Levine, S. C. (2011). Some types of parent number talk count more than others: Relations between parents' input and children's cardinal-number knowledge. *Developmental Science, 14*(5), 1021–1032. https://doi.org/10.1111/j.1467-7687.2011.01050.x

Gunnar, M. R. (2020). Early adversity, stress, and neurobehavioral development. *Development and Psychopathology, 32*(5), 1555–1562. https://doi.org/10.1017/s0954579420001649

Gupta, A. (2011). Play and pedagogy framed within India's historical, socio-cultural and pedagogical context. In S. Rogers (Ed.), *Rethinking play and pedagogy in early childhood education: Concepts, contexts and cultures* (pp. 86–99). Routledge.

Gutiérrez, K. D., Cortes, K., Cortez, A., DiGiacomo, D., Higgs, J., Johnson, P., Ramón Lizárraga, J., Mendoza, E., Tien, J., & Vakil, S. (2017). Replacing representation with imagination: Finding ingenuity in everyday practices. *Review of Research in Education, 41*(1), 30–60. https://www.jstor.org/stable/44668686

Gutiérrez, K. D., & Rogoff, B. (2003). Cultural ways of learning: Individual traits or repertoires of practice. *Educational Researcher, 32*(5), 19–25. https://doi.org/10.3102/0013189X032005019

Hackman, D. A., Gallop, R., Evans, G. W., & Farah, M. J. (2015). Socioeconomic status and executive function: Developmental trajectories and mediation. *Developmental Science, 18*(5), 686–702. https://doi.org/10.1111/desc.12246

Haight, W. L., Wang, X. L., Fung, H. H., Williams, K., & Mintz, J. (1999). Universal, developmental, and variable aspects of young children's play: A cross-cultural comparison of pretending at home. *Child Development, 70*(6), 1477–1488. https://doi.org/10.1111/1467-8624.00107

Harris, P., Koenig, M., Corriveau, K., & Jaswal, V. (2018). Cognitive foundations of learning from testimony. *Annual Review of Psychology, 69*, 1–23. https://doi.org/10.1146/annurev-psych-122216-011710

Harris, P. L. (2012). *Trusting what you're told: How children learn from others*. Harvard University Press.

Hassrick, E. M., Raudenbush, S. W., & Rosen, L. (2017). *The ambitious elementary school: Its conception, design and contribution to educational equity*. University of Chicago Press.

Hawes, Z., & Ansari, D. (2020). What explains the relationship between spatial and mathematical skills? A review of evidence from brain and behavior. *Psychonomic Bulletin & Review, 27*(3), 465–482. https://doi.org/10.3758/s13423-019-01694-7

Hawes, Z., Tepylo, D., & Moss, J. (2015). Developing spatial thinking: Implications for early mathematics education. In B. Davis & Spatial Reasoning Study Group (Eds.), *Spatial reasoning in the early years: Principles, assertions and speculations* (pp. 29–44). Routledge.

Hirsh-Pasek, K., Blinkoff, E., Golinkoff, R., & Hadani, H. (2020). *A new path to education reform: Playful learning promotes 21st-century skills in schools and beyond*. Brookings. https://www.brookings.edu/articles/a-new-path-to-education-reform-playful-learning-promotes-21st-century-skills-in-schools-and-beyond

Hirsh-Pasek, K., Golinkoff, R., Berk, L. E., & Singer, D. (2008). *A mandate for playful learning in preschool: Presenting the evidence*. Oxford University Press.

Hirsh-Pasek, K., Golinkoff, R. M., Nesbitt, K., Lautenbach, C., Blinkoff, E., & Fifer, G. (2022). *Making schools work: Bringing the science of learning to joyful classroom practice*. Teachers College Press.

Hobson, R. P. (1993). The emotional origins of social understanding. *Philosophical Psychology,* 6(3), 227–249. https://doi.org/10.1080/09515089308573090

Howard, L. H., Henderson, A. M., Carrazza, C., & Woodward, A. L. (2015). Infants' and young children's imitation of linguistic in-group and out-group informants. *Child Development,* 86(1), 259–275. https://doi.org/10.1111/cdev.12299

Hughes, F. P. (1999). *Children, play and development.* Allyn & Bacon.

Hunter, J., Hunter, R., Tupouniua, J., & Leach, G. (2022). Bringing the home into school: Learning and connecting through mathematics education during the time of a pandemic. *Educational Studies in Mathematics, 111*(2), 207–224. https://doi.org/10.1007/s10649-022-10157-1

Huttenlocher, J., Haight, W., Bryk, A., Seltzer, M., & Lyons, T. (1991). Early vocabulary growth: Relation to language input and gender. *Developmental Psychology,* 27(2), 236–248. https://doi.org/10.1037/0012-1649.27.2.236

Huttenlocher, J., Vasilyeva, M., Cymerman, E., & Levine, S. (2002). Language input and child syntax. *Cognitive Psychology,* 45(3), 337–374. https://doi.org/10.1016/S0010-0285(02)00500-5

Izard, C. E., Woodburn, E. M., Finlon, K. J., Krauthamer-Ewing, E. S., Grossman, S. R., & Seidenfeld, A. (2011). Emotion knowledge, emotion utilization, and emotion regulation. *Emotion Review,* 3(1), 44–52. https://doi.org/10.1177/1754073910380972

Izard, V., & Spelke, E. S. (2009). Development of sensitivity to geometry in visual forms. *Human Evolution,* 23(3), 213–248. https://www.ncbi.nlm.nih.gov/pmc/articles/PMC3045057/

Jimerson, S., Egeland, B., Sroufe, L. A., & Carlson, B. (2000). A prospective longitudinal study of high school dropouts examining multiple predictors across development. *Journal of School Psychology,* 38(6), 525–549. https://doi.org/10.1016/S0022-4405(00)00051-0

Kinzler, K. D., & Spelke, E. S. (2011). Do infants show social preferences for people differing in race? *Cognition,* 119(1), 1–9. https://doi.org/10.1016/j.cognition.2010.10.019

Kinzler, K. D., Dupoux, E., & Spelke, E. S. (2007). The native language of social cognition. *Proceedings of the National Academy of Sciences,* 104(30), 12577–12580. https://doi.org/10.1073/pnas.0705345104

Klahr, D., & Nigam, M. (2004). The equivalence of learning paths in early science instruction: Effects of direct instruction and discovery learning. *Psychological Science,* 15(10), 661–667. https://psycnet.apa.org/doi/10.1111/j.0956-7976.2004.00737.x

Klibanoff, R. S., Levine, S. C., Huttenlocher, J., Vasilyeva, M., & Hedges, L. V. (2006). Preschool children's mathematical knowledge: The effect of teacher "math talk." *Developmental Psychology,* 42(1), 59–69. https://doi.org/10.1037/0012-1649.42.1.59

Klingberg, T., Fernell, E., Olesen, P., Johnson, M., Gustafsson, P., Dahlström, K., Gillberg, C., Forssberg, H., & Westerberg, H. (2005). Computerized training of working memory in children with ADHD—A randomized, controlled trial. *Journal of the American Academy of Child and Adolescent Psychiatry,* 44, 177–186. https://doi.org/10.1097/00004583-200502000-00010

Koenig, M. A., & Echols, C. H. (2003). Infants' understanding of false labeling events: The referential roles of words and the speakers who use them. *Cognition,* 87(3), 179–208. https://doi.org/10.1016/s0010-0277(03)00002-7

Koenig, M. A., Clément, F., & Harris, P. L. (2004). Trust in testimony: Children's use of true and false statements. *Psychological Science,* 15(10), 694–698. https://doi.org/10.1111/j.0956-7976.2004.00742.x

Koşkulu-Sancar, S., van de Weijer-Bergsma, E., Mulder, H., & Blom, E. (2023). Examining the role of parents and teachers in executive function development in early and middle childhood: A systematic review. *Developmental Review,* 67, https://doi.org/10.1016/j.dr.2022.101063

Kuhl, P. K., Conboy, B. T., Padden, D., Nelson, T., & Pruitt, J. (2005). Early speech perception and later language development: Implications for the "critical period." *Language Learning and Development,* 1(3–4), 237–264. https://doi.org/10.1207/s15473341lld0103&4_2

Kuhl, P. K., Stevens, E., Hayashi, A., Deguchi, T., Kiritani, S., & Iverson, P. (2006). Infants show a facilitation effect for native language phonetic perception between 6 and 12 months. *Developmental Science*, 9(2), F13–F21.

Kuhl, P. K., Williams, K. A., Lacerda, F., Stevens, K. N., & Lindblom, B. (1992). Linguistic experience alters phonetic perception in infants by 6 months of age. *Science (New York)*, 255(5044), 606–608. https://doi.org/10.1126/science.1736364

Kuhn, D. (2012). The development of causal reasoning. *Wiley Interdisciplinary Reviews: Cognitive Science*, 3(3), 327–335. http://dx.doi.org/10.1002/wcs.1160

Kumar, N. N., Chan, Y. L., Chen, H., & Oliver, B. G. (2023). Editorial: Effects of environmental toxins on brain health and development. *Frontiers in Molecular Neuroscience*, 16, 1149776. https://doi.org/10.3389/fnmol.2023.1149776

Kuwabara, M., & Smith, L. B. (2012). Cross-cultural differences in cognitive development: Attention to relations and objects. *Journal of Experimental Child Psychology*, 113(1), 20–35. https://doi.org/10.1016/j.jecp.2012.04.009

Ladson-Billings, G. (2014). Culturally relevant pedagogy 2.0: A.k.a. the remix. *Harvard Educational Review*, 84(1), 74–84. https://doi.org/10.17763/haer.84.1.p2rj13148 5484751

Lanphear, B. P. (2015). The impact of toxins on the developing brain. *Annual Review of Public Health*, 36, 211–230. https://doi.org/10.1146/annurev-publhealth-031912-114413

Lapidow, E., & Walker, C. M. (2020). Informative experimentation in intuitive science: Children select and learn from their own causal interventions. *Cognition*, 201, 104315. https://psycnet.apa.org/doi/10.1016/j.cognition.2020.104315

Lawson, G. M., & Farah, M. J. (2017). Executive function as a mediator between SES and academic achievement throughout childhood. *International Journal of Behavioral Development*, 41(1), 94–104. https://doi.org/10.1177/0165025415603489

Lawson, G. M., Hook, C. J., & Farah, M. J. (2018). A meta-analysis of the relationship between socioeconomic status and executive function performance among children. *Developmental Science*, 21(2). https://doi.org/10.1111/desc.12529

Le Corre, M., & Carey, S. (2007). One, two, three, four, nothing more: An investigation of the conceptual sources of the verbal counting principles. *Cognition*, 105(2), 395–438. https://doi.org/10.1016/j.cognition.2006.10.005

Lee, J. Y., Wright, C. A., Golinkoff, R. M., & Hirsh-Pasek, K. (2023). Another case of the theory to practice gap: South Korean early childhood education and care. *Early Childhood Research Quarterly*, 65, 385–395. https://doi.org/10.1016/j.ecresq.2023.07.008

LeFevre, J.-A., Skwarchuk, S.-L., Smith-Chant, B., Fast, L., Kamawar, D., & Bisanz, J. (2009). Home numeracy experiences and children's math performance in the early school years. *Canadian Journal of Behavioural Science*, 41, 55–66. https://doi.org/10.1037/a0014532

Leslie, A. M., & Keeble, S. (1987). Do six-month-old infants perceive causality? *Cognition*, 25(3), 265–288. https://doi.org/10.1016/S0010-0277(87)80006-9

Levine, S. C., Huttenlocher, J., Taylor, A., & Langrock, A. (1999). Early sex differences in spatial skill. *Developmental Psychology*, 35(4), 940–949. https://doi.org/10.1037//0012-1649.35.4.940

Levine, S. C., Suriyakham, L. W., Rowe, M. L., Huttenlocher, J., & Gunderson, E. A. (2010). What counts in the development of young children's number knowledge? *Developmental Psychology*, 46(5), 1309–1319. https://doi.org/10.1037/a0019671

Lillard, A., & Else-Quest, N. (2006). Evaluating Montessori education. *Science*, 313(5795), 1893–1894. https://psycnet.apa.org/doi/10.1126/science.1132362

Lindquist, K. A., Satpute, A. B., & Gendron, M. (2015). Does language do more than communicate emotion? *Current Directions in Psychological Science*, 24(2), 99–108. https://doi.org/10.1177/0963721414553440

Liquin, E. G., & Gopnik, A. (2022). Children are more exploratory and learn more than adults in an approach-avoid task. *Cognition, 218*(C), 104940. https://doi.org/10.1016/j.cognition.2021.104940

Litkowski, E. C., Duncan, R. J., Logan, J. A. R., & Purpua, D. J. (2020). When do preschoolers learn specific mathematics skills? Mapping the development of early numeracy knowledge. *Journal of Experimental Child Psychology, 195*, 104846. https://doi.org/10.1016/j.jecp.2020.104846

Lupien, S. J., Maheu, F., Tu, M., Fiocco, A., & Schramek, T. E. (2007). The effects of stress and stress hormones on human cognition: Implications for the field of brain and cognition. *Brain and Cognition, 65*(3), 209–237. https://doi.org/10.1016/j.bandc.2007.02.007

Markus, H. R., & Kitayama, S. (1991). Culture and the self: Implications for cognition, emotion, and motivation. *Psychological Review, 98*, 224–253. https://doi.org/10.1037/0033-295X.98.2.224

Masuda, T., & Nisbett, R. E. (2001). Attending holistically versus analytically: Comparing the context sensitivity of Japanese and Americans. *Journal of Personality and Social Psychology, 81*(5), 922–934. https://doi.org/10.1037/0022-3514.81.5.922

McClelland, M. M., Cameron, C. E., Duncan, R., Bowles, R. P., Acock, A. C., Miao, A., & Pratt, M. E. (2014). Predictors of early growth in academic achievement: The head-toes-knees-shoulders task. *Frontiers in Psychology, 5*, 81720. https://doi.org/10.3389%2Ffpsyg.2014.00599

McCormick, R. (2017). Does access to green space impact the mental well-being of children?: A systematic review. *Journal of Pediatric Nursing, 37*, 3–7. https://doi.org/10.1016/j.pedn.2017.08.027

McEwen, B. S., & Morrison, J. H. (2013). The brain on stress: Vulnerability and plasticity of the prefrontal cortex over the life course. *Neuron, 79*(1), 16–29. https://doi.org/10.1016/j.neuron.2013.06.028

McLaughlin, K. A., & Sheridan, M. A. (2016). Beyond cumulative risk: A dimensional approach to childhood adversity. *Current Directions in Psychological Science, 25*(4), 239–245. https://doi.org/10.1177/0963721416655883

Meltzoff, A. N. (1988). Infant imitation after a 1-week delay: Long-term memory for novel acts and multiple stimuli. *Developmental Psychology, 24*(4), 470–476. https://doi.org/10.1037/0012-1649.24.4.470

———. (1995). Understanding the intentions of others: Re-enactment of intended acts by 18-month-old children. *Developmental Psychology, 31*(5), 838–850. https://doi.org/10.1037/0012-1649.31.5.838

Metaferia, B. K., Futo, J., & Takacs, Z. K. (2021). Parents' views on play and the goal of early childhood education in relation to children's home activity and executive functions: A cross-cultural investigation. *Frontiers in Psychology, 12*, 646074. https://doi.org/10.3389%2Ffpsyg.2021.646074

Mills, C. M. (2013). Knowing when to doubt: Developing a critical stance when learning from others. *Developmental Psychology, 49*(3), 404. https://doi.org/10.1037%2Fa0029500

Miranda, M. L., Maxson, P., & Edwards, S. (2009). Environmental contributions to disparities in pregnancy outcomes. *Epidemiologic Reviews, 31*, 67–83. https://doi.org/10.1093/epirev/mxp011

Mix, K. S., Levine, S. C., Cheng, Y.-L., Stockton, J. D., & Bower, C. (2021). Effects of spatial training on mathematics in first and sixth grade children. *Journal of Educational Psychology, 113*(2), 304–314. https://doi.org/10.1037/edu0000494

Mix, K. S., Levine, S. C., Cheng, Y.-L., Young, C., Hambrick, D. Z., Ping, R., & Konstantopoulos, S. (2016). Separate but correlated: The latent structure of space and mathematics across development. *Journal of Experimental Psychology: General, 145*(9), 1206–1227. https://doi.org/10.1037/xge0000182

Mix, K. S., Sandhofer, C. M., Moore, J. A., & Russell, C. (2012). Acquisition of the cardinal word principle: The role of input. *Early Childhood Research Quarterly, 27*(2), 274–283. https://psycnet.apa.org/doi/10.1016/j.ecresq.2011.10.003

Miyake, A., Friedman, N., Emerson, M., Witzki, A., Howerter, A., & Wager, T. (2000). The unity and diversity of executive functions ad their psychological contributions to complex "frontal lobe" tasks: A latent variable analysis. *Cognitive Psychology, 41*(1), 49–100. https://doi.org/10.1006/cogp.1999.0734

Moffitt, T. E., Arseneault, L., Belsky, D., Dickson, N., Hancox, R.J., Harrington, H., Houts, R., Poulton, R., Roberts, B. W., Ross, S., & Sears, M. R. (2011). A gradient of childhood self-control predicts health, wealth, and public safety. *Proceedings of the National Academy of Sciences, 108*(7), 2693–2698. https://doi.org/10.1016/j.ecresq.2011.10.003

Monette, S., Bigras, M., & Guay, M. C. (2011). The role of the executive functions in school achievement at the end of grade 1. *Journal of Experimental Child Psychology, 109*(2), 158–173. https://doi.org/10.1016/j.jecp.2011.01.008

Montag, J. L., Jones, M. N., & Smith, L. B. (2015). The words children hear: Picture books and the statistics for language learning. *Psychological Science, 26*(9), 1489–1496. https://doi.org/10.1177/0956797615594361

Narayan, R., Rodriguez, C., Araujo, J., Shaqlaih, A., & Moss, G. (2013). Constructivism: Constructivist learning theory. In B. J. Irby, G. Brown, R. Lara-Alecio, & S. Jackson (Eds.), *The handbook of educational theories* (pp. 169–183). Information Age Publishing.

National Academies of Sciences, Engineering, and Medicine (National Academies). (2017). *Promoting the educational success of children and youth learning English: Promising futures.* National Academies Press. https://doi.org/10.17226/24677

———. (2019). *Vibrant and healthy kids: Aligning science, practice, and policy to advance health equity.* National Academies Press. https://doi.org/10.17226/25466

———. (2022). *Science and engineering in preschool through elementary grades: The brilliance of children and the strengths of educators.* National Academies Press. https://doi.org/10.17226/26215.

———. (2023). *Closing the opportunity gap for young children.* National Academies Press. https://doi.org/10.17226/26743

National Research Council (NRC). (2009). *Mathematics learning in early childhood: Paths toward excellence and equity.* National Academies Press. https://doi.org/10.17226/12519

National Research Council (NRC) & Institute of Medicine (IOM). (2000). *From neurons to neighborhoods: The science of early childhood development.* National Academies Press. https://doi.org/10.17226/9824

Nelson, K. (2007). *Young minds in social worlds: Experience, meaning, and memory.* Harvard University Press. https://doi.org/10.4159/9780674041400

Newcombe, N. S., & Huttenlocher, J. (2003). *Making space: The development of spatial representation and reasoning.* MIT Press.

Nisbett, R. E., Peng, K., Choi, I., & Norenzayan, A. (2001). Culture and systems of thought: Holistic versus analytic cognition. *Psychological Review, 108*(2), 291–310. https://doi.org/10.1037/0033-295X.108.2.291

Noble, K. G., McCandliss, B. D., & Farah, M. J. (2007). Socioeconomic gradients predict individual differences in neurocognitive abilities. *Developmental Science, 10*(4), 464–480. https://doi.org/10.1111/j.1467-7687.2007.00600.x

Oswald, M., Goldin-Meadow, S., & Levine, S. C. (2023). *Iconic number gestures increase talk about cardinal number.* Mathematics Cognition and Learning Society.

Pellegrini, A. D. (2009). *The role of play in human development.* Oxford University Press. https://doi.org/10.1093/acprof:oso/9780195367324.001.0001

Pellegrini, A. D., & Galda, L. (1990). Children's play, language, and early literacy. *Topics in Language Disorders, 10*(3), 76.

Perez, J., & Feigenson, L. (2022). Violations of expectation trigger infants to search for explanations. *Cognition, 218*, 104942. https://doi.org/10.1016/j.cognition.2021.104942

Piaget, J. (1962). *Play, dreams and imitation*. Norton.

———. (1970). *Science of education and the psychology of the child*. Orion Press.

Pruden, S. M., Levine, S. C., & Huttenlocher, J. (2011). Children's spatial thinking: Does talk about the spatial world matter? *Developmental Science, 14*(6), 1417–1430. https://doi.org/10.1111/j.1467-7687.2011.01088.x

Ramani, G. B., & Siegler, R. S. (2008). Promoting broad and stable improvements in low-income children's numerical knowledge through playing number board games. *Child Development, 79*(2), 375–394. https://doi.org/10.1111/j.1467-8624.2007.01131.x

Ramani, G. B., Rowe, M. L., Eason, S. H., & Leech, K. A. (2015). Math talk during informal learning activities in Head Start families. *Cognitive Development, 35*, 15–33. https://doi.org/10.1016/j.cogdev.2014.11.002

Raudenbush, S. W., Hernandez, M., Goldin-Meadow, S., Carrazza, C., Foley, A., Leslie, D., Sorkin, J. E., & Levine, S. C. (2020). Longitudinally adaptive assessment and instruction increase numerical skills of preschool children. *Proceedings of the National Academy of Sciences, 117*(45), 27945–27953. https://doi.org/10.1073/pnas.2002883117

Reid, J. L., & Kagan, S. L. (2022). Reaching for consensus about preschool curricula. *Phi Delta Kappan, 104*(2), 50–55. https://doi.org/10.1177/00317217221130634

Rhodes, M., Leslie, S. J., Yee, K. M., & Saunders, K. (2019). Subtle linguistic cues increase girls' engagement in science. *Psychological Science, 30*(3), 455–466. https://doi.org/10.1177/0956797618823670

Richland, L. E., Chan, T. K., Morrison, R. G., & Au, T. K. F. (2010). Young children's analogical reasoning across cultures: Similarities and differences. *Journal of Experimental Child Psychology, 105*(1–2), 146–153. https://doi.org/10.1177/0956797618823670

Ritchie, S. J., & Bates, T. C. (2013). Enduring links from childhood mathematics and reading achievement to adult socioeconomic status. *Psychological Science, 24*(7), 1301–1308. https://doi.org/10.1177/0956797612466268

Rogoff, B. (2016). Culture and participation: A paradigm shift. *Current Opinion in Psychology, 8*, 182–189. https://doi.org/10.1016/j.copsyc.2015.12.002

Rogoff, B., Dahl, A., & Callanan, M. (2018). The importance of understanding children's lived experience. *Developmental Review, 50*. https://doi.org/10.1016/j.dr.2018.05.006

Rogoff, B., & Mejía-Arauz, R. (2022). The key role of community in Learning by Observing and Pitching In to family and community endeavours (El papel clave de la comunidad en Aprender por medio de Observar y Acomedirse en las actividades de la familia y la comunidad). *Journal for the Study of Education and Development, 45*(3), 494–548. https://doi.org/10.1080/02103702.2022.2086770

Rogoff, B., Mejía-Arauz, R., & Correa-Chávez, M. (2015). A cultural paradigm—Learning by observing and pitching in. *Advances in Child Development and Behavior, 49*, 1–22. https://doi.org/10.1016/bs.acdb.2015.10.008

Romeo, R. R., Segaran, J., Leonard, J. A., Robinson, S. T., West, M. R., Mackey, A. P., Yendiki, A., Rowe, M. L., & Gabrieli, J. D. E. (2018). Language exposure relates to structural neural connectivity in childhood. *Journal of Neuroscience, 38*(36), 7870–7877. https://doi.org/10.1523/JNEUROSCI.0484-18.2018

Roopnarine, J., Laskar, J., Sacks, M., & Stores, M. (1998). The cultural contexts of children's play. In O. N. Saracho & B. Spodek (Eds.), *Multiple perspectives on play in early childhood education* (pp. 194–219). State University of New York Press.

Roskos, K., & Christie, J. (2001). Examining the play–literacy interface: A critical review and future directions. *Journal of Early Childhood Literacy, 1*(1), 59–89. https://doi.org/10.1177/14687984010011004

Rowe, M. L., Leech, K. A., & Cabrera, N. (2016). Going beyond input quantity: *Wh*-questions matter for toddlers' language and cognitive development. *Cognitive Science, 41*(Suppl 1), 162–179. https://doi.org/10.1111/cogs.12349

Ruggeri, A., Xu, F., & Lombrozo, T. (2019). Effects of explanation on children's question asking. *Cognition, 191*, 103966. https://psycnet.apa.org/doi/10.1016/j.cognition.2019.05.003

Salmon, K., O'Kearney, R., Reese, E., & Fortune, C. A. (2016). The role of language skill in child psychopathology: Implications for intervention in the early years. *Clinical Child and Family Psychology Review, 19*, 352–367. https://doi.org/10.1007/s10567-016-0214-1

Sarama, J., & Clements, D. (2009). *Early childhood mathematics education research: Learning trajectories for young children.* Routledge. https://doi.org/10.4324/9780203883785

Sarama, J., & Clements, D. H. (2003). Building blocks of early childhood mathematics. *Teaching Children Mathematics, 9*, 480–485. http://dx.doi.org/10.1016/j.ecresq.2004.01.014

Sarama, J., Lange, A. A., Clements, D. H., & Wolfe, C. B. (2012). The impacts of an early mathematics curriculum on oral language and literacy. *Early Childhood Research Quarterly, 27*, 489–502. https://psycnet.apa.org/doi/10.1016/j.ecresq.2011.12.002

Schiff, M., Duyme, M., Dumaret, A., & Tomkiewicz, S. (1982). How much could we boost scholastic achievement and IQ scores? A direct answer from a French adoption study. *Cognition, 12*(2), 165–196. https://doi.org/10.1016/0010-0277(82)90011-7

Schmidt, H., Daseking, M., Gawrilow, C., Karbach, J., & Kerner auch Koerner, J. (2022). Self-regulation in preschool: Are executive function and effortful control overlapping constructs? *Developmental Science, 25*(6), e13272.

Schulz, L. (2012). The origins of inquiry: Inductive inference and exploration in early childhood. *Trends in Cognitive Sciences, 16*(7), 382–389.

Schwab, J. F., & Lew-Williams, C. (2016). Language learning, socioeconomic status, and child-directed speech. *WIREs Cognitive Science, 7*(4), 264–275. https://doi.org/10.1002/wcs.1393

Seo, K.-H., & Ginsburg, H. P. (2004). What is developmentally appropriate in early childhood mathematics education. Lessons from new research. In D. H. Clements, J. Sarama, & A. M. Dibiase (Eds.), *Engaging young children in mathematics: Standards for early childhood mathematics.* Lawrence Erlbaum Associates.

Shah, P. E., Weeks, H. M., Richards, B., & Kaciroti, N. (2018). Early childhood curiosity and kindergarten reading and math academic achievement. *Pediatric Research, 84*(3), 3. https://doi.org/10.1038/s41390-018-0039-3

Shneidman, L. A., & Goldin-Meadow, S. (2012). Language input and acquisition in a Mayan village: How important is directed speech? *Developmental Science, 15*(5), 659–673. https://doi.org/10.1111/j.1467-7687.2012.01168.x

Shneidman, L. A., Arroyo, M. E., Levine, S. C., & Goldin-Meadow, S. (2013). What counts as effective input for word learning? *Journal of Child Language, 40*(3), 672–686. https://doi.org/10.1017/S0305000912000141

Shonkoff, J. P., & Fisher, P. A. (2013). Rethinking evidence-based practice and two-generation programs to create the future of early childhood policy. *Development and Psychopathology, 25*, 1635–1653.

Shonkoff, J. P., Slopen, N., & Williams, D. R. (2021). Early childhood adversity, toxic stress, and the impacts of racism on the foundations of health. *Annual Review of Public Health, 42*, 115–134. https://doi.org/10.1146/annurev-publhealth-090419-101940

Shtulman, A., & Walker, C. (2020). Developing an understanding of science. *Annual Review of Developmental Psychology, 2*, 111–132. http://dx.doi.org/10.1146/annurev-devpsych-060320-092346

Siegler, R., & Ramani, G. (2008). Playing linear numerical board games promotes low-income children's numerical development. *Developmental Science, 11*, 655–661. https://doi.org/10.1111/j.1467-7687.2008.00714.x

Silva, K., Correa-Chávez, M., & Rogoff, B. (2010). Mexican-heritage children's attention and learning from interactions directed to others. *Child Development, 81*, 898–912. https://doi.org/10.1111/j.1467-8624.2010.01441.x

Singarajah, A., Chanley, J., Gutierrez, Y., Cordon, Y., Nguyen, B., Burakowski, L., & Johnson, S. P. (2017). Infant attention to same- and other-race faces. *Cognition, 159*, 76–84. https://doi.org/https://doi.org/10.1016/j.cognition.2016.11.006

Sobel, D. M., & Legare, C. H. (2014). Causal learning in children. *Wiley Interdisciplinary Reviews: Cognitive Science, 5*(4), 413–427. http://dx.doi.org/10.1002/wcs.1291

Sommer, K., Slaughter, V., Wiles, J., Owen, K., Chiba, A. A., Forster, D., Malmir, M. and Nielsen, M. (2021). Can a robot teach me that? Children's ability to imitate robots. *Journal of Experimental Child Psychology, 203*, 105040. https://psycnet.apa.org/doi/10.1016/j.jecp.2020.105040

Spelke, E. S. (1990). Principles of object perception. *Cognitive Science, 14*(1), 29–56. https://doi.org/10.1207/s15516709cog1401_3

———. (2022). *What babies know: Core knowledge and composition* (Vol. 1). Oxford University Press.

Spelke, E. S., & Kinzler, K. D. (2007). Core knowledge. *Developmental Science, 10*(1), 89–96. https://doi.org/10.1111/j.1467-7687.2007.00569.x

Spelke, E. S., Phillips, A., & Woodward, A. L. (1995). Infants' knowledge of object motion and human action. In D. Sperber, D. Premack, & A. J. Premack (Eds.), *Causal cognition: A multidisciplinary debate* (pp. 44–78). Clarendon Press/Oxford University Press.

Spencer, R. M. C., Walker, M. P., & Stickgold, R. (2017). Sleep and memory consolidation. In S. Chokroverty (Ed.), *Sleep disorders medicine: Basic Science, technical considerations and clinical aspects* (pp. 205–223). Springer. https://doi.org/10.1007/978-1-4939-6578-6_13

Stahl, A. E., & Feigenson, L. (2015). Observing the unexpected enhances infants' learning and exploration. *Science, 348*(6230), 91–94. https://doi.org/10.1126/science.aaa3799

Stavans, M., & Csibra, G. (2023). The observation of social interactions helps infants track agents across contexts. https://doi.org/10.31234/osf.io/p5aue

Stevens, C., Lauinger, B., & Neville, H. (2009). Differences in the neural mechanisms of selective attention in children from different socioeconomic backgrounds: An event-related brain potential study. *Developmental Science, 12*(4), 634–646. https://doi.org/10.1111/j.1467-7687.2009.00807.x

Susperreguy, M. I., & Davis-Kean, P. E. (2016). Maternal math talk in the home and math skills in preschool children. *Early Education and Development, 27*(6), 841–857. https://doi.org/10.1080/10409289.2016.1148480

Tamis-LeMonda, C. S., Bornstein, M. H., & Baumwell, L. (2001). Maternal responsiveness and children's achievement of language milestones. *Child Development, 72*(3), 748–767. https://doi.org/10.1111/1467-8624.00313

Tamis-LeMonda, C. S., Kuchirko, Y., & Song, L. (2014). Why is infant language learning facilitated by parental responsiveness? *Current Directions in Psychological Science, 23*(2), 121–126. https://doi.org/10.1177/0963721414522813

Tennie, C., Call, J., & Tomasello, M. (2009). Ratcheting up the ratchet: On the evolution of cumulative culture. *Philosophical Transactions of the Royal Society of London, Series B: Biological Sciences, 364*(1528), 2405–2415. https://doi.org/10.1098/rstb.2009.0052

Tomasello, M. (2000). Culture and cognitive development. *Current Directions in Psychological Science, 9*(2), 37–40. https://doi.org/10.1111/1467-8721.00056

———. (2003). *Constructing a language: A usage-based theory of language acquisition*. Harvard University Press.

———. (2020). The adaptive origins of uniquely human sociality. *Philosophical Transactions of the Royal Society B: Biological Sciences, 375*(1803), 20190493. https://doi.org/10.1098/rstb.2019.0493

Tomasello, M., Kruger, A. C., & Ratner, H. H. (1993). Cultural learning. *Behavioral and Brain Sciences*, *16*(3), 495–511. https://doi.org/10.1017/S0140525X0003123X

Tominey, S. L., & McClelland, M. M. (2011). Red light, purple light: Findings from a randomized trial using circle time games to improve behavioral self-regulation in preschool. *Early Education and Development*, *22*(3), 489–519. https://doi.org/10.1080/10409289.2011.574258

Tong, Y., Wang, F., & Danovitch, J. (2020). The role of epistemic and social characteristics in children's selective trust: Three meta-analyses. *Developmental Science*, *23*(2), e12895. https://doi.org/10.1111/desc.12895

Toub, T. S., Hassinger-Das, B., Nesbitt, K. T., Ilgaz, H., Weisberg, D. S., Hirsh-Pasek, K., Golinkoff, R. M., Nicolopoulou, A., & Dickinson, D. K. (2018). The language of play: Developing preschool vocabulary through play following shared book-reading. *Early Childhood Research Quarterly*, *45*, 1–17. https://doi.org/10.1016/j.ecresq.2018.01.010

Umberson, D., Olson, J. S., Crosnoe, R., Liu, H., Pudrovska, T., & Donnelly, R. (2017). Death of family members as an overlooked source of racial disadvantage in the United States. *Proceedings of the National Academy of Sciences*, *114*(5), 915–920. https://doi.org/10.1073/pnas.1605599114

Van der Ven, S. H., Kroesbergen, E. H., Boom, J., & Leseman, P. P. (2012). The development of executive functions and early mathematics: A dynamic relationship. *British Journal of Educational Psychology*, *82*(1), 100–119. https://doi.org/10.1111/j.2044-8279.2011.02035.x

Vandermaas-Peeler, M. (2002). Variations in parent support of children's play. *Psychology and Culture*, *6*(1). https://doi.org/10.2307-0919.1054

Verdine, B. N., Golinkoff, R. M., Hirsh-Pasek, K., & Newcombe, N. S. (2017). Spatial skills, their development, and their links to mathematics. *Monographs of the Society for Research in Child Development*, *82*(1), 7–30. https://doi.org/10.1111/mono.12280

Vygotsky, L. S. (1967). Play and its role in the mental development of the child. *Soviet Psychology*, *5*(3), 6–18. https://doi.org/10.2753/RPO1061-040505036

———. (1978). *Mind in society*. Cambridge University Press.

Vygotsky, L. S., & Cole, M. (1978). *Mind in society: Development of higher psychological processes*. Harvard University Press.

Wai, J., Lubinski, D., & Benbow, C. P. (2009). Spatial ability for STEM domains: Aligning over 50 years of cumulative psychological knowledge solidifies its importance. *Journal of Educational Psychology*, *101*(4), 817. https://psycnet.apa.org/doi/10.1037/a0016127

Wang, Y., Williams, R., Dilley, L., & Houston, D. M. (2020). A meta-analysis of the predictability of LENATM automated measures for child language development. *Developmental Review*, *57*, 100921. https://doi.org/10.1016/j.dr.2020.100921

Waters, N. E., Ahmed, S. F., Tang, S., Morrison, F. J., & Davis-Kean, P. E. (2021). Pathways from socioeconomic status to early academic achievement: The role of specific executive functions. *Early Childhood Research Quarterly*, *54*, 321–331. https://doi.org/10.1016/j.ecresq.2020.09.008

Watts, T. W., Duncan, G. J., Clements, D. H., & Sarama, J. (2018). What is the long-run impact of learning mathematics during preschool? *Child Development*, *89*(2), 539–555. https://doi.org/10.1111/cdev.12713

Watts, T. W., Duncan, G. J., Siegler, R. S., & Davis-Kean, P. E. (2014). What's past is prologue: Relations between early mathematics knowledge and high school achievement. *Educational Researcher (Washington, DC, 1972)*, *43*(7), 352–360. https://doi.org/10.3102/0013189X14553660

Werker, J. F., & Hensch, T. K. (2015). Critical periods in speech perception: New directions. *Annual Review of Psychology*, *66*(1), 173–196. https://doi.org/10.1146/annurev-psych-010814-015104

Werker, J. F., & Tees, R. C. (1984). Phonemic and phonetic factors in adult cross-language speech perception. *Journal of the Acoustical Society of America, 75*(6), 1866–1878. https://doi.org/10.1121/1.390988

Whitehurst, G. J., Falco, F. L., Lonigan, C. J., Fischel, J. E., DeBaryshe, B. D., Valdez-Menchaca, M. C., & Caulfield, M. (1988). Accelerating language development through picture book reading. *Developmental Psychology, 24*(4), 552–559. https://doi.org/10.1037/0012-1649.24.4.552

Wiebe, S. A., Sheffield, T., Nelson, J. M., Clark, C. A., Chevalier, N., & Espy, K. A. (2011). The structure of executive function in 3-year-olds. *Journal of Experimental Child Psychology, 108*(3), 436–452. https://doi.org/10.1016/j.jecp.2010.08.008

Woodard, K., & Pollak, S. D. (2020). Is there evidence for sensitive periods in emotional development? *Current Opinion in Behavioral Sciences, 36*, 1–6. https://doi.org/10.1016/j.cobeha.2020.05.004

Woodward, A. L. (2009). Infants' grasp of others' intentions. *Current Directions in Psychological Science, 18*(1), 53–57. https://doi.org/10.1111/j.1467-8721.2009.01605.x

Wynn, K. (1992). Children's acquisition of the number words and the counting system. *Cognitive Psychology, 24*, 220–251. https://psycnet.apa.org/doi/10.1016/0010-0285(92)90008-P

Xu, F. (2019). Towards a rational constructivist theory of cognitive development. *Psychological Review, 126*(6), 841. https://psycnet.apa.org/doi/10.1037/rev0000153

Xu, F., & Kushnir, T. (2013). Infants are rational constructivist learners. *Current Directions in Psychological Science, 22*(1), 28–32. https://psycnet.apa.org/doi/10.1177/0963721412469396

Yee, L. J., Radzi, N. M. M., & Mamat, N. (2022). Learning through play in early childhood: A systematic review. *International Journal of Academic Research in Progressive Education and Development, 11*(4), 985–1031. https://doi.org/10.3389%2Ffpsyg.2022.995164

Zelazo, P. D., Carter, A., Reznick, J. S., & Frye, D. (1997). Early development of executive function: A problem-solving framework. *Review of General Psychology, 1*(2), 198–226. https://doi.org/10.1037/1089-2680.1.2.198

Zevenbergen, A. A., Whitehurst, G. J., & Zevenbergen, J. A. (2003). Effects of a shared-reading intervention on the inclusion of evaluative devices in narratives of children from low-income families. *Journal of Applied Developmental Psychology, 24*(1), 1–15. https://doi.org/10.1016/S0193-3973(03)00021-2

Zosh, J. M., Hirsh-Pasek, K., Hopkins, E. J., Jensen, H., Liu, C., Neale, D., Solis, S. L., & Whitebread, D. (2018). Accessing the inaccessible: Redefining play as a spectrum. *Frontiers in Psychology, 9.* https://www.frontiersin.org/articles/10.3389/fpsyg.2018.01124

4

Developing High-Quality, Equitable Preschool Curricula

As summarized in Chapters 2 and 3, preschool curriculum plays a critical role in shaping instructional quality, classroom processes, and children's early learning during a unique window of opportunity for development. Curriculum identifies the content children are to learn, the goals for children's learning and development, intentional teaching strategies, and needed instructional materials. Although there is clear agreement that children should engage in reading, writing, mathematics, science, and social studies beginning in the primary grades (Bruner, 1985; Council of Chief State School Officers & National Governors Association [CCSSO & NGA], 2010; National Council for the Social Studies, 2013), debate is ongoing about the amount of attention that should be given to learning academic content in these subject matter areas in preschool (Zigler et al., 2011). During the preschool years, strong foundational skills that affect developmental trajectories can be built; however, many children face societal inequities during this period. As stressed throughout this report, the available research evidence points to the importance of adopting strengths-based approaches to understanding the varied backgrounds and experiences of young children and the ways in which those contexts shape the way they learn and establish a strong foundation for lifelong learning.

This chapter identifies the essential components and characteristics of equitable preschool curriculum for all children based on the strongest available evidence of the efficacy of existing curricula. In essence, these criteria constitute the committee's new vision for high-quality preschool curriculum. The chapter describes the criteria in detail, along with a list of key questions for decision makers to consider. Importantly, the committee calls for early childhood educators to reject the false dichotomies that plague the field and broaden their perspectives on curriculum and its potential benefits. A summary of research on different curriculum types and approaches is included. The chapter then presents a continuum of curriculum types and the roles of educators in implementing them. A major purpose of this chapter is to provide guidance for curriculum developers, in order to increase the quality and availability of research-based, validated curricula necessary for achieving the committee's new vision for every child. The chapter considers who develops curriculum, how the process varies according to curriculum type, and specific considerations for developing curriculum in the content domains. A description of "educative curriculum" follows. Such curricula are designed to support the learning and development of teachers as well as children, particularly in the content domains. Educative curricula are especially valuable because children from minoritized communities too often have less qualified teachers who may not have been prepared to teach the content domains, a situation that perpetuates inequitable opportunities to learn. The chapter concludes with a discussion of research-based and validated preschool curricula, followed by a framework for curriculum development and evaluation.

MOVING BEYOND FALSE DICHOTOMIES

False dichotomies are common in the early education field (e.g., Clements & Sarama, 2014b; Merkley & Ansari, 2018). Many discussions, even by experts (e.g., Kagan & Reid, 2022), tend to phrase issues as tensions between two mutually exclusive alternatives, such as play versus content or teaching academics versus teaching the "whole child" (Zigler et al., 2011). Other such dichotomies include scripts versus teacher autonomy; constrained versus nonconstrained goals, lower- versus higher-level skills, family-to-classroom versus classroom-to-family engagement (Kagan & Reid, 2022), and those listed below:

Play——Academics
Emergent——Highly scripted
Child-initiated——Teacher-directed
Exploratory——Content-focused
Comprehensive/whole child——Domain-specific
Active learning——Passive acquisition
Investigatory——Didactic
Social-emotional——Cognitive
Spontaneous——Deliberate
Out-of-school language and reasoning——School-based language and reasoning

These dichotomies may overgeneralize simple contrasts without considering compromise or even a positive synthesis.

False dichotomies such as these are based on *either/or* thinking, which assumes there is one right answer to highly complex questions. Resolving the tensions and complexities inherent in educational decisions requires rejecting these false dichotomies and moving from *either/or* to *both/and* thinking (Bredekamp & Willer, 2022) and considering multiple ways of thinking among different cultural groups as well as individual children (Boutte, 2015; Souto-Manning, 2023; Souto-Manning et al., 2019; Wright & Counsell, 2018). *Both/and* thinking requires applying diverse perspectives and considering several possible answers to complex questions.

Perhaps the most unfortunate false dichotomy is "play versus academics." As described in Chapter 3, children learn a great deal through play (Hirsh-Pasek & Golinkoff, 2008; Hirsh-Pasek et al., 2009), including social skills and emotional competencies, language, literacy, STEM (science, technology, engineering, mathematics), and other content areas (e.g., Sarama & Clements, 2009a; Weisberg et al., 2015; Zosh et al., 2018). Although play is widely understood to be beneficial, a research review investigated whether pretend play is critical for the development of various domains, or if it is but one of many routes to positive development or simply an epiphenomenon of other routes (Lillard et al., 2013). For executive functioning and social skills, for example, research did not strongly support the critical cause view, but does not differentiate between the other two. For other domains, such as reasoning and problem solving, there was little to suggest that play is the causal factor. More research on play's specific role is needed (Lillard et al., 2013). A more recent experiment, however, provided evidence that pretend play *tutoring* (teacher involvement outside of, or commenting on, and inside of, play) led to gains in social behavior skills but not social-emotional development (Jaggy et al., 2023). This study illustrates that play may be powerful developmentally if the environment, interactions, and specific activities are introduced or guided by teachers.

Supplementing this approach with awareness of systemic bias may be more effective. Such playful learning can include whole- and small-group activities, specific learning centers, and outdoor play. Introducing such intentionality through curricula has been shown statistically and practically to have significant positive effects on preschoolers learning in the United States and internationally (e.g., Clements et al., 2020; Dockett & Perry, 2010; Fisher et al., 2013; Helenius, 2018; Lewis Presser et al., 2015; Sarama & Clements, 2009a; Schmitt et al., 2018; Størksen et al., 2023; Taner Derman et al., 2020). In many instances, however, teaching academics is pitted against developmentally appropriate practice, underestimating children's competence and denying them challenging curriculum (Bredekamp & Joseph, 2024, p. 140; see also Sullivan et al., 2015). The key is to make academic content meaningful and engaging for young children—but content often lacks these qualities, particularly for children living in low-income communities and those who are members of historically marginalized groups (Adair & Colegrove, 2021; Boutte, 2024; Early et al., 2010; Malik et al., 2018; National Academies of Sciences, Engineering, and Medicine, 2023; Souto-Manning & Rabadi-Raol, 2018; Wright & Counsell, 2018).

Families and early childhood educators alike express concern that young children's opportunities for play and social-emotional learning (SEL) may be stifled when early education experiences focus on academic content. These concerns are legitimate when methods for supporting content learning are inappropriate for young children. Inappropriate methods can lead to missed opportunities in preschool for children to explore and learn content through engaging, playful learning experiences in which children have autonomy and agency to approach problems and seek solutions, and in ways that integrate different content areas into interdisciplinary learning experiences. To leverage these opportunities, educators and developers need to move beyond dichotomizing complex issues and embrace *both/and* thinking (Bredekamp & Willer, 2022), while also integrating other views and perspectives beyond Eurocentric notions. Research makes clear that, given such appropriate pedagogy, tailored for young children's optimal ways of learning, preschoolers can learn across academic domains throughout early childhood with no negative effects on other developmental domains (e.g., Le et al., 2019).

During the first 5 years of life, then, content learning can occur in ways that are aligned with developmentally appropriate practice (National Association for the Education of Young Children [NAEYC], 2022) and can include opportunities for play and playful activities (Hirsh-Pasek et al., 2009; Weisberg et al., 2015; Zosh et al., 2018). Because content instruction has too often been limited, neglected, or conducted inappropriately in the years before formal schooling (e.g., Brosterman, 1997; Clements et al., 2019a; National Academies, 2022; Zigler et al., 2011), research points to the importance of intentional teaching for children aged 3–5 years (Burchinal et al., 2022).

Another dichotomy, constrained versus nonconstrained goals, also termed "lower- versus higher-level skills," further illustrates the need for synthesis. For example, important constrained goals in preschool include attaining alphabet knowledge and phonological awareness; an example of a nonconstrained goal is learning vocabulary. Teaching *only* nonconstrained, higher-level skills may be counterproductive given that lower-level knowledge may be necessary for the effective learning and use of higher-level processes, perhaps especially in hierarchical content domains such as mathematics (e.g., Clements & Sarama, 2021; Hartman et al., 2023; Piasta, 2023; Xu et al., 2023) and early literacy (Roberts et al., 2019). Further, researchers of color have argued that privileging higher- over lower-level skills and knowledge may not serve the needs of some communities because they have not had equitable opportunities to learn those skills and attain that knowledge (Delpit, 1988, 2013). Therefore, it is crucial for developers of high-quality preschool curricula to consider how they can support both differentiation and meaningful synthesis of goals and skills when appropriate (Clements et al., 2011; Mulligan et al., 2020), with a focus on specific goals for individual children when appropriate. An important caveat is that content hierarchies intrinsic to the domains' structures do not privilege "school-based" ways of representing and processing content but recognize knowledge gained from everyday and out-of-school environments and experiences (Banks, 1993, 1995). Different cultural groups' and individuals' ways of understanding and building knowledge are not only valid but may also be complementary. Thus it is critical to consider the hierarchical process of learning in some domains and the continuum of learning in varied contexts.

Finally, a pedagogical false dichotomy lies between direct, or teacher-initiated, instruction and other approaches to teaching, such as inquiry. A research review in *Science* suggested that the latter are more effective in teaching concepts, but that the choice of a pedagogical strategy should depend on the goals of instruction and the learners' needs (de Jong et al., 2023). (See Chapter 3 for a discussion of the ways in which children learn.) Most of the time, moreover, a combination of approaches featuring active thinking and learning on the part of the child and intentional, direct instruction where required is recommended (de Jong et al., 2023):

> Theoretical purity is less important than a consideration of all relevant theories and empirical work. The complexity of the field often creates a Babel of disciplines . . . in which the lack of communication prevents progress. This is one conceit curriculum developers can ill afford. Instead, they must meld academic issues and practical teaching demands no less than a serious consideration of what researchers and teachers from other philosophical positions experience and report. This does not imply inconsistent positions. It does imply that overzealous applications (often misinterpretations and overgeneralizations) can limit practical effectiveness. As merely one illustration, constructivism does not imply that practice is not necessary and does not dictate specific pedagogical practices. (Clements, 2008, p. 615)

CHARACTERISTICS OF HIGH-QUALITY, EQUITABLE PRESCHOOL CURRICULUM

Effective use of curricula is one of the most important determinants of quality in preschool education (Yoshikawa et al., 2013). This section describes the committee's vision for high-quality, equitable pre-K curriculum. These criteria derive from the committee's review of the evidence, with special consideration of the needs of historically marginalized groups of children, including Black, Latine, and Indigenous children; multilingual learners; children with disabilities or developmental delays; and children experiencing poverty. To some extent, the committee's criteria are consistent with the Office of Head Start's criteria for effective, comprehensive curricula. Head Start's online *Curriculum Consumer Report* evaluates and rates curriculum (Head Start Early Childhood Learning and Knowledge Center [ECLKC], 2020). And a recent guide from the U.S. Department of Education's What Works Clearinghouse contains recommendations relevant to the development of high-quality curricula (Burchinal et al., 2022).

Ensuring Equity

The overarching goal of this report is to provide guidance for achieving equitable learning and developmental outcomes for all preschool children (Curenton et al., 2017; also see Chapters 1, 5, 6, and 7). The committee defines "equity" as the goal and process of ensuring that everyone has a fair opportunity to thrive, which requires valuing all individuals' and populations' equality; fully recognizing systemic racism and oppression; rectifying historical and contemporary structural injustices, systemic biases, and oppression; and providing resources and supports accordingly (Curenton et al., 2017; Jones, 2014; Muhammad, 2023). In short, equity does not mean *equal* or the *same*. Rather, achieving equitable outcomes for young children, especially for the historically marginalized groups listed above, requires that educators have high expectations for every child and that curriculum itself meets high standards and addresses historical patterns of bias and other forms of inequity. Curricula must promote growth and achievement in all content and developmental domains, as well as children's positive self-identity, sense of belonging, and agency across domains (Wagner, 2023). To this end, curriculum must be developed for the rich diversity of the population of preschool children and adaptable for the unique strengths and needs of each individual child. Importantly, preschool curricula whose key characteristic is effectively promoting high-quality teaching and learning have been validated as achieving equitable outcomes (e.g., Clements et al., 2011; Lillard et al., 2023).

Of primary concern, therefore, is that equity be a fundamental, substantive component of any high-quality curriculum. Accordingly, it is essential for curriculum developers to ensure that curriculum is designed for and accessible to all children and their teachers (Clements et al., 2021a; Gersten et al., 2005; Hebbeler & Spiker, 2016; National Academies, 2017, 2018a, 2022; National Research Council [NRC], 2001b, 2009; Sanders et al., 2007; Yoon & Martin, 2019).

Children Living in Poverty

Children from communities that have been historically marginalized, including those living in poverty, do not have the same type of access to high-quality preschool and program experiences as their peers (National Academies, 2023). For example, previous research has shown that low-income children are less likely than their peers from higher-income households to be enrolled in high-quality preschool (i.e., 18% compared with 29%; Nores & Barnett, 2014). And additional evidence points to the likelihood that classrooms with lower quality (i.e., structural and process measures) will serve a higher percentage of children from low-income communities and families (Aguiar & Aguiar, 2020; Bassok & Galdo, 2016; Friedman-Krauss et al., 2014; Valentino, 2018). Therefore, curricula development must consider the accessibility of content as well as the resources available to all children and teachers.

Children with Disabilities

High-quality curricula are designed for inclusive settings with evidence-based adaptations and accommodations embedded throughout to facilitate the active engagement and learning of children with disabilities. Therefore, adaptations and effective supports for children with identified disabilities need to be incorporated from the earliest stages of curriculum development (Clements et al., 2021a; Steinbrenner et al., 2022). Accomplishing this can be challenging for early childhood curriculum development and teaching, however, because historically, the emphasis has been on creating general supportive environments that facilitate and enhance children's development (Grisham & Hemmeter, 2017), whereas special education has sometimes emphasized individualized approaches to children with disabilities. Instead, high-quality curricula include and provide support for teachers taking a blended approach—integrating practices that address the needs of all children in inclusive settings. That is, the needs of individual children with disabilities are integrated into the classroom's activities and routines so that all children can be meaningfully included in each educational experience (Grisham & Hemmeter, 2017).

Beyond inclusion, it is critical to attend to the inequities in special education from an intersectional perspective, such as the overcategorization of Black and Latine children into special education (Harry & Klingner, 2014), particularly those categories viewed as low status (e.g., intellectual disability) versus high status (e.g., autism, ADHD; Skrtic et al., 2021). In addition, the role of bias in procedures or assessments used to make those decisions must be attended to.

Culturally Responsive and Linguistically Affirming Pedagogy

Culturally responsive and linguistically affirming pedagogy and discourse practices are considered foundational (e.g., Durden & Curenton, 2018; Ladson-Billings, 1994, 1995; Lee et al., 1990; O'Brien et al., 2023; Sanders et al., 2007). High-quality curricula achieve this goal by including all children and cultures, thus having universal impact while reducing disparities in outcomes across groups based on advantage (Watts et al., 2023).

Essential to equity-driven preschool classrooms are culturally and linguistically responsive, relevant, and affirming educational materials. A recent report entitled *The Representation of Social Groups in U.S. Educational Materials and Why It Matters* (Armstrong, 2021) synthesizes the results of 160 studies on this topic. Although most involved older children and youth, the results have implications for developers of pre-K curricula as well. For example, culturally responsive materials have been found to improve self-identity and enhance active engagement and motivation to learn. Use of culturally relevant picture books and children's literature with children in the primary grades has been found to positively support children's language and literacy development (Brooks & Browne, 2012; Fleming et al., 2015; Lohfink & Loya, 2010).

Multilingual Learners

High-quality curricula address the specific strengths and needs of multilingual learners and promote early bilingualism (Durán et al., 2010; National Academies, 2017; Sandhofer & Uchikoshi, 2013). For example, a study found that Spanish-speaking preschoolers made significant gains in their emergent literacy skills in both Spanish and English in a domain-specific language and literacy curriculum; these gains were greater than those of a control group using a comprehensive curriculum. English-only and Spanish-to-English transitional versions of the curriculum were equally effective for English language outcomes, but for Spanish language outcomes, only the transitional model was effective (Farver et al., 2009). Similarly, a two-way immersion program, using a comprehensive curriculum and alternating between English and Spanish weekly, led to similar gains in language, literacy, and mathematics as a comparison English immersion program (Barnett et al., 2007). However, the two-way immersion program also improved the Spanish language development of multilingual learners and native English-speaking children without losses in English language learning (Barnett et al., 2007). Supportive curricula include goals of emergent bilingualism for multilingual learners and adaptations of instructional practices that scaffold language development and comprehension, as well as materials and learning experiences that accurately reflect and build on the cultures and languages of multilingual children and their families.

Antibias Pedagogy

Although some curricula are designed to promote culturally responsive instruction, recent literature highlights the need to go further and actively practice antibias and antiracist pedagogy (Derman-Sparks & Edwards, 2020; NAEYC, 2019; see Chapter 5 of this report). Antibias education extends beyond celebrating diversity, infusing everything that happens in a program—including interactions among teachers, children, families, and administrators—and shaping how the curriculum is implemented every day (Derman-Sparks & Edwards, 2020). Antibias instruction fulfills four distinct goals: (1) support for children's development of a confident sense of identity without needing to feel superior to others, (2) ease with and respect for human diversity, (3) a sense of fairness and justice, and (4) the skills of empowerment and taking action and standing up for oneself or others (NAEYC, 2019).

In concert with antibias education, antiracist education seeks to interrogate White privilege, power, and epistemology in learning by "acknowledging and addressing the primacy of race in education and social relations" (Escayg, 2020, p. 5). Escayg (2020) underscores three core principles of antiracist education: (1) acknowledging the dominant discourse and power in centering one perspective in early childhood systems, which influences teaching curricula and guidelines; (2) using a strengths-based perspective embedded with historical and cultural knowledge about practices related to families and parenting; and (3) "unsettling and unmasking the white racial frame" by acknowledging the role of Eurocentric perspectives on knowledge and interactions "that operate on intellectual, emotional, and social levels, including within institutional contexts such as the media and schools" (Escyag, 2020, p. 10). Curricula can support such goals, but achieving antibias instruction requires the inclusion of nondominant perspectives, voices, and knowledge in the conceptualization of teaching, learning, guidelines, and what constitutes best practices (Allen et al., 2021; Escayg, 2020; Iruka et al., 2023).

Beyond curriculum per se, achieving culturally responsive instruction requires comprehensive interventions that involve all parties and all aspects of schools and homes. For example, an intervention in elementary grades (not pre-K) that emphasizes professional development and school-wide planning and implementation successfully decreased racial disparities in school discipline for Black students (McIntosh et al., 2021). Likewise, a preschool intervention using the Pyramid Model[1] (described later in this chapter)

---

[1] The Pyramid Model for Promoting Social Emotional Competence in Infants and Young Children is a "positive behavioral intervention and support framework to help early educators build skills for supporting nurturing and responsive caregiving, create learning environments, provide targeted social-emotional skills, and support children with challenging behavior" (National Center for Pyramid Model Innovations, n.d.).

addressed behavioral issues without the use of suspension and expulsion, which affect Black children at more than three times the rate experienced by other children (Fox et al., 2021; see also Vinh et al., 2016). Again, professional development and school leadership and teamwork were the core of the intervention, layered onto extant curricula. There is a critical need for research to explore whether such interventions can be supported by and incorporated into preschool curricula. For example, a specific curriculum for reducing exclusionary discipline practices was implemented successfully with middle school students, but there is little evidence that such systemic problems can be addressed in preschool curricula (Nese et al., 2021).

Language and Early Literacy

Although interactive book reading is one of the most effective ways to promote young children's language learning and early literacy (Institute of Education Sciences [IES], 2007; Zucker et al., 2013), the quality and cultural relevance of the materials matter. Rudine Sims Bishop (1990) first identified the critical need for books and curriculum materials that, metaphorically, provide children with "mirrors, windows, and sliding glass doors." In *mirror* books, children see all their identities—their race, ethnicity, culture, language, socioeconomic background, abilities/disabilities, families, and communities—represented positively and accurately (Trotman Scott et al., 2018; Wright et al., 2022). In mirror books, diverse characters exercise agency and effect change in the world around them (Fleming et al., 2015). *Window* books provide windows on the world, enabling all children to learn about people, places, and events. Every child needs to read books that fully depict the diversity of the world and the accomplishments and agency of diverse people. Books can also provide *sliding glass doors* for children to exercise their imaginations, envision new experiences, enter the world created by the author, and gain vital background information—all necessary abilities for later reading comprehension (Duke, 2019).

Books and other curriculum resources communicate who is valued and how people ought to be treated. Children from historically marginalized groups, especially those who are Black, Indigenous, and Latine, need books and materials with positive images that counteract the racism, stereotypes, and biases they experience every day. By contrast, books and other curriculum resources can reinforce biases by omitting, devaluing, or presenting negative images of children, their families, and communities (Armstrong, 2021). Recently, a team of researchers developed rubrics for curriculum review that can be used by educators or school leaders to determine whether a curriculum includes a culturally responsive and racial equity focus and whether the literacy materials, and the storybooks in particular, exemplify this focus (Curenton et al., 2023).

Further emphasizing the importance of diverse resources, First Book conducted a pilot study to assess educators' perspectives on diverse books and their impact on student outcomes. First, the group surveyed almost 4,000 educators from every state working in Title 1 or Title 1–eligible schools, 18% of whom were preschool teachers (First Book Research & Insights, 2023). Teachers agreed that diverse books are important but not many are available. First Book then conducted in-depth interviews with a small sample of ethnically and racially diverse students: 16.2% were Black, 31.7% were Latine, and 21.8% were White. The study found that increasing access to diverse books resulted in students' spending more time reading; it also found that a majority chose "mirror" books with characters like themselves. A promising finding was a positive impact on student reading outcomes with reading gains highest among 4- to 6-year-old students. As a pilot, the study has numerous limitations but will be replicated with a larger sample and control group.

Research shows that children's literature has not achieved the goal of promoting equity and inclusion (Adukia et al., 2021). Annually, the Cooperative Children's Book Center, in the School of Education at the University of Wisconsin–Madison, documents the books it receives by and about Black, Indigenous, and People of Color (BIPOC). Although such books have become more numerous, they are still a small percentage of the overall number of books published (Cooperative Children's Book Center [CCBC], n.d.). In 2022, of the total 3,451 books analyzed, the center reported the following percentages of books with at least one Black, Indigenous, or Person of Color as a primary character or subject: 12% Black/African, 9% Asian, 0.3% Pacific Islander, 6% Latine, 7% BIPOC Unspecified (e.g., brown-skinned character), 0.6% Arab, and 1% Indigenous (CCBC, n.d.). The 6% share of books about Latine characters is far from equitable, given that more than 26% of young children in the United States are Latine (Fernando, 2021).

Supporting Active and Interactive Learners

Educators' (often unconscious and implicit) racism may negatively impact young children's agency in educational contexts, at least according to teachers' ratings (Adair et al., 2017, 2018, 2024). Opportunities to experience agency are important to children's ability to learn and show their capabilities (Adair, 2014), which is a key characteristic of an active learner. "Active learners" are children who initiate explorations of and interactions with the surrounding world and with both adults and peers (Brosterman, 1997; Cobb, 2000; DeVries et al., 2002; Fröbel, 1885; Gelman, 1994; NRC, 2001b; Piaget, 1973; Samuelsson et al., 2006). Thus it is important that developers of high-quality curricula avoid a preponderance of passive "reception" of knowledge, recognizing that children construct knowledge and understanding from a wide variety of experiences (Clements, 1997).

Further, curricula can support teachers in ensuring that classroom experiences promote learning and development and minimize time wasted in passive experiences, such as waiting during transitions between activities (Early et al., 2010; La Paro et al., 2009).

High-quality curricula can also help teachers achieve other critical characteristics of early education, such as stimulating and supportive interactions between teachers and children (Yoshikawa et al., 2013) and, particularly, among teachers and children and content (Clements & Wright, 2022). Communication and supportive interaction are key factors in children's learning and development (Burchinal et al., 2022), and children have the right to communicate and interact (Samuelsson et al., 2006). Developers can ensure multiple opportunities for children to talk with, not just listen to, teachers and interact with peers by applying research on productive dialogues and "think-pair-share" strategies, incorporating the best of such interactions between teachers and children, as well as interactions among children (e.g., Fraivillig et al., 1999; Palincsar, 1986). They can support teachers in using an equity lens, such as ensuring they are aware of their own implicit bias based on children's sociodemographic background and providing varied opportunities for children, especially those from marginalized groups, to express their ideas (Delpit, 1988; Iruka et al., 2023). High-quality curricula support teachers in better understanding children by observing, interacting, and being reflective (Burchinal et al., 2022; Samuelsson et al., 2006). Curricula will be inadequate if they simply provide activities without guidance for teachers to support the thinking and learning for which those activities are designed.

Addressing Goals

High-quality curricula (whether comprehensive or combinations) are intentional and purposeful in addressing goals in all developmental and content domains, including multiple, developmentally sequenced experiences to both support new learning and reinforce and expand previously acquired competencies (Diamond et al., 2013). We return to content domains in a succeeding section. Here, we emphasize that content areas and developmental domains—including social, emotional, and physical—need to be addressed systematically and sequentially (Burchinal et al., 2022; Clements, 2007). Most important, high-quality curricula promote joyful, engaged learning for all children (Bohart & Procopio, 2022).

Involving Families

High-quality curricula promote reciprocal partnerships and engagement with families (Beleslin et al., 2022; Samuelsson et al., 2006). To provide culturally and linguistically relevant curricula and ensure equity, developers and teachers need to engage with and learn from families and communities (González et al., 2005; Reyes et al., 2016). A new vision for curriculum development includes a collaboration between developers and evaluations with communities and racially, culturally, and linguistically diverse families within them. Educators need to incorporate and build on families' funds of knowledge—the experiences, traditions, resources, and rich cultures they bring with them. Curricula need to build in communication supports to promote ongoing, two-way partnerships to bring the home into the school and vice versa (Sanders et al., 2007). Parents' knowledge of children's development predicts positive outcomes for their children, so two-way communication and sharing are critical (e.g., National Academies, 2016). Every chapter of this report discusses families and their involvement. This brief section is simply a reminder of their role in the development, selection, and implementation of preschool curriculum.

Supporting Excellence and Fidelity in Teaching the Curriculum

Teaching a curriculum well requires implementing it with fidelity. Although an aspect of fidelity is compliance or adherence to a curriculum's instructional activities, it may be as or more important to be true to the vision of the young children experiencing the curriculum and what happens in each classroom (Clements et al., 2011). Therefore, high-quality curricula are developed to be supportive; adaptable; and, especially, educative for teachers—the latter is a critical issue to which this chapter returns. In a similar vein, instruments that measure fidelity, whether curriculum specific or more general, must assess more than just adherence or dosage, but the *quality* of the environment and teaching, including those characteristics empirically connected to children's learning and development (e.g., Clements et al., 2011; Sarama & Clements, 2021; see Chapters 2 and 9). Similarly, the measures must use models that consider the way "quality" is defined; research notes that definitions of quality often fail to address issues of equity and the lived experiences of children from marginalized communities (García Coll et al.; Iruka et al., 2022; Marks & García Coll, 2018; Phillips et al., 2022).

All of these considerations lead to a final and critical characteristic: a high-quality curriculum provides strong guidance and support for teaching effectively and sensitively while being flexible and adaptable. Brown & Campione (1996) contrast two ways to flexibly adapt a curriculum. The first, a "lethal mutation," no longer captures the pedagogical essence of the intervention and can be harmful. For example, simplifying a game by removing a step in which children turn to their partner and ask, "I am right?," limits peer interaction and removes an opportunity for productive disagreement (Clements & Sarama, 2021). In contrast, a "productive adaptation" positively reinterprets a curriculum, preserving its essence while tailoring the learning experience to the strengths, needs, and characteristics of particular classrooms and children (Brown & Campione, 1996). An example is giving some children a number cube with only 1, 2, 3, 1, 2, 3 on the six faces and other children a cube with numbers from 5 to 10, depending on the children's level of thinking (Clements & Sarama, 2021). Ideally, such formative assessment is built into a curriculum; regardless, any adaptation that serves the needs of children, within the written curriculum or not, is a sign of fidelity to high-quality teaching practice.

Two types of adaptations need to be included in a curriculum, with specific, easy-to-implement suggestions. "Micro-adaptations" occur *during* a lesson to maximize engagement and learning. In the previous example, changing the number cube could be done during a lesson to meet each child's needs. "Macro-adaptations" involve reflecting on teaching and learning episodes so as to adjust future instruction. A teacher might plan a completely new activity for the following lesson for a child who excels in the activity (detailed examples can be found in the studied curricular reviewed here or at LearningTrajectories.org). Such adaptations can be of many types, such as modifying activities to be culturally responsive or responsive to the needs of a child with disabilities.

High-quality curricula provide research-based guidance that benefits everyone. In contrast to the notion that individual teachers create all aspects of the curriculum, systematic, evidence-based practice is more effective than private, idiosyncratic practice (Raudenbush, 2009). This does not imply use of a narrowly "scripted" curriculum; rather, focusing on the shared scientific base is a more effective and efficient way to improve education. Further, such scientifically grounded, shared practice is, somewhat paradoxically, more likely to generate creative contributions. Teachers may modify shared practices, and those modifications will be accessible to discussion and further research. And, more extensively, productive adaptations and flexible curriculum planning are necessary for teachers and children in different sociocultural contexts and with different individual strengths, assets, interests, and needs (Bredekamp & Joseph, 2024). From this perspective, fidelity is being true to the research guidance and the vision of the curriculum as supporting all children's development, not compliance with a rigid script. Curriculum developers need to incorporate both of these critical aspects.

Summary: Characteristics of High-Quality, Equity-Driven Preschool Curriculum

This chapter describes the components and criteria of high-quality preschool curricula that support equity and promote positive learning and developmental outcomes. Table 4-1 summarizes characteristics proposed by the committee that can be incorporated into the development of high-quality, equitable curricula.

TABLE 4-1 Characteristics of High-Quality, Equity-Driven Preschool Curriculum

Curriculum Characteristic	Key Considerations for Decision Makers
Research-based	Is it based on current research on content and teaching practices that support children's development and learning? Are essential principles of how children develop and learn reflected in the curriculum's philosophy and planned experiences?
Evidenced-based for child outcomes	Has the curriculum been rigorously validated? Does research show positive learning outcomes from its use with children of racially, ethnically, linguistically, culturally, and socioeconomically diverse backgrounds?
Scope and sequence	Does the curriculum provide an organized framework and sequence to guide teachers' decision making and children's development and learning?
Focus is across developmental domains and content areas or coherently incorporates domain-specific curriculum	Does the curriculum address "the whole child"—all domains of development (cognitive, social, emotional, and physical)—and content areas, such as literacy, mathematics, science, social studies, health and physical education, and the arts? *Or* are domain-specific curricula, such as focused literacy and mathematics, coherently organized to guide educators' implementation?
Covers content and learning domains in depth	Is there an organized scope and sequence in each of the learning domains that describes progressive steps and individual learning experiences? Does the curriculum build on children's prior learning and experiences?
Clearly defines specific developmentally appropriate learning goals	Does the curriculum address important goals such as the standards of the disciplines (e.g., mathematics, literacy, science) and/or the state or federal early learning standards? Are the goals reasonable expectations for most 3- to 5-year-old children?
Includes well-designed learning experiences and interactions	Does the curriculum provide opportunities for children to be active and engaged both mentally and physically?
Emphasizes responsive, intentional teaching	Do learning experiences include both child-focused exploration and investigation and teacher-guided instruction? Is the curriculum responsive to children's strengths and interests? Does it promote positive interactions among teachers and children?
Provides guidance on preparing developmentally appropriate, engaging learning environments, materials, and schedules	Does the curriculum provide flexible guidance on daily, weekly, and/or monthly schedules? Is there guidance on needed age-appropriate and culturally and linguistically relevant books, equipment, and materials for children and teachers that are flexible to support children' interests and progress over time? Is there guidance on organizing the environment, including using diverse learning contexts designed to meet important, meaningful goals—such as centers, small and large groups, and individual experiences?

(continued)

TABLE 4-1 Continued

Curriculum Characteristic	Key Considerations for Decision Makers
Supports culturally relevant, responsive, and sustaining teaching and learning	Does the curriculum promote a strengths-based approach, recognizing that all development and learning is a product of cultural experiences? Does the curriculum positively promote children's cultural and racial identities and home languages, and recognize and build on their prior knowledge and competence acquired in their families and communities?
Supports multilingual learners and various language systems	Does the curriculum provide instructional support for teachers to scaffold children's English language development while also supporting multilingual learners' home languages or their language system (e.g., African American Vernacular English)? Is emergent bilingualism for multilingual learners a goal? Are there linguistically affirming and culturally responsive materials and activities in children's home languages and language system that support multilingual/multidialectal learners' development?
Provides individuation and effective supports for children with identified disabilities	Does the curriculum provide for adaptations, accommodations, modifications, and effective supports for children with identified disabilities or developmental delays?
Supports individualized instruction for every child	Does the curriculum offer guidance for teachers to adapt recommended teaching strategies and learning experiences according to individual children's strengths, interests, abilities, needs, and continuing learning progress? Is the guidance detailed and easy to use, including both key components of high-quality formative assessment, assessing to understand children's level of thinking, strategies, etc., and modifying tasks and teaching strategies based on this understanding?
Supports family engagement	Does the curriculum promote reciprocal partnerships with families? Are materials and strategies provided for families in their preferred languages so they can engage in school experiences and decisions and extend children's learning at home?
Includes ongoing assessment tools and strategies aligned with goals and experiences	Is there support for teachers to collect, analyze, and use information from both formative and summative assessments to adapt and individualize instruction and to help children make continued progress?
Provides professional development	Are there initial and ongoing professional learning opportunities to ensure that teachers implement the curriculum with fidelity (often a balance of compliance fidelity with fidelity of vision)?

SOURCE: Adapted from the Preschool Curriculum Consumer Report Criteria (ECLKC, 2020).

In summary, high-quality curricula are coherent, equitable, culturally relevant, linguistically supportive and affirming, flexible, and adaptable (Clements & Sarama, 2002a; National Academies, 2022; Sanders et al., 2007). Full development of high-quality curricula includes establishing evidence that supports their effectiveness (National Academies, 2022), meaning that the curriculum is both research based *and* empirically validated (Clements, 2007). Meeting these criteria places substantial demands on curriculum developers, who work in interdisciplinary areas (Clements, 2007), often as part of diverse interdisciplinary teams that include experts in serving children from historically marginalized groups and of diverse races, ethnicities, languages, abilities/disabilities, and socioeconomic backgrounds.

WHO DEVELOPS VARIOUS CURRICULUM TYPES AND APPROACHES

Curriculum development requires broad and deep knowledge, experience, and expertise. Therefore, it is important to ask who develops curricula for preschool currently and who would ideally. Preschool teachers cannot be expected to create curriculum resources independently (Ball & Cohen, 1996; National Academies, 2020, 2022); in addition to expertise, the task requires substantial time and teamwork. Some educators champion the individual teacher's interpretation and even creation of curriculum. As noted earlier, however, research suggests that implementing systematic, evidence-based practice is more pedagogically powerful and more equitable than individual teachers' private practice (Raudenbush, 2009).

Nevertheless, although it varies by curriculum type and approach, teachers always are cocreators of curriculum when it is implemented (Burkhardt et al., 1989). Although their role is limited in certain types of highly structured, direct instruction–based approaches, high-quality implementation always considers children's culture and language, strengths and assets, interests, personalities, individual abilities, and knowledge (Castagno & Brayboy, 2008; Sanders et al., 2007). Another example is the implementation of learning trajectories—asset-based approaches that integrate goals, child-centered developmental progressions, and teaching practices (described fully in later sections). Learning trajectories are hypothetical in that they are realized educationally only when instantiated by teachers and the children in their classrooms, with modifications being inherent in the approach. Learning trajectories approaches are asset based because they always start with and build on the strengths of each child—what they know and can do. In this way, a high-quality curriculum supports teachers' agency to imbue curriculum implementation with sovereignty, self-determination, and cultural relevance (see Castagno & Brayboy, 2008). Although research in this area is limited, one study showed the success of involving teachers in developing a problem-based STEM curriculum for preschool children (John et al., 2018). The teachers perceived increased knowledge and self-efficacy in teaching STEM in their classrooms, supporting use of a participatory curriculum design approach to empower teachers and enhance their self-efficacy in teaching STEM to young children.

Several other approaches to planning and implementing curriculum are frequently used in preschool programs. For example, early childhood education has a long tradition of emergent curriculum in which educational experiences are derived from the interests and experiences of the learners as the school year proceeds (Jones & Nimmo, 1994). "Although emergent curriculum places considerable emphasis on following children's interests, this approach does not mean that nothing is planned and that everything emerges solely from the children" (Bredekamp & Joseph, 2024, p. 367). Instead, emergent curriculum can be described as a planning process in which teachers and children create webs of possibilities that become tentative plans (Jones & Nimmo, 1994). Depending on children's initiatives and responses, the teacher observes, assesses, and adapts plans and experiences to meet learning goals. Such a child-centered approach supports flexibility and creativity. At the same time, however, implementers of emergent curricula benefit from knowledge such as that embodied in learning trajectories and developmental progressions. Rather than dichotomize curriculum as either completely teacher planned and emerging from children's interests or commercially published, a more complex range of curriculum options can be considered.

In some cases, then, curriculum is developed very close to the classroom. Depending on the quality of the curriculum, it can potentially be highly open ended, flexible, and responsive to the individual children in the classroom and their cultural and linguistic contexts (Sanders et al., 2007), and to the class as a whole. The curriculum can also build on and respond to individual children's strengths, interests, motivation, understanding, and abilities. Increasingly, however, curriculum is developed at a distance from the classroom and is much more prescribed. Teachers pace instruction to ensure that the scope and sequence of the curriculum are covered so that children are exposed to and learn concepts and continue to make progress on important learning goals and expectations.

In reality, curriculum development lies somewhere between these two alternatives, and rather than dichotomizing curriculum as either completely teacher planned and emerging from children's interests or commercially published, one can consider a more complex range of curriculum options. Table 4-2 describes the teacher's role in implementing a continuum of curriculum types (Bredekamp & Joseph, 2024). Even this cursory description reveals the relationship between curriculum and teaching. At one extreme, teachers using an emergent curriculum have tremendous responsibilities

TABLE 4-2 Preschool Curriculum Types and the Teacher's Role in Implementation

Emergent Curriculum (based on children's interests, hypotheses, and investigations)	Curriculum Model with Linked Assessment Tools and Professional Development	Researcher-Developed and Validated Curriculum with Teachers' Guide and Professional Development	Published Curriculum with Resources and Materials; Proprietary or Open Source (by agency, school district, or system of child care programs)	Published, Highly Scripted Curriculum with Materials; May Be Researcher Developed
Identify developmental and learning goals.				
Prepare the environment, and obtain materials and resources.	Provide materials, environment, and learning experiences within the curriculum.			
Plan interest-based curriculum and learning experiences (such as guided play and projects) with children.	Use intentional child- and teacher-guided strategies.	Implement curriculum closely to ensure fidelity to program.	Reference teacher's guide to identify scope and sequence, implement learning experiences, and use recommended strategies.	Implement curriculum closely to ensure fidelity to program. This may be compliance fidelity (e.g., with direct instruction approaches) or fidelity to a vision, depending on the curriculum goals.
Know learning trajectories of skills and knowledge in each curriculum area.			Make decisions about how to use or adapt suggested learning plans.	Remain sensitive to children's responses and plan for needs.
Observe and assess children's strengths, interests, and progress.	Use program's assessment tools to assess children's strengths, interests, and progress.	Observe and assess children's strengths, interests, and progress.	Observe and assess children's interests and progress.	Use program's assessment tools to track children's progress.
Adapt teaching to help individual children, including children with disabilities, make progress.	Adapt teaching to help individual children, including children with disabilities, make progress.	Adapt teaching to help individual children, including those with disabilities, make progress.	Adapt teaching, including lessons, scripts, and prompts, to help individual children make progress.	Adapt teaching as much as possible to engage individual children (including those with disabilities), build on their strengths, and help them make progress.

SOURCE: Adapted from Bredekamp & Joseph, 2024, Table 10.1, p. 359.

and are expected to create almost everything in the curriculum, all while ensuring that children achieve important learning outcomes. At the other extreme, teachers' expertise may be underestimated, and adaptation for individual differences may be limited if administrators do not permit deviation from the script.

CURRICULUM FOR SEL

SEL involves developing knowledge and skills in emotion recognition and regulation, positive self-image, compassion, positive relationships with adults and other children, and effective social problem solving and decision making. Such learning begins in infancy and continues throughout the early childhood years (Institute of Medicine [IOM] & NRC, 2015). Positive SEL and social-emotional development can be promoted in preschool programs in which teachers provide learning opportunities that are engaging and educative. However, children living in poverty are more likely to experience lower-quality early education, even with the availability and funding of programs such as Head Start and public pre-K (National Academies, 2023). The intersection of other marginalizing factors can produce further negative impacts on a child's early educational experiences and development.

The Foundational Importance of SEL

Children who develop social-emotional competencies are more likely to have more positive experiences and academic trajectories beyond their preschool years (e.g., Bierman et al., 2008; Burchinal et al., 2022; Flook et al., 2015; IOM & NRC, 2015). Furthermore, social-emotional competencies support early learning. For example, they provide security and support that enables and contributes to learning in all domains (e.g., Starnes, 2017). This can involve "apprenticeship in thinking" that develops general and specific cognitive abilities through interactions in everyday social contexts (Rogoff, 1990).

In summary, SEL is and must be a major domain in preschool curriculum (IOM & NRC, 2015). Positive social-emotional experiences are critical and increasingly important given recent social-cultural changes and stresses due to the pandemic (Gunter et al., 2012). However, "scholars and practitioners have raised important questions about whether guiding frameworks, prominent programs, and associated assessments adequately reflect, cultivate, and leverage cultural assets and promote the optimal well-being of young people, especially those from communities of color and underresourced backgrounds" (Jagers et al., 2019, p. 162), bringing attention to the concept of "transformative SEL," which is "the potential of SEL to mitigate the educational, social, and economic inequities that derive from the interrelated legacies of racialized cultural oppression in the United States and globally" (Jagers et al., 2019, p. 163). This means that SEL must also attend to the structure of power by ensuring that children, including children with privilege, are aware of their identity and others and that they co-create a community of agency and belonging.

SEL Curricula and Interventions

Preschool experiences impact children's social-emotional development (see, e.g., Goldstein et al., 2013; IOM & NRC, 2015, p. 7341; Shure & Spivack, 1980), as well as their social preferences, such as being more egalitarian (List et al., 2020). High-quality interventions and curricula are based mainly on models of SEL and target malleable factors identified through research (Domitrovich et al., 2012; IOM & NRC, 2010). Such theory- and evidenced-based interventions with high-quality implementations from introduction to sustainability can have a positive effect on young children's SEL (see, e.g., Bierman et al., 2008; Domitrovich et al., 2012; Myran et al., 2009), including children with disabilities (Vaughn et al., 2003), although overall evaluations of SEL programs have been mixed (Zhai et al., 2015). A review of research on early childhood SEL interventions concludes that the more effective programs include professional development of educators, stress management for educators, and embedding strategies in everyday classroom activities (McClelland et al., 2017). This section reviews research on evidence-based, focused SEL curricula and interventions with implications for developing and evaluating preschool curricula.

The *I Can Problem Solve* (ICPS) curriculum was designed to decrease disruptive behaviors by teaching interpersonal cognitive problem-solving skills. ICPS includes lessons in recognizing children's own and others' emotions, perspective taking, and practice in thinking of multiple solutions to social problems before they arise (Shure & Spivack, 1982). A randomized controlled trial (RCT) involving 4-year-old African American children in a low-income community found improvements in children's social problem-solving skills—especially the ability to think of alternative solutions to interpersonal problems—and decreases in physical and verbal aggression, inability to cope with frustrations, and social withdrawal (Shure & Spivack, 1982). Feis & Simons (1985) replicated the study in an RCT with rural preschoolers, finding decreases in problem behaviors and fewer referrals to a mental health consultant in children experiencing ICPS compared with those in the control group.

More research has been conducted on *Preschool Promoting Alternative Thinking Strategies* (PATHS), a universal elementary school prevention curriculum aimed at reducing aggression and behavior problems by promoting the development of social-emotional competence. The curriculum first teaches emotional competencies, considered to develop first, and then cognition and behavior. As an example, it teaches verbal mediation and inhibitory control with lessons using a traffic signal, with the red light signaling "Stop—Calm Down," yellow signaling children to "Slow Down—Think," and green signaling "Go—Try My Plan." Feeling Face cards teach identifying and verbally labeling feelings and emotions, in order to manage them. Multiple studies have been conducted on PATHS, such as one reporting support for its effectiveness in promoting inhibitory control and verbal fluency and partial mediation of behavioral outcomes of inhibitory control (Riggs et al., 2006). The authors argue that developers of social-emotional prevention programs should consider developing integration for executive function, verbal processing, and emotional awareness. The conservative review process of the What Works Clearinghouse, on the other hand, concluded that PATHS had no discernable effects (effect size = 0) on academic achievement, social interactions, observed individual behavior, or emotional status for students in elementary school (What Works Clearinghouse [WWC], n.d.). However, the large Head Start CARES[2] project reported that PATHS showed small to moderate improvements in children's knowledge and understanding of emotion (emotion knowledge), social problem-solving skills, and social behaviors (Morris et al., 2014).

Furthermore, positive effects were found in a more extensive intervention project using PATHS as one component. The Head Start Research-based, Developmentally Informed (REDI) was not a curriculum but an enrichment intervention designed to promote social-emotional competence (PATHS), language, and literacy development. These components were designed to be integrated and implemented with *The Creative Curriculum* and *HighScope*, which Head Start programs were already using (Nix et al., 2013). REDI included brief lessons, extension activities, and teaching strategies, all supported by professional development and mentoring (Bierman et al., 2008). In that study, significant differences favored children in REDI classrooms on vocabulary, emergent literacy, emotional understanding, social problem solving, social behavior, and engagement. In another study, REDI substantially decreased teacher-reported and independent observations of children's internalizing and externalizing behavior problems, with the most potent effects for Latine girls (Raver et al., 2009). Another study testing REDI's logic model found that preschool gains in the social-emotional and language and emergent literacy skills mediated three important kindergarten outcomes: reading, learning engagement, and positive social behavior. Importantly, this was after accounting for preschool gains in vocabulary and emergent literacy skills (Nix et al., 2013). Also noteworthy,

---

[2]CARES stands for Classroom-based Approaches and Resources for Emotion and Social skill promotion.

REDI's social-emotional benefits were the most sustainable of the domain effects (Sanford DeRousie & Bierman, 2012; see also Welsh et al., 2020).

Al's Pals Kids Making Healthy Choices is a social-emotional curriculum designed to promote positive relationships, self-control, problem solving, and healthy decision making, and reduce problem behaviors such as aggression and social withdrawal (Lynch, 1998). The curriculum includes guided play, puppets, songs, and teacher-led lessons. An RCT in a large Head Start program found significant positive effects on children's social-emotional competence and coping skills and less aggression in the intervention group compared with the control group (Lynch et al., 2004).

Mindfulness and/or yoga is embedded in some SEL interventions (McClelland et al., 2017). For example, in an RCT of the *Kindness Curriculum*, children who participated significantly improved in cognitive regulation and prosocial behavior compared with the control group (Flook et al., 2015). As in many such studies, larger gains were found for children initially lower in social competence.

The Pyramid Model for Promoting Social and Emotional Competence in Infants and Young Children has been particularly influential in preschool programs across the United States. It is designed to improve social-emotional development and reduce challenging behavior in preschool settings (Fox et al., 2010; Hemmeter et al., 2006, 2013). The U.S. Department of Education's Office of Civil Rights (U.S. Department of Education, 2021) reported that over 2,800 children received one or more suspensions from public preschool programs in 2017–2018, with Black children representing the highest proportion of those suspensions. Data from 2017–2018 also indicated that preschoolers served under the Individuals with Disabilities Education Act were expelled at rates 2.5 times their share of the total preschool population (U.S. Department of Education, 2021). A recent policy statement offers guidance about decreasing inappropriate discipline practices and increasing promotion and prevention practices to foster social-emotional competence (U.S. Department of Health and Human Services & U.S. Department of Education, 2014). The statement encourages programs to consider implementing the Pyramid Model (Fox et al., 2003; Hemmeter et al., 2006).

The Pyramid Model is a multitiered framework for identifying and implementing evidence-based practices in early education programs and classrooms to promote social skills and emotional competencies in all children, including those with developmental disabilities. The Pyramid Model was designed to be an efficient classroom-wide approach for supporting all young children's social-emotional development and preventing challenging behaviors. In this model, social-emotional teaching practices are implemented within and across classroom activities and routines, not only during small-group instruction.

The Pyramid Model includes four components: (1) building positive relationships with children, families, and colleagues; (2) designing supportive and engaging environments; (3) teaching social-emotional skills intentionally; and (4) developing individualized interventions for children with the most challenging behaviors. Key components include embedded instructional strategies, such as emotional literacy (acquiring vocabulary to communicate feelings, friendship skills, behavior regulation [e.g., calming strategies]) and problem solving.

The model is designed to be implemented by classroom educators with support from behavior or mental health consultants and is based on two primary assumptions. The first assumption is that there is a relationship between children's social-emotional development, communication skills, and problem behavior. The second is that to address the needs of all children in early childhood settings, professionals need a range of strategies for addressing the myriad factors that might cause challenging behaviors.[3]

Research from a randomized study on implementing the Pyramid Model within public preschool classrooms indicated that teachers who implemented the model rated children as having fewer challenging behaviors and improved social skills (Hemmeter et al., 2016). Outcomes for children were not statistically significant, but effect sizes were of moderate size; the study met the rigorous What Works Clearinghouse standards without reservations (see Hemmeter et al., 2016). A later evaluation extended the Pyramid Model with components based on current research related to implicit bias, culturally responsive practices, and what is known about the use of inappropriate discipline practices in early childhood programs (Fox et al., 2021). Although not an experimental evaluation of the approach's effect on inappropriate discipline practices, it did illustrate how early education programs can address diverse populations' social, emotional, and behavioral needs without using suspension and expulsion (Fox et al., 2021).

The Pyramid Model aims to support all children's social-emotional development and reduce the intensity or likelihood of significant and persistent problem behaviors. The Pyramid Model mirrors elements in the tiered Positive Behavior Interventions and Supports framework used in K–12 schools (McIntosh & Goodman, 2016). Both frameworks reflect a three-tiered model of classroom strategies for promoting the social-emotional development of all children and addressing the needs of children at risk for or who have challenging behaviors (Fox et al., 2003). Tier 1 represents universal practices implemented to support all children's SEL and behavior. Tier 2 practices are implemented with children identified as at risk for persistent challenging behaviors. Tier 3 provides individualized planning

---

[3]For more information, see "Teaching Social-Emotional Skills" (https://challengingbehavior.org/implementation/classroom/practical-strategies).

and support for children with the most persistent challenging behaviors (Dunlap et al., 2014; Lewis et al., 2013). Children with disabilities often require explicit social skills instruction. Under this model, teachers are offered a significant level of support to offer targeted and effective social-emotional skill-building lessons and interventions that decrease challenging behavior and improve a child's ability to learn. This is particularly important in inclusive settings, since children with disabilities are 2.5 times more likely than typically developing peers to be expelled from preschool based on behavioral issues (U.S. Department of Education, 2023). The Pyramid Model has also led the field in scaling and disseminating the model, and it is currently implemented at some level in nearly every state in the United States and has been adopted broadly by Head Start.

Evaluations of the *Tools of the Mind* curriculum, designed to promote self-regulation, have been mixed, with some studies showing positive effects (e.g., Barnett et al., 2008; Baron et al., 2017), followed most often by null effects at the preschool level (Baron et al., 2017; Nesbitt & Farran, 2021), as reviewed in an upcoming section. The large CARES research reported that Tools did not demonstrate expected impacts on executive function or self-regulation, producing positive impacts only on emotional knowledge (Morris et al., 2014).

Another SEL curriculum, Strong Start Pre-K, which includes "booster lessons," significantly decreased internalizing behaviors and improved child–teacher relationships (Gunter et al., 2012). Part of an evidence-based SEL series designed to be developmentally appropriate and reduce students' internalizing problem behaviors, the Pre-K program is highly structured and partly scripted to teach a vocabulary of feelings and social-emotional competencies that prevent mental health problems. Literature, puppets, and familiar situations are included in brief, repeated lessons. Other studies in kindergarten and grades 1 and 2 similarly yielded positive effects (Kramer et al., 2010; Whitcomb & Merrell, 2012).

The Incredible Years includes a preschool classroom curriculum entitled Dina Dinosaur and training programs for both parents and educators. The Dinosaur program includes whole-group lessons, small-group activities, materials such as puppets and a Calm Down thermometer, and skills development embedded throughout the day.[4] Its training programs for different contexts are designed to prevent and reduce behavior problems and improve emotional self-regulation and social competence. Ideally, contexts are combined, involving parent, teachers, and child from infancy through elementary grades. Videos and vignettes portray adults from different backgrounds modeling social-emotional coaching and positive discipline, and children engaged in social problem solving. Studies on different programs

---

[4]See www.incredibleyears.com

and outcomes are available (Webster-Stratton & Bywater, 2019). An RCT with a sample of children in Head Start found that the children experiencing Incredible Years demonstrated fewer conduct problems than children in the Head Start program that did not use the curriculum (Webster-Stratton et al., 2001). Another RCT found that compared with the control group, children experiencing Incredible Years showed greater gains in emotion regulation and social competence and greater decreases in conduct problems (Webster-Stratton et al., 2008). A recent study reported positive effects on preschoolers' social competencies with decreased behavior problems (Major et al., 2024). Caveats include the quasi-experimental structure and the use of any teacher reports (which may be more subjective, a caveat for many studies in this sphere). (Positive effects were also found in studies in which the curriculum was combined with, and thus confounded by, other curriculum and extracurricular components [e.g., Zhai et al., 2012].) The large CARES research project reported that Incredible Years improved children's emotional knowledge, social problem–solving skills, and social behaviors but failed to produce expected impacts on children's problem behaviors and executive function. As an exception, however, children with the highest levels of behavior problems at the beginning of the year experienced some benefit (Morris et al., 2014).

Finally, consistent with the results of these studies, a meta-analysis that included many of these curricula and approaches indicated that early social-behavioral interventions emphasizing intentional teaching of social skills have a substantial benefit for children with emotional and behavioral problems (Dong et al., 2023a). Curriculum and intervention fidelity were significant moderators of these effects, with important implications for SEL preschool curricula. The effects of curriculum-based interventions were smaller than interventions without curriculum. Thus, a written curriculum may not ameliorate preschoolers' social behavioral problems as effectively as programs in other forms. Interventions integrated throughout the day were smaller than those delivered during scheduled times, suggesting the importance of intentional teaching of SEL for preschoolers and, thus, professional development for teachers (Dong et al., 2023a).

The CARES study concluded that some evidence-based approaches can improve preschoolers' social-emotional competence when implemented at scale with appropriate support. However, it also found no facilitative effects on academic competencies, and, importantly, no impacts on outcomes in kindergarten as reported by teachers and parents. Fadeout is a pervasive phenomenon, but little about social-emotional skill persistence is known. A meta-analysis reported that at 1- to 2-year follow-ups, persistence rates were larger for cognitive skills than for social-emotional skills, and they demonstrated similar patterns of fadeout (Hart et al., 2023). In contrast to many studies that show that children with lower entry skills benefit the most from curricular interventions, follow-up quantile treatment effect analyses found that students with greater emotional knowledge and problem-solving skills gained more from the social-emotional curricula studied in CARES (Shea & Jenkins, 2021).

Although much has been learned, more research on SEL curricula would benefit the field. Studies of some SEL-oriented curricula—such as *Second Step*, designed to reduce impulsive, high-risk, and aggressive behaviors—are often limited methodologically (e.g., WWC, 2013). However, pilot studies have been promising (Upshur et al., 2013). A follow-up efficacy evaluation also found promising results, with marginal effects on the social-emotional domain and significant effects on measures of executive function (Upshur et al., 2017). However, Latine children appeared to have fewer gains in executive function than White students.

SEL: Implications for Preschool Curricula

Existing research identifies SEL as critical to the preschool educational experience. Further, theory- and evidenced-based interventions with high-quality implementations from introduction to sustainability can have a positive effect on young children's SEL (e.g., Bierman et al., 2008; Domitrovich et al., 2012; Myran et al., 2009). Features of the curricula, approaches, and interventions in the research corpus offer helpful guidelines for high-quality preschool education. However, many successful projects constituted specific interventions or broader approaches that go well beyond providing a curriculum, with many of them not encapsulated in a written curriculum at all. Further, at least one meta-analysis found that approaches or interventions using a written curriculum had smaller effects than those that did not (this review focused on children with emotional and behavioral problems [Dong et al., 2023a]). Therefore, while the implications drawn from research are empirically supported, not all effective programs are (or are entirely) encapsulated into written curricular objects. Nevertheless, several guidelines are suggested by the research:

- Effective curricula and approaches promote incremental and sequential SEL; theme-based curriculum need to be supplemented with a curriculum or approach that provides such learning experiences (Burchinal et al., 2022). A suggested progression is to begin with identifying and labeling feelings such as happy, sad, mad, and scared and then progress to others, such as frustrated, jealous, or disappointed (Burchinal et al., 2022).
- Children learn about how people feel and interact by observing, asking questions, and discussing peoples' feelings and interactions with trusted adults. They also learn from lessons in understanding others and their perspectives, taking turns cooperating, and dealing with conflict. They develop social-emotional understanding and

competencies better when teachers use classroom experiences intentionally to discuss feelings, strategies for resolving conflicts, or collaborative decision making (Burchinal et al., 2022; IOM & NRC, 2015).
- Intentionally teaching social-emotional skills, including scheduled, sequenced lessons emphasizing small-group work, develops preschoolers' social problem solving (Burchinal et al., 2022), their ability to identify and discuss feelings, and their use of verbal mediation. Such teaching may include individualized interventions for children with challenging behaviors (especially those that use functional assessment of the relationship between the challenging behaviors and the child's environment and that adapt the environment [Dunlap et al., 2006]). Literature, videos, photographs, puppet shows, familiar situations, role playing, and specific classroom incidents can help provide educational experiences. Supplements following these guidelines may also promote general cognitive skills. For example, a cost-effective intervention using scheduled, sequenced (across increasing difficulty) movement and music games developed working memory, attentional flexibility, and inhibitory control for Head Start children, with multilingual learners also benefiting (Schmitt et al., 2015).
- New understandings and skills need to be implemented in staged activities and within and across classroom activities and routines to provide repeated experiences and generalization.
- Similarly, effective social-emotional development is fostered by wide-ranging efforts to build positive relationships among educators and children, families, and colleagues and to design supportive and engaging environments (Blewitt et al., 2020).
- Recognizing and incorporating children's backgrounds, languages, and experiences fosters positive social-emotional experiences and makes learning more relevant and engaging (Burchinal et al., 2022).
- Strategies that nurture the academic and social development of young Black children in low-socioeconomic communities include building strong positive relationships with students, creating a safe and supportive learning environment, fostering teacher–family partnerships, building confidence, providing education resources, and holding students to high expectations (Karaya, 2022). New approaches to addressing inequities and injustices have been proposed for curriculum, teaching, and research that need to be explored and investigated (e.g., Souto-Manning, 2023).
- The success of the Pyramid Model is relevant to integrated multitiered systems of support. Approaches that focus on not only academics or social-emotional development but both simultaneously recognize

that social-emotional skills provide an essential foundation for learning (Wackerle-Hollman et al., 2021) In a new vision for curriculum, skills would be integrated, and teachers would not be able to focus solely on social-emotional development, language and literacy, or mathematics. Rather curricula would encompass the whole child and recognize the interconnectedness of learning and development.
- As in all domains, professional development and support from administrators and behavior or mental health consultants are important, if not requisite, supports for teachers in high-quality implementations of social-emotional curricula.

SEL and the Content Domains

Although results are mixed, interventions addressing social-emotional development can facilitate, and will not harm, preschoolers' learning of content domains. On the other hand, some educators express concern that SEL might be stifled when early education experiences focus on academic content. Although these concerns may be legitimate when methods for supporting content learning are inappropriate for young children, research is clear that, given appropriate pedagogy, young children can learn across academic domains throughout early childhood with no adverse effects on other developmental domains (Le et al., 2019). Teaching of those content domains that aligns with research can have positive effects on the development of social-emotional and other general competencies, such as executive function and self-regulation (e.g., Burchinal et al., 2022; Chernyak et al., 2022). For example, social interactions have been shown to support children's math explorations, and greater math knowledge has been shown to support social interactions (e.g., Chernyak et al., 2022; Zippert et al., 2019).

CURRICULUM IN THE CONTENT DOMAINS

High-quality curriculum is especially important for the subject-matter content domains. Teaching and learning subject matter requires curriculum materials that build toward a vision of excellence; are true to the subject, developmentally appropriate, and engaging; and are supported by evidence of their success (Bohart & Procopio, 2022; Clements & Sarama, 2002a; National Academies, 2022; Nyisztor & Marcus, 2008). Research indicates that effective use of curricula that focus on content such as language and literacy, mathematics, science, and social-emotional development contributes substantially to children's learning and development (Clements & Wright, 2022; Justice et al., 2015; Yoshikawa et al., 2013). Curricula may play a particularly important role given that general quality ratings (e.g., Quality

Rating and Improvement System) have not proven predictive of, and may not assess what is needed to support, learning in subject-matter content domains (Finders et al., 2023). Furthermore, approaches such as incidental experiences and teachable moments are valuable but inadequate if used exclusively (Ginsburg et al., 2008).

Guidelines for the Content Domains

Teaching content is necessary for teaching the "whole child." Children have the capability and natural motivation to investigate and learn subject-matter content. Developers of high-quality curricula are aware of the need for attention to all content domains, even if they are developing a domain-specific curriculum (Burchinal et al., 2022; Clements & Wright, 2022; National Academies, 2022).

Goals for all domains encompass concepts; procedures; information and facts; productive disposition; practices such as problem solving, problem posing, and investigation; and transfer to other domains, including social-emotional development, executive function and self-regulation, learning to learn, and approaches to learning. These components, along with domain-general processes, predict success in school and in life (e.g., Amukune & Józsa, 2023; Clements et al., 2016; Haywood, 2004; McClelland et al., 2019; Morgan et al., 2018; National Academies, 2018b; Sung & Wickrama, 2018; Vitiello & Greenfield, 2017; Zelazo et al., 2004). Developers of effective, equitable curricula use research to build those components into learning experiences, including formative assessment, and scaffolding within a context of a caring community (Banse et al., 2021; Clements et al., 2016; Haywood, 2004; National Academies, 2022). Advancing equity requires comprehensive support from the entire educational context in which teachers work, including their communities, social service agencies, professional development providers, and public policies (NAEYC, 2019).

Effective teaching of content is based on an understanding of children's thinking and learning (see Chapter 3). As discussed previously, curriculum developers support instruction that begins with and proceeds from a deep and reflective understanding of the thinking and learning of groups and individuals, specific to the domain. Research within each domain provides suggestions that are often unique to that content. For STEM, for example, teachers using curricula that include scientific kits and materials are more likely to teach accurate content (National Academies, 2022; Nowicki et al., 2013). As another example, teachers' modeling of math materials before an activity or transition is more effective than following general class organization suggestions (Moffett et al., 2021).

Curricular supports for teachers that enable them to develop deep knowledge of the fundamentals of the content domains are essential for understanding what one is teaching. Without such knowledge of the goals and big ideas of the domain, it is difficult for teachers to recognize their nascent forms in children's everyday activities, play, and other representations (Broderick & Hong, 2020; Edwards et al., 1993, 2012), and in turn, teachers may be unable to build on children's prior knowledge and effectively implement an approach focused on asset-based learning trajectories. Given the limited preservice and in-service experiences offered to many preschool teachers, this requires considerable effort on the part of curriculum developers (see, later in this chapter, Educative Curricula: Teaching Both Children and Their Teachers).

Teaching content to young children takes place mainly in playful contexts, ranging from intentional small- and large-group and individual work, to everyday routines, to child-initiated play and teachable moments (Diamond et al., 2013). Content instruction includes both incidental and intentional approaches. For curriculum developers, it is important to consider the goals, the children, and the range of teaching approaches to determine pedagogical practices (Burchinal et al., 2022). For example, naturalistic language scaffolding embedded in play and everyday routines positively supports children's receptive and expressive language development, especially for children with disabilities (e.g., Schreibman et al., 2015).

Literacy and Language

A substantial evidence base exists on teaching early literacy and language to inform curriculum development (International Literacy Association, 2018; National Institute for Literacy, 2008; Snow et al., 1998). For example, the large-scale meta-analysis of research on early literacy development conducted by the National Early Literacy Panel (National Institute for Literacy, 2008) identified foundational knowledge and skills that are the forerunners of conventional reading and writing. Among these predictors are alphabet knowledge, phonological awareness, concepts of print, early writing, and oral language. Continuing research with diverse populations of children on interventions to improve these and other early literacy and language outcomes, such as comprehension and background knowledge, has important implications for the development of high-quality preschool curriculum.

Compared with earlier views of the science of reading that focused on formal instruction in reading in elementary school, recent work emphasizes complexities beyond the "simple view of reading" and focuses on the substantial development of foundational literacy skills in the early years, especially in families and in preschool (Cabell et al., 2023; Zucker et al., 2022). Essential foundations such as language comprehension and production, print knowledge (Piasta et al., 2012), and content knowledge can develop early. This recent research also moves beyond studying only typically developing, monolingual English-speaking children to include those who are multilingual leaners, are racially diverse, live in diverse cultures, and have disabilities (Cabell et al., 2023).

Teaching Letter Names and Sounds

This research corpus provides detailed guidance for curriculum developers. For example, teaching letter sounds explicitly using mnemonics (e.g., embedding letters in familiar actions, objects, or characters) and embedding letters and their sounds within words in interesting and imaginative stories facilitates positive motivation and learning outcomes (Roberts & Sadler, 2019).

Some curricula teach primarily letter names or teach letter names before letter sounds (phonics), but research shows that teaching letter names and sounds simultaneously leads to greater learning (Piasta, 2023; Piasta et al., 2010). Some curricula develop letters through whole-group instruction; however, differentiating teaching based on formative assessment and teaching primarily in small groups is more effective (Piasta, 2014, 2023). Such instruction also is more effective if targeted to each child's letter and sound knowledge and if sequenced to teach easier letters (e.g., letters in a child's name; note that letter sounds are not so sequenced), such as A, B, and X, before more difficult letters, such as Q, U, and V (Piasta, 2023; Piasta et al., 2022).

Some curricula teach all uppercase letters before any lowercase letters. Children do recognize uppercase letters more easily, but once they can name one, they can learn the lowercase version without waiting to learn the full uppercase alphabet (Piasta, 2023).

In summary, research supports combining brief (approximately 10–15 minutes), fast-paced, explicit letter-name and letter-sound teaching that includes embedded mnemonics. Unfortunately, this approach is not used frequently. Research does not support other popular approaches, such as teaching using multisensory techniques, letters within contexts, or combined alphabet and phonological awareness (Piasta, 2023).

By contrast, some preschool curricula use large-group lessons and move all children through the same activities (e.g., "letter of the week" approaches), minimizing individualization. As described previously, effective curricula embed consistent formative assessment to adapt instruction to children's current level of knowledge and skill.

Book Reading

In a similar vein, specific language scaffolds during book-reading activities promote children's development of language and literacy, especially for populations who have experienced being marginalized (Pentimonti &

Justice, 2010; Pentimonti et al., 2010, 2017). For example, teachers might reduce the number of possible choices, as in, "What is this part of the animal called? Is it the teeth or the jaw?" (Pentimonti & Justice, 2010, p. 247). Preschool teachers' use of such scaffolds is infrequent, however, so curricula could build them into lessons, emphasizing flexible use based on formative assessment (Pentimonti et al., 2017). For example, to teach the competence of predicting future events in a story, teachers might present possible choices for children just developing the ability, such as, "Do you think Juan will dress up as an animal or superhero for the party?" For children who are further along in developing the ability, the teacher might challenge them to reason and hypothesize by asking, "Why do you think so?" or "Why is it helpful to predict what will happen?"

Similarly, specific pedagogical practices in shared book reading improve a range of language and literacy competencies in young children, including those with or at risk for learning disabilities (Murphy et al., 2023). Preschoolers can also learn more than simply "names." For example, experimental and quasi-experimental studies of the *World of Words* curriculum found that both word knowledge and conceptual development were taught successfully by engaging children with new vocabulary through taxonomic categories, such as scientific or health concepts and content (Neuman & Kaefer, 2018; Neuman et al., 2011). In one study, statistically significant effects were found in the intervention group on children's curriculum-related expressive vocabulary, content knowledge, and knowledge of information texts compared with the control group (Neuman et al., 2016). Although *World of Words* is a language curriculum designed to increase children's vocabulary and world knowledge through content-rich units of study, the curriculum is available only in English.

Young children benefit from integrated and interdisciplinary approaches to teaching content. Arguably, integration is most important for language and literacy, as it gives meaning to their use, develops disciplinary literacy, and develops content knowledge, all with effectiveness equal to that of more siloed approaches (Purpura et al., 2021; Wright & Gotwals, 2023). However, developers consider the focus and interrelationship of curricula and curricular components with the subject and the children in mind (National Academies, 2022; see the section Integrated and Interdisciplinary Curricula later in this chapter). In literacy, for example, explicit, structured activities targeting awareness of the written language and phonological features of language help children develop early literacy competencies more than informal storybook reading (Justice et al., 2015).

To develop language skills, curricula encourage replacing simple "right or wrong" feedback with discussion of the ideas and strategies that underlie answers. In multiturn conversations, for example, teachers ask several children about their interpretation of a storybook or how they solved a problem and then ask others if they agree with the solution, always inviting multiple children to respond (Justice et al., 2015).

One of the most effective ways to build children's language and literacy skills is an interactive picture book–reading technique called "dialogic reading" (IES, 2007). While reading books with children individually or in small groups, the teacher uses five types of increasingly complex prompts or questioning strategies that stimulate the children's language interaction. Research on dialogic reading demonstrates that it enhances the language skills of children from middle- and upper-income families more than does typical picture book reading (IES, 2007). Likewise, studies of dialogic reading with children experiencing poverty and children with disabilities found substantial positive effects on language learning (Towson et al., 2016).

Dialogic reading is a key component of *Literacy Express*, a comprehensive curriculum including units on oral language, literacy, basic mathematics, science, general knowledge, and social-emotional development (Lonigan et al., 2005). What Works Clearinghouse standards found positive effects on print knowledge and phonological awareness and promising effects on oral language (IES, 2007; Lonigan et al., 2011).

Both interactive book reading and oral storytelling are proven strategies for promoting preschool children's language and early literacy development (IES, 2007; Johnson et al., 2019; Wright et al., 2022; Zucker et al., 2013). Interactive book reading, in which teachers engage children in conversation about the story before, during, and after reading the book, has enormous power to capitalize on the stories that books convey and images they depict to positively represent and support children's identities, cultural experiences, and backgrounds, and to promote equity and inclusion (Armstrong, 2021; Bishop, 1990).

Storytelling

It is important to note, however, that such a focus on the written word neglects the value of oral storytelling traditions among diverse cultural groups. Oral storytelling is an especially rich aspect of Black American culture (Gardner-Neblett & Iruka, 2015; Gardner-Neblett et al., 2017; Heath, 1983/1996, 1989). An analysis of the Early Childhood Longitudinal Study, which used a large, nationally representative sample of children born in the United States in 2001, demonstrated for the first time that Black preschoolers' oral-storytelling abilities are positively related to their kindergarten early literacy skills (Gardner-Neblett & Iruka, 2015). The study found that storytelling abilities in preschool predicted early literacy in kindergarten for Black children from both low- and higher-income families, but not for children from other racial and ethnic groups.

Oral storytelling is also an important part of the histories and present-day life of children of other races, ethnicities, and cultural groups, including Native Americans and Pacific Islanders (Tharp, 1982; Tharp & Gallimore, 1988; Tharp et al., 2003). For example, "talk story" is an essential part of the enduring oral traditions of Hawaii. During talk story, people share ideas, opinions, and daily events with others in groups in an overlapping fashion. Talk story was one of the key elements of the Kamehameha Early Education Program (KEEP), which produced positive effects on children's reading comprehension. KEEP was thoroughly evaluated and has been described as providing the strongest evidence for the efficacy of culturally based educational practice (Demmert & Towner, 2003). Oral storytelling and its presence in children's literature supports the development of a healthy, positive self-identity in Black children (Johnson et al., 2019; Wright & Counsell, 2018).

Another research-validated curriculum component is storytelling and story acting (STSA), a structured practice that exemplifies child-centered, play-based, and constructivist approaches that can operate as a module in various curricula. During learning center or free play times, any child can choose to dictate a story to a teacher or assistant teacher, who records it. Later, the teacher reads each story to the class as the author, and other children they choose, act out the story. In an experiment, the addition of an STSA component increased preschoolers' narrative comprehension, print and word awareness, pretend abilities, and self-regulation; it also reduced play disruption (Nicolopoulou et al., 2015).

Available Curricula

Opening the World of Learning (OWL) curriculum is focused on language and early literacy but is described by its publisher as comprehensive because it teaches these skills in the context of content areas such as science, mathematics, social studies, and the arts (Savvas Learning Company, 2014). OWL is available in English and Spanish. As discussed in Chapter 2, the curriculum was used successfully in the earliest iteration of the Boston public pre-K program (Weiland, 2016; Weiland & Yoshikawa, 2013). As part of Early Reading First, the Enhanced Language and Literacy Success (ELLS) study evaluated OWL with additional supports for emergent writing and dual language learners (Wilson et al., 2013). The ELLS study found positive effects on some language and literacy outcomes for both monolingual English speakers and dual language learners. In the Georgia Summer Transition program using the Spanish–English version of OWL, children had statistically significant higher Spanish and English vocabulary skills (Early et al., 2016; Maxwell et al., 2013).

Another preschool literacy curriculum, *Doors to Discovery*, uses eight thematic units to build oral language, phonological awareness, concepts of print, alphabet knowledge, writing, and comprehension. Topics of study include nature, friendship, communities, and health. The What Works Clearinghouse identified three studies on *Doors to Discovery* that meet its evidence standards (IES, 2013), showing potentially positive, substantively important effects for oral language and print knowledge (Christie et al., 2003; IES, 2013).

Conclusion

Finally, research suggests that high-quality language and literacy in curricula may also promote children's development of general cognitive competencies, such as self-regulation and executive function, possibly more so than curricular approaches targeting such competencies directly (Blair & Raver, 2014; Marti et al., 2018; Mattera et al., 2021b). We return to these issues in the following section.

These are only some of many examples that could be cited. As stated, there is a large base of studies beyond the scope of this chapter, and multiple resources based on this research provide substantial guidance and specific practices (e.g., Cabell et al., 2023; Clements & Wright, 2022). For example, the Michigan Association of Intermediate School Administrators' General Education Leadership Network Early Literacy Task Force (General Education Leadership Network [GELN], 2023) produced a strongly referenced, research-based guide to essential practices for preschool. Among the 10 practices are "intentional use of literacy artifacts in dramatic play and throughout the learning environment" and "brief, clear, systematic, and explicit instruction in letter names, the sound(s) associated with the letters, and how the letters are shaped and formed," along with others on read-alouds with reference to print, vocabulary, and comprehension; writing; rich conversations; assessment; abundant materials; and collaboration with families (GELN, 2023, pp. 3, 5).

The entire recent literacy research corpus also emphasizes explicit support for teaching subject-matter content as a critical foundation for the development of background knowledge that is essential for reading comprehension.

Mathematics

As in language and literacy, there is a large research corpus on teaching early mathematics (Baroody et al., 2019; Burchinal et al., 2022; Clements & Sarama, 2021; Clements et al., 2023a; Frye et al., 2013; NRC, 2009; Nunes et al., 2016; Sarama & Clements, 2009b). High-quality curricula build on that base. For example, curricula that support teachers in structuring lessons involving mathematics that are challenging but achievable for each child promote children's learning in important and often neglected ways (Sullivan et al., 2015). Curriculum developers know and apply domain-specific research in designing and creating curricula. High-quality curricula help teachers understand developmental progressions in each domain and ways to assess and understand children's level of thinking and learning in each (Clements & Wright, 2022; National Academies, 2022; NRC, 2009). Furthermore, such curricula support multiple ways of representing, expressing, and strategizing mathematics, encouraging mathematical thinking for diverse cultures and individuals.

Differences in goals can give the false impression that research on curriculum and teaching in early mathematics is contradictory; however, different pedagogical approaches can be effective for different goals (Hiebert & Grouws, 2007). For example, when the goal is only learning facts, procedures, and skills (instrumental understanding, or rules without reasons [Skemp, 1976]), certain curriculum elements—such as whole-group organization, clear directions and explanations with modeling, fast pace, emphasis on mastery, and careful review—can be effective (Agodini et al., 2010; Carnine et al., 1997; Clark et al., 2012; Gersten, 1985; Heasty et al., 2012). In contrast, goals focused on relational understanding (knowing both what to do and why [Skemp, 1976]) include skills and competencies such as conceptual knowledge, mathematical practices, general cognitive competencies (e.g., executive function), and positive dispositions (NRC, 2001a). Here, effective teaching strategies include attending explicitly to concepts and connections among facts, skills, and key mathematical ideas with consistent math talk among all participants; creating a shared coherent mathematical structure; and focusing on children struggling with key math ideas (Hiebert & Grouws, 2007; here, "struggle" does not indicate frustration but rather an effort to make sense of mathematics and figure out how to understand or solve a problem without following prescribed procedures). Mathematical processes, such as problem solving (CCSSO & NGA, 2010), are developed simultaneously. A recent survey of U.S. parents, teachers, and adults revealed opinions consistent with relevant, creative, problem solving–based education. Surprisingly, in this survey, mathematics was also identified as the most important subject for school and later life (Global Strategy Group, 2023). Comparing domain importance—all domains are important and tightly interrelated—is not the point, but previous research indicated the same groups spent less time and attributed less importance to mathematics (Sarama & Clements, 2009b), so this survey may indicate that opinions are changing, with STEM education seen as appropriate for all children.

Relational Understanding

Research supports addressing relational understanding, as it promotes more complete mathematical learning and development (Clements &

Sarama, 2021; Fuson & Briars, 1990; Gilmore et al., 2017; National Mathematics Advisory Panel, 2008; Özcan & Doğan, 2017) and supports skill fluency, while focusing mainly on skill acquisition (Blöte et al., 2001; Hiebert & Grouws, 2007; Knapp et al., 1992). As one example of these benefits, urban first and second graders living in poverty learned to use the standard arithmetic algorithms skillfully and to understand them conceptually, when taught conceptually, by connecting place-value blocks and written representations. Second graders and high-ability first graders performed better than third graders who received traditional skills-based instruction (Fuson & Briars, 1990). Essential general cognitive competencies, such as executive function, are strongly related to mathematical learning and achievement (more than to other content domains, in some studies [Clements et al., 2016]). Research suggests that curricula that attend to these relations and build specific supports for developing both general cognitive competences and mathematics yield multiple benefits simultaneously (Blair & Raver, 2014; Clements & Sarama, 2015b; Deaño et al., 2023; Deflorio et al., 2019; Marti et al., 2018; Mulcahy et al., 2021), particularly for populations that have been historically marginalized (Byers et al., 2018; Clements et al., 2023a; Dong et al., 2021). This is consistent with work by African-centered education scholars, who call for giving Black learners of science, technology, engineering, arts, and mathematics (STEAM) "an educational experience that is relatable, relevant and engaging" (Bailey et al., 2023, p. 8), but also argue the importance of not seeing mathematics and STEM writ large as neutral because of European epistemology centered in mathematics and science (e.g., Bailey et al., 2023; Martin, 2009; Wright et al., 2016). Thus, high-quality content learning in mathematics, as well as in literacy and science, may promote both learning of content and executive functioning competencies, and do so more effectively than other general approaches, such as the *Tools of the Mind* curriculum, whose theoretical core of scaffolding of play has shown small and more often no or a negative effect on executive function in multiple studies (Barnett et al., 2008; Clements et al., 2016, 2023a; Farran & Wilson, 2014; Lonigan & Phillips, 2012; Mattera et al., 2021b; Nesbitt & Farran, 2021). In sum, teaching for relational goals is research validated and important to do in collaboration with marginalized families (Sonnenschein et al., 2005).

Free and Guided Play

The discussion of false dichotomies and a continuum of instruction approaches applies to learning in mathematics as well as in language and literacy. Starting with the most unstructured approach, mathematics arises naturally and frequently from children's free play across a range of topics (Campbell et al., 2018; Seo & Ginsburg, 2004) and in children as young as toddlers (Reikerås, 2016; Sim & Xu, 2017). The effects on learning are less well known but remain promising. More striking, children in classrooms emphasizing mathematics were found to be likelier to be engaged at a higher-quality level during free-choice (play) time (Aydogan et al., 2005). Thus, high-quality mathematics and free play need not compete for time; doing both makes each richer. On the other hand, research in multiple countries shows minimal math learning during free play (Clements & Sarama, 2021); without guidance, children may build experiential foundations for later math learning but not explicit math concepts (Sarama & Clements, 2009a). Other research shows that talking to children about mathematics in their play promotes learning (Helenius et al., 2016; van Oers, 2010). Specifically, interactions that are a good fit with what children are playing and those that engage children's thinking and include discussions about math topics promote math achievement with no detriment to their play (Trawick-Smith et al., 2016). Therefore, it is effective for educators to seek and use teachable moments in everyday play and routines (Lehrl et al., 2017) and attend to all children, including very young children, who may not be seen as "doing mathematics" (Björklund & Barendregt, 2016), while recognizing that these moments will constitute only a small portion of the math activities needed in most cases.

Other approaches to play help children learn mathematics reliably. A systematic review of free play, guided play, and direct instruction found that guided play was particularly important in mathematics, with a greater positive effect than direct instruction on early math learning overall and shape recognition specifically, and greater positive effect than free play on spatial vocabulary (Skene et al., 2022). This finding is consistent with research-validated experiments showing that guided play and playful teaching approaches are more effective than unguided play (Clements & Sarama, 2007), especially for children with fewer previous opportunities to learn mathematics (Clements et al., 2021b; Lewis Presser et al., 2015). Indeed, the guided approach supports equitable education (Fidjeland et al., 2023; Finders et al., 2023; Gawthorpe & Davidson, 2023).

Furthermore, programs based only on an "everyday" or "play"[5] approach to math education frequently show negligible gains. In comparison, approaches that focus on subject-matter content have strong, consistent, positive effects (Fuller et al., 2017) without impeding social-emotional development (Le et al., 2019). High-quality guided play (see Pound, 2017; van Oers & Poland, 2012) includes having a clear learning goal; ensuring that children have a degree of choice and agency; and using an understanding

---

[5]The quotation marks used here denote the researchers' use of the terms, possibly indicating a lack of intentional teaching and dichotomizing approaches so that the benefit of well-designed everyday play and experiences to promote learning would not be detected.

of children's thinking and interests to choose strategies, such as open-ended questions, hints, prompts, and modeling (see also Gawthorpe & Davidson, 2023; Gervasoni, 2018; Skene et al., 2022).

Finally, a playful but intentional teaching approach is more effective in promoting math learning than are laissez-faire approaches or teaching based only on "teachable moments" (Ginsburg et al., 2008; Helenius, 2017; Knaus, 2017; Lai et al., 2018; Lehrl et al., 2017), including in free-play contexts such as block centers (Schmitt et al., 2018; Trawick-Smith et al., 2016). This is especially true for children with disabilities (Hojnoski et al., 2018). Later sections address intentional teaching.

Unsurprisingly, these issues and suggestions mirror similar findings in the debates on discovery learning. Guided discovery has been found more effective than unguided discovery teaching (Baroody et al., 2014, 2019; Paliwal & Baroody, 2020; but see also Clark et al., 2012) and better at developing concepts compared with direct instruction alone (de Jong et al., 2023).

Direct Instruction

Despite the benefits of less structured approaches, however, direct instruction is important in a multidimensional pedagogical toolkit, including at appropriate junctures with discovery- or inquiry-based learning contexts (de Jong et al., 2023; Geary et al., 2019). As a simple example, direct instruction is necessary and efficient for Piaget's category of social-conventional knowledge, such as spelling "four," writing "4" or other mathematical symbols, and following conventions or procedures. Physical knowledge is learned through acting on objects; in contrast, logical-math knowledge is learned through thinking about one's actions on objects (Piaget, 1964). Intentional, playful experiences and guided discovery approaches develop deep understanding and transfer to new situations that are needed for relational understanding in all math topics (Clements & Sarama, 2021; Weisberg et al., 2015), such that children engage with mathematics beyond interactions with teachers (Gawthorpe & Davidson, 2023). While strategies from the pedagogical toolkit are best deployed depending on the content, context, and children, those who explore math ideas playfully before intentional instruction use a greater variety of strategies and attend to the features of problems more than do those instructed first (DeCaro & Rittle-Johnson, 2012). Some preschool math curricula include such play-based sessions.

Big Math for Little Kids (Ginsburg, 2003) is a comprehensive math program for 4- and 5-year-olds. It uses activities and stories to develop ideas about key topics in mathematics, as well as mathematical language, thinking strategies, and curiosity and positive affect.

In summary, educators teaching for relational understanding view children as active learners who initiate explorations of and interactions with the surrounding world and both adults and peers (Burchinal et al., 2022; Cobb, 2000; DeVries et al., 2002; Fröbel, 1885; Gelman, 1994; NRC, 2001b; Piaget, 1973; Samuelsson et al., 2006; Yoshikawa et al., 2013). They avoid a preponderance of passive "reception" of knowledge, understanding that children construct knowledge from a wide variety of experiences (Clements, 1997), including direct instruction, when it contributes to their learning. Such experiences support learning and development and minimize time wasted in passive experiences, such as waiting (La Paro et al., 2009). Teachers support learning by using an equity lens to watch and listen to children and the way they express their ideas (Delpit, 1988, 2006). Encouraging teachers to see the strengths of all children, even if it includes ideas and expressions that are unfamiliar, allows them to build mathematics from each child's experiences and ideas. This is complemented by using a learning trajectories approach, along with culturally responsive teaching, to support the construction of math ideas (Wright et al., 2016; see also the following section). By observing, interacting, and being reflective, they base interactions and activities on children's thinking and learning (Burchinal et al., 2022; Samuelsson et al., 2006). In these ways, they promote joyful, engaged learning for all children (Bohart & Procopio, 2022).

Learning Trajectories

A critical feature of teaching approaches that develop relational thinking is that they base teaching on an understanding of children's thinking and learning. A research-validated approach that does so and seamlessly integrates goals, children's thinking, and the teacher is the learning trajectories construct (Clements & Sarama, 2014a, 2021; Sarama & Clements, 2009b). The use of learning trajectories has been research validated in multiple studies (Clements & Sarama, 2007; Clements et al., 2023b; Dumas et al., 2019; Gray-Lobe et al., 2021; Mattera et al., 2021a; Orcan-Kacan et al., 2023; Sarama & Clements, 2019b; Stites & Rakes, 2019; Verschaffel et al., 2019). Teachers in these studies used all the strategies in the previously described multidimensional pedagogical toolkit. Furthermore, they combined brief, active, whole-group sessions; individual work (sometimes using educational technology); incidental learning throughout the day; and small-group sessions. The last were especially important because of the personal involvement and close interactions involved, supporting the understanding and use of children's thinking to differentiate instruction. Such formative assessment is one of the most strongly empirically supported teaching approaches (Jiang et al., 2023; National Mathematics Advisory Panel, 2008; Shepard, 2005). Formative assessment entails using an ongoing understanding of children's thinking and learning to inform and adapt instruction for groups and individuals. However, formative assessment is not useful unless teaching is adapted according to what is learned through the assessment (Hill, 2020; National Mathematics Advisory Panel, 2008).

Effective teachers ask and answer the following questions: What do children need to learn?, Where are children now?, and How do I help them progress? (Shepard, 2005). Importantly, these questions align with the three components of learning trajectories: goal, developmental progression, and linked teaching activities and strategies; this may be why learning trajectories support and contribute to teachers' professional development and teaching prowess (Bardsley, 2006; Sarama et al., 2016b, 2017b) and children's learning (Clements & Sarama, 2007; Clements et al., 2023b; Hanby, 2018; Koç et al., 2023; Sarama & Clements, 2019b).

Considering the validating studies cited, it is important to note that most have involved a specific curriculum, so that effects from the learning trajectories may have been confounded by other differences between the compared groups. Therefore, in order to address the specific contribution of learning trajectories, studies were needed that rigorously compared learning trajectory–based instruction with the same instruction lacking a critical aspect of learning trajectories. In most cases, these experiments validated the learning trajectory approach (Baroody et al., 2022, under review; Clements et al., 2019b, 2020b, 2021a; Sarama et al., 2021). In Baroody et al. (2021), which showed no significant difference, the learning trajectory itself—patterning (i.e., the recognition, duplication, and extension of repeating patterns)—may have been underresearched.

In summary, teachers who know how to use the three components of a learning trajectory are more effective in supporting children's learning (NRC, 2009). Without such knowledge, teachers of young children may offer tasks that are either too easy or too difficult for young children, and this mismatch may limit the children's learning (Clements & Sarama, 2021; Cooper et al., 2007).

Playful, meaningful, content-rich education based on learning trajectories benefits all children and is especially important for children with disabilities (Clements et al., 2021b). Children with various disabilities may operate at levels different from those of their peers and at quite different levels in one topic (say, counting) than in others (such as geometry). Learning trajectories offer different ways to introduce math topics, such as arithmetic (e.g., counting, subitizing, partitioning), so children can build on their individual strengths. The levels of learning trajectories are clusters of ideas and processes, not just skills, so children can both learn and show competence using a variety of modalities and representations. Finally, learning trajectories can be aligned with formative assessment and the Individualized Education Program or Individualized Family Service Plan process. For all children with disabilities or math difficulties, tiered support is important and has been validated as effective (Doabler et al., 2014; Klein et al., 2019).

Finally, teaching with the learning trajectory approach, which is asset-based at its core, while emphasizing culturally responsive teaching and the role of families and of out-of-school experiences, increases identity construction and meaning-making practices for Black boys, supporting their construction of math ideas (Wright et al., 2016). Such efforts are especially important given evidence that Black boys are often considered as less able than their White peers in mathematics (Martin, 2007). Further, the approach has direct empirical support. Black preschoolers engaged in a conceptually grounded, learning trajectories curriculum gained more than other groups (Clements et al., 2011) and their gains persisted into fifth grade (Clements et al., 2023b).

Although it is beyond the scope of this chapter, there is also a substantial body of research on teaching strategies for relational understanding. For example, research has demonstrated how to structure curricula in such areas as teacher expectations; group size and structure; math talk, discussions, and connections; adapting activities; implementation; formative assessment; examples and nonexamples; collaboration with families and assurance of positive experiences for children from culturally and linguistically diverse backgrounds; and, of course, specific teaching strategies for each math topic (Baroody et al., 2019; Clements & Sarama, 2012, 2021; Clements et al., 2023a; Durden & Curenton, 2018; Ma & Kessel, 2018; NRC, 2009; Nunes et al., 2016; Sarama & Clements, 2019b). As an example, a research review found that multilingual learners with learning disabilities succeed in learning mathematical problem solving when culturally relevant scaffolding, including visual models, is integral to the teaching–learning process (Lei & Xin, 2023).

Given the importance of the learning trajectories approach in many research reviews and projects (Baroody et al., 2019; Burchinal et al., 2022; Clements & Sarama, 2021; Frye et al., 2013; NRC, 2009), and because they are relevant to all domains, this approach is addressed further in a subsequent section.

Science and Engineering

In science, engineering, and aspects of other domains, curriculum developers are still working to achieve the vision of the Framework for K–12 Science Education (NRC, 2012) and to demonstrate genuine alignment with that framework and the Next Generation Science Standards (NRC, 2013). Curricula that do align with these promote and support investigation and design (Broderick & Hong, 2020; National Academies, 2022). Such materials can provide information and guidance on science and engineering topics that many preschool teachers have not had the opportunity to learn about (National Academies, 2022).

Developers of high-quality science and engineering curricula ensure that the materials include substantive investigation and design; are conceptually and pedagogically coherent; support teachers' noticing and understanding of children's learning and development; and provide for flexibility (National Academies, 2022), including suggestions for incorporations from local cultures and adaptations for all children (the former is particularly important, given the marginalization of groups for both scientists and children [Burbanks et al., 2020; National Academies, 2022]). They help orient children to phenomena and design challenges, including collecting, analyzing, and making sense of data. They support children's development of explanations, discourse, and design solutions, the last of which is particularly challenging for preschool teachers (Domínguez & Goldstein, 2020). A promising approach is building science and engineering instruction into activities already taking place in the classroom, thus providing contextualized experiences that make learning engaging and meaningful (Bustamante et al., 2018). A research review identified categories of activities that have potential for developing children's learning and engagement with STEM fields: educational robots, educational games, argumentative interactions, inquiry-based learning and engineering design, drawing and telling about engineers, free play and pretend play, and group membership (Ha et al., 2023).

Although the number of studies of preschool science and engineering curricula is limited, some studies provide direct evidence for the benefits of following these guidelines. An early study of a preschool science curriculum emphasizing coherence and sequential development of science concepts in four modules, along with careful integration with other domains, showed that children were highly engaged with science, socially active, and rarely disruptive (French, 2004). They also made significant gains of approximately 0.5 standard deviation on the Peabody Picture Vocabulary Test (French, 2004).[6] Informational texts promote preschoolers' knowledge of literacy forms and can make valuable contributions to all phases of learning science and engineering (Clements & Wright, 2022; Hwang & Duke, 2020; Sarama et al., 2017a). High-quality curricula provide tools that help teachers elicit and guide classroom discussions, facilitating

---

[6]The committee cautions against using gains made on norm-referenced and individually administered measures of receptive vocabulary based on words in Standard American English (e.g., Peabody Picture Vocabulary Test) as the sole marker/measure of children's academic achievement. Research has pointed to the potential of such tools to be susceptible to bias if they do not adequately capture the experiences, familiar concepts, and cultural nuances of children from racially, culturally, and linguistically minoritized children, as well as children from households with lower incomes and children with disabilities (Champion et al., 2003; Restrepo et al., 2006).

children's cognitive and affective engagement with both literacy and science (Mantzicopoulos & Patrick, 2011); they can also support preschoolers' basic concept acquisition and general cognitive competencies (Greenfield et al., 2017; RISE Project, n.d.; Toran et al., 2019).

In one study, a curriculum consisting of science games provided high-quality instructional support to teachers, including affordances for interactions that develop concepts, analysis, and reasoning (Guarrella et al., 2021); it thus provided teachers with a structure for transforming pedagogical prompts into effective teaching practice. Similarly, another study found that an early STEM program contributed to teachers' skills in teaching STEM concepts, as well as to students' competencies in STEM and recognition of its applications. A challenge in the program's implementation was the need for more classroom time (Mesutoglu & Corlu, 2023). And, although not a curriculum study per se, a STEM intervention in preschool increased creativity and problem-solving scores (Yalçın & Erden, 2021).

Furthermore, for STEM especially, high-quality curricula help all children, especially those who are members of marginalized groups, to identify with the STEM fields by including a wide range of people working in the field and meaningful STEM topics. For example, culturally based learning experiences may focus on care for the environment, such as recycling and caring for plant and animal life, including the specific places and environments where children live (National Academies, 2022). Vignettes from a Head Start Center on the White Earth reservation in northwest Minnesota, which incorporates cultural themes, show children's engagement, interest, and curiosity about animal tracks (Dubosarsky et al., 2011). In another instance, Conscious Ingenuity, a K–8 African-centered program uses STEAM to build Black children's character, confidence, and capabilities. Conscious Ingenuity uses African-centered cultural practices, such as call and response, affirmation recitals, communication styles, cultural imagery, and problem-solving lessons aligned with their community (Bailey et al., 2023). Although Conscious Ingenuity is a promising approach and is being implemented in schools such as Baltimore City Public Schools, more rigorous evidence is needed to further substantiate this program's effects on children's capabilities and learning outcomes. High-quality STEM experiences have the potential to ensure that children's sociodemographics, such as their race, gender, place, ability, or class, do not determine their ability to meaningfully engage in and contribute to others' learning. This is possible when curricula do not center solely on the dominant groups' experiences, resources, language, and ability but meaningfully strengthen children's domain-general skills, such as their approaches to learning and executive function (Bustamante et al., 2018). As in other domains, engaging families in STEM experiences is an important aspect of preschool education. Although interventions often yield small effects, providing materials and resources for home use appears to be a promising feature (Zucker et al., 2022).

All children have the right to benefit from high-quality STEM experiences that have strong potential to help to develop science and engineering and other domains, as well as approaches to learning and executive functioning strategies (Bustamante et al., 2018). Culturally responsive, asset-based approaches emphasizing the importance of families and of leveraging out-of-school practices help African American males build positive identity and provide meaning-making practices that promote stronger STEM learning (Wright et al., 2016). Although little research has been done in this area, investigating social justice issues such as toxins and other problems in specific, low-resource areas could be pursued in future curriculum development projects.

Other Domains

Briefly, the committee notes that although other domains, including SEL, are not often discussed as "content" domains, they do have conceptual or "content" aspects. These include the recognition, understanding, and appropriate expression of emotions, known as emotional literacy and language, and emotional self-regulation (Joseph et al., 2021), as well as cognitive problem-solving strategies that teach children to think about consequences and alternatives before acting (Fox & Hemmeter, 2009; Joseph & Strain, 2010; Sarama et al., 2017a; Webster-Stratton et al., 2001). These are important aspects of social-emotional development and the learning of social studies—the latter needs more research. In addition, the Head Start Early Learning Outcomes Framework and state learning standards often include other domains such as the visual and performing arts, physical development and education, health and safety, approaches to learning, and social studies (e.g., Head Start, 2023; Maryland State Department of Education, 2024).

Educators' Roles

Educators vary in their sustained use of a curriculum. To support invested, improved implementation, it is crucial for developers and publishers of high-quality curricula to consider how to effectively promote teachers' autonomy in choosing and implementing a curriculum (making productive adaptations [Brown & Campione, 1996]). High-quality curricula also need to promote teachers' access to resources and support for teachers from program administrators (Lieber et al., 2010; Sarama & Clements, 2021; Sarama et al., 2016b). See the section Educative Curricula: Teaching Both Children and Their Teachers.

CURRICULUM TYPES AND APPROACHES

This section provides additional information about the two general types of curricula discussed previously, comprehensive and domain specific, and then describes integrated and interdisciplinary curricula, which can fall into either of those categories. Next, it gives an example of culturally relevant and sustaining Indigenous curriculum approaches. The section then discusses frequently used approaches to delivering curriculum content: the project approach, the Reggio Emilia approach, the Cycle of Inquiry, and the learning trajectories approach. Although these approaches are not curricula, they are designed to promote children's deep engagement in thinking and learning about interesting and relevant topics of study and questions to investigate and may also be part of a comprehensive curriculum. Next the section describes and presents research on Montessori education, one of the oldest approaches to early education. Finally, the section reviews technology for children and their teachers.

Comprehensive and Domain-Specific Curricula

As this chapter has described, research reviews suggest that curricula focused on one domain have greater positive effects on those targeted domains than comprehensive curricula (Chaudry et al., 2017; Jenkins et al., 2018; Weiland et al., 2018; Yoshikawa et al., 2013, 2016). That is, domain-specific (developed by experts in a given domain [Chaudry et al., 2017]), play-infused curricula supported by professional development and coaching for teachers have been identified as the most likely to increase instructional quality in large-scale preschool programs (Jenkins et al., 2018). There are also examples of empirically validated efforts to incorporate a domain-specific component into a comprehensive curriculum (an approach strongly supported by state leaders [Little & Gragson, 2023]). Initially, the Boston public pre-K program, for example, included curricula on language and literacy, as well as mathematics, in its *Focus on PreK* curriculum, and multiple rigorous studies validated this approach as improving literacy, especially vocabulary, and math skills (Clements et al., 2011; Weiland & Yoshikawa, 2013). It is important to point out that in addition to having well-qualified certified teachers, Boston pre-K sites were accredited by the National Association for the Education of Young Children as having a baseline of high-quality program provision. The substantial and meaningful gains were complemented by an increase in executive functioning abilities due to the two domain-specific curricula. While all groups benefited, Latine children benefited particularly (Weiland & Yoshikawa, 2013). A different math curriculum, *Numbers Plus Preschool Mathematics,* added to a comprehensive *HighScope* curriculum also led to greater math learning, although the effects were small (Wakabayashi et al., 2020).

A review across five large-scale evaluations identified six potentially important features of both comprehensive and domain-specific curricula: a significant focus on specific instructional content, inclusion of detailed prompts or suggestions for the lesson while also incorporating teacher voice (described below), time for planning, real-time data, and early childhood training for administrators (Weiland et al., 2018). An example of detailed prompts is explicit illustrations of goals to be achieved when reading aloud a book; such goals range from basic comprehension and recall to high-level inference making and depend on which book is being read. Such prompts are not intended to be repeated as given, but are reminders of key pedagogical strategies, vocabulary, and so forth that teachers can read in advance or have in front of them as they teach. "Soft-scripted" prompts preserve teacher voice by providing guidance but not requiring compliance. Those providing professional development need to remind teachers that soft scripts are intended as two-way communication with professionals. This perspective is grounded in the assumption that the teacher–curriculum relationship is interactive and dynamic (Drake et al., 2014).

Integrated and Interdisciplinary Curricula

Integrated curricula simultaneously address learning goals across content areas or developmental domains, helping meet the challenge of covering many learning goals with limited instructional time. Such curricula can also help children make meaningful connections between topics of study. For example, literacy and social-emotional goals might be addressed within a single experience or lesson, such as reading books about friendship or conflict resolution.

Integrated curricula can also support antibias education and other inclusive practices (Derman-Sparks & A.B.C. Task Force, 1989; Derman-Sparks & Edwards, 2020) by incorporating reading or writing of stories that promote (1) positive identity for children of all races, ethnicities, languages, and abilities; (2) respect for differences; and (3) examples of fairness, agency, and actions that promote social justice (Brooks & Browne, 2012; Fleming et al., 2015; Lohfink & Loya, 2010).

The terms *interdisciplinary* and *integrated* both describe approaches that connect learning across content domains, but the terms are rarely distinguished. Integration can be partial, where one domain plays a supporting role, or full, where all domains are combined in major lessons, instructional activities, or projects. In contrast, interdisciplinary curricula are selective: domains are connected only when doing so serves each domain, so that each retains its core conceptual and epistemological structures (National Academies, 2022).

Although designed for slightly older children (kindergarten to second grade), the evidence-based curriculum *Science, Oral Language, and Literacy Development from the Start of School* (*SOLID Start*; Wright & Gotwals,

2017) includes topics of study based on scientific phenomena that children can observe and investigate, such as insects or birds on the playground. Playful learning experiences, relevant informational books, and teacher-scaffolded discussions are included. Children draw and write to represent and record their ideas and findings. Because the authors do not consider literacy (reading, writing, speaking, listening, images, representations, etc.) a "discipline," one could view this curriculum as fully integrated or even interdisciplinary for the focal competencies in literacy, language, and science (National Academies, 2022), each of which showed improved outcomes for children (Wright & Gotwals, 2017).

Another example, the *Connect4Learning* (C4L) preschool curriculum, is based explicitly on an interdisciplinary approach to literacy, language, mathematics, science, engineering, and social-emotional development (Sarama et al., 2016a, 2017a). When appropriate, children might concentrate mainly on a mathematical exploration. Even then, development of the language and social-emotional domains is always involved. All components of C4L are drawn from research-validated curricula, and pilot studies have shown improvements in all included domains. Larger-scale studies are under way (Sarama et al., 2017a).

Approaches to Curriculum Implementation

Curriculum content and early learning standards often come directly from the subject-matter disciplines: what children need to know and be able to do in mathematics, science, language, literacy, health, social studies, and the arts. Such content teaches accurate information about the world and how to obtain new knowledge. Because the content knowledge is often removed from children's direct, cultural experiences, however, pre-K curriculum is typically organized conceptually. Conceptual organizers can make content knowledge more meaningful, engaging, and understandable for young children, particularly for children from culturally and linguistically minoritized groups.

Many curricula, including those that are comprehensive, interdisciplinary, and domain specific, incorporate a concept- or theme-based approach in which in-depth learning experiences are designed around a broad topic of study or meaningful conceptual organizers, such as the classroom community, families, the environment, or building structures (Sarama & Clements, 2015a; Sarama et al., 2017a; Schickedanz et al., 2005). Boston's *Focus on PreK* for 3-year-olds, for example, includes 6- to 8-week units of study such as "World of Color" and "Family and Friends." Eight-week-long topics for 4-year-olds include "Together in our Community" and "Building Our Working City."[7] Culturally responsive and affirming curriculum, such as that for Native Americans described in Box 4-1, may be conceptually

---

[7] https://www.bpsearlylearning.org/focus-on-prek

BOX 4-1
Indigenous Curricula and Pedagogy

A review of culturally responsive approaches to curriculum implementation found that approaches were most comprehensive and responsive to the community in curricula designed for and implemented among Indigenous families. These curricula (e.g., *Growing and Learning with Young Native Children*, *Doors to Discovery*, *Food Resource Equity and Sustainability for Health* [*FRESH*], *Emotion-Based Prevention Program*, *I Can Problem Solve*) tend to be codeveloped by teachers and communities, with a heavy emphasis on cultural significance, meaningful learning, and community engagement (Burstein et al., 2014; Gilliard & Moore, 2007; Wetherill et al., 2021). Increasingly, Indigenous early learning programs, such as Walatowa Head Start in New Mexico, are transitioning their curricula and programming to support local Indigenous worldviews and language immersion.

In their curriculum for Indigenous children, Gilliard & Moore (2007) describe "teaching within a culturally relevant context, building a sense of belongingness and community through ritual, and respecting children, families, and community [as] were essential to defining the Native American Indian culture within these early learning programs" (p. 251). Similarly, the approach of Graue et al. (2014) to cultural relevance is described as family based. Burstein and colleagues (2014) also describe adaptations of early reading curricula (e.g., *Doors to Discovery, Opening the World of Learning*) through cultural wraparound adaptations designed specifically for Indigenous children and families (e.g., changing examples to make them contextually relevant, including words in Indigenous languages, adding culturally relevant artifacts and props, creating thematic unit books that align with Indigenous cultures). Thompson et al. (2008) designed a curriculum toolkit for Indigenous communities, with the curriculum designed to change according to the community's needs. The curriculum is "centered in each child's heritage," and children make contributions to the heritage (Thompson et al., 2008, p. 399). Wetherill and colleagues (2021) described *FRESH*, a tribally led gardening curriculum for Indigenous preschool children intended to mirror and match Indigenous concepts. For instance, the authors describe a lesson on butter bean, squash, and corn, reflecting the Indigenous concept of the Three Sisters Crops (i.e., growing the three crops alongside one another).

These curricula represent a unique, community-informed approach to preschool curriculum that offers possibilities for increasing the cultural responsiveness of curricula in other communities. Nonetheless, relatively few research studies of the implementation and outcomes of Indigenous curricula have been conducted. This limited presence of research likely reflects limitations in collecting valid and reliable measures of cultural concepts on which such curricula focus, the curricula's orientation toward benefit to local community context rather than generalizability, and the time needed to overcome historical and enduring impacts of colonization aimed at dismantling the very cultural teachings that Indigenous communities strive to sustain and revitalize through culturally grounded curriculum today.

organized and place based around children's family and community cultural traditions and lived experiences.

Frequently used general approaches to curriculum implementation—including the project approach (Helm & Katz, 2016; Katz et al., 2014), the Reggio Emilia approach, the Cycle of Inquiry (Broderick & Hong, 2020; Edwards et al., 1993, 2012; Rinaldi, 2021), and learning trajectories approaches—represent ways of conceptually organizing and deeply engaging children with curriculum content. Developers of high-quality curricula are aware of these approaches to creating and implementing curriculum, especially their similarities and differences and the empirical research on each. Each of these approaches is described in the next sections, followed by a discussion of Montessori education.

The Project Approach

The project approach for preschool children has long been widely valued and used in early childhood education (Helm & Katz, 2016; Katz et al., 2014). This approach is a way of engaging children over an extended period in investigations within the social and cultural contexts of their lived experiences. The project approach organizes curriculum around an in-depth investigation of a real-world topic, focused on questions posed by children, the teacher, or the teacher and children together (see Box 4-2).

Projects are effective ways of integrating curriculum content and promoting children's understanding and thinking (Duke, 2015; Snider & Vartuli, 2020). Well-planned and well-implemented projects engage children's interests and eagerness to learn, focus their attention, require higher-order thinking, and are joyful. The teacher needs to build on children's interests or to cultivate their interest in a topic worth learning about, as well as to decide whether a topic is important, practical, and consistent with the learning standards and goals of the larger curriculum (Helm & Katz, 2016; Helm & Snider, 2020).

A project has three phases. Phase 1 occurs when a possible topic emerges either from children's interest or from an idea initiated by the teacher. During this phase, the class generates ideas, thoughts, and questions about the topic. Good topics offer opportunities for firsthand experiences, observation, interaction with experts, and research. During Phase 2, children engage in an investigation of the topic. The questions the children want to answer need to be broad enough to allow for substantive research. Children might take field trips, hear from visiting experts, or conduct experiments. Phase 3 is a culminating event during which children communicate, share, and present their work and findings to others, usually families, the community, or peers in their class or school. The project approach draws on and cultivates children's interests and motivation to learn.

> **BOX 4-2**
> **Children Discovering Their World**
>
> The project approach is the basis for a digital pre-K curriculum supported by the state of Maryland. The Maryland State Department of Education's Division of Early Childhood funded researchers at the University of Maryland to develop Children Discovering Their World, which includes two fully digital comprehensive project-based curricula—*Children Explore Their World* for 3-year-olds and *Children Study Their World* for 4-year-olds.* The curricula are distributed to licensed child care centers in Maryland without charge, under a grant from the state. Programs apply, and if they are accepted, the lead teacher receives an iPad loaded with the 3- or 4-year-old curriculum (eight project guides with lesson plans across content areas), all the children's books in the lessons (not digital), and an array of content materials, plus professional development and coaching. Embedded are literacy and math scope and sequence, strategies for supporting multilingual learners, guidance on instructing children with Individualized Education Programs, and strategies for differentiating instruction and implementing universal design for learning. The Maryland Early Learning Assessment is the formative assessment. The curricula are research based, but a large-scale evaluation of *Children Study Their World* for 4-year-olds in Head Start was interrupted by the COVID-19 pandemic. Given that the program is fully digital, lessons can be updated as new research is published, especially on literacy and social-emotional development.
>
> *https://education.umd.edu/cdw

Projects need to engage children in thinking and problem solving; finding answers to their questions; and building comprehension, background content knowledge, and skills. Research on the project approach finds that although it is challenging to implement, it is most effective when teachers have content knowledge themselves (National Academies, 2018b). For example, Project ABC2, the project approach plus coaching focused on content, was implemented in five Kansas City area Head Start and community programs (Snider et al., 2017). Project approach fidelity plus content coaching significantly improved teachers' Classroom Assessment Scoring System (CLASS) instructional support scores on concept development, quality of feedback, and language modeling, which are persistently the lowest of CLASS scores in all programs. Another study in Head Start classrooms (Vartuli et al., 2014) found that coaching resulted in higher project approach fidelity scores, which predicted higher scores for the CLASS Instructional Support, Emotional Support, and Classroom Organization domains.

Project-based learning holds promise for enhancing learning outcomes for children from low-income families. Although it was conducted with children older than pre-K, one study developed and successfully implemented two project-based units based on state social studies standards and content area literacy in four second grade classrooms in low-income school districts (Halvorsen et al., 2012). The achievement of students in the low-income districts was then compared with that of students in higher-income districts. Results showed no statistically significant differences on standards-based assessments of social studies and literacy between the children from lower- and higher-income families.

The Reggio Emilia Approach

The Reggio Emilia approach originated in the exemplary, municipally run preschools and infant–toddler centers in the city of Reggio Emilia, Italy. Since the approach first became widely known in the early 1990s, it has inspired educators throughout the United States and the world (Broderick & Hong, 2020; Edwards et al., 1993, 2012; Rinaldi, 2021). Loris Malaguzzi, founder of the approach, used the metaphor "the hundred languages of children" to communicate the genius of every child. The "hundred languages" refer to the many ways children learn using various forms of media, such as drawing, painting, sculpting, writing, photography, video, music, dance, words, and numbers. These are used to engage, build, and display children's understanding of the world. The approach emanates from the image of the child as rich in potential, strong, and powerful—and as a citizen with rights. In Reggio, "children with special rights" (in the United States called "children with special needs" or "children with disabilities") are given priority in enrollment (Smith, 1998).

The Reggio Emilia approach is not a curriculum, nor is it a model. It involves collaborative project work among small groups of children and co-construction of knowledge and understanding between teachers and children (Edwards et al., 2012; Rinaldi, 2021). In addition, teachers and children place themselves in zones of proximal development, continually scaffolding each other's learning. Curriculum is a process of inviting and sustaining learning. In Reggio-inspired schools, the curriculum emerges from children's interests in topics or questions and their desire to find out more or to solve a problem. However, teachers plan in advance for possible directions the work will take to achieve goals. They listen carefully to children and meet regularly to discuss how to further the children's involvement and deepen their understanding. The Reggio approach is described as a "pedagogy of listening" (Rinaldi, 2021).

In Reggio, schools have a special teacher, called an *atelierista*, who is knowledgeable about the visual arts and media and works closely with teachers and children. A specially equipped studio space contains a wide range of materials used by children to represent their ideas and thinking in projects. Short- and long-term projects are a major teaching and learning strategy in Reggio schools. Facilitated by teachers, children work in small groups on a topic or a project of interest to them that emerges from the children's experiences (Vecchi, 2002).

The growth in children's thinking that occurs through project work is captured in one of the most compelling aspects of the approach—documentation. As a project proceeds, educators compile and display representations of the children's thinking and learning using various media (photographs of them at work, drawings, sculptures, constructions, writing, and transcripts of their discussions). Documentation is not merely for display; it is used for children to revisit, reflect on, and deepen their thinking (Rinaldi, 2021).

Although there is a dearth of research on the efficacy of the Reggio approach in the United States, the approach has inspired educators throughout the country and the world since first becoming widely known in the early 1990s. A survey of California state preschools conducted by the Deputy Superintendent of Public Instruction found that 40% of preschool programs reported using a locally developed curriculum. Of those, 6% of public and 12% of community-based programs reported using the Reggio Emilia approach.[8] In addition, a large-scale, longitudinal RCT on this approach was carried out in Colombia. The study examined the impact of high-quality, project- and play-based, Reggio-inspired programs on young children from infancy to age 5 (Bernal et al., 2022; Nores et al., 2018). The programs incorporated positive teacher–child interactions, integration of multiple content and developmental domains, and intense professional development. Among preschoolers, large effects were found in the areas of mathematics, language, literacy, executive function, and health (Bernal et al., 2022).

Cycle of Inquiry (COI)

Although similar, the project approach and COI approach are not the same (Broderick & Hong, 2020). The COI approach also starts with children's interests, but teachers and children continually redesign the curriculum together as it develops (Broderick & Hong, 2020). This approach was initially inspired by researchers' encounters with Reggio Emilia.

COI involves six steps, beginning with teachers' systematic observations and documentation of children's play and questions. Teachers then interpret children's thinking and create a curriculum action plan based on their observations and interpretations of the children's play. Next, they create plans to provoke children's thinking and inquiry, set up and facilitate play, and finally reflect on and evaluate children's learning and standards met.

---

[8]Reported by Neville-Morgan in a March 27, 2023, listening session with the committee.

As with the Reggio approach, teachers engage children in representing and rerepresenting their ideas related to the topic of study using various media and documentation of their learning. Although COI is not a curriculum, case studies of the COI approach have found that it supports productive discussions between preschool teachers and children (Broderick et al., 2022) and could be incorporated into broader curricula (Hong et al., 2021).

Learning Trajectories Approaches

As described previously, learning trajectories describe the paths of children's thinking and learning in a specific domain (STEM or literacy), called a *developmental progression*, and a related, conjectured route through a set of instructional tasks, whose purpose is to support the development of a curriculum or a curriculum component (Clements & Sarama, 2014a; Simon, 1995). Thus, learning trajectories have three interrelated components, (1) a goal, (2) a developmental progression of levels of thinking, and (3) instructional activities correlated with each level. To attain a certain competence in a given topic or domain (the goal), students learn each successive level (the developmental progression), aided by tasks (instructional activities) designed to build the mental actions-on-objects that enable thinking at each higher level (Clements & Sarama, 2014a; Maloney et al., 2014).

Although they have been created and studied most commonly in the area of math education, learning trajectories have been developed and shown to be beneficial in many domains, such as language, communication, and literacy; social-emotional development; physical development; and executive function (Jen et al., 2023). Across domains, these benefits include encouraging deep, gradual learning and unpacking the complexity of each domain (Jen et al., 2023).

All curriculum approaches benefit from the infusion of knowledge of the domains, children's thinking and learning in the domains, and effective strategies for guiding and supporting this thinking and learning. Learning trajectories approaches provide that guidance and can thus contribute to most other curriculum approaches (Broderick & Hong, 2020; Clements & Sarama, 2021; Dorr, 2017; Duke et al., 2016; Edwards et al., 1993, 2012; Helm & Katz, 2016; Hendrick, 1997; Karademir & Akman, 2021; Katz et al., 2014; Leung, 2023; Sarama & Clements, 2009b; Sarama et al., 2021; Tullis, 2011; Wellen, 2018). Research shows that children experiencing a learning trajectories–based curriculum learn more mathematics and learn at a faster rate than other groups (Clements et al., 2011, 2013). Other analyses have found that all children who experience learning trajectories–based instruction have steeper growth curves than control groups, but that this significant improvement in learning rate appears to benefit Black and Latine students most, "highlighting the critical societal need for research-based mathematics curricula in preschool" (Dumas et al., 2019, p. 1). The use of learning trajectories as a basis for curricula in multiple content domains has received broad empirical support (e.g., Baroody et al., 2022; Burchinal et al., 2022; Clements et al., 2019b; Ebby et al., 2020; Maloney et al., 2014; Mattera et al., 2021a; NRC, 2009; Sarama et al., 2021; Wu et al., 2023). However, given the continued concern that White children and their outcomes are deemed the norm, which is especially problematic because of the historical roots of the achievement gap, what outcomes are used to determine competency, and the theoretical basis for teaching and learning, more culturally grounded research and a critical lens are needed to ensure the approaches and outcomes being used are not centering solely White, English-speaking, middle-class, and able-bodied epistemologies (Ascenzi-Moreno & Seltzer, 2021; Gardner-Neblet et al., 2023).

Montessori Education

Originating more than 100 years ago, the Montessori educational approach was designed by Maria Montessori during her work with young children who were considered to have cognitive disabilities and lived in the impoverished areas of Rome, Italy. The Montessori method is a whole-child, comprehensive curriculum and instructional approach incorporating independent, hands-on, child-directed experiences, as well as academic content, with teachers acting as guides and facilitators as opposed to direct instructors (Lillard, 2013). Two professional organizations, the American Montessori Society (AMS) and Association Montessori Internationale, establish standards for teacher preparation and accreditation of schools, which determine fidelity of implementation. Montessori preschools must meet specific criteria, including multiage classrooms serving 3- to 6-year-olds; certified teachers who complete an approved course of study; well-organized classrooms that include numerous, specially designed multisensory, self-correcting materials; 3-hour periods of independent work time; small-group and individual lessons; positive discipline; and no grades. During work time, children are free to choose constructive activities that promote learning in language, writing and reading, mathematics, geography, culture, music, and art. The Montessori curriculum also emphasizes practical life skills that promote positive social relationships, as well as correct steps for performing practical tasks, such as rolling up a work mat. In keeping with Montessori's philosophy that education is necessary for peace, AMS promotes peace and social justice, including an emphasis on antibias, antiracist practices with a 12-week certificate program for teachers.[9] Debs & Brown (2017) describe challenges to ensuring that Montessori programs

---

[9]learn.amshq.org

serve students of color, and also ways Montessori applies to implementing culturally responsive and sustaining practices. Among their examples are integration of Montessori with Hawaiian language and culture-based programs (Schonleber, 2011) and Native American Montessori programs aligned with cultural preservation goals (e.g., Ayer, 2016; Johnston, 2018).

There are approximately 5,000 Montessori schools in the United States. Despite its historical origins of serving children living in poverty, most Montessori schools in the United States serve middle- to high-income families in private schools. However, the number of public Montessori schools, primarily magnet or charter schools, has increased from 300 in 2014 to 500 in 2023 (American Montessori Society, 2024), with students of color comprising a majority (Debs & Brown, 2017). Public schools typically use a random lottery for admission. However, a study conducted by Child Trends (Hilty et al., 2021) found several barriers to equitable access, including that lotteries are not truly random and that programs are located in majority-White communities. Studies of Montessori have produced mixed results, which can be attributed to limitations such as selection bias and lack of fidelity (Hilty et al., 2021).

To address the lack of control for fidelity of implementation, one study (Lillard, 2012) compared outcomes for preschool children in three conditions: high-fidelity, classic Montessori programs; lower-fidelity Montessori, supplemented with conventional preschool materials and activities; and conventional preschool with no Montessori. Assessments at the beginning of the year did not differ on a range of children's social and academic outcomes. At the end of the year, children in classic Montessori demonstrated statistically significant gains on measures of executive function, reading, mathematics, vocabulary, and social problem solving, with the largest effect sizes for executive function. However, important limitations of the study include lack of random assignment to programs and a well-educated, middle-income, mostly White sample.

By contrast, a more recent longitudinal study was conducted in a high-poverty city, utilizing a randomized lottery (Lillard et al., 2017). Half the sample "won" the lottery and were placed in Montessori, while the other half attended public and private "business as usual" schools. Children were assessed four times over the 3 years of Montessori preschool (ages 3–6) on a range of measures, including academic ability, theory of mind, social problem solving, executive function, mastery orientation, school enjoyment, and creativity. Although the samples did not differ at the outset, over time the Montessori children demonstrated better outcomes on academic achievement, social understanding, mastery orientation, and school enjoyment. The most promising finding was that over time, scores of lower-income children in the Montessori group converged with scores of higher-income children in the other schools, demonstrating potential to lessen the income opportunity gap.

Nevertheless, a major limitation is that the study using a lottery sample is not an RCT and further research is needed.

In ten states, Montessori education is on the approved list of prekindergarten curricula (see Chapter 8). South Carolina, the state with the largest percentage of Montessori public schools in the United States (serving preschool through 8th grade), conducted a large-scale, multiyear, mixed-methods evaluation to inform future investment (Culclasure et al., 2018). The study examined fidelity, demographic makeup of schools, effects on academic and behavior outcomes, and teachers' attitudes. Rather than primarily serving White, middle-income students, as is often the case, public Montessori in South Carolina was found to serve a diverse population of students, with 54% from low-income families and 45% children of color. To evaluate impact, Montessori students were matched to non-Montessori students with the same demographics and baseline performance. Montessori students demonstrated greater achievement in language arts, mathematics, and social studies, and improved attendance and behavior, with higher levels of creativity and executive function found in some years (Culclasure et al., 2018). Despite limitations, including variations in fidelity and possible selection bias, the South Carolina study is the largest comprehensive, longitudinal evaluation of public Montessori to date.

Technology for Children and Their Teachers

Educational technology has the potential to make positive contributions to early education, and decades of research has found that technology can provide developmentally appropriate experiences for young children (Clements & Swaminathan, 1995; Hsin et al., 2014; Sigdel, 2017). However, some organizations firmly oppose young children's technology use, and some teachers retain a bias against technology (Lee & Ginsburg, 2007; Sargent, 2017) that often contradicts research evidence (Herodotou, 2018; Hsin et al., 2014; Lindahl & Folkesson, 2012; Reeves et al., 2017). Research has refuted most of these criticisms, while accepting that not all uses are beneficial (Clements & Sarama, 2003; Lentz et al., 2014; Sarama & Clements, 2019a). For example, homes with more access to technology better support mathematics learning (e.g., Li et al., 2006; Navarro et al., 2012), and this is particularly so for certain children (e.g., African American children; Judge, 2005).

This is not to say that the more media children engage with the better. However, it does suggest a miscommunication about "media." That is, large consumptions of media in all forms and of any content can be harmful. Children who use more *entertainment* media, for example, have smaller gains in assertiveness, social skills, and task orientation; these effects emerge mainly at high rather than moderate levels of use of such media (Dore et al., 2023). In contrast, children who use more *educational* technology have larger gains in task orientation and assertiveness, and those using technology that focuses on social-emotional content have larger gains in task orientation and behavioral control (Dore et al., 2023).

Thus, it is important to state that this section addresses educational technology specifically, as it has the potential to make multiple contributions to early education. However, whether this potential is realized depends on which technology is used and how—especially how it relates to the adopted curriculum. Research on different models of educational technology—technology-assisted instruction (including practice, tutorials, tasks, tools, and games); e-books, word processing and other tools, digital manipulatives, exploratory environments, and scientific tools and simulations; programming, coding, and robotics; and combinations of these—has identified the specific benefits of each. These benefits may be especially promising for children with disabilities. Unfortunately, reality often falls short of realizing this promise. To realize these benefits, teachers require resources, support, and professional development. Fortunately, there is a growing research base for providing each.

Technology for Children

To begin, debates regarding how technology can be useful in improving learning often involve false dichotomies. For example, some educators focus solely on drill and practice approaches, which, if used alone, can be ineffective and even miseducative (Dewey, 1997). Other educators tolerate only "open-ended" or (narrowly defined) developmentally appropriate technology applications. Evidence counters such dichotomous thinking for key domains: social-emotional development; literacy and language; STEM subjects; and general cognitive competences, such as executive function and creativity (e.g., Clements & Sarama, 2003).

Types of software and pedagogical approaches that have shown benefits range widely. They include, for example, practice; technological manipulatives; simulations; exploratory environments; programming (coding); digital books; games; and creative development of text, art, music, and videos. And high-quality software, implemented well, similarly shows that technology can contribute to the curriculum (e.g., Burnett, 2010; Clements & Sarama, 2003; Cuban, 2001; Hartle, 2020; Herodotou, 2018; Hsin et al., 2014; Larkin et al., 2022). Young children prefer technology that differentiates tasks, offering more support or more challenge when indicated for individuals, and that provides children with choices and autonomy (LeSage & Ruttenberg-Rozen, 2021). Technology also can make special contributions for children with disabilities, including and beyond assistive technologies (Clements et al., 2021b).

Although such benefits of educational technology are generally seen with high-quality software, a caution is that most easily available software is not of high quality (see Callaghan & Reich, 2018). In the development of high-quality curricula, it is important to avoid common limitations on quality, such as missing instructions, poor feedback (corrective only, not informative), ineffective guidance and modeling on how to solve a problem that children could not solve, and lack of responsiveness to children's individual levels of thinking. Young children prefer technology that differentiates tasks, offering more support or more challenge when indicated for individuals, and that provides children with choices and autonomy (LeSage & Ruttenberg-Rozen, 2021). Building such formative assessment into digital curricula and then doing fine-grained research to evaluate and refine it continually is a promising avenue for educational technology. As a research example, missing even one important characteristic, such as individualizing according to children's needs, resulted in the lack of any gains from a digital program in literacy for children entering with low literacy scores (Kreskey & Truscott, 2016). Although positive characteristics of high-quality software are less well defined, research provides some guidance. Some characteristics apply across different software types and pedagogical approaches, while others are unique to an approach. In general, as with any curriculum component, the choice of software needs to serve the goal for learning and be based on evidence.

Finally, high-quality technology experiences can facilitate positive social-emotional development (Clements & Sarama, 2003). According to a review of 87 studies, most studies showed that technology use enhances children's collaboration and interaction with others and, for some, their development of cultural identity (Hsin et al., 2014).

Technology for Teachers

There is a growing literature on what professional development teachers want and need in order to implement technology well, as well as how technology can enhance the implementation of professional development (Clements & Sarama, 2002b; Ikram, 2017; Kim et al., 2017; Langub & Warner, 2018; Marklund, 2015; Papadakis & Kalogiannakis, 2019; Sarama & Clements, 2019a; Sundqvist, 2017). For example, coaching teachers virtually has been successful and is more scalable than other approaches (Kinzie et al., 2014; Whittaker et al., 2015). Web-based tools can offer multimedia that contribute to the understanding of children's learning, as well as teaching strategies consistent with children's needs (Clements & Sarama, 2017/2023). Furthermore, the design and content of software, even that for children, may contribute to teachers' professional development. This point applies to all components of a curriculum, an issue discussed in the next section.

Digital curriculum resources, compared with traditional text versions, offer curriculum developers a wide variety of ways to support teachers in interacting with children around domains and implementing curricula in new ways, providing personalized learning, and melding formative and summative assessments (Pepin et al., 2017).

EDUCATIVE CURRICULA: TEACHING BOTH CHILDREN AND THEIR TEACHERS

Created with this purpose in mind, curriculum materials can contribute to a change in the educational system writ large and particularly to professional development (Ball & Cohen, 1996; Beyer & Davis, 2015). That is, they are part of educative curricula, materials designed to support both teacher and child learning (Drake et al., 2014), including resources and structures that help teachers gain profound knowledge of the content to be taught (Cabell et al., 2023; Ma, 1999), as well as knowledge of children's thinking and learning and how to support their learning (Clements & Sarama, 2021). Arguably, no category of the workforce is more in need of educative curricula than early childhood, populated with teachers and staff who are given insufficient professional preparation, resources, and pay (IOM & NRC, 2015). This critical feature of a high-quality curriculum requires a concerted effort by developers to build in specific structures and content, including the domain content, how children think and learn about that content, and how pedagogical strategies can support children's thinking and learning—a challenging task. This curriculum feature may be particularly important in the STEM domains. Even when provided training in STEM education, preschool teachers have difficulty planning and implementing STEM activities, often because they lack content knowledge (Cevikbas et al., 2024; Leung, 2023; Yıldırım, 2020).

Although many curricula provide instructional activities without supporting explanations and other forms of professional support (Zangori & Forbes, 2014), the potential for professional development is real and critical. Curricular interventions are a potentially stronger lever for change than other approaches commonly adopted in the education system (Whitehurst, 2009). This advantage is important in content areas, especially those with which teachers are unfamiliar, such as the STEM domains (Clements & Wright, 2022; National Academies, 2022; one report dedicates a chapter to content knowledge in mathematics, NRC, 2009). But it is also important even in familiar areas such as literacy and language (notably multilingual learning), in which there have been many historical practices not in line with current research or a focus on equity (e.g., Duke & Martin, 2010; see also Chapters 1 and 7 in this volume).

A synthesis of a research project designed to describe what is and is not known about educative curricular materials reports implications relevant to developers of preschool curricula (Davis et al., 2017). Educative curricula have the following features. First, because teachers will adapt curricula, motivated by concerns about time and students' competencies, educative materials suggest adaptations of lessons that would take different amounts of time and meet a range of students' needs while meeting goals (e.g., narratives describing alternatives that reduce time needed but providing opportunities for learning). Second, because different teachers will need and use different educative features, especially regarding discourse and explanations (Broderick et al., 2022), curriculum designers develop a variety of such features (e.g., narratives; boxes on content and pedagogical knowledge, including generative questions and rubrics) and help teachers recognize any new practices. Languages and vocabulary that teachers can comprehend comfortably are essential. Third, because teacher learning is situated in everyday work, educative materials provide representations of practice, such as rubrics illustrating key concepts with student work examples or learning stories. Fourth, because content can be new, educative curricula provide multiple supports for teachers' understanding of the content, especially the big ideas of the domain (e.g., Clements & Conference Working Group, 2004; National Academies, 2022), through content storylines, visuals, and children's own definitions of concepts.

The structure and content of supports for teachers may lead to different types of learning (Beyer & Davis, 2015). Beyer and Davis found that lesson-specific narrative supports helped preservice teachers understand and use specific adaptations. Teachers considered those supports to be useful, relevant, and motivating. In contrast, general expository supports helped teachers identify and use principles of practice in analyzing lesson plans (Beyer & Davis, 2015). Both types of supports may therefore be valuable; however, it is noteworthy that the lesson-specific supports for adaptations are critical for effective formative assessment and inclusive education. Materials need to help teachers attend to children's level of thinking in creating small groups (Jiang et al., 2023).

DEVELOPING RESEARCH-BASED AND EMPIRICALLY VALIDATED CURRICULA: A FRAMEWORK

While challenging, developing a high-quality curriculum is an opportunity to attend to and help educators leverage the multilayered contexts and experiences that shape all children's development and learning. Developing a high-quality early childhood curriculum entails ensuring that the curriculum is individually, culturally, and linguistically affirming; supportive; and interactive (National Academies, 2020; Sanders et al., 2007; Steffe & Cobb, 1988). Indeed, developing high-quality, research-based, and empirically validated early childhood curricula is so demanding of both expertise and effort that it is rare. Yet this is what the early childhood field needs. Fortunately, research, grounded in rigorous, asset-based and community-rooted principles, can provide knowledge and resources necessary to guide this development, expansion, and sustainability.

Although studies in this area exist, the field needs more consistent, comprehensive, and cogent research on specific curricula. The large Preschool Curriculum Evaluation Research (PCER) initiative identified ten curricula that showed no statistically significant impacts on any of the student-level measures and five that showed significant impacts on some measures (Preschool Curriculum Evaluation Research Consortium, 2008). Familiarity with these findings is critical for developers of high-quality curricula, including the strengths and shortcomings of the design of the research. They also need to be familiar with other studies like these (usually of a single curriculum) and the characteristics of each of these curriculum studies, including the majority that did not include equity concerns.

Equity must be considered in all phases of research and development (Iruka, 2024). For example, what are the theoretical approaches and framing of the studies? Do existing studies include marginalized groups? Does any original research that is to be conducted do so? Convenience samples are usually inadequate and inappropriate. Similarly, do reviews and original work include funds of knowledge from various cultures (Civil, 2002; Moll et al., 1992; Presmeg, 2007)? For example, a culturally based math curriculum, the Design and Build It module of the *Adapting Yup'ik Elders' Knowledge* project, increased 6th-grade students' math understanding (Lipka & Adams, 2002). As another example, developing students' spatial abilities through art and design (e.g., tilings or tessellations) as well as puzzles (e.g., tangrams) can be based in art found in most cultures (Danesi, 2009). Research is needed on similar approaches with preschool children. Such activities are engaging and can increase students' self-efficacy in mathematics (Casey et al., 2011; Cheng & Mix, 2012). Importantly, mathematics is a particularly challenging domain in which to incorporate funds of knowledge compared with all other domains (González et al., 2001).

Other issues are underresearched and underdeveloped, such as the relative lack of Spanish versions of curricula and the absence of curricula and other resources in any other languages (Park et al., 2017), which is a vital gap for multilingual learners' development and achievement (see Chapter 7). Another such issue is the tension between creating locally specific, culturally relevant curricula and curricula that are adaptable but also can be widely disseminated. Curricula that are developed by and for members of a specific group may benefit from using published research on and involving consultants with expertise in the various content domains. For curricula that are to be widely disseminated, the converse is true: literature and writing partners or consultants from all communities intended as audiences for the curricula need to be involved in all phases of research and development.

At the same time, there are many pressures and constraints on curriculum developers. Preschool standards, especially accumulated across states and organizations, can lead to an overwhelming list of topics and outcomes (not all of which are consistent with research or the wisdom of expert practice, such as considerable time spent on the calendar or on bodies in outer space). Curriculum developers must determine how to incorporate the standards without overwhelming teachers and children. Another constraint derives from assessment systems, especially mandated ones, that can have the same weaknesses. These are sociopolitical issues that must be considered in curriculum development.

Research indicates that curriculum research and development complement one another when designed and conducted together (Battista & Clements, 2000; Clements, 2007, 2008; Clements & Battista, 2000; Doabler et al., 2014; Lagemann, 1997; Lloyd et al., 2017; Sarama & Clements, 2008). Unfortunately, most publishers claim that their curricula are based on research. However, few document even these claims, and those that do tend to list theories or research evidence generally without specific connections to the curriculum (Battista & Clements, 2000; Chard et al., 2008; Clements, 2007, 2008; Doabler et al., 2014; Lagemann, 1997; Lloyd et al., 2017; Sarama & Clements, 2008). Further, little distinction is made between that which is research based and that which is empirically validated.

On the positive side, more instances of the synthesis of research and curriculum development have recently become available. This literature includes the creation and evaluation of theoretical and practical frameworks for such work. Several such frameworks have been proposed and used (e.g., Bannan-Ritland, 2003; Boerst et al., 2010; Burkhardt, 2006; The Design-Based Research Collective, 2003; Kimpston & Rogers, 1986; Lewis et al., 2006); most are general, and many deal with evaluation, not development, of curricula (e.g., Carnine et al., 1997; Darling-Hammond & Snyder, 1992; Heck et al., 2012; Lloyd et al., 2017; NRC, 2004; Schoenfeld, 2016; Senk & Thompson, 2003; Walker, 1992).

One framework, the Curriculum Research Framework (CRF; Clements, 2007; Clements & Sarama, 2013), has been used to develop research-based and empirically validated curricula in early childhood education (e.g., Blanton et al., 2019; Bojorquea et al., 2018; Clements & Sarama, 2007, 2008; Doabler et al., 2019; Foster et al., 2016; Gavin et al., 2013; Ghalichi & Roehrig, 2017; Herrmann-Abell et al., 2016; Li et al., 2021; Sarama et al., 2017a; Superfine et al., 2010; Zucker et al., 2019) or cited as providing useful guidelines (e.g., Duschl et al., 2011; Hjalmarson & Baker, 2020; Kinzie et al., 2015; Moore et al., 2018; Munter et al., 2016; Solem et al., 2015).

These proposal frameworks include goals and strategies. Because it constitutes one-way translations of research results, however, a framework limited to research-to-practice strategies is flawed in its presumptions, insensitive to changing goals in the content area, and unable to contribute to a revision of the theory and knowledge on which it is built—the second critical goal of a scientific curriculum research program. Instead, a valid scientific curriculum development program needs to address two basic issues—effect and conditions—in the three domains of practice, policy, and theory (see Table 4-3).

TABLE 4-3 Goals of Curriculum Research

	Practice	Policy	Theory
Effects	• Is the curriculum effective in helping children achieve specific learning goals? Are goals culturally and linguistically affirming? Are the intended and unintended consequences positive for children? (What is the quality of the evidence [construct and internal validity]?) (6–10)* • Is there credible documentation of both a priori research and research performed on the curriculum, indicating the efficacy of the approach as compared with alternative approaches? (all)	• Are the curriculum goals important? (1, 5, 10) • What is the effect size for students? (9, 10) • What effects does it have on teachers? (10)	• Why is the curriculum effective? (all) • What were the theoretical bases? (1, 2, 3) • What cognitive changes occurred, and what processes were responsible? That is, what specific components and features (e.g., instructional procedures, materials) account for its impact and why? (4, 6, 7)
Conditions	• When and where?— Under what conditions is the curriculum effective? (Do findings generalize to communities/groups of interest [external validity]? (8, 10)	• What are the support requirements (7) for various contexts? What are the costs and available resources? (8–10)	• Why do certain sets of conditions decrease or increase the curriculum's effectiveness? (6–10) • How do specific strategies produce previously unattained results and why? (6–10)

*Numbers in parentheses refer to the specific research and development phases described in Table 4-4.
SOURCE: Adapted from Clements, 2007, p. 39.

The CRF is intended to guide the process by including three broad categories of research and development work, within which there are ten phases. The three categories involve (1) reviewing existing research (a priori foundations), (2) building models of children's thinking and learning in a domain (learning trajectories), and (3) appraising the effectiveness and general worth of the result (evaluation: formative [leading to revisions] and summative [to determine the effects of the completed curriculum]). Specific phases describing how research and curriculum development are integrated to their mutual benefit are provided in Table 4-4 (for full details, see Clements, 2007; Clements & Sarama, 2013). Note that all phases include scientific research, but only the last two focus on quantitative data; all ten include qualitative data. This framework was intended for curriculum developers and researchers but can also guide the creation of criteria for any evaluation.

CURRICULA BEYOND PRESCHOOL

Although this committee was charged only with addressing high-quality preschool curriculum, we would be remiss to ignore one of the most important determinants of the long-range benefits of such a curriculum: without high-quality curricula in later grades, the benefits of preschool are often lost (Clements et al., 2013, 2023b; Kang et al., 2019; McCormick et al., 2019; Wu et al., 2023). With follow-through, children's learning and development are more likely to continue on a positive trajectory (Ansari & Pianta, 2018; but see cautions in Bailey et al., 2019; Carr, 2021; Carr et al., 2019; Jenkins et al., 2018; Pearman et al., 2019; Sarama & Clements, 2015b; Unterman & Weiland, 2019). Developing consistency in curricula across early childhood programs, including both horizontal and vertical alignment, is a key consideration for policy makers (Little & Gragson, 2023).

In summary, traditional research is conservative; it studies "what is" rather than "what could be." When research is an integral component of the design process, when it helps uncover and invent models of children's thinking and builds these into a creative product, it moves to the vanguard in innovation and reform in education. Early childhood education is not an "implication" tagged onto the end of studies from developmental and cognitive psychology. Educational research and curriculum research and development need be interwoven with other domains of study for progress in the field and for the benefit of all children (see also Clements & Sarama, 2015a, p. 251).

TABLE 4-4 Categories and Phases of the Curriculum Research Framework

Categories	Questions Asked	Phases
Research reviews: A priori foundations. In variants of the research-to-practice model, extant research is reviewed and implications for the curriculum drawn.	What is already known that can be applied to the anticipated curriculum? How can the needs of all groups and all individuals be addressed?	Content analyses of standards, organizations, and domain experts are conducted to gather knowledge concerning the specific subject-matter content, including the role it would play in children's learning (phase 1); reviews of relevant curricular issues for preschool are garnered from fields such as educational psychology, education, and early childhood (phase 2); and similar reviews of pedagogy are conducted, including the effectiveness of certain types of educational structures, experiences, and activities (phase 3). Equity concerns are addressed in these and all other phases (Meaney, 2018).
Learning trajectories. Curriculum components are created and sequenced in accordance with empirically based models of children's thinking and learning.	How might the curriculum be constructed to be consistent with what is known about children's thinking and learning?	In phase 4, the nature and content of all components of the curriculum are tailored based on what is known about children's thinking and learning in all domains, as well as what is known about educational environments and pedagogical methods. This includes assessments, which must equitably measure the thinking and learning of all children, for example, children from linguistically marginalized communities. That is, all assessments—whether curriculum-embedded assessments built into a curriculum or separate measures accompanying the curriculum—must document all forms of validity, especially *consequential validity* (Dong & Clements, 2023; Dong et al., 2023b; Messick, 1989). Adaptations for children with disabilities and consideration of cultural responsiveness, multilingual learners, and other equity issues are foundational for all components. This research is applied and revised (or, not infrequently, created anew) dynamically, simultaneously with the development of instructional tasks, using grounded theory methods, clinical interviews, teaching experiments, and design experiments.
Evaluation: Formative and summative. In these phases, empirical evidence is collected with which to evaluate the curriculum,	How can the curriculum be appropriate, accessible, easy to use, and effective for all adults and children?	Phase 5 focuses on marketability, using strategies such as gathering information about educators and families from all societal groups, representation of which is carefully designed. More important, phase 5 focuses on full community collaboration, involving the community in creating the curriculum collaboratively (for all phases).

(continued)

TABLE 4-4 Continued

Categories	Questions Asked	Phases
realized in some form. The goal is to evaluate the appeal, usability, and effectiveness of an instantiation of the curriculum.	Is the curriculum usable by, and effective with, diverse groups of children and teachers?	Formative phases 6 to 8 are aimed at understanding the meaning that children and teachers give to the curriculum components and activities in progressively expanding, diverse social contexts so as to improve the curriculum. For example, the usability and effectiveness of specific components and characteristics of the curriculum are evaluated as implemented by a teacher who is familiar with the materials. The evaluation begins with implementation among individuals or small groups (phase 6), then continues with whole classes (phase 7), and finally focuses on implementation by a diverse group of teachers (phase 8). The curriculum is frequently, in cycles, altered based on empirical results, with the focus expanding to include aspects of support for teachers. Methods include interpretive work using a mix of model testing and model generation strategies, including design experiments and microgenetic, microethnographic, and phenomenological approaches (phase 6); classroom-based teaching experiments and ethnographic participant observation (phase 7); and these plus content analyses (phase 8). The curriculum is altered based on empirical results, with the focus expanding to include aspects of support for teachers.
	What is the effectiveness of the curriculum in diverse, realistic contexts?	Summative phases 9 and 10 are intended to assess whether the goals of the curriculum have been met. (Note that these evaluations can lead to curricular revisions, for example, between editions.)

SOURCE: Adapted from Clements, 2007.

CONCLUSION

The development and implementation of high-quality, equitable curriculum is a highly creative, complex enterprise that requires input and support across family, community, and educational contexts and diverse experts and expertise that does not rely solely on Eurocentric epistemology and models of teaching approaches, learning, and outcomes.

- High-quality curricula are coherent, equitable, culturally relevant, and linguistically affirming, and have the flexibility to be adapted. To support their effectiveness, such curricula would also be research based and empirically validated as part of their development.

- Theoretical purity is less important for developing and evaluating high-quality curricula than considering all relevant theories and empirical work. Similarly, research designs and methods are suited for specific investigations and questions, but a complete research and development program requires multiple methodologies.
- The development and evaluation of high-quality curricula are resource intensive. Although progressing through multiple stages is demanding and producing satisfactory evaluation data is costly, given the potential financial and human costs of inadequate curricula, it is actually impractical to avoid careful, long-range development and evaluation of high-quality curricula.
- Curriculum has a significant effect on teaching and learning. Curricula can be educative, supporting teachers' acquisition of content knowledge and implementation of new approaches that support all children's thinking and learning.

As noted in this and previous chapters, a key challenge to advancing a new vision for preschool curriculum, particularly for children facing the greatest educational disparities, is the development of policy levers for curriculum choice and implementation that are closely aligned with empirical evidence. The committee recognizes that these considerations impose significant challenges for curriculum developers who work across disciplinary areas; however, it is essential for high-quality, equitable preschool curricula to be developed to meet the needs of the diverse population of preschool children and be able to suit the unique strengths and needs of every child.

REFERENCES

Adair, J. K. (2014). Agency and expanding capabilities in early grade classrooms: What it could mean for young children. *Harvard Educational Review*, 84(2), 217–241. https://doi.org/10.17763/haer.84.2.y46vh546h41l2144

———. (in review). The related impact of agency and racism on young children's development: Evidence from three large-scale, multi-sited studies. *Child Development*.

Adair, J. K., & Colgrove, K. S. (2021). *Segregation by experience: Agency, learning, and racism in the early grades*. University of Chicago Press.

Adair, J. K., Colgrove, K. S.-S., & Mcmanus, M. E. (2017). How the word gap argument negatively impacts young children of Latinx immigrants' conceptualizations of learning. *Harvard Educational Review*, 87(3), 309–334. https://eric.ed.gov/?id=EJ1164890

Adair, J. K., Colgrove, K. S. S., & Mcmanus, M. E. (2018). Troubling messages: Agency and learning in the early schooling experiences of children of Latinx immigrants. *Teachers College Record*, 120(6), 1–40. https://doi.org/10.1177/016146811812000608

Adair, J. K., Park, S., Alonzo, M., McManus, M. E., Odim, N., Lee, S., Jones, N. N., Payne, K. A., & Colgrove, K. S. S. (2024). Equitable access to agency-supportive early schooling contexts for young children of color. *Early Childhood Research Quarterly*, 69, 49–64. https://doi.org/10.1016/j.ecresq.2024.06.003

Adukia, A., Eble, A., Harrison, E., Runesha, H. B., & Szasz, T. (2021). *What we teach about race and gender: Representation in images and text of children's books.* https://bfi.uchicago.edu/working-paper/2021-44

Agodini, R., Harris, B., Thomas, M., Murphy, R., Gallagher, L., & Pendleton, A. (2010). *Achievement effects of four early elementary school math curricula: Findings for first and second graders.* National Center for Education Evaluation and Regional Assistance, Institute of Education Sciences, U.S. Department of Education.

Aguiar, A. L., & Aguiar, C. (2020). Classroom composition and quality in early childhood education: A systematic review. *Children and Youth Services Review, 115*, 105086. https://psycnet.apa.org/doi/10.1016/j.childyouth.2020.105086

Allen, R., Shapland, D. L., Neitzel, J., & Iruka, I. U. (2021). Creating antiracist early childhood spaces. *Young Children, 76*(2), 49–54. https://fpg.unc.edu/publications/viewpoint-creating-anti-racist-early-childhood-spaces

American Montessori Society. (2024). *Montessori public schools.* https://amshq.org/Educators/Montessori-Schools/Montessori-Public-Schools

Amukune, S., & Józsa, K. (2023). Approaches to learning in elementary classrooms: Contribution of mastery motivation and executive functions on academic achievement. *International Journal of Instruction, 16*(2), 389–412. http://dx.doi.org/10.29333/iji.2023.16222a

Ansari, A., & Pianta, R. C. (2018). The role of elementary school quality in the persistence of preschool effects. *Children and Youth Services Review, 86*, 120–127. https://doi.org/10.1016/j.childyouth.2018.01.025

Armstrong, A. L. (2021). *The representation of social groups in U.S. education materials and why it matters: A research overview.* New America. https://www.newamerica.org/education-policy/reports/the-representation-of-social-groups-in-u-s-educational-materials-and-why-it-matter/

Ascenzi-Moreno, L., & Seltzer, K. (2021). Always at the bottom: Ideologies in assessment of emergent bilinguals. *Journal of Literacy Research, 53*(4), 468–490. https://doi.org/10.1177/1086296x211052255

Aydogan, C., Plummer, C., Kang, S. J., Bilbrey, C., Farran, D. C., & Lipsey, M. W. (2005, June 5–8). *An investigation of prekindergarten curricula: Influences on classroom characteristics and child engagement.* Paper presented at the National Association for the Education of Young Children. Washington, DC.

Ayer, D. (2016, May 16). Native Montessori project revived. *Montessori Public.* https://www.montessoripublic.org/2016/05/native-montessori-project

Bailey, D. D. E., Holly, J., Jr., & West, R. (2023). Proposing African-centered education in STEM for African (American) STEM learners. *Journal of Black Excellence in Engineering, Science, & Technology, 1*, 1–20. https://nsbejournal.scholasticahq.com/article/90617-proposing-african-centered-education-in-stem-for-african-american-stem-learners

Bailey, D. H., Jenkins, J. M., & Alvarez-Vargas, D. (2019). *Complementarities between early educational intervention and later educational quality? A systematic review of the sustaining environments hypothesis* (EdWorkingPaper No. 19-99). Annenberg Institute at Brown University. http://www.edworkingpapers.com/ai19-99

Ball, D. L., & Cohen, D. K. (1996). Reform by the book: What is—or might be—the role of curriculum materials in teacher learning and instructional reform? *Educational Researcher, 25*(9), 6–8, 14. https://doi.org/10.2307/1177151

Banks, J. A. (1993). The canon debate, knowledge construction, and multicultural education. *Educational Researcher, 22*(5), 4–14. https://doi.org/10.3102/0013189X022005004

———. (1995). Multicultural education and curriculum transformation. *The Journal of Negro Education, 64*(4), 390–400. https://doi.org/10.2307/2967262

Bannan-Ritland, B. (2003). The role of design in research: The integrative learning design framework. *Educational Researcher, 32*(1), 21–24. http://dx.doi.org/10.3102/0013189X032001021

Banse, H. W., Clements, D. H., Sarama, J., Day-Hess, C. A., & Joswick, C. (2021). Intentional teaching moments: Supporting executive function development and early mathematics through a geometry activity. *Young Children, 76*(3), 75–82. https://www.naeyc.org/resources/pubs/yc/fall2021/geometry-activity

Bardsley, M. E. (2006). Pre-kindergarten teachers' use and understanding of hypothetical learning trajectories in mathematics education. [Doctoral dissertation, SUNY at Buffalo]. *Proquest.*

Barnett, W. S., Jung, K., Yarosz, D. J., Thomas, J., Hornbeck, A., Stechuk, R., & Burns, S. (2008). Educational effects of the Tools of the Mind curriculum: A randomized trial. *Early Childhood Research Quarterly, 23*(3), 299–313. https://doi.org/10.1016/j.ecresq.2008.03.001

Barnett, W. S., Yarosz, D. J., Thomas, J., Jung, K., & Blanco, D. (2007). Two-way and monolingual English immersion in preschool education: An experimental comparison. *Early Childhood Research Quarterly, 22*(3), 277–293. https://doi.org/10.1016/j.ecresq.2007.03.003

Baron, A., Evangelou, M., Malmberg, L.-E., & Melendex-Torres, G. J. (2017). The Tools of the Mind curriculum for improving self-regulation in early childhood: A systematic review. *Campbell Systematic Reviews, 13*(1), 1–77. https://doi.org/10.4073/csr.2017.10

Baroody, A. J., Clements, D. H., & Sarama, J. (2019). Teaching and learning mathematics in early childhood programs. In C. P. Brown, M. B. McMullen, & N. File (Eds.), *The Wiley Handbook of Early Childhood Care and Education* (pp. 329–353). Wiley Blackwell Publishing. https://doi.org/10.1002/9781119148104

Baroody, A. J., Clements, D. H., & Sarama, J. (2022). Lessons learned from 10 experiments that tested the efficacy and assumptions of hypothetical learning trajectories. *Education Sciences, 12*, 195. https://doi.org/10.3390/educsci12030195

Baroody, A. J., Purpura, D. J., Eiland, M. D., & Reid, E. E. (2014). Fostering first graders' fluency with basic subtraction and larger addition combinations via computer-assisted instruction. *Cognition and Instruction, 32*(2), 159–197. https://doi.org/10.1080/07370008.2014.887084

Baroody, A. J., Yilmaz, N., Clements, D. H., & Sarama, J. (2021). Evaluating a basic assumption of learning trajectories: The case of early patterning learning. *Journal of Mathematics Education, 13*(2), 8–32. https://doi.org/10.1007/s11858-019-01122-z

Bassok, D., & Galdo, E. (2016). Inequality in preschool quality? Community-level disparities in access to high-quality learning environments. *Early Education and Development, 27*(1), 128–144. https://psycnet.apa.org/doi/10.1080/10409289.2015.1057463

Battista, M. T., & Clements, D. H. (2000). Mathematics curriculum development as a scientific endeavor. In A. E. Kelly & R. A. Lesh (Eds.), *Handbook of research design in mathematics and science education* (pp. 737–760). Erlbaum.

Beleslin, T. P., Lepičnik-Vodopivec, J., Partalo, S., & Šindić, A. (2022). Where does mathematics education start? Connecting the preschool curriculum and the home environment. *Our School, 6*(1), 119–140. https://doi.org/10.7251/NSK2201119B

Bernal, R., Giannola, M., & Nores, M. (2022). The effects of a project and play-based early education program on medium term developmental trajectories of young children in a low-income setting. *SSRN*, 4191995. https://dx.doi.org/10.2139/ssrn.4191995

Beyer, C. J., & Davis, E. A. (2015). Using educative curriculum materials to support preservice elementary teachers' curricular planning: A comparison between two different forms of support. *Curriculum Inquiry, 39*(5), 679–703. https://doi.org/10.1111/j.1467-873X.2009.00464.x

Bierman, K. L., Domitrovich, C. E., Nix, R. L., Gest, S. D., Welsh, J. A., Greenberg, M. T., Blair, C. B., Nelson, K. E., & Gill, S. (2008). Promoting academic and social-emotional school readiness: The Head Start REDI Program. *Child Development, 79*(6), 1802–1817. https://doi.org/10.1111/j.1467-8624.2008.01227.x

Bishop, R. S. (1990). Mirrors, windows, and sliding glass doors. *Perspectives: Choosing and Using Books for the Classroom*, 6(3). https://digitalscholarship.unlv.edu/cgi/viewcontent.cgi?article=1153&context=taboo

Björklund, C., & Barendregt, W. (2016). Teachers' pedagogical mathematical awareness in diverse child-age-groups. *Nordic Studies in Mathematics Education*, 21(4), 115–133. http://ncm.gu.se/nomad

Blair, C. B., & Raver, C. C. (2014). Closing the achievement gap through modification of neurocognitive and neuroendocrine function: Results from a cluster randomized controlled trial of an innovative approach to the education of children in kindergarten. *PLoS One*, 9(11), e112393. https://doi.org/10.1371/journal.pone.0112393

Blanton, M., Stroud, R., Stephens, A., Gardiner, A. M., Stylianou, D. A., Knuth, E., Isler-Baykal, I., & Strachota, S. (2019). Does early algebra matter? The effectiveness of an early algebra intervention in grades 3 to 5. *American Educational Research Journal*, 56(5), 1930–1972. https://doi.org/10.3102/0002831219832301

Blewitt, C., O'Connor, A., Morris, H., Mousa, A., Bergmeier, H., Nolan, A., Jackson, K., Barrett, H., & Skouteris, H. (2020). Do curriculum-based social and emotional learning programs in early childhood education and care strengthen teacher outcomes? A systematic literature review. *International Journal of Environmental Research and Public Health*, 17(3), 1049. https://doi.org/10.3390/ijerph17031049

Blöte, A. W., van der Burg, E., & Klein, A. S. (2001). Students' flexibility in solving two-digit addition and subtraction problems: Instruction effects. *Journal of Educational Psychology*, 93, 627–638. https://psycnet.apa.org/doi/10.1037/0022-0663.93.3.627

Boerst, T., Lambdin, D. V., Confrey, J., White, D., Heck, D., Baltzley, P. C., Knuth, E., & Quander, J. R. (2010). Strengthening research by designing for coherence and connections to practice. *Journal for Research in Mathematics Education*, 41(3), 216–235. https://eric.ed.gov/?id=EJ883114

Bohart, H., & Procopio, R. (Eds.). (2022). *Developmentally appropriate practice in early childhood programs serving children from birth through age 8* (4th ed.). National Association for the Education of Young Children.

Bojorquea, G., Torbeyns, J., Van Hoof, J., Van Nijlen, D., & Verschaffel, L. (2018). Effectiveness of the Building Blocks program for enhancing Ecuadorian kindergartners' numerical competencies. *Early Childhood Research Quarterly*, 44(3), 231–241. https://doi.org/10.1016/j.ecresq.2017.12.009

Boutte, G. S. (2015). Kindergarten through grade 3: Four things to remember about African American language: Examples from children's books. *YC Young Children*, 70(4), 38–45.

Boutte, G. S., Wynter-Hoyte, K., & Bryan, N. (2024). *Revolutionary love for early childhood classrooms: Nurturing the brilliance of young Black children*. Scholastic.

Bredekamp, S., & Joseph, G. E. (2024). *Effective practices in early childhood education: Building a foundation* (5th ed.). Pearson Education.

Bredekamp, S., & Willer, B. (2022). Intentional teaching: Complex decision making and the core considerations. In H. Bohart & R. Procopio (Eds.), *Developmentally appropriate practice in early childhood programs serving children from birth through age 8* (4th ed., pp. 5–23). National Association for the Education of Young Children.

Broderick, J. T., & Hong, S. B. (2020). *From children's interests to children's thinking: Using a cycle of inquiry to plan curriculum*. National Association for the Education of Young Children.

Broderick, J. T., Sareh, N., & Aggrey, P. M.-B. (2022). Teaching preschool teachers to converse productively with children: A single case design. *Early Childhood Education Journal*, 51(1), 165–178. https://doi.org/10.1007/s10643-021-01284-0

Brooks, W., & Browne, S. (2012). Towards a culturally situated reader responsive theory. *Children's Literature in Education*, 43(1), 74–85. https://eric.ed.gov/?id=EJ957036

Brosterman, N. (1997). *Inventing kindergarten.* Harry N. Abrams.

Brown, A. L., & Campione, J. C. (1996). Psychological theory and the design of innovative learning environments: On procedures, principles, and systems. In R. Glaser (Ed.), *Innovations in learning: New environments for education* (pp. 289–325). Erlbaum.

Bruner, J. S. (1985). Models of the learner. *Educational Researcher, 14*(6), 5–8. https://doi.org/10.3102/0013189X014006005

Burbanks, S. M., IV, Shockley, K. G., & LeNiles, K. (2020). The need for African centered education in STEM programs for Black youth. *Journal of African American Males in Education, 11*(2), 12–24. https://jaamejournal.scholasticahq.com/article/18091-the-need-for-african-centered-education-in-stem-programs-for-black-youth

Burchinal, M. R., Bierman, K., Gonzalez, J., McClelland, M. M., Nelson, K., Pentimonti, J., Purpura, D. J., Sachs, J., Sarama, J., Schlesinger-Devlin, E., & Washington, J. (2022). *Preparing young children for school* (WWC No. 2022009). National Center for Education Evaluation and Regional Assistance, Institute of Education Sciences, U.S. Department of Education. https://whatworks.ed.gov

Burkhardt, H. (2006). From design research to large-scale impact: Engineering research in education. In J. V. d. Akker, K. P. E. Gravemeijer, S. McKenney, & N. Nieveen (Eds.), *Educational design research* (pp. 133–162). Routledge.

Burkhardt, H., Fraser, R., & Ridgway, J. (1989). The dynamics of curriculum change. In J. Malone, H. Burkhardt, & C. Keitel (Eds.), *The mathematics curriculum: Towards the year 2000.* Science and Mathematics Education Centre, Curtin University.

Burnett, C. (2010). Technology and literacy in early childhood educational settings: A review of research. *Journal of Early Childhood Literacy, 10*(3), 247–270. https://doi.org/10.1177/1468798410372154

Burstein, K., Zamudio, I., Otto, C., Rodgers, J., Yellowman, I., Clark, G., Guy, M., Blanchard, J., & Christie, J. (2014). *Advancing early literacy achievement: A longitudinal study of an American Indian early childhood education program.* http://swifamilies.org/wp-content/uploads/2015/05/Advancing-Early-Literacy-Achievement.pdf

Bustamante, A. S., Greenfield, D., & Nayfeld, I. (2018). Early childhood science and engineering: Engaging platforms for fostering domain-general learning skills. *Education Sciences, 8*(3), 144. https://doi.org/10.3390/educsci8030144

Byers, A. I., Cottone, E. A., & Cameron, C. E. (2018). From design copying to mathematics in the early childhood classroom. *Young Children, 73*(1), 80–85. https://www.naeyc.org/resources/pubs/yc/mar2018/design-copying-mathematics

Cabell, S. Q., Neuman, S. B., & Terry, N. P. (Eds.). (2023). *Handbook on the science of early literacy.* Guilford.

Callaghan, M. N., & Reich, S. M. (2018). Are educational preschool apps designed to teach? An analysis of the app market. *Learning, Media and Technology, 43*(3), 280–293. https://doi.org/10.1080/17439884.2018.1498355

Campbell, C., Speldewinde, C., Howitt, C., & MacDonald, A. (2018). STEM practice in the early years. *Creative Education, 9*(01), 11–25. https://doi.org/10.4236/ce.2018.91002

Carnine, D. W., Jitendra, A. K., & Silbert, J. (1997). A descriptive analysis of mathematics curricular materials from a pedagogical perspective: A case study of fractions. *Remedial and Special Education, 18*(2), 66–81. http://dx.doi.org/10.1177/074193259701800201

Carr, R. C. (2021). *The benefits of early childhood education can persist in the long run.* Hunt Institute and Duke University. https://hunt-institute.org/wp-content/uploads/2021/10/HI-Duke-Brief-Carr_v2.pdf

Carr, R. C., Mokrova, I. L., Vernon-Feagans, L., & Burchinal, M. R. (2019). Cumulative classroom quality during pre-kindergarten and kindergarten and children's language, literacy, and mathematics skills. *Early Childhood Research Quarterly, 47,* 218–228. https://psycnet.apa.org/doi/10.1016/j.ecresq.2018.12.010

Casey, B. M., Dearing, E., Vasilyeva, M., Ganley, C. M., & Tine, M. (2011). Spatial and numerical predictors of measurement performance: The moderating effects of community income and gender. *Journal of Educational Psychology*, 103(2), 296–311. https://doi.org/10.1037/a0022516

Castagno, A. E., & Brayboy, B. M. (2008). Culturally responsive schooling for indigenous youth: A review of the literature. *Review of Educational Research*, 78, 941–993. http://dx.doi.org/10.3102/0034654308323036

Cevikbas, M., König, J., & Rothland, M. (2024). Empirical research on teacher competence in mathematics lesson planning: Recent developments. *ZDM Mathematics Education*, 56, 101–113. https://doi.org/10.1007/s11858-023-01487-2

Champion, T. B., Hyter, Y. D., McCabe, A., & Bland-Stewart, L. M. (2003). "A matter of vocabulary" performances of low-income African American Head Start children on the Peabody Picture Vocabulary Test—III. *Communication Disorders Quarterly*, 24(3), 121–127. https://psycnet.apa.org/doi/10.1177/15257401030240030301

Chard, D. J., Baker, S. K., Clarke, B., Jungjohann, K., Davis, K., & Smolkowski, K. (2008). Preventing early mathematics difficulties: The feasibility of a rigorous kindergarten mathematics curriculum. *Learning Disability Quarterly*, 31, 11–20. https://doi.org/10.2307/30035522

Chaudry, A., Morrissey, T., Weiland, C., & Yoshikawa, H. (2017). *Cradle to kindergarten: A new plan to combat inequality.* Russell Sage.

Cheng, Y.-L., & Mix, K. S. (2012). Spatial training improves children's mathematics ability. *Journal of Cognition and Development*, 15(1), 2–11. https://doi.org/10.1080/15248372.2012.725186

Chernyak, N., Harris, P. L., & Cordes, S. (2022). A counting intervention promotes fair sharing in preschoolers. *Child Development*, 93(5). https://doi.org/10.1111/cdev.13775

Christie, J., Roskos, K., Vukelich, C., & Han, M. (2003). The effects of a well-designed literacy program on young children's language and literacy development. In F. Lamb-Parker, J. Hagen, R. Robinson, & H. Rhee (Eds.), *The first eight years: Pathways to the future: Implications for research, policy, and practice* (pp. 447–448). Proceedings of the Head Start National Research Conference. Mailman School of Public Health, Columbia University.

Civil, M. (2002). Culture and mathematics: A community approach. *Journal of Intercultural Studies*, 23(2), 133–148. http://dx.doi.org/10.1080/07256860220151050A

Clark, R. E., Kirschner, P. A., & Sweller, J. (2012). Putting students on the path to learning: The case for fully guided instruction. *American Educator*, 36(1), 6–11. https://www.aft.org/sites/default/files/Clark.pdf

Clements, D. H. (1997). (Mis?)Constructing constructivism. *Teaching Children Mathematics*, 4(4), 198–200. https://www.researchgate.net/profile/Douglas_Clements/publication/234715059_MisConstructing_Constructivism/links/5c00686492851c63cab04bb5/MisConstructing-Constructivism.pdf

———. (2007). Curriculum research: Toward a framework for research-based curricula. *Journal for Research in Mathematics Education*, 38(1), 35–70. https://doi.org/10.2307/30034927

———. (2008). Linking research and curriculum development. In L. D. English (Ed.), *Handbook of international research in mathematics education* (2nd ed., pp. 589–625). Taylor & Francis.

Clements, D. H., & Battista, M. T. (2000). Designing effective software. In A. E. Kelly & R. A. Lesh (Eds.), *Handbook of research design in mathematics and science education* (pp. 761–776). Erlbaum.

Clements, D. H., & Conference Working Group. (2004). Part one: Major themes and recommendations. In D. H. Clements, J. Sarama, & A.-M. DiBiase (Eds.), *Engaging young children in mathematics: Standards for early childhood mathematics education* (pp. 1–72). Erlbaum.

Clements, D. H., & Sarama, J. (2002a). Mathematics curricula in early childhood. *Teaching Children Mathematics, 9*(3), 163–166. http://dx.doi.org/10.5951/TCM.9.3.0163
———. (2002b). Teaching with computers in early childhood education: Strategies and professional development. *Journal of Early Childhood Teacher Education, 23*(3), 215–226. http://dx.doi.org/10.1080/1090102020230305
———. (2003). Strip mining for gold: Research and policy in educational technology—A response to "Fool's Gold". *Educational Technology Review, 11*(1), 7–69. www.editlib.org/index.cfm?fuseaction=Reader.ViewAbstract&paper_id=17793
———. (2007). Effects of a preschool mathematics curriculum: Summative research on the Building Blocks project. *Journal for Research in Mathematics Education, 38*(2), 136–163. https://doi.org/10.2307/748360
———. (2008). Experimental evaluation of the effects of a research-based preschool mathematics curriculum. *American Educational Research Journal, 45*(2), 443–494. https://doi.org/10.3102/0002831207312908
———. (2012). Learning and teaching early and elementary mathematics. In J. S. Carlson & J. R. Levine (Eds.), *Instructional strategies for improving student learning: Focus on early mathematics and reading* (Vol. 3, pp. 107–162). Information Age.
———. (2013). Rethinking early mathematics: What is research-based curriculum for young children? In L. D. English & J. T. Mulligan (Eds.), *Reconceptualizing early mathematics learning* (pp. 121–147). Springer. https://doi.org/10.1007/978-94-007-6440-8_7
———. (2014a). Learning trajectories: Foundations for effective, research-based education. In A. P. Maloney, J. Confrey, & K. H. Nguyen (Eds.), *Learning over time: Learning trajectories in mathematics education* (pp. 1–30). Information Age.
———. (2014b, March 3). Play, mathematics, and false dichotomies. *Preschool matters . . . today!* https://nieer.wordpress.com/2014/03/03/play-mathematics-and-false-dichotomies
———. (2015a). Discussion from a mathematics education perspective. *Mathematical Thinking and Learning, 17*(2–3), 244–252. https://doi.org/10.1080/10986065.2015.1016826
———. (2015b). Learning executive function and early mathematics. In C. Kurose & N. Albert (Eds.), *Mathematical instruction for perseverance collected papers* (p. 20). Spencer Foundation. http://hub.mspnet.org/index.cfm/28129
———. (2017/2023). *Learning and teaching with learning trajectories ([LT]²)*. Marsico Institute, Morgridge College of Education, University of Denver. www.learningtrajectories.org
———. (2021). *Learning and teaching early math: The learning trajectories approach* (3rd ed.). Routledge. https://doi.org/10.4324/9781003083528
Clements, D. H., & Swaminathan, S. (1995). Technology and school change new lamps for old? *Childhood Education, 71*(5), 275–281. http://dx.doi.org/10.1080/00094056.1995.10522619
Clements, D. H., & Wright, T. S. (2022). Teaching content in early childhood education. In H. Bohart & R. Procopio (Eds.), *Developmentally appropriate practice in early childhood programs serving children from birth through age 8* (4th ed., pp. 63–80). National Association for the Education of Young Children.
Clements, D. H., Fuson, K. C., & Sarama, J. (2019a). Critiques of the Common Core in early math: A research-based response. *Journal for Research in Mathematics Education, 50*(1), 11–22. https://doi.org/10.5951/jresematheduc.50.1.0011
Clements, D. H., Lizcano, R., & Sarama, J. (2023a). Research and pedagogies for early math. *Education Sciences, 13*(8), 839. https://doi.org/10.3390/educsci13080839
Clements, D. H., Sarama, J., & Germeroth, C. (2016). Learning executive function and early mathematics: Directions of causal relations. *Early Childhood Research Quarterly, 36*(3), 79–90. https://doi.org/10.1016/j.ecresq.2015.12.009
Clements, D. H., Sarama, J., Baroody, A. J., Joswick, C., & Wolfe, C. B. (2019b). Evaluating the efficacy of a learning trajectory for early shape composition. *American Educational Research Journal, 56*(6), 2509–2530. https://doi.org/10.3102/0002831219842788

Clements, D. H., Sarama, J., Baroody, A. J., Kutaka, T. S., Chernyavskiy, P., Joswick, C., Cong, M., & Joseph, E. (2021a). Comparing the efficacy of early arithmetic instruction based on a learning trajectory and teaching-to-a-target. *Journal of Educational Psychology, 113*(7), 1323–1337. https://doi.org/doi.org/10.1037/edu0000633

Clements, D. H., Sarama, J., Layzer, C., & Unlu, F. (2023b). Implementation of a scale-up model in early childhood: Long-term impacts on mathematics achievement. *Journal for Research in Mathematics Education, 54*(1), 64–88. https://doi.org/10.5951/jresematheduc-2020-0245

Clements, D. H., Sarama, J., Layzer, C., Unlu, F., & Fesler, L. (2020). Effects on mathematics and executive function of a mathematics and play intervention versus mathematics alone. *Journal for Research in Mathematics Education, 51*(3), 301–333. https://doi.org/10.5951/jresemtheduc-2019-0069

Clements, D. H., Sarama, J., Spitler, M. E., Lange, A. A., & Wolfe, C. B. (2011). Mathematics learned by young children in an intervention based on learning trajectories: A large-scale cluster randomized trial. *Journal for Research in Mathematics Education, 42*(2), 127–166. https://doi.org/10.5951/jresematheduc.42.2.0127

Clements, D. H., Sarama, J., Wolfe, C. B., & Spitler, M. E. (2013). Longitudinal evaluation of a scale-up model for teaching mathematics with trajectories and technologies: Persistence of effects in the third year. *American Educational Research Journal, 50*(4), 812–850. https://doi.org/10.3102/0002831212469270

Clements, D. H., Vinh, M., Lim, C.-I., & Sarama, J. (2021b). STEM for inclusive excellence and equity. *Early Education and Development, 32*(1), 148–171. https://doi.org/10.1080/10409289.2020.1755776

Cobb, P. (2000). Constructivism in social context. In L. P. Steffe & P. W. Thompson (Eds.), *Radical constructivism in action: Building on the pioneering work of Ernst von Glasersfeld* (pp. 152–178). RoutledgeFalmer.

Cooper, J. O., Heron, T. E., & Heward, W. L. (2007). *Applied behavior analysis* (2nd ed.). Pearson Prentice Hall.

Cooperative Children's Book Center. (n.d.). *Books by and/or about Black, Indigenous and people of color (all years)*. University of Wisconsin–Madison School of Education. https://ccbc.education.wisc.edu/literature-resources/ccbc-diversity-statistics/books-by-about-poc-fnn

Council of Chief State School Officers & National Governors Association. (2010). *Common core state standards*. http://corestandards.org/

Cuban, L. (2001). *Oversold and underused*. Harvard University Press.

Culclasure, B. T., Fleming, D. J., & Riga, G. (2018). An evaluation of Montessori education in South Carolina's public schools. *Online Submission*.

Curenton, S. M., Franco-Jenkins, X., Nazaire, O. R., Huang, C., & Miller, E. K. (2023). *Literacy for social justice, equity diversity, and inclusion: Curriculum audit & book review audit*. Center on the Ecology of Early Development.

Curenton, S. M., Iruka, I., & Durden, T. (2017). Introduction. In S. M. Curenton, I. Iruka, & T. Durden (Eds.), *African American children in early childhood education: Making the case for policy investments in families, schools, and communities advances in race and ethnicity in education* (Vol. 5, pp. 3–13). Emerald Group Publishing Limited. https://doi.org/10.1108/S2051-231720170000005001

Danesi, M. (2009, April 24). *Puzzles and the brain*. https://www.psychologytoday.com/us/blog/brain-workout/200904/puzzles-and-the-brain

Darling-Hammond, L., & Snyder, J. (1992). Curriculum studies and the traditions of inquiry: The scientific tradition. In P. W. Jackson (Ed.), *Handbook of research on curriculum* (pp. 41–78). Macmillan.

Davis, E. A., Palincsar, A. S., Smith, P. S., Arias, A. M., & Kademian, S. M. (2017). Educative curriculum materials: Uptake, impact, and implications for research and design. *Educational Researcher, 46*(6), 293–304. https://doi.org/10.3102/0013189x17727502

de Jong, T., Lazonder, A. W., Chinn, C. A., Fischer, F., Gobert, J., Hmelo-Silver, C. E., Koedinger, K. R., Krajcik, J. S., Kyza, E. A., Linn, M. C., Pedaste, M., Scheiter, K., & Zacharia, Z. C. (2023). Let's talk evidence—The case for combining inquiry-based and direct instruction. *Educational Research Review*. https://doi.org/10.1016/j.edurev.2023.100536

Deaño, M., Alfonso, S., Diniz, A. M., Iglesias-Sarmiento, V., & Das, J. P. (2023). Math Modules Training improves math achievement & associated cognitive processing. *Psychology*, 14(6), 1053–1069. https://doi.org/10.4236/psych.2023.146057

Debs, M. C., & Brown, K. E. (2017). Students of color and public Montessori schools: A review of the literature. *Journal of Montessori Research*, 3(1). https://files.eric.ed.gov/fulltext/EJ1161350.pdf

DeCaro, M. S., & Rittle-Johnson, B. (2012). Exploring mathematics problems prepares children to learn from instruction. *Journal of Experimental Child Psychology*, 113(4), 552–568. https://doi.org/10.1016/j.jecp.2012.06.009

Deflorio, L., Klein, A., Starkey, P., Swank, P. R., Taylor, H. B., Halliday, S. E., Beliakoff, A., & Mulcahy, C. (2019). A study of the developing relations between self-regulation and mathematical knowledge in the context of an early math intervention. *Early Childhood Research Quarterly*, 46, 33–48. https://doi.org/10.1016/j.ecresq.2018.06.008

Delpit, L. (1988). The silenced dialogue: Power and pedagogy in educating other people's children. *Harvard Educational Review*, 58(3), 280–298. http://lmcreadinglist.pbworks.com/f/Delpit+(1988).pdf

———. (2006). Lessons from teachers. *Journal of Teacher Education*, 57(3), 220–231. https://doi.org/10.1177/0022487105285966

———. (2013). *"Multiplication is for white people": Raising expectations for other people's children*. The New Press.

Demmert, W. G., Jr., & Towner, J. C. (2003). *A review of the research literature on the influences of culturally based education on the academic performance of Native American students*. Northwest Regional Educational Laboratory. https://educationnorthwest.org/sites/default/files/cbe.pdf

Derman-Sparks, L., & A.B.C. Task Force. (1989). *Anti-bias curriculum: Tools for empowering young children*. National Association for the Education of Young Children.

Derman-Sparks, L., & Edwards, J. O. (2020). *Anti-bias education for young children and ourselves* (2nd rev ed.). National Association for the Education of Young Children.

The Design-Based Research Collective. (2003). Design-based research: An emerging paradigm for educational inquiry. *Educational Researcher*, 32(1), 5–8. https://doi.org/10.3102/0013189X032001005

DeVries, R., Zan, B., Hildebrandt, C., Edmiaston, R., & Sales, C. (2002). *Developing constructivist early childhood curriculum: Practical principles and activities*. Teachers College.

Dewey, J. (1997). *Experience and education*. Simon & Schuster.

Diamond, K. E., Justice, L. M., Siegler, R. S., & Snyder, P. A. (2013). *Synthesis of IES research on early intervention and early childhood education* (NCSER No. 2013-3001). National Center for Special Education Research, Institute of Education Sciences, U.S. Department of Education. http://ies.ed.gov/ncser/pubs/20133001/pdf/20133001.pdf

Doabler, C. T., Clarke, B., Fien, H., Baker, S. K., Kosty, D. B., & Cary, M. S. (2014). The science behind curriculum development and evaluation: Taking a design science approach in the production of a tier 2 mathematics curriculum. *Learning Disability Quarterly*, 38(2), 97–111. https://doi.org/10.1177/0731948713520555

Doabler, C. T., Clarke, B., Firestone, A. R., Turtura, J. E., Jungjohann, K. J., Brafford, T. L., Sutherland, M., Nelson, N. J., & Fien, H. (2019). Applying the Curriculum Research Framework in the design and development of a technology-based tier 2 mathematics intervention. *Journal of Special Education Technology*, 34(3), 176–189. https://doi.org/10.1177/0162643418812051

Dockett, S., & Perry, B. (2010). What makes mathematics play? In L. Sparrow, B. Kissane, & C. Hurst (Eds.), *MERGA 33: Shaping the future of mathematics education* (pp. 715–718). Mathematics Education Research Group of Australasia.

Domínguez, X., & Goldstein, M. (2020). *Next generation preschool science: Findings from design-based research to inform iterative development of an innovative curricular program and a field study to examine implementation and efficacy.* Society for Research on Educational Effectiveness.

Domitrovich, C. E., Moore, J. E., & Greenberg, M. T. (2012). Maximizing the effectiveness of social-emotional interventions for young children through high-quality implementation of evidence-based interventions. In B. Kelly & D. F. Perkins (Eds.), *Handbook of implementation science for psychology in education* (pp. 207–229). Cambridge University Press.

Dong, X., Burke, M. D., Ramirez, G., Xu, Z., & Bowman-Perrott, L. (2023a). A meta-analysis of social skills interventions for preschoolers with or at risk of early emotional and behavioral problems. *Behavioral Sciences, 13*(11). https://doi.org/10.3390/bs13110940

Dong, Y., & Clements, D. H. (2023). Consequential validity of early childhood assessments. In *Handbook of research methods in early childhood education.* Information Age.

Dong, Y., Clements, D. H., Sarama, J., Dumas, D. G., Banse, H. W., & Day-Hess, C. A. (2021). Mathematics and executive function competencies in the context of interventions: A quantile regression analysis. *Journal of Experimental Education, 90*(2), 297–318. https://doi.org/10.1080/00220973.2020.1777070

Dong, Y., Dumas, D. G., Clements, D. H., Day-Hess, C. A., & Sarama, J. (2023b). Evaluating the consequential validity of the Research-Based Early Mathematics Assessment. *Journal of Psychoeducational Assessment, 41*(5), 575–582. https://doi.org/10.1177/07342829231165812

Dore, R., Xiao, N., Sayers, R., Purtell, K., & Justice, L. (2023). Does home media use predict preschoolers' skill gains? A time diary study. *Translational Issues in Psychological Science.*

Dorr, M. (2017). *The effectiveness of project-based learning using digital storytelling technology on improving second-grade students' performance of science standards.* [Master's thesis, University of Central Florida]. Orlando, Florida. http://stars.library.ucf.edu/cgi/viewcontent.cgi?article=6664&context=etd

Drake, C., Land, T. J., & Tyminski, A. M. (2014). Using educative curriculum materials to support the development of prospective teachers' knowledge. *Educational Researcher, 43*(3), 154–162. https://doi.org/10.3102/0013189X14528039

Dubosarsky, M., Murphy, B., Roehrig, G., Frost, L. C., Jones, J., Carlson, S. P., Londo, N., Melchert, C. J. B., Gettel, C., & Bement, J. (2011). Incorporating cultural themes to promote preschoolers' critical thinking in American Indian Head Start classrooms. *Young Children, 66*(5), 20–29. https://www.researchgate.net/publication/281656318_Incorporating_cultural_themes_to_promote_preschoolers'_critical_thinking_in_American_Indian_head_start_classrooms

Duke, N. K. (2015). Project based learning in Michigan. *Michigan Reading Journal, 48*(1). https://scholarworks.gvsu.edu/mrj/vol48/iss1/6

———. (2019). *Making the most of informational text.* NAEYC. https://www.naeyc.org/resources/blog/making-most-informational-text

Duke, N. K., & Martin, N. M. (2010). 10 things every literacy educator should know about research. *The Reading Teacher, 66*(1), 9–22. http://dx.doi.org/10.1598/RT.65.1.2

Duke, N. K., Halvorsen, A.-L., & Strachan, S. (2016). Project-based learning: Not just for STEM anymore. *Phi Delta Kappan, 98*(1), 15–19.

Dumas, D. G., McNeish, D., Sarama, J., & Clements, D. H. (2019). Preschool mathematics intervention can significantly improve student learning trajectories through elementary school. *AERA Open, 5*(4), 1–5. https://doi.org/10.1177/2332858419879446

Dunlap, G., Kincaid, D., Horner, R. H., Knoster, T., & Bradshaw, C. P. (2014). A comment on the term "positive behavior support". *Journal of Positive Behavior Interventions*, 16(3), 133–136. https://doi.org/10.1177/1098300715604826

Dunlap, G., Strain, P. S., Fox, L., Carta, J. J., Conroy, M., Smith, B. J., Less, K., Hemmeter, M. L., Timm, M. A., McCart, A. B., Sailor, W., Markey, U., Markey, D. J., Lardieri, S., & Sowell, C. (2006). Prevention and intervention with young children's challenging behavior: Perspectives regarding current knowledge. *Behavioral Disorders*, 32, 29–45.

Durán, L. K., Roseth, C. J., & Hoffman, P. (2010). An experimental study comparing English-only and Transitional Bilingual Education on Spanish-speaking preschoolers' early literacy development. *Early Childhood Research Quarterly*, 25(2), 207–217. https://doi.org/10.1016/j.ecresq.2009.10.002

Durden, T., & Curenton, S. M. (2018). Pathways to excellence—What we know works for nurturing Black children's success. In I. U. Iruka, S. M. Curenton, & T. R. Durden (Eds.), *African American children in early childhood education: Making the case for policy investments in families, schools, and communities* (Vol. 5, pp. 35–55). Emerald Publishing Limited. https://doi.org/10.1108/S2051-231720170000005003

Duschl, R., Maeng, S., & Sezen, A. (2011). Learning progressions and teaching sequences: A review and analysis. *Studies in Science Education*, 47(2), 123–182. https://doi.org/10.1080/03057267.2011.604476

Early, D. M., Iruka, I. U., Ritchie, S., Barbarin, O. A., Winn, D.-M. C., Crawford, G. M., Frome, P. M., Clifford, R. M., Burchinal, M. R., Howes, C., Bryant, D. M., & Pianta, R. C. (2010). How do pre-kindergarteners spend their time? Gender, ethnicity, and income as predictors of experiences in pre-kindergarten classrooms. *Early Childhood Research Quarterly*, 25(2), 177–193. https://doi.org/http://dx.doi.org/10.1016/j.ecresq.2009.10.003

Early, D. M., LaForett, D. R., Kraus, S., & Hume, K. (2016). *Evaluation findings from Georgia's 2015 summer Transition Program*. The University of North Carolina at Chapel Hill, FPG Child Development Institute. https://www.decal.ga.gov/documents/attachments/STP2015Report.pdf

Ebby, C. B., Hulbert, E. T., & Broadhead, R. M. (2020). *A focus on addition and subtraction: Bringing mathematics education research to the classroom*. Routledge.

Edwards, C., Gandini, L., & Forman, G. E. (1993). *The hundred languages of children: The Reggio Emilia approach to early childhood education*. Ablex Publishing Corp.

———. (2012). *The hundred languages of children: The Reggio Emilia experience in transformation* (3rd ed.). Praeger.

Escayg, K.-A. (2020). Anti-racism in U.S. early childhood education: Foundational principles. *Sociology Compass*, 14(4), e12764. https://doi.org/https://doi.org/10.1111/soc4.12764

Farran, D. C., & Wilson, S. J. (2014). *Achievement and self-regulation in pre-kindergarten classrooms: Effects of the Tools of the Mind curriculum*. Peabody Research Institute.

Farver, J. A. M., Lonigan, C. J., & Eppe, S. (2009). Effective early literacy skill development for young Spanish-speaking English language learners: An experimental study of two methods. *Child Development*, 80(3), 703–719. https://doi.org/10.1111/j.1467-8624.2009.01292.x

Feis, C. L., & Simons, C. (1985). Training preschool children in interpersonal cognitive problem solving skills: A replication. *Prevention in the Human Services*, 4, 59–70. https://doi.org/10.1300/J293v03n04_07

Fernando, C. (2021, March 16). Racial diversity in children's books grew but slowly. *Associated Press News*. https://apnews.com/article/race-andethnicity-wisconsin-madison-childrens-books-480e49bd32ef45e163d372201df163ee

Fidjeland, A., Rege, M., Solli, I. F., & Størksen, I. (2023). Reducing the gender gap in early learning: Evidence from a field experiment in Norwegian preschools. *European Economic Review*, 154. https://doi.org/10.1016/j.euroecorev.2023.104413

Finders, J. K., Duncan, R. J., Purpura, D. J., Elicker, J., & Schmitt, S. A. (2023). Testing theoretical explanations for heterogeneity in associations between a state quality rating and improvement system and prekindergarten children's academic performance. *Contemporary Educational Psychology, 73*, 102174. https://doi.org/10.1016/j.cedpsych.2023.102174

First Book Research & Insights. (2023). *The impact of a diverse classroom library*. https://firstbook.org

Fisher, K. R., Hirsh-Pasek, K., Newcombe, N., & Golinkoff, R. M. (2013). Taking shape: Supporting preschoolers' acquisition of geometric knowledge through guided play. *Child Development, 84*(6), 1872–1878. https://doi.org/10.1111/cdev.12091

Fleming, J., Catapano, S., Thompson, M., & Carrillo, S. (2015). *More mirrors in the classroom: Using urban children's literature to increase literacy*. Rowman & Littlefield.

Flook, L., Goldberg, S. B., Pinger, L., & Davidson, R. J. (2015). Promoting prosocial behavior and self-regulatory skills in preschool children through a mindfulness-based kindness curriculum. *Developmental Psychology, 51*(1), 44–51. https://doi.org/10.1037/a0038256

Foster, M. E., Anthony, J. L., Clements, D. H., & Sarama, J. (2016). Improving mathematics learning of kindergarten students through computer assisted instruction. *Journal for Research in Mathematics Education, 47*(3), 206–232. https://doi.org/https://doi.org/10.5951/jresematheduc.47.3.0206

Fox, L., & Hemmeter, M. L. (2009). A program-wide model for supporting social emotional development and addressing challenging behavior in early childhood settings. In W. Sailor, G. Dunlop, G. Sugai, & R. Horner (Eds.), *Handbook of positive behavior support* (pp. 177–202). Springer Publishing Co.

Fox, L., Carta, J., Stain, P. S., Dunlap, G., & Hemmeter, M. L. (2010). Response-to-intervention and the pyramid model. *Infants and Young Children, 23*, 3–14. https://files.eric.ed.gov/fulltext/ED577843.pdf

Fox, L., Dunlap, G., Hemmeter, M. L., Joseph, G. E., & Strain, P. S. (2003). The teaching pyramid: A model for supporting social competence and preventing challenging behavior in young children. *Young Children, 58*(4), 48–52. https://challengingbehavior.org/docs/TeachingPyramid_yc_article_7_2003.pdf

Fox, L., Strain, P. S., & Dunlap, G. (2021). Preventing the use of preschool suspension and expulsion: Implementing the pyramid model. *Preventing School Failure: Alternative Education for Children and Youth, 65*(4), 312–322. https://doi.org/10.1080/1045988x.2021.1937026

Fraivillig, J. L., Murphy, L. A., & Fuson, K. C. (1999). Advancing children's mathematical thinking in Everyday Mathematics classrooms. *Journal for Research in Mathematics Education, 30*(2), 148–170. https://psycnet.apa.org/doi/10.2307/749608

French, L. (2004). Science as the center of a coherent, integrated early childhood curriculum. *Early Childhood Research Quarterly, 19*(1), 138–149. https://doi.org/http://dx.doi.org/10.1016/j.ecresq.2004.01.004

Friedman-Krauss, A. H., Raver, C. C., Morris, P. A., & Jones, S. M. (2014). The role of classroom-level child behavior problems in predicting preschool teacher stress and classroom emotional climate. *Early Education and Development, 25*(4), 530–552. https://psycnet.apa.org/doi/10.1080/10409289.2013.817030

Fröbel, F. W. A. (1885). *The education of man*. A. Lovell and Co.

Frye, D., Baroody, A. J., Burchinal, M. R., Carver, S., Jordan, N. C., & McDowell, J. (2013). *Teaching math to young children: A practice guide*. National Center for Education Evaluation and Regional Assistance, Institute of Education Sciences, U.S. Department of Education. https://ies.ed.gov/ncee/wwc/PracticeGuide/18

Fuller, B., Bein, E., Bridges, M., Kim, Y., & Rabe-Hesketh, S. (2017). Do academic preschools yield stronger benefits? Cognitive emphasis, dosage, and early learning. *Journal of Applied Developmental Psychology, 52*, 1–11. https://doi.org/10.1016/j.appdev.2017.05.001

Fuson, K. C., & Briars, D. J. (1990). Using a base-ten blocks learning/teaching approach for first- and second-grade place-value and multidigit addition and subtraction. *Journal for Research in Mathematics Education, 21*(3), 180–206. https://psycnet.apa.org/doi/10.2307/749373

García Coll, C., Lamberty, G., Jenkins, R., McAdoo, H. P., Crnic, K., Wasik, B. H., & Vázquez García, H. (1996). An integrative model for the study of developmental competencies in minority children. *Child Development, 67*(5), 1891–1914.

Gardner-Neblett, N., & Iruka, I. U. (2015). Oral narrative skills: Explaining the language-emergent literacy link by race/ethnicity and SES. *Developmental Psychology, 51*(7), 889–904. https://doi.org/10.1037/a0039274

Gardner-Neblett, N., Curenton, S. M., & Blitch, K. (2017). Viewing African American children's oral language skills as a strength. In I. U. Iruka, S. M. Curenton, & T. R. Durden (Eds.), *African American children in early childhood education (Advances in race and ethnicity in education)* (Vol. 5, pp. 123–141). Emerald Group Publishing Limited.

Gardner-Neblett, N., Iruka, I. U., & Humphries, M. (2023). Dismantling the Black–White achievement gap paradigm: Why and how we need to focus instead on systemic change. *Journal of Education, 203*(2), 433–441. https://doi.org/10.1177/00220574211031958

Gavin, M. K., Casa, T. M., Adelson, J. L., & Firmender, J. M. (2013). The impact of challenging geometry and measurement units on the achievement of grade 2 students. *Journal for Research in Mathematics Education, 44*(3), 478–509. https://eric.ed.gov/?id=EJ1017790

Gawthorpe, A., & Davidson, K. C. (2023). Active learners in numeracy: Implementing guided play for early numeracy learning. *Research in Teacher Education, 13*(1), 13–20. https://doi.org/10.15123/uel.8w731

Geary, D. C., Berch, D. B., & Koepke, K. M. (2019). Introduction: Cognitive foundations for improving mathematical learning. In D. C. Geary, D. B. Berch, & K. M. Koepke (Eds.), *Cognitive foundations for improving mathematical learning* (Vol. 5, pp. 1–36). Academic Press. https://doi.org/10.1016/B978-0-12-815952-1.00001-3

Gelman, R. (1994). Constructivism and supporting environments. In D. Tirosh (Ed.), *Implicit and explicit knowledge: An educational approach* (Vol. 6, pp. 55–82). Ablex.

General Education Leadership Network. (2023). *Essential instructional practices in early literacy: Prekindergarten.* GELN. https://literacyessentials.org/downloads/gelndocs/pre-k_literacy_essentials.pdf

Gersten, R. (1985). Direct instruction with special education students: A review of evaluation research. *Journal of Special Education, 19*(1), 41–58. https://psycnet.apa.org/doi/10.1177/002246698501900104

Gersten, R., Jordan, N. C., & Flojo, J. R. (2005). Early identification and interventions for students with mathematical difficulties. *Journal of Learning Disabilities, 38*, 293–304. https://doi.org/10.1177/00222194050380040301

Gervasoni, A. (2018). The impact and challenges of early mathematics intervention in an Australian context. In G. Kaiser, H. Forgasz, M. Gravenm, A. Kuzniak, E. Simmt, & B. Xu (Eds.), *13th International Congress on Mathematical Education* (pp. 115–133). Springer International Publishing. https://doi.org/10.1007/978-3-319-72170-5

Ghalichi, N., & Roehrig, G. (2017). The role of research-based curricular unit on students' systems understanding of human impact on the environment. *Eurasia Proceedings of Educational and Social Sciences, 7*, 147–154. https://epess.net/index.php/epess/article/view/352

Gilliard, J. L., & Moore, R. A. (2007). An investigation of how culture shapes curriculum in early care and education programs on a Native American Indian reservation. *Early Childhood Education Journal, 34*(4), 251–258. https://eric.ed.gov/?id=EJ757633

Gilmore, C., Keeble, S., Richardson, S., & Cragg, L. (2017). The interaction of procedural skill, conceptual understanding and working memory in early mathematics achievement. *Journal of Numerical Cognition, 3*(2), 400–416. https://doi.org/10.5964/jnc.v3i2.51

Ginsburg, H. (2003). *Big math for little kids*. Pearson Learning Group.

Ginsburg, H. P., Lee, J. S., & Stevenson-Boyd, J. (2008). Mathematics education for young children: What it is and how to promote it. *Social Policy Report, 22*(1), 1–24. https://eric.ed.gov/?id=ED521700

Global Strategy Group. (2023). *The need to make math more relevant and engaging for K–12 students*. GSG. https://gatesfoundation.org/-/media/1dc7905be1334a7abfa8ae5ba1355217.ashx

Goldstein, P., Warde, B., & Peluso, P. (2013). *Children's readiness gains in publically funded, community-based pre-kindergarten programs for 4 year olds and preschool for 3 year olds*. Child & Youth Care Forum. https://doi.org/10.1007/s10566-013-9215-0

González, N., Andrade, R., Civil, M., & Moll, L. (2001). Bridging funds of distributed knowledge: Creating zones of practices in mathematics. *Journal of Education for Students Placed at Risk, 6*(1–2), 115–132. https://doi.org/10.1207/S15327671ESPR0601-2_7

González, N., Moll, L. C., & Amanti, C. (Eds.). (2005). *Funds of knowledge: Theorizing practices in households, communities, and classrooms*. Routledge.

Graue, E., Whyte, K., & Delaney, K. K. (2014). Fostering culturally and developmentally responsive teaching through improvisational practice. *Journal of Early Childhood Teacher Education, 35*(4), 297–317. https://eric.ed.gov/?id=EJ1044965

Gray-Lobe, G., Pathak, P., & Walters, C. (2021). *The long-term effects of universal preschool in Boston* (Discussion Paper No. 2021.05). MIT Department of Economics and National Bureau of Economic Research. https://seii.mit.edu/wp-content/uploads/2021/05/210503_Boston-Pre-K_One-Pager_v12.pdf

Greenfield, D. B., Alexander, A., & Frechette, E. (2017). Unleashing the power of science in early childhood. *Zero to Three, 37*(5), 13–21. http://www.mothergooseprograms.org/wp-content/uploads/2017/07/Unleashing-the-Power-of-Science-Zero-to-Three.pdf

Grisham, J., & Hemmeter, M. L. (2017). *Blended practices for teaching young children in inclusive settings*. Brookes Publishing. http://ebookcentral.proquest.com/lib/du/detail.action?docID=4787826

Guarrella, C., Cohrssen, C., & van Driel, J. (2021). The quality of teacher–child interactions during the enactment of playful science games in preschool. *Early Education and Development, 33*(4), 634–654. https://doi.org/10.1080/10409289.2021.1900993

Gunter, L., Caldarella, P., Korth, B., & Young, K. R. (2012). Promoting social and emotional learning in preschool students: A study of Strong Start Pre-K. *Early Childhood Education Journal, 40*(3), 151–159. https://doi.org/10.1007/s10643-012-0507-z

Ha, V. T., Hai, B. M., Mai, D. T. T., & Van Hanh, N. (2023). Preschool STEM activities and associated outcomes: A scoping review. *International Journal of Engineering Pedagogy, 13*(8). https://doi.org/10.3991/ijep.v13i8.42177

Halvorsen, A.-L., Duke, N. K., Brugar, K. A., Block, M. K., Strachan, S. L., Berka, M. B., & Brown, J. M. (2012). Narrowing the achievement gap in second-grade social studies and content area literacy: The promise of a project-based approach. *Theory & Research in Social Education, 40*(3), 198–229. https://doi.org/10.1080/00933104.2012.705954

Hanby, K. (2018). *Teachers' formative assessment practices for early addition and subtraction: Is teachers' awareness of a learning trajectory related to how they respond to students?* [Doctoral dissertation, University of Michigan]. Ann Arbor, MI.

Harry, B., & Klingner, J. (2014). *Why are so many minority students in special education?: Understanding race and disability in schools*. Teachers College Press.

Hart, E. R., Bailey, D. H., Luo, S., Sengupta, P., & Watts, T. W. (2023). *Do intervention impacts on social-emotional skills persist at higher rates than impacts on cognitive skills? A meta-analysis of educational RCTs with follow-up* (EdWorkingPaper No. 23-782). Annenberg Institute at Brown University. https://doi.org/10.26300/7j8s-dy98

Hartle, L. C. (2020). Technology and young children. In L. Cohen & S. Waite-Stupiansky (Eds.), *STEM in early childhood education: How science, technology, engineering, and mathematics strengthen learning* (pp. 22–45). Routledge.

Hartman, J. R., Hart, S., Nelson, E. A., & Kirschner, P. A. (2023). Designing mathematics standards in agreement with science. *International Electronic Journal of Mathematics Education, 18*(3), em0739. https://doi.org/10.29333/iejme/13179

Haywood, H. C. (2004). Thinking in, around, and about the curriculum: The role of cognitive education. *International Journal of Disability Development and Education, 51*(3), 231–252.

Head Start Early Childhood Learning & Knowledge Center (ECLKC). (2020). *Curriculum consumer report: Preschool.* National Center on Early Childhood Development, Teaching, and Learning. https://eclkc.ohs.acf.hhs.gov/sites/default/files/featured_file/preschool-curriculum-consumer-report-032519.pdf

———. (2023). *Head Start Early Learning Outcomes Framework: Ages Birth to Five.* U.S. Department of Health & Human Services, Administration for Children & Families. https://eclkc.ohs.acf.hhs.gov/school-readiness/article/head-start-early-learning-outcomes-framework

Heasty, M., McLaughlin, T. F., Williams, R. L., & Keenan, B. (2012). The effects of using direct instruction mathematics formats to teach basic math skills to a third grade student with a learning disability. *Academic Research International, 2*(3), 382–387. http://www.savap.org.pk/journals/ARInt./Vol.2(3)/2012(2.3-47).pdf

Heath, S. B. (1983/1996). *Ways with words: Language, life, and work in communities and classrooms.* Cambridge University Press.

———. (1989). Oral and literate traditions among Black Americans living in poverty. *American Psychologist, 44*(2), 367–373. https://psycnet.apa.org/doi/10.1037/0003-066X.44.2.367

Hebbeler, K., & Spiker, D. (2016). Supporting young children with disabilities. *The Future of Children, 26*(2), 185–205. https://eric.ed.gov/?id=EJ1118562

Heck, D. J., Chval, K. B., Weiss, I. R., & Ziebarth, S. W. (Eds.). (2012). *Approaches to studying the enacted mathematics curriculum.* Information Age.

Helenius, O. (2017). *Theorizing professional modes of action for teaching preschool mathematics.* 17th Nordic Conference on Mathematics Education, Stockholm, Sweden.

Helenius, O. (2018). Explicating professional modes of action for teaching preschool mathematics. *Research in Mathematics Education, 20*(2), 183–199. https://doi.org/10.1080/14794802.2018.1473161

Helenius, O., Johansson, M. L., Lange, T., Meaney, T., & Wernberg, A. (2016). Measuring temperature within the didaktic space of preschool. *Nordic Studies in Mathematics Education, 21*(4), 155–176. http://ncm.gu.se/nomad

Helm, J. H., & Katz, L. G. (2016). *Young investigators: The project approach in the early years* (3rd ed.). Teachers College Press.

Helm, J. H., & Snider, K. A. (Eds.). (2020). *Growing child intellect: The manifesto for engaged learning in the early years.* Teachers College Press.

Hemmeter, M. L., Fox, L., & Snyder, P. (2013). A tiered model for promoting social-emotional competence and addressing challenging behavior. In V. Buysse & E. Peisner-Feinberg (Eds.), *Handbook of response to intervention in early childhood* (pp. 85–101). Brookes Publishing.

Hemmeter, M. L., Ostrosky, M., & Fox, L. (2006). Social and emotional foundations for early learning: A conceptual model for intervention. *School Psychology Review, 35*(4), 583–601. https://psycnet.apa.org/record/2006-22260-005

Hemmeter, M., Snyder, P., Fox, L., & Algina, J. (2016). Evaluating the implementation of the "Pyramid Model for Promoting Social-Emotional Competence" in early childhood classrooms. *Topics in Early Childhood Special Education, 36*(3), 133–146. https://eric.ed.gov/?id=EJ1117049

Hendrick, J. (Ed.). (1997). *First steps toward teaching the Reggio way.* Prentice Hall.

Herodotou, C. (2018). Young children and tablets: A systematic review of effects on learning and development. *Journal of Computer Assisted Learning, 34*(1), 1–9. https://doi.org/10.1111/jcal.12220

Herrmann-Abell, C. F., Koppal, M., & Roseman, J. E. (2016). Toward high school biology: Helping middle school students understand chemical reactions and conservation of mass in non-living and living systems. *CBE—Life Sciences Education, 15*(ar74), 1–21. https://doi.org/10.1187/cbe.16-03-0112

Hiebert, J. C., & Grouws, D. A. (2007). The effects of classroom mathematics teaching on students' learning. In F. K. Lester, Jr. (Ed.), *Second handbook of research on mathematics teaching and learning* (Vol. 1, pp. 371–404). Information Age.

Hill, H. C. (2020). Does studying student data really raise test scores? *EdWeek*. https://www.edweek.org/technology/opinion-does-studying-student-data-really-raise-test-scores/2020/02

Hilty, R., Boddicker-Young, P., Hegseth, D., Thompson, J., Bultinck, E., Fojut, J., & Early, D. (2021). *Understanding equitable access to public Montessori pre-K: A case study of Montessori recruitment and enrollment practices*. Child Trends.

Hirsh-Pasek, K., & Golinkoff, R. M. (2008). Why play = learning. In R. E. Tremblay, R. G. Barr, R. D. Peters, & M. Boivin (Eds.), *Encyclopedia on early childhood development* (pp. 1–7). Centre of Excellence for Early Childhood Development. www.child-encyclopedia.com/pages/PDF/Hirsh-Pasek-GolinkoffANGxp.pdf

Hirsh-Pasek, K., Golinkoff, R. M., Berk, L. E., & Singer, D. G. (2009). *A mandate for playful learning in preschool: Presenting the evidence*. Oxford University Press.

Hjalmarson, M. A., & Baker, C. K. (2020). Mathematics specialists as the hidden players in professional development: Researchable questions and methodological considerations. *International Journal of Science and Mathematics Education*, 18, 51–66. https://doi.org/10.1007/s10763-020-10077-7

Hojnoski, R. L., Caskie, G. I. L., & Miller Young, R. (2018). Early numeracy trajectories: Baseline performance levels and growth rates in young children by disability status. *Topics in Early Childhood Special Education*, 37(4), 206–218. https://doi.org/10.1177/0271121417735901

Hong, S. B., Broderick, J. T., & McAuliffe, C. M. (2021). Drawing to learn: A classroom case study. *Early Childhood Education Journal*, 49, 15–25. https://eric.ed.gov/?id=EJ1280218

Hsin, C.-T., Li, M.-C., & Tsai, C.-C. (2014). The influence of young children's use of technology on their learning: A review. *Educational Technology & Society*, 17(4), 85–99. https://eric.ed.gov/?id=EJ1045554

Hwang, H., & Duke, N. K. (2020). Content counts and motivation matters: Reading comprehension in third-grade students who are English Learners. *AERA Open*, 6(1). https://doi.org/10.1177/2332858419899075

Ikram, H. (2017). Effect of teachers' professional development in media technology on preschoolers learning in rural settings. In J. Johnston (Ed.), *Proceedings of EdMedia 2017* (pp. 509–513). Association for the Advancement of Computing in Education. https://www.learntechlib.org/primary/p/178355/

Institute of Education Sciences (IES). (2007). *Dialogic reading: WWC Intervention Report*. What Works Clearinghouse; U.S. Department of Education. https://ies.ed.gov/ncee/wwc/Docs/InterventionReports/WWC_Dialogic_Reading_020807.pdf

———. (2013). *Doors to Discovery: WWC Intervention Report*. What Works Clearinghouse; U.S. Department of Education. https://ies.ed.gov/ncee/WWC/Docs/InterventionReports/wwc_doors_062513.pdf

Institute of Medicine (IOM) & National Research Council (NRC). (2010). *Preventing mental, emotional, and behavioral disorders among young people: Progress and possibilities*. The National Academies Press.

———. (2015). *Transforming the workforce for children birth through age 8: A unifying foundation*. The National Academies Press. www.nap.edu/catalog/19401/transforming-the-workforce-for-children-birth-through-age-8-a

International Literacy Association. (2018). *What effective pre-K literacy instruction looks like: Literacy leadership brief*. International Literacy Association. https://www.literacyworldwide.org/docs/default-source/where-we-stand/ila-what-effective-pre-k-literacy-instruction-looks-like.pdf

Iruka, I. U. (2024). Advancing equity in early childhood education research. In J. J. Mueller, N. File, A. J. Stremmel, I. U. Iruka, & K. L. Whyte, *Understanding research in early childhood education* (p. 12). Routledge. https://doi.org/10.4324/9781003354499-4

Iruka, I. U., Gardner-Neblett, N., Telfer, N. A., Ibekwe-Okafor, N., Curenton, S. M., Sims, J., Sansbury, A. B., & Neblett, E. W. (2022). Effects of racism on child development: Advancing antiracist developmental science. *Annual Review of Developmental Psychology, 4*, 109–132. https://doi.org/10.1146/annurev-devpsych-121020-031339

Iruka, I. U., Kainz, K., Kuhn, L., Guss, S., Tokarz, S., Yazejian, N., & Niño, S. (2023). Early education program racial and ethnic composition and associations with quality and children's language and social-emotional development. *Early Education and Development, 34*(6), 1341–1360. https://doi.org/10.1080/10409289.2022.2139553

Jagers, R., Rivas-Drake, D., & Williams, B. (2019). Transformative social and emotional learning (SEL): Toward SEL in service of educational equity and excellence. *Educational Psychologist, 54*(3), 162–184. https://doi.org/10.1080/00461520.2019.1623032

Jaggy, A. K., Kalkusch, I., Bossi, C. B., Weiss, B., Sticca, F., & Perren, S. (2023). The impact of social pretend play on preschoolers' social development: Results of an experimental study. *Early Childhood Research Quarterly, 64*, 13–25. https://psycnet.apa.org/doi/10.1016/j.ecresq.2023.01.012

Jen, J., Oscar, K., & Anna, R. (2023). *Early childhood learning trajectories: The evidence base.* Australian Education Research Organisation. https://doi.org/https://doi.org/APO-323253

Jenkins, J. M., Duncan, G. J., Auger, A., Bitler, M. P., Domina, T., & Burchinal, M. R. (2018). Boosting school readiness: Should preschool teachers target skills or the whole child? *Economic of Education Review, 65*, 107–125. https://doi.org/10.1016/j.econedurev.2018.05.001

Jiang, H., Justice, L. M., Lin, T.-J., Purtell, K. M., & Sun, J. (2023). Peer experiences in the preschool classroom: Contribution to Children's academic development. *Journal of Applied Developmental Psychology, 86*, 101542. https://doi.org/10.1016/j.appdev.2023.101542

John, M.-S., Sibuma, B., Wunnava, S., Anggoro, F., & Dubosarsky, M. (2018). An iterative participatory approach to developing an early childhood problem-based STEM curriculum. *European Journal of STEM Education, 3*(3), 7. https://doi.org/10.20897/ejsteme/3867

Johnson, L. L., Boutte, G., Greene, G., & Smith, D. (Eds.). (2019). *African diaspora literacy: The heart of transformation in K-12 schools and teacher education.* Lexington Books.

Johnston, L. J. (2018). *Education self-determination superstars: Cochiti Pueblo takes on language-learning.* Indian Country Media Network.

Jones, C. P. (2014). Systems of power, axes of inequity: Parallels, intersections, braiding the strands. *Medical Care, 52*(10), S71–S75. http://www.jstor.org/stable/24465890

Jones, E., & Nimmo, J. (1994). *Emergent curriculum.* National Association for the Education of Young Children.

Joseph, G. E., & Strain, P. S. (2010). Teaching young children interpersonal problem-solving skills. *Young Exceptional Children, 13*(3), 28–40.

Joseph, G. E., Yates, T., & Ostrosky, M. (2021). Strategies to foster emotional literacy. In M. L. Hemmeter, M. M. Ostrosky, & L. Fox (Eds.), *Unpacking the Pyramid Model: A practical guide for preschool teachers* (pp. 131–140). Brookes Publishing.

Judge, S. (2005). The impact of computer technology on academic achievement of young African American children. *Journal of Research in Childhood Education, 20*(2), 91–101.

Justice, L. M., Chow, S.-M., Capellini, C., Flanigan, K., & Colton, S. (2015). Emergent literacy intervention for vulnerable preschoolers: Relative effects of two approaches. *Journal of Educational Psychology, 107*(2), 558–576. https://doi.org/10.1037/edu0000007

Kagan, S. L., & Reid, J. L. (2022). Reaching for consensus about preschool curricula. *Kappan, 104*(2), 50–55. https://kappanonline.org/consensus-preschool-curricula-reid-kagan/

Kang, C. Y., Duncan, G. J., Clements, D. H., Sarama, J., & Bailey, D. H. (2019). The roles of transfer of learning and forgetting in the persistence and fadeout of early childhood mathematics interventions. *Journal of Educational Psychology*, *111*(4), 590–603. https://doi.org/10.1037/edu0000297

Karademir, A., & Akman, B. (2021). Preschool inquiry-based mathematics in practice: Perspectives of teachers and parents. *Journal of Qualitative Research in Education*, *25*, 151–178. https://doi.org/10.14689/enad.25.7

Karaya, N. N. (2022). *A case study examining how teachers and parents provide strategies that nurture the academic and social development of young Black children in low-socioeconomic communities* [Doctoral dissertation, Liberty University]. Lynchburg, VA.

Katz, L. G., Chard, S. C., & Kogan, Y. (2014). *Engaging children's minds: The project approach* (3rd ed.). Praeger. http://publisher.abc-clio.com/9781440828447

Kim, C., Yuan, J., Gleasman, C., Shin, M., & Hill, R. B. (2017). Preparing pre-service early childhood teachers to teach mathematics with robots. In B. K. Smith, M. Borge, E. Mercier, & K. Y. Lim (Eds.), *Making a difference: Prioritizing equity and access in CSCL* (Vol. 2). 12th International Conference on Computer Supported Collaborative Learning, Philadelphia, PA. International Society of the Learning Sciences. https://doi.org/10.22318/cscl2017.92

Kimpston, R. D., & Rogers, K. B. (1986). A framework for curriculum research. *Curriculum Inquiry*, *16*(4), 463–474. https://eric.ed.gov/?id=EJ343797

Kinzie, M. B., Whittaker, J. V., McGuire, P., Lee, Y., & Kilday, C. (2015). Research on curricular development for pre-kindergarten mathematics and science. *Teachers College Record*, *117*(7), 1–40. https://doi.org/10.1177/016146811511700705

Kinzie, M. B., Whittaker, J. V., Williford, A. P., DeCoster, J., McGuire, P., Lee, Y., & Kilday, C. R. (2014). "MyTeachingPartner—Math/Science" pre-kindergarten curricula and teacher supports: Associations with children's mathematics and science learning. *Grantee Submission*, *29*, 586–599.

Klein, A., Starkey, P., & Deflorio, L. (2019). Improving the mathematical knowledge of at-risk preschool children: Two approaches to intensifying early math intervention. In D. C. Geary, D. B. Berch, & K. M. Koepke (Eds.), *Cognitive foundations for improving mathematical learning* (Vol. 5, pp. 215–245). Elsevier. https://doi.org/10.1016/B978-0-12-815952-1.00009-8

Knapp, M. S., Shields, P. M., & Turnbull, B. J. (1992). *Academic challenge for the children of poverty*. U.S. Department of Education. https://eric.ed.gov/?id=ED353355

Knaus, M. J. (2017). Supporting early mathematics learning in early childhood settings. *Australasian Journal of Early Childhood*, *42*(3), 4–13. https://doi.org/10.23965/AJEC.42.3.01

Koç, K., Koç, Y., & Albayrak, S. B. (2023). Exploring early childhood teachers' differentiation practices in teaching mathematics with learning trajectories. In M. Licardo, J. Mezak, & I. E. Gencel (Eds.), *Teaching for the future in early childhood education* (pp. 77–94). University of Maribor University Press. https://doi.org/10.18690/um.pef.2.2023

Kramer, T., Caldarella, P., Christensen, L., & Shatzer, R. (2010). Social and emotional learning in the kindergarten classroom: Evaluation of the strong start curriculum. *Early Childhood Education Journal*, *37*(4), 303–309. https://doi.org/10.1007/s10643-009-0354-8

Kreskey, D. D., & Truscott, S. D. (2016). Is computer-aided instruction an effective tier-one intervention for kindergarten students at risk for reading failure in an applied setting? *Contemporary School Psychology*, *20*(2), 142–151. https://eric.ed.gov/?id=EJ1099524

La Paro, K. M., Hamre, B. K., Locasale-Crouch, J., Pianta, R. C., Bryant, D., Early, D. M., Clifford, R. M., Barbarin, O. A., Howes, C., & Burchinal, M. R. (2009). Quality in kindergarten classrooms: Observational evidence for the need to increase children's learning opportunities in early education classrooms. *Early Education and Development*, *20*(4), 657–692. https://doi.org/10.1080/10409280802541965

Ladson-Billings, G. (1994). *The dreamkeepers: Successful teachers of African American children*. Jossey-Bass.

———. (1995). But that's just good teaching! The case for culturally relevant pedagogy. *Theory Into Practice*, 34(3), 159–165. https://theavarnagroup.com/wp-content/uploads/2015/11/But-thats-just-good-teaching.pdf

Lagemann, E. C. (1997). Contested terrain: A history of education research in the United States, 1890–1990. *Educational Researcher*, 26(9), 5–17. http://www.jstor.org/stable/1176271

Lai, Y., Carlson, M. A., & Heaton, R. M. (2018). Giving reason and giving purpose. In Y. Li, W. J. Lewis, & J. J. Madden (Eds.), *Mathematics matters in education: Essays in honor of Roger E. Howe* (pp. 149–171). Springer International Publishing. https://doi.org/10.1007/978-3-319-61434-2_7

Langub, L., & Warner, M. (2018). *Fostering digital literacy development with elementary & early childhood educators*. Society for Information Technology & Teacher Education International Conference, Washington, DC.

Larkin, K., Lommatsch, C., Resnick, I., & Lowrie, T. (2022). The design and use of a digital tool to support the development of preschool children's logical reasoning. *Journal of Research on Technology in Education*, 55(6), 1080–1093. https://doi.org/10.1080/15391523.2022.2107590

Le, V.-N., Schaack, D., Neishi, K., Hernandez, M. W., & Blank, R. K. (2019). Advanced content coverage at kindergarten: Are there trade-offs between academic achievement and social-emotional skills? *American Educational Research Journal*, 56(4), 1254–1280. https://doi.org/10.3102/0002831218813913

Lee, C. D., Lomotey, K., & Shujaa, M. J. (1990). How shall we sing our sacred song in a strange land? The dilemma of double-consciousness and the complexities of an African-center pedagogy. *Journal of Education*, 172(2), 45–61.

Lee, J. S., & Ginsburg, H. P. (2007). Preschool teachers' beliefs about appropriate early literacy and mathematics education for low-and middle-socioeconomic status children. *Early Education and Development*, 18(1), 111–143. https://psycnet.apa.org/doi/10.1080/10409280701274758

Lehrl, S., Kluczniok, K., Rossbach, H.-G., & Anders, Y. (2017). Longer-term effects of a high-quality preschool intervention on children's mathematical development through age 12: Results from the German model project Kindergarten of the Future in Bavaria. *Global Education Review*, 4(3), 70–87. https://files.eric.ed.gov/fulltext/EJ1158198.pdf

Lei, Q., & Xin, Y. P. (2023). A synthesis of mathematical word problem-solving instructions for English learners with learning disabilities in mathematics. *Review of Education*, 11(2), e3396. https://doi.org/10.1002/rev3.3396

Lentz, C. L., Seo, K. K. J., & Gruner, B. (2014). Revisiting the early use of technology: A critical shift from "how young is too young?" to "how much is 'just right'?" *Dimensions of Early Childhood*, 42(1), 15–23. https://www.learntechlib.org/p/154937/

LeSage, A., & Ruttenberg-Rozen, R. (2021). "More gooder": Children evaluate early numeracy apps. In M. van den Heuvel-Panhuizen & A. Kullberg (Eds.), *Mathematics education at preschool level: Proceedings of the 14th International Congress on Mathematical Education* (pp. 89–93). https://www.icme14.org/ueditor/jsp/upload/file/20210718/1626607224969048865.pdf

Leung, W. M. V. (2023). STEM education in early years: Challenges and opportunities in changing teachers' pedagogical strategies. *Education Sciences*, 13(5), 490. https://doi.org/10.3390/educsci13050490

Lewis, C. C., Perry, R., & Murata, A. (2006). How should research contribute to instructional improvement? The case of lesson study. *Educational Researcher*, 35(3), 3–14. http://dx.doi.org/10.3102/0013189X035003003

Lewis, T. J., Adamson, R., Mitchell, B. S., & Lembke, E. S. (2013). An overview of program-wide positive behavior supports: Building a comprehensive continuum of early social behavior supports for at-risk children. In V. Buysse & E. S. Peisner-Feinberg (Eds.), *Handbook of response to intervention in early childhood* (pp. 57–68). Brookes Publishing.

Lewis Presser, A., Clements, M., Ginsburg, H. P., & Ertle, B. (2015). Big Math for Little Kids: The effectiveness of a preschool and kindergarten mathematics curriculum. *Early Education and Development, 26*(3), 399–426. https://doi.org/10.1080/10409289.2015.994451

Li, X., Atkins, M. S., & Stanton, B. (2006). Effects of home and school computer use on school readiness and cognitive development among Head Start children: A randomized controlled pilot trial. *Merrill-Palmer Quarterly, 52*(2), 239–263. http://dx.doi.org/10.1353/mpq.2006.0010

Li, Y., Howe, R. E., Lewis, W. J., & Madden, J. J. (Eds.). (2021). *Developing mathematical proficiency for elementary instruction*. Springer. https://doi.org/10.1007/978-3-030-68956-8

Lieber, J., Hanson, M., Butera, G., Palmer, S., Horn, E., & Czaja, C. (2010). Do preschool teachers sustain their use of a new curriculum? *NHSA Dialog: A Research-to-Practice Journal for the Early Intervention Field, 13*(4), 248–252. https://eric.ed.gov/?id=EJ904198

Lillard, A. S. (2012). Preschool children's development in classic Montessori, supplemented Montessori, and conventional programs. *Journal of School Psychology, 50*, 379–401. https://doi.org/10.1016/j.jsp.2012.01.001

———. (2013). Playful learning and Montessori education. *American Journal of Play, 5*(2), 157–186. https://files.eric.ed.gov/fulltext/EJ1077161.pdf

Lillard, A. S., Heise, M. J., Richey, E. M., Tong, X., Hart, A., & Bry, P. M. (2017). Montessori preschool elevates and equalizes child outcomes: A longitudinal study. *Frontiers in Psychology, 8*, 1783. https://doi.org/10.3389/fpsyg.2017.01783

Lillard, A. S., Lerner, M. D., Hopkins, E. J., Dore, R. A., Smith, E. D., & Palmquist, C. M. (2013). The impact of pretend play on children's development: A review of the evidence. *Psychological Bulletin, 139*(1), 1. https://psycnet.apa.org/doi/10.1037/a0029321

Lillard, A. S., Tong, X., & Bray, P. M. (2023). Seeking racial and ethnic parity in preschool outcomes: An exploratory study of public Montessori schools vs. business-as-usual schools. *Journal of Montessori Research, 9*(1), 16–36. https://files.eric.ed.gov/fulltext/EJ1390782.pdf

Lindahl, M. G., & Folkesson, A. M. (2012). Can we let computers change practice? Educators' interpretations of preschool tradition. *Computers in Human Behavior, 28*(5), 1728–1737. http://dx.doi.org/10.1016/j.chb.2012.04.012

Lipka, J., & Adams, B. (2002). *Improving Alaska Native rural and urban students' mathematical understanding of perimeter and area* [Unpublished manuscript]. Alaska School Research Fund.

List, J., Cappelen, A. W., Tungodden, B., & Samek, A. (2020). The effect of early childhood education on social preferences. *Journal of Political Economy, 128*(7). https://doi.org/10.1086/706858

Little, M., & Gragson, A. (2023). State leaders in early childhood education: Perspectives on instructional policy supports and alignment. *Early Childhood Research Quarterly, 63*, 288–298. https://doi.org/10.1016/j.ecresq.2022.12.016

Lloyd, G. M., Cai, J., & Tarr, J. E. (2017). Issues in curriculum studies: Evidence-based insights and future directions. In J. Cai (Ed.), *Compendium for research in mathematics education* (pp. 824–852). National Council of Teachers of Mathematics.

Lohfink, G., & Loya, J. (2010). The nature of Mexican American third graders' engagement with culturally relevant picture books. *Bilingual Research Journal, 3*(3), 346–363. https://eric.ed.gov/?id=EJ907099

Lonigan, C. J., & Phillips, B. M. (2012, March). *Comparing skills-focused and self-regulation focused preschool curricula: Impacts on academic and self-regulatory skills*. Paper presented at the Society for Research on Educational Effectiveness, Washington, DC.

Lonigan, C. J., Farver, J. M., Clancy-Menchetti, J., & Phillips, B. M. (2005). Promoting the development of preschool children's emergent literacy skills: A randomized evaluation of a literacy-focused curriculum and two professional development models. *Child Development, 80*(3), 703–719. http://dx.doi.org/10.1007/s11145-009-9214-6

Lonigan, C. J., Farver, J. M., Phillips, B.M., & Clancy-Menchetti, J. (2011). Promoting the development of preschool children's emergent literacy skills: A randomized evaluation of literacy-focused curriculum and two professional development models. *Reading and Writing: An Interdisciplinary Journal, 24*, 305–337. http://dx.doi.org/10.1007/s11145-009-9214-6

Lynch, K. B. (1998). *Results of Michigan Replication Study 1996-97: Child outcomes.* Al's Pals: Kids Making Healthy Choices. Virginia Institute for Development Disabilities, Virginia Commonwealth University.

Lynch, K. B., Geller, S. R., & Schmidt, M. G. (2004). Multi-year evaluation of the effectiveness of a resilience-based prevention program for young children. *Journal of Primary Prevention, 24*(3), 335–353. https://psycnet.apa.org/doi/10.1023/B:JOPP.0000018052.12488.d1

Ma, L. (1999). *Knowing and teaching elementary mathematics: Teachers' understanding of fundamental mathematics in China and the United States.* Erlbaum.

Ma, L., & Kessel, C. (2018). The theory of school arithmetic: Whole numbers. In M. G. Bartolini Bussi & X. H. Sun (Eds.), *Building the foundation: Whole numbers in the primary grades: The 23rd ICMI study* (pp. 439–463). Springer International Publishing. https://doi.org/10.1007/978-3-319-63555-2_9

Major, S. O., Gaspar, M. F., Palos, A. C., & Pereira, M. D. (2024). Effectiveness of the Incredible Years® Teacher Classroom Management program: Preschool children's outcomes. *Journal of Applied Developmental Psychology, 90*. https://doi.org/10.1016/j.appdev.2023.101616

Malik, R., Hamm, K., Schochet, L., Novoa, C., Workman, S., & Jessen-Howard, S. (2018). *America's child care deserts in 2018.* Center for American Progress. https://www.americanprogress.org/article/americas-child-care-deserts-2018

Maloney, A. P., Confrey, J., & Nguyen, K. H. (Eds.). (2014). *Learning over time: Learning trajectories in mathematics education.* Information Age.

Mantzicopoulos, P., & Patrick, H. (2011). Reading picture books and learning science: Engaging young children with informational text. *Theory Into Practice, 50*(4), 269–276. www.tandfonline.com/doi/abs/10.1080/00405841.2011.607372

Marklund, L. (2015). Preschool teachers' informal online professional development in relation to educational use of tablets in Swedish preschools. *Professional Development in Education, 41*(2), 236–253. http://dx.doi.org/10.1080/19415257.2014.999380

Marks, A. K., & García Coll, C. (2018). Education and developmental competencies of ethnic minority children: Recent theoretical and methodological advances. *Developmental Review, 50*, 90–98. http://dx.doi.org/10.1016/j.dr.2018.05.004

Marti, M., Melvin, S., Noble, K. G., & Duch, H. (2018). Intervention fidelity of Getting Ready for School: Associations with classroom and teacher characteristics and preschooler's school readiness skills. *Early Childhood Research Quarterly, 44*, 55–71. https://doi.org/10.1016/j.ecresq.2018.02.010

Martin, D. B. (2007). Mathematics learning and participation in the African American context: The co-construction of identity in two intersecting realms of experience. In N. S. Nasir & P. Cobb (Eds.), *Improving access to mathematics: Diversity and equity in the classroom* (pp. 146–158). Teachers College Press.

———. (2009). Researching race in mathematics education. *Teachers College Record, 111*(2), 295–338. http://dx.doi.org/10.1177/016146810911100208

Maryland State Department of Education. (2024). *Maryland early learning standards.* https://marylandpublicschools.org/Documents/MD-EarlyLearning-Standards-2024-a.pdf

Mattera, S. K., Jacob, R., MacDowell, C., & Morris, P. A. (2021a). *Long-term effects of enhanced early childhood math instruction: The impacts of Making Pre-K Count and High 5s on third-grade outcomes.* MDRC. https://www.mdrc.org/publication/long-term-effects-enhanced-early-childhood-math-instruction

Mattera, S. K., Rojas, N. M., Morris, P. A., & Bierman, K. (2021b). Promoting EF with preschool interventions: Lessons learned from 15 years of conducting large-scale studies. *Frontiers in Psychology, 12,* 1–20. https://doi.org/10.3389/fpsyg.2021.640702

Maxwell, K., Yi, P., Kraus, S., & Hume, K. (2013). *Evaluation findings from Georgia's 2012 Pre-K Summer Transition Program.* FPG Child Development Institute, The University of North Carolina at Chapel Hill. https://www.decal.ga.gov/documents/attachments/2012STPReport.pdf

McClelland, M. M., Tominey, S. L., Schmitt, S. A., & Duncan, R. (2017). SEL interventions in early childhood. *The Future of Children, 27*(1), 33–48. https://files.eric.ed.gov/fulltext/EJ1145093.pdf

McClelland, M. M., Tominey, S. L., Schmitt, S. A., Hatfield, B. E., Purpura, D. J., Gonzales, C. R., & Tracy, A. N. (2019). Red light, purple light! Results of an intervention to promote school readiness for children from low-income backgrounds. *Frontiers in Psychology, 10,* 2365. https://doi.org/10.3389/fpsyg.2019.02365

McCormick, M. P., Weiland, C., Hsueh, J., Maier, M. F., Hagos, R., Snow, C. E., Leacock, N., & Schick, L. (2019). Promoting content-enriched alignment across the early grades: A study of policies & practices in the Boston Public Schools. *Early Childhood Research Quarterly, 52,* 57–73. https://doi.org/https://doi.org/10.1016/j.ecresq.2019.06.012

McIntosh, K., & Goodman, S. (2016). *Integrated multi-tiered systems of support: Blending RTI and PBIS.* Guilford Publications.

McIntosh, K., Girvan, E. J., Fairbanks Falcon, S., McDaniel, S. C., Smolkowski, K., Bastable, E., Santiago-Rosario, M. R., Izzard, S., Austin, S. C., Nese, R. N. T., & Baldy, T. S. (2021). Equity-focused PBIS approach reduces racial inequities in school discipline: A randomized controlled trial. *School Psychology, 36*(6), 433–444. https://doi.org/10.1037/spq0000466

Meaney, T. (2018). Mathematics curricula: Issues of access and quality. In M. Jurdak & R. Vithal (Eds.), *Sociopolitical dimensions of mathematics education: From the margin to mainstream* (pp. 171–189). Springer International Publishing. https://doi.org/10.1007/978-3-319-72610-6_10

Merkley, R., & Ansari, D. (2018). *Foundations for learning: Guided play for early years maths education.* Chartered College of Teaching. https://my.chartered.college/impact_article/foundations-for-learning-guided-play-for-early-years-maths-education/

Messick, S. (1989). Validity. In R. L. Linn (Ed.), *Educational measurement* (3rd ed., pp. 13–103). Macmillan.

Mesutoglu, C., & Corlu, M. S. (2023). The earlySTEM Program: An evaluation through teacher perceptions. *Canadian Journal of Science, Mathematics and Technology Education, 23,* 145–160. https://doi.org/10.1007/s42330-023-00264-3

Moffett, L., Weissman, A., Weiland, C., McCormick, M., Hsueh, J., Snow, C., & Sachs, J. (2021). Unpacking pre-K classroom organization: Types, variation, and links to school readiness gains. *Journal of Applied Developmental Psychology, 77,* 101346. https://doi.org/10.1016/j.appdev.2021.101346

Moll, L. C., Amanti, C., Neff, D., & Gonzalez, N. (1992). Funds of knowledge for teaching: Using a qualitative approach to connect homes and classrooms. *Theory Into Practice, 31,* 132–141. https://doi.org/10.1080/00405849209543534

Moore, T. J., Selcen Guzey, S., Roehrig, G. H., & Lesh, R. A. (2018). Representational fluency: A means for students to develop STEM literacy. In K. L. Daniel (Ed.), *Towards a framework for representational competence in science education* (pp. 13–30). Springer International Publishing. https://doi.org/10.1007/978-3-319-89945-9_2

Morgan, P. L., Farkas, G., Hillemeier, M. M., Pun, W. H., & Maczuga, S. (2018). Kindergarten children's executive functions predict their second-grade academic achievement and behavior. *Child Development*, 90(5), 1802–1816. https://doi.org/10.1111/cdev.13095

Morris, P. A., Mattera, S. K., Castells, N., Bangser, M., Bierman, K. L., & Raver, C. C. (2014). *Impact findings from the Head Start CARES Demonstration: National evaluation of three approaches to improving preschoolers' social and emotional competence* (OPRE Report No. 2014-44). Office of Planning, Research and Evaluation, Administration for Children and Families, U.S. Department of Health and Human Services.

Muhammad, G. (2023). *Unearthing joy: A guide to culturally and historically responsive teaching and learning*. Scholastic.

Mulcahy, C., Day Hess, C. A., Clements, D. H., Ernst, J. R., Pan, S. E., Mazzocco, M. M. M., & Sarama, J. (2021). Supporting young children's development of executive function through early mathematics. *Policy Insights from the Behavioral and Brain Sciences*, 8(2), 192–199. https://doi.org/10.1177/23727322211033005

Mulligan, J. T., Oslington, G., & English, L. D. (2020). Supporting early mathematical development through a "pattern and structure" intervention program. *ZDM Mathematics Education*, 52(4), 663–676. https://doi.org/10.1007/s11858-020-01147-9

Munter, C., Cobb, P., & Shekell, C. (2016). The role of program theory in evaluation research: A consideration of the What Works Clearinghouse standards in the case of mathematics education. *American Journal of Evaluation*, 37(1), 7–26. https://doi.org/10.1177/1098214015571122

Murphy, K. A., Pentimonti, J. M., & Chow, J. C. (2023). Supporting children's language and literacy through collaborative shared book reading. *Intervention in School and Clinic*, 58(3), 155–163. http://dx.doi.org/10.1177/10534512221081218

Myran, S. P., Richardson, R. C., & Stonelson, S. (2009). Teaching social and emotional competence in early childhood. *International Journal of Special Education*, 24(3), 143–149. https://digitalcommons.odu.edu/cdse_pubs/2

National Academies of Sciences, Engineering, and Medicine (National Academies). (2016). *Parenting matters: Supporting parents of children ages 0–8*. The National Academies Press. https://doi.org/10.17226/21868

———. (2017). *Promoting the educational success of children and youth learning English: Promising futures*. National Academies Press. https://doi.org/10.17226/24677

———. (2018a). *English learners in STEM subjects: Transforming classrooms, schools, and lives*. National Academies Press. https://doi.org/10.17226/25182

———. (2018b). *How people learn II: Learners, contexts, and cultures*. National Academies Press. https://doi.org/10.17226/24783

———. (2020). *Changing expectations for the K-12 teacher workforce: Policies, preservice education, professional development, and the workplace*. National Academies Press. https://doi.org/10.17226/25603

———. (2022). *Science and engineering in preschool through elementary grades: The brilliance of children and the strengths of educators*. National Academies Press. https://doi.org/10.17226/25912

———. (2023). *Reducing intergenerational poverty*. National Academies Press. https://doi.org/10.17226/27058

National Association for the Education of Young Children (NAEYC). (2019). *Advancing equity in early childhood education: Position statement*. NAEYC. https://www.naeyc.org/resources/position-statements/equity

National Center for Pyramid Model Innovations. (n.d.). *Practice strategies: Teaching social-emotional skills*. https://challengingbehavior.org/implementation/classroom/practical-strategies/

National Council for the Social Studies. (2013). *The college, career, and civic life (C3) framework for social studies state standards: Guidance for enhancing the rigor of K-12 civics, economics, geography, and history*. https://www.socialstudies.org/standards/c3

National Institute for Literacy. (2008). *Developing early literacy: Report of the National Early Literacy Panel, A Scientific Synthesis of Early Literacy Development and Implications for Intervention.* U.S. Government Printing Office.

National Mathematics Advisory Panel. (2008). *Foundations for success: The final report of the National Mathematics Advisory Panel.* U.S. Department of Education, Office of Planning, Evaluation and Policy Development. https://eric.ed.gov/?id=ED500486

National Research Council (NRC). (2001a). *Adding it up: Helping children learn mathematics.* National Academies Press. https://doi.org/10.17226/9822.

———. (2001b). *Eager to learn: Educating our preschoolers.* National Academies Press.

———. (2004). *On evaluating curricular effectiveness: Judging the quality of K-12 mathematics evaluations.* National Academies Press.

———. (2009). *Mathematics learning in early childhood: Paths toward excellence and equity.* National Academies Press.

———. (2012). *A framework for K-12 science education: Practices, crosscutting concepts, and core ideas.* National Academies Press.

———. (2013). *Next generation science standards: For states, by states.* National Academies Press.

Navarro, J. I., Aguilar, M., Marchena, E., Ruiz, G., Menacho, I., & Van Luit, J. E. (2012). Longitudinal study of low and high achievers in early mathematics. *British Journal of Educational Psychology, 82*(1), 28–41. https://doi.org/10.1111/j.2044-8279.2011.02043.x

Nesbitt, K. T., & Farran, D. C. (2021). Effects of prekindergarten curricula: Tools of the Mind as a case study. *Monographs of the Society for Research in Child Development, 86*(1). https://doi.org/10.1111/mono.12425

Nese, R. N. T., Santiago-Rosario, M. R., Malose, S., Hamilton, J., Nese, J. F. T., & Horner, R. (2021). Improving a universal intervention for reducing exclusionary discipline practices using student and teacher guidance. *Psychology in the Schools, 59*(10), 2042–2061. https://doi.org/10.1002/pits.22576

Neuman, S. B., & Kaefer, T. (2018). Developing low-income children's vocabulary and content knowledge through a shared book reading program. *Contemporary Educational Psychology, 52*, 15–24. https://doi.org/10.1016/j.cedpsych.2017.12.001

Neuman, S. B., Kaefer, T., & Pinkham, A. M. (2016). Improving low-income preschoolers' word and world knowledge: The effects of content-rich instruction. *Elementary School Journal, 116*(4), 652–674. https://eric.ed.gov/?id=EJ1103949

Neuman, S. B., Newman, E. H., & Dwyer, J. (2011). Educational effects of a vocabulary intervention on preschoolers' word knowledge and conceptual development: A cluster-randomized trial. *Reading Research Quarterly, 46*(3), 249–272. https://doi.org/10.1598/rrq.46.3.3

Nicolopoulou, A., Cortina, K. S., Ilgaz, H., Cates, C. B., & de Sa, A. B. (2015). Using a narrative- and play-based activity to promote low-income preschoolers' oral language, emergent literacy, and social competence. *Early Child Research Quarterly, 31*, 147–162. https://doi.org/10.1016/j.ecresq.2015.01.006

Nix, R. L., Bierman, K. L., Domitrovich, C. E., & Gill, S. (2013). Promoting children's social-emotional skills in preschool can enhance academic and behavioral functioning in kindergarten: Findings from Head Start REDI. *Early Education and Development, 24*(7), 1000–1019. https://doi.org/10.1080/10409289.2013.825565

Nores, M., & Barnett, W. S. (2014). Access to high quality early care and education: Readiness and opportunity gaps in America. *National Institute for Early Education and Center on Enhancing Early Learning Policy report.* Center on Enhancing Early Learning Outcomes.

Nores, M., Figueras-Daniel, A., Lopez, M. A., & Bernal, R. (2018). Implementing aeioTU: Quality improvement alongside an efficacy study—Learning while growing. *Annals of the New York Academy of Sciences (Special Issue: Implementation Research and Practice for Early Childhood Development), 1419*(1), 201–217. https://doi.org/10.1111/nyas.13662

Nowicki, B., Sullivan-Watts, B., Shim, M., Young, B., & Pockalny, R. (2013). Factors influencing science content accuracy in elementary inquiry science lessons. *Research in Science Education*, *43*, 1135–1154. https://eric.ed.gov/?id=EJ1003070

Nunes, T., Dorneles, B. V., Lin, P.-J., & Rathgeb-Schnierer, E. (2016). *Teaching and learning about whole numbers in primary school.* Springer. https://doi.org/10.1007/978-3-319-45113-8_1

Nyisztor, D., & Marcus, B. (2008). Concepts and content belong in early childhood curriculum. *Canadian Children*, *33*(2), 16–19. https://doi.org/10.1177/183693911604100208

O'Brien, L. M., Paratore, J. R., Salinas, A., & Blodgett, S. (2023). Using connected teaching and learning to deepen children's interdisciplinary learning. *Journal of Early Childhood Research*, *21*(2), 181–197. https://doi.org/10.1177/1476718X221145503

Orcan-Kacan, M., Karacelik, S., Aktug, N. D., Clements, D. H., & Sarama, J. (2023). The effect of the Building Blocks education program on Turkish preschool children's recognition of geometrical shapes. *European Journal of Educational Sciences*, *10*(1), 53–68. https://doi.org/10.19044/ejes.v10no1a53

Özcan, Z. Ç., & Doğan, H. (2017). A longitudinal study of early math skills, reading comprehension and mathematical problem solving. *Pegem Eğitim ve Öğretim Dergisi*, *8*(1), 1–18. https://doi.org/10.14527/pegegog.2018.001

Palincsar, A. S. (1986). The role of dialogue in providing scaffolded instruction. *Educational Psychologist*, *21*(1–2), 73–98. http://dx.doi.org/10.1080/00461520.1986.9653025

Paliwal, V., & Baroody, A. J. (2020). Fostering the learning of subtraction concepts and the subtraction-as-addition reasoning strategy. *Early Childhood Research Quarterly*, *51*, 403–415. https://psycnet.apa.org/doi/10.1016/j.ecresq.2019.05.008

Papadakis, S., & Kalogiannakis, M. (2019). Evaluating a course for teaching introductory programming with Scratch to pre-service kindergarten teachers. *International Journal of Technology Enhanced Learning*, *11*(3), 231–246. https://doi.org/10.1504/IJTEL.2019.100478

Park, M., O'Toole, A., & Katsiaficas, C. (2017). *Dual language learners: A national demographic and policy profile.* Migration Policy Institute. https://eric.ed.gov/?id=ED589153

Pearman, F. A., II, Springer, M., Lipsey, M., Lachowicz, M., Swain, W., & Farran, D. (2019). *Teachers, schools, and pre-K effect persistence: An examination of the sustaining environment hypothesis* (EdWorkingPaper No. 19-85). Annenberg Institute at Brown University. http://www.edworkingpapers.com/ai19-85

Pentimonti, J. M., & Justice, L. M. (2010). Teachers' use of scaffolding strategies during read alouds in the preschool classroom. *Early Childhood Education Journal*, *37*(4), 241–248. https://psycnet.apa.org/doi/10.1007/s10643-009-0348-6

Pentimonti, J. M., Justice, L. M., Yeomans-Maldonado, G., McGinty, A. S., Slocum, L., & O'Connell, A. (2017). Teachers' use of high- and low-support scaffolding strategies to differentiate language instruction in high-risk/economically disadvantaged settings. *Journal of Early Intervention*, *39*(2), 125–146. https://doi.org/https://doi.org/10.1177/1053815117700865

Pentimonti, J. M., Zucker, T. A., Justice, L. M., & Kaderavek, J. N. (2010). Information text use in preschool read alouds. *The Reading Teacher*, *63*(8), 656–665. https://doi.org/10.1598/RT.63.8.4

Pepin, B., Choppin, J. M., Ruthven, K., & Sinclair, N. (2017). Digital curriculum resources in mathematics education: Foundations for change. *ZDM Mathematics Education*, *49*(5), 645–661. https://doi.org/10.1007/s11858-017-0879-z

Phillips, D. A., Johnson, A. D., & Iruka, I. U. (2022). Early care and education settings as contexts for socialization: New directions for quality assessment. *Child Development Perspectives*, *16*(3), 127–133. https://doi.org/10.1111/cdep.12460

Piaget, J. (1964). Development and learning. In R. E. Ripple & V. N. Rockcastle (Eds.), *Piaget rediscovered* (pp. 7–20). Cornell University.

———. (1973). *To understand is to invent: The future of education*. Grossman.

Piasta, S. B. (2014). Moving to assessment-guided differentiated instruction to support young children's alphabet knowledge. *The Reading Teacher, 68*(3), 202–211. https://doi.org/10.1002/trtr.1316

———. (2023). The science of early alphabet instruction: What we do and do not know. In S. Q. Cabell, S. B. Neuman, & N. P. Terry (Eds.), *Handbook on the science of early literacy* (pp. 83–94). Guilford.

Piasta, S. B., Justice, L. M., McGinty, A. S., & Kaderavek, J. N. (2012). Increasing young children's contact with print during shared reading: Longitudinal effects on literacy achievement. *Child Development, 83*(3), 810–820. https://doi.org/10.1111/j.1467-8624.2012.01754.x

Piasta, S. B., Park, S., Fitzgerald, L. R., & Libnoch, H. A. (2022). Young children's alphabet learning as a function of instruction and letter difficulty. *Learning and Individual Differences, 93*, 102113. https://doi.org/10.1016/j.lindif.2021.102113

Piasta, S. B., Purpura, D. J., & Wager, R. K. (2010). Fostering alphabet knowledge development: A comparison of two instructional approaches. *Reading & Writing, 23*(6), 607–626. https://doi.org/10.1007%2Fs11145-009-9174-x

Pound, L. (2017). Count on play: The importance of play in making sense of mathematics. In G. Goodliff, N. Canning, J. Parry, & L. Miller (Eds.), *Young children's play and creativity: Multiple voices* (pp. 220–228). Routledge.

Preschool Curriculum Evaluation Research Consortium. (2008). *Effects of preschool curriculum programs on school readiness* (NCER No. 2008-2009). National Center for Education Research, Institute of Education Sciences, U.S. Department of Education. U.S. Government Printing Office.

Presmeg, N. C. (2007). The role of culture in teaching and learning mathematics. In F. K. Lester, Jr. (Ed.), *Second handbook of research on mathematics teaching and learning* (Vol. 1, pp. 435–458). Information Age.

Purpura, D. J., Schmitt, S. A., Napoli, A. R., Dobbs-Oates, J., King, Y. A., Hornburg, C. B., Westerberg, L., Borriello, G. A., Bryant, L. M., Anaya, L. Y., Kung, M., Litkowski, E., Lin, J., & Rolan, E. (2021). Engaging caregivers and children in picture books: A family-implemented mathematical language intervention. *Journal of Educational Psychology, 113*(7), 1338–1353. https://doi.org/10.1037/edu0000662

Raudenbush, S. W. (2009). The Brown legacy and the O'Connor challenge: Transforming schools in the images of children's potential. *Educational Researcher, 38*(3), 169–180. https://doi.org/10.3102/0013189X09334840

Raver, C. C., Jones, S. M., Li-Grining, C., Zhai, F., Metzger, M. W., & Solomon, B. (2009). Targeting children's behavior problems in preschool classrooms: A cluster-randomized controlled trial. *Journal of Consulting and Clinical Psychology, 77*(2), 302–316. https://doi.org/10.1037/a0015302

Reeves, J. L., Gunter, G. A., & Lacey, C. (2017). Mobile learning in pre-kindergarten: Using student feedback to inform practice. *Journal of Educational Technology & Society, 20*(1), 37–44. https://psycnet.apa.org/record/2017-03609-004

Reikerås, E. (2016). Central skills in toddlers' and pre-schoolers' mathematical development, observed in play and everyday activities. *Nordic Studies in Mathematics Education, 21*(4), 57–77. http://ncm.gu.se/nomad

Restrepo, M. A., Schwanenflugel, P. J., Blake, J., Neuharth-Pritchett, S., Cramer, S. E., & Ruston, H. P. (2006). Performance on the PPVT–III and the EVT: Applicability of the measures with African American and European American preschool children. *Language, Speech, and Hearing Services in Schools, 37*(1), 17–27. https://doi.org/10.1044/0161-1461(2006/003)

Reyes, I., Da Silva Iddings, A. C., & Feller, N. (2016). Building relationships with diverse students and families: A funds of knowledge perspective. *Journal of Early Childhood Literacy, 16*(1), 8–33. https://doi.org/10.1177/1468798415584692

Riggs, N. R., Greenberg, M. T., Kusché, C. A., & Pentz, M. A. (2006). The mediational role of neurocognition in the behavioral outcomes of a social-emotional prevention program in elementary school students: Effects of the PATHS curriculum. *Prevention Science*, 7(1), 91–102. https://doi.org/10.1007/s11121-005-0022-1

Rinaldi, C. (2021). *In dialogue with Reggio Emilia: Listening, researching and learning* (2nd ed.). Routledge.

RISE Project. (n.d.). *The RISE project: Readiness Through Integrative Science and Engineering*. Tufts University. http://rise.as.tufts.edu

Roberts, T. A., & Sadler, C. D. (2019). Letter sound characters and imaginary narratives: Can they enhance motivation and letter sound learning? *Early Childhood Research Quarterly*, 46, 97–111. https://doi.org/10.1016/j.ecresq.2018.04.002

Roberts, T. A., Vadasy, P. F., & Sanders, E. A. (2019). Preschool instruction in letter names and sounds: Does contextualized or decontextualized instruction matter? *Reading Research Quarterly*, 55(4), 573–600. https://doi.org/10.1002/rrq.284

Rogoff, B. (1990). *Apprenticeship in thinking: Cognitive development in social context*. Oxford University Press.

Samuelsson, I. P., Sheridan, S., & Williams, P. (2006). Five preschool curricula—Comparative perspective. *International Journal of Early Childhood*, 38(1), 11–30. http://dx.doi.org/10.1007/BF03165975

Sanders, K. E., Deihl, A., & Kyler, A. (2007). DAP in the 'hood: Perceptions of child care practices by African American child care directors caring for children of color. *Early Childhood Research Quarterly*, 22(3), 394–406. https://doi.org/10.1016/j.ecresq.2007.03.002

Sandhofer, C. M., & Uchikoshi, Y. (2013). Cognitive consequences of dual language learning: Cognitive function, language and literacy, science and mathematics, and social–emotional development. In Governor's State Advisory Council on Early Learning and Care (Ed.), *California's best practices for young dual language learners research overview papers* (pp. 51–89). Department of Education.

Sanford DeRousie, R. M., & Bierman, K. L. (2012). Examining the sustainability of an evidence-based preschool curriculum: The REDI program. *Early Childhood Research Quarterly*, 27(1), 55–56. https://doi.org/10.1016%2Fj.ecresq.2011.07.003

Sarama, J., & Clements, D. H. (2008). Linking research and software development. In G. W. Blume & M. K. Heid (Eds.), *Research on technology and the teaching and learning of mathematics* (Vol. 2, *Cases and perspectives*, pp. 113–130). Information Age.

———. (2009a). Building blocks and cognitive building blocks: Playing to know the world mathematically. *American Journal of Play*, 1(3), 313–337.

———. (2009b). *Early childhood mathematics education research: Learning trajectories for young children*. Routledge. https://doi.org/10.4324/9780203883785

———. (2015a). Preschoolers getting in shape. In Teaching Young Children (Ed.), *Exploring math and science in preschool* (pp. 35–37). National Association for the Education of Young Children.

———. (2015b). Scaling up early mathematics interventions: Transitioning with trajectories and technologies. In B. Perry, A. MacDonald, & A. Gervasoni (Eds.), *Mathematics and transition to school: International perspectives* (pp. 153–169). Springer. https://doi.org/10.1007/978-98 t -287 215-9_ 10

———. (2019a). Technology in early childhood education. In O. N. Saracho (Ed.), *Handbook of research on the education of young children* (pp. 183–198). Routledge.

———. (2019b). The Building Blocks and TRIAD projects. In P. Sztajn & P. H. Wilson (Eds.), *Learning trajectories for teachers: Designing effective professional development for math instruction* (pp. 104–131). Teachers College Press.

———. (2021). Long-range impact of a scale-up model on mathematics teaching and learning: Persistence, sustainability, and diffusion. *Journal of Cognitive Education and Psychology*, 20(1). https://doi.org/10.1891/JCEP-D-20-00005

Sarama, J., Brenneman, K., Clements, D. H., Duke, N. K., & Hemmeter, M. L. (2016a). *Connect4Learning: The pre-K curriculum*. Connect4Learning. https://www.connect4learning.com/pdfs/C4L_White_Paper_Overview_REV_10_16.pdf

———. (2017a). Interdisciplinary teaching across multiple domains: The C4L (Connect4Learning) curriculum. In L. B. Bailey (Ed.), *Implementing a standards-based curriculum in the early childhood classroom* (pp. 1–53). Routledge.

Sarama, J., Clements, D. H., Baroody, A. J., Kutaka, T. S., Chernyavskiy, P., Shi, J., & Cong, M. (2021). Testing a theoretical assumption of a learning-trajectories approach in teaching length measurement to kindergartners. *AERA Open, 7*(1), 1–15. https://doi.org/10.1177/23328584211026657

Sarama, J., Clements, D. H., & Spitler, M. E. (2017b). Evidence of teacher change after participating in TRIAD's learning trajectories-based professional development and after implementing learning trajectory-based mathematics. *Mathematics Teacher Education and Development, 19*(3), 58–75. https://eric.ed.gov/?id=EJ1163880

Sarama, J., Clements, D. H., Wolfe, C. B., & Spitler, M. E. (2016b). Professional development in early mathematics: Effects of an intervention based on learning trajectories on teachers' practices. *Nordic Studies in Mathematics Education, 21*(4), 29–55.

Sargent, A. R. (2017). *Urban preschool teachers' instructional technology integration perceptions and practices*. Hampton University.

Savvas Learning Company. (2014). *Opening the World of Learning (OWL) program overview*. https://doi.org/mysavvastraining.com.

Schickedanz, J., Dickinson, D. K., & Charlotte-Mecklenburg Schools. (2005). *Opening the world of learning: A comprehensive literacy program*. Pearson Early Learning.

Schmitt, S. A., Korucu, I., Napoli, A. R., Bryant, L. M., & Purpura, D. J. (2018). Using block play to enhance preschool children's mathematics and executive functioning: A randomized controlled trial. *Early Childhood Research Quarterly, 44*, 181–191. https://doi.org/10.1016/j.ecresq.2018.04.006

Schmitt, S. A., McClelland, M. M., Tominey, S. L., & Acock, A. C. (2015). Strengthening school readiness for Head Start children: Evaluation of a self-regulation intervention. *Early Childhood Research Quarterly, 30*, 20–31. https://psycnet.apa.org/doi/10.1016/j.ecresq.2014.08.001

Schoenfeld, A. H. (2016). 100 years of curriculum history, theory, and research. *Educational Researcher, 45*(2), 105–111. https://doi.org/10.3102/0013189X16639025

Schonleber, N. (2011). Hawaiian culture-based education and the Montessori approach: Overlapping teaching practices values, and worldview. *Journal of American Indian Education, 50*(3), 5–25. https://doi.org/10.1353/jaie.2011.a798449

Schreibman, L., Dawson, G., Stahmer, A. C., Landa, R., Rogers, S. J., McGee, G. G., Kasari, C., Ingersoll, B., Kaiser, A. P., Bruinsma, Y., McNerney, E., Wetherby, A., & Halladay, A. (2015). Naturalistic developmental behavioral interventions: Empirically validated treatments for autism spectrum disorder. *Journal of Autism and Developmental Disorders, 45*(8), 2411–2428. https://doi.org/10.1007/s10803-015-2407-8

Senk, S. L., & Thompson, D. R. (2003). *Standards-based school mathematics curricula. What are they? What do students learn?* Erlbaum.

Seo, K.-H., & Ginsburg, H. P. (2004). What is developmentally appropriate in early childhood mathematics education? In D. H. Clements, J. Sarama, & A.-M. DiBiase (Eds.), *Engaging young children in mathematics: Standards for early childhood mathematics education* (pp. 91–104). Erlbaum.

Shea, Z. M., & Jenkins, J. M. (2021). Examining heterogeneity in the impacts of socioemotional curricula in preschool: A quantile treatment effect approach. *Frontiers in Psychology, 12*, 624320. https://doi.org/10.3389/fpsyg.2021.624320

Shepard, L. A. (2005). Assessment. In L. Darling-Hammond & J. Bransford (Eds.), *Preparing teachers for a changing world* (pp. 275–326). Jossey-Bass.
Shure, M. B., & Spivack, G. (1980). Interpersonal problem solving as a mediator of behavioral adjustment in preschool and kindergarten children. *Journal of Applied Developmental Psychology, 1*(1), 29–44. https://psycnet.apa.org/doi/10.1016/0193-3973(80)90060-X
———. (1982). Interpersonal problem-solving in young children: A cognitive approach to prevention. *American Journal of Community Psychology, 10*(3), 341. https://psycnet.apa.org/doi/10.1007/BF00896500
Sigdel, S. (2017). Technology and learning capacity of children: A positive impact of technology in early childhood. *MBA Student Scholarship*, 56. https://scholarsarchive.jwu.edu/mba_student/56
Sim, Z. L., & Xu, F. (2017). Learning higher-order generalizations through free play: Evidence from 2- and 3-year-old children. *Developmental Psychology, 53*(4), 642–651. https://doi.org/10.1037/dev0000278
Simon, M. A. (1995). Reconstructing mathematics pedagogy from a constructivist perspective. *Journal for Research in Mathematics Education, 26*(2), 114–145. https://doi.org/10.2307/749205
Skemp, R. (1976). Relational understanding and instrumental understanding. *Mathematics Teaching, 77*, 20–26.
Skene, K., O'Farrelly, C. M., Byrne, E. M., Kirby, N., Stevens, E. C., & Ramchandani, P. G. (2022). Can guidance during play enhance children's learning and development in educational contexts? A systematic review and meta-analysis. *Child Development, 93*(4), 1162–1180. https://doi.org/10.1111/cdev.13730
Skrtic, T. M., Saatcioglu, A., & Nichols, A. (2021). Disability as status competition: The role of race in classifying children. *Socius: Sociological Research for a Dynamic World, 7*. https://doi.org/10.1177/23780231211024398
Smith, C. (1998). Children with "special rights" in the preprimary and infant-toddler centers of Reggio Emilia. In C. Edwards, G. L. Gandini, & G. Forman (Eds.), *The hundred languages of children: The Reggio Emilia approach—advanced reflections* (2nd ed., pp. 199–214). Ablex Publishing.
Snider, K., & Vartuli, S. (2020). Curriculum research on the project approach: Illuminating the "what" and the "how" of teaching and learning. In J. H. Helm & K. A. Snider (Eds.), *Growing child intellect: The manifesto for engaged learning in the early years.* Teachers College Press.
Snider, K., Holley, M., & Usman, A. (2017). *Final report: Project ABC2—Adults building capacities for young children. Commissioned program evaluation report for Project ABC2—Adults building capacities for young children.* Mid-America Head Start Metropolitan Council on Early Learning.
Snow, C. E., Burns, M. S., & Griffin, P. (Eds.) (1998). *Preventing reading difficulties in young children.* The National Academies Press.
Solem, M., Huynh, N. T., & Boehm, R. (Eds.). (2015). *Learning progressions for maps, geospatial technology, and spatial thinking: A research handbook.* National Center for Research in Geography Education.
Sonnenschein, S., Baker, L., Moyer, A., & LeFevre, S. (2005, April). *Parental beliefs about children's reading and math development and relations with subsequent achievement.* Biennial Meeting of the Society for Research in Child Development, Atlanta, GA.
Souto-Manning, M. (2023). *Justice for young children: (Re)considering the role of the research community. Social justice for young children conversation series.* Foundation for Child Development. https://www.fcd-us.org/blog-justice-for-young-children-reconsidering-the-role-of-the-research-community/
Souto-Manning, M., & Rabadi-Raol, A. (2018). (Re)centering quality in early childhood education: Toward intersectional justice for minoritized children. *Review of Research in Education, 42*(1), 203–225. https://doi.org/10.3102/0091732X18759550

Souto-Manning, M., Rabadi-Raol, A., Robinson, D., & Perez, A. (2019). What stories do my classroom and its materials tell? Preparing early childhood teachers to engage in equitable and inclusive teaching. *Young Exceptional Children*, 22(2), 62-73. https://doi.org/10.1177/1096250618811619

Starnes, L. P. (2017). *Effects of social-emotional education on pre-kindergarten student academic achievement* [Doctoral Dissertation, Liberty University]. http://digitalcommons.liberty.edu/cgi/viewcontent.cgi?article=2681&context=doctoral

Steffe, L. P., & Cobb, P. (1988). *Construction of arithmetical meanings and strategies*. Springer-Verlag.

Steinbrenner, J. R., McIntyre, N., Rentschler, L. F., Pearson, J. N., Luelmo, P., Jaramillo, M. E., Boyd, B. A., Wong, C., Nowell, S. W., Odom, S. L., & Hume, K. A. (2022). Patterns in reporting and participant inclusion related to race and ethnicity in autism intervention literature: Data from a large-scale systematic review of evidence-based practices. *Autism: The International Journal of Research and Practice*, 26(8), 2026-2040. https://doi.org/10.1177/13623613211072593

Stites, M. L., & Rakes, C. R. (2019, October). *Mathematical interventions for young children: One size does not fit all*. Paper presented at the Division for Early Childhood Annual Conference, Dallas, TX.

Størksen, I., Rege, M., Solli, I. F., ten Braak, D., Lenes, R., & Geldhof, G. J. (2023). The playful learning curriculum: A randomized controlled trial. *Early Childhood Research Quarterly*, 64, 36-46. https://doi.org/10.1016/j.ecresq.2023.01.015

Sullivan, P., Askew, M., Cheeseman, J., Clarke, D., Mornane, A., Roche, A., & Walker, N. (2015). Supporting teachers in structuring mathematics lessons involving challenging tasks. *Journal of Mathematics Teacher Education*, 18(2), 123-140. https://doi.org/10.1007/s10857-014-9279-2

Sundqvist, P. (2017, October 8-10). *Challenges of teaching technology in the preschool*. TENZ-ICTE Conference, Christchurch, New Zealand.

Sung, J., & Wickrama, K. A. S. (2018). Longitudinal relationship between early academic achievement and executive function: Mediating role of approaches to learning. *Contemporary Educational Psychology*, 54, 171-183. https://doi.org/https://doi.org/10.1016/j.cedpsych.2018.06.010

Superfine, A. C., Kelso, C. R., & Beal, S. (2010). Examining the process of developing a research-based mathematics curriculum and its policy implications. *Educational Policy*, 24(6), 908-934. https://doi.org/10.1177/0895904809351690

Taner Derman, M., Şahin Zeteroğlu, E., & Ergişi Birgül, A. (2020). The effect of play-based math activities on different areas of development in children 48 to 60 months of age. *SAGE Open*, 10(2). https://doi.org/10.1177/2158244020919531

Tharp, R. G. (1982). The effective instruction of comprehension: Results and description of the Kamehameha Early Education Program. *Reading Research Quarterly*, 71(4), 503-527. https://eric.ed.gov/?id=EJ267019

Tharp, R. G., & Gallimore, R. (1988). *Rousing minds to life: Teaching, learning, and schooling in social contexts*. Cambridge University Press.

Tharp, R. G., Estrada, P., Dalton, S. S., & Yamauchi, L. A. (2003). *Research evidence: Five standards for effective pedagogy and student outcomes* (Technical Report No. GJ). Center for Research on Education, Diversity & Excellence. University of California.

Thompson, N. L., Hare, D., Sempier, T. T., & Grace, C. (2008). The development of a curriculum toolkit with American Indian and Alaska Native communities. *Early Childhood Education Journal*, 35(5), 397-404. http://www.joycerain.com/uploads/2/3/2/0/23207256/curriculum_toolkit_early_education.pdf

Toran, M., Aydin, E., & Etguer, D. (2019). Investigating the effects of STEM enriched implementations on school readiness and concept acquisition of children. *Elementary Education Online*, 19(1), 299-309. https://doi.org/10.17051/ilkonline.2020.656873

Towson, J. A., Gallagher, P. A., & Bingham, G. A. (2016). Dialogic reading: Language and preliteracy outcomes for young children with disabilities. *Journal of Early Intervention*, 38(4), 230–246. https://doi.org/10.1177/1053815116668643

Trawick-Smith, J., Swaminathan, S., & Liu, X. (2016). The relationship of teacher child play interactions to mathematics learning in preschool. *Early Child Development and Care*, 186(5), 716–733. https://doi.org/10.1080/03004430.2015.1054818

Trotman Scott, M., Wright, B. L., & Ford, D. Y. (2018). The book matters: Using the color-coded Bloom-Banks matrix to support the literacy and engagement of Black boys. In E. Moore, Jr., A. Michael, & M. W. Penick-Parks (Eds.), *The guide for White women who teach Black boys* (pp. 358–364). Corwin.

Tullis, P. (2011). The death of preschool. *Scientific American Mind*, 22(5), 36–41. https://www.scientificamerican.com/article/the-death-of-preschool/

U.S. Department of Education. (2021). *Discipline practices in preschool*. https://civilrightsdata.ed.gov/assets/downloads/crdc-DOE-Discipline-Practices-in-Preschool-part1.pdf

———. (2023). Discipline discussions: Suspension, expulsion & informal removals: Unexpected realities in preschool. *Office of Special Education and Rehabilitative Services Blog*. https://sites.ed.gov/osers/2023/05/suspension-expulsion-informal-removals-unexpected-realities-in-preschool/#:~:text=7%25%20of%20the%20nation's%201.5,of%20the%20total%20preschool%20population

U.S. Department of Health and Human Services, & U.S. Department of Education. (2014). *Expulsion and suspension policy statement, information memorandum* (No. CCDF-ACF-IM-2016-03). https://www.acf.hhs.gov/occ/policy-guidance/expulsion-and-suspension-policy-statement

Unterman, R., & Weiland, C. (2019). *Quantifying and predicting variation in the medium-term effects of oversubscribed prekindergarten programs*. MDRC. https://doi.org/10.1111/cdev.13308

Upshur, C. C., Heyman, M., & Wenz-Gross, M. (2017). Efficacy trial of the Second Step Early Learning (SSEL) curriculum: Preliminary outcomes. *Journal of Applied Developmental Psychology*, 50, 15–25. https://doi.org/10.1016/j.appdev.2017.03.004

Upshur, C. C., Wenz-Gross, M., & Reed, G. (2013). A pilot study of a primary prevention curriculum to address preschool behavior problems. *Journal of Primary Prevention*. https://doi.org/10.1007/s10935-013-0316-1

Valentino, R. (2018). Will public pre-K really close achievement gaps? Gaps in prekindergarten quality between students and across states. *American Educational Research Journal*, 55(1), 79–116. https://files.eric.ed.gov/fulltext/EJ1167066.pdf

van Oers, B. (2010). Emergent mathematical thinking in the context of play. *Educational Studies in Mathematics*, 74(1), 23–37. https://doi.org/10.1007/s10649-009-9225-x

van Oers, B., & Poland, M. (2012). Promoting abstract thinking in young children's play. In B. van Oers (Ed.), *Developmental education for young children* (Vol. 7, pp. 121–136). Springer. https://doi.org/10.1007/978-94-007-4617-6_8

Vartuli, S., Bolz, C., & Wilson, S. (2014). A learning combination: Coaching with CLASS and the project approach. *Early Childhood Research & Practice*, 16(1). https://ecrp.illinois.edu/v16n1/vartuli.html

Vaughn, S., Kim, A.-H., Sloan, C. V. M., Hughes, M. T., Elbaum, B., & Sridhar, D. (2003). Social skills interventions for young children with disabilities: A synthesis of group design studies. *Remedial and Special Education*, 24, 2–15. https://psycnet.apa.org/doi/10.1177/074193250302400101

Vecchi, V. (2002). *Theater curtain: The ring of transformations*. Reggio Children.

Verschaffel, L., Bojorquea, G., Torbeyns, J., & Van Hoof, J. (2019). *Persistence of the Building Blocks' impact on Ecuadorian children's early numerical abilities* [Paper presentation]. EARLI 2019, Aachen University, Germany.

Vinh, M., Strain, P., Davidon, S., & Smith, B. J. (2016). One state's systems change efforts to reduce child care expulsion. *Topics in Early Childhood Special Education*, 36(3), 159–164. https://doi.org/10.1177/0271121415626130

Vitiello, V. E., & Greenfield, D. B. (2017). Executive functions and approaches to learning in predicting school readiness. *Journal of Applied Developmental Psychology*, 53(Suppl C), 1–9. https://doi.org/10.1016/j.appdev.2017.08.004

Wackerle-Hollman, A., Spencer, T. D., Artman-Meeker, K., Kelley, E. S., Durán, L., & Foster, M. E. (2021). Multi-tiered system of supports in early childhood: Identifying gaps, considerations for application, and solutions. *Early Childhood Research Quarterly*, 56, 201–212. https://psycnet.apa.org/doi/10.1016/j.ecresq.2021.03.010

Wagner, C. J. (2023). Toward a shared conception of children's content area identities in literacy, math, and science: A systematic integrative review. *Review of Educational Research*. https://doi.org/10.3102/00346543231184888

Wakabayashi, T., Andrade-Adaniya, F., Schweinhart, L. J., Xiang, Z., Marshall, B. A., & Markley, C. A. (2020). The impact of a supplementary preschool mathematics curriculum on children's early mathematics learning. *Early Childhood Research Quarterly*, 53, 329–342. https://doi.org/10.1016/j.ecresq.2020.04.002

Walker, D. F. (1992). Methodological issues in curriculum research. In P. W. Jackson (Ed.), *Handbook of research on curriculum* (pp. 98–118). Macmillan.

Watts, T. W., Jenkins, J. M., & Dodge, K. A. (2023). Understanding heterogeneity of the impact of public preschool programs. *Monographs of the Society for Research in Child Development*, 88(1). https://doi.org/10.1111/mono.12456

Webster-Stratton, C., & Bywater, T. (2019). The Incredible Years® series: An internationally evidenced multimodal approach to enhancing child outcomes. In *APA handbook of contemporary family psychology: Family therapy and training* (Vol. 3, pp. 343–359). https://doi.org/10.1037/0000101-021

Webster-Stratton, C., Reid, J. M., & Hammond, M. (2001). Preventing conduct problems, promoting social competence: A parent and teacher training partnership in Head Start. *Journal of Clinical Child Psychology*, 30, 283–302. https://doi.org/10.1207/s15374424jccp3003_2

Webster-Stratton, C., Reid, M. J., & Stoolmiller, M. (2008). Preventing conduct problems and improving school readiness: Evaluation of the Incredible Years teacher and child training programs in high-rissk schools. *Journal of Child Psychology and Psychiatry*, 49, 471–488. https://psycnet.apa.org/doi/10.1111/j.1469-7610.2007.01861.x

Weiland, C. (2016). Impacts of the Boston prekindergarten program on the school readiness of young children with special needs. *Developmental Psychology*, 52(11), 1763–1776. https://doi.org/10.1037/dev0000168

Weiland, C., & Yoshikawa, H. (2013). Impacts of a prekindergarten program on children's mathematics, language, literacy, executive function, and emotional skills. *Child Development*, 84(6), 2112–2130. https://doi.org/10.1111/cdev.12099

Weiland, C., McCormick, M., Mattera, S., Maier, M., & Morris, P. (2018). Preschool curricula and professional development features for getting to high-quality implementation at scale: A comparative review across five trials. *AERA Open*, 4(1). https://doi.org/10.1177/2332858418757735

Weisberg, D. S., Kittredge, A. K., Hirsh-Pasek, K., Golinkoff, R. M., & Klahr, D. (2015). Making play work for education. *Phi Delta Kappan*, 96(8), 8–13. https://doi.org/10.1177/0031721715583955

Wellen, L. (2018). A classroom for all students: Project-based learning. *Lutheran Education Journal*, Spring 2018, 10. https://lej.cuchicago.edu/files/2018/05/LEJ_Spring_2018_Final_Draft_W-Cover.pdf

Welsh, J. A., Bierman, K. L., Nix, R. L., & Heinrichs, B. N. (2020). Sustained effects of a school readiness intervention: 5th grade outcomes of the Head Start REDI program. *Early Childhood Research Quarterly*, 53, 151–160. https://doi.org/10.1016/j.ecresq.2020.03.009

Wetherill, M. S., Bourque, E. E., Taniguchi, T., Love, C. V., Sisk, M., & Jernigan, V. B. B. (2021). Development of a tribally-led gardening curriculum for indigenous preschool children: The FRESH study. *Journal of Nutrition Education and Behavior, 53*(11), 991–995. https://www.jneb.org/article/S1499-4046(21)00754-5/fulltext

What Works Clearinghouse (WWC). (n.d.). *Promoting Alternative THinking Strategies (PATHS): Supportive learning environment interventions review protocol.* Institute of Education Sciences, U.S. Department of Education. https://ies.ed.gov/ncee/wwc/InterventionReport/712

———. (2013). *Second step.* Institute of Education Sciences. https://ies.ed.gov/ncee/wwc/Intervention/792

Whitcomb, S. A., & Merrell, K. W. (2012). Understanding implementation and effectiveness of Strong Start K-2 on social-emotional behavior. *Early Childhood Education Journal, 40*(1), 63–71. https://doi.org/10.1007/s10643-011-0490-9

Whitehurst, G. J. (2009). *Don't forget curriculum.* Brown Center on Education Policy, Brookings Institution. https://www.brookings.edu/articles/dont-forget-curriculum

Whittaker, J. V., Kinzie, M. B., Williford, A., & DeCoster, J. (2015). Effects of MyTeachingPartner–Math/Science on teacher–child interactions in prekindergarten classrooms. *Early Education and Development, 27*(1), 110–127. https://doi.org/10.1080/10409289.2015.1047711

Wilson, S. J., Dickinson, D. K., & Rowe, D. W. (2013). Impact of an Early Reading First program on the language and literacy achievement of children from diverse language backgrounds. *Early Childhood Research Quarterly, 28*(3), 578–592. https://psycnet.apa.org/doi/10.1016/j.ecresq.2013.03.006

Wright, B. L., & Counsell, S. L. (2018). *The brilliance of Black boys: Cultivating school success in the early grades.* Teachers College Press.

Wright, B. L., Counsell, S. L., Goings, R. B., Freeman, H., & Peat, F. (2016). Creating access and opportunity: Preparing African-American male students for STEM trajectories PreK-12. *Journal for Multicultural Education, 10*(3), 384–404. https://eric.ed.gov/?id=EJ1165581

Wright, B. L., Ford, D. Y., & Moore, J. L. (2022). *Black boys are lit: Engaging preK-3 gifted and talented Black boys using multicultural literature and Ford's Bloom-Banks Matrix.* Information Age.

Wright, T. S., & Gotwals, A. W. (2017). Supporting disciplinary talk from the start of school: Teaching students to think and talk like scientists. *The Reading Teacher, 71*(2), 189–197. https://doi.org/10.1002/trtr.1602

———. (2023). Supporting integrated instruction in science and literacy in K–2 classrooms. In S. Q. Cabell, S. B. Neuman, & N. P. Terry (Eds.), *Handbook on the science of early literacy.* Guilford.

Wu, T., McCormick, M., Weiland, C., Hsueh, J., Sachs, J., & Snow, C. (2023). *What sustains the pre-K boost? New evidence from Boston Public Schools.* Boston Early Childhood Research Practice Partnership.

Xu, C., Di Lonardo Burr, S., & LeFevre, J.-A. (2023). The hierarchical relations among mathematical competencies: From fundamental numeracy to complex mathematical skills. *Canadian Journal of Experimental Psychology, 77*(4), 284–295. https://doi.org/10.1037/cep0000311

Yalçın, V., & Erden, Ş. (2021). The effect of STEM activities prepared according to the design thinking model on preschool children's creativity and problem-solving skills. *Thinking Skills and Creativity, 41*, 100864. https://doi.org/10.1016/j.tsc.2021.100864

Yıldırım, B. (2020). Preschool STEM activities: Preschool teachers' preparation and views. *Early Childhood Education Journal, 49*, 149–162. https://doi.org/10.1007/s10643-020-01056-2

Yoon, J., & Martin, L. A. (2019). Infusing culturally responsive science curriculum into early childhood teacher preparation. *Research in Science Education, 49*, 697–710. https://doi.org/10.1007/s11165-017-9647-x

Yoshikawa, H., Weiland, C., & Brooks-Gunn, J. (2016). When does preschool matter? *The Future of Children*, 26(2), 21–35. www.futureofchildren.org/publications/journals/journal_details/index.xml?journalid=87

Yoshikawa, H., Weiland, C., Brooks-Gunn, J., Burchinal, M. R., Espinosa, L. M., Gormley, W. T., Ludwig, J., Magnuson, K. A., Phillips, D. A., & Zaslow, M. J. (2013). *Investing in our future: The evidence base on preschool education*. Foundation for Child Development and Society for Research in Child Development. http://fcd-us.org/resources/evidence-base-preschool www.srcd.org/policy-media/policy-updates/meetings-briefings/investing-our-future-evidence-base-preschool

Zangori, L., & Forbes, C. T. (2014). Scientific practices in elementary classrooms: Third-grade students' scientific explanations for seed structure and function. *Science Education*, 98(4), 614–639. https://doi.org/10.1002/sce.21121

Zelazo, P. D., Craik, F. I. M., & Booth, L. (2004). Executive function across the life span. *Acta Psychologica*, 115(2–3), 167–183. https://doi.org/10.1016/j.actpsy.2003.12.005

Zhai, F., Raver, C. C., & Jones, S. M. (2012). Academic performance of subsequent schools and impacts of early interventions: Evidence from a randomized controlled trial in Head Start settings. *Children and Youth Services Review*, 34(5), 946–954. https://doi.org/10.1016%2Fj.childyouth.2012.01.026

———. (2015). Social and emotional learning services and child outcomes in third grade: Evidence from a cohort of Head Start participants. *Child and Youth Services Review*, 56, 42–51. https://doi.org/10.1016/j.childyouth.2015.06.016

Zigler, E., Gilliam, W. S., & Barnett, W. S. (Eds.). (2011). *The pre-K debates: Current controversies and issues*. Brookes Publishing.

Zippert, E. L., Eason, S. H., Marshall, S., & Ramani, G. B. (2019). Preschool children's math exploration during play with peers. *Journal of Applied Developmental Psychology*, 65. https://doi.org/10.1016/j.appdev.2019.101072

Zosh, J. M., Hirsh-Pasek, K., & Golinkoff, R. M. (2018). Playing to learn mathematics. In A. Pyle (Ed.), *Play-based learning* (pp. 33–37). *Encyclopedia on Early Childhood Development*. http://www.child-encyclopedia.com/sites/default/files/dossiers-complets/en/play-based-learning.pdf

Zucker, T. A., Cabell, S. Q., Justice, L. M., Pentimonti, J. M., & Kaderavek, J. N. (2013). The role of frequent, interactive prekindergarten shared reading in the longitudinal development of language and literacy skills. *Developmental Psychology*, 49(8), 1425–1439. https://doi.org/10.1037/a0030347

Zucker, T. A., Carlo, M. S., Landry, S. H., Masood-Saleem, S. S., Williams, J. M., & Bhavsar, V. (2019). Iterative design and pilot testing of the Developing Talkers tiered academic language curriculum for pre-kindergarten and kindergarten. *Journal of Research on Educational Effectiveness*, 12(2), 274–306. https://doi.org/10.1080/19345747.2018.1519623

Zucker, T. A., Maldonado, G. Y., Assel, M., McCallum, C., Elias, C., Swint, J. M., & Lal, L. (2022). Informal science, technology, engineering and math learning conditions to increase parent involvement with young children experiencing poverty. *Frontiers in Psychology*, 13. https://www.frontiersin.org/articles/10.3389/fpsyg.2022.1015590

5

Optimizing the Learning Environment for Effective and Equitable Curriculum Delivery

Curricula provide a guide for educator–child interactions aimed at imparting skills and knowledge, as well as excitement about learning and views of oneself as a strong learner. These interactions occur within a broader context that can either facilitate or undermine these immediate instructional goals and thus the promise of early education. At stake is the growth of knowledge and essential life skills for all children who are coming of age in a historically diverse society in which racism, discrimination, and segregation persist. The extent to which this context is sensitive to and celebrates young children's backgrounds and individual differences and ensures equitable access to high-quality learning opportunities is central to effective curriculum delivery and associated learning outcomes.

Earlier chapters of this report focus on the child and summarize the evidence on how children learn and thrive in the early childhood years, as well as the components and characteristics of high-quality equitable preschool curricula. This chapter focuses on creating learning environments that support educators' efforts to utilize curricula in support of all young children's learning and well-being. In accordance with this report's central focus on issues of equity, the chapter calls attention to the urgent need for bias-free, antiracist, and culturally responsive learning environments as a precondition for learning. Both streams of knowledge—on the developing child and on developmentally enriching environments—are foundational to ensuring equitable access to effective curricula for all children. The chapter begins with a discussion of overall quality in early childhood education and curriculum effectiveness and equity. The sections that follow explore the importance of the educator–child relationship in promoting learning, and peer interactions and peer-related adversity. Next, the chapter describes educator approaches to classroom management, including creation of a sense of belonging and the effects of disciplinary practices. This is followed by a discussion of teacher well-being and professional development. The chapter concludes with a discussion of inclusive early childhood learning environments that foster high-quality, equitable educational experiences for all children.

OVERALL QUALITY OF EARLY CHILDHOOD SETTINGS AND EFFECTIVENESS AND EQUITY OF CURRICULUM

It is now widely documented that high-quality early childhood education—especially public programs, such as Head Start and public pre-K, designed to prepare children experiencing poverty and children with disabilities for school entry—can help close early income-based opportunity gaps in school achievement and generate strong academic outcomes for minoritized children, multilingual learners, and those with identified disabilities (National Academies of Sciences, Engineering, and Medicine, 2023; Phillips et al., 2017; Yoshikawa et al., 2013). Decades of academic research on variation in quality in both center- and home-based early education settings—defined primarily in terms of educator–child interactions—have shown further that children experience stronger growth in cognitive and social-emotional development when quality is higher, especially when it approaches the upper end of commonly used observational measures of quality (Burchinal et al., 2016; Johnson, 2017). However, it is important to note that these associations between quality and child outcomes are generally small, arguing for expansion of more culturally and linguistically centered and inclusive observational measures and clarifying culturally meaningful child outcomes (Burchinal, 2018; Curenton et al., 2019; Iruka et al., 2022a).

Unfortunately, none of this research has examined how the quality of the early education setting affects variation in the implementation of specific curricula, whether a published package, locally developed, or teacher designed. Nor have studies examined either the influence of ingredients of high-quality early education on curriculum effectiveness or learning outcomes linked to reliance on specific curricula. As discussed in Chapter 4, there is replicated evidence that both comprehensive and domain-specific curricula can have positive effects on time on instruction and educator–child interactions. And yet, for comprehensive curricula, associated impacts on children's learning or other outcomes have been elusive (see Chapter 2).

Here, the focus is on the inverse relationship, namely the role played by the quality of the broader learning environment in curriculum design, delivery, and outcomes. It is reasonable to expect that the broader context in which a curriculum is utilized by educators and received by children will affect the fidelity, quality, and equity of implementation and thus curriculum-specific child learning outcomes. Suggestive evidence is provided by findings that stronger relations between teachers' instructional support and students' academic achievement occur in higher-quality preschool classrooms, defined as classrooms in the top decile of the quality distribution (Burchinal et al., 2010). Similarly, Burchinal and colleagues (2016) found that more time in math instruction predicted gains in math skills when overall instructional support was higher.

This gap in knowledge about links between the quality of early childhood education settings and effective, equitable curriculum use (and outcomes) highlights the need to identify dimensions of early education environments that support effective and equitable curriculum delivery and, specifically, that offer learning opportunities that center minority children's experiences, needs, and assets, thus providing all children with access to developmentally supportive learning opportunities (Phillips et al., 2022a). These dimensions can then be the focus of professional development and other efforts to improve early learning through curriculum reform. While existing curriculum-specific evidence is sparse at best, one can examine the science on how young children learn and thrive (including evidence specific to the subgroups of children on which this report focuses; see, e.g., Stern et al., 2024), summarized in Chapter 3, to propose elements of learning environments that likely undermine or facilitate educators' effective and equitable use of curricula to support learning for all children.

The urgency of this task is underscored by growing evidence that children from minoritized and other historically marginalized populations experience inequitable access to inclusive and higher-quality early childhood education settings and have disproportionally less developmentally supportive experiences within such settings (National Academies, 2023). The evidence that this systemic exclusion and biased treatment interfere with children's access to effective curricula warrants focused attention by the research community. Further, in light of this report's emphasis on high-quality, equity-driven curriculum, it is essential that such efforts draw on integrative models that bring factors essential to understanding the growth and development of racially, ethnically, and linguistically minoritized children to traditional ecological models, as well as to the specific ways in which "quality" is operationalized by commonly used assessment instruments (García Coll et al., 1996; Iruka et al., 2022a; Marks & García Coll, 2018), as reflected in the conceptual framework of this report (see Chapter 1). These theoretical frameworks emphasize the importance of considering the impact of experiences of systematic exclusion, unequal access to crucial supports, and biased treatment on the development of minoritized children, with implications for all historically marginalized children, including those with identified disabilities. As noted in Chapter 1, the committee's conceptual framework emphasizes that understanding the realities of the lives of children and awareness of historical and current inequities, and addressing historic and systemic barriers to opportunities is a critical step in creating high-quality curricula that are centered on equity to ensure the health, well-being, and achievement of every child, regardless of their race, class, ability, language, and gender.

Using a critical lens, the committee draws on the developmental and neuroscience literatures reviewed in Chapter 3 to consider setting-level processes that likely bear on the success with which early education environments support curriculum reform that maximizes learning outcomes for all children. Ample evidence, reviewed in this chapter and in Chapter 7, shows the importance of the dosage and rigor of instructional content; reliance on a variety of instructional modalities; the provision of substantive feedback; and frequent educator–child interactions that extend conversational exchanges, urge children to explain their thinking, and are linguistically rich (Burchinal et al., 2016; Nguyen et al., 2020; Weiland, 2018). This chapter focuses on the broader environment within which these instructional exchanges occur.

THE EDUCATOR–CHILD RELATIONSHIP AS FOUNDATIONAL TO LEARNING

Perhaps the most fundamental element of early childhood education settings affecting children's ability to learn from any curricula is the extent to which the setting enables children to feel safe and secure (Phillips, 2016; Shonkoff, 2011). Avoidance of adverse experiences that undermine these basic needs is central to establishing early education settings that support effective and equitable curriculum delivery. Adversity arises from experiences that produce frequent or prolonged activation of the body's stress management system, many of which are more prevalent in the lives of the children who are the focus of this report. These experiences include the unpredictability and social exclusion that are often due to the impact of poverty, racism, and other sources of systemic inequities. The downstream impacts of such experiences can compromise the developing brain structures and functioning on which children's receptivity to and capacity for learning and remembering—and thus curriculum effectiveness—depend (see Chapter 3).

The vast majority of young children learn and thrive in early childhood education settings, as documented by the large literature on the positive developmental impacts of child care, Head Start, and pre-K (Johnson, 2017; Phillips et al., 2017; Yoshikawa et al., 2013). The central source of such positive outcomes—beyond the many child-, family-, and culturally based assets that children bring—is the relationships young children forge with the adults in early education environments (Hamre, 2014).

One of the most robust findings in the child development literature is the protective role that sensitive, warm, and responsive relationships with adults play in the healthy development of children of all ages (Institute of Medicine [IOM] & National Research Center [NRC], 2000; National Academies, 2019). Children's essential sense of emotional and physical safety and security is acquired in the context of close adult–child relationships. Indeed, these close relationships can buffer children who are exposed to adversity, including adversity arising from marginalization and discrimination, from harmful impacts (National Academies, 2016; Redding, 2019).

The highly consequential role of adult–child relationships is no less applicable to early childhood education settings (Pianta & Steinberg, 1992; Verschueren & Koomen, 2012). The relationship an educator establishes with each child is among the most potent predictors of children's early learning and behavior in these settings. The warmth and responsiveness that characterize the educator–child relationship set the stage for the child's receptivity to learning from that educator. Herein lies the importance of this relationship for the success of curriculum reform efforts. Indeed, the defining feature of positive adult–child relationships reflects dynamics in which children can reliably receive comfort and reassurance from the adult, allowing them to engage with their environment in a self-directed manner that enables exploration and learning (National Academies, 2023). Manifestations of agency or self-efficacy, as this behavior is often called, are central to a child's ability to learn, even in the early childhood years (Adair & Colgrove, 2021). A close educator–child relationship may also provide a child with elevated levels of positive teacher attention; enhanced feelings of acceptance, affirmation, and belonging; and extra instructional support for learning that can boost knowledge and skill development (O'Connor et al., 2011).

In early childhood education research, the educator–child relationship has commonly been captured through educators' ratings of their closeness and conflict with individual children in their classrooms (Pianta, 2001). This research affirms that academic learning, engagement, and self-regulation skills are predicted by the extent to which students' relationships with their preschool or kindergarten educator are characterized by warmth, trust, and positive affect (closeness) or by disagreement, negative affect, and lack of dyadic rapport (conflict). Children's closeness to (Cadima et al., 2016; Jones et al., 2013; Lee & Bierman, 2015; Nguyen et al., 2020; Vitiello et al., 2022) and conflict with (Berry, 2012; Jones et al., 2013; Li & Lau, 2019; McKinnon & Blair, 2019; Nguyen et al., 2020) educators predict change over time in such outcomes as literacy skills, attention, inhibitory control, cognitive flexibility, working memory, learning engagement, and behavioral regulation. This association has recently been affirmed for dual language/multilingual learners, for whom teachers have been found to report closer relationships than for English speakers in the same classroom (Luchtel et al., 2010; Oades-Sese & Li, 2011; Winsler et al., 2014). Recent evidence further demonstrates that a close educator–child relationship is more strongly predictive of children's early learning capacities and skills than are classroom-level assessments of the quality of teacher–child interactions (Wright, 2024). This implies that setting-wide quality ratings may bypass developmentally influential elements of child-specific educator–child relationships and individual differences in the experiences children have with their educators.

Alongside evidence of the potent role played by young children's close relationships with their early educators in their adjustment to and functioning within education settings is documentation that close, conflict-free educator–child relationships are not shared equally by all children. In particular, evidence is mounting that teachers rate their relationships with Black children—and Black boys, in particular—and children from lower-income families as more conflictual across the elementary years regardless of academic performance or behavior (Jerome et al., 2009; Wood et al., 2020). Black preschoolers are also more likely to experience higher conflict as reported by educators, as well as lower classroom educator–child interaction quality than children of other races, and boys also experience higher conflict than girls (Goldberg & Iruka, 2022; Paschall et al., 2023). Especially concerning is evidence that educator–child conflict in pre-K settings, as reported by teachers, may be more damaging for Black boys' behavior compared with that of boys of other races (Essien & Wood, 2022; Goldberg & Iruka, 2022; Iruka et al., 2022b; Wood et al., 2020), calling attention to how teacher perceptions can impact children's behavior and sense of safety and protection (Alanis, 2004; Wright & Counsell, 2018).

Conflictual relationships manifest as harsh, intrusive, and punitive educator responses to young children's behavior and can set in motion a cascade of negative interactions that further entrench educators' perceptions of a child as difficult and thus as a source of conflict. Such responses are commonly observed in studies of early childhood classroom interactions. In one recent study of a relatively high-quality pre-K program, for example, half of the children were exposed directly or indirectly to instances of harsh treatment, including yelling or cursing, ignoring a child in physical or emotional need, or physically redirecting or disciplining a child (Phillips et al., 2022b). These negative, reactive disciplinary actions are far from innocuous. They have been found to be associated with increases in stress-induced cortisol levels, impaired self-regulation, and higher rates of anxious-vigilant and externalizing behaviors (Degol & Bachman, 2015; Gunnar et al., 2010; Phillips et al., 2022b).

Emerging evidence suggests that such exposures to harsh and controlling educator interactions are experienced disproportionately by minoritized children and those with disabilities (Barnett et al., 2013; Gilliam et al., 2016; Wymer et al., 2022). Children at the intersection of race and gender, and notably Black boys, are the subject of especially negative and harsh treatment by educators across age groups, despite being no more likely than White children to engage in behaviors that prompt such responses (Gilliam et al., 2016; Pigott & Cowen, 2000; Skiba et al., 2011). Children internalize these perceptions; this was evidenced in a sample of fourth graders in Quebec who reported less supportive and more discriminatory relationships with their teachers, even when earlier classroom behavior and academic achievement were taken into account (Fitzpatrick et al., 2015).

The biases reflected in this pattern of results are powerfully demonstrated by a study of pre-K educators who watched videos of two Black and two White children in a classroom and were primed to expect challenging behavior and were asked to identify which children would require the most attention (Gilliam et al., 2016). In addition, eye-tracking technology was used to record which children were watched the most. Both Black and White teachers reported spending more time watching Black children during the video in anticipation of problems and rated them as needing more attention (Gilliam et al., 2016).

ADDRESSING PEER-RELATED ADVERSITY WITHIN THE CLASSROOM

Within early childhood education settings, a common threat to feelings of safety and security arises from negative encounters with peers, including those that lead to social exclusion (Fabes et al., 2003; Phillips et al., 2022a). These encounters, in turn, can undermine children's exploratory behaviors, self-regulation capacities, and receptivity to feedback—all of which are foundational to early learning. For many children, entry into an early childhood education setting constitutes their first encounter with unfamiliar peers at a time when social-emotional skills are in a formative stage of development. These settings have thus been characterized appropriately as crucibles for social development and as proving grounds for the development of trust, empathy, acceptance, and tolerance (Howes, 2014; IOM & NRC, 2000; Vandell et al., 2006). Interactions characterized by these positive qualities foster children's emotional security, sense of belonging in the early education setting, and positive identity development. Their neglect or absence has the opposite effect, as is amply illustrated by research on the emergence of social hierarchies in groups of young children.

Boyce et al. (2012) document the emergence of social hierarchies, in which specific children fall into dominant and subordinate positions within peer groups, in early childhood classrooms serving 5-year-olds. Specifically, certain children were observed to experience disproportionate teasing, controlling and directing, and threatening physical and relational aggression—and thus rejection and marginalization. Children who experienced such "social subordination" were significantly more likely than their peers to exhibit classroom inattention, concerning symptomatology (e.g., anxiety, sadness, acting out), and lower academic competence. Experiences of subordination and exclusion were also associated with altered neurobiological stress responses that, in turn, contributed to detrimental behavioral impacts. While the socioeconomic status of the children's families did not predict experiences of subordination, children from families of lower socioeconomic status exhibited more adverse impacts from such experiences, suggesting heightened vulnerability to social rejection. Olson (1992) documented similar phenomena among preschoolers in her work on the origins and dynamics of peer aggression in Head Start classrooms. More broadly, this evidence informs the broader and growing literature on social exclusion in childhood, which operates at both the individual and group levels (Killen et al., 2013).

A closely related literature documents the social exclusion experienced by children with disabilities, who struggle mightily with peer relationships (Guralnick, 1998). While these children, like all children, seek to play with and befriend typically developing peers, their attempts are all too often rejected. And while inclusive classrooms can promote interactions between children with disabilities and their typically developing peers, with benefits to all (see Chapter 6), these settings do not necessarily enhance sustained social exchanges or friendships for the children with disabilities (Guralnick et al., 1996). There is no reason to believe that the developmental impacts of experiences of exclusion would be any less harmful for children with disabilities than for others who are the targets of subordination and rejection, but pertinent empirical evidence in this regard is lacking.

Multilingual learners can also experience social challenges when interacting with their English-speaking peers. In a landmark ethnographic study of preschool multilingual learners, Tabors (1997) describes the double bind faced by multilingual learners when they enter preschool classrooms in which English is the dominant language. They do not have the English skills to interact and engage with their English-speaking peers, and yet these social interactions are essential to learning the new language and developing the social skills needed to function in group settings. Consequently, multilingual learners are at risk of becoming "omega children," characterized as those who have lower standing in the social dominance hierarchy of their peer group because of their lack of the communication skills necessary for social competence (Garnica, 1981). Thus, without linguistic scaffolding and social facilitation by preschool teachers (see Chapter 7), multilingual learners are at risk of becoming socially isolated because they do not speak the same language as their peers and teachers.

Educators can play a highly influential role—sometimes portrayed as the "invisible hand"—in preventing such instances of social exclusion, promoting positive peer interaction, and thus alleviating threatening or exclusionary peer interactions (Farmer et al., 2011). Indeed, the Pyramid Model discussed in Chapters 4 and 6 rests on a foundation of nurturing and responsive relationships on which subsequent tiers of the pyramid, and thus the prosocial development of all children, depend (National Center for Pyramid Model Innovations, n.d.). By engaging in proactive social scaffolding in which children are helped to enter a peer group, resolve conflicts constructively, and learn to take turns and share, educators facilitate more harmonious and complex peer interactions (Acar et al., 2017; Williams et al., 2010). Classrooms with an explicit focus on fostering egalitarian interactions among the children (collaborative learning), respecting and supporting the unique developmental and cultural differences of each child, and encouraging all children to contribute actively to the learning process can counteract the emergence of peer hierarchies (Boyce et al., 2012). Evidence in this regard comes from a recent intervention with preschoolers (most of whom were Latine) that relied on teachers' promotion of intergroup contact via intentional peer pairings and support for engagement in cooperative activities, which effectively promoted preschoolers' cross-gender peer relationships in the classroom (Hanish et al., 2021). Efforts to apply these findings toward the goal of enhancing other forms of cross-group collaboration, friendship, and understanding are urgently needed.

EDUCATORS' APPROACHES TO CLASSROOM MANAGEMENT

Virtually all comprehensive assessment tools for capturing early childhood education quality include the dimension of classroom management. It is in this domain that harsh educator–child interactions and instances of educator–child conflict are most apparent, insofar as they are typically manifested in the service of maintaining order in the classroom, ensuring that children follow rules and routines, and stopping behavior perceived to be disruptive (Huston et al., 2015; Moffett et al., 2021). The Model of the Prosocial Classroom (Jennings & Greenberg, 2009) and the Teaching Through Interactions framework (Hamre et al., 2013) emphasize teacher–child interactions that establish the emotional and organizational climate of the early education setting as foundational to children's receptivity to learning. The emotional climate of the classroom or home (extent of warmth, positive emotions) plays the same supportive role for all children. Beyond the emotional tone of the setting, substantial evidence now highlights the contribution of a well-managed classroom to children's ability to learn

(Domitrovich et al., 2009; Fishman & Wille, 2014; Hsueh et al., 2014; Lieber et al., 2009; Odom et al., 2010). Educators are, effectively, managers of the classroom social system.

At the classroom level, consistent routines and predictable, proactively implemented expectations for behavior serve to assure children of their safety and security, and enable them gradually to regulate their own behavior, including learning to pay attention despite distractions and follow increasingly complex instructions that facilitate learning. To the extent that these routines and expectations draw on the diversity of children's experiences, backgrounds, languages, and funds of knowledge, all children's sense of belonging will be enhanced.

These practices may be especially important for children who are more challenged than others by social interaction, including those with disabilities and those who may be excluded because of their cultural, racial, linguistic, and economic backgrounds. They are also the focus of guidance on inclusive educational practice and, increasingly, of efforts to ensure that teacher biases and associated discriminatory treatment of marginalized groups of children are addressed as part of professional development. Attending to educator strategies for managing the classroom social system is an integral element of ensuring that teachers can devote their time to supporting learning and that all children in an early education setting are receptive to acquiring the lessons that curricula are designed to impart.

At the extreme, the more conflictual and harsh disciplinary treatment experienced by historically marginalized young children, discussed above, that is captured in assessments of classroom management has been suggested as one reason for disproportionality in suspensions and expulsions (Goldberg & Iruka, 2022; Wymer et al., 2022). Teacher biases and the negative, reactive responses to behavior that teachers disproportionally perceive to be disruptive when enacted by minoritized children are strong candidates as sources of this treatment (Barnett et al., 2013; Gilliam et al., 2016) and warrant immediate attention in teacher training and professional development efforts. For example, kindergarten teachers have been reported to view Black boys as demonstrating poor self-regulation and social skills (Williford et al., 2021; Wood et al., 2020). These views, in turn, have been associated with teachers' reliance on exclusionary discipline practices (Williford et al., 2021). The consequences are devastating: the U.S. Office for Civil Rights (2016) reports that Black children make up 18% of preschool enrollments but almost half of children being suspended or expelled. Children with disabilities are also at risk of systemic exclusionary practices; they are twice as likely as children without disabilities to be suspended and expelled (U.S. Office for Civil Rights, 2016). And Black boys from low-income backgrounds receiving special education services are suspended at higher rates than any other subgroup of children (National Center for Learning Disabilities, 2020). In addition to inflicting discriminatory exclusion from access to a curriculum on a young child, with accompanying detrimental impacts on early learning, early experiences of suspension, expulsion, and other exclusionary practices increase the likelihood of suspension and expulsion in later grades, leading to what some call the school-to-prison pipeline (Skiba et al., 2014).

As children proceed through school, their experiences of exclusionary discipline practices can continue, with highly consequential adverse impacts. For example, according to a recent report from the Adolescent Brain Cognitive Development study, Black 9- to 10-year-olds were 4.7 times more likely to receive a detention or suspension than their White peers, as were children of "other" race/ethnicity, in models that controlled for externalizing behavior problems, family conflict, household income, and other demographic characteristics (Fadus et al., 2021). These exclusionary practices also increase the odds of long-term emotional, mental, and educational harm (Chu & Ready, 2018). In samples of older children, for example, perceived discrimination from teachers has been associated with drops in grades, lower academic self-concept, and less persistence (Neblett et al., 2006; Wong et al., 2003). If internalized, these attitudes can lead to lower self-esteem and psychological distress, and higher levels of alcohol consumption and obesity (Kwate & Meyer, 2011; Williams & Mohammed, 2009, 2013). Youth internalize these biased and racialized perceptions and practices, as evidenced by their own reports of less supportive and more discriminatory relationships with their teachers, even when earlier classroom behavior and academic achievement are taken into account (Fitzpatrick et al., 2015). Identifying the earliest age at which children begin to expect, internalize, and show behavioral manifestations of their experiences with educator bias and unequal treatment—which may be as early as preschool (Gansen, 2021)—is essential for preventive interventions.

THE ESSENTIAL ROLE OF TEACHER WELL-BEING

As of 2019, approximately 2.73 million early childhood educators cared for more than 10 million children in center-based and listed (licensed, registered, regulated, or license-exempt) home-based settings in the United States (Office of Planning, Research & Evaluation, n.d.). This workforce consisted largely of women (92%), and in many child care sectors, largely of members of racial and ethnic minority groups (40%), immigrants (22%), and low-income individuals (average annual salary of $17,725, 67% below the national average; Chang, 2020; Deloitte, n.d.). Early childhood teachers earn, on average, two-thirds of what kindergarten teachers with the same levels of higher education earn (Whitebook et al., 2014). Nearly half of all early childhood educators rely on some form of government assistance (Whitebook et al., 2018), and many struggle to pay for health care, utilities, and food (Whitaker et al., 2015).

This essential workforce also faces challenging working conditions, including long hours and physical and emotional demands (Kwon et al., 2021), leading to staff turnover, absenteeism, poor physical health conditions, high rates of burnout, emotional exhaustion, stress, and mental health problems (Haberman, 2005). For example, early childhood teachers in high-poverty schools or Head Start programs have reported rates of depression ranging from 25% to 50% (Hamre & Pianta, 2004; Whitaker et al., 2013). And close to half of teachers in the acclaimed Tulsa pre-K program reported concerning levels of depressive symptomatology (Johnson et al., 2021). Early childhood teachers also report high levels of workplace stress (De Schipper et al., 2009; Groeneveld et al., 2012; Jeon et al, 2014; Li-Grining et al., 2010). Additionally, reports indicate that early childhood educators' mental health problems have been exacerbated by the COVID-19 pandemic (Palomino et al., 2023).

A growing body of evidence demonstrates that educators' ability to offer stable, stimulating, and inclusive education settings for young children is affected by their own well-being (see Chapter 11 in IOM & NRC, 2015). Well-being in this context emphasizes freedom from stress that is psychosocial (e.g., depression), economic (e.g., low wages, material hardship), or job related (e.g., burnout). High levels of stress can impede educators' concentration and planning abilities, interfere with their own emotion regulation, and give rise to unchecked implicit bias. These compromised and consequential adult outcomes can carry negative consequences for the classroom management and instructional interactions that undergird educators' ability to deliver a curriculum effectively and equitably. Replicated empirical evidence has found that both preschool educators' depression and low wages predict more reactive, punitive, and intrusive educator–child interactions, as well as lower quality of instruction (e.g., Buettner et al., 2016; Hindman & Bustamante, 2019; Johnson et al., 2021). In two samples of Head Start educators, for example, both teacher depression and teacher workplace stress predicted poorer quality of teacher–child interaction and, specifically, more teacher–child conflict (Li-Grining et al., 2010; Whitaker et al., 2015). Teachers with higher levels of depression are also more likely to request that a child be expelled from their care (Silver & Zinsser, 2020).

This chain of associations from educator stress and depression to compromised teacher–child relationships also has implications for child outcomes, primarily with regard to social-emotional development (Buettner et al., 2016; Hindman & Bustamante, 2019; Jeon et al., 2014,

2019; Whitaker et al., 2015). In one study, for example, educator depression predicted increased problem behavior over the course of a Head Start year (Roberts et al., 2016). Other studies, however, have found that despite high rates of depression and food insecurity, educators are able to compartmentalize or absorb their stress such that their students are protected from its impacts (Johnson et al., 2020). While laudable, the toll it likely takes on teachers is another reminder of the critical need to support them socially, emotionally, and economically to ensure they give all children their best selves.

In light of the chronic work overload, job strain, and poor compensation—yet high expectations—that characterize the early childhood education workforce, there is an urgent need to address educators' well-being as a basic precondition for high-quality early education. Fortunately, promising evidence offers guidance for promoting educator well-being—early childhood intervention programs, as well as parenting interventions, can target adult stress and equip participants with supportive behavior management strategies, directly address teachers' own experiences of stress, and provide in-classroom coaching and consultation from mental health professionals (see IOM & NRC, 2015). A key next step is to apply these approaches to routinely available professional development for early educators, including those aimed at promoting the effective and equitable use of high-quality curriculum.

PROFESSIONAL DEVELOPMENT OF THE EARLY EDUCATION WORKFORCE

Professional development is key to implementing curriculum to support child outcomes. In its review of the research evidence, the committee found that coaching, training, and/or mentoring that accompany a well-structured, sequenced curriculum are key factors for ensuring curriculum quality and effectiveness (e.g., Clements et al., 2011; Goodrich et al., 2017; Marietta & Marietta, 2013; Upshur et al., 2017; Weiland, 2016; Wenz-Gross et al., 2018). Professional development (including coaching and training) can serve many purposes, including training in student skills and capacities in certain content areas and training in effectively providing instruction that nurtures those skills (Clements & Sarama, 2021; Goodrich et al., 2017; Weiland et al., 2018).

Mentoring, which may involve the mentor's spending time in the classroom observing instruction, modeling teaching strategies, and providing feedback, is another opportunity for teachers to strengthen their instructional skills and the implementation fidelity of a curriculum (Assel et al., 2007; Domitrovich et al., 2009; Goodrich et al., 2017). Some of the literature reviewed by the committee underscores the importance of frequent and/or intensive training and coaching as integral to building teacher skills—for example, receiving coaching at least twice a month from an experienced teacher who is steeped in early childhood education content knowledge and possesses sophisticated pedagogical practices grounded in teaching/learning and child development (Weiland et al., 2018); receiving ongoing teacher training and in-classroom coaching (Portilla et al., 2020); or having long-term, multiyear professional development opportunities (Sarama et al., 2021). Overall, having access to training and resources that support teachers' understanding of how curricular content, instructional techniques, assessments, and pedagogy align benefits teachers' implementation of curricula and subsequently promotes student outcomes (Cohen-Vogel et al., 2020; Portilla et al., 2020).

The availability of and access to professional learning supports vary widely across professional roles, programs, and settings. For example, a family child care provider may have access to different types and amounts of support from those that can be accessed by professionals in a Head Start program. Additionally, the availability of and access to professional learning supports can vary greatly from place to place. During site visits conducted by the committee that authored the 2015 report *Transforming the Workforce for Children Birth Through Age 8: A Unifying Foundation* (IOM & NRC, 2015), interviews with individuals and organizations working with young children conducted in Chicago, Illinois; Tulsa, Oklahoma; and Washington State identified potential barriers to professional learning that included lack of time, lack of funding to pay for professional learning opportunities, isolation from their professional community, high rates of staff turnover, and lack of available opportunities for professional development; these barriers were especially common in rural and resource-constrained areas (IOM & NRC, 2015). It is important to address these barriers to professional development in order to ensure that all early childhood educators have the opportunity to develop their knowledge and skills and to provide the best possible care and education for young children (IOM & NRC, 2015).

In addition to individual training and development, IOM & NRC (2015) identified other systemic factors that are important for supporting high-quality early childhood practice (Figure 5-1). These factors, often influenced by elements outside the control of educators, include the following:

- **Practice environment:** working conditions, staffing structures, staff-to-child ratios
- **Resources:** curricular materials, instructional tools, child assessment resources, supplies

OPTIMIZING THE LEARNING ENVIRONMENT 229

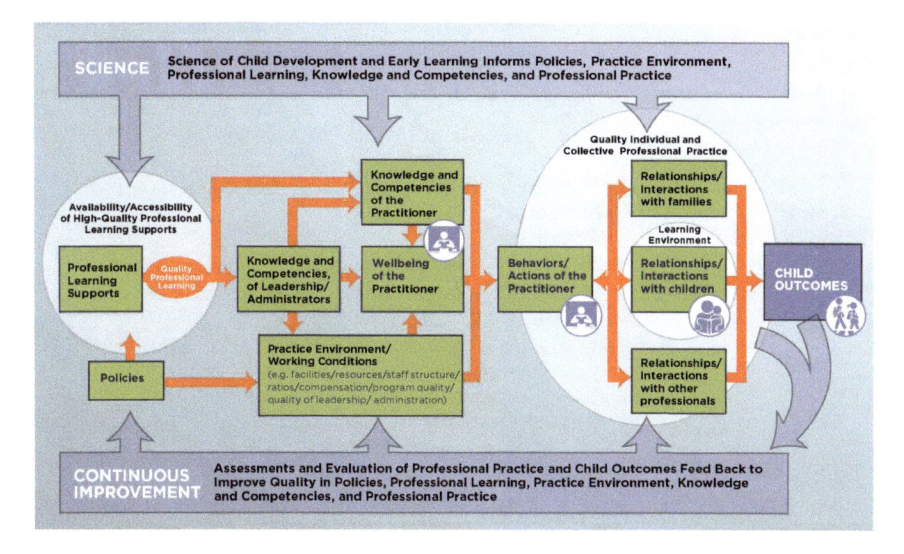

FIGURE 5-1 Factors that contribute to the quality of professional practice and ultimately to improving child outcomes.
SOURCE: IOM & NRC, 2015, p. 359.

- **Policies:** professional requirements, opportunities for advancement, evaluation systems, quality improvement systems
- **Status and well-being of professionals:** incentives to attract and retain teachers, perceptions of the profession, compensation, stress management support

Ideally, all of these factors work together to create an environment where children can thrive. For this to happen, professional learning and workforce development must be driven by the science of child development and supported by coherent evaluation and assessment systems. The 2015 IOM & NRC report also identifies key features of effective professional learning for instructional practices (Box 5-1).

In summary, early childhood educators need to have the right skills and knowledge, but they also need to work in an environment that supports them and gives them the resources they need to succeed. This means having supportive policies, adequate staffing, and access to high-quality professional development opportunities (see IOM & NRC, 2015, for an in-depth discussion of factors that contribute to quality professional practice and an overview of ongoing professional learning for early childhood educators). More research is needed on supports for successful implementation of preschool curricula, including integrated professional development.

> **BOX 5-1**
> **Key Features of Effective Professional**
> **Learning for Instructional Practices**
>
> Research suggests that effective professional learning for instructional practices has several key features:
>
> - Develops knowledge of the specific content to be taught, including deep conceptual knowledge of the subject and its processes (Blömeke et al., 2011; Brendefur et al., 2013; Garet et al., 2001).
> - Gives corresponding attention to specific pedagogical content knowledge, including all three aspects of learning trajectories: the goal, the developmental progression of levels of thinking, and the instructional activities corresponding to each level—and especially their connections. This feature of professional learning also helps build a common language for educators in working with each other and other groups (Brendefur et al., 2013; Bryk et al., 2010).
> - Includes active learning involving the details of setting up, conducting, and formatively evaluating subject-specific experiences and activities for children, including a focus on reviewing student work and small-group instructional activities (Brendefur et al., 2013; Garet et al., 2001).
> - Focuses on common actions and problems of practice, which, to the extent possible, should be situated in the classroom.
> - Grounds experiences in particular curriculum materials and allows educators to learn and reflect on that curriculum, implement it, and discuss their implementation.
> - Includes in-classroom coaching. The knowledge and skill of coaches are of critical importance. Coaches also must have knowledge of the content, general pedagogical knowledge, and pedagogical content knowledge, as well as knowledge of and competencies in effective coaching.
> - Employs peer study groups or networks for collective participation by educators who work together (Garet et al., 2001).
> - Incorporates sustained and intensive professional learning experiences and networks rather than stand-alone professional learning activities (Garet et al., 2001).
> - Ensures that all professional learning activities (e.g., trainings, adoption of new curricula, implementation of new standards) are interconnected and consistent in content and approach (Brendefur et al., 2013; Garet et al., 2001). This consistency also involves a shared language and goal structure that promote peer communication and collaboration.
> - Ties professional learning to the science of adult learning. There is now increasing recognition of the importance of multiple, comprehensive domains of knowledge and learning for adults (NRC, 2012).
> - Addresses equity and diversity concerns in access to and participation in professional learning.
> - Addresses economic, institutional, and regulatory barriers to implementing professional learning.
>
> SOURCE: Excerpted from IOM & NRC, 2015, pp. 398–399.

FOSTERING INCLUSIVE AND EQUITABLE EARLY CHILDHOOD LEARNING ENVIRONMENTS

There is an urgent need to ensure that children—especially racially, ethnically, and linguistically minoritized children; children living in poverty; and children with disabilities—are provided equitable, inclusive, culturally affirming experiences in early childhood education settings (Meek et al., 2020). The urgency that surrounds this need is motivated by examples of the structural inequities, unequal treatment, and acts of racism that add to the adversities experienced by minoritized children and families. The National Academies (2023) report *Closing the Opportunity Gap for Young Children from Birth to Age 8* provides a comprehensive analysis of these experiences and their developmental impacts. Within early education, these experiences start with the basic landscape of access to high-quality settings (National Academies, 2023).

Minoritized children are more likely than their peers to experience biased treatment and, ultimately, suspensions and expulsions in early education settings, as described previously in this chapter. The critical importance of identifying effective approaches to addressing educator biases and exclusionary practices in early education classrooms, and their pernicious impacts on young children's learning and development, is clear. Absent focused attention to establishing learning environments that protect children from the adverse impacts of stressful encounters with peers and educators, support their feelings of safety and security, and celebrate their diverse backgrounds, even the best-designed curricula will fall short of desired impacts.

Beyond eliminating biased treatment of children, these approaches need to foster full appreciation and incorporation of the many strengths and assets that minoritized children and families bring to early education settings. Fortunately, promising models exist—often focused on older children—that are ripe for adaptation to pre-K settings and for scale-up, accompanied by multimethods research designs that will permit identification of the active ingredients of various approaches, their causal impacts, and the extent to which they generalize across circumstances and populations. These models are often grounded in the literature on culturally responsive classrooms, as well as newer conceptualizations of antibias or antiracist pedagogy.

Culturally Responsive Classrooms

Culturally responsive classrooms adopt an asset-based approach that draws on children's cultures, languages, abilities, and experiences to make learning meaningful and relevant; help build positive and healthy racial, ethnic, and linguistic identity; support inclusive classroom practices; and help children achieve success in school (Ladson-Billings, 1995b). Relevant classroom practices are based on two fundamental principles of learning:

(1) new learning builds on prior learning, and (2) what people learn and how they learn are a product of their experiences in multiple social and cultural contexts (National Academies, 2018). Simply put, children make sense of new experiences in relation to what they already know (Delpit, 2006; Ladson-Billings, 2009, 2014; National Academies, 2018). Especially for young children, learning is acquired primarily in the social, cultural, and linguistic contexts of their families and communities. By valuing and embracing a multiplicity of cultural and linguistic assets—including both culturally grounded content and values—students' feeling of belonging and connectedness to school will be strengthened, as will engagement and motivation to learn (Armstrong, 2022; Byrd, 2016; Krasnoff, 2016).

The terms "culturally relevant," "culturally responsive," and "culturally affirming" are often used interchangeably today. These terms communicate the essential role of culture in children's development and the need to view children's cultures as strengths on which to build. Culturally relevant pedagogy, first promulgated by Ladson-Billings (1995a,b, 2014), accepts and affirms children's identities, especially those of children whose experiences and cultures have historically been excluded, based on three tenets: academic achievement, cultural competence, and sociopolitical critique. Gay (2018) developed a framework of culturally responsive teaching, emphasizing that specific strategies and classroom practices must connect to and build on children's cultural knowledge and experiences in their families and communities to support their identities and promote new learning.

Recently, culturally and linguistically sustaining pedagogy has been emphasized, building and extending asset-based approaches and calling for practices within schools that sustain, rather than ignore or eradicate, cultural ways of being in communities of color (Paris, 2012; Paris & Alim, 2017). Educators value and sustain the cultural and linguistic practices of the community while providing access to the dominant culture (White, middle class, and standard-English speaking). In practice, this means that children's languages and cultures are centered meaningfully in classroom experiences instead of being considered "add-ons." As examples, these practices include teaching heritage languages and including Native culture and traditions throughout the curriculum, as well as African-centered curricula and pedagogy (Box 5-2).

A body of research conducted by the Center for Research on Education, Diversity, and Excellence (n.d.) demonstrates that curriculum and teaching built on children's cultural backgrounds and strengths can contribute to school readiness and academic achievement across age groups (see also Doherty et al., 2003; Tharp et al., 2003). Culturally responsive practices have positive effects on students' engagement, attention, and motivation—all of which are prerequisites for successful learning (Krasnoff, 2016; National Academies, 2018). Using culturally relevant examples in curriculum

BOX 5-2
African-Centered Curricula and Pedagogy

An important literature strand has explored Afrocentric approaches and culturally relevant practices for Black preschoolers. In the United States, there are private preschools (e.g., Little Sun People, Seneca Village Montessori School) and charter schools (e.g., Sankofa Freedom Academy, Betty Shabazz International Charter Schools) that concentrate on serving and empowering Black children. These schools generally use Afrocentric curricula, which elevate the perspectives of people of color and emphasize the histories and cultures of people of African descent.

The goal of African-centered pedagogy and curriculum is to mitigate the effects of institutional racism and teachers' biases in the classroom and schools, and to provide a healthy, healing, and culturally grounded space for Black children who have had their identity and self-worth challenged since the beginning of colonization (Iruka et al., 2023; Shockley, 2011; Shockley & Lomotey, 2020). African-centered early childhood curricula are focused on "identity—the importance of identifying the Black child as an African; pan Africanism—the idea that all Black people in the world are Africans; African culture—the long-standing tradition of Blacks using African culture and language to sustain themselves and bring order to their lives and communities; African values adoption and transmission—the inclusion of an African ethos into educational process for Black children; and Black nationalism—the idea that Blacks, regardless of their specific location, constitute a nation" (Shockley, 2011, p. 1032). Afrocentric schools and their curricula often promote cooperation and teamwork to achieve goals while rejecting the hyperindividualism that many European-centered curricula and schools endorse (Rotenberg, 2020). Asante (1991) notes that African-centered education allows children to be centered in their cultural information, which results in their being better students, more disciplined, and more motivated for schoolwork. Unlike the current and predominant teaching pedagogy in preschool, African-centered teaching practices allow Black children to experience cultural congruity between their lived realities and learning experiences in the classroom; develop a healthy racial and diasporic Black identity; enable critical consciousness surrounding issues of race, racism, and fairness; improve academic outcomes; and cultivate strong collective ties with their local and diasporic communities.

Tracing the origins of African-centered sites of learning in the United States, Durden (2007) stated, "since the 1700's Blacks have designed independent schools to meet the cultural and intellectual needs of their children" (p. 24). Afrocentricity provides the theoretical framings of African-centered education (Shockley & Lomotey, 2020). African-centered education refers to teaching and learning practices that use African ways of knowing and being (King & Swartz, 2015) to foster Black children's healthy racial identity development, self-knowledge, and agency (Shockley & Lomotey, 2020). Specifically, in the classroom, "children are taught about events, places, people and things, with crucial reference to and in the critical context of the historical trajectory of people of African descent" (Shockley & Cleveland, 2011, p. 55). In essence, the classroom functions as a space where children can receive accurate historical knowledge about their African ancestry, thereby disrupting the adverse psychological effects of anti-Blackness on children's developing sense of self and identity.

(continued)

> **BOX 5-2 Continued**
>
> There has been some examination of African-centered education, primarily for older students, showing positive effects on students' knowledge and attitudes toward science, technology, engineering, and mathematics (Burbanks et al., 2020), higher test scores (Dei & Kempf, 2013), racial pride (Johnson, 2016), self-esteem and sense of belonging (Foston, 2004; Hancock, 2017; Watson, 2015), and adolescent girls' mental health (Constantine et al., 2006). However, there is a lack of empirical data focused on African-centered early childhood education. There are some emerging African-centered curricula, such as *Education for Life Academy*, *Sankofa Science Solutions*, *The Historic Journey Curriculum*, *Oh Freedom!*, *Kamali Academy*, and *Kwanzaa 365*, to name a few. Unfortunately, African-centered teaching and pedagogy has been pushed out of or absent from traditional education training and preparation programs for educators to the detriment of Black children's learning and achievement (Akua, 2020); these emerging African-centered curricula provide some options for further exploration.
>
> Another strategy for better serving Black children is to leverage their cultural and linguistic practices—including using African American English—in classroom instruction (Gardner-Neblett et al., 2017). Yet research has seldom explored how these practices can be intentionally integrated into an existing curriculum, and there is relatively little evidence on the impact of these practices on preschoolers' development (an exception is Jackson, 2017).

and teaching has also been found to have positive effects on the academic achievement of racially, ethnically, culturally, and linguistically diverse students. These effects have been demonstrated for Native Hawaiians, but evidence also exists for the effectiveness of culturally relevant practice for older elementary and high school students who are Black, Latine, and Alaska Native (Krasnoff, 2016).

New America recently identified eight educator competencies needed for culturally responsive teaching that are consistent with lessons from this body of research (Muñiz, 2019, 2020). The first is for educators to become self-aware of their own cultural lens. They need to recognize the historical and current destructive effects of discrimination and bias based on ethnicity, race, socioeconomic background, gender, sexual orientation, religion, ability/disability, or family structure. They need to reflect on their own biases and how those biases may affect judgments about the competence of children and their subsequent behavior toward them. Other competencies are consistent with those previously discussed: drawing on children's cultures to shape curriculum and teaching, bringing real-world issues into the classroom, modeling high expectations for all children, promoting respect for differences, collaborating with families and communities, and communicating in linguistically and culturally responsive ways. These principles are also consistent with evidence regarding the effectiveness of culturally responsive teaching (Krasnoff, 2016).

When preschool programs incorporate children's cultures and languages/dialects in meaningful ways, children are more likely to engage in classroom activities, develop both social-emotional and academic skills, and improve their self-concept (Craig & Washington, 2006; Gort & Sembiante, 2015; Hancock, 2017). Additionally, culturally responsive programs can promote multigenerational learning and strengthen communities. For example, Head Start program staff in Region XI—which serves primarily Indigenous children—often use local Indigenous languages and encourage both families and children to engage with Native language and cultural practices, which helps create bonds among elders, parents, and children (Sarche et al., 2020). To facilitate these efforts, in 2018, Head Start released *Making It Work! Connecting Cultural Learning Experiences in American Indian and Alaska Native Classrooms and Communities* with the Head Start Child Development and Early Learning Framework (Head Start Early Childhood Learning and Knowledge Center [ECLKC], 2024). Materials are available online to help programs align expectations for child outcomes with traditional cultural skills, values, beliefs, and ways of knowing, including examples of cultural lessons. Children's participation in heritage practices, such as traditional storytelling, not only promotes Indigenous communities' wellness (Hodge et al., 2002), but also facilitates children's acquisition of literacy and math skills (McKeough et al., 2008; Riser et al., 2020). Recognizing these potential benefits, Head Start and several states emphasize cultural responsiveness in their early learning program standards (National Center on Early Childhood Development, Teaching, and Learning, 2020).

A 2022 report based on interviews with 31 early childhood education leaders documents broad consensus that early childhood curricula and classroom practices should be culturally relevant (Reid & Kagan, 2022). The leaders agreed that children's learning is maximized when curricula provide learning opportunities that build on the children's cultural experiences at home and in their communities. Nevertheless, Krasnoff (2016) points out that there are limitations to the evidence on culturally responsive educational practices. Although the literature identifies characteristics and examples of culturally responsive practices, there is a lack of experimental or quasi-experimental research demonstrating the link between these practices and learning outcomes (apart from the Kamehameha Early Education Program described in Chapter 4). Krasnoff (2016) concludes that "the lack of experimental studies points more to the difficulty in conducting such studies in public schools than to the validity of culturally responsive practices" (p. 20).

Antiracist Pedagogy

Kishimoto (2018) describes antiracist pedagogy as being "about how one teaches" (p. 540), not about a specific curriculum. It is expressed in routine teacher–child and peer interactions and learning materials, approaches, and routines, rather than as a separate focus of classroom instruction. Unfortunately, there is a paucity of research on antiracist pedagogy in early childhood education settings (Curenton et al., 2022). However, observational measures, such as the Assessing Classroom Sociocultural Equity Scale (ACSES; Curenton et al., 2019), described below, not only provides an assessment tool for measuring the extent to which early childhood classroom interactions reflect antiracist pedagogy, but also offers a comprehensive operationalization of this construct as it applies to young children. The guiding framework for the ACSES emphasizes the importance of bidirectional interactions between teachers and children and in children's peer-to-peer interactions that (1) encourage children to express their knowledge and cultural identities; (2) connect children's home and school languages; (3) provide a nurturing and affirming classroom climate in which children can express their unique personalities, emotions, abilities, and ideas; (4) offer instruction that is connected to children's lived experiences at home and in their communities; (5) explicitly and intentionally emphasize building positive cultural and bias-free interactions between teachers and children and between peers that value diversity and strive for social justice; (6) include equitable discipline based on redirection and encouragement for positive behavior; and (7) incorporate intellectually stimulating instructional content, curriculum, and viewpoints that challenge the status quo of present-day knowledge and social hierarchy and show minoritized learners in positions of authority and agency (Curenton et al., 2022).

As with the state of evidence around culturally responsive instruction as it affects children's outcomes (Krasnoff, 2016), research on specific strategies for reducing implicit and explicit racial biases and their harmful manifestations in early education settings is sparse. Promising findings are emerging, however, that the intergroup attitudes of young children (under 8 years, although seldom studied in preschool-age students) about children of differing races and ethnicities and children with disabilities can be positively affected by actual contact or that which is media based (including books; Aboud et al., 2012) or imagined (Birtel et al., 2019). Impacts on behavior, such as peer relationships and friendship choices, appear to be more difficult to produce. A successful intervention focused on fostering cross-gender interactions among preschool-age children (Hanish et al., 2021) may also offer lessons for strategies focused on facilitating other cross-group interactions.

A 2019 National Academies report noted that implicit bias training offers an opportunity to mitigate prejudices; however, research also emphasizes the need for these interventions to take an antiracist approach that addresses discrimination affecting racially minoritized populations, such as ethnocentrism, internalized biases, and both overt and covert forms of discrimination. The report also notes that early childhood education is a unique context in which to address these concerns (National Academies, 2019). For example, actively incorporating cultural competence into curriculum and cultivating partnerships with families can help bridge the gap between a child's home environment and educational setting. Such an approach acknowledges the diverse cultural and linguistic backgrounds of children and the potential influence these backgrounds have on receptivity to various pedagogical approaches. For example, some communities may emphasize child-directed play while others may emphasize more indirect approaches such as observation without direct involvement. Recognizing these nuances allows educators to tailor their methods to affirm and resonate with children's lived experiences to foster a more inclusive learning environment (National Academies, 2019). More research is needed on interventions to reduce implicit biases in preschool settings when evidence of racial prejudice emerges, and educators' needs in addressing these biases.

Observational Measures of Culturally Responsive and Inclusive Classrooms

Most commonly used quality assessment tools pay no attention to whether early childhood education environments are free from bias, inclusive, and culturally and linguistically responsive (Phillips et al., 2022a). Some available measures, such as the Inclusive Classroom Profile (Soukakou et al., 2012), which captures early education quality features of importance for children with disabilities and their classmates, and the Classroom Assessment of Supports for Emergent Bilingual Acquisition (Freedson et al., 2011), which captures the quality of language supports and cultural inclusion for multilingual learners, are rarely used by investigators not focused on these populations, despite their prevalence in early education settings.

As introduced above, the ACSES focuses explicitly on antibias, culturally responsive practices and thus offers an essential supplement to existing early education quality assessment instruments by attending to how teachers actively navigate issues of racial inequity and help foster connections between school and children's culture and language (Curenton et al., 2019). The ACSES captures the frequency with which classroom interactions (1) challenge status quo knowledge, (2) provide equitable learning opportunities for minoritized children, (3) utilize discipline practices equitably, (4) make connections to home life, and (5) offer personalized learning opportunities. Challenging the status quo was recently found to be the most consistent predictor of preschoolers' skills, showing positive associations with children's math, executive functioning, and social skills (Curenton et al., 2022). Executive functioning skills were also positively predicted by connections to home life and personalized learning opportunities. Curenton et al. (2022) recommend an experimental study of a professional development intervention related to antiracist pedagogy as the next step toward identifying its causal impacts on children's learning and development. In addition, Head Start has developed a program quality assessment tool—the Native Culture & Language in the Classroom Observation (American Indian and Alaska Native Head Start Family and Child Experiences Survey 2019 Workgroup, 2021)—to observe the degree to which Native culture and language are used in programs serving American Indian and Alaska Native children and families. Head Start also has developed the Dual Language Learners Program Assessment (ECLKC, 2021), which evaluates the degree to which culturally and linguistically responsive practices are provided for multilingual learners.

These observational measures provide a lens through which to examine whether early education environments center equity. An essential next step is to produce a next-generation quality assessment instrument that incorporates these newer, equity- and inclusion-focused assessments so that, rather than serving as add-ons to commonly used instruments such as the Classroom Assessment Scoring System (CLASS) and Early Childhood Environment Rating Scale (ECERS), they become fully integrated into the quality measures used by early education researchers.

CONCLUSION

Effective educators of young children are not only pedagogical leaders but also sources of safety, protection, security, scaffolding, validation, and inclusion in their roles as leaders of the early childhood education setting. Effective enactment of the pedagogical role is inextricably intertwined with educators' attention to these other roles. The committee's review of the literature identified key themes related to creating optimal environments for learning and effective and equitable curriculum delivery:

- Stressful encounters with other children and educators that threaten children's feelings of safety and security compromise their capacities and motivation to learn. Close relationships with teachers and predictable, supportive, and proactive classroom management practices buffer children from the adverse consequences of such encounters. Absent attention to these broader dynamics of early education settings, even the best-designed curricula will fall short of desired impacts.

- Scaffolding inclusive peer interactions; eliminating biases that undermine the development of close, affirming educator–child relationships; and relying on warm, consistent, and proactive classroom management strategies are essential to the effective delivery of equitable curriculum. These strategies need to be incorporated into the core elements of both curriculum design and professional development.
- Educators' capacity to establish warm, predictable, and accepting learning environments—and thus to deliver effective and equitable curriculum—is deeply affected by their own well-being, which has been defined in terms of mental health, economic security, and freedom from workplace burnout.
- Efforts to ensure the provision of effective and equitable curriculum need to incorporate supports for teacher well-being. First and foremost, equity in pay for preschool educators with comparably educated K–12 teachers is an essential foundation for any effort aimed at reducing the detrimental impacts of stress among early childhood educators. In addition, both within-program coaching and consultation focused on stress management as it affects classroom practices, and access to mental health supports are necessary to enable early childhood educators to implement developmentally enhancing classroom practices.
- Culturally and linguistically responsive curriculum and teaching are an essential component of high-quality, equity-focused curriculum. A small, but growing body of research exists for its efficacy with preschoolers, although more evidence is available for its effectiveness with older children and youth. Early evidence suggests that young children benefit from opportunities to see themselves, their identities, their experiences, and their communities in positive ways.
- Research on early childhood education quality and curriculum has developed in silos. As a result, little is known about the reciprocal relationship between the quality of the setting in which curriculum is delivered and the features of curricula and curriculum implementation that support early learning for all children.

Providing educators with the training and supports they need to develop warm and affirming relationships with all children; ensure inclusive, prosocial peer interactions; and provide consistent, supportive, and proactive management of the overall classroom social environment is an integral component of curriculum reform. Practices and policies aimed at effective curriculum delivery need to embrace this broader context within which educators teach and children learn.

REFERENCES

Aboud, F. E., Tredoux, C., Tropp, L., Brown, C. S., Niens, U., Noor, N. M., & Una Global Evaluation Group. (2012). Interventions to reduce prejudice and enhance inclusion and respect for ethnic differences in early childhood: A systematic review. *Developmental Review*, 32, 307–336. https://doi.org/10.1016/j.dr.2012.05.001

Acar, I. H., Hong, S.-Y., & Wu, C. (2017). Examining the role of teacher presence and scaffolding in preschoolers' peer interactions. *European Early Childhood Education Research Journal*, 25(6), 866–884. https://doi.org/10.1080/1350293X.2017.1380884

Adair, J. K., & Colgrove, K. S. (2021). *Segregation by experience: Agency, learning, and racism in the early grades*. University of Chicago Press.

AIAN FACES 2019 Workgroup. (2021). *Native culture & language in the classroom observation* (OPRE Report No. 2021-38). Office of Planning, Research, and Evaluation, Administration for Children and Families, U.S. Department of Health and Human Services. https://www.acf.hhs.gov/sites/default/files/documents/opre/nclco-stand-alone_2019-updates_january2021_508.pdf

Akua, C. (2020). Standards of Afrocentric education for school leaders and teachers. *Journal of Black Studies*, 51(2), 107–127. https://doi.org/10.1177/0021934719893572

Alanis, I. (2004). Effective instruction: Integrating language and literacy. In *Scholars in the field: The challenges of migrant education*. AEL, Inc. https://eric.ed.gov/?id=ED481649

Armstrong, A. L. (2022, February 16). *The representation of social groups in U.S. educational materials and why it matters: A research review*. New America. https://www.newamerica.org/education-policy/briefs/the-representation-of-social-groups-in-us-education-materials-and-why-it-matters

Asante, M. K. (1991). The Afrocentric idea in education. *Journal of Negro Education*, 60(2), 170–180. https://doi.org/10.2307/2295608

Assel, M. A., Landry, S. H., Swank, P. R., & Gunnewig, S. (2007). An evaluation of curriculum, setting, and mentoring on the performance of children enrolled in pre-kindergarten. *Reading and Writing*, 20, 463–494. https://psycnet.apa.org/doi/10.1007/s11145-006-9039-5

Barnett, S., Carolan, M., & Johns, D. (2013). *Equity and excellence: African-American children's access to quality preschool*. Center on Enhancing Early Learning Outcomes; National Institute for Early Education Research; White House Initiative on Educational Excellence for African Americans. http://ceelo.org/wp-content/uploads/2017/05/Equity-ExcellenceAfrican-AmericanChildren.pdf

Berry, D. (2012). Inhibitory control and teacher–child conflict: Reciprocal associations across the elementary-school years. *Journal of Applied Developmental Psychology*, 33(1), 66–76. https://doi.org/10.1016/j.appdev.2011.10.002

Birtel, M. D., Di Bernardo, G. A., Stathi, S., Crisp, R. J., Cadamuro, A., & Vezzali, L. (2019). Imaging contact reduces prejudice in preschool children. *Social Development*, 28, 1054–1073. https://psycnet.apa.org/doi/10.1111/sode.12374

Blömeke, S., Suhl, U., & Kaiser, G. (2011). Teacher education effectiveness: Quality and equity of future primary teachers' mathematics and mathematics pedagogical content knowledge. *Journal of Teacher Education*, 62(2), 154–171. https://eric.ed.gov/?id=EJ920445

Boyce, W. T., Obradovic, J., Bush, N. R., Stamperdahl, J., Kim, Y. S., & Alder, N. (2012). Social stratification, classroom climate, and the behavioral adaptation of kindergarten children. *Proceedings of the National Academy of Sciences*, 109(Suppl 2), 17168–17173. https://psycnet.apa.org/doi/10.1073/pnas.1201730109

Brendefur, J., Strother, S., Thiede, K., Lane, C., & Surges-Prokop, M. (2013). A professional development program to improve math skills among preschool children in Head Start. *Early Childhood Education Journal*, 41(3), 187–195. https://eric.ed.gov/?id=EJ998750

Bryk, A. S., Sebring, P. B., Allensworth, E., Suppescu, S., & Easton, J. Q. (2010). *Organizing schools for improvement: Lessons from Chicago*. University of Chicago Press.

Buettner, C. K., Jeon, L., Hur, E., & Garcia, R. E. (2016). Teachers' social–emotional capacity: Factors associated with teachers' responsiveness and professional commitment. *Early Education and Development, 27*(7), 1018–1039. https://psycnet.apa.org/doi/10.1080/1 0409289.2016.1168227

Burbanks, S. M., Shockley, K. G., & LeNiles, K. (2020). The need for African centered education in STEM programs for black youth. *Journal of African American Males in Education, 11*(2). https://jaamejournal.scholasticahq.com/article/18091-the-need-for-african-centered-education-in-stem-programs-for-black-youth

Burchinal, M. (2018). Measuring early care and education quality. *Child Development Perspectives, 12*(1), 3–9. https://doi.org/10.1111/cdep.12260

Burchinal, M., Vandergrift, N., Pianta, R., & Mashburn, A. (2010). Threshold analysis of association between child care quality and child outcomes for low-income children in prekindergarten programs. *Early Childhood Research Quarterly, 25*(2), 166–176. https://doi.org/10.1016/j.ecresq.2009.10.004

Burchinal, M., Zaslow, M., & Tarullo, L. (2016). Quality thresholds, features and dosage in early care and education: Secondary data analyses of child outcomes. *Monographs of the Society for Research in Child Development, 81*(2), 1–128. https://doi.org/10.1111/mono.12236

Byrd, C. M. (2016). Does culturally relevant teaching work? An examination from student perspectives. *SAGE Open, 6,* 1–10. https://journals.sagepub.com/doi/epub/10.1177/2158244016660744

Cadima, J., Verschueren, K., Leal, T., & Guedes, C. (2016). Classroom interactions, dyadic teacher-child relationships, and self-regulation in socially disadvantaged young children. *Journal of Abnormal Child Psychology, 44*(1), 7–17. https://doi.org/10.1007/s10802-015-0060-5

Center for Research on Education, Diversity, and Excellence. (n.d.). *The CREDE standards.* https://manoa.hawaii.edu/coe/crede

Chang, D. I. (2020). Connecting the dots: Improving child care workers' conditions leads to better health, economic stability, and greater equity. *Health Affairs Forefront.* https://www.healthaffairs.org/do/10.1377/forefront.20201019.28108/full

Chu, E. M., & Ready, D. D. (2018). Exclusion and urban public high schools: Short- and long-term consequences of school suspensions. *American Journal of Education, 124*(4), 479–509. http://dx.doi.org/10.1086/698454

Clements, D. H., & Sarama, J. (2021). Sustainable, scalable professional development in early mathematics: Strategies, evaluation, and tools. In Y. Li, R. E. Howe, W. J. Lewis, & J. J. Madden (Eds.), *Developing mathematical proficiency for elementary instruction* (pp. 221–238). Springer International Publishing.

Clements, D. H., Sarama, J., Spitler, M. E., Lange, A. A., & Wolfe, C. B. (2011). Mathematics learned by young children in an intervention based on learning trajectories: A large-scale cluster randomized trial. *Journal for Research in Mathematics Education, 42*(2), 127–166. http://dx.doi.org/10.5951/jresematheduc.42.2.0127

Cohen-Vogel, L., Sadler, J. R., Little, M., & Merrill, B. (2020). (Mis)Alignment of instructional policy supports in Pre-K and kindergarten: Evidence from rural districts in North Carolina. *Early Childhood Research Quarterly, 52,* 30–43. https://earlylearningnetwork.unl.edu/wp-content/uploads/2020/06/Mis-Alignment-of-instructional-policy-supports-in-Pre-_2020_Early-Childhood.pdf

Constantine, M. G., Alleyne, V. L., Wallace, B. C., & Franklin-Jackson, D. C. (2006). Africentric cultural values: Their relation to positive mental health in African American adolescent girls. *Journal of Black Psychology, 32*(2), 141–154. https://psycnet.apa.org/doi/10.1177/0095798406286801

Craig, H. K., & Washington, J. A. (2006). *Malik goes to school: Examining the language skills of African American students from preschool–5th grade.* Psychology Press.

Curenton, S. M., Iruka, I. U., Humphries, M., Jensen, B., Durden, T., Rochester, S. E., Sims, J., Whittaker, J. V., & Kinzie, M. B. (2019). Validity for the Assessing Classroom Sociocultural Equity Scale (ACSES) in early childhood classrooms. *Early Education and Development, 31*(2), 284–303. https://doi.org/10.1080/10409289.2019.1611331

Curenton, S. M., Rochester, S. E., Sims, J., Ibekwe-Okafor, N., Iruka, I. U., Garcia-Miranda, A. G., & Whitaker, J. (2022). Antiracism defined as equitable sociocultural interactions in prekindergarten: Classroom racial composition makes a difference. *Child Development, 93*(3), 681–698. https://psycnet.apa.org/doi/10.1111/cdev.13779

De Schipper, E. J., Riksen-Walraven, J. M., Geurts, S. A., & de Weerth, C. (2009). Cortisol levels of caregivers in child care centers as related to the quality of their caregiving. *Early Childhood Research Quarterly, 24*(1), 55–63. https://doi.org/10.1016/j.ecresq.2008.10.004

Degol, J. L., & Bachman, H. J. (2015). Preschool teachers' classroom behavioral socialization practices and low-income children's self-regulation skills. *Early Childhood Research Quarterly, 31*, 89–100. https://doi.org/10.1016/j.ecresq.2015.01.002

Dei, G. J. S., & Kempf, A. (2013). *New perspectives on African-centred education in Canada.* Canadian Scholars' Press.

Deloitte. (n.d.). *Data USA: childcare workers.* https://datausa.io/profile/soc/childcare-workers

Delpit, L. (2006). Lessons from teachers. *Journal of Teacher Education, 57*(3), 220–231. https://doi.org/10.1177/0022487105285966

Doherty, R. W., Hilberg, R. S., Pinal, A., & Tharp, R. G. (2003). Five standards and student achievement. *NABE Journal of Research and Practice, 1*(1), 1–24. https://eric.ed.gov/?id=EJ666287

Domitrovich, C. E., Gest, S. D., Gill, S., Bierman, K. L., Welsh, J. A., & Jones, D. (2009). Fostering high-quality teaching with an enriched curriculum and professional development support: The Head Start REDI program. *American Educational Research Journal, 46*(2), 567–597. https://doi.org/10.3102%2F0002831208328089

Durden, T. R. (2007). African centered schooling: Facilitating holistic excellence for Black children. *Faculty Publications from Nebraska Center for Research on Children, Youth, Families, and Schools, 16.* https://digitalcommons.unl.edu/cyfsfacpub/16

Essien, I., & Wood, J. L. (2022). Suspected, surveilled, singled-out, and sentenced: An assumption of criminality for Black males in early learning. *Journal of Negro Education, 91*(1), 65–82.

Fabes, R. A., Hanish, L. D., & Martin, C. L. (2003). Children at play: The role of peers in understanding the effects of child care. *Child Development, 74*(4), 1039–1043. https://doi.org/10.1111/1467-8624.00586

Fadus, M. C., Valadez, E. A., Bryant, B. E., Garcia, A. M., Neelon, B., Tomko, R. L., & Squeglia, L. M. (2021). Racial disparities in elementary school disciplinary actions: Findings from the ABCD study. *Journal of the American Academy of Child & Adolescent Psychiatry, 60*(8), 998–1009. https://psycnet.apa.org/doi/10.1016/j.jaac.2020.11.017

Farmer, T. W., Lines, M. M., & Hamm, J. V. (2011). Revealing the invisible hand: The role of teachers in children's peer experiences. *Journal of Applied Developmental Psychology, 32*(5), 247–256. https://doi.org/10.1016/j.appdev.2011.04.006

Fishman, M., & Wille, J. (2014). *Head Start CARES for migrant and seasonal families: Adapting a preschool social-emotional curriculum* (OPRE Report 2014-43). Office of Planning, Research and Evaluation, Administration for Children and Families, U.S. Department of Health and Human Services.

Fitzpatrick, C., Côté-Lussier, C., Pagani, L. S., & Blair, C. (2015). I don't think you like me very much: Child minority status and disadvantage predict relationship quality with teachers. *Youth & Society, 47*(5), 727–743. https://doi.org/10.1177/0044118X13508962

Foston, N. A. (2004). Preparing for preschool: Making the best choice for your child. *Ebony, 59*(10), 120–124.

Freedson, M., Figueras-Daniel, A., Frede, E., Jung, K., & Sideris, J. (2011). The Classroom Assessment of Supports for Emergent Bilingual Acquisition (CASEBA): Psychometric properties and initial findings from New Jersey's Abbott Preschool Program. In C. Howes, J. Downer, & R. Pianta (Eds.), *Dual language learners in the early childhood classroom*. Brookes Publishing.

Gansen, H. M. (2021). Disciplining difference(s): Reproducing inequalities through disciplinary interactions in preschool. *Social Problems*, 68(3), 740–760. http://dx.doi.org/10.1093/socpro/spaa011

García Coll, C., Lamberty, G., Jenkins, R., McAdoo, H. P., Crnic, K., Wasik, B. H., & Garcia, H. V. (1996). An integrative model for the study of developmental competencies in minority children. *Child Development*, 67, 1891–1914. https://pubmed.ncbi.nlm.nih.gov/9022222/

Gardner-Neblett, N., Curenton, S. M., & Blitch, K. (2017). Viewing African American children's oral language skills as a strength. In I. U. Iruka, S. M. Curenton, & T. R. Durden (Eds.), *African American children in early childhood education* (Advances in race and ethnicity in education; Vol. 5, pp. 123–141). Emerald.

Garet, M. S., Porter, A. C., Desimone, L., Birman, B. F., & Yoon, K. S. (2001). What makes professional development effective? Results from a national sample of teachers. *American Educational Research Journal*, 38, 915–945. https://journals.sagepub.com/doi/pdf/10.3102/00028312038004915

Garnica, O. K. (1981). Social dominance and conversational interaction—The omega child. In J. Green & C. Wallat (Eds.), *Ethnography and language in educational settings* (pp. 229–252). Ablex Publishing Corporation.

Gay, G. (2018). *Culturally responsive teaching: Theory, research, and practice* (3rd ed.). Teachers College Press.

Gilliam, W. S., Maupin, A. N., Reyes, C. R., Accavitti, M., & Shic, F. (2016). Do early educators' implicit biases regarding sex and race relate to behavior expectations and recommendations for preschool expulsions and suspensions? *Yale Child Study Center*, 18. https://medicine.yale.edu/childstudy/zigler/publications/Preschool%20Implicit%20Bias%20Policy%20Brief_final_9_26_276766_5379_v1.pdf

Goldberg, M. J., & Iruka, I. U. (2022). The role of teacher-child relationship quality in Black and Latino boys' positive development. *Early Childhood Education Journal*, 51, 301–315. https://doi.org/10.1007/s10643-021-01300-3

Goodrich, J. M., Lonigan, C. J., & Farver, J. A. M. (2017). Impacts of a literacy-focused preschool curriculum on the early literacy skills of language-minority children. *Early Childhood Research Quarterly*, 40, 13–24. https://doi.org/10.1016/j.ecresq.2017.02.001

Gort, M., & Sembiante, S. F. (2015). Navigating hybridized language learning spaces through translanguaging pedagogy: Dual language preschool teachers' languaging practices in support of emergent bilingual children's performance of academic discourse. *International Multilingual Research Journal*, 9(1), 7–25. http://dx.doi.org/10.1080/19313152.2014.981775

Groeneveld, M. G., Vermeer, H. J., van IJzendoorn, M. H., & Linting, M. (2012). Caregivers' cortisol levels and perceived stress in home-based and center-based childcare. *Early Childhood Research Quarterly*, 27(1), 166–170. https://doi.org/10.1016/j.ecresq.2011.05.003

Gunnar, M. R., Kryzer, E., Van Ryzin, M. J., & Phillips, D. A. (2010). The rise in cortisol in family daycare: Associations with aspects of care quality, child behavior, and child sex. *Child Development*, 81(3), 851–869. https://doi.org/10.1111/j.1467-8624.2010.01438.x

Guralnick, M. G. (1998). Social competence with peers and early childhood inclusion. In M. J. Guralnick (Ed.), *Early childhood inclusion: Focus on change* (pp. 3–35). Brookes Publishing.

Guralnick, M. J., Gottman, J. M., & Hammond, M. A. (1996). Effects of social setting on the friendship formation of young children differing in developmental status. *Journal of Applied Developmental Psychology, 17*(4), 625–651. https://psycnet.apa.org/doi/10.1016/S0193-3973(96)90019-2

Haberman, M. (2005). Teacher burnout in black and white. *New Educator, 1*(3), 153–175. https://doi.org/10.1080/15476880590966303

Hamre, B. K. (2014). Teachers' daily interactions with children: An essential ingredient in effective early childhood programs. *Child Development Perspectives, 8*(4), 223–230. https://psycnet.apa.org/doi/10.1111/cdep.12090

Hamre, B. K., & Pianta, R. C. (2004). Self-reported depression in nonfamilial caregivers: Prevalence and associations with caregiver behavior in childcare settings. *Early Childhood Research Quarterly, 19*, 297–318. https://doi.org/10.1111/cdep.12090

Hamre, B. K., Pianta, R. C., Downer, J. T., DeCoster, J., Mashburn, A. J., Jones, S. M., Brown, J. L., Cappella, E., Atkins, M., Rivers, S. E., Brackett, M. A., & Hamagami, A. (2013). Teaching through interactions: Testing a developmental framework of teacher effectiveness in over 4,000 classrooms. *Elementary School Journal, 113*(4), 461–487. https://doi.org/10.1086/669616

Hancock, R. E. (2017). Global citizenship education: Emancipatory practice in a New York preschool. *Journal of Research in Childhood Education, 31*(4), 571–580.

Hanish, L. D., Martin, C. L., Cook, R., DeLay, D., Lecheile, B., Fabes, R. A., Goble, P., & Bryce, C. (2021). Building integrated peer relationships in preschool classrooms: The potential of buddies. *Journal of Applied Developmental Psychology, 73*(March–April), 1–12. https://doi.org/10.1016/j.appdev.2021.101257

Head Start Early Childhood Learning and Knowledge Center (ECLKC). (2021). *Dual language learners program assessment.* https://eclkc.ohs.acf.hhs.gov/form/dll-program-assessment

———. (2024). *Making it work: Implementing cultural learning experiences in American Indian and Alaska Native early learning settings for children ages birth to 5.* https://eclkc.ohs.acf.hhs.gov/culture-language/article/making-it-work-implementing-cultural-learning-experiences-american-indian-alaska-native-early

Hindman, A. H., & Bustamante, A. S. (2019). Teacher depression as a dynamic variable: Exploring the nature and predictors of change over the head start year. *Journal of Applied Developmental Psychology, 61*, 43–55. https://doi.org/10.1016/j.appdev.2018.09.004

Hodge, F. S., Pasqua, A., Marquez, C. A., & Geishirt-Cantrell, B. (2002). Utilizing traditional storytelling to promote wellness in American Indian communities. *Journal of Transcultural Nursing, 13*, 6–11. https://doi.org/10.1177/104365960201300102

Howes, C. (2014). Children's social development within the socialization context of child care and early childhood education. In P. K. Smith & C. H. Hard (Eds.), *The Wiley Blackwell handbook of childhood social development* (2nd ed., pp. 246–262). Wiley.

Hsueh, J., Lowenstein, A., Morris, P., Mattera, S., & Bangser, M. (2014). *Impacts of social-emotional curricula on three-year-olds: Exploratory findings from the Head Start Cares demonstration.* Social Science Research Network.

Huston, A. C., Bobbitt, K. C., & Bentley, A. (2015). Time spent in child care: How and why does it affect social development? *Developmental Psychology, 51*(5), 621–634. https://doi.org/10.1037/a0038951

Institute of Medicine (IOM) & National Research Council (NRC). (2015). *Transforming the workforce or children birth through age 8.* National Academies Press.

———. (2000). *From neurons to neighborhoods: The science of early childhood development.* The National Academies Press. https://doi.org/10.17226/9824

Iruka, I. U., Kainz, K., Kuhn, L., Guss, S. S., Tokarz, S., Yazejian, N., & Niño, S. (2022a). Early education program racial and ethnic composition and associations with quality and children's language and social-emotional development. *Early Education and Development, 34*(6), 1341–1360. https://doi.org/10.1080/10409289.2022.2139553

Iruka, I. U., Musa, T., & Allen, D. J. (2023). African-centered education (ACE): Strategies to advance culturally responsive pedagogy and equitable learning opportunities for young Black children. *Theory into Practice*, 1–17. https://doi.org/10.1080/00405841.2023.2258732

Iruka, I. U., Sheridan, S., Koziol, N., Schumacher, R., Kerby, H., Prokasky, A., & Choi, D.-h. (2022b). Examining malleable factors that explain the end-of-kindergarten racial/ethnic gaps. *Elementary School Journal*, 122(3), 378–410. https://doi.org/10.1086/718072

Jackson, A. L. (2017). *Exploring the use of African American Vernacular English to foster phonemic awareness development in African American preschoolers who are at-risk*. (Order No. 10747181). ProQuest Central; ProQuest Dissertations & Theses Global. http://libproxy.lib.unc.edu/login?url=https://www.proquest.com/dissertations-theses/exploring-use-african-american-vernacular-english/docview/2068609366/se-2

Jennings, P. A., & Greenberg, M. T. (2009). The prosocial classroom: Teacher social and emotional competence in relation to student and classroom outcomes. *Review of Educational Research*, 79, 491–525. https://doi.org/10.3102/ 0034654308325693

Jeon, L., Buettner, C. K., Grant, A. A., & Lang, S. N. (2019). Early childhood teachers' stress and children's social, emotional, and behavioral functioning. *Journal of Applied Developmental Psychology*, 61, 21–32. https://doi.org/10.1016/j.appdev.2018.02.002

Jeon, L., Buettner, C. K., & Snyder, A. R. (2014). Pathways from teacher depression and childcare quality to child behavioral problems. *Journal of Consulting and Clinical Psychology*, 82(2), 225. https://doi.org/10.1037/a0035720

Jerome, E. M., Hamre, B. K., & Pianta, R. C. (2009). Teacher-child relationships from kindergarten to sixth grade: Early childhood predictors of teacher-perceived conflict and closeness. *Social Development*, 18(4), 915–945. https://doi.org/10.1111%2Fj.1467-9507.2008.00508.x

Johnson, A. D. (2017). Child care and child development in the United States: Where have we come from, what do we know now, and where are we going? In E. Votruba-Drzal & E. Dearing (Eds.), *The Wiley handbook of early childhood development programs, practices, and policies* (pp. 261–285). John Wiley & Sons.

Johnson, A. D., Phillips, D. A., Partika, A., The Tulsa SEED Study Team, & Castle, S. (2020). Everyday heroes: The personal and economic stressors of Early Care and Education teachers serving low-income children. *Early Education and Development*, 31, 973–993. https://doi.org/10.1080/10409289.2020.1785266

Johnson, A. D., Phillips, D. A., Schochet, O. N., Martin, A., Castle, S., & The Tulsa SEED Study Team. (2021). To whom little is given, much is expected: ECE teacher stressors and supports as determinants of classroom quality. *Early Childhood Research Quarterly*, 54, 13–30. https://doi.org/10.1016/j.ecresq.2020.07.002

Johnson, T. A. (2016). "I walk a bit bigger now": Lessons from students in an African-centered after school program. *Journal of Negro Education*, 85(2), 143–155. http://dx.doi.org/10.1108/SSRP-12-2019-0058

Jones, S. M., Bub, K. L., & Raver, C. C. (2013). Unpacking the black box of the Chicago School Readiness Project intervention: The mediating roles of teacher–child relationship quality and self-regulation. *Early Education & Development*, 24(7), 1043–1064. https://doi.org/10.1080%2F10409289.2013.825188

Killen, M., Mulvey, K. L., & Hitti, A. (2013). Social exclusion in childhood: A developmental intergroup perspective. *Child Development*, 84(3), 772–790. https://doi.org/10.1111/cdev.12012

King, J. E., & Swartz, E. E. (2015). *The Afrocentric praxis of teaching for freedom: Connecting culture to learning*. Routledge.

Kishimoto, K. (2018). Anti-racist pedagogy: From faculty's self-reflection to organizing within and beyond the classroom. *Race Ethnicity and Education*, 21(4), 540–554. https://doi.org/10.1080/13613324.2016.1248824

Krasnoff, B. (2016). *Culturally responsive teaching: A guide to evidence-based practices for teaching all students equitably.* Region X Equity Assistance Center. https://educationnorthwest.org

Kwate, N. O. A., & Meyer, I. H. (2011). On sticks and stones and broken bones: Stereotypes and African American health. *Du Bois Review: Social Science Research on Race, 8*(1), 191–198. https://doi.org/10.1017/S1742058X11000014

Kwon, K.-A., Horm, D. M., & Amirault, C. (2021). Early childhood teachers' well-being: What we know and why we should care. *Zero to Three Journal, 41*(3), 35–44. https://www.zerotothree.org/resource/journal/early-childhood-teachers-well-being-what-we-know-and-why-we-should-care/

Ladson-Billings, G. (1995a). But that's just good teaching! The case for culturally relevant pedagogy. *Theory into Practice, 34*(3), 159–165. https://theavarnagroup.com/wp-content/uploads/2015/11/But-thats-just-good-teaching.pdf

Ladson-Billings, G. (1995b). Toward a theory of culturally relevant pedagogy. *American Educational Research Journal, 32*(3), 465–491. https://doi.org/10.3102/00028312032003465

Ladson-Billings, G. (2009). *The dreamkeepers: Successful teachers of African American children* (2nd ed.). Jossey-Bass.

Ladson-Billings, G. (2014). Culturally relevant pedagogy 2.0: A.K.A. the remix. *Harvard Educational Review, 84*(1), 74–84. https://www.teachingworks.org/images/files/CRP_remix_HER.pdf

Lee, P., & Bierman, K. L. (2015). Classroom and teacher support in kindergarten: Associations with the behavioral and academic adjustment of low-income students. *Merrill-Palmer Quarterly, 61*(3), 383–411. https://doi.org/10.13110/merrpalmquar1982.61.3.0383

Li, J.-B., & Lau, E. Y. H. (2019). Teacher–student conflict and preschoolers' adjustment in the transition to primary school: The role of child self-regulation and parents' positive relations with others. *Early Education and Development, 30*(3), 423–437. https://doi.org/10.1080/10409289.2018.1535227

Li-Grining, C., Raver, C. C., Champion, K., Sardin, L., Metzger, M., & Jones, S. M. (2010). Understanding and improving classroom emotional climate and behavior management in the real world: The role of Head Start teachers' psychosocial stressors. *Early Education and Development, 21*, 65–94. https://doi.org/10.1080/10409280902783350

Lieber, J., Butera, G., Hanson, M., Palmer, S., Horn, E., Czaja, C., Diamond, K., Goodman-Jansen, G., Daniels, J., Gupta, S., & Odom, S. (2009). Factors that influence the implementation of a new preschool curriculum: Implications for professional development. *Early Education and Development, 20*(3), 456–481. https://psycnet.apa.org/record/2009-08600-005

Luchtel, M., Hughes, K., Luze, G., Bruna, K. R., & Peterson, C. (2010). A comparison of teacher-rated classroom conduct, social skills, and teacher–child relationship quality between preschool English learners and preschool English speakers. *NHSA Dialog, 13*(2), 92–111. https://doi.org/10.1080/15240 751003737877

Marietta, G., & Marietta, S. (2013). *PreK-3rd's Lasting Architecture.* Foundation for Child Development. https://www.fcd-us.org/wp-content/uploads/2013/09/FCDCaseStdyUnionCity-2.pdf

Marks, A. K., & García Coll, C. (2018). Education and developmental competencies of ethnic minority children: Recent theoretical and methodological advances. *Developmental Review, 50*(A), 90–98. https://psycnet.apa.org/record/2018-32030-001

McKeough, A., Bird, S., Tourigny, E., Romaine, A., Graham, S., Ottmann, J., & Jeary, J. (2008). Storytelling as a foundation to literacy development for Aboriginal children: Culturally and developmentally appropriate practices. *Canadian Psychology/Psychologie Canadienne, 49*(2), 148. https://psycnet.apa.org/record/2008-07437-011

McKinnon, R. D., & Blair, C. (2019). Bidirectional relations among executive function, teacher–child relationships, and early reading and math achievement: A cross-lagged panel analysis. *Early Childhood Research Quarterly, 46*, 152–165. https://doi.org/10.1016/j.ecresq.2018.03.011

Meek, S., Iruka, I. U., Allen, R., Yazzie, D., Fernandez, V., Catherine, E., McIntosh, K., Gordon, L., Gilliam, W., Hemmeter, M. L., Blevins, D., & Powell, T. (2020). *Start with equity: Fourteen priorities to dismantle systemic racism in early care and education.* The Children's Equity Project. https://childandfamilysuccess.asu.edu/cep

Moffett, L., Weissman, A., Weiland, C., McCormick, M., Hsueh, J., Snow, C., & Sachs, J. (2021). Unpacking pre-K classroom organization: Types, variation, and links to school readiness gains. *Journal of Applied Developmental Psychology, 77*, 101346.

Muñiz, J. (2019). *Culturally responsive teaching: A 50-state survey of teaching standards.* New America.

———. (2020). *Culturally responsive teaching: A reflection guide.* New America.

National Academies of Sciences, Engineering, and Medicine (National Academies). (2016). *Parenting matters: Supporting parents of children ages 0-8.* National Academies Press.

———. (2018). *How people learn II: Learners, contexts, and cultures.* National Academies Press.

———. (2019). *Vibrant and healthy kids: Aligning Science, practice, and policy to advance health equity.* National Academies Press.

———. (2023). *Closing the opportunity gap for young children from birth to age 8.* National Academies Press.

National Center for Learning Disabilities. (2020). *Significant disproportionality in special education. Current trends and actions for impact.* https://www.ncld.org/wp-content/uploads/2020/10/2020-NCLD-Disproportionality_Trends-and-Actions-for-Impact_FINAL-1.pdf

National Center for Pyramid Model Innovations. (n.d.). *Pyramid Model overview.* https://challengingbehavior.org/pyramid-model/overview/basics/

National Center on Early Childhood Development, Teaching, and Learning. (2020). *Preschool curriculum consumer report.* Office of Head Start, U.S. Department of Health and Human Services. https://eclkc.ohs.acf.hhs.gov/sites/default/files/featured_file/preschool-curriculum-consumer-report-032519.pdf

National Research Council. (2012). *Education for life and work: Developing transferable knowledge and skills in the 21st century.* The National Academies Press.

Neblett, E. W., Philips, C. L., Cogburn, C. D., & Sellers, R. M. (2006). African American adolescents' discrimination experiences and academic achievement: Racial socialization as a cultural compensatory and protective factor. *Journal of Black Psychology, 32*(2), 199–218. https://eric.ed.gov/?id=EJ735003

Nguyen, T., Ansari, A., Pianta, R. C., Whittaker, J. V., Vitiello, V. E., & Ruzek, E. (2020). The classroom relational environment and children's early development in preschool. *Social Development, 29*(4), 1071–1091. https://doi.org/10.1111/sode.12447

O'Connor, E. E., Dearing, E., & Collins, B. A. (2011). Teacher-child relationships and behavior problem trajectories in elementary school. *American Educational Research Journal, 48*(1), 120–162. https://psycnet.apa.org/record/2011-00608-004

Oades-Sese, G. V., & Li, Y. (2011). Attachment relationships as predictors of language skills for at-risk bilingual preschool children. *Psychology in the Schools, 48*(7), 707–722. https://doi.org/10.1002/pits.20583

Odom, S. L., Fleming, K., Diamond, K., Lieber, J., Hanson, M., Butera, G., Horn, E., Palmer, S., & Marquis, J. (2010). Examining different forms of implementation and in early childhood curriculum research. *Early Childhood Research Quarterly, 25*(3), 314–328. https://doi.org/10.1016%2Fj.ecresq.2010.03.001

Office of Planning, Research & Evaluation. (n.d.). *National Survey of Early Care and Education 2019.* Administration for Children & Families, U.S. Department of Health and Human Services. https://www.acf.hhs.gov/opre/project/national-survey-early-care-and-education-2019-2017-2022

Olson, S. L. (1992). Development of conduct problems and peer rejection in preschool children: A social systems analysis. *Journal of Abnormal Child Psychology, 20*, 327–350. https://doi.org/10.1007/bf00916696

Palomino, C., Cabanoglu, A., Oppenheim, J., Catherine, E., Meek, S., Gilliam, W., & Bucher, E. (2023). *Examining the mental health of early childhood professionals and children early in the pandemic*. Children's Equity Project. https://cep.asu.edu/sites/default/files/2023-05/mh-report_051623.pdf

Paris, D. (2012). Culturally sustaining pedagogy: A needed change in stance, terminology, and practice. *Educational Researcher, 41*(3), 93–97. https://doi.org/10.3102/0013189X12441244

Paris, D., & Alim, H. S. (Eds.). (2017). *Culturally sustaining pedagogies: Teaching and learning for justice in a changing world*. Teachers College Press.

Paschall, K. W., Barnett, M. A., Mastergeorge, A. M., Li, X., & Vasquez, M.B. (2023). A new look at teacher interactional quality: Profiles of individual teacher–child relationship and classroom teaching quality among Head Start students. *Early Education and Development, 34*(5), 1172–1190. https://doi.org/10.1080/10409289.2022.2094159

Phillips, D. (2016). Integrating enriched learning and protection from toxic stress in early education settings. In S. Jones & N. Leseau (Eds.), *Leading edge in early childhood education* (pp. 7–28). Harvard University Press.

Phillips, D. A., Hutchison, J., Martin, A., Castle, S., & Johnson, A. D. (2022b). First do no harm: How teachers support or undermine children's self-regulation. *Early Childhood Research Quarterly, 59*, 172–185. https://doi.org/10.1016/j.ecresq.2021.12.001

Phillips, D. A., Johnson, A. D., & Iruka, I. (2022a). Early care and education settings as contexts for socialization: New directions for quality assessment. *Child Development Perspectives, 16*(3), 127–133. https://doi.org/10.1111/cdep.12460

Phillips, D. A., Lipsey, M. W., Dodge, K. A., Haskins, R., Bassok, D., Burchinal, M. R., Duncan, G. J., Dynarski, M., Magnuson, K. A., & Weiland, C. (2017). *Puzzling it out: The current state of scientific knowledge on pre-kindergarten effects: A consensus statement*. Brookings Institution. https://www.brookings.edu/wp-content/uploads/2017/04/consensus-statement_final.pdf

Pianta, R. (2001). *Student–teacher relationship scale–short form*. Psychological Assessment Resources, Inc.

Pianta, R. C., & Steinberg, M. (1992). Teacher-child relationships and the process of adjusting to school. *New Directions for Child and Adolescent Development, 1992*(57), 61–80. https://doi.org/10.1002/cd.23219925706

Pigott, R. L., & Cowen, E. L. (2000). Teacher race, child race, racial congruence, and teacher ratings of children's school adjustment. *Journal of School Psychology, 38*(2), 177–196. https://psycnet.apa.org/record/2000-15512-004

Portilla, X. A., Mattera, S., & Wulfsohn, S. (2020). *Supporting the implementation of high-quality early childhood curricula in preschool programs: Lessons from the field: Policy Brief*. MDRC. https://www.mdrc.org/work/publications/supporting-implementation-high-quality-early-childhood-curricula-preschool

Redding, C. (2019). A teacher like me: A review of the effect of student-teacher racial/ethnic matching on teacher perceptions of students and student academic and behavioral outcomes. *Review of Educational Research, 89*(4), 499–535. https://doi.org/10.3102/0034654319853545

Reid, J. L., & Kagan, S. L. (2022). Reaching for consensus about preschool curricula. *Phi Delta Kappan, 104*(2), 50–55. https://kappanonline.org/consensus-preschool-curricula-reid-kagan/

Riser, Q. H., Rouse, H. L., Choi, J. Y., & Ku, S. (2020). The contribution of home literacy context to preschool academic competencies for American Indian and Alaska native children. *Child & Youth Care Forum, 49*, 303–323. https://psycnet.apa.org/record/2019-62764-001

Roberts, A., LoCasale-Crouch, J., Hamre, B., & DeCoster, J. (2016). Exploring teachers' depressive symptoms, interaction quality, and children's social-emotional development in Head Start. *Early Education and Development, 27*(5), 1–13. https://doi.org/10.1080/10409289.2016.1127088

Rotenberg, C. (2020). The path less traveled: Afrocentric schools and their potential for improving Black Student achievement while upholding Brown. *Fordham Urban Law Journal, 47,* 1173. https://ir.lawnet.fordham.edu/cgi/viewcontent.cgi?article=2813&context=ulj

Sarama, J., Clements, D. H., & Guss, S. S. (2021). Longitudinal evaluation of a scale-up model for professional development in early mathematics. In S. Dunekacke, A. Jegodtka, T. Koinzer, K. Eilerts, & L. Jenßen (Eds.), *Early childhood teachers professional competence in mathematics* (pp. 163–186). Routledge.

Sarche, M., Barnes-Najor, J., Abramson-Martin, L., Amaya-Thompson, J., Cameron, A., Charles, T.., Godfrey, A., Kaufman, C. E., Petticrew, E., Richardson, M., Sauve, M., Shuey, D., & Whitaker, J. (2020). *Native language and culture experiences among children in Region XI Head Start classrooms and programs: Findings from the American Indian and Alaska Native Head Start Family and Child Experiences Survey 2015* (OPRE Report No. 2020-01). U.S. Office of Planning, Research, and Evaluation. https://www.acf.hhs.gov/sites/default/files/documents/opre/aian_faces_culture_and_language_in_classroom_and_program_508.pdf

Shockley, K. G. (2011). The complexity of developing properly trained education professionals for African American children: Exploring an African indigenous socialization process. *Urban Review, 43*(3), 379–395. https://doi.org/10.1007/s11256-010-0157-7

Shockley, K. G., & Cleveland, D. (2011). Culture, power, and education: The philosophies and pedagogy of African centered educators. *International Journal of Critical Pedagogy, 3*(3). https://libjournal.uncg.edu/ijcp/article/view/263

Shockley, K. G., & Lomotey, K. (2020). *African-centered education: Theory and practice.* Myers Education Press.

Shonkoff, J. P. (2011). Protecting brains, not simply stimulating minds. *Science, 333,* 982–983. https://doi.org/10.1126/science.1206014

Shonkoff, J. P., Slopen, N., & Williams, D. R. (2021). Early childhood adversity, toxic stress, and the impacts of racism on the foundations of health. *Annual Review of Public Health, 42,* 115–134. https://doi.org/10.1146/annurev-publhealth-090419-101940

Silver, H. C., & Zinsser, K. M. (2020). The interplay among early childhood teachers' social and emotional well-being, mental health consultation, and preschool expulsion. *Early Education and Development, 31*(7), 1133–1150. https://psycnet.apa.org/record/2020-52143-001

Skiba, R. J., Arredondo, M. I., & Williams, N. T. (2014). More than a metaphor: The contribution of exclusionary discipline to a school-to-prison pipeline. *Equity & Excellence in Education, 47*(4), 546–564. https://psycnet.apa.org/record/2014-49218-012

Skiba, R. J., Horner, R. H., Chung, C. G., Rausch, M. K., May, S. L., & Tobin, T. (2011). Race is not neutral: A national investigation of African American and Latino disproportionality in school discipline. *School Psychology Review, 40*(1), 85–107. https://eric.ed.gov/?id=EJ921466

Soukakou, E., Winton, P., & Weest, T. (2012). *The Inclusive Classroom Profile (ICP): Report on preliminary findings of demonstration study in North Carolina.* National Professional Development Center on Inclusion. https://fpg.unc.edu/publications/inclusive-classroom-profile-icp-preliinary-findings-demonstration-study-north-carolina

Stern, J. A., Coard, S. I., Barbarin, O. A., & Cassidy, J. (2024). What attachment scholars can learn from research on Black family resilience. *Child Development Perspectives, 18,* 10–18. https://doi.org/10.1111/ cdep.12492

Tabors, P. (1997). *One child, two languages.* Brookes Publishing.

Tharp, R. G., Estrada, P., Dalton, S. S., & Yamauchi, L. A. (2003). *Research evidence: Five standards for effective pedagogy and student outcomes* (Technical Report No. GJ). Center for Research on Education, Diversity & Excellence. University of California, Santa Cruz.

U.S. Office for Civil Rights. (2016). *Data snapshot: School discipline* (Issue Brief No. 1). Civil Rights Data Collection. https://ocrda ta.ed.gov/assets/downloads/CRDC-School-Discipline-Snaps hot.pdf

Upshur, C. C., Heyman, M., & Wenz-Gross, M. (2017). Efficacy trial of the Second Step Early Learning (SSEL) curriculum: Preliminary outcomes. *Journal of Applied Developmental Psychology*, 50, 15–25. https://www.cfchildren.org/wp-content/uploads/research/upshur-et-al-2017.pdf

Vandell, D. L., Nenide, L., & VanWinkle, S. G. (2006). Peer relationships in early childhood. In K. McCartney & D. Phillips (Eds.), *Blackwell handbook of early childhood development* (pp. 455–470). Blackwell.

Verschueren, K., & Koomen, H. M. Y. (2012). Teacher-child relationships from an attachment perspective. *Attachment and Human Development*, 14(3), 205–211. https://psycnet.apa.org/record/2012-11615-001

Vitiello, V. E., Nguyen, T., Ruzek, E., Pianta, R. C., & Whittaker, J. V. (2022). Differences between pre-K and kindergarten classroom experiences: Do they predict children's social-emotional skills and self-regulation across the transition to kindergarten? *Early Childhood Research Quarterly*, 59, 287–299. https://doi.org/10.1016/j.ecresq.2021.11.009

Watson, M. J. (2015). Afrocentricity for all: A case study examining the self-healing power of alternative curricula as a mediating tool of inclusion. *Charlotte: UNC Charlotte Electronic Theses and Dissertations*. https://repository.uncc.edu/islandora/object/etd%3A1738

Weiland, C. (2016). Launching preschool 2.0: A road map to high-quality public programs at scale. *Behavioral Science & Policy*, 2(1), 37–46. https://behavioralpolicy.org/wp-content/uploads/2017/05/BSP_vol1is1_Weiland.pdf

———. (2018). Pivoting to the "how": Moving preschool policy, practice, and research forward. *Early Childhood Research Quarterly*, 45(2018), 188–192. https://www.sciencedirect.com/science/article/abs/pii/S0885200618300371

Weiland, C., McCormick, M., Mattera, S., Maier, M., & Morris, P. (2018). Preschool curricula and professional development features for getting to high-quality implementation at scale: A comparative review across five trials. *AERA Open*, 4(1). https://journals.sagepub.com/doi/full/10.1177/2332858418757735

Wenz-Gross, M., Yoo, Y., Upshur, C. C., & Gambino, A. J. (2018). Pathways to kindergarten readiness: The roles of Second Step early learning curriculum and social emotional, executive functioning, preschool academic and task behavior skills. *Frontiers in Psychology*, 9, 1886. https://psycnet.apa.org/record/2018-52628-001

Whitaker, R. C., Becker, B. D., Herman, A. N., & Gooze, R. A. (2013). The physical and mental health of Head Start staff: The Pennsylvania Head Start Staff Wellness Survey, 2012. *Preventing Chronic Disease*, 10. https://doi.org/10.5888/pcd10.130171

Whitaker, R. C., Dearth-Wesley, T., & Gooze, R. A. (2015). Workplace stress and the quality of teacher–children relationships in Head Start. *Early Childhood Research Quarterly*, 30, 57–69. https://doi.org/10.1016/j.ecresq.2014.08.008

Whitebook, M., McLean, C., Austin, L. J. E., & Edwards, B. (2018). *The early childhood workforce index—2018*. Center for the Study of Child Care Employment, University of California, Berkeley. Accessed January 15, 2022. https://cscce.berkeley.edu/wp-content/uploads/2022/04/Early-Childhood-Workforce-Index-2018.pdf

Whitebook, M., Phillips, D., & Howes, C. (2014). *Worthy work, still unlivable wages: The early childhood workforce 25 years after the National Child Care Staffing Study*. First Five Years Fund. https://www.ffyf.org/wp-content/uploads/2014/11/Child-Care-Employment-Report-11.18.14.pdf

Williams, D. R., & Mohammed, S. A. (2009). Discrimination and racial disparities in health: Evidence and needed research. *Journal of Behavioral Medicine*, *32*, 20–47. https://doi.org/10.1007%2Fs10865-008-9185-0

———. (2013). Racism and health I: Pathways and scientific evidence. *American Behavioral Science*, *57*, 1152–1173. https://doi.org/10.1177%2F0002764213487340

Williams, S. T., Mastergeorge, A. M., & Ontai, L. L. (2010). Caregiver involvement in infant peer interactions: Scaffolding in a social context. *Early Childhood Research Quarterly*, *25*(2), 251–266. https://doi.org/10.1016/j.ecrq.2009.11.004

Williford, A. P., Alamos, P., Whittacker, J. E., & Accavotta, M. R. (2021). *Who's left out of learning? Racial disparities in teachers' reports of exclusionary discipline strategies beyond suspensions and expulsions*. (EdWorkingPaper No. 21-472). Annenberg Institute at Brown University. https://doi.org/10.26300/pep2-w676

Winsler, A., Kim, Y. K., & Richard, E. R. (2014). Social-emotional skills, behavior problems, and Spanish competence predict the acquisition of English among English language learners in poverty. *Developmental Psychology*, *50*(9), 2242–2254. https://doi.org/10.1037/a0037161

Wong, C. A., Eccles, J., & Sameroff, A. J. (2003). The influence of ethnic discrimination and ethnic identification on African American adolescents' school and socioemotional adjustment. *Journal of Personality*, *71*, 1197–1232. https://doi.org/10.1111/1467-6494.7106012

Wood, J. L., Essien, I., & Blevins, D. (2020). Black males in kindergarten: The effect of social skills on close and conflictual relationships with teachers. *Journal of African American Males in Education (JAAME)*, *8*(2), 30–50. https://jaamejournal.scholasticahq.com/article/18490-black-males-in-kindergarten-the-effect-of-social-skills-on-close-and-conflictual-relationships-with-teachers

Wright, B. L. (2018). *The brilliance of Black boys: Cultivating school success in the early grades*. Teachers College Press.

Wright, B. L., & Counsell, S. L. (2018). *The brilliance of Black boys: Cultivating school success in the early grades*. Teachers College Press.

Wright, A., Martin, A., Castle, S., Phillips, D. A., Johnson, A. D., & Tulsa SEED Study Team. (2024). The roles of student-teacher relationship quality and classroom self-regulatory supports for children's self-regulatory skills in kindergarten and first grade. *Early Education and Development*, 1–25. https://doi.org/10.1080/10409289.2024.2360870

Wymer, S. C., Corbin, C. M., & Williford, A. P. (2022). The relation between teacher and child race, teacher perceptions of disruptive behavior, and exclusionary discipline in preschool. *Journal of School psychology*, *90*, 33–42. https://doi.org/10.1016/j.jsp.2021.10.003

Yoshikawa, H., Weiland, C., Brooks-Gunn, J., Burchinal, M. R., Espinosa, L. M., Gormley, W. T., Ludwig, J., Magnuson, K., Phillips, D., & Zaslow, M. J. (2013). *Investing in our future: The evidence base on preschool education*. Foundation for Child Development. https://www.fcd-us.org/the-evidence-base-on-preschool/

6

Specialized and Targeted Curricula and Practices for Supporting Children with Disabilities

Providing equitable educational experiences for children with disabilities centers on offering access to learning opportunities that enhance their ability to achieve personal goals throughout their lifespan, their eventual economic stability, and their equal status in society (Cole, 2022; Hehir, 2012). The inclusion of children with disabilities in general early learning and education settings constitutes a fundamental civil right upheld by both legal precedent and a large body of research evidence. However, inclusion of young children with disabilities in preschool settings has not significantly improved for several decades. In addition, children with specific diagnoses, such as intellectual disability or emotional disturbance, and children with multiple diagnoses are less likely to be included in early education settings (Meek et al., 2020b).

The fields of early intervention and early childhood special education (ECSE) are based on the premise that maximizing growth and development early on can avoid further delays and disability diagnoses (Early Childhood Technical Assistance Center, n.d.). Although many options for general early childhood curricula are available in preschool settings, they often lack sufficient dosage, intensity, and focus to meaningfully improve the progress of children who are experiencing moderate to significant developmental delays (Hebbeler & Spiker, 2016; National Academies of Sciences, Engineering, and Medicine, 2023). Targeted and scaffolded approaches to instruction have been found to be necessary to enhance the developmental trajectories of children with disabilities (Division for Early Childhood [DEC], 2014). Status quo educational practices and access to inclusive educational environments can vary significantly across and within states and by factors such as age, race and ethnicity, home language, and family income (Meek et al., 2020a,b; National Academies, 2023). These variations can affect opportunities to meaningfully improve growth trajectories; give attention to children's individualized goals; and provide developmental supports to address intellectual, language, social-emotional, or motor delays. This is especially true for children facing multiple risk factors. The Individuals with Disabilities Education Act (IDEA) guarantees a child's right to a free and appropriate public education in the least restrictive environment with a focus on individualized goals and objectives that directly address areas of need identified through an evaluation process. Given the mandate of individualization in IDEA, general curricula may not provide adequate supports for teachers to individualize and effectively address the specialized needs of young children identified with delays or disabilities.

This chapter focuses on the various curricula that fill a gap in educational practices for serving preschool children with disabilities effectively. The chapter begins with a brief overview of special education, followed by a discussion of contextual factors related to race, discrimination, and disability and inclusionary practices. Next is a discussion of curricula designed for children with disabilities, including activity-based curricula, curricula with integrated assessment, curricular approaches for children with autism spectrum disorder, and curricular approaches for multilingual learners with disabilities. Importantly, this report is focused on curricula and not individual strategies, practices, or approaches focused solely on parent training. A long line of research in these areas falls outside of the scope of this report. Specialized curricula available for children with disabilities are limited; however, those identified by the committee, along with the evidence base for their use and their intended purposes, are described in this chapter.

THE NEEDS OF CHILDREN WITH DISABILITIES

Research shows that children with disabilities benefit from being educated in inclusive settings that provide them with access to engaging early education experiences in natural settings (i.e., educational settings that are typical for a child of the same age without a disability) with typically developing peers (Frazeur Cross et al., 2004; Rafferty et al., 2003). Indeed, inclusion in high-quality preschool programs has been shown to promote positive academic, developmental, and social outcomes (National Academies, 2023). To meet the range of needs of all children with disabilities, special education services are designed to be delivered across a variety of settings, including at home, in child care settings, in general early education programs, and in self-contained ECSE classrooms. This continuum of services is designed to meet the identified individualized needs of children by addressing their goals and objectives in the least restrictive environments—a requirement by law (IDEA, 1995).

Children with disabilities require curricula that provide specific strategies and approaches for teaching developmental skills across all areas of development (Barton & Smith, 2015; DEC, 2014). It is important for curricula and pedagogical approaches to embed strategies that are most likely to improve specific developmental outcomes. For example, children with autism will likely require specialized intervention focused on language and social skills development (Fuller & Kaiser, 2020; Landa, 2018; Pasco; 2018). Likewise, children with Down syndrome will require focused support for gross and fine motor development, as well as attention to cognitive development (Bull, 2020; Marchal et al., 2016).

A Brief Overview of Special Education

The Education for All Handicapped Children Act (EHA), enacted by Congress in 1975, formally supported states and localities in upholding the rights of children with disabilities and their families in order to effectively meet their needs and promote positive learning and developmental outcomes. Prior to the EHA, many children were excluded from opportunities to attend public school. For example, in 1970, laws in many states excluded children with intellectual disability, emotional disturbances, and children who were deaf or blind. In 1986, the law was updated to address early intervention and mandate provision of services to children with disabilities from birth, which had previously not been a requirement until 3 years of age. A 1990 reauthorization renamed this law the Individuals with Disabilities Education Act (IDEA). This update to the law extended mandated services to children from birth to 5 years of age who met criteria for developmental delay. This update also added traumatic brain injury and autism as new disability categories (U.S. Department of Education [ED], 2024).

Children in the birth–5 age group generally qualify for special education under the criteria for developmental delay or speech and language impairment (Office of Special Education Programs [OSEP], 2020). For example, to qualify for special education services under the developmental delay criteria, children must perform at least 1.5 standard deviations below the mean in two or more developmental areas on standardized tests (IDEA, 2017). Once children qualify, they are provided with an Individualized Family Service Plan (IFSP) or Individualized Education Program (IEP) that specifies the educational goals for the child and objectives for achieving mastery under each goal. IFSPs are generally for children aged 0–3 years, and they emphasize family and community supports. IEPs are generally for children aged 3 years and above, and they emphasize services delivered in preschool settings.

IDEA also requires the delivery of services in the least restrictive environment, which calls for a range of options to meet a child's educational needs in settings with typically developing peers (IDEA, 2004). A premise of this mandate is to include children with disabilities with their typically developing peers to the maximum extent possible. To this end, children with disabilities must be provided with effective supports to facilitate their meaningful inclusion in general education preschool settings and in community-based care. The special education team must explore all options for including the child in preschools and early care settings before deciding on more restrictive options, such as a self-contained special education preschool classroom.

Currently about 70% of children aged 3–5 who are identified as having a disability attend a general early education program (OSEP, 2020); however, 3-year-olds have lower rates of inclusion in general early learning programs compared with their older peers. Research suggests that early exposure to segregated educational settings can increase the likelihood of children remaining in such settings throughout their academic career (Meek et al., 2020b). Curricula that are designed to support the learning, development, and inclusion of children with disabilities are a key element of creating equitable educational experiences for all children.

Research has documented that children with disabilities may need specific supports to address developmental delays in areas such as language and literacy (Dennis et al., 2012; Gillon, 2005; Green et al., 2014; Hindson et al., 2005; O'Connor et al., 1993). The development of language and communication skills lays a crucial foundation for children's emergent literacy and successful social interactions. Children with disabilities frequently face challenges in their interactions with both peers and the adults who are teaching them these skills, hindering their full participation in typical learning environments. Yet, preschool curricula created for typically developing children have largely not been studied to see whether they are effective for children with disabilities, and most research on interventions has focused on children in either clinical or small-group settings rather than classroom settings (Hebbeler & Spiker, 2016). The committee's review of the literature found a dearth of curricula that focus specifically on effectively supporting inclusion and provide appropriate supports for children with disabilities that can maximize the benefits of early education for this population.

Prevalence and Incidence of Categorial Disabilities and Access to Services

IDEA Part B, Section 619, ensures that children aged 3–5 years who have disabilities have equitable opportunity for full participation in free and appropriate education and receive supports and services to address their individual needs. In 2018, 6.75% of all children in the United States in this age range were served by IDEA. Of these, 30.53% are female, and 69.47% are male; 50.61% are White, 26.53% are Hispanic/Latine, 12.86% are Black, 4.08% are Asian, 1.17% are American Indian or Alaska Native, 0.29% are Native Hawaiian or other Pacific Islander, and 4.46% are two or more races. And 8.43% were identified as English learners (ED et al., 2020).

IDEA covers 13 disability categories. The percentage of students in the 3–5 years age group that receive special education and/or related services under IDEA Part B, Section 619, in each of these categories are as follows: speech or language impairment 41.44%, developmental delay 37.71%, autism 11.41%, intellectual disability 1.64%, specific learning disability 1.09%, hearing impairment 1.09%, orthopedic impairment 0.63%, emotional disturbance 0.35%, visual impairment 0.33%, traumatic brain injury 0.14%, deaf-blindness 0.02%, multiple disabilities 0.95%, and other health impairment 3.2% (ED et al., 2020; OSEP, 2021a).

Barriers to access to early intervention and special education services are the result of multiple structural factors, including persistent underfunding and uneven service distribution across states and localities—particularly in rural areas and underserved communities of color. In addition, the scarcity of qualified and certified professionals conducting evaluations, interventions, and other services creates barriers to timely evaluation and high-quality support for children with disabilities. Furthermore, policy and technical considerations that influence access, such as eligibility criteria and screening for disabilities, can vary from state to state (Hirai et al., 2018; Macy et al., 2014; National Academies, 2019, 2023; National Research Council, 2002; OSEP, 2021a). Indeed, eligibility criteria for special education in preschool—and the effect on access—has been noted as an area of particular concern. States determine how to define "developmental delay"—one of the most prevalent categories for eligibility for this age group. These state-to-state variations include differences in the number of areas of delay needed to qualify as well as the extent of delay that must be met in order to meet eligibility criteria (i.e., 1.5 versus 2.0 standard deviations below the mean). As a result, children who meet eligibility criteria in one state may not be eligible in another (OSEP, 2021a).

Race, Discrimination, and Disability

A large and growing number of children are born into families who have been marginalized because of race, linguistic background, culture, low socioeconomic status, or undocumented immigration status. These populations in the United States have historically experienced discrimination and diminished opportunities for school success (National Academies, 2023; National Center for Education Statistics, 2023).

While minimal data about the languages spoken at home are available for young children receiving early intervention and ECSE services, 8.43% of children aged 3–5 years served under Part B were identified as English learners, as noted in the previous section (ED et al., 2020). In addition to issues of race and home language, about 35% of U.S. children born to immigrants have parents who are unauthorized (Annie E. Casey Foundation, 2021). This compromised immigration status can create additional vulnerabilities and barriers to parents' ability to access services for their children with disabilities because of fears of forced deportation and family separation (Cycyk & Durán, 2020).

When considering the unique needs of children with disabilities, it is critical that providers be prepared to cultivate an intersectional lens that acknowledges and addresses the stark inequities that exist for Black and Brown children receiving early intervention and ECSE services (Blanchard et al., 2021; Love & Beneke 2021). In general, the success of children who have been marginalized in the United States has long been impeded by factors related to bias and structural racism (Iruka et al., 2022). Historically, many laws and policies in the United States have disadvantaged and inequitably supported marginalized communities across multiple sectors and settings, including educational settings (National Academies, 2023). Accordingly, children from populations that have been historically marginalized disproportionately experience poverty and limited access to high-quality early childhood education and health care, leading to poorer performance on measures of language, literacy, and math at the time of preschool entry as compared with their White peers (National Assessment of Educational Progress, 2019). These academic challenges are amplified for Black and Latine children with disabilities (Graves & Ye, 2017; Rios & Burke, 2021).

Young children operate within social contexts in which factors such as racism, ableism, and other types of oppression can intersect and perpetuate inequitable systems. The negative impact of bias and discrimination on the basis of multiple marginalizing identities on child development must be considered. These biases—both implicit and explicit—can have both psychological and social-emotional consequences for young children that affect how they learn, develop, and thrive as members of their communities (Beneke et al., 2021). Garbarino & Ganzel (2000) developed a model that describes how the convergence of multiple risk factors over time jeopardizes child outcomes. In other words, the many inequities experienced by children with disabilities can be compounded when other identity intersections (e.g., race, ethnicity, class, nativity) are taken into account, which can affect their development profoundly (National Academies, 2023). These effects are magnified by inequitable practices within the education system. It has been found, for example, that Black children are overidentified with emotional-behavioral disorders and as early as preschool are being expelled at significantly higher rates compared with White children (Gilliam & Reyes, 2018; Gilliam et al., 2016; National Academies, 2023). There are also widespread trends of English learners being overidentified for learning disabilities in the United States since the 1960s, which disproportionately affects Latine children (National Center for Learning Disabilities, 2020; Rodríguez & Rodríguez, 2017). Curricula designed for children with disabilities that provide supports for implementing equitable, antibias, and antiracist teaching practices have the potential to help ameliorate the negative impacts of biases on children's opportunities and academic outcomes.

Inclusionary Practices

Receiving services in inclusive settings has been found to promote a variety of positive academic and social outcomes for children with disabilities, as well as positive social outcomes for children without disabilities (National Academies, 2023). There is wide variation between the states with the most and least inclusive classroom settings. In 2020, 34.8% of children aged 3–5 years received the majority of their services in regular early childhood classrooms. More than a quarter (27.7%) of children receiving services were in a separate classroom (i.e., a classroom that included less than 50% children without disabilities), and the number of children in separate classrooms varied by race and ethnicity: Asian 40.4%, Native Hawaiian or other Pacific Islander 33.4%, Black 31.5%, Hispanic/Latine 31.3%, two or more races 30.5%, White 23.5%, and American Indian or Alaska Native 21.8%. In five states, the percentage of children served by IDEA Part B in separate classrooms was more than 50% (OSEP, 2022a). Data also show that 3-year-olds are most likely to receive special education services in settings that are less inclusive (Meek et al., 2020b).

Head Start is the largest federally funded preschool program in the United States, and it provides one of the primary contexts for inclusion (Administration for Children and Families, n.d.). It is mandated that at least 10% of Head Start enrollment include children with disabilities (U.S. Department of Health and Human Services, 2007). Inclusionary practices afford children with disabilities the opportunity to be educated alongside their typically developing peers and are broadly supported by leading national organizations focused on the education of young children, such as the Division for Early Childhood (DEC) and National Association for the Education of Young Children (NAEYC; 2009; see also IDEA, 2004). Evidence also shows that inclusion improves the developmental outcomes of children with disabilities (Barton & Smith, 2015; Lawrence et al., 2016). Research indicates that young children with disabilities enrolled in inclusive, high-quality early childhood programs demonstrate greater developmental gains in cognitive, communicative, and social-emotional domains compared with their peers who are in more segregated learning environments. The realization of these benefits is contingent upon consistent inclusion throughout the week that spans diverse social and learning experiences, combined with the provision of individualized instructional strategies in inclusive learning environments (Holahan & Costenbader, 2000; Justice et al., 2014; Meek et al., 2020b; Strain, 1983). Moreover, including individuals with disabilities promotes equity, and disability rights advocates have long argued that excluding children with disabilities from general education settings is discriminatory (Arduin, 2015; White House, 2021). However, despite expansion of public pre-K programs, there has not been a corresponding increase in inclusive learning opportunities for children with disabilities, highlighting the underutilization of public pre-K as a potential vehicle for promoting inclusion (Meek et al., 2020b).

Importantly, however, inclusion does not mean that children with disabilities are simply placed in general education settings; the spirit of inclusion is to meaningfully engage children with disabilities in classroom activities and provide opportunities for them to develop to their full potential alongside their same-age, typically developing peers (DEC & NAEYC, 2009). Within programs, commonly identified barriers to inclusion include negative attitudes and beliefs held by teachers and administrators, limited teacher self-efficacy regarding instruction of children with disabilities, perceived or real policy or financial constraints, inadequate workforce preparation, disjointed services and systems, a lack of oversight and accountability mechanisms, and a pervasive reluctance to alter the status quo (Meek et al., 2020b). It has been well documented that general education teachers need specialized professional development and adequate supports to teach young children with disabilities effectively (D'Agostino & Douglas, 2021; Stites et al., 2021). While positive attitudes toward inclusion are prevalent among many teachers, a study of Head Start and public pre-K teachers found that many of the educators did not have a strong sense of self-efficacy in implementing inclusive practices such as individualized instruction and alternative communication methods. They also identified priority areas for professional development, particularly in managing behavioral issues, positioning children with motor impairments, and teaching communication strategies (Bruns & Mogharreban, 2007; Meek et al., 2020b). Families of children with disabilities have also reported barriers to inclusion such as limited child care options, rejections from programs, and unstable child care arrangements (Booth-LaForce & Kelly, 2004; Grisham-Brown et al., 2010; Knoche et al., 2006; Meek et al., 2020b; Weglarz-Ward & Santos, 2018).

Despite compelling evidence supporting inclusion, research highlights several persistent barriers. These include the intersection of race, disability, and other identity categories, and the effect of this intersection on placement decisions, which can potentially lead to inequitable access for specific groups. Ableism, misinformed perceptions held by educators and administrators, lack of professional development opportunities, and insufficient coordination between early childhood programs and local special education service providers further hinder inclusion efforts (Meek et al., 2020b).

SOCIAL AND EMOTIONAL DEVELOPMENT

There is well-documented evidence concerning the needs of children with disabilities with respect to social-emotional development and the potential vulnerabilities that this population faces in terms of social exclusion and peer victimization—both are discussed in this section.

Social Inclusion

Despite ongoing efforts to foster diversity and social inclusion in preschool classrooms, research finds that simply increasing classroom diversity is insufficient to realize the full benefits of inclusive education for children with disabilities (Chen et al., 2017; Diamond, 2001; Kwon et al., 2011). Rather, these benefits are contingent upon opportunities for positive and productive social interactions. A 2019 study on peer interactions explored the influence of pragmatic language and self-regulation skills on play interactions. The findings of this study revealed that skill in both pragmatic language and self-regulation was a positive predictor of cross-status play (i.e., interactions between children with disabilities and their typically developing peers), and that pragmatic language appeared to be more crucial for children with disabilities in fostering these cross-status interactions than it was for children without disabilities—highlighting a challenge in forming interactions across disability groups (Lin et al., 2019). These findings underscore the need for educators to have supports that allow them to tailor their inclusion practices to individual students' needs in these domains. Given the established link between these skills and children's academic and social success (Duncan et al., 2007), these findings also suggest that educational programs promoting these skills—for instance, collaborative small-group activities fostering high-quality social interactions—could have a synergistic effect on the overall development of all children (Lin et al., 2019).

Studies have also shown a relationship between specific social-communicative skills and social acceptance in preschoolers. Research suggests that children who can effectively demonstrate skills such as initiating conversation with peers, taking turns during social interactions, and adapting responses based on their peers' communication are preferred communication partners for their peers. In a study of children with varying language abilities, children with specific language impairments tended to interact more with adults and had fewer interactions with their peers. These findings highlight the importance of early intervention programs that can enhance both social and communicative skills in children with disabilities. Although numerous interventions exist to improve the social skills of this population, often using direct instruction approaches (Stanton-Chapman & Snell, 2011), a growing body of evidence suggests that interventions incorporating multiple domains (social, language, cognitive) are more effective in promoting positive social outcomes and contributing to children's future academic success (Caprara et al., 2000; Guralnick, 1992; Stanton-Chapman & Snell, 2011).

Social Behavior and Social Competence

Delays in social-emotional development in early childhood can have lasting effects across all developmental domains. Children with disabilities may sometimes require additional supports to help develop skills in social communication and interaction. These skills are essential for establishing and cultivating relationships across the lifespan. When opportunities to develop social skills early in childhood are absent or constrained, children with disabilities do not have an equal opportunity to achieve full inclusion (McCollow & Hoffman, 2019). And when social-emotional development is not adequately supported, young children's opportunities to learn can be impeded, and they may have increased risk of being excluded from educational settings (Brown et al., 2012).

Researchers have documented that children exhibiting emotional and behavioral problems may experience a variety of challenges in preschool classrooms that affect their peer relationships and their ability to learn (Bulotsky-Shearer et al., 2008; Lee et al., 2016). Children with disabilities may need more supports than their typically developing peers to achieve positive social-emotional outcomes (Lee et al., 2016).

Many school systems have adopted multitiered systems of support (MTSS) for those experiencing learning and behavioral difficulties, and many early childhood programs are beginning to adopt this approach (Buysse & Peisner-Feinberg, 2013; Hebbeler & Spiker, 2016). MTSS has four key components: (1) leadership teams that plan and support the delivery of tiered interventions; (2) universal screening; (3) delivery of increasingly intensive instruction for learners identified as needing extra support, where Tier 1 is universal instruction, Tier 2 is targeted support, and Tier 3 is intensive support; and (4) monitoring of progress (Al Otaiba et al., 2023; Fletcher et al., 2014).

One MTSS model, the Pyramid Model for Promoting Social Emotional Competence in Infants and Young Children, is a highly influential model implemented in preschool programs across the United States to improve social-emotional development and reduce challenging behavior in preschool settings for all children, including those with developmental disabilities (Fox et al., 2010; Hebbeler & Spiker, 2016; Hemmeter et al., 2006, 2013). (See Chapter 4 for a more detailed description of the Pyramid Model.)

Children with disabilities often require explicit instruction in social skills. The Pyramid Model provides educators with substantial support in facilitating social-emotional skill development. These interventions mitigate disruptive behaviors and enhance a child's ability to learn. This is especially critical in inclusive environments, as children with disabilities are 2.5 times more likely than their typically developing peers to be expelled from preschool because of behavioral concerns (ED, 2023). The Pyramid Model may also provide insights that could be applied to developing integrated MTSS approaches that would focus not just on academics or social-emotional development but on both simultaneously, recognizing that social-emotional skills provide the foundation for learning (Wackerle-Hollman et al., 2021). While emerging evidence suggests that this approach can help to achieve both positive academic and behavioral outcomes, further research is needed to better understand the implementation of MTSS across diverse program settings (Hebbeler & Spiker, 2016).

Peer Victimization

A 2016 study by the National Academies on bullying prevention in youth found that students with disabilities were at increased risk for bullying and that this disproportionate risk begins in preschool (National Academies, 2016; Son et al., 2012). The preschool years offer an opportunity for the cultivation of essential competencies necessary for navigating peer relationships throughout life. Existing research indicates that children with disabilities are more susceptible to and experience peer victimization with greater frequency than their nondisabled peers (Son et al., 2012).

There is considerable evidence that peer victimization constitutes a significant social issue with deleterious potential impacts on children's psychosocial well-being and educational outcomes, often with lasting effects such as depression, social withdrawal, poor academic performance, low self-esteem, and school absence or avoidance (Brunstein-Klomek et al., 2007; Fekkes et al., 2006; Glew et al., 2005; Hawker & Boulton, 2000; Sourander et al., 2006).

A 2012 study examining preschool peer victimization, using data from the Pre-Elementary Education Longitudinal Study, discovered that approximately one-fifth to one-third of children with disabilities experienced physical (e.g., tripping, kicking, hitting, punching) and verbal (e.g., teasing, threatening harm, name-calling) victimization. These findings emphasize the urgent need for proactive strategies and supports in preschool classrooms to prevent the bullying of children with disabilities (Son et al., 2012).

CURRICULA DESIGNED FOR CHILDREN WITH DISABILITIES

This section describes curricula that are commonly implemented in settings that include or have been designed specifically for children with disabilities. It is important to note that many lack adequate research findings to describe them as "evidence based." The committee's commissioned literature review on preschool curriculum quality (School Readiness Consulting [SRC], 2022) found that children with disabilities are largely underrepresented in the reviewed studies related to curriculum effectiveness, impact on child outcomes, and curriculum scalability. Ratings of 17 curricula reported in the Curriculum Consumer Report (National Center on Early Childhood Development, Teaching, and Learning [NCECDTL], 2020), which reviews selected curricula used by Head Start grantees,[1] found that only 4 had full evidence for individualization for children with disabilities and developmental delays (NCECDTL, 2020; SRC, 2022). Taken as a whole, the literature reviewed did not offer sufficient empirical evidence to make valid inferences about how well most of the extant curricula work for children with disabilities (SRC, 2022). This area is ripe for growth.

More research is needed to test the efficacy of these curricula across the diverse populations of children served by IDEA Part B programs. Hebbeler & Spiker (2016) note some of the challenges in conducting research on interventions for children with disabilities. For example, the legal entitlement to individually determined services makes it impossible to use random assignments or control groups that receive no treatment. In addition, the population of children with disabilities is very diverse both across and within disability categories; many assessment tools have not been validated for use with this population, and sample sizes are limited for some disability categories.

The curricula included in this chapter include activity-based curricula, curricula with integrated assessment and intervention planning systems, and curricular approaches for children with autism. It should be noted that the committee was not asked to evaluate individual curricula, isolated strategies, or parent training programs as part of this study. The curricula

---

[1] The *Curriculum Consumer Report*'s ratings are based on criteria of effective, comprehensive curricula. The criterion for *Individualization for Children with Disabilities, Suspected Delays, or Other Special Needs* notes that "individualization for children with disabilities, suspected delays, or other special needs includes providing more specialized supports for children to access and participate in learning, social experiences, and activities. The curriculum's guidance for specialized supports includes specific teaching practices and ways of interacting with children, as well as adaptations to daily schedules, learning activities, and the learning environment. Individualizing for children with disabilities, suspected delays, or other special needs enables all children to access, participate, and thrive in early learning settings" (NCECDTL, 2020; see https://eclkc.ohs.acf.hhs.gov/curriculum/consumer-report/criteria/individualization-children-disabilities-suspected-delays-or-other-special-needs).

described in this section have not been evaluated or endorsed by the committee. They are included as examples of existing curricula that are intended for use with children with disabilities, have been widely used in the field, and have been influential in teaching practices.

Activity-Based Curricula

Building Blocks for Teaching Preschoolers with Special Needs (Sandall et al., 2019) is an activity-based curriculum that allows teachers to develop activity matrices that systematically incorporate children's special education objectives and strategies for addressing their developmental needs into classroom routines. The idea behind *Building Blocks* is that teachers can learn to target children's specific learning needs during all classroom routine activities, thereby facilitating inclusion with a systematic and intentional focus throughout the school day (Sandall et al., 2019). *Building Blocks*[2] can be used in conjunction with any early childhood curriculum, making it a versatile tool for supporting inclusion across a diverse array of early education settings. The curriculum provides a host of recommended accommodations to help teachers consider ways to adapt their instruction and the classroom environment to meet each child's educational needs.

The *Building Blocks* curriculum provides a roadmap for meaningfully addressing the needs of children with disabilities throughout a typical preschool day while also maintaining the structure of a general education preschool classroom. It provides forms that can be completed to help teachers create an activity matrix, which includes the classroom's daily schedule. During each activity, teachers specify in writing exactly how they will target the objectives in children's IFSPs/IEPs during the activity and what specific accommodations or adaptations they will use. This process requires teachers to plan ahead and intentionally incorporate the needs of children with disabilities into classroom routines and activities on a daily basis. *Building Blocks* also provides a significant array of suggested adaptations and accommodations that teachers can draw upon in their planning. Although no research has specifically measured the effects of the *Building Blocks* curriculum, it is widely used and follows the practices supported by the 2009 DEC/NAEYC joint position statement (DEC & NAEYC, 2009) on early childhood inclusion, which was affirmed by the U.S. Department of Health and Human Services (2018).

---

[2]*Building Blocks for Teaching Preschoolers with Special Needs* is published by Brookes Publishing and is a separate curriculum from *Building Blocks™ Pre-K* published by McGraw-Hill, which is discussed in other parts of this report.

Curricula with Integrated Assessment

Specific curricula have been developed for children with disabilities that include criterion-referenced assessments with companion curricula. These approaches allow teachers to measure children's developmental needs in small increments of change across the core areas of development, including receptive and expressive language, fine and gross motor skills, adaptive development, and social-emotional development. With baseline data for each child, teachers can use the companion curriculum to target their instruction specifically to the child's level in that developmental domain. The criterion-referenced assessments provide a scope and sequence of skills to be mastered so that teachers receive concrete guidance on what to teach next. These curricula can also be particularly informative for IFSP/IEP goal planning and monitoring of children's progress.

The Assessment, Evaluation, and Programming System (AEPS-3)

AEPS-3, available for use with children aged 0–6 years, is a widely used, curriculum-based, seamless assessment and educational planning system (Bagnato et al., 2010; Bricker et al., 2022). It is appropriate for use with all young children, including those who are developing typically, are learning English, have resettled from other countries, are at risk for or have developmental delays, and have documented disabilities. It is also available in Spanish. The AEPS-3 test covers the development of young children in eight major developmental areas: fine motor, gross motor, adaptive, social-emotional, social-communication, cognitive, literacy, and math. The assessment portion of the integrated system has been found to have good score agreement and test–retest score reliability (Grisham et al., 2021). Hsia (1993) found that the AEPS Test for Three to Six Years was sensitive to differences in performance between children with disabilities and those without, as well as among children of different ages. This result provided evidence for the hierarchical nature of the AEPS test, which is intended to be sensitive to differences in performance among various age groups. As goals and objectives become progressively more difficult, the AEPS test can identify children at risk for developmental delays if they cannot perform skills within the average range of their age bracket. Additional, federally funded studies of the instructional validity of the AEPS test indicated that its use was conducive to writing more functional IFSPs and IEPs (Bricker et al., 2022). For use after the AEPS test, the *AEPS-3* curriculum is an activity-based, multitiered curriculum that helps professionals support children's development with differentiated instruction in the same eight developmental areas addressed by the assessment.

A modest amount of evidence points to the psychometric properties of the *AEPS-3*. Studies on its utility show that participants find it useful for monitoring progress and planning—a finding consistent with studies of earlier versions (Bailey & Bricker, 1986; Gao & Grisham-Brown, 2008; Grisham et al., 2021; Hamilton, 1995). Studies also found that the assessment could be carried out with relatively high levels of interrater reliability (≥ 80%; Grisham et al., 2021). Although a 2021 study noted positive results on the utility and feasibility of *AEPS-3*, the results of that study were based on a small number of participants (11 teachers/providers), who participated in the study during the 2020–2021 school year (Grisham et al., 2021). These teachers were provided with 3 hours of training on using the curriculum correctly with three focal children for 8–10 weeks; the teachers then participated in focus groups. They perceived that the *AEPS-3* curriculum helped them to implement recommended practices with young children with disabilities. Other studies of treatment validity of AEPS have used similarly small samples of teachers/providers and students (Grisham et al., 2021).

Hawaii Early Learning Profile (HELP)

HELP is an integrated, observational assessment tool and intervention system that applies to diverse settings and can be completed by educators, parents, specialists, and other professionals with expertise in early childhood development (Halle et al., 2011). HELP allows early educators to assess children's development and then design effective interventions to target their developmental needs. HELP 3–6 (2nd edition)[3] for preschoolers, an extension of the version that focuses on children from birth to age 3 years, covers six primary domains: cognitive, language, gross motor, fine motor, social, and self-help. The assessment portion of HELP 3–6 is divided into three books: the HELP 3–6 Assessment Manual; the Curriculum Guide; and Activities at Home, which offers suggestions for at-home activities that can be incorporated into daily routines to help support the child's development (Texas Education Agency, 2019). While the version for younger children has been shown to be valid and reliable (Li et al., 2019), there is still limited research on the use and efficacy of either version of HELP (Manfra et al., 2021).

The Carolina Curriculum for Preschoolers with Special Needs (CCPSN)

CCPSN (Johnson-Martin et al., 2004) is a curriculum-based observational measure designed to provide a systematic approach for developing intervention plans for children with mild to moderate disabilities who are

---

[3]More information about HELP products is available at https://shineearly.store/collections/help-3-6-years-2nd-ed-extends-beyond-help-0-3

functioning within the 24- to 60-month developmental range. It includes a criterion-referenced assessment for determining the child's mastery of five domains: social adaptation, cognitive, language, gross motor, and fine motor skills (Castro et al., 2011). CCPSN can offer valuable data for intervention planning and assessment procedures and aligns with widely recognized recommendations advocating for a strong linkage between these two elements. Establishing this linkage can foster continuity and predictability of improvement in performance for children with disabilities (Castro et al., 2011).

Once the assessment has been completed, the curriculum maps onto the areas of need it has identified. CCPSN allows professionals to work closely with the child's teachers, family members, and other service providers to document the child's skills across all areas of development. Each item on the assessment tool is linked directly to a curriculum item that describes procedures for teaching the assessed skill, providing a framework for moving smoothly from assessment to intervention. General modifications of the items in each developmental domain are also suggested so that a child's sensory or motor limitations can be accommodated. While CCPSN provides rich data on children's behavior, and the general approach is congruent with DEC-recommended practices, it is important to acknowledge its limited focus on environmental characteristics (physical, social, attitudinal). This potential gap necessitates the integration of complementary assessment tools to illuminate the impact of environmental factors on children's development and learning (Bagnato et al., 2010; Castro et al., 2011).

Curriculum Overview

Overall, the AEPS, HELP, and CCPSN provide similar approaches to linking assessment data with interventions. They provide teachers with a process for integrating assessment data with intervention planning for children with disabilities. While more research is needed on all three approaches, they provide a roadmap for designing curricula that integrate curriculum-based assessments, support data-based decision making, and enhance teachers' abilities to deliver differentiated and targeted instruction. In a new vision for curriculum, these approaches provide excellent examples of how researchers might consider building linked assessment and curriculum systems.

Curricular Approaches for Children with Autism Spectrum Disorder

Generally, curricula are not designed for specific disabilities; as described earlier in this chapter, they target various development domains that are often impacted by disability in early childhood development. However, autism is a notable exception. This section describes curricular approaches designed specifically for children with autism that have been broadly influential in the field of early childhood education. (For a thorough review of evidence-based practices for children with autism see Steinbrenner et al. [2020].)

Dramatically increasing prevalence rates of autism have prompted the development of curricula focused in this area. Since 2000, the prevalence of autism in the United States has nearly tripled, from 0.67% of all children to 1.85% (Johns Hopkins Bloomberg School of Public Health, 2020). Children with autism are increasingly included in general education preschool settings, but early childhood teachers need adequate and targeted supports for teaching children with autism effectively, given that, by definition, many of these children have significant delays in communication and social interaction and can engage in disruptive and challenging behaviors (D'Agostino & Douglas, 2021). Early educators have been found to benefit from training in and access to approaches directed at improving the joint attention, functional play, communication, and social skills of children with autism (D'Agostino & Douglas, 2021). These approaches are often designed to be delivered one-on-one or in small groups to maximize the individualized instructional supports and reinforcements offered. Many of the effective early intervention approaches for autism are based on the principles of applied behavior analysis (ABA; Behavior Analyst Certification Board [BACB], 2023). Principles of ABA include a prompt to the child (discriminant stimulus), a behavior from the child (response), and a consequence that is likely to reinforce the desired behavior (BACB, 2023). The differences among the various approaches that are grounded in ABA lie primarily in the types of rewards used and whether instructors deliver the therapy using a highly structured format or natural routines and play. In this section, the committee describes the intervention approaches for children with autism based on ABA techniques.

Discrete Trial Training (DTT)

DTT is the best-known and most widely used structured ABA technique for teaching children with autism; it has a broad research base demonstrating its efficacy specifically with preschool-aged children (Cohen et al., 2006; Howard et al., 2005; Remington et al., 2007; Smith et al., 2000a; Whalen & Schreibman, 2003). DTT was one of the first interventions developed for teaching children with autism, and it is still widely implemented in homes, schools, and community-based settings (e.g., Lerman et al., 2016). In preschool settings, DTT requires the teacher to divide skills into small, "discrete" components. The therapist teaches these skills systematically and one by one to the child. Tangible rewards are used to reinforce desired behavior. For a child, this might include a favorite food or access to a preferred toy or activity. For example, a teacher might start teaching colors by having the child point to the color blue and rewarding the behavior before moving on to the next color. After the child has receptively learned all his or her colors, the teacher might teach the child to say the name of each color.

It is important to note, however, that some have criticized DTT and its lack of naturalistic interactions, as well as the limited evidence that children can generalize the skills learned in these controlled, one-on-one settings (Charlop-Christy et al., 1999). DTT sessions are in fact most often conducted in isolated cubicles to reduce distractions. Nevertheless, researchers have recently begun conducting DTT sessions in more naturalistic settings, during functional daily routines, while allowing more progressive approaches that include flexible feedback to children based on their individual responses to the prompts or stimuli (Haq & Aranki, 2019; Steinbrenner et al., 2020).

In a new vision for early childhood curriculum, early childhood educators teaching children with autism who are receiving DTT therapy will need practical guidance for supporting the generalization of skills learned in DTT sessions during naturally occurring preschool routines. Teachers will need specific guidance and support on helping children with increasing engagement with peers, functional communication, and symbolic play. Although general education teachers should not be responsible for conducting DTT sessions, it is important that they be aware of this approach, as caregivers may have opted for this type of therapy for their child. Early childhood teachers need access to accurate information about the benefits and limitations of DTT and their role in supporting the development of children with autism who are participating in DTT therapy.

Pivotal Response Treatment (PRT)

PRT is also based on the principles of ABA, but unlike DTT, PRT is a child-directed, naturalistic teaching strategy. The technique of PRT was developed by Drs. Lynn and Robert Koegel at the University of California, Santa Barbara, in 1987 (Simpson, 2005). With PRT, learning opportunities are determined by the child's interests, and the adult follows the child's lead during sessions. Learning opportunities are created based on the interests the child displays during the session. For example, a child who is enjoying playing with blocks might be asked to identify a red block and then asked to place it on the structure when she points to it correctly. The reinforcers offered are also naturalistic and based on the situation. For example, if the learning opportunity is based on getting the child to ask for bubbles, the bubbles become the natural reinforcer for a correct response rather than contrived reinforcers such as edibles.

More than 200 peer-reviewed journal articles and 30 books and manuals are based on PRT (Uljarević et al., 2022). The committee included PRT in this chapter because general education preschool teachers will likely need to use PRT techniques if children with autism are to realize the benefits of this approach. It is often recommended that teachers in inclusive settings continue the process for generalization to optimize its effects. To support implementation, researchers have developed a manualized approach to implementing PRT strategies with young children in a classroom setting: Strategies for Teaching based on Autism Research (STAR; Arick et al., 2004). STAR includes three levels: basic skills in verbal communication and following directions (Level 1); increasing language skills, play skills, and basic letter and number understanding (Level 2); and academic-focused interventions for expanding vocabulary, following complex routines, story recall, addition, and subtraction (Level 3). The STAR program's goal is to develop the child's skills in a highly structured environment and then use those skills in the child's natural environments (Stahmer et al., 2015). The curriculum is divided into six main areas: expressive language, receptive language, spontaneous language, functional routines, preacademic concepts, and play and social interaction skills (Arick et al., 2004). STAR uses three teaching strategies: DTT, PRT, and functional routines.

Studies of the STAR program have found positive effects (Arick et al., 2003; Bacon et al., 2014). For example, a relatively large-scale randomized controlled trial involving 302 preschoolers with autism in 84 classrooms found positive effects on children's receptive language (effect size of 0.13) and on their social skills as rated by teachers (effect size of 0.19; Young et al., 2016). Studies have also shown that teachers can learn to implement STAR strategies, but that they require intensive training, coaching, and time for achieving and maintaining the fidelity of the curriculum's implementation (Stahmer et al., 2015; Suhrheinrich, 2015).

Therefore, in a new vision for preschool curriculum development, general education teachers would have access to specialized curriculum for children with autism and ongoing training and coaching to support the implementation of the more specialized and targeted supports needed by these children. Collaborating with ECSE personnel would also be necessary, along with administrative support.

MULTILINGUAL LEARNERS WITH DISABILITIES

Today, a growing population of young children speak languages other than English at home. This report refers to these children as "multilingual learners"; they are also called "English learners" (National Academies, 2017; Park et al., 2018). English learners are specifically defined as students who have limited English proficiency upon school entry, as determined by performance on mandated English proficiency tests (Elementary and Secondary Education Act [ESEA], 2015). Despite awareness that language barriers can negatively impact the academic achievement of English learners, they are educated primarily in English-only contexts with limited educational supports (National Academies, 2017). Research also suggests that children who speak different dialects of English (e.g., African American English or Appalachian English), which are language systems in and of themselves, are unlikely to have access to preschool environments where their home dialect is recognized or supported (Wheeler, 2016). As described in Chapter 7, educators may endorse common misconceptions that multilingual learners should abandon their home language to improve their English proficiency; however, this notion is not supported by evidence, and it negatively impacts family relationships and identity development (National Academies, 2017; Portes and Hao, 1998).

Multilingual Children with Disabilities

The intersectionality of being a multilingual learner with disabilities presents unique challenges in today's preschool systems (Waitoller & Lubienski, 2019). Although research highlights the importance of home language development for academic and social-emotional success, the limited supply of curricular resources in other languages reduces opportunities for children of linguistically diverse backgrounds to access and effectively engage in instructional content. Reading begins with language development, and preschools have a critical role in scaffolding and fostering the language development of the young children they serve (Deshmukh et al., 2022). This responsibility and the critical need in the field demand that curricula designed for use in classrooms serving multilingual students have features that directly address their language learning needs in both their home language(s) and English. Moreover, in inclusive settings there will also be children who both are multilingual and have disabilities. These children will arguably need even more support to address their unique developmental needs.

Research provides evidence that children designated as English learners are actually underidentified for ECSE (Morgan et al., 2012; National Academies, 2023). This may be the result of confusion about how to identify multilingual children with special education needs and accurately differentiate between language delay or disorder and language characteristics that are also common in second language acquisition. In addition, for children who speak dialects other than General American English, language assessments may not accurately capture language and literacy skills, leading to incorrect identification of speech and language disabilities (Harris & Schroeder,

2013; Smith et al., 2000b). There are also issues related to conducting adequate and effective outreach in communities that speak languages other than English to inform families about the availability of services for children with delays and disabilities (The Education Trust, 2021). Both Child Find[4] and special education evaluation practices need to improve with respect to young multilinguals to ensure equity in access to services (Cycyk et al., 2022; Durán et al., 2023).

Importantly, however, once children enter kindergarten and have been identified as English learners, they tend to be overidentified with a special learning disability by third grade (NCLD, 2020; Rodríguez & Rodríguez, 2017), and 45% of the Latine students served under IDEA are served under the learning disability category (OSEP, 2022b). These trends suggest that general education settings are not meeting the instructional needs of English learners and are thereby contributing to these children's persistent reading problems throughout the early elementary grades that result in overidentification for special education (Waitoller et al., 2010). Even when these students receive special education services, they have been found to not experience the intended benefits of extra and individualized services (Hanson & Espinosa, 2016; Huang et al., 2021).

Promising Models for Multilingual Learners with Disabilities

Integrated models using the MTSS framework (discussed earlier in this chapter) have been proposed for children in preschool through second grade but are not implemented routinely in preschool settings (Carta & Miller Young, 2019; Wackerle-Hollman et al., 2021). In elementary grades, most states use MTSS approaches to identify and provide interventions for students with or at risk for special learning disabilities (Schiller et al., 2020). MTSS models are beneficial for multilingual learners (Balu et al., 2015) because they support early identification and preventive approaches (Al Otaiba et al., 2023; Doabler et al., 2019).

The U.S. Department of Education has funded three model demonstration projects to develop MTSS approaches specifically for English learners with and without disabilities (OSEP, 2018, 2021b). These projects provide important roadmaps for implementing MTSS successfully with English

---

[4]Part of IDEA Part B, Child Find mandates that states have policies and procedures to ensure that all children with disabilities who are residing in the state, including children with disabilities who are homeless, are wards of the state, or are attending private schools—regardless of the severity of their disability—and are in need of special education and related services are identified, located, and evaluated, and that a practical method is developed and implemented to determine which children are currently receiving needed special education and related services (IDEA, 2017).

learners, as well as maximizing early intervention delivery and reducing the misidentification of disabilities in the English learners population.

MTSS models in early childhood settings are gaining traction (Carta & Miller Young, 2019), but there are important considerations in designing these models for multilingual preschoolers. MTSS can be beneficial for all students, but the comprehensive and preventive approach may be particularly beneficial for students designated as English learners upon kindergarten entry. Attention to young children's varying levels of English proficiency is needed to ensure that practices are fair, equitable, accurate, and effective. Attention is also needed for the development of their home languages and the foundation this provides for English development and academic achievement (OSEP, 2018).

Another promising model is the *Vocabulary, Oral Language, and Academic Readiness* (VOLAR) intervention (Gutierrez-Clellen et al., 2014), which focuses on teaching vocabulary and oral language through shared book reading using common trade books with Spanish and English support. The curriculum was designed specifically for Spanish–English bilingual children experiencing language delays. Results indicate that participating in the VOLAR curriculum supports meaningful gains in vocabulary and oral language in English and Spanish for children who have identified speech and language disabilities (Simon-Cereijido, 2015). The curriculum is somewhat dated at this point, and the books that form the basis for the curriculum are no longer readily available, highlighting a pressing need to develop more curricula specifically for multilingual children with disabilities. Given that the vast majority of children served under IDEA Part B who are identified as English learners speak Spanish at home, Spanish is a priority language on which to focus for developing new multilingual curricula. However, this need not preclude efforts in communities to address the needs of all multilingual learners, particularly other large and growing populations, such as Mandarin-speaking children in San Francisco or Somali-speaking children in Minneapolis.

For multilingual learners, bilingual instruction yields better academic, social-emotional, and identity development outcomes than English-only instruction (Bialystok, 2018). Bilingual instruction has also been found to benefit young children with disabilities (Cheatham et al., 2012). In its position statement on advancing equity in early childhood education, NAEYC (2019) recommended that early childhood educators "design and implement learning activities using language(s) that the children understand" (p. 7). Bilingualism research shows that developing the home language(s) helps promote children's emotional well-being (Collins et al., 2011), their identity development through positive impacts on family relationships (Bialystok, 2018; Tseng & Fuligni 2000), and a host of academic skills (Winsler et al., 2014; see Chapter 7). Yet young multilingual learners whose home language differs from the language of instruction tend to shift from using their home language to using English as they enter preschool (Fillmore, 1991; Kan & Kohnert, 2005), and this shift continues in later years (Gibson et al., 2012; Mancilla-Martinez & Lesaux, 2011; Portes & Hao, 1998). According to Cummins's (1979) threshold hypothesis, a transfer of foundational academic skills from the first to the second language occurs once the learner has achieved high proficiency in the first language. Conversely, children learning in a second language before having developed proficiency in a first language face a host of challenges, including being unable to express oneself in the classroom, reduced opportunities for communication at home, having fewer opportunities for learning, and being at risk of being misdiagnosed for learning disabilities. Still, currently published dual language curricula are available only in Spanish, and even those are limited. Additionally, no evidence-based, published curricula have been developed in languages other than English or Spanish (Park et al., 2018).

As part of the committee's new vision, curricula would be developed in languages other than English from inception to foster language and concept development in children's home language, in order to build a strong foundation for academic success for all children. Ideally these curricula would be designed for inclusive settings with specific and targeted supports for children identified as having disabilities or delays. For children who are multilingual learners and have disabilities, limited and largely ineffective early education supports can inhibit their academic progress. Much more research and development are needed to provide curricula that effectively support their learning and development, reduce bias in practice, and elevate cultural and linguistic features for addressing these children's early education needs.

CONCLUSION

The inclusion of children with disabilities continues to be a pressing issue in early childhood education. It has been widely documented that early childhood educators are largely unprepared to meet the needs of children with disabilities and that more focused attention is needed on both preservice and in-service professional development to help teachers embrace inclusion, increase feelings of efficacy, and experience less burnout (D'Agostino & Douglas, 2021; Stites et al., 2021). To promote equity for young children with disabilities, strategies need to be embedded in curricula, with a focus on implementing inclusion and meeting individualized needs. Many existing models, including activity-based curricula and curricula with integrated assessment, can inform future curriculum development for children with disabilities. Children with autism present unique learning needs, and it is likely that specialized approaches for them will continue to be warranted.

Children who are multilingual learners and have disabilities are also a growing population, and curricula need to be developed in languages other than English, especially Spanish, to address these children's specific learning needs more equitably. The nearly exclusive focus on English instruction that prevails today runs counter to current evidence on multilingual development and increases the risk already incurred by young children with disabilities who have limited English proficiency.

MTSS holds promise in early childhood education for preventing the development of learning disabilities by enabling the early identification of children who may be falling behind in benchmark levels of performance, particularly in social-emotional and language and literacy development. Differentiated instruction, including MTSS for English learners, using evidence-based practices and data-based decision making is evolving as an integrated and comprehensive solution for preventing learning disability and improving educational outcomes. Tiered instruction offers a promising approach for providing structured support for both general and differentiated instruction.

Focusing on the needs of children with disabilities has the potential to improve the educational experiences of all children. All children require some level of individualized support and accommodation, and while these needs may be more pronounced for children with disabilities, the skills that general education teachers develop to teach children with disabilities more effectively will ultimately benefit all children.

REFERENCES

Administration for Children and Families. (n.d.). *ECD programs*. https://www.acf.hhs.gov/ecd/programs

Al Otaiba, S., McMaster, K., Wanzek, J., & Zaru, M. W. (2023). What we know and need to know about literacy interventions for elementary students with reading difficulties and disabilities, including dyslexia. *Reading Research Quarterly, 58*(2), 313–332. https://doi.org/10.1002/rrq.458

Annie E. Casey Foundation. (2021). *Understanding the children of immigrant families*. https://www.aecf.org/blog/who-are-the-children-in-immigrant-families

Arduin, S. (2015). A review of the values that underpin the structure of an education system and its approach to disability and inclusion. *Oxford Review of Education, 41*(1), 105–121. https://doi.org/10.1080/03054985.2015.1006614

Arick, J. R., Loos, L., Falco, R., & Krug, D. A. (2004). *The STAR program: Strategies for teaching based on autism research*. Pro-Ed. https://starautismsupport.com

Arick, J. R., Young, H. E., Falco, R. A., Loos, L. M., Krug, D. A., Gense, M. H., & Johnson, S. B. (2003). Designing an outcome study to monitor the progress of students with autism spectrum disorders. *Focus on Autism and Other Developmental Disabilities, 18*(2), 75–87. https://psycnet.apa.org/record/2003-06153-002

Bacon, E. C., Dufek, S., Schreibman, L., Stahmer, A. C., Pierce, K., & Courchesne, E. (2014). Measuring outcome in an early intervention program for toddlers with autism spectrum disorder: Use of a curriculum-based assessment. *Autism Research and Treatment*. https://doi.org/10.1155/2014/964704

Bagnato, S. J., Neisworth, J. T., & Pretti-Frontczak, K. (2010). *LINKing authentic assessment and early childhood intervention: Best measures for best practices* (2nd ed.). Brookes Publishing.

Bailey, E., & Bricker, D. (1986). A psychometric study of a criterion-referenced assessment instrument designed for infants and young children. *Journal of the Division of Early Childhood, 10*(2), 124–134. https://doi.org/10.1177/105381518601000204

Balu, R., Zhu, P., Doolittle, F., Schiller, E., Jenkins, J., & Gersten, R. M. (2015). *Evaluation of response to intervention practices for elementary school reading.* National Center for Education Evaluation and Regional Assistance, Institute of Education Sciences, U.S. Department of Education. http://files.eric.ed.gov/fulltext/ED560820.pdf

Barton, E. E., & Smith, B. (2015). Advancing high-quality preschool inclusion: A discussion and recommendations for the field. *Topics in Early Childhood Special Education, 35*(2), 69–78. https://doi.org/10.1177/0271121415583048

Behavior Analyst Certification Board (BACB). (2023). *BACB fact sheet.* https://www.bacb.com/about-behavior-analysis/treatment-of-autism-and-other-developmental-disabilities

Beneke, M., Blanchard, S. B., Vinh, M., & Barton, E. E. (2021). Counteracting bias and advancing justice in early childhood. *Topics in Early Childhood Special Education, 41*(1), 4–5. https://doi.org/10.1177/02711214211007068

Bialystok, E. (2018). Bilingual education for young children: Review of the effects and consequences. *International Journal of Bilingual Education and Bilingualism, 21*(6), 666–679. https://doi.org/10.1080%2F13670050.2016.1203859

Blanchard, S. B., Newton, J., Didericksen, K., Daniels, M., & Glosson, K. (2021). Confronting racism and bias within early intervention: The responsibility of systems and individuals to influence change and advance equity. *Topics in Early Childhood Special Education, 41*(1), 6–17. https://doi.org/10.1177/0271121421992470

Booth-LaForce, C., & Kelly, J. F. (2004). Childcare patterns and issues for families of preschool children with disabilities. *Infants and Young Children, 17*(1), 5–16. https://citeseerx.ist.psu.edu/document?repid=rep1&type=pdf&doi=4b24714cd3afd376e6ac1ba3dbf37a8464f29a07

Bricker, D. D., Waddell, M., Capt, B., Johnson, J., Pretti-Frontczak, K., Slentz, K., & Sstraka, E. (2002). *AEPS assessment, evaluation, and programming system for infants and children* (2nd ed.). Brookes Publishing.

Brown, C. M., Copeland, K. A., Sucharew, H., & Kahn, R. S. (2012). Social-emotional problems in preschool-aged children: Opportunities for prevention and early intervention. *Archives of Pediatrics & Adolescent Medicine, 166*(10), 926–932. https://doi.org/10.1001/archpediatrics.2012.793

Bruns, D. A., & Mogharreban, C. C. (2007). The gap between beliefs and practices: Early childhood practitioners' perceptions about inclusion. *Journal of Research in Childhood Education, 21*(3), 229–241. https://eric.ed.gov/?id=EJ764545

Brunstein-Klomek, A., Marrocco, F., Kleinman, M., Schonfeld, I. S., & Gould, M. S. (2007). Bullying, depression, and suicidality in adolescents. *Journal of the American Academy of Child & Adolescent Psychiatry, 46*(1), 40–49. https://doi.org/10.1097/01.chi.0000242237.84925.18

Bull, M. J. (2020). Down syndrome. *New England Journal of Medicine, 382*(24), 2344–2352. https://doi.org/10.1056/nejmra1706537

Bulotsky-Shearer, R., Fantuzzo, J. W., & McDermott, P. A. (2008). An investigation of classroom situational dimensions of emotional and behavioral adjustment and cognitive and social outcomes for head start children. *Developmental Psychology, 44*, 139–154. https://doi.org/10.1037/0012-1649.44.1.13

Buysse, V., & Peisner-Feinberg, E. (Eds.). (2013). *Handbook of response to intervention in early childhood.* Brookes Publishing.

Caprara, G. V., Barbaranelli, C., Pastorelli, C., Bandura, A., & Zimbardo, P. G. (2000). Prosocial foundations of children's academic achievement. *Psychological Science, 11*(4), 302–306. https://doi.org/10.1111/1467-9280.00260

Carta, J. J., & Young, M. (2019). *Multi-tiered systems of support for young children*. Brookes Publishing.

Castro, S., Pinto, A. I., & Maia, M. (2011). Linking the Carolina curriculum for preschoolers with special needs to the ICF-CY. *British Journal of Development Disabilities*, 57(113), 133–146. https://efisiopediatric.com/wp-content/uploads/2017/06/Castro-Pinto-Maia_2011.pdf

Charlop-Christy, M. H., LeBlanc, L. A., & Carpenter, M. H. (1999). Naturalistic teaching strategies (NaTS) to teach speech to children with autism: Historical perspective, development, and current practice. *California School Psychologist*, 4, 30–46. https://doi.org/10.1007/BF03340868

Cheatham, G. A., Milagros Santos, R., & Kerkutluoglu, A. (2012). Review of comparison studies investigating bilingualism and bilingual instruction for students with disabilities. *Focus on Exceptional Children*, 45(3), 1–12. https://doi.org/10.17161/foec.v45i3.6681

Chen, J., Lin T.-J., Justice, L., & Sawyer, B. (2017). The social networks of children with and without disabilities in early childhood special education classrooms. *Journal of Autism and Developmental Disorders*. Advance online publication. https://doi.org/10.1007/s10803-017-3272-4

Cohen, H., Amerine-Dickens, M., & Smith, T. (2006). Early intensive behavioral treatment: Replication of the UCLA model in a community setting. *Journal of Developmental and Behavioral Pediatrics*, 27(2), 145–155. https://doi.org/10.1097/00004703-200604002-00013

Cole, M. 2022. *Education, equality and human rights: Issues of Gender, 'race', sexuality, disability and social class*. Taylor & Francis. https://www.taylorfrancis.com/books/edit/10.4324/9781003177142/education-equality-human-rights-mike-cole

Collins, B. A., Toppelberg, C., Suárez-Orozco, C., O'Connor, E., & Nieto-Castañon, A. (2011). Cross-sectional associations of Spanish and English competence and well-being in Latino children of immigrants in kindergarten. *International Journal of the Sociology of Language*, 2011(208), 5–23. https://doi.org/10.1515/ijsl.2011.010

Cummins, J. (1979). Linguistic interdependence and the educational development of bilingual children. *Review of Educational Research*, 49(2), 222–251. https://doi.org/10.3102/00346543049002222

Cycyk, L. M., & Durán, L. (2020). Supporting young children with disabilities and their families from undocumented immigrant backgrounds: Recommendations for program leaders and practitioners. *Young Exceptional Children*, 23(4), 212–224. https://eric.ed.gov/?id=EJ1280077

Cycyk, L. M., De Anda, S., Ramsey, K., Sheppard, B., & Zuckerman, K. (2022). Moving through the pipeline: Ethnic and linguistic disparities in special education from birth through age five. *Educational Researcher*, 51(7), 451–464. https://doi.org/10.3102/0013189X221120262

D'Agostino, S. R., & Douglas, S. N. (2021). Early childhood educators' perceptions of inclusion for children with autism spectrum disorder. *Early Childhood Education Journal*, 49, 725–737. https://doi.org/10.1007/s10643-020-01108-7

D'Agostino, S. R., & Douglas, S. N. (2022). Preparation experiences of pre-service inclusive preschool teachers: A qualitative metasynthesis. *Journal of Early Childhood Teacher Education*, 43(2), 307–326. https://eric.ed.gov/?id=EJ1349128

Dennis, L. R., Lynch, S. A., & Stockall, N. (2012). Planning literacy environments for diverse preschoolers. *Young Exceptional Children*, 15(3), 3–19. https://eric.ed.gov/?id=EJ976955

Deshmukh, R. S., Pentimonti, J. M., Zucker, T. A., & Curry, B. (2022). Teachers' use of scaffolds within conversations during shared book reading. *Language, Speech, and Hearing Services in Schools*, 53(1), 150–166. https://doi.org/10.1044/2021_lshss-21-00020

Diamond, K. E. (2001). Relationships among young children's ideas, emotion understanding and social contact with classmates with disabilities. *Topics in Early Childhood Special Education*, 21, 104–113. https://doi.org/10.1177/027112140102100204

Division for Early Childhood (DEC). (2014). *DEC recommended practices in early intervention/ early childhood special education.* https://www.dec-sped.org/dec-recommended-practices

Division for Early Childhood & National Association for the Education of Young Children. (2009). *Early childhood inclusion: A joint position statement of the Division for Early Childhood (DEC) and the National Association for the Education of Young Children (NAEYC).* https://www.decdocs.org/position-statement-inclusion

Doabler, C. T., Clarke, B., Kosty, D., Smolkowski, S., Kurtz Nelson, E., Fien, H., & Baker, S. (2019). Building number sense among English learners: A multisite randomized controlled trial of a tier 2 kindergarten mathematics intervention. *Early Childhood Research Quarterly, 47,* 432–444. https://doi.org/10.1016/j.ecresq.2018.08.004

Duncan, G. J., Dowsett, C. J., Claessens, A., Magnuson, K., Huston, A. C., Klebanov, P., Pagani, L. S., Feinstein, L., Engel, M., Brooks-Gunn, J., & Sexton, H. (2007). School readiness and later achievement. *Developmental Psychology, 43*(6), 1428. https://doi.org/10.1037/0012-1649.43.6.1428

Durán, L., Cycyk, L., & Batz, R. (2023). Voces de la gente: Spanish-speaking families' perspectives on early childhood special education. *Journal of Early Intervention, 45*(3), 285–305. https://doi.org/10.1177/10538151221131514

Early Childhood Technical Assistance Center. (n.d.). *The Individuals with Disabilities Education Act (IDEA).* https://ectacenter.org/idea.asp

The Education Trust. (2021). *Our youngest learners. Increasing equity in early intervention.* https://edtrust.org/increasing-equity-in-early-intervention

Elementary and Secondary Education Act of 1965, Pub. L. No. 89-10, 79 Stat. 27 (1965). https://www.govinfo.gov/content/pkg/STATUTE-79/pdf/STATUTE-79-Pg27.pdf

Fekkes, M., Pijpers, F. I., & Verloove-Vanhorick, S. P. (2006). Effects of antibullying school program on bullying and health complaints. *Archives of Pediatrics & Adolescent Medicine, 160*(6), 638–644. https://doi.org/10.1001/archpedi.160.6.638

Fillmore, L. W. (1991). When learning a second language means losing the first. *Early Childhood Research Quarterly, 6*(3), 323–346. https://doi.org/10.1016/S0885-2006(05)80059-6

Fletcher, J. M., Stuebing, K., Barth, A., Miciak, J., Francis, D., & Denton, C. (2014). Agreement and coverage of indicators of response to intervention: A multimethod comparison and simulation. *Topics in Language Disorders, 34*(1), 74–89. https://doi.org/10.1097/TLD.0000000000000004

Fox, L., Carta, J., Strain, P. S., Dunlap, G., & Hemmeter, M. L. (2010). Response to intervention and the pyramid model. *Infants & Young Children, 23*(1), 3–13. https://psycnet.apa.org/record/2010-06077-002

Frazeur Cross, A., Traub, E., Hutter-Pishgahi, L., & Shelton, G. (2004). Elements of successful inclusion for children with significant disabilities. *Topics in Early Childhood Special Education, 24*(3), 169–183. https://doi.org/10.1177/02711214040240030401

Fuller, E. A., & Kaiser, A. P. (2020). The effects of early intervention on social communication outcomes for children with autism spectrum disorder: A meta-analysis. *Journal of Autism and Developmental Disorders, 50,* 1683–1700. https://doi.org/10.1007/s10803-019-03927-z

Gao, X., & Grisham-Brown, J. (2011). The use of authentic assessment to report accountability data on young children's language, literacy and pre-math competency. *International Educational Studies, 4*(2), 41–53. https://files.eric.ed.gov/fulltext/EJ1066453.pdf

Garbarino, J., & Ganzel, B. (2000). The human ecology of early risk. In J. P. Shonkoff & S. J. Meisels (Eds.), *Handbook of early childhood intervention* (2nd ed., pp. 76–93). Cambridge University Press. https://doi.org/10.1017/CBO9780511529320.006

Gibson, T. A., Oller, D. K., Jarmulowicz, L., & Ethington, C. (2012). The receptive-expressive gap in the vocabulary of young second-language learners: Robustness and possible mechanisms. *Bilingualism: Language and Cognition, 15*(1), 102–116. https://doi.org/10.1017/s1366728910000490

Gilliam, W. S., & Reyes, C. R. (2018). Teacher decision factors that lead to preschool expulsion. *Infants & Young Children*, *31*(2), 93–108. https://doi.org/10.1097/IYC.0000000000000113

Gilliam, W. S., Maupin, A. N., Reyes, C. R., Accavitti, M., & Shic, F. (2016). Do early educators' implicit biases regarding sex and race relate to behavior expectations and recommendations of preschool expulsions and suspensions. *Yale University Child Study Center*, *9*(28), 1–16. https://marylandfamiliesengage.org/wp-content/uploads/2019/07/Preschool-Implicit-Bias-Policy-Brief.pdf

Gillon, G. T. (2005). Facilitating phoneme awareness development in 3- and 4-year-old children with speech impairment. *Language, Speech, and Hearing Services in Schools*, *36*(4), 308–324. https://doi.org/10.1044/0161-1461(2005/031)

Glew, G. M., Fan, M. Y., Katon, W., Rivara, F. P., & Kernic, M. A. (2005). Bullying, psychosocial adjustment, and academic performance in elementary school. *Archives of Pediatrics & Adolescent Medicine*, *159*(11), 1026–1031. https://doi.org/10.1001/archpedi.159.11.1026

Graves, S. L., Jr., & Ye, F. F. (2017). Are special education labels accurate for Black children? Racial differences in academic trajectories of youth diagnosed with specific learning and intellectual disabilities. *Journal of Black Psychology*, *43*(2), 192–213. https://psycnet.apa.org/record/2017-07068-004

Green, K. B., Terry, N. P., & Gallagher, P. A. (2014). Progress in language and literacy skills among children with disabilities in inclusive early reading first classrooms. *Topics in Early Childhood Special Education*, *33*(4), 249–259. https://psycnet.apa.org/record/2014-00232-006

Grisham, J., Waddell, M., Crawford, R., & Toland, M. (2021). Psychometric properties of the Assessment, Evaluation, and Programming System for Infants and Children–Third Edition (AEPS-3). *Journal of Early Intervention*, *43*(1), 24–37. https://doi.org/10.1177/1053815120967359

Grisham-Brown, J., Cox, M., Gravil, M., & Missall, K. (2010). Differences in child care quality for children with and without disabilities. *Early Education and Development*, *21*(1), 21–37. https://eric.ed.gov/?id=EJ877205

Guralnick, M. J. (1992). A hierarchical model for understanding children's peer-related social competence. In S. L. Odom, S. R. McConnel, & M. A. McEvoy (Eds.), *Social competence of young children with disabilities: Issues and strategies for intervention* (pp. 37–64). Brookes Publishing. https://depts.washington.edu/chdd/guralnick/pdfs/Guralnick_A_Heiarchical_Model-BB-1992.pdf

Gutierrez-Clellen, V., Simon-Cerejido, G., & Restrepo, M. A. (2014). *Improving vocabulary and oral language of bilingual Latino preschoolers: An intervention for speech-language pathologists*. Plural Publishing, Inc.

Halle, T., Zaslow, M., Wessel, J., Moodie, S., & Darling-Churchill, K. (2011). *Understanding and choosing assessments and developmental screeners for young children ages 3-5: Profiles of selected measures* (OPRE Report No. 2011-23). Administration for Children & Families.

Hamilton, D. (1995). *The utility of the assessment, evaluation, and programming system in the development of quality IEP goals and objectives for young children, birth to three, with visual impairments* [Unpublished doctoral dissertation]. University of Oregon.

Hanson, M., & Espinosa, L. (2016). Culture, ethnicity, and linguistic diversity: Implications for early childhood special education. In B. Reichow, B. A. Boyd, E. E. Barton, & S. L. Odom (Eds.), *Handbook of early childhood special education* (pp. 455–471). https://doi.org/10.1007/978-3-319-28492-7

Haq, S. S., & Aranki, J. (2019). Comparison of traditional and embedded DTT on problem behavior and responding to instructional targets. *Behavior Analysis in Practice*, *12*(2), 396–400. https://doi.org/10.1007/s40617-018-00324-3

Harris, Y. R., & Schroeder, V. M. (2013). Language deficits or differences: What we know about African American Vernacular English in the 21st century. *International Education Studies, 6*(4), 194–204. http://dx.doi.org/10.5539/ies.v6n4p194

Hawker, D. S., & Boulton, M. J. (2000). Twenty years' research on peer victimization and psychosocial maladjustment: A meta-analytic review of cross-sectional studies. *Journal of Child Psychology and Psychiatry and Allied Disciplines, 41*(4), 441–455. https://pubmed.ncbi.nlm.nih.gov/10836674/

Hebbeler, K., & Spiker, D. (2016). Supporting young children with disabilities. *Future of Children, 26*(2), 185–205. https://eric.ed.gov/?id=EJ1118562

Hehir, T. (2012). Looking forward: Toward a new role in promoting educational equity for students with disabilities from low-income backgrounds. In G. Sykes, B. Schneider, & D. Plank (Eds.), *Handbook of education policy research* (pp. 831–841). Routledge.

Hemmeter, M. L., Fox, L., & Snyder, P. (2013). A tiered model for promoting social-emotional competence and addressing challenging behavior. In V. Buysee & E. S. Peisner-Feinberg (Eds.), *Handbook of response to intervention in early childhood*. Paul H. Brookes Publishing.

Hemmeter, M. L., Ostrosky, M., & Fox, L. (2006). Social and emotional foundations for early learning: A conceptual model for intervention. *School Psychology Review, 35*(4), 583–601. https://psycnet.apa.org/record/2006-22260-005

Hindson, B., Byrne, B., Fielding-Barnsley, R., Newman, C., Hine, D. W., & Shankweiler, D. (2005). Assessment and early instruction of preschool children at risk for reading disability. *Journal of Educational Psychology, 97*(4), 687. https://psycnet.apa.org/record/2005-15839-015

Hirai, A. H., Kogan, M. D., Kandasamy, V., Reuland, C., & Bethell, C. (2018). Prevalence and variation of developmental screening and surveillance in early childhood. *JAMA Pediatrics, 172*(9), 857–66. https://doi.org/10.1001/jamapediatrics.2018.1524

Holahan, A., & Costenbader, V. (2000). A comparison of developmental gains for preschool children with disabilities in inclusive and self-contained classrooms. *Topics in Early Childhood Special Education, 20*(4), 224–235. https://doi.org/10.1177/027112140002000403

Howard, J. S., Sparkman, C. R., Cohen, H. G., Green, G., & Stanislaw, H. (2005). A comparison of intensive behavior analytic and eclectic treatments for young children with autism. *Research in Developmental Disabilities, 26*(4), 359–383. https://doi.org/10.1016/j.ridd.2004.09.005

Hsia, T. (1993). *Evaluating the psychometric properties of the assessment, evaluation, and programming system for 3 to 6 years: AEPS test 3 to 6 years (AEPS test)*. [Dissertation]. University of Oregon. https://www.proquest.com/openview/03539c9cd2a7b84ca19561a9ab1a56e6/1?pq-origsite=gscholar&cbl=18750&diss=y

Huang, B. H., Bedore, L., Niu, L., Wang, Y., & Wicha, N. (2021). The contributions of oral language to English reading outcomes among young bilingual students in the United States. *International Journal of Bilingualism, 25*(1), 40–57. https://doi.org/10.1177/1367006920938136

Individuals with Disabilities Education Act, Continuum of alternative placements, 20 U.S.C. § 1400, 1995.

Individuals with Disabilities Education Act, 20 U.S.C. § 1412(a)(5), 2004.

Individuals with Disabilities Education Act, 20 U.S.C. § 1400, 2007.

Individuals with Disabilities Education Act, 34 C.F.R. § 300.8(b), 2017. https://sites.ed.gov/idea/regs/b/a/300.8/b

Iruka, I. U., Gardner-Neblett, N., Telfer, N. A., Ibekwe-Okafor, N., Curenton, S. M., Sims, J., Sansbury, A. B., & Neblett, E. W. (2022). Effects of racism on child development: Advancing ant-racist developmental science. *Annual Review for Developmental Psychology, 4*, 109–132. https://www.annualreviews.org/doi/full/10.1146/annurev-devpsych-121020-031339

Johns Hopkins Bloomberg School of Public Health. (2020). *U.S. autism rates up 10 percent in new CDC report*. https://publichealth.jhu.edu/2020/us-autism-rates-up-10-percent-in-new-cdc-report

Johnson-Martin, N. M., Hacker, B., & Attermeier, S. (2004). *The Carolina curriculum for preschoolers with special needs (CCPSN)* (2nd ed.). Brookes Publishing.

Justice, L. M., Logan, J. A., Lin, T. J., & Kaderavek, J. N. (2014). Peer effects in early childhood education: Testing the assumptions of special-education inclusion. *Psychological Science, 25*(9), 1722–1729. https://doi.org/10.1177/0956797614538978

Kan, P. F., & Kohnert, K. (2005). Preschoolers learning Hmong and English. *Journal of Speech, Language, and Hearing Research, 48*(2), 372–383. https://doi.org/10.1044/1092-4388(2005/026)

Knoche, L., Peterson, C. A., Edwards, C. P., & Jeon, H. J. (2006). Child care for children with and without disabilities: The provider, observer, and parent perspectives. *Early Childhood Research Quarterly, 21*(1), 93–109. https://digitalcommons.unl.edu/cgi/viewcontent.cgi?article=1073&context=famconfacpub

Kwon, K.-A., Elicker, J., & Kontos, S. (2011). Social IEP objectives, teacher talk, and peer interaction in inclusive and segregated preschool settings. *Early Childhood Education Journal, 39*, 267–277. https://doi.org/10.1007/s10643-011-0469-6

Landa, R. J. (2018). Efficacy of early interventions for infants and young children with, and at risk for, autism spectrum disorders. *International Review of Psychiatry, 30*(1), 25–39. https://doi.org/10.1080/09540261.2018.1432574

Lawrence, S. M., Smith, S., & Banerjee, R. (2016). *Preschool inclusion: Key findings from research and implications for policy.* National Center for Children in Poverty: Child Care & Early Education Research Connections. https://doi.org/10.7916/D8571C1C

Lee, K., Calkins, A., & Shin, T. S. (2016). Head Start impact on social–emotional outcomes for children with disabilities. *Research on Social Work Practice, 26*(7), 790–802. https://psycnet.apa.org/record/2016-47026-005

Lerman, D. C., Valentino, A. L., & LeBlanc, L. A. (2016). Discrete trial training. In R. Lang, T. B. Hancock, & N. N Singh (Eds.), *Early intervention for young children with autism spectrum disorder* (pp. 47–83). Springer.

Li, Z., Gooden, C., & Toland, M. D. (2019). Reliability and validity evidence for the Hawaii Early Learning Profile, Birth-3 Years. *Journal of Early Intervention, 41*(1), 62–83. https://eric.ed.gov/?id=EJ1203678

Lin, T.-J., Chen, J., Justice, L. M., & Sawyer, B. (2019). Peer interactions in preschool inclusive classrooms: The roles of pragmatic language and self-regulation. *Exceptional Children, 85*(4), 432–452. https://doi.org/10.1177/0014402919828364

Love, H. R., & Beneke, M. R. (2021). Pursuing justice-driven inclusive education research: Disability critical race theory (DisCrit) in early childhood. *Topics in Early Childhood Special Education, 41*(1), 31–44. https://doi.org/10.1177/0271121421990833

Macy, M., Marks, K., & Towle, A. (2014). Missed, misused, or mismanaged: Improving early detection systems to optimize child outcomes. *Topics in Early Childhood Special Education, 34*(2), 94–105. https://doi.org/10.1177/0271121414525997

Mancilla-Martinez, J., & Lesaux, N. K. (2011). Early home language use and later vocabulary development. *Journal of Educational Psychology, 103*, 535–546. https://doi.org/10.1037/a0023655

Manfra, L., Larsen, J. A., & Turley, D. (2021). *Testing the structure of HELP 3-6 Assessment among Head Start children using confirmatory factor analysis.* https://documents.shineearly.store/HELP_3-6-FactorAnalysis-Manfra.pdf

Marchal, J. P., Maurice-Stam, H., Houtzager, B. A., van Rozenburg-Marres, S. L. R., Oostrom, K. J., Grootenhuis, M. A., & van Trotsenburg, A. P. (2016). Growing up with Down syndrome: Development from 6 months to 10.7 years. *Research in Developmental Disabilities, 59*, 437–450. https://doi.org/10.1016/j.ridd.2016.09.019

McCollow, M. M., & Hoffman, H. H. (2019). Supporting social development in young children with disabilities: Building a practitioner's toolkit. *Early Childhood Education Journal, 47*(3), 309–320. https://eric.ed.gov/?id=EJ1211331

Meek, S., Iruka, I. U., Allen, R., Yazzie, D., Fernandez, V., Catherine, E., McIntosh, K., Gordon, L., Gilliam, W., Hemmeter, M. L., Blevins, D., & Powell, T. (2020a). *Start with equity: Fourteen priorities to dismantle systemic racism in early care and education.* The Children's Equity Project. https://childandfamilysuccess.asu.edu/cep

Meek, S., Smith, L., Allen, R., Catherine, E., Edyburn, K., Williams, C., Fabes, R., McIntosh, K., Garcia, E., Takanishi, R., Gordon, L., Jimenez-Castellanos, O., Hemmester, M. L., Gilliam, W., & Pointier, R. (2020b). *Start with equity: From the early years to the early grades.* Children's Equity Project and Bipartisan Policy Center. https://childandfamilysuccess.asu.edu/sites/default/files/2020-07/CEP-report-071520-FINAL.pdf

Morgan, P. L., Farkas, G., Hillemeier, M., & Maczuga, S. (2012). Are minority children disproportionately represented in early intervention and early childhood special education? *Education Research, 41*(9), 339–351. https://doi.org/10.3102/0013189x12459678

National Academies of Sciences, Engineering, and Medicine (National Academies). (2016). *Preventing bullying through science, policy, and practice.* The National Academies Press. https://doi.org/10.17226/23482

———. (2017). *Promoting the educational success of children and youth learning English: Promising futures.* The National Academies Press. https://doi.org/10.17226/24677

———. (2019). *Monitoring educational equity.* The National Academies Press. https://doi.org/10.17226/25389

———. (2023). *Closing the opportunity gap for young children.* The National Academies Press. https://doi.org/10.17226/26743

National Assessment of Educational Progress. (2019). *Results from the 2019 mathematics and reading assessments.* National Center for Education Statistics, U.S. Department of Education, Institute of Education Sciences. https://www.nationsreportcard.gov/mathematics?grade=4

National Association for the Education of Young Children. (2019). *Advancing equity in early childhood education: Position statement.* https://www.naeyc.org/sites/default/files/globally-shared/downloads/PDFs/resources/position-statements/advancingequitypositionstatement.pdf

National Center for Education Statistics. (2023). *Achievement gaps.* U.S. Department of Education. https://nces.ed.gov/nationsreportcard/studies/gaps

National Center for Learning Disabilities. (2020). *The state of LD: Introduction.*

National Center on Early Childhood Development, Teaching, and Learning (NCECDTL). (2020). *Preschool curriculum consumer report.* Office of Head Start, U.S. Department of Health and Human Services. https://eclkc.ohs.acf.hhs.gov/sites/default/files/featured_file/preschool-curriculum-consumer-report-032519.pdf

National Research Council. (2002). *Minority students in special and gifted education.* The National Academies Press.

O'Connor, R. E., Jenkins, J. R., Leicester, N., & Slocum, T. A. (1993). Teaching phonological awareness to young children with learning disabilities. *Exceptional Children, 59*(6), 532–546.

Office of Special Education Programs (OSEP). (2018). *Meeting the needs of English learners with and without disabilities: Brief 1.* U.S. Department of Education. https://www.txel.org/media/ei3pnf2d/series2-brief3_final.pdf

———. (2020). *OSEP fast facts: Children 3 through 5 served under Part B, Section 619 of the IDEA.* U.S. Department of Education. https://sites.ed.gov/idea/osep-fast-facts-children-3-5-20

———. (2021a). *43rd annual report to Congress on the implementation of the Individuals with Disabilities Education Act.* U.S. Department of Education. https://sites.ed.gov/idea/2021-individuals-with-disabilities-education-act-annual-report-to-congress

———. (2021b). *Meeting the needs of English learners with and without disabilities: Brief 3.* U.S. Department of Education. https://www.txel.org/media/ei3pnf2d/series2-brief3_final.pdf

———. (2022a). *Annual report to Congress on the implementation of the Individuals with Disabilities Education Act*. U.S. Department of Education. https://sites.ed.gov/idea/files/44th-arc-for-idea.pdf

———. (2022b). *OSEP fast facts: Students with disabilities who are English learners (ELs) served under IDEA Part B*. U.S. Department of Education. https://sites.ed.gov/idea/osep-fast-facts-students-with-disabilities-english-learners

Park, M., Zong, J., & Batalova, J. (2018). *Growing superdiversity among young U.S. dual language learners and its implications*. Migration Policy Institute. https://www.migrationpolicy.org/research/growing-superdiversity-among-young-us-dual-language-learners-and-its-implications

Pasco, G. (2018). The value of early intervention for children with autism. *Paediatrics and Child Health*, *28*(8), 364–367. http://dx.doi.org/10.1016/j.paed.2018.06.001

Portes, A., & Hao, L. (1998). E pluribus unum: Bilingualism and loss of language in the second generation. *Sociology of Education*, *71*(4), 269–294. https://doi.org/10.2307/2673171

Rafferty, Y., Piscitelli, V., & Boettcher, C. (2003). The impact of inclusion on language development and social competence among preschoolers with disabilities. *Exceptional Children*, *69*, 467–479. https://doi.org/10.1177/001440290306900405

Remington, B., Hastings, R. P., Kovshoff, H., Degli Espinosa, F., Jahr, E., Brown T., Alsford, P., Lemaic, M., & Ward, N. (2007). Early intensive behavioral intervention: Outcomes for children with autism and their parents after two years. *American Journal on Mental Retardation*, *112*(6), 418–438. https://doi.org/10.1352/0895-8017(2007)112[418:EIBIOF]2.0.CO;2

Rios, K., & Burke, M. M. (2021). Facilitators and barriers to positive special education experiences and health among Latino families of children with disabilities: Two systematic literature reviews. *Review Journal of Autism and Developmental Disorders*, *8*, 299–311. https://link.springer.com/article/10.1007/s40489-020-00220-z

Rodríguez, A., & Rodríguez, D. (2017). English learners with learning disabilities: What is the current state? *Insights into Learning Disabilities*, *14*(1), 97–112. https://files.eric.ed.gov/fulltext/EJ1165743.pdf

Sandall, S. R., Scwartz, I., Joseph, G., & Gauvreau, A. (2019). *Building blocks for teaching preschoolers with special needs* (3rd ed.). Brookes Publishing.

Schiller, E., Chow, K., Thayer, S., Nakamura, J., Wilkerson, S. B., & Puma, M. (2020). *What tools have states developed or adapted to assess schools' implementation of a multi-tiered system of supports/response to intervention framework?*. Regional Educational Laboratory Appalachia. Institute of Education Sciences. http://files.eric.ed.gov/fulltext/ED603782.pdf

School Readiness Consulting. (2022). [Literature review on preschool curriculum quality]. Literature review commissioned by the Committee on a New Vision for High-Quality Pre-K Curriculum.

Simon-Cereijido, G. (2015). Preschool language interventions for Latino dual language learners with language disorders: What, in what language, and how. *Seminars in Speech Language*, *36*(2), 154–164. https://doi.org/10.1055/s-0035-1549110

Simpson, R. L. (2005). Evidence-based practices and students with autism spectrum disorders. *Focus on Autism and Other Developmental Disabilities*, *20*(3), 140–149. https://doi.org/10.1177/10883576050200030201

Smith, T., Groen, A., & Wynn, J. W. (2000a). Randomized trial of intensive early intervention for children with pervasive developmental disorder. *American Journal on Mental Retardation*, *105*(4), 269–285. https://doi.org/10.1352/0895-8017(2000)105<0269:RTOIEI>2.0.CO;2

Smith, T. T., Myers-Jennings, C., & Coleman, T. (2000b). Assessment of language skills in rural preschool children. *Communication Disorders Quarterly*, *21*(2), 98–113. https://eric.ed.gov/?id=EJ603370

Son, E., Parish, S. L., & Peterson, N. A. (2012). National prevalence of peer victimization among young children with disabilities in the United States. *Children and Youth Services Review*, 34(8), 1540–1545. http://dx.doi.org/10.1016/j.childyouth.2012.04.014

Sourander, A., Aromaa, M., Pihlakoski, L., Haavisto, A., Rautava, P., Helenius, H., & Sillanpää, M. (2006). Early predictors of deliberate self-harm among adolescents. A prospective follow-up study from age 3 to age 15. *Journal of Affective Disorders*, 93(1–3), 87–96. https://doi.org/10.1016/j.jad.2006.02.015

Stahmer, A. C., Reed, S., Lee, E., Reisinger, E. M., Connell, J. E., & Mandell, D. S. (2015). Training teachers to use evidence-based practices for autism: Examining procedural implementation fidelity. *Psychology in the Schools*, 52(2), 181–195. https://doi.org/10.1002%2Fpits.21815

Stanton-Chapman, T. L., & Snell, M. E. (2011). Promoting turn-taking skills in preschool children with disabilities: The effects of a peer-based social communication intervention. *Early Childhood Research Quarterly*, 26(3), 303–319. http://dx.doi.org/10.1016/j.ecresq.2010.11.002

Steinbrenner, J. R., Hume, K., Odom, S. L., Morin, K. L., Nowell, S. W., Tomaszewski, B., Szendrey, S., McIntyre, N. S., Yücesoy-Özkan, S., & Savage, M. N. (2020). *Evidence-based practices for children, youth, and young adults with autism*. The University of North Carolina at Chapel Hill, Frank Porter Graham Child Development Institute, National Clearinghouse on Autism Evidence and Practice Review Team.

Stites, M. L., Walter, H. L., & Krikorian, J. G. (2021). These aren't the kids I signed up for: The lived experience of general education, early childhood preservice teachers in classrooms for children with special needs. *Journal of Early Childhood Teacher Education*, 42(1), 1–19. https://doi.org/10.1080/10901027.2020.1718806

Strain, P. S. (1983). Generalization of autistic children's social behavior change: Effects of developmentally integrated and segregated settings. *Analysis and Intervention in Developmental Disabilities*, 3(1), 23–34. https://doi.org/10.1016/0270-4684(83)90024-1

Suhrheinrich, J. (2015). A sustainable model for training teachers to use pivotal response training. *Autism*, 19(6), 713–723. https://doi.org/10.1177/1362361314552200

Texas Education Agency. (2019). *Hawaii Early Learning Profile*. https://www.txautism.net/evaluations/hawaii-early-learning-profile

Tseng, V., & Fuligni, A. J. (2000). Parent-adolescent language use and relationships among immigrant families with East Asian, Filipino, and Latin American backgrounds. *Journal of Marriage and Family*, 62(2), 465–476. https://doi.org/0.1111/j.1741-3737.2000.00465.x

Uljarević, M., Billingham, W., Cooper, M. N., Condron, P., & Hardan, A. Y. (2022). Examining effectiveness and predictors of treatment response of pivotal response treatment in autism: An umbrella review and a meta-analysis. *Frontiers in Psychiatry*, 12, 766150. https://doi.org/10.3389/fpsyt.2021.766150

U.S. Department of Education (ED). (2023). *Discipline discussions: Suspension, expulsion & informal removals: Unexpected realities in preschool*. Blog. Office of Special Education and Rehabilitative Services. https://sites.ed.gov/osers/2023/05/suspension-expulsion-informal-removals-unexpected-realities-in-preschool

———. (2024). *A history of the Individuals with Disabilities Education Act*. https://sites.ed.gov/idea/IDEA-History#Pre-EHA-IDEA

U.S. Department of Education, Office of Special Education and Rehabilitative Services, & Office of Special Education Programs. (2020). *41st annual report to Congress on the implementation of the Individuals with Disabilities Education Act, 2019*. https://sites.ed.gov/idea/files/41st-arc-for-idea.pdf

U.S. Department of Health and Human Services. (2007). *Head Start program performance standards*. Early Childhood Learning & Knowledge Center. https://eclkc.ohs.acf.hhs.gov/policy/45-cfr-chap-xiii

———. (2018). *Early childhood inclusion position statement*. https://eclkc.ohs.acf.hhs.gov/children-disabilities/article/early-childhood-inclusion-position-statement

Wackerle-Hollman, A., Spencer, T., Meeker, K., Kelley, E., Durán, L., & Foster, M. (2021). Multi-tiered system of supports in early childhood: Identifying gaps, considerations for application, and solutions. *Early Childhood Research Quarterly, 56*(3), 201–212. https://doi.org/10.1016/j.ecresq.2021.03.010

Waitoller, F. R., & Lubienski, C. (2019). Disability, race, and the geography of school choice: Toward an intersectional analytical framework. *American Educational Research Association Open, 5*(1), 2332858418822505. https://doi.org/10.1177/2332858418822505

Waitoller, F. R., Artiles, A. J., & Cheney, D. A. (2010). The miner's canary: A review of overrepresentation research and explanations. *Journal of Special Education, 44*(1), 29–49. http://dx.doi.org/10.1177/0022466908329226

Weglarz-Ward, J. M., & Santos, R. M. (2018). Parent and professional perceptions of inclusion in childcare: A literature review. *Infants & Young Children, 31*(2), 128–143. https://doi.org/10.1097/IYC.0000000000000115

Whalen, C., & Schreibman, L. (2003). Joint attention training for children with autism using behavior modification procedures. *Journal of Child Psychology & Psychiatry, 44*(3), 456–468. https://doi.org/10.1111/1469-7610.00135

Wheeler, R. (2016). "So much research, so little change": Teaching standard English in African American classrooms. *Annual Review of Linguistics, 2,* 367–390. http://dx.doi.org/10.1146/annurev-linguistics-011415-040434

White House. (2021). *Fact sheet: Advancing disability inclusive democracy in the United States and globally* [Press release]. https://www.whitehouse.gov/briefing-room/statements-releases/2021/12/03/fact-sheet-advancing-disability-inclusive-democracy-in-the-united-states-and-globally

Winsler, A., Kim, Y., & Richard, E. (2014). Social-emotional skills, behavior problems, and Spanish competence predict the acquisition of English among English language learners in poverty. *Developmental Psychology, 50,* 2242–2254. https://doi.org/10.1037/a0037161

Young, H. E., Falco, R. A., & Hanita, M. (2016). Randomized, controlled trial of a comprehensive program for young students with autism spectrum disorder. *Journal of Autism and Developmental Disorders, 46,* 544–560. https://doi.org/10.1007/s10803-015-2597-0

7

High-Quality Early Childhood Curriculum for Multilingual Learners

The need for a new vision for high-quality early childhood curriculum that addresses equity, diversity, and inclusion, and cultural and linguistic responsiveness is urgent for young children who speak one or more languages other than English in the home, or multilingual learners. The science and evidence base surrounding the process of first, second, or multiple language acquisition in children aged 0–5 years has greatly expanded in the last 10–15 years from research in the fields of psycholinguistics, cognitive neuroscience, developmental psychology, educational research, and program evaluation (National Academies of Sciences, Engineering, and Medicine, 2017). Despite this greater scientific understanding of how young children learn a first and second language and educational approaches that promote enhanced language and cognitive development for multilingual learners, however, the application of practices based on this knowledge in early childhood education has not kept pace (Figueras-Daniel & Li, 2021; Martin et al., 2022b; Sembiante et al., 2022). This gap between what is known about how curriculum can best meet the needs of multilingual learners and what occurs in early education programs is influenced by multiple factors:

- misperceptions about the value of languages other than English leading to a "deficit" view of multilingual learners;
- misconceptions about the capacity of all young children to learn and benefit from exposure to multiple languages from birth;
- inadequate and inconsistent methods for identifying who is a multilingual learner during the preschool years;

- insufficient access to early childhood curricula available in languages other than in English, with little attention to needs of multilingual learners;
- educational goals that do not include the importance of early bilingualism;
- lack of widespread, common understanding of practical instructional methods and strategies in early childhood education (ECE) that promote early bilingualism and academic skills;
- inappropriate assessment instruments and methods that do not include the language competencies or knowledge of multilingual learners in languages other than English;
- lack of qualified bilingual ECE professionals; and
- flawed research on the development and achievement of multilingual learners.

As the size, diversity, and proportion of young multilingual learners continue to grow across the country and are increasingly represented in ECE settings, a shared vision of high-quality curriculum that can guide instructional and assessment practices for multilingual learners is crucial. Approximately one-third of all children aged 0–8 years are currently exposed to more than one language in the home, according to the U.S. Census Bureau (Park et al., 2018). And the Office of Head Start reports that at least one-third of preschool children in its programs are considered multilingual learners (Early Childhood Learning & Knowledge Center [ECLKC], 2022); in many states multilingual learners make up a majority or sizeable proportion of children attending preschool (e.g., 60% of children in California aged 0–5 years are so identified; 50% in Texas; 46% in New Jersey; and 44% in New Mexico, New York, and Nevada [Lazarín & Park, 2021]). More than 140 languages have been identified within the Head Start child population, with nearly 90% of all Head Start classrooms serving multilingual learners and many serving a population representing more than three different home languages (ECLKC, 2022). Unfortunately, early care and education teachers who are able to speak more than one language remain in short supply, making up roughly 15% of the early childhood educator workforce (Park et al., 2015).

While Spanish-speaking multilingual learners constitute the majority of this population in the United States, it is important to note the growing number of children whose home language(s) may not be supported by any existing curricula or who may be less likely than their peers to attend early education settings where home language support is possible. For example, data on the top 10 states for numbers of all multilingual learners versus Black multilingual learners in the K–12 system show that these two sets of states did not overlap, with the exception of Connecticut, suggesting that Black multilingual learners may encounter less access to opportunities to support their home language (Villegas & Velazco, 2021). In addition, although the top language spoken by Black multilingual learners was Spanish, the next four most commonly spoken languages for Black multilingual learners (French Creole, French, Cushite, and Kru/Ibo/Yoruba) were not among the remaining (after Spanish) top languages spoken among all multilingual learners (Arabic, Chinese, Vietnamese, and Somali).[1] These students may also be misidentified or underidentified for services to support their home language (Villegas & Velazco, 2021).

To ensure equity, it is critical to provide high-quality early care and education for multilingual learners, including effective program language models, well-designed curriculum with instructional practices that scaffold language interactions, and appropriate ongoing assessment instruments and methods. Relevant qualifications for early childhood teachers also need to be defined and put into practice. This chapter reviews current evidence on specific curricula, teaching strategies, environmental supports, and instructional practices that are associated with improved outcomes and long-term achievement for multilingual learners.

SHIFTING FROM DEFICIT-BASED TO ASSET-BASED APPROACHES

A critical first step in providing equitable, high-quality early care and education for multilingual learners is to recognize and build upon their linguistic, cultural, and social assets and talents. Historically, research that examines the growth, progress, or achievement of multilingual learners has focused on their differences from monolingual peers, judging their development based on standards or norms designed for English-only populations, without considering the unique linguistic and developmental trajectories of children whose first language is not English (Center for Early Care and Education Research-Dual Language Learners, 2011; Espinosa & Crandell, 2020). This approach can lead to a "deficit perspective" that views multilingual learners as having less academic potential and abilities than monolingual English-speaking peers because of their lack of proficiency in English (Foundation for Child Development, 2020). As such, policy makers in the past have referred to "the extra burden" of learning two languages during the early years, sending the message that learning more than one language during a child's early years is difficult and imposes an added learning burden on young children. This perspective has led to some misguided state policies for young multilingual learners, restricting exposure to multiple languages until after kindergarten. Viewing the learning and achievement

---

[1] Data on languages most common among all English learners are from fall 2017, and data for languages spoken among Black English learners are from 2013.

of multilingual learners through this deficit lens has often led educators to underestimate what multilingual learners know and to form inaccurate assumptions about their potential.

What is more, research has demonstrated that learning two or more languages during a child's early years is possible for all children and can be associated with enhanced cognitive abilities as well as the potential for higher achievement in both spoken languages relative to monolingual students (Halle et al., 2012; Ramirez & Kuhl, 2017; Thompson, 2015). The current scientific consensus is that children who achieve fluency in both their home language(s)[2] and English are likely to experience advantages in cognitive, social, academic, and professional outcomes, as well as to be protected from cognitive decline at older ages (Bialystok, 2017; National Academies, 2017).

These findings suggest that early childhood educators and curriculum developers need to understand the benefits of early bi- and multilingualism and view the development of multilingual learners through the lens of the powerful advantages of having more than one language instead of viewing these children as deficient because of limited English skills. In fact, across the globe, many countries explicitly require all young children to become bilingual or multilingual, with most adults speaking more than one language (Klingert, 2023); these include European Union countries, which require that all children learn at least two languages in addition to their home language (European Parliament, 2023). In the United States, by contrast, only about 20% of the adult population is fluent in more than one language, and of adults born in the United States, only 6.5% speak more than one language (Chiswick & Miller, 2016; Dietrich & Hernandez, 2022). While much of the world understands the benefits of becoming bi- or multilingual, policies in the United States have been slow to reflect the scientific evidence on the immediate and long-term advantages of multilingualism.

Educators who work with children who speak a language other than English at home recognize that the development of multilingual learners differs from that of their native English-speaking peers because of differences in the context and societal circumstances of their upbringing. For example, although the vast majority of multilingual learners are born in the United States (95%; Park et al., 2018), they often have one or more parents born outside of the United States. Many of these families immigrated to the United States recently and are not familiar with societal and cultural norms, nor with school expectations. Some families of multilingual learners have undergone traumatic experiences related to their migration

---

[2] The term "home language" is used throughout this report to refer to the primary language that is spoken in the home. Other terms used synonymously are "mother tongue," "heritage language," "first language," and "L1."

to the United States, which can have adverse cognitive and social effects on their children's development (Yoshikawa, 2011). Moreover, by definition, the families of multilingual learners speak a language other than English in the home, which could lead to social isolation, and in some cases, generate mixed feelings or even a sense of shame for the children (Halgunseth et al., 2013; Motaghi-Tabar, 2016).

Variation in culture-specific parenting goals, values, and practices across racial and ethnic groups can contribute to inaccurate perceptions of multilingual learners' early social, language, and literacy potential. For instance, culturally specified parenting concepts such as *familismo* (family), *respeto* (respect), and being *bien educado* (well educated) among Latine families (Halgunseth et al., 2013; Tamis-LeMonda et al., 2020) and concepts such as *chiao shun* among Chinese families (Chao, 1994) emphasize the importance of "having harmonious relationships with others, respecting adult authority, prioritizing the needs of the family, and conducting oneself in a manner that does not bring shame on the family or community" (Foundation for Child Development, 2020, p. 136). Other values to which children are exposed early in life may include valuing the group or collective well-being, which contrasts with individualistic cultures, including many cultures in the United States, which value independence and self-reliance—values that are commonly effected in American schools (Small, 2002). These contrasting early socialization values and practices can lead to patterns of behavior in the early education setting that are inconsistent with program goals—for instance, a child may be reluctant to stand out as the only one who knows the answer—and can inaccurately influence teachers' judgment of the knowledge levels of multilingual learners.

Family members' beliefs differ as to how exposure to English and continued use of the home language affects their children's language learning and academic success (Ladson-Billings, 1994). Some may view their children's development of the home language as critical for maintaining ties to the family's cultural heritage and the connection with family members in their countries of origin. Alternatively, newly arrived immigrant families may prioritize the swift acquisition of English over maintaining their heritage language and may encourage their children to use English exclusively. Consequently, differing beliefs and objectives related to cultural and language preservation significantly influence the extent of exposure and opportunities for children to utilize both languages (Foundation for Child Development, 2020).

Given multilingual learners' wide variety of family contexts and early learning environments, they ought not to be viewed as a homogeneous group or only in comparison with their English-only peers (see Box 7-1). These sociocultural and demographic variations, such as language spoken in the home, age at first exposure to English, family socioeconomic status,

> **BOX 7-1**
> **Dual Language/Multilingual Curricula and Pedagogy**
>
> Families value curricula and instructional practices that respond to their home culture and language(s), but available research on their perceptions of specific curricular modifications is insufficient. Research does show that families want programs, teachers, and curriculum materials that respect their cultural beliefs and practices, and that they consider cultural and linguistic responsiveness as a key factor when choosing a preschool program for their children (Cleveland et al., 2013). When preschool professionals and curricula use children's home language(s), multilingual families are more likely to engage in their children's schooling and build partnerships with preschool programs (Harvey & Wennerstrom, 2023). And the vast majority of multilingual families—including many Indigenous families—consider it important or very important that their children learn the family's heritage language(s) (Meek et al., 2020; Sánchez Walker & Montrul, 2021; Sarche et al., 2020, 2021). However, few studies have examined how families experience specific cultural and linguistic modifications of curricula (especially in private preschool settings). In general, Head Start parents have reported feeling satisfied with the cultural responsiveness of their program; when surveyed, most Head Start parents (71%) reported that their local program provided their children with curricular materials that reflected their cultural background (Reid et al., 2022). Future studies are needed to determine how curricular modifications can support children's multilingual and multicultural development, as well as family engagement.

race, and country of origin, all can influence the child's proficiency and early literacy skills in both the home language and English (National Academies, 2017). Thus, to understand each multilingual learner's language status and educational needs, it is important for early childhood teachers to gather in-depth knowledge of the circumstances, values, and culture of multilingual children and their families (Halgunseth et al., 2013). To better understand the behaviors and language competencies of multilingual learners, early childhood educators will need to expand their thinking beyond simple comparisons between multilingual and English-only children. Language and literacy development will look different for multilingual learners, so educators need to use norms and learning trajectories that differ from those based on children who speak English only. Early childhood curriculum that is responsive to the needs of multilingual learners will include tools and methods for collecting important contextual information about multilingual learners (e.g., age of acquisition of each language, extent and nature of exposure to each language, and key family characteristics), as well as family histories that go beyond the typical home language survey.

Finally, the extent to which early childhood curricula provide learning experiences in multilingual learners' languages is an important feature of their early development that impacts later school success. Several research studies have indicated that the exposure of preschoolers and school-age children to their home language contributes to the enhancement of their language development (Barnett et al., 2007; Hammer et al., 2012; Spencer et al., 2020; Tamis-LeMonda et al., 2019). Moreover, use of the child's first language in the home or in the school setting does not appear to affect the rate or level of English acquisition. However, an emphasis on English in the early education setting does appear to impact multilingual learners' continued development of the home language negatively (Barnett et al., 2007; National Academies, 2017), likely because of the higher value placed on English proficiency within the school and broader social context. Given research findings about the impact of multilingual learners' exposure to their languages through their parents and teachers, attention is needed to the amount and quality of exposure multilingual learners experience in each language.

The next section reviews recent findings and conclusions about dual language development in early childhood, along with particular classroom practices that empirical evidence has shown to be effective for linguistically diverse children. It is the committee's hope that the insights into how young children acquire and benefit from exposure to multiple languages, as well as identified promising pedagogical practices, will pave the way for more equitable and high-quality early childhood curriculum for multilingual learners, as well as fruitful lines of inquiry for future research.

CURRENT RESEARCH ON EARLY BILINGUAL DEVELOPMENT

As the knowledge base concerning the language development of multilingual learners has continued to expand, it is increasingly being used as a foundation to support and guide the development of early childhood curriculum. Several strands of research from multiple disciplines have illuminated the process of early bilingualism.

First, studies on early brain development indicate that infants have the capacity to learn two languages simultaneously, and the early years are considered the optimal period for bilingual acquisition (Berken et al., 2017; Ramirez & Kuhl, 2017). Research from cognitive neuroscientists provides evidence suggesting that the bilingual brain exhibits higher neurological activity than the monolingual brain, attributed to the necessity of processing two languages (Bialystok, 2017), and is associated with greater control of focused attention and self-regulatory behavior (Conboy, 2013), skills that are associated with enhanced executive function in multilingual learners.

Indeed, National Academies (2017) notes that "children given the opportunity to develop competence in two or more languages early in life benefit from their capacity to communicate in more than one language and may show enhancement in certain cognitive skills, as well as improved academic outcomes in school" (p. 147). Recent research is also exploring whether children who speak two dialects of the same language—bi-dialecticalism—may also experience similar cognitive benefits as those experienced by children who speak two or more different languages (Antoniou et al., 2016). This research may provide a foundation for how we think about ways to support home dialect for children in the United States who speak rule-governed dialects of General American English, such as African American English or Chicano English dialects. Next, findings from psycholinguistic research indicate that, while multilingual learners generally exhibit a language development trajectory similar to that of monolingual children, their progress displays distinctive features due to the acquisition of two languages (Foundation for Child Development, 2020). These unique characteristics encompass language mixing (i.e., mixing languages within sentences), reduced vocabularies in each language (Bedore et al., 2005), and variations in the emergence of specific linguistic milestones (National Academies, 2017).

A National Academies report, *Promoting the Educational Success of Children and Youth Learning English,* provides a synthesis of research on the development and achievement of dual language learners from birth to age 21 (National Academies, 2017). This consensus study yielded a comprehensive view of language development, school practices, and educational policies that impact multilingual learners' growth and school success. The report offers four major interrelated conclusions that can guide efforts to improve educational outcomes for multilingual learners. First, *all* children are capable of learning more than one language from the earliest months of life and benefit from early exposure to multiple languages. Second, high levels of proficiency in both the home language and English are linked to the best academic and social outcomes. Third, the earlier children are exposed to a second language, the greater are their chances for full bilingualism. And fourth, home language loss is currently the norm for multilingual learners, particularly once they enter English-speaking early education settings, which subverts the possibility of full bilingualism and may place the child at risk for disrupted family relations, including estrangement from their cultural heritage (see Box 7-2).

While multilingual learners bring critical linguistic and cultural strengths to their educational experiences, research has found that their experiences in school are not supporting them in reaching their full potential (Espinosa & Crandall, 2020; Holtzman et al., 2022; Spencer et al., 2020). The results of many statewide kindergarten entry assessments show multilingual learners

BOX 7-2
Summary of Research Findings for Multilingual Learners from Birth to Age 5

The major findings about the development of dual language learners (DLLs) aged 0–5 from the 2017 National Academies report *Promoting the Educational Success of Children and Youth Learning English* include the following:

Benefits of Early Bilingualism

- All young children, if given adequate exposure to two languages, can acquire full competence in both languages;
- Early bilingualism confers benefits such as improved academic outcomes in school as well as enhancement of certain cognitive skills such as executive functioning;
- Early exposure to a second language—before three years of age—is related to better language skills in second language, English;
- The cognitive, cultural, and economic benefits of bilingualism are tied to high levels of competence including listening, speaking, reading, and writing in both languages, e.g., balanced bilingualism at kindergarten entry predicts best long-term outcomes.

Process of Dual Language Development

- "The language development of DLLs often differs from that of monolingual children: they may take longer to learn some aspects of language that differ between the two languages and their level of proficiency reflects variations of amount and quality of language input" (Espinosa, 2018, p.11);
- There is wide variation in the language competency among DLLs that is due to multiple social and cultural factors such as parents' immigration status and number of years in U.S., family Socio-Economic Status, status of home language in the community, resources and amount of support and for both languages.

Strategies for Supporting Dual Language Development

- While learning English, DLLs should also be supported in maintaining their home language in preschool and early school years with the goal of achieving full proficiency in both languages;
- The language development of DLLs improves when adults engage in frequent, responsive, and diverse language interactions. This includes incorporating a wide range of diverse words and sentence structures. For many DLL families, this implies the importance of consistently using their native language in daily interactions, storytelling, singing, and reading books.

SOURCE: Excerpted from Foundation for Child Development, 2020, p. 138.

ranked at the bottom of "school readiness" (Ackerman & Tazi, 2015)—results that often are a by-product of being assessed only in English. A large percentage of multilingual learners never reach full proficiency in English and become long-term English language learners,[3] which puts them at risk for having lower academic achievement and dropping out of high school. In California, the state with the largest number and proportion of multilingual learners in the country, more than half of all multilingual learners are never designated as fully English proficient, which means that the language programs they experienced did not provide them with essential language and literacy skills needed for the 21st century. Sadly, many of these children also have lost proficiency in their home language by the time they are in elementary school (National Academies, 2017). Thus, while most multilingual learners have the capacity to excel in school by becoming fully bilingual and biliterate, few receive the educational experiences necessary to realize that potential.

Research on Early Bilingualism

All young children (including multilingual learners) need "responsive, sensitive, trusting, and nurturing relationships with adults to develop the social-emotional competencies that underlie all future learning" (Espinosa & Crandell, 2020, p. 197; see Chapter 3 in this report for fuller discussion of the learning needs of all children). The features described in Chapter 4 as essential elements of high-quality equitable curricula in early childhood education are as necessary for multilingual learners as for their monolingual English-speaking peers. For all children, both the quantity and quality of adult language directed to them, as well as the language diversity, influence future language and cognitive outcomes (Adamson et al., 2021). As such, adults can pose questions to children that are interesting, give them enough time to respond, engage in turn taking in an extended conversation, and expose children to a vocabulary that is rich in content and contains diverse sentence structures (Espinosa & Crandell, 2020).

Age of Exposure

As noted earlier, research has found that infants, from all language, social, and economic backgrounds, including those with disabilities (see Chapter 6), have the ability to learn more than one language and that the early years are an ideal time to be exposed to multiple languages (Conboy,

---

[3] The term "long-term English language learners" refers to a "formal educational classification" designated to students "who have been enrolled in American schools for more than six years, who are not progressing toward English proficiency, and who are struggling academically due to their limited English skills" (Grazzini, 2019, p. x).

2013; Ramirez & Kuhl, 2017). The influence of the age at which a child is first exposed to a second language has been studied extensively. Research has shown that during the first year of life, multilingual learners can distinguish between two different languages and learn the features of each language (Kuhl et al., 2006). An enriching language environment during the first years of life influences the "brain architecture" of infants (Espinosa & Crandell, 2020). Noninvasive brain-imaging techniques have allowed researchers to study how early bilingualism impacts brain functioning. For example, magnetoencephalography is being used to study the language processing of infants and toddlers (Institute for Learning and Brain Sciences, n.d.). This sophisticated method of studying how the human brain processes language during a child's early years provides insight into how specific experiences with more than one language can influence the "organization of the language processing systems of the brains of young multilingual learners" (Espinosa, 2015b, p. 43). Based on research from cognitive neuroscientists, it is now known that from their earliest days, human babies have an innate and extensive ability to hear, process, and learn multiple languages. In fact, even the youngest babies can sort the unique phonology (or sounds) of each language perceived into separate language categories, and by the preschool years, bilingual children are skilled in interpreting contextual cues to direct their utterances in the appropriate language to the appropriate person (Byers-Heinlein et al., 2010; Kuhl et al., 2006). Additional research has found that during the last trimester of pregnancy, fetuses are actively processing the unique characteristics of different languages and beginning to make distinctions among them (Conboy, 2013; Kisilevsky et al., 2009).

Research in cognitive neuroscience indicates that the bilingual brain exhibits greater neurological activity than the monolingual brain because of the necessity of processing two languages (Bialystok, 2017). This increased neurological activity is linked to improved control of focused attention and self-regulatory behavior (Conboy, 2013), skills that, in turn, contribute to enhanced executive function in individuals learning multiple languages. The National Academies 2017 report emphasizes that children who have the opportunity to develop proficiency in two or more languages early in life gain the ability to communicate in multiple languages and may experience advancements in certain cognitive skills, leading to improved academic outcomes in school (National Academies, 2017, p. 147). These cognitive benefits are observable even in the first year of life. Bilingual infants as young as 7 months old have demonstrated superior mental flexibility when faced with changing learning tasks. Compared with their monolingual counterparts, bilingual infants exhibited greater ability to quickly adapt to shifts in learning conditions and modify their responses (Barac et al., 2014; Kovács & Mehler, 2009; Sandhofer & Uchikoshi, 2013). This specific skill—the capacity to suppress prior learning when conditions change—is generally considered a facet of executive function and constitutes an essential element of school readiness.

Early bilingualism has also been linked to various aspects of executive function, including working memory, inhibitory control, and the ability to focus on relevant task cues while disregarding irrelevant ones, along with enhanced language skills (Sandhofer & Uchikoshi, 2013). As mentioned earlier, these executive functioning abilities are recognized as fundamental to kindergarten readiness and overall academic success (Espinosa, 2013). As infants progress and become preschoolers, these benefits in executive functioning skills become even more evident, particularly in tasks that necessitate selectively attending to competing options and the capability to suppress interfering information (Sandhofer & Uchikoshi, 2013).

Further studies indicate that infants exhibit heightened sensitivity to the distinct sounds of various languages during their initial year of life. It has been observed that sometime in the latter half of their first year, their perceptual sensitivity to unfamiliar language sounds begins to decrease (Kuhl et al., 2003). Other research has discovered that individuals learning multiple languages simultaneously or from a very early age tend to achieve significant language milestones in each language around the same ages and acquire both languages at similar rates (Petitto & Holowka, 2002). Additionally, certain studies suggest that the most favorable age for grasping the morphology and syntax of a second language is before reaching the age of 5 years. The "language sensitivities" identified in infants are noted to diminish after the age of 3 or 4 years (Meisel, 2008).

Type and Amount of Exposure

The quantity and quality of speech directed toward multilingual learners directly impact their language development, as per the findings of the National Academies (2017). Several studies indicate that multilingual learners who receive at least 40–60% of their language exposure in each language demonstrate progress comparable to that of monolingual individuals with 100% exposure to one language (Thordardottir, 2011). Moreover, multilingual learners with over 70% exposure to English do not show significant differences in English language skills compared with monolingual children with 100% exposure (Hoff et al., 2012). In summary, this research implies that multilingual learners benefit from frequent, responsive, and enriched language interactions. Early, balanced exposure to dual languages, with at least 40% of the time dedicated to each language, is linked to high proficiency in both languages and improved long-term academic achievement for multilingual learners.

From an educational standpoint, this research suggests that very young children can acquire proficiency in two languages earlier than previously believed (Kuhl, 2011). Additionally, early exposure to more than one language shapes the neural architecture of the brain, enhancing specific cognitive processing abilities in all young children.

Preschool and Multilingual Learners

As multilingual learners progress into preschool, they frequently exhibit heightened executive functioning advantages over monolingual learners, surpassing those advantages observed in multilingual infants. These advantages are evident across various racial, cultural, and socioeconomic backgrounds, as well as with different language pairings. Nonetheless, the extent of these cognitive benefits relies on the degree of bilingualism in the child. Those children who maintain a more balanced proficiency in both languages demonstrate more significant advantages than those who exhibit stronger dominance in a single language (Bialystok & Barac, 2012; Yow & Li, 2015).

The preschool years are critical for language development and especially for building the foundations for future literacy for all children, including multilingual learners. While multilingual learners exhibit a similar overall language development pattern to monolingual children, their bilingualism introduces unique variations, such as language mixing, smaller vocabularies in each language, and differences in the timing of specific linguistic milestones. These variations stem from the inherent complexities of acquiring two languages simultaneously. (National Academies, 2017). For example, Sandhofer & Uchikoshi (2013) emphasize that research consistently indicates a delay in word recall and slower word retrieval times during picture-naming tasks among bilingual children. Additionally, these children tend to score lower on verbal fluency tasks. This implies that early childhood educators might consider providing additional waiting time for responses, recognizing the heightened linguistic processing challenge faced by young multilingual learners, especially in their non-dominant language. Many studies have found that bilingual preschoolers tend to have smaller vocabularies in each language when compared with English- and Spanish-speaking monolinguals (Hoff, 2021; Pearson et al., 1993). However, when both languages are considered together, their vocabulary size is often comparable to that of monolinguals. As Conboy (2013) points out, "bilingual lexical learning leads to initially smaller vocabularies in *each separate language* than for monolingual learners of those same languages, and that *total vocabulary sizes* (the sum of what children know in both their languages) in bilinguals are similar to those of monolingual toddlers" (p. 19).

Given that the size of vocabulary is a significant objective in preschool education and plays a crucial role in future reading comprehension, it is essential for curriculum designers and preschool teachers to grasp the variations in dual language learning. This discrepancy in vocabulary growth typically does not signify language delays or potential learning difficulties; instead, it is a common aspect of early bilingualism. For instance, if a preschooler learning multiple languages is unfamiliar with the English term "window," the child may still comprehend the concept learned at home and know the word for "window" in their home language (e.g., *ventana* in Spanish).

Oral language skills (e.g., vocabulary skills, listening comprehension, grammatical knowledge, and expressive vocabulary) are especially important for multilingual learners' future reading comprehension abilities (Espinosa & Zepeda, 2019; Lesaux, 2013). In general, multilingual learners have shown phonics and decoding skills comparable to those of monolingual English speakers early in the reading process but have shown much lower levels of reading comprehension. Although with effective instruction, multilingual learners are able to master the building blocks of word decoding, many do not have sufficient oral language skills to understand what they are reading (National Academies, 2017). This research underscores the significance of fostering oral language development and employing instructional approaches that offer immersive and compelling language encounters in both languages. Simultaneously, there should be a concentrated effort on cultivating early literacy skills. Keeping this in mind, it becomes imperative for preschool curricula to prioritize the enhancement of oral language and vocabulary development for young learners who are multilingual.

Numerous studies have emphasized the significance of purposeful exposure to English during the preschool years as important to future school performance for multilingual learners. For example, research has indicated that lower levels of English proficiency upon entering kindergarten are linked to subsequent challenges in school, particularly difficulties in English language reading (Galindo, 2010; Halle et al., 2012). Moreover, recent studies examining the duration required for dual language learners to achieve full proficiency in English have highlighted the importance of robust language skills in both the home language and English at the onset of kindergarten. These skills are deemed essential for the successful academic advancement in the second language and may decrease the likelihood of children becoming long-term English language learners (Thompson, 2015; Winsler et al., 2016).

In summary, multiple factors are known to affect language and literacy growth for multilingual learners, including age of acquisition of each language, the quality and quantity of their exposure to each language, the amount of time multilingual learners spend in each of their languages, and the language practices used in their early schooling.

Importance of Home Language Maintenance and Development

While early exposure to English promotes multilingual learners' eventual bilingualism, it also carries some risks. Frequently, when multilingual learners are introduced to English as the primary language of instruction in preschool, there is a tendency for them to develop a preference for speaking only English and become hesitant to use their home language (Oller & Eilers, 2002; Wong-Filmore, 1991). The early abandonment of a child's first or home language is linked to enduring language challenges and the potential risk of losing connection with their cultural and linguistic heritage (National Academies, 2017). If children are unable to communicate in their home language with their parents, other family members, and members of their linguistic community, there is a potential loss of identity and ties to their ethnic, cultural, and linguistic roots (Espinosa, 2013). To prevent the premature erosion of home language skills, early childhood education curriculum needs to incorporate strategies that actively support, intentionally encourage, and regularly assess the development of multilingual learners in both their home language and English.

To best serve multilingual learners, the goal of helping them achieve high levels of English proficiency cannot come at the expense of their home language proficiency. To thrive in a global, multilingual world while also forming a positive self-identity and maintaining and sustaining strong bonds with their immediate and extended families, preschool multilingual learners need a strong foundation in their home language, as well as high levels of English proficiency (Espinosa & Crandell, 2020; Halle et al., 2012). This goal is possible when early childhood curriculum includes language scaffolds, specific strategies that focus on home language maintenance, and English acquisition, as well as methods and tools for monitoring growth in both languages (National Academies, 2017).

RESEARCH-BASED PRINCIPLES FOR ECE CURRICULUM FOR MULTILINGUAL LEARNERS

ECE that is culturally and linguistically responsive to multilingual learners is essential for them to achieve their full potential cognitively, academically, and socially. The research presented earlier in this chapter affirms two major findings: (1) Acquiring two or more languages in early childhood is advantageous, not a weakness; and (2) robust proficiency in the home language, coupled with English language skills, seems to be the most effective groundwork for success in both early and later stages of schooling. The findings also provide insights into early bilingual learning that have implications for important elements of high-quality early childhood curricula for multilingual learners. Research is also emerging on ways to support children who speak dialects other than General American English at home (Box 7-3). One consistent finding across many studies is that *all* young children benefit from early learning opportunities that support emergent bilingualism; therefore, early education goals can be strengthened by immediately including bilingualism as an explicit goal for multilingual learners and eventually expanding to all children. Further, 50 states and the District of Columbia award qualifying high school seniors the Seal of

---

BOX 7-3
African American English (AAE): An Example of a Variation of the English Language

Although some have described this language system a restricted, deficient code, unable to support logical thought (Bereiter & Engelmann, 1966), AAE is a systematic and rule-governed language with its own linguistic structure, vocabulary, and grammar (Baker-Bell, 2020; Green, 2002; Pearson et al., 2013). "Some of the phonological patterns [of AAE . . .] include vowelization of final r-colored vowels, substituting initial voiced 'th' /ð/ with /d/, and changing final /Iŋ/ to /In/ [. . .] common grammatical patterns [. . .] include omission of plural morphemes when a quantifier is present, omission of possessives, and omission of regular past tense 'ed'" (Pearson et al., 2013, p. 220). This variation is a major dialect of English spoken by a large majority of African American children or use these patterns of AAE in their speech in the preschool years (Pearson et al., 2013), indicating that many young AAE-speaking children are learning two or more language varieties, making them bidialectal (Washington et al., 2023). Additionally, children in Black immigrant families may be multidialectal or multilingual as they speak AAE, General American English (GAE), and another English dialect or language.

In their seminal work, Craig & Washington (2006) synthesized a decade of research on African American children's oral language and literacy skills from preschool to fifth grade. Studies indicate that not all African American or Black children are AAE speakers; children's use of AAE depends on the density of AAE used in their community. "Approximately nine out of 10 African American children growing up in poverty will be AAE speakers when they enter school" (Washington et al., 2023, p. 766). African American children who frequently use AAE, also called high-density dialect speakers, struggle the most with reading because there is a great distance between their oral language repertoire and written print (Washington & Seidenberg, 2021). High-density AAE speakers' reading struggles are not a reflection of their cognitive and academic capabilities but rather an indication of anti-Black systemic racism and linguicism that judges Black people's language and culture as substandard compared with that of White people, resulting in them not embracing this linguistic capital and integrating it into the classroom and teaching (Baker-Bell, 2020). Furthermore, AAE speakers are likely to experience opportunity gaps from living in low-income families and communities and internalized racism and emotional challenges. For example, AAE speakers may avoid speaking and monitor their speech because of distress experienced with the use of AAE in standard American English environments (Washington & Seidenberg, 2021).

Biliteracy, "an award given by a school, district, or state in recognition of students who have studied and attained proficiency in two or more languages by high school graduation" (Seal of Biliteracy, 2024). No statistics are currently available on the percentage of multilingual learners who enter early education programs with a home language other than English and achieve a Seal of Biliteracy at graduation; however, it makes sense to track these early pathways to full biliteracy.

> While research on how best to support AAE speakers is limited, there is some indication that increased professionals' knowledge, strategies for instruction, and practice coupled with a change in attitude about AAE could support the reading and overall learning of AAE speakers (Blackburn, 2012). In their randomized controlled study with 73 mainly White teachers (78% White, 12% Black, 7% Hispanic, and 3% Asian) in a master's-level teacher education program, Fogel & Ehri (2006) found that teachers in the exposure, strategy, and practice group, which required them translating sentences from GAE into AAE, showed improvement in their instruction method compared with those who were in the exposure and strategy instruction group, which required reviewing the rules of AAE and reviewing translations from GAE to AAE along with the exposure task and the exposure only group which required reading three short stories written in AAE. The effect sizes were large, in the range of 1.90–2.20. However, there were no significant differences between the groups in their attitudes toward AAE, although the trend moved from negative to neutral. The authors conclude that exposure and direct practice are essential to improve instructional approaches for AAE speakers. Still, there is a need to address "positive attitudes toward AAE [. . . as] attitude shifts require more than simple knowledge acquisition. Teachers may also need to be sensitized to the difficulties that dialect-speaking students face in learning new dialect forms in the classroom" (Fogel & Ehri, 2006, p. 475). These findings mirror the conclusions from the National Academies report (2017) about the most effective educational practices for multilingual learners.
>
> Thus, a shift in professional preparation, classroom support, and instructional practices is needed to transform from a deficit orientation to one that attends to Black children's and their families' strengths and assets and the impact of racism and biases. Washington et al. (2023) recommend the following approaches to meet the needs of AAE-speaking children: (1) learn about the sophisticated and complex system of AAE; (2) learn about the general oral language development and AAE, such as milestones and the impact of poverty, and the opportunity gaps in accurately identifying children with language disorders; (3) learn about the science of reading that "promotes structured literacy approaches that [a] differentiate instruction based on the outcomes of assessment and progress monitoring data; [b] deliver systematic reading instruction, following a logical scope and sequence; and [c] provide direct, intentional, and explicit reading instruction" (Washington et al., 2023, pp. 768–770). Most importantly, it will be critical for educators to go beyond the structured literacy approach to one that supports mastery in decoding, critical analyses, and insights for children whose oral code may differ from print. This approach will require building on children's language repertoire and systems rather than ignoring or castigating it as "bad English" (Washington & Iruka, forthcoming).

RESEARCH-SUPPORTED CURRICULUM, STRATEGIES, AND PRACTICES FOR MULTILINGUAL LEARNERS

Early childhood curricula in the United States are rarely developed specifically for multilingual learners; more commonly, they are developed for English-speaking children and then translated into other languages with supplementary materials that are culturally responsive to the community in which the program is located, and sometimes include suggested adaptations for different groups of multilingual learners. Consequently, the research literature on effective curricula for multilingual learners is focused primarily on studies of amounts of home language and English used (Figueras-Daniel & Li, 2021; Hammer et al., 2014; Raikes et al., 2019; Sembiante et al., 2022; White et al., 2023), the purposes and quality of language used in pre-K classrooms (Jacoby & Lesaux, 2017; Limlingan et al., 2020; Méndez et al., 2015; Miller, 2017), or a set of practices and adaptations designed to scaffold English language comprehension while also providing home language support for multilingual learners (Center for Equity for English Learners [CEEL], 2020; Espinosa, 2015a; Hsin et al., 2022; Lindholm-Leary, 2015).

Translating Curricula into Other Languages

Some widely used early childhood curricula have been translated into other languages, most commonly Spanish (e.g., *The Creative Curriculum*, *CIRCLE Pre-K Curriculum*, *Tools of the Mind*, *Opening the Word of Learning* [OWL]), but most are available only in English with some materials or suggestions for multilingual learners (e.g., *HighScope*, *Curiosity Corner*, *Galileo*, *Connect4Learning*). While the translated versions of early childhood curricula offer to multilingual learners opportunities to experience bilingual instruction and better comprehend the content of the instruction, challenges arise when taking material developed in English and directly translating the curriculum into other languages. The translated versions have been developed with attention to ensuring comparability in the conceptual, linguistic, or semantic content, and/or level of difficulty of the translated material across languages. What is more, the meaning and vocabulary of some content may not be the same between the non-English and English versions of the same material. Words in one language may have multiple meanings or may be used idiomatically in very specific ways that cannot be translated directly into another language (García et al., 2006). If the content for a given lesson or activity has not been developed in both English and the second language simultaneously, the translation or adaptation process may inadvertently change the content or meaning of the text, or the linguistic complexity of the desired skill or ability that is being taught.

Some curriculum developers have minimized the errors in direct translations by *back translating* their materials. This double translation process involves first translating from English to a different language (most often Spanish) and then translating it back to English by a separate translator to check for correct meaning, tone, and content. It is very difficult to have exact translations across languages because of differences in idioms, shades of meanings, and grammar (Zhang & Gao, 2014). In addition to being skilled translators, translators need some background in early childhood education, so they understand the terminology commonly used in this field.

Programs and Policies for Identifying Multilingual Learners

While several federal programs encourage states to collect data on multilingual learners and establish home language survey policies, most states lack policies or consistent procedures for identifying who is and who is not a multilingual learner during the preschool years. The federal Head Start program requires programs to provide data on the linguistic background of the children and families they serve and offers guidance on how to collect important information from families (Lazarín & Park, 2021). The Child Care and Development Fund also requires states to collect and report data on the primary home language of families served by the program, but no consistent or standardized method is provided. Few states require state preschool or other publicly funded early childhood programs to use a standard process for identifying multilingual learners. Consequently, although U.S. Census Bureau data indicate that an estimated 33% of all children under age 5 years speak a language other than English in the home (Lazarín & Park, 2021), very little is known about the numbers of children across the United States, their specific languages spoken, their communities of residence, or their learning needs.

Further complicating the challenges of accurately identifying multilingual learners during the preschool years is the disjointed system of public and private providers of early education (see Chapter 8), which lacks consensus about the process and criteria for defining multilingual learners. Across states and sometimes even across cities, the same child may be identified as a multilingual learner in one program and not in another (Lazarín & Park, 2021). Without proper identification of individual children, it is difficult to design appropriate language goals and determine the child's specific learning needs. Without some knowledge of the multilingual preschool population in communities and states, it is difficult to allocate resources, design targeted professional development for early childhood educators, and effectively support multilingual learners' emergent bilingualism. However, a few states have recently enacted policies that outline specific methods for identifying multilingual learners during the preschool years: Illinois, New York, Pennsylvania, and Minnesota have guidelines for gathering information from families that profiles the child's early language exposure in the home.

In 2022, California passed a bill (California Assembly Bill No. 1363, 2021) that went into effect January 2023 and requires that all California State Preschool Program providers, including those operating Family Child Care Home Education Networks, "to identify and collect data on multilingual learners; language characteristics of preschool programs, such as whether the program uses the home language for instruction or offers a dual language immersion program; and the language composition of program staff" (Villegas, 2022). This landmark legislation is the first of its kind that frames the child's home language and culture as assets to be valued and embraced by preschool educators. The identification process includes two steps: a Family Language Survey administered to all children enrolled and a Family Languages and Interest Interview for those children identified as potential multilingual learners. Specifically, the legislation reads,[4]

> It is the intent of the Legislature for the state preschool contractors, teachers, and staff to better understand the language and developmental needs of dual language learners enrolled in publicly funded preschool programs by identifying them through a family language instrument and a family language and interest interview. The identification of dual language learners will help improve program quality and inform the allocation and use of state and program resources to better support them and their linguistic and developmental needs for success in school and in life.

The legislation also instructs early education providers to help families understand the benefits of multilingualism and the important role of the home language in supporting English development; it also encourages families to continue supporting the ongoing development of the home language, with additional resources available to families in multiple languages. Following the enactment of this legislation, California's preschool programs reported slightly higher enrollment rates of multilingual learners (Villegas, 2022). The state is now focused on building a qualified bilingual workforce with high-quality materials to meet the needs of multilingual children (Villegas, 2022).

The Migration Policy Institute has recommended that state and local early education programs engage in the following steps to accurately identify and meet the educational needs of multilingual learners (Lazarín & Park, 2021, p. 23):

> (1) initial determination of whether young children have significant exposure to a language other than English in their home environment; (2) collection of accurate data about DLLs' linguistic environment and experiences; and (3) determination of DLLs' evolving language and literacy skills in English and in the home language, as well as language dominance.

---

[4]California Assembly Bill 1363, Chapter 498.

Thus, while several states have made progress in developing systems for identifying multilingual learners during the preschool years, no state yet has designed a coordinated data system that identifies and monitors multilingual learners from birth to age 5 and on to the K–12 system. Early identification of multilingual learners is a critical first step in high-quality educational services, as it enables understanding of students' linguistic assets and learning needs.

Classroom Language Models for Multilingual Learners

Typically, state early childhood education program guidelines and Head Start recommend one of four classroom language models for multilingual learners. A classroom language model outlines which language(s) will be spoken intentionally during which times of the day to achieve the language goals for each child and program. The language models are

- *English only*: This model is acceptable when all the children and staff speak English. The limitations of this language model are that it restricts children from early bilingualism and may overlook the cultural diversity of the children and families enrolled.
- *English with home language support*: This classroom language model is appropriate when most teachers and staff speak English primarily and some of the children speak languages other than English in the home as their first language. In this model, the language of instruction is mostly English, but the staff make intentional efforts to bring the children's different languages and cultures into the classroom. This is the most common classroom language model for pre-K programs that have multilingual learners enrolled; it is a method for respecting and reflecting the languages and cultures of all children while not having the language capacity or class composition to implement a full dual language program. Several instructional approaches have been designed that offer early childhood educators specific strategies and professional development to support the multiple languages of children when staff are monolingual (e.g., Personalized Oral Language Learning and Sobrato Early Academic Language), with varying levels of research evidence on their effectiveness for multilingual learners, as described below.
- *Dual language models*: In this classroom language model, the educators communicate and deliver instruction in two languages. Each language is "spoken during designated, equal, and predictable periods" (Office of Head Start, 2015, p. 11). The goals include emergent bilingualism for all the children, as well as learning

to value different cultures and languages. Early childhood dual language classroom models often allocate equal amounts of time and equitable content in each language, which is consistent with the research cited above; however, some have decided on a 90/10 approach, where 90% of the time instruction is delivered in one language (typically home language) and 10% of instructional time is in English. Still other programs decide on varying amounts of English/home language, such as 80/20 or 70/30.

- *Home/heritage language immersion*: In this classroom language model, all the children speak a language other than English in the home—or as in the case of many Native American/tribal communities, programs are designed to revitalize a language essential to a community's identity and cultural values (Box 7-4). Goals of this model include "develop[ing] strong language skills that serve as a foundation for second language development, supporting age-level development in English over time. [. . .] Experienc[ing] their home language as a positive source of strength and knowledge and as a connection between home and school" (Office of Head Start, 2015, p. 15). In addition, this model will "promote their development of a language that is central to MLs [multilingual learners'] family, culture, and identity and promote their overall language development by building on the knowledge and skills they have developed in their home language" (Espinosa & Crandell, 2020, p. 214).

Early childhood education programs usually state explicitly the classroom language models they use and provide the organizing structure for classroom language usage. However, in many cases, amounts of English used throughout the day and during targeted instructional activities vary substantially from the official language policy (Figueras-Daniel & Li, 2021; Martin et al., 2022a).

Evaluations of Curricula for Multilingual Learners

Other than positing that the elements of high-quality early childhood curriculum also apply to multilingual learners but require linguistic and instructional adaptations, the contributions of specific curricula to the growth and development of multilingual learners has not been studied independently from the impacts of specific language practices or instructional strategies (Castro et al., 2011; López & Paez, 2020; see Chapter 4 for more detailed information). Research efforts have not focused on specific curricula for multilingual learners and the quality of their implementation to the same extent that language usage and specific instructional strategies have been examined for child impacts. However, a few studies have found that early

BOX 7-4
Heritage Language Revitalization Programs

For Indigenous communities facing the threat of language extinction, heritage language revitalization efforts are not just urgent—they are seen as vital to cultural identity and community well-being. While acknowledging the importance of essential skills and English proficiency for academic advancement, community members recognize the unique role their language plays in maintaining and restoring their heritage.

Bringing children together with fluent speakers for language acquisition is crucial. The question of who can teach these endangered languages in schools remains a pressing issue. There is often a lack of qualified instructors fluent in the community's heritage language, and in cases where remaining speakers are elderly or in poor health, this issue becomes even more complex. Incorporating culture into the curriculum presents another layer of complexity. The question of how best to incorporate Indigenous languages and culture into education extends beyond mere curriculum materials, such as history, songs, and stories. A broader perspective recognizes the intricate web of relationships between teachers and students, the learning environment itself, and the underlying philosophies about education and knowledge acquisition. This holistic approach, often referred to as "culture-based education," holds immense potential for improving educational outcomes for Indigenous students.

While research on the effectiveness of language revitalization programs continues to be limited, particularly because of the difficulty of measuring outcomes in small tribal populations, promising findings do exist. Research suggests promising benefits from well-designed programs. Studies highlight the positive impact of "strong, additive, and academically rigorous" programs on language maintenance and achievement. Evidence shows that strong programs do not hinder English acquisition and can even enhance student performance mirroring the research on emergent bilingualism. Most importantly, community-driven programs with local control contribute to student motivation, self-esteem, and cultural pride, strengthening the school–community bond. However, limitations such as teacher availability and program design persist.

Further research is needed to continue examining the potential benefit of language revitalization on language maintenance, academic achievement, and cultural identities. Successful revitalization of endangered languages in education will require addressing teacher shortages, embracing a broader view of cultural integration, and implementing well-designed programs with community involvement. Despite the challenges, research findings indicate positive impacts on language, academic achievement, and cultural identity, making this pursuit an endeavor in alignment with the committee's vision.

SOURCE: Summarized from National Academies, 2017.

childhood curricula centered around child-led activities, which support children's agency and allow them to make decisions and explore their environments, are associated with greater social, language, and academic gains for multilingual learners than other types of curricula (Alamillo et al., 2016; Ansari & Winsler, 2014; Rodriguez et al., 2003). These studies suggest that when young multilingual learners have opportunities to engage with their peers, select activities of interest to them, use all of their linguistic skills when communicating, and direct some of their learning experiences, they make greater academic gains than when they are in more restricted settings.

A small, but growing number of studies is examining the impacts of preschool bilingual programs on multilingual learners' academic and social outcomes (Barnett et al., 2007; Serafini et al., 2022; Steele et al., 2017). Two studies focused on the impacts of bilingual preschool compared with English immersion on preschoolers' early language, literacy, and math skills (Barnett et al., 2007; Oliva-Olson, 2019). Barnett and colleagues (2007) found that all preschoolers made comparable gains in English, but that only the children in dual language models made gains in their Spanish language and academic skills—and they did so without compromising their gains in English. These findings echo earlier studies of ECE bilingual education that also found that children who attended bilingual preschool "showed significant and parallel gains in Spanish language development as well as significant and greater increases in English language proficiency over time" (Winsler et al., 1999, p. 349). These results are significant given the conclusion by the National Academies (2017) that the best preparation for school success is language skills in both the home language and English, as well as longitudinal studies that have shown that strong bilingual skills are associated with higher academic performance in English. Similarly, Oliva-Olson (2019) also found that children who attended a two-way bilingual program had higher Spanish and English skills than those who attended primarily English immersion programs with some amount of support for home language. These results were moderated by the quality of teacher–child language interactions. All of these studies included samples of preschoolers who speak Spanish and English. These questions about bilingual classroom language models are clearly needed for children with native languages other than Spanish, particularly for children whose home languages are nonphonetic and dissimilar to English.

Based on the studies discussed in this chapter, it is clear that multilingual learners attending bilingual preschool can learn a second language (e.g., English) without losing their first or home language when the classroom language model provides sufficient high-quality exposure to both languages. These findings can be contrasted with other studies (Barnett et al., 2007) that have shown that when preschool multilingual learners attend English-immersion settings, their English language skills do not grow at faster rates than when they attend bilingual programs and that their first or home language skills decline. Thus, for multilingual preschoolers, English-immersion programs have been shown to impede their potential for early bilingualism while not accelerating their English acquisition.

Teaching Strategies and Instructional Practices for Multilingual Learners

The most frequently used classroom language model in early childhood classrooms serving multilingual learners is primarily English with some amount of home language support (Oliva-Olson, 2019). Therefore, recent studies have examined the effectiveness of sets of strategies and practices that all early childhood educators can implement whether or not they are fluent in their students' home languages (Brodziak de los Reyes et al., 2022; CEEL, 2020; Méndez et al., 2015; Pollard-Durodola et al., 2016). These specific strategies include

- Partnering with families to collaboratively develop language goals and integrating vocabulary, customs, values, and home languages into classroom routines.
- Supplying books and environmental text, such as labels, in the native languages of students, along with educational and play resources (such as dolls and food items) that reflect the diverse backgrounds of multilingual learners. These actions illustrate the appreciation of children's language and cultural heritage within the educational setting (Espinosa & Crandell, 2020). Additionally, studies reveal that incorporating books in the home language can enhance language development in multilingual learners, particularly when coupled with purposeful instruction in the home language (Gutierrez-Clellen et al., 2014).
- Preparing educators with basic words and phrases, such as greetings, in the multilingual learners' home languages and singing songs and chants in children's home languages (Espinosa & Crandell, 2020).
- Using multiple methods of communicating meanings of words—such as hand and body gestures, pictorial representations, concrete objects or realia—and connecting instructional content to children's cultural backgrounds and family traditions (Brodziak de los Reyes et al., 2022; National Academies, 2017).
- Providing opportunities for multilingual learners to interact with their English-speaking peers during open-ended activities and Spanish-speaking[5] peers during teacher-led small-group activities (Espinosa & Crandell, 2020).

---

[5]As previously discussed, most studies of preschool multilingual learners conducted in the United States have included samples of native Spanish speakers, although some recent studies have included native speakers of Cantonese, Vietnamese, and Mandarin.

- Encouraging multilingual preschoolers to use all of their linguistic knowledge when communicating (e.g., emphasize the content of the interaction and do not discourage multilingual learners from using their home language throughout the day). This is often referred to as *translanguaging* or code-switching when multilingual learners use a mixture of home language and English to communicate (Seltzer et al., 2020).

While these specific instructional strategies for English with home language support have some evidence of positive impacts on language and literacy growth for multilingual learners (Castro et al., 2017), the Oliva-Olson study (2019) of Head Start preschool classrooms found that children who attended the dual language classrooms gained more in Spanish and English fluency outcomes than those in the English with home language supports, such as those described above. Thus, it appears that when early childhood educators are not proficient in multilingual learners' home languages and unfamiliar with their family cultures, English with home language support strategies promote better language and literacy growth than English only, but balanced dual language programs promote the most growth in both English and multilingual learners' home languages.

Teacher–Child Relationships

Central to all preschool children's feelings of security and safety are the nature and quality of their relationships with the important adults in their lives, namely parents and teachers. Research has shown that close teacher–child relationships characterized by warmth, comfort, and openness are positively associated with children's engagement and achievement, whereas conflictual relationships characterized by negativity and friction can undermine children's school performance (Li et al., 2022). For multilingual learners, close, nonconflictual relationships with their teachers provide opportunities for verbal interactions, where they can engage with others, practice current language and social skills, and learn new vocabulary and concepts (Limlingan et al., 2020). The quality of the interactions between teachers and multilingual learners has been shown to be critical to acquiring a new language, as well as to developing social-emotional, math, and literacy skills (Downer et al., 2012; Hammer et al., 2014). Daily conversations between teachers and children have also been described as meaningful interchanges that promote culture-specific values and ideas (Rogoff et al., 2017).

A recent, large study of 162 Head Start classrooms (Limlingan et al., 2020) that used the Family and Child Experiences Survey 2009 dataset found positive associations between teachers' amount of Spanish use and emotionally supportive teacher–child interactions. In those Head Start classrooms where teachers spoke to the children more often in their home language (in this case, Spanish), the children also showed larger gains in Spanish language learning and positive approaches to learning. These results were similar to a multistate study of state-wide pre-K programs (Downer et al., 2012), in which children from more emotionally supportive classrooms showed larger gains in social competence and letter naming. The conclusions of these studies highlight the value of teachers using multilingual learners' home languages during everyday interactions and providing emotionally supportive learning environments. This also indicates the need for the early education field to organize around providing more bilingual educators who are qualified to provide high-quality linguistically responsive services for multilingual learners.

ASSESSMENT PRACTICES FOR MULTILINGUAL LEARNERS

The valid and comprehensive assessment of young multilingual learners' development and achievement is essential—but often challenging—for early care and education professionals (Espinosa & García, 2012). Knowledge of linguistically appropriate assessment practices is particularly crucial to high-quality, individualized instruction for multilingual learners. Individualized instruction recognizes and builds on the child's current language strengths and targets specific learning needs, thus promoting the important developmental and achievement outcomes necessary for success in school and later in life. Individualizing instruction for multilingual learners requires comprehensive, ongoing assessments that are fair; valid; and linguistically, culturally, and developmentally appropriate. Such assessments show how multilingual learners are progressing and what educational decisions and adjustments are needed.

The first issue facing educators who work with multilingual learners is to determine their students' proficiency in each language, as well as the distribution of their knowledge across the two languages. Assessment experts in academia, the Office of Head Start, and several states widely agree that multilingual learners need to be assessed in both their home or native language and in English (Espinosa & Gutiérrez-Clellen, 2013; Friedman-Krauss et al., 2021; Office of Head Start, 2015; Peña & Halle, 2011). Young multilingual learners who are exposed to multiple languages are likely to develop a dominant language, even though the distinctions may be subtle, as indicated by Paradis et al. (2011). Before educators can assess a child's developmental status, educational progress, or the need for intervention, it is crucial to identify the language in which the child is more proficient. Typically, an emergent bilingual will exhibit a larger or more specialized vocabulary, along with greater grammatical proficiency and mastery of the linguistic structure, in one of their languages. This is the language that the child has been exposed to the most, uses more fluently, and often prefers to communicate in (Paradis et al., 2011; Pearson, 2002).

When multilingual learners are assessed only in English, which is most often their weaker language, as is the case in most early language and kindergarten readiness assessments, they will score significantly lower in language, literacy, and math tasks than their English-only peers (Espinosa & García, 2012). However, these scores may be typical for a child who is in the early stages of second-language acquisition and not represent any language delays or be a cause for concern. An emergent bilingual may know many vocabulary words in their home language but have limited knowledge of English vocabulary, grammatical rules, or idioms (Hammer et al., 2011; Páez et al., 2007). For example, young multilingual learners may know the names of objects in the kitchen in their home language but not in English. They may also know words such as "recess," and "scissors" in English because these are the words they are exposed to at school (Espinosa & Gutiérrez-Clellen, 2013). They may not learn the same words in Spanish because there was no opportunity to do so at home. In those cases, the child may appear to have a limited vocabulary in each language. However, as discussed previously in this chapter, when the total number of words the child knows in both languages is considered, it is often comparable to the number and range of vocabulary words that monolingual children know (Espinosa & Gutiérrez-Clellen, 2013).

Therefore, any conclusions about the developmental progress or need for special services need to be based on knowledge about the multilingual child's abilities in both their home language and English. It is also essential that early childhood educators understand the process of second-language acquisition during the preschool years and the characteristics of the multilingual learners' home languages and cultural practices so they can make judgments about each students' progress and whether a referral for in-depth language assessment is warranted.

An appropriate approach to the assessment of multilingual learners consists of both formal and informal methods (Espinosa & Zepeda, 2019). Initial assessment needs to include "a formal family interview or questionnaire about the languages spoken in the home and by which family members; this will provide information on each multilingual learners' early language-learning opportunities" (Espinosa & Zepeda, 2019, p. 14). In addition, early childhood educators need to know the child's level of English language skills. Many programs use formal assessments such as the preLAS, an English language proficiency assessment for early learners (Duncan & De Avila, 1985), which early education personnel can administer to individuals to gain more specific information about a child's receptive and expressive English language abilities. Many other standardized English-proficiency assessments have been validated for multilingual learners who speak Spanish in the home (Barrueco et al., 2012), but few that have been validated with other language groups.

In addition to formal assessment, ongoing informal observational assessment that is both structured and unstructured provides early childhood teachers with important information about each multilingual learners' progress and learning needs. Regular and continuous evaluation for the enhancement and adaptation of instruction involve the examination of each child's performance through observations, checklists, rating scales, work samples, and portfolios incorporated into everyday activities (Espinosa & Gutiérrez-Clellen, 2013; Stefanakis & Meier, 2010). These assessments need to align with the goals of the curriculum, be based on accurate developmental trajectories for multilingual learners, and include information from families (National Academies, 2017).

TEACHER COMPETENCIES FOR MULTILINGUAL LEARNERS

Early childhood educators who work with multilingual learners need the skills and competencies required of all early childhood educators, in addition to specialized knowledge about the development and learning needs of multilingual preschoolers. In a recent briefing paper for the state of California, Espinosa & Zepeda (2019) argue that in order to be effective with young multilingual learners, early childhood educators need some essential dispositions that undergird affirming and appropriate instruction. They need to

a. **Possess a strengths-based perspective toward multilingual learners.** In other words, they need to believe that the ability to speak more than one language during the early childhood years is a strength that will yield lifelong benefits.
b. **Possess an essential dispositional quality to effective teaching** and the development of warm and accepting relationships with multilingual learners.
c. **Maintain an openness to multilingual learners' culture and an understanding of the contexts in which they live.** In other words, they need to be able to converse "with families about their child-rearing beliefs, practices, and expectations and integrate culturally responsive practices into their programmatic goals and objectives" (Espinosa & Zepeda, 2019, p. 3).
d. **Continuously self-monitor and reflect on how personal beliefs and values interact and influence their teaching.** In other words, they need to be able to self-reflect on how their linguistic and cultural background interact with their perceptions and classroom practices and remain open to confronting their own biases and possible misperceptions.

In addition, after reviewing the literature on early childhood teacher competencies and the success of multilingual preschool learners, Espinosa & Zepeda (2019) suggested the following competencies:

- Can articulate the main features of high-quality early childhood education and why they compose the foundation for early education for multilingual learners.
- Understand and can describe the two main classroom language models for multilingual learners—(1) balanced English and home language, and (2) English language development with home language support—and their structures and strategies.
- Demonstrate the ability to successfully implement at least one classroom language model.
- Know and can articulate the importance of implementing specific strategies for supporting the ongoing development of multilingual learners' first or home language, while also intentionally and systematically exposing multilingual learners to English.
- Know how to select and implement technology and interactive media for use in educating multilingual learners.

Finally, Espinosa & Zepeda (2019) suggested that all early childhood educators who work with multilingual learners receive professional development and become competent in the following areas (p. 12):

- "Understand that all young children have the capacity to become bi/multilingual with sufficient language and social supports
- Can discuss the neurological impacts of early bilingualism
- Can describe the stages of second-language acquisition
- Know the components of language
- Can describe the interdependence theory of first-language influence on second-language acquisition
- Understand the multiple paths to bilingualism
- Can identify and differentiate between simultaneous and sequential bilingualism[6]
- Can articulate the influences on rate of second-language acquisition; individual differences
- Understand the role of code-switching for multilingual learners

---

[6]Children exposed to proficient speakers of their first and second language (L1 and L2) before 3 years of age are referred to as simultaneous bilinguals. Children whose onset of L2 exposure occurs later than age 3 are often referred to as sequential bilinguals (National Academies, 2017).

- Can select and administer culturally and linguistically appropriate formal and informal assessments
- Can establish positive and respectful reciprocal relationships with multilingual families"

CONCLUSION

High-quality, equitable curriculum development and implementation for multilingual learners will require a shift in the field of early childhood education, as well as in education in general, from a deficits-based to an assets-based perspective. Instead of being viewed through the lens of what they do not know in English, multilingual learners need to be appreciated, affirmed, and celebrated for what they do know and for their bilingual potential, regardless of the language they speak. Future research on the impacts of early childhood curriculum on the growth and achievement of multilingual learners will need to recognize that emergent bilingualism is a goal for all multilingual learners and desirable for English-speaking preschoolers, because of the cognitive, linguistic, and social benefits of full bilingualism and biliteracy.

Most states, school districts, and local programs have yet to develop a standard procedure for identifying multilingual learners during the preschool years; thus, they miss the opportunity to document community contexts, language distribution patterns, and educational needs. Identifying multilingual learners during the preschool years and providing targeted, linguistically and culturally affirming services will enable program implementers and policy makers to demonstrate the benefits of a strengths-based approach that celebrates and values home language abilities and cultural knowledge as assets rather than liabilities.

As the field of early childhood education is populated primarily with English-speaking teachers and administrators, it will be critical to provide professional development on the methods and strategies that all staff can implement to support both home language maintenance and intentional systematic English language development. As discussed in this chapter, research demonstrates the linguistic advantages of multilingual learners attending balanced dual language classrooms—and providing these classrooms requires qualified bilingual staff, who are currently in short supply. Consequently, there is an urgent need to prepare more bilingual early childhood teachers across a range of languages, extending the possibility of dual language classrooms to languages beyond Spanish and English.

Most early childhood curricula have been developed in English, although some have created Spanish translations and made adaptations for children who are multilingual. A concentrated effort to develop instructional materials that take into consideration the learning trajectories of multilingual learners, adjust benchmarks for children who are learning through two languages, include representations of children's cultures and values, and embed assessments recognizing a range of developmental patterns common to multilingual learners will help to improve educational practices to children from diverse backgrounds.

Researchers and policy makers are slowly documenting the core competencies of all early childhood educators who work with multilingual learners. These qualifications to educate young multilingual learners effectively need to be clearly articulated and embedded into early childhood teacher preparation programs, as well as comprehensive professional development systems. The future educational success of the increasingly diverse population of students relies on the knowledge, dispositions, and skills of a workforce that is well prepared, well supported, and respected.

REFERENCES

Ackerman, D. J., & Tazi, Z. (2015). Enhancing young Hispanic dual language learners' achievement: Exploring strategies and addressing challenges. *ETS Research Report Series*, *2015*(1), 1–39. https://files.eric.ed.gov/fulltext/EJ1109677.pdf

Adamson, L. B., Caughy, M. O. B., Bakeman, R., Rojas, R., Owen, M. T., Tamis-LeMonda, C. S., Pacheco, D., Pace, A., & Suma, K. (2021). The quality of mother-toddler communication predicts language and early literacy in Mexican American children from low-income households. *Early Childhood Research Quarterly*, *56*, 167–179. https://doi.org/10.1016/j.ecresq.2021.03.006

Alamillo, L., Yun, C., & Bennett, L. R. (2016). Translanguaging in a Reggio-inspired Spanish dual-language immersion programme. *Early Child Development and Care*, *187*(3-4), 469–486. https://doi.org/10.1080/03004430.2016.1236091

Ansari, A., & Winsler, A. (2014). Montessori public school pre-K programs and the school readiness of low-income Black and Latino children. *Journal of Educational Psychology*, *106*(4), 1066–1079. https://doi.org/10.1037/a0036799

Antoniou, K., Grohmann, K. K., Kambanaros, M., & Katsos, N. (2016). The effect of childhood bilectalism and multilingualism on executive control. *Cognition*, *149*, 18–30. https://doi.org/10.1016/j.cognition.2015.12.002

Baker-Bell, A. (2020). Dismantling anti-Black linguistic racism in English language arts classrooms: Toward an anti-racist black language pedagogy. *Theory Into Practice*, *59*(1), 8–21. https://doi.org/10.1080/00405841.2019.1665415

Barac, R., Bialystok, E., Castro, D. C., & Sanchez, M. (2014). The cognitive development of young dual language learners: A critical review. *Early Childhood Research Quarterly*, *29*(4), 699–714. https://doi.org/10.1016%2Fj.ecresq.2014.02.003

Barnett, W. S., Yarosz, D. J., Thomas, J., Jung, K., & Blanco, D. (2007). Two-way and monolingual English immersion in preschool education: An experimental comparison. *Early Childhood Research Quarterly*, *22*(3), 277–293. https://doi.org/10.1016/j.ecresq.2007.03.003

Barrueco, S., Lopez, M., Ong, C., & Lozano, P. (2012). *Assessing Spanish-English bilingual preschoolers: A guide to best approaches and measures*. Brookes Publishing.

Bedore, L., Pena, E., García, M., & Cortez, C. (2005). Conceptual versus monolingual scoring: When does it make a difference? *Language Speech and Hearing Services in Schools*, *36*(3), 188–200. https://pubmed.ncbi.nlm.nih.gov/16175883/

Bereiter, C., & Engelmann, S. (1966). *Language learning activities for the disadvantaged child*. Prentice Hall.

Berken, J. A., Gracco, V. L., & Klein, D. (2017). Early bilingualism, language attainment, and brain development. *Neuropsychologia, 98*, 220–227. https://doi.org/10.1016/j.neuropsychologia.2016.08.031

Bialystok, E. (2017). The bilingual adaptation: How minds accommodate experience. *Psychological Bulletin, 143*(3), 233–262. https://doi.org/10.1037/bul0000099

Bialystok, E., & Barac, R. (2012). Emerging bilingualism: Dissociating advantages for metalinguistic awareness and executive control. *Cognition, 122*(1), 67–73. https://doi.org/10.1016/j.cognition.2011.08.003

Blackburn, J. F. (2012). The effect of dialect instruction on student knowledge of and attitudes toward African American English. *Communication Disorders Quarterly, 33*(4), 220–229. http://dx.doi.org/10.1177/1525740111430524

Brodziak de los Reyes, I., Holtzman, D. J., White, L., Carbuccia-Abbott, M., Manship, K., & Quick, H. (2022). *Promising strategies for supporting dual language learners, regardless of the languages teachers speak (First 5 California Dual Language Learner Pilot Study, Brief 3)*. American Institutes for Research. https://www.air.org/sites/default/files/2022-06/First-5-DLL-Instruction-Brief-3-Language-Independent-Strategies-June-2022.pdf

Byers-Heinlein, K., Burns, T., & Werker, J. F. (2010). The roots of bilingualism in newborns. *Psychological Science, 21*(3), 343–348. https://doi.org/10.1177/0956797609360758

California Assembly Bill No. 1363, Chapter 498 (2021). https://leginfo.legislature.ca.gov/faces/billTextClient.xhtml?bill_id=202120220AB1363

Castro, D. C., Espinosa, L., & Páez, M. (2011). Defining and measuring quality early childhood practices that promote dual language learners' development and learning. In M. Zaslow, I. Martinez-Beck, K. Tout, & T. Halle (Eds.), *Quality measurement in early childhood settings* (pp. 257–280). Brookes Publishing.

Castro, D. C., Gillanders, C., Franco, X., Bryant, D. M., Zepeda, M., Willoughby, M. T., & Méndez, L. I. (2017). Early education of dual language learners: An efficacy study of the Nuestros Niños School Readiness professional development program. *Early Childhood Research Quarterly, 40*, 188–203. http://dx.doi.org/10.1016/j.ecresq.2017.03.002

Center for Early Care and Education Research-Dual Language Learners. (2011). *Early care and education quality measures: A critical review of the research related to dual language learners* (Research Brief No. 5). The University of North Carolina, FPG Child Development Institute, Center for Early Care and Education Research—Dual Language Learners. https://mncoe.org/cs/groups/communications/documents/basic/y29l/mdaw/~edisp/mncoe000209.pdf

Center for Equity for English Learners. (2020). *Sobrato Early Academic Language (SEAL) model: Final report of findings from a four-year study*. Loyola Marymount University and Wexford Institute. https://doi.org/10.15365/ceel.seal2020

Chao, R. K. (1994). Beyond parental control and authoritarian parenting style: Understanding Chinese parenting through the cultural notion of training. *Child Development, 65*(4), 1111–1119. https://doi.org/10.2307/1131308

Chiswick, B. R., & Miller, P. W. (2017). Do native-born bilinguals in the US earn more? *Review of Economics of the Household, 16*(3), 563–583. https://doi.org/10.1007/s11150-017-9398-5

Cleveland, J., Susman-Stillman, A., & Halle, T. (2013). *Parental perceptions of quality in early care and education* (Publication No. 2013-44). Child Trends; University of Minnesota; Amherst H. Wilder Foundation. https://cms.childtrends.org/wp-content/uploads/2013/12/2013-44ParentalPerceptionsofQuality.pdf

Conboy, B. (2013). Neuroscience research: How experience with one or multiple languages affects the developing brain. In Governor's State Advisory Council on Early Learning and Care (Ed.), *California's best practices for young dual language learners research overview papers* (pp. 1–50). Child Development Division, California Department of Education. https://www.cde.ca.gov/sp/cd/Re/documents/dllresearchpapers.pdf

Craig, H. K., & Washington, J. A. (2006). *Malik goes to school: Examining the language skills of African American students from preschool-5th grade.* Psychology Press.

Dietrich, S., & Hernandez, E. (2022, December 6). *Nearly 68 million people spoke a language other than English at home in 2019.* U.S. Census Bureau. https://www.census.gov/library/stories/2022/12/languages-we-speak-in-united-states.html

Downer, J. T., López, M., Grimm, K. J., Hamagami, A., Pianta, R. C., & Howes, C. (2012). Observations of teacher–child interactions in classrooms serving Latinos and dual language learners: Applicability of the Classroom Assessment Scoring System in diverse settings. *Early Childhood Research Quarterly, 27*(1), 21–32. https://doi.org/10.1016/j.ecresq.2011.07.005

Duncan, S. E., & De Avila, E. A. (1985). *Pre-LAS English: Pre-Language assessment scales.* CTB/McGraw-Hill.

Early Childhood Learning & Knowledge Center. (2022). *Home language support.* Administration for Children and Families, U.S. Department of Health and Human Services. https://eclkc.ohs.acf.hhs.gov/culture-language/article/home-language-support

Espinosa, L. (2015a). Challenges and benefits of early bilingualism in the United States' context. *Global Education Review, 2*(1), 40–53. https://files.eric.ed.gov/fulltext/EJ1055271.pdf

———. (2015b). *Getting it right for young children from diverse backgrounds: Applying research to improve practice with a focus on dual language learners* (2nd Ed.). Pearson.

Espinosa, L., & Crandell, J. (2020). Early learning and care for multilingual and dual language learners ages zero to five. In P. Krizo & A. Calinsky (Eds.), *Improving education for multilingual and English learner students: Research to practice* (pp. 189–250). California Department of Education. https://www.cde.ca.gov/sp/el/er/documents/mleleducation.pdf

Espinosa, L., & García, E. (2012). *Developmental assessment of young dual language learners with a focus on kindergarten entry assessments: Implications for state policies* (Working Paper No. 1). Center for Early Care and Education Research–Dual Language Learners. University of North Carolina, Frank Porter Graham Child Development Institute.

Espinosa, L., & Gutiérrez-Clellen, V. (2013). Assessment of young dual language learners in preschool. In Governor's State Advisory Council on Early Learning and Care (Ed.), *California's best practices for young dual language learners research overview papers* (pp. 172–201). Child Development Division, California Department of Education. https://www.cde.ca.gov/sp/cd/Re/documents/dllresearchpapers.pdf

Espinosa, L., & Zepeda, M. (2019). *ECE dual language learner essential competencies for working with dual language learners.* https://earlyedgecalifornia.org/wp-content/uploads/2019/12/Faculty-Initiative-Project-Dual-Language-Learners-PD-2020.pdf

Espinosa, L. M. (2013). Challenging common myths about dual language learners. *Policy to Action Brief, 10*(8), 1–26. https://www.fcd-us.org/wp-content/uploads/2016/04/Challenging-Common-Myths-Update.pdf

———. (2018). Encouraging the development and achievement of dual language learners in early childhood. *American Educator, 42*(3), 10. https://files.eric.ed.gov/fulltext/EJ1192671.pdf

European Parliament. (2023). *Language policy.* https://www.europarl.europa.eu/erpl-app-public/factsheets/pdf/en/FTU_3.6.6.pdf

Figueras-Daniel, A., & Li, Z. (2021). Evidence of support for dual language learners in a study of bilingual staffing patterns using the Classroom Assessment of Supports for Emergent Bilingual Acquisition (CASEBA). *Early Childhood Research Quarterly, 54,* 271–285. https://doi.org/10.1016/j.ecresq.2020.09.011

Fillmore, L. W. (1991). When learning a second language means losing the first. *Early Childhood Research Quarterly, 6*(3), 323–346. https://doi.org/10.1016/S0885-2006(05)80059-6

Fogel, H., & Ehri, L. C. (2006). Teaching African American English forms to standard American English-speaking teachers: Effects on acquisition, attitudes, and responses to student use. *Journal of Teacher Education, 57*(5), 464–480. https://doi.org/10.1177/0022487106294088

Foundation for Child Development (2020). *Getting it right: Using implementation research to improve outcomes in early care and education.* https://www.fcd-us.org/getting-it-right-using-implementation-research-to-improve-outcomes-in-early-care-and-education/

Friedman-Krauss, A. H., Barnett, W. S., Garver, K. A., Hodges, K. S., Weisenfeld, G. G., & Gardiner, B. A. (2021). *The state of preschool 2020: State preschool yearbook.* National Institute for Early Education Research. https://nieer.org/research-library/state-preschool-yearbook-2021

Galindo, C. (2010). English language learners' math and reading achievement trajectories in the elementary grades. In E. E. Garcia & E. C. Frede (Eds.), *Young English language learners: Current research and emerging directions for practice and policy.* Teachers College Press.

García, G. E., McKoon, G., & August, D. (2006). Language and literacy assessment of language-minority students. In D. August & T. Shanahan (Eds.), *Developing literacy in second-language learners: Report of the National Literacy Panel on Language-Minority Children and Youth* (pp. 597–624). Lawrence Erlbaum Associates Publishers.

Grazzini, A. (2019). *Advocating for one-way dual language programs in high school, academia bilingue.* [Doctoral dissertation, National Louis University]. Digital Commons@NLU. https://core.ac.uk/download/pdf/267938639.pdf

Green, L. J. (2002). *African American English: A linguistic introduction.* Cambridge University Press.

Gutierrez-Clellen, V., Simon-Cereijido, G., & Restrepo, M. A. (2014). *Improving the vocabulary and oral language skills of bilingual Latino preschoolers: An intervention for speech-language pathologists.* Plural Publishing.

Halgunseth, L., Jia, G., & Barbarin, O. (2013). Family engagement in early childhood programs: Serving families of young dual language learners. In Governor's State Advisory Council on Early Learning and Care (Ed.), *California's best practices for young dual language learners research overview papers* (pp. 119–171). Child Development Division, California Department of Education. https://www.cde.ca.gov/sp/cd/Re/documents/dllresearchpapers.pdf

Halle, T., Hair, E. C., Wandner, L. D., McNamara, M., & Chien, N. (2012). Predictors and outcomes of early versus later English language proficiency among English language learners. *Early Childhood Research Quarterly, 27*(1), 1–20. https://doi.org/10.1016/j.ecresq.2011.07.004

Hammer, C. S., Hoff, E., Uchikoshi, Y., Gillanders, C., Castro, D., & Sandilos, L. E. (2014). The language and literacy development of young dual language learners: A critical review. *Early Childhood Research Quarterly, 29*(4), 715–733. https://doi.org/10.1016/j.ecresq.2014.05.008

Hammer, C. S., Komaroff, E., Rodriguez, B. L., Lopez, L. M., Scarpino, S. E., & Goldstein, B. (2012). Predicting Spanish-English bilingual children's language abilities. *Journal of Speech, Language, and Hearing Research, 55*(5), 1251–1264. https://doi.org/10.1044/1092-4388(2012/11-0016)

Hammer, C. S., Scarpino, S., & Davison, M. D. (2011). Beginning with language: Spanish-English bilingual preschoolers' early literacy development. In S. B. Neuman & D. K. Dickinson (Eds.), *Handbook of early literacy research* (Vol. 3, pp. 118–135). Guilford Press.

Harvey, H., & Wennerstrom, E. K. (2021). Hearing their voices: Parents' perceptions of preschool special education evaluations with dual-language learners. *Topics in Early Childhood Special Education, 43*(1), 46–59. https://doi.org/10.1177/02711214211005853

Hoff, E. (2021). Why bilingual development is not easy. *Advances in Child Development and Behavior, 61*, 129–167. https://doi.org/10.1016/bs.acdb.2021.03.002

Hoff, E., Core, C., Place, S., Rumiche, R., Señor, M., & Parra, M. (2012). Dual language exposure and early bilingual development. *Journal of Child Language, 39*(1), 1–27. https://doi.org/10.1017/S0305000910000759

Holtzman, D. J., de los Reyes, I. B., White, L., Carbuccia-Abbott, M., Manship, K., & Quick, H. (2022). *A deeper look at classroom language approaches and how they relate to language skills and other outcomes for dual language learners (Brief 2)*. First 5 California, American Institutes for Research. https://www.air.org/sites/default/files/2022-06/First-5-DLL-Instruction-Brief-2-Classroom-Language-Approaches-June-2022.pdf

Hsin, L. B., Holtzman, D. J., White, L., de los Reyes, I. B., Manship, K., & Quick, H. (2022). *Relationships between classroom practices and language and development among dual language learner infants and toddlers (Brief 4)*. First 5 California, American Institutes for Research. https://www.air.org/sites/default/files/2022-06/First-5-DLL-Instruction-Brief-4-Infants-Toddlers-June-2022.pdf

Institute for Learning and Brain Sciences. (n.d.). *MEG Brain Imaging at I-LABS*. University of Washington. https://ilabs.uw.edu/meg-brain-imaging-i-labs/

Jacoby, J. W., & Lesaux, N. K. (2017). Language and literacy instruction in preschool classes that serve Latino dual language learners. *Early Childhood Research Quarterly, 40*, 77–86. https://doi.org/10.1016/j.ecresq.2016.10.001

Kisilevsky, B. S., Hains, S. M., Brown, C. A., Lee, C. T., Cowperthwaite, B., Stutzman, S. S., Swansburg, M. L., Lee, K., Xie, X., Huang, H., Ye, H.-H., Zhang, K., & Wang, Z. (2009). Fetal sensitivity to properties of maternal speech and language. *Infant Behavior and Development, 32*(1), 59–71. https://doi.org/10.1016/j.infbeh.2008.10.002

Klingert, L. (2023, February 13). Multilingualism strong among Europeans, less so among native English speakers. *The Brussels Times*. https://www.brusselstimes.com/365877/multilingualism-strong-among-europeans-less-so-among-native-english-speakers

Kovács, Á. M., & Mehler, J. (2009). Cognitive gains in 7-month-old bilingual infants. *Proceedings of the National Academy of Sciences, 106*(16), 6556–6560. https://doi.org/10.1073/pnas.0811323106

Kuhl, P. K. (2011). Early language learning and literacy: Neuroscience implications for education. *Mind, Brain, and Education, 5*(3), 128–142. https://doi.org/10.1111/j.1751-228x.2011.01121.x

Kuhl, P. K., Stevens, E. B., Hayashi, A., Deguchi, T., Kiritani, S., & Iverson, P. (2006). Infants show a facilitation effect for native language phonetic perception between 6 and 12 months. *Developmental Science, 9*(2). https://doi.org/10.1111/j.1467-7687.2006.00468.x

Kuhl, P. K., Tsao, F. M., & Liu, H. M. (2003). Foreign-language experience in infancy: Effects of short-term exposure and social interaction on phonetic learning. *Proceedings of the National Academy of Sciences, 100*(15), 9096–9101. https://doi.org/10.1073%2Fpnas.1532872100

Ladson-Billings, G. (1994). *The dreamkeepers: Successful teachers of African American children*. Jossey-Bass.

Lazarín, M., & Park, M. (2021). *Taking stock of dual language learner identification and strengthening procedures and policies*. Migration Policy Institute. https://www.migrationpolicy.org/research/dual-language-learner-identification-procedures-policies

Lesaux, N. K. (2013). Reading and reading instruction for children from low-income and non-English-speaking households. *The Future of Children, 23*(2), 73–88. https://doi.org/10.1353/foc.2012.0010

Li, L., Valiente, C., Eisenberg, N., Spinrad, T. L., Johns, S. K., Berger, R. H., Thompson, M. S., Southworth, J., Piña, A., Hernández, M. M., & Gal-Szabo, D. E. (2022). Longitudinal associations among teacher-child relationship quality, behavioral engagement, and academic achievement. *Early Childhood Research Quarterly, 61*, 25–35. https://doi.org/10.1016/j.ecresq.2022.05.006

Limlingan, M. C., McWayne, C. M., Sanders, E. A., & López, M. (2020). Classroom language contexts as predictors of Latinx preschool dual language learners' school readiness. *American Educational Research Journal, 57*(1), 339–370. https://doi.org/10.3102/0002831219855694

Lindholm-Leary, K. (2015). *Sobrato Family Foundation, Early Academic and Literacy Project, after five full years of implementation: Final research report.* San Jose Unified School District; Redwood City School District. https://assets-global.website-files.com/65f9b0 3347c6e70853aa5f66/6656abc2bb53ba28e80816d8_SEAL_Report_Final_9Mar2015_ LindholmLeary%20(1)%20(2).pdf

López, L., & Páez, M. (2020). *Teaching dual language learners: What early childhood educators need to know.* Brookes Publishing.

Martin, A., White, L., Quick, H., & Manship, K. (2022a). *First 5 California Dual Language Learner Pilot Study.* AIR. https://www.air.org/project/first-5-california-dual-language-learner-pilot-study

Martin, K., Ketchabaw, W. T., & Turkeltaub, P. E. (2022b). Plasticity of the language system in children and adults. In A. Quartarone, M. F. Ghilardi, & F. Boller (Eds.), *Handbook of clinical neurology* (Vol. 184, pp. 397–414). https://doi.org/10.1016/b978-0-12-819410-2.00021-7

Meek, S., Iruka, I. U., Allen, R., Yazzie, D., Fernandez, V., Catherine, E., McIntosh, K., Gordon, L., Gilliam, W., Hemmeter, M. L., Blevins, D., & Powell, T. (2020). *Start with equity: Fourteen priorities to dismantle systemic racism in early care and education.* The Children's Equity Project. https://childandfamilysuccess.asu.edu/cep.

Meisel, J. M. (2008). Child second language acquisition or successive first language acquisition. In B. Haznedar & E. Gavruseva (Eds.), *Current trends in child second language acquisition: A generative perspective* (Vol. 45, pp. 55–80). John Benjamins Publishing Company.

Méndez, L. I., Crais, E. R., Castro, D. C., & Kainz, K. (2015). A culturally and linguistically responsive vocabulary approach for young Latino dual language learners. *Journal of Speech, Language, and Hearing Research, 58*(1), 93–106. https://doi.org/10.1044%2F2014_JSLHR-L-12-0221

Miller, E. (2017). Spanish instruction in head start and dual language learners' academic achievement. *Journal of Applied Developmental Psychology, 52,* 159–169. https://doi.org/10.1016/j.appdev.2017.07.008

Motaghi-Tabar, S. (2016). *Bidirectional language learning in migrant families* [Doctoral dissertation, Macquarie University]. https://www.languageonthemove.com/wp-content/uploads/2017/03/Thesis_Shiva_Motaghi-Tabari_BidirectionalLanguageLearning.pdf

National Academies of Sciences, Engineering, and Medicine. (2017). *Promoting the educational success of children and youth learning English: Promising futures.* The National Academies Press.

Office of Head Start. (2015). *Classroom language models: A leader's implementation manual.* Department of Health and Human Services, National Center on Cultural and Linguistic Responsiveness. https://eclkc.ohs.acf.hhs.gov/sites/default/files/pdf/pps-language-models.pdf

Oliva-Olson, C. (2019). Dos Métodos: *Two classroom language models in Head Start. Strengthening the diversity and quality of the early care and education workforce.* Urban Institute. www.urban.org/sites/default/files/publication/101242/dos_metodos_two_ classroom_language_models_in_head_start_1.pdf

Oller, D. K., & Eilers, R. E. (Eds.). (2002). *Language and literacy in bilingual children.* Faculty and Staff Multilingual Matters.

Páez, M., Tabors, P. O., & López, L. M. (2007). Dual language and literacy development of Spanish-speaking preschool children. *Journal of Applied Developmental Psychology, 28*(2), 85–102. https://doi.org/10.1016/j.appdev.2006.12.007

Paradis, J., Genesee, F., & Crago, M. B. (2011). *Dual language development and disorders: A handbook on bilingualism and second language learning* (3rd ed.). Brookes Publishing.

Park, M., McHugh, M., Batalova, J., & Zong, J. (2015). *Immigrant and refugee workers in the early childhood field: Taking a closer look.* Migration Policy Institute. https://www.migrationpolicy.org/research/immigrant-and-refugee-workers-early-childhood-field-taking-closer-look

Park, M., Zong, J., & Batalova, J. (2018). *Growing superdiversity among young US dual language learners and its implications*. Migration Policy Institute. https://www.migrationpolicy.org/research/growing-superdiversity-among-young-us-dual-language-learners-and-its-implications

Pearson, B. Z. (2002). Bilingual infants: Mapping the research agenda. In M. Suárez-Orozco & M. M. Páez (Eds.), *Latinos remaking America* (pp. 306–320). University of California Press.

Pearson, B. Z., Conner, T., & Jackson, J. E. (2013). Removing obstacles for African American English-speaking children through greater understanding of language difference. *Developmental Psychology, 49*(1), 31. https://doi.org/10.1037/a0028248

Pearson, B. Z., Fernández, S. C., & Oller, D. K. (1993). Lexical development in bilingual infants and toddlers: Comparison to monolingual norms. *Language Learning, 43*(1), 93–120. https://scholarworks.umass.edu/cgi/viewcontent.cgi?referer=&httpsredir=1&article=1006&context=adjunct_sw

Peña, E. D., & Halle, T. (2011). Assessing preschool dual language learners: Traveling a multiforked road. *Child Development Perspectives, 5*(1), 28–32. https://doi.org/10.1111/j.1750-8606.2010.00143.x

Petitto, L. A., & Holowka, S. (2002). Evaluating attributions of delay and confusion in young bilinguals: Special insights from infants acquiring a signed and a spoken language. *Sign Language Studies, 3*(1), 4–33. https://www.jstor.org/stable/26204891

Pollard-Durodola, S. D., González, J. E., Sáenz, L., Soares, D., Resendez, N., Kwok, O., Davis, H., & Zhu, L. (2016). The effects of content-related shared book reading on the language development of preschool dual language learners. *Early Childhood Research Quarterly, 36*, 106–121. https://doi.org/10.1016/j.ecresq.2015.12.004

Raikes, H. H., White, L. J., Green, S., Burchinal, M., Kainz, K., Horm, D., Bingham, G. E., Cobo-Lewis, A. B., St Clair, L., Greenfield, D. B., & Esteraich, J. (2019). Use of the home language in preschool classrooms and first- and second-language development among dual-language learners. *Early Childhood Research Quarterly, 47*, 145–158. https://doi.org/10.1016/j.ecresq.2018.06.012

Ramirez, N. F., & Kuhl, P. (2017). The brain science of bilingualism. *Young Children, 72*(2), 38–44. https://ilabs.uw.edu/sites/default/files/2017_FerjanRamirez_Kuhl_NAEYC.pdf

Reid, N., Aikens, N., Larson, A., Tarullo, L., Cannon, J., & Malone, L. (2022). *Head Start families' program and selection experiences* (OPRE Report No. 2022-09). Office of Planning, Research, and Evaluation, Administration for Children and Families, U.S. Department of Health and Human Services. https://www.acf.hhs.gov/sites/default/files/documents/opre/headstart-families-experiences-feb-2022_0.pdf

Rodriguez, L., Irby, B. J., Brown, G., Lara-Alecio, R., & Galloway, M. (2003). *An analysis of a public school prekindergarten bilingual Montessori program* [Presentation]. Paper presented at the Annual Meeting of the American Educational Research Association, Chicago. https://files.eric.ed.gov/fulltext/ED478568.pdf

Rogoff, B., Coppens, A. D., Alcalá, L., Aceves-Azuara, I., Ruvalcaba, O., López, A., & Dayton, A. (2017). Noticing learners' strengths through cultural research. *Perspectives on Psychological Science, 12*(5), 876–888. https://doi.org/10.1177/1745691617718355

Sánchez Walker, N., & Montrul, S. (2020). Language experience affects comprehension of Spanish passive clauses: A study of heritage speakers and second language learners. *Languages, 6*(1), 2. https://doi.org/10.3390/languages6010002

Sandhofer, C., & Uchikoshi, Y. (2013). Cognitive consequences of dual language learning: Cognitive function, language and literacy, science and mathematics and socioemotional development. In State Advisory Council on Early Learning and Care (Ed.), *California's best practices for young dual language learners: Research overview papers* (pp. 51–89). California Department of Education Press.

Sarche, M., Barnes-Najor, J., Abramson-Martin, L., Amaya-Thompson, J., Cameron, A., Charles, T., Godfrey, A., Kaufman, C. E., Petticrew, E., Richardson, M., Sauve, M., Shuey, D., & Whitaker, J. (2020). *Native language and culture experiences among children in Region XI Head Start classrooms and programs: Findings from the American Indian and Alaska Native Head Start Family and Child Experiences Survey 2015* (OPRE Report No. 2020-01). Office of Planning, Research, and Evaluation, Administration for Children and Families, U.S. Department of Health and Human Services.

Sarche, M., Malone, L., Hoard, L., Barnes-Najor, J., Cameron, A., West, J., & Barofsky, M. Y. (2021). Perspectives of Region XI Head Start federal, research, and program partners in carrying out a national study of American Indian and Alaska Native Head Start children, families, and programs. *American Journal of Community Psychology, 69*(1–2), 239–253. https://doi.org/10.1002/ajcp.12542

Seal of Biliteracy. (2024). *Seal of Biliteracy: Frequently asked questions*. https://sealofbiliteracy.org/faq

Seltzer, K., Ascenzi-Moreno, L., & Aconite, G. (2020). Translanguaging and early childhood education in the USA: Insights from the CUNY-NYSIEB Project. In I. Diehm, J. A. Panagiotopoulou, & P. Stosić (Eds.), *Inclusion, education and translanguaging. Inklusion und Bildung in Migrationsgesellschaften*. Spring VS. https://doi.org/10.1007/978-3-658-28128-1_3

Sembiante, S. F., Bengochea, A., & Gort, M. (2022). Morning circle as a community of practice: Co-teachers' transmodality in a dual language bilingual education preschool classroom. *Journal of Early Childhood Literacy*. https://doi.org/10.1177/14687984221144232

Serafini, E. J., Rozell, N., & Winsler, A. (2022). Academic and English language outcomes for DLLs as a function of school bilingual education model: The role of two-way immersion and home language support. *International Journal of Bilingual Education and Bilingualism, 25*(2), 552–570. https://doi.org/10.1080/13670050.2019.1707477

Small, M. F. (2002). *Kids: How biology and culture shape the way we raise young children*. Anchor Books.

Spencer, T. D., Moran, M., Thompson, M. S., Petersen, D. B., & Restrepo, M. A. (2020). Early efficacy of multitiered dual-language instruction: Promoting preschoolers' Spanish and English oral language. *AERA Open, 6*(1). https://doi.org/10.1177/2332858419897886

Steele, J. L., Slater, R. O., Zamarro, G., Miller, T., Li, J., Burkhauser, S., & Bacon, M. (2017). Effects of dual-language immersion programs on student achievement: Evidence from lottery data. *American Educational Research Journal, 54*(1), 282S–306S. https://doi.org/10.3102/0002831216634463

Stefanakis, E. H., & Meier, D. (2010). *Differentiated assessment: How to assess the learning potential of every student (Grades 6-12)*. Jossey-Bass.

Tamis-LeMonda, C. S., Caughy, M. O., Rojas, R., Bakeman, R., Adamson, L. B., Pacheco, D., Owen, M. T., Suma, K., & Pace, A. (2019). Culture, parenting, and language: Respeto in Latine mother–child interactions. *Social Development, 29*(3), 689–712. https://doi.org/10.1111/sode.12430

Thompson, K. D. (2015). English learners' time to reclassification. *Educational Policy, 31*(3), 330–363. https://doi.org/10.1177/0895904815598394

Thordardottir, E. (2011). The relationship between bilingual exposure and vocabulary development. *International Journal of Bilingualism, 15*(4), 426–445. https://doi.org/10.1177/1367006911403202

Villegas, L. (2022, August 25). Dual language learner identification in California moves one step closer to reality. *New America*. https://www.newamerica.org/education-policy/edcentral/dual-language-learner-identification-in-california-moves-one-step-closer-to-reality/

Villegas, L., & Velazco, E. (2021, April 5). *Looking beyond the 'typical' English learner: The intersectionality of Black English learners in U.S. public schools*. New America. https://www.newamerica.org/education-policy/edcentral/looking-beyond-the-typical-english-learner-the-intersectionality-of-black-english-learners-in-us-public-schools/

Washington, J. & Iruka, I. U. (forthcoming). Linguistic justice: Addressing linguistic variation of Black children in teaching and learning. *Linguistics and Education*.

Washington, J. A., & Seidenberg, M. S. (2021). Teaching reading to African American children: When home and school language differ. *American Educator*, 45(2), 26. https://files.eric.ed.gov/fulltext/EJ1304333.pdf

Washington, J. A., Lee-James, R., & Stanford, C. B. (2023). Teaching phonemic and phonological awareness to children who speak African American English. *The Reading Teacher*, 76(6), 765–774. https://eric.ed.gov/?id=EJ1377704

White, H., Galloway, E. P., & Jiménez, R. T. (2023). Bridging theory to practice: Exploring the role of an educative translingual curriculum to support linguistically diverse classroom practices. *TESOL Quarterly*. https://doi.org/10.1002/tesq.3258

Winsler, A., Díaz, R. M., Espinosa, L., & Rodríguez, J. L. (1999). When learning a second language does not mean losing the first: Bilingual language development in low-income, Spanish-speaking children attending bilingual preschool. *Child Development*, 70(2), 349–362. https://doi.org/10.1111/1467-8624.t01-1-00026

Yoshikawa, H. (2011). *Immigrants raising citizens: Undocumented parents and their children*. Russell Sage Foundation.

Yow, W. Q., & Li, X. (2015). Balanced bilingualism and early age of second language acquisition as the underlying mechanisms of a bilingual executive control advantage: Why variations in bilingual experiences matter. *Frontiers in Psychology*, 6, 123975. https://doi.org/10.3389/fpsyg.2015.00164

Zhang, Y., & Gao, C. (2014). *Back translating: An integrated approach to focus learners' attention on their L2 knowledge gaps*. English Teaching Forum. U.S. Department of State. https://eric.ed.gov/?id=EJ1029177

8

State- and Program-Level Curriculum Decision Making and Selection

Across the country, curriculum is selected, adopted, and implemented in multiple ways. From state policy makers to family child care providers, curriculum is researched, developed, and piloted with the goal of enriching children's early learning experiences. Specifically, how curriculum is developed and implemented varies from state to state. Many states have adopted standards, and commercial curriculum is developed based on those standards. In some cases, curriculum may also be developed locally by teachers or child care providers to meet the needs of their students and their specific communities.

Preschool children, aged 3–5 years, participate in a variety of program types. The United States has a mixed delivery system for early childhood programs. A mixed delivery system combines different program types, such as center-based programs, which may be located in schools or community programs, and home-based programs. Each type of program is governed with different polices, regulations, and funding mechanisms, including private-pay tuition; foundation grants or university sponsorship; publicly funded prekindergarten, Head Start, and child care subsidies; and other public funding streams. Programs are blended together in order to maximize access or enhance quality (Morris & Smith, 2021). In 2016, 49% of preschool-age children were in center-based care, 8% were in home-based care, 2% had multiple care arrangements, and the remaining 41% were cared for by parents or relatives (National Center for Education Statistics, 2017). Funding streams are complex to describe because many programs receive more than one type of funding. In 2019, 76% of center-based programs and 62% of licensed home-based programs received some form of public funding (Datta et al., 2021a,b). The complexity of the early childhood system and the diversity of program options lead to great variability in children's preschool experiences.

This chapter presents evidence on the stakeholders involved in the selection and adoption of preschool curriculum; the criteria used, as well as early learning standards and how they inform implementation and fidelity; and implications for assessment. Data examined in this chapter include information reported in the National Institute for Early Education Research's (NIEER's) annual State of Preschool surveys (e.g., Friedman-Krauss et al., 2023) about the supports that states have in place around curriculum selection and implementation in state-funded pre-K. The chapter includes discussion on which states meet NIEER's Curriculum Supports quality standards benchmarks and how these standards are met.[1] It is worth noting that the data are more limited for family child care settings—a key area for future research; when possible, information from these contexts is included.

HOW ARE CURRICULUM DECISIONS MADE?

Preschool programs differ in the standards and requirements they are subject to, with important implications for preschool quality. Given the complexity of the early childhood system, the specific program standards and requirements that apply to a program are largely determined by the program's type, location, and funding sources. Operational requirements are often determined by the state in which a program is located—exceptions being preschool programs located in tribal jurisdictions that adhere to tribal and federal requirements, and Head Start programs.

Broader Curriculum Selection and Standards

Curriculum standards and requirements, as well as broader early childhood systems and structures, vary by location and program funding stream. Preschool programs are often free to select any curriculum they choose or develop their own curriculum, although their curriculum decisions may be impacted by funding requirements or other program standards they are subject to. These standards may include state or federal early learning standards, which identify developmental and learning goals for preschool in several content domains. For instance, Head Start programs must align their curricula with funding requirements in the Head Start Program Performance Standards and the Head Start Early Learning Outcomes Framework.[2]

---

[1] Portions of this chapter are adapted from a paper commissioned by the committee for this study (Friedman-Krauss, 2023).

[2] For more information, see https://eclkc.ohs.acf.hhs.gov/school-readiness/article/head-start-early-learning-outcomes-framework

State-Level Selection

Each state has unique rules about program licensing or registration, as well as which types of programs are required to have a license or registration to operate. Licensing or registration requirements typically focus on facilities, health and safety, staffing requirements, and other basic operating rules, and they are mainly aimed at protecting children from harm rather than advancing child development and early learning (see National Center on Early Childhood Quality Assurance [NCECQA], 2020a). Programs are also required to comply with regulations and standards specific to initiatives they participate in and receive funding from, including federal initiatives (such as Head Start), state initiatives (such as prekindergarten), and other grants or entitlements. Requirements for these initiatives typically go beyond licensing standards and often focus on programming and quality of care and instruction; however, the specific content and requirements of these standards varies by initiative (Friedman-Krauss et al., 2022). For an example of statewide requirements, the California Preschool Learning Foundations outline key knowledge and skills that most developing children can achieve when provided with the kinds of interactions, instruction, and environments that research has shown will promote early learning and development. The foundations can provide early childhood educators, parents, and the public with a clear understanding of the wide range of knowledge and skills that preschool children typically attain when given the benefits of a high-quality preschool program.[3]

Many states also offer quality rating and improvement systems that rate programs according to quality standards and provide supports for increasing ratings over time; participation is usually voluntary or is required only for programs receiving certain types of public funding (NCECQA, 2020b). As a result of different program locations and funding streams, some preschool programs in the United States are exempt from any requirements or standards; others must meet basic licensing requirements related to staffing and safety but no other standards, and still others are required to meet program quality standards related to instruction and other aspects of programming. This variability in program standards and requirements has important implications for program quality.

NIEER's *State of Preschool Yearbook* (Friedman-Krauss et al., 2023) assesses each state-funded public preschool program's policies around supports for curriculum selection and implementation. To meet this quality standards benchmark, which NIEER considers a minimum for programs that support children's development and learning, programs must provide at least one support for selecting a curriculum and at least one support for

---

[3]For more information, see https://www.cde.ca.gov/sp/cd/re/psfoundations.asp

implementing the chosen curriculum. Supports for curriculum implementation include, for example, offering guidance on selecting evidence-based curriculum model(s), offering a list of state-approved and/or recommended curricula, requiring programs to adopt a specific curriculum, and requiring alignment of the chosen curriculum with the state's early learning and development standards. Examples of state supports for curriculum implementation include training on the selected curriculum, ongoing technical assistance on curriculum implementation, and specific funding to support curriculum implementation or training.

During the 2021–2022 school year, 56 out of 62 (90%) state-funded pre-K programs met NIEER's Curriculum Supports benchmark (Friedman-Krauss et al., 2023). State preschool programs have made some progress in providing more supports for curriculum implementation over the last 7 years (when NIEER started tracking it; see Figure 8-1). During the 2015–2016 school year—the first year this benchmark was assessed—46 out of 58 (79%) of state-funded preschool programs met the Curriculum Supports benchmark (Barnett et al., 2017). Among the six state-funded preschool programs that currently do not meet NIEER's Curriculum Supports benchmark, all do provide supports for selecting a curriculum but do not provide support for implementation.

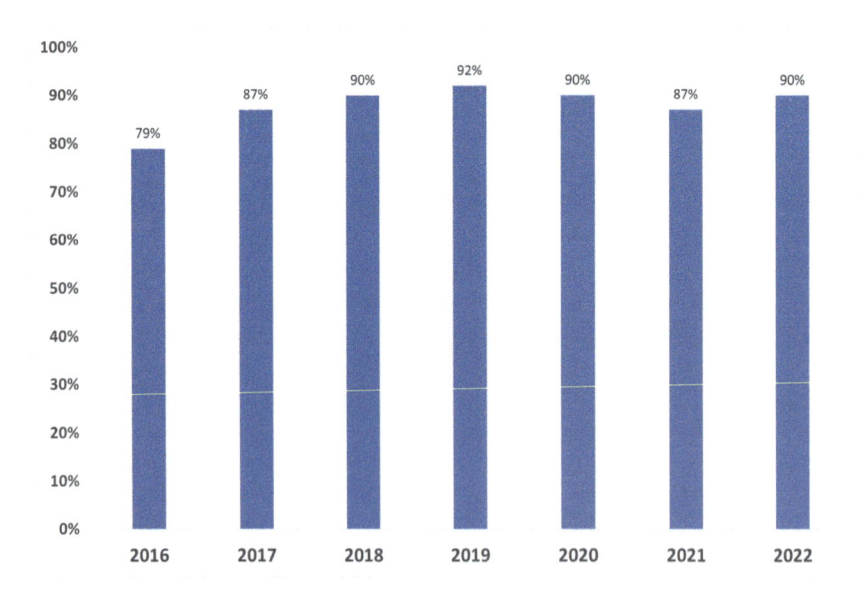

FIGURE 8-1 Percent of state-funded preschool programs meeting the Curriculum Supports benchmark each year.
NOTE: The total number of state-funded programs and the actual programs change each year so lower percentages do not necessarily mean programs are losing benchmarks.
SOURCE: Friedman-Krauss et al., 2023.

Turning first to supports for selecting a curriculum, in 2021–2022, 55 out of 62 (89%) state-funded preschool programs reported offering guidance on criteria for selecting an evidence-based curriculum for preschool classrooms. This was the most commonly reported type of support (see Table 8-1). Fifty-three (85%) programs require that the selected curriculum is aligned with the state's early learning and development standards. Thirty-three (53%) reported providing a list of either state-approved or recommended curricula (or both). Only 14 (23%) require all sites to use a specific curriculum.

Table 8-1 also shows which state-funded preschool programs reported providing three different supports for curriculum implementation. Forty-four (71%) programs reported that a state's office of early learning or department of education provided training on the curriculum. Forty-four (71%) states also reported providing funding specifically to support curriculum implementation and/or training on implementing the curriculum. And 43 (69%) programs reported that the state delivers ongoing technical assistance on curriculum implementation.

Overall, in most states, even preschool programs that are subject to state or federal program standards have significant flexibility in their curriculum choices. Furthermore, states and localities vary in their structural and systems-level determinants of program quality and access, such as program funding, child eligibility requirements, and early childhood systems design and leadership.

Selection by Family Child Care Providers

Family child care providers are generally less likely than centers and schools to use a published curriculum, which may lead to disparities in learning opportunities. The National Survey of Early Care and Education showed that family child care homes are far less likely than centers to use published curricula, with usage by these two groups at 55% and 74%, respectively (National Survey of Early Care and Education Project Team [NSECEPT], 2015). Similarly, in a qualitative survey, Forry & Wessel (2012) found that none of the 30 participating family child care providers reported using a published, state-recommended curriculum. Instead of commercial curricula, the family child care providers often create their own curricula (i.e., "local" or "homegrown" curricula), based on what they believe children should learn and combining different learning activities (Forry & Wessel, 2012; Freeman & Karlsson, 2012). And when using a published curriculum (often, *The Creative Curriculum*), family child care providers supplement it with locally developed curricula or with less well-known resources (Forry & Wessel, 2012; Fuligni et al., 2012). Qualitative research (e.g., Forry & Wessel, 2012) suggests that family child care providers believe providers' creativity to plan or customize activities, particularly to supplement curricula, is a key resource in supporting children's school readiness. However, variations in curriculum

TABLE 8-1 Supports for Curriculum Selection and Implementation Used by State-Funded Preschool Programs, 2021–2022

State/Program	Supports for Curriculum Selection					Supports for Curriculum Implementation			Other Supports*
	Provides guidance on criteria for selecting evidence-based curriculum models	Provides a list of state-approved curricula	Provides a list of state-recommended curricula	Requires adoption of specific curricula by all programs and sites	Requires alignment of curricula with early learning and development standards	Provides training sponsored by state education agency/office of early learning	Delivers ongoing technical assistance on curriculum implementation	Provides funding to support curriculum implementation or training	
Alabama	Yes				Yes	Yes	Yes	Yes	Yes
Alaska					Yes				
Arizona					Yes		Yes	Yes	Yes
Arkansas	Yes	Yes			Yes	Yes	Yes	Yes	Yes
California CSPP	Yes					Yes	Yes		Yes
California TK								Yes	
Colorado	Yes								
Connecticut CDCC	Yes				Yes	Yes	Yes		Yes
Connecticut SRP	Yes				Yes	Yes	Yes	Yes	Yes
Connecticut Smart Start	Yes				Yes	Yes	Yes		Yes
Delaware	Yes	Yes				Yes	Yes	Yes	
District of Columbia	Yes	Yes	Yes			Yes	Yes	Yes	Yes

333

Florida	Yes				Yes	
Georgia	Yes	Yes	Yes		Yes	
Hawaii DOE	Yes				Yes	Yes
Hawaii HPCSC	Yes				Yes	Yes
Illinois	Yes		Yes		Yes	Yes
Iowa Shared Visions	Yes				Yes	Yes
Iowa SWVPP	Yes				Yes	
Kansas	Yes				Yes	Yes
Kentucky	Yes			Yes	Yes	Yes
Louisiana 8(g)	Yes	Yes	Yes	Yes	Yes	
Louisiana LA 4	Yes	Yes	Yes	Yes	Yes	
Louisiana NSECD	Yes	Yes	Yes	Yes	Yes	
Maine	Yes			Yes	Yes	Yes
Maryland	Yes		Yes	Yes	Yes	Yes
Massachusetts CPPI	Yes					
Massachusetts Ch. 70	Yes			Yes	Yes	Yes
Michigan	Yes	Yes		Yes		
Minnesota Head Start	Yes	Yes	Yes	Yes	Yes	Yes

(*continued*)

TABLE 8-1 (Continued)

State/Program	Supports for Curriculum Selection					Supports for Curriculum Implementation				Other Supports*
	Provides guidance on criteria for selecting evidence-based curriculum models	Provides a list of state-approved curricula	Provides a list of state-recommended curricula	Requires adoption of specific curricula by all programs and sites	Requires alignment of curricula with early learning and development standards	Provides training sponsored by state education agency/office of early learning	Delivers ongoing technical assistance on curriculum implementation	Provides funding to support curriculum implementation or training		
Minnesota VPK & SRP	Yes	Yes	Yes	Yes	Yes	Yes	Yes	Yes	Yes
Mississippi	Yes	Yes		Yes	Yes	Yes	Yes	Yes	
Missouri		Yes	Yes			Yes			
Montana									
Nebraska					Yes	Yes		Yes	
Nevada	Yes				Yes	Yes	Yes		
New Jersey Abbott	Yes		Yes		Yes	Yes		Yes	
New Jersey ECPA	Yes		Yes		Yes	Yes		Yes	
New Jersey ELLI	Yes		Yes		Yes	Yes		Yes	
New Mexico	Yes				Yes	Yes	Yes	Yes	Yes
New York	Yes				Yes	Yes	Yes	Yes	Yes

North Carolina	Yes				Yes	Yes	Yes
North Dakota	Yes	Yes			Yes	Yes	Yes
Ohio	Yes				Yes	Yes	Yes
Oklahoma	Yes	Yes			Yes	Yes	Yes
Oregon Pre-K	Yes				Yes	Yes	Yes
Oregon Preschool Promise	Yes		Yes		Yes	Yes	Yes
Pennsylvania RTL	Yes		Yes		Yes		Yes
Pennsylvania HSSAP	Yes	Yes	Yes		Yes	Yes	
Pennsylvania K4 & SBPK	Yes		Yes		Yes		
Pennsylvania Pre-K Counts	Yes	Yes	Yes		Yes	Yes	
Rhode Island	Yes	Yes	Yes	Yes	Yes	Yes	
South Carolina	Yes		Yes		Yes	Yes	
Tennessee	Yes	Yes		Yes		Yes	Yes
Texas	Yes	Yes	Yes		Yes		
Utah			Yes				
Vermont	Yes				Yes	Yes	Yes
Virginia VPI	Yes	Yes	Yes	Yes	Yes	Yes	Yes
Virginia Mixed Delivery	Yes	Yes	Yes	Yes	Yes	Yes	

(continued)

TABLE 8-1 (Continued)

State/Program	Supports for Curriculum Selection					Supports for Curriculum Implementation			Other Supports*
	Provides guidance on criteria for selecting evidence-based curriculum models	Provides a list of state-approved curricula	Provides a list of state-recommended curricula	Requires adoption of specific curricula by all programs and sites	Requires alignment of curricula with early learning and development standards	Provides training sponsored by state education agency/office of early learning	Delivers ongoing technical assistance on curriculum implementation	Provides funding to support curriculum implementation or training	
Washington ECEAP	Yes	Yes	Yes	Yes	Yes	Yes	Yes	Yes	Yes
Washington TK	Yes		Yes				Yes		
West Virginia	Yes	Yes		Yes	Yes		Yes	Yes	
Wisconsin	Yes					Yes	Yes		Yes
Total	55	25	24	14	53	44	43	44	30

* In some states, "other supports" provided results in the state meeting the benchmark. This is determined based on what the other supports are.

NOTE: CDCC = Child Day Care Contracts; CPPI = Commonwealth Preschool Partnership Initiative; CSPP = California State Preschool Program; DOE = Department of Education; ECEAP = Early Childhood Education and Assistance Program; ECPA = Early Childhood Program Aid; ELLI = Early Launch to Learning Initiative; HPCSC = Hawaii Public Charter School Commission; HSSAP = Head Start Supplemental Assistance Program; NSECD = Nonpublic School Early Childhood Development; RTL = Ready to Learn; SBPK = School-Based Prekindergarten; SRP = School Readiness Program/Plus; SWVPP = Statewide Voluntary Preschool Program; TK = Transitional Kindergarten; VPI = Virginia Preschool Initiative; VPK = Voluntary Prekindergarten.

implementation or differences between published and locally developed curricula may contribute to unequal learning opportunities and outcomes (Jenkins et al., 2018). These disparities could have important equity implications, especially given that a large proportion of children enrolled in family child care homes are from racially marginalized populations and families experiencing poverty (NSECEPT, 2016).

CRITERIA FOR SELECTION AND ADOPTION

As articulated throughout this report, curriculum encompasses the totality of student experiences that occur in the educational process. Selecting a curriculum is more than choosing printed materials—it is designing an environment rich in experiences and activities to enhance a child's physical well-being and motor development, social-emotional development, approaches to learning, language development, cognition, and general knowledge. With a solid understanding of child development and how children learn, the design process must include teachers and child care providers, administrators, policy makers, and parents. Most importantly, children need to be at the heart of the design. The building blocks for adopting a curriculum include using program standards to establish goals and a vision, creating student outcomes, selecting instructional materials, and providing professional development, all while working within budgetary constraints. These building blocks occur at the federal, state, and local levels.

Adopting curricula is part of a complex budget system that includes multiple decision makers. Federal, state, and local budgets are the result of negotiations, advocacy, and setting priorities. Programs funded with public dollars require the early education field to ensure that decision makers understand the benefits of high-quality early education and care. Approval of the program, including funding instructional materials and professional development, is the responsibility of the board of education. Typically, instructional materials are piloted by teachers before being adopted formally. The board also approves the district budgets that fund the programs. A given district may adopt multiple programs, each with their own funding source (federal, state, and local) and program requirements. Because program requirements do not always align, teacher, administrator, and districts need accountability and must submit extra paperwork.[4]

At the federal level, Head Start programs support children's growth from birth to age 5 years through services centered around early learning and development, physical and mental health, and family well-being.

---

[4]For an example, see guidance provided by the Los Angeles Unified School District that articulates the vision, goals, curriculum, and instructional materials to be used in the classroom to differentiate instruction to meet the needs of all children: https://www.lausd.org/cms/lib/CA01000043/Centricity/Domain/593/2015%20REVISED%20TK%20REFERENCE%20GUIDE%205777.3.pdf

The federal government funds Head Start programs through the Administration for Children and Families, which is part of the U.S. Department of Health and Human Services. Across the country, school districts, nonprofit and for-profit groups, faith-based institutions, tribal councils, and other organizations qualify to become Head Start recipients and receive federal funding.[5] Many programs combine funding from federal, state, and local sources to maximize service delivery and continuity.

EARLY LEARNING STANDARDS

Curricula are closely related to early learning standards. Early learning standards encapsulate learning goals, or expectations for what children will know and be able to do; curricula provide the means of supporting children in achieving these goals. While standards are usually created by national organizations or state departments of education, curricula are often selected by local boards of education, officials, administrators, and teachers.

The National Association for the Education of Young Children (NAEYC) and National Association of Early Childhood Specialists in State Departments of Education (NAECS; 2009) recommend that the development of early learning standards involve conversations with families, teachers, and the early childhood professional community writ large. However, the committee found little evidence of the impact of those conversations in the actual development of standards. Teachers' and families' voices are mainly used to illustrate standards. New York, for instance, includes teacher quotes in the state's early learning guidelines, but only to demonstrate how the standards can be implemented successfully. Other states, such as Maine, included parents or family advocates in the task force groups that developed the standards, but the direct contribution of parents and teachers to standards is not always clear. Most standards are intended to serve as guides for both families and practitioners as they support child development; however, families and practitioners do not typically have the opportunity to decide on the goals and expectations for development, which can contribute to mismatches between standards, curricula, and instructional practices.

Although many publishers report that their preschool curricula are aligned with Head Start standards, the alignment was not always clearly explained in the reviewed literature. Head Start programs are required to use curricula that are research-based and promote measurable progress toward the learning indicators laid out in the Head Start Early Learning Outcomes Framework (HSELOF). However, on publishers' websites as well as in research articles, the committee found only a few in-depth descriptions of how the various existing curricula contributed to HSELOF's developmental

---

[5]https://eclkc.ohs.acf.hhs.gov/grant-application

progressions and measurable outcomes. This gap is important because, as explained later, Head Start programs need to be able to assess curriculum alignment against these standards and sometimes also to their state's early learning standards.

Aligning Curricula to State-Level Standards

The landscape of the state-level early learning standards is somewhat fragmented. Each state has its own standards, and the committee did not find any documents that showed the alignment of all the states' early learning standards. In our own review of the standards, the committee noted that most states' standards recommend that curricula be research based, developmentally appropriate, comprehensive, and sequenced toward achieving specific learning goals. However, states differ in their learning goals and curriculum content expectations (DeBruin-Parecki & Slutzky 2016; Whitaker et al., 2022). Mainly, then, it is up to the publishers/developers, administrators, and teachers to determine how well a given curriculum aligns with the state's learning standards.

To facilitate comparisons of curricula with learning standards, some publishers and state agencies provide curriculum crosswalks—charts that juxtapose state-level standards and curriculum components. For example, Missouri developed a document to show correspondence between its standards and the HSELOF (see Missouri Department of Elementary and Secondary Education, 2021). These alignment efforts help educators and families better understand what their children should be learning and how the taught curriculum aligns with standards from the state and from national organizations. Still, it is challenging for educators, child care providers, administrators, and families to navigate the multiple learning standards and connect them to curriculum implementation. It is also challenging and time-consuming for publishers or state agencies to create crosswalks between each curriculum and the early learning standards of each state.

Successful alignment between the curricula and instructional strategies from preschool through third grade is theorized to lead to better organization of services and learning opportunities for children, as well as enhanced school–family partnerships (Bogard & Takanishi, 2005; Brooks-Gunn, 2003; Reynolds & Temple, 2008; Stipek et al., 2017). When there is not alignment, as discussed in Chapter 4, there are detrimental effects on children's outcomes. Curricular alignment for preschool through third grade could be particularly beneficial in reducing opportunity gaps and disparities in learning outcomes for multilingual learners, children with disabilities, and children from families with low income (Demanchick et al., 2009; Garland, 2011; Jacobson, 2009; National Academies, 2023; Rice, 2008; Severns, 2012).

Discrepancies in Alignment to State Standards

There are important curricular discrepancies in how districts and programs incorporate state standards into their curriculum choices. For example, McMahon & Whyte (2020) found curricular differences between two Californian districts that had made large investments to align their math curriculum with the state's standards. These authors found that one district's math curriculum consistently offered challenging tasks across pre-K through third grade, while the other district used a math curriculum with tasks that were less cognitively demanding. The prevalence of more challenging activities across grades suggests that children in the first district would be exposed to more advanced content and learning opportunities, but both districts had made efforts to align with the state standards; this suggests that more guidance is needed (McMahon & Whyte, 2020). This study and similar studies indicate that there may be a lack of agreement within and across districts on how to connect state standards to the preschool curriculum.

Discrepancies between state standards and school districts' curriculum choices may lead to inequitable learning opportunities. For instance, as family advocates, administrators, and teachers in Tennessee's Jackson-Madison County School System looked for ways to increase equitable outcomes in their schools, they engaged in a deep curriculum review process and found that the district-selected curricula were outdated and insufficient to comply with state standards (Stewart, 2020). Because of the misalignment, teachers did not use the curriculum consistently and supplemented it heavily with materials that they created or found online. As a result, children had access to materials of varying quality and content, and their learning opportunities were unequally distributed (Stewart, 2020). To address the disparities, the school district purchased new curricula that closely aligned with the state standards and created spaces for district leaders, administrators, and teachers to discuss how the curricula mapped with their goals, vision, and practice. After implementing the curricula, children's literacy scores on state assessments increased by 77% (Stewart, 2020).

Acknowledging the key role of district policies and practices in mediating the effect of state policies on teaching, Stipek et al. (2017) recommended developing clear curriculum guidelines and instructional framework for pre-K through grade 3 at the district and school levels. Still, there is an ongoing debate over how to best incorporate early learning standards into early learning curricula and how to align these standards with K–12 standards (National Research Council [NRC], 2015). It is important to consider that alignment between curriculum and standards is only helpful insofar as the early learning and development standards set appropriate targets for skills and competencies. Many, if not most, do not include important outcomes for children such as positive racial and cultural identity, resilience, curiosity, and some of the other outcomes mentioned throughout this report.

WHAT CURRICULA DO STATES APPROVE AND SUPPORT?

In 2020–2021, 30 state-funded preschool programs reported having a list of either approved or recommended comprehensive curricula from which local districts/programs could select a curriculum (Friedman-Krauss et al., 2022). Out of the 30 state-funded programs, all but three are required to select a curriculum from the approved or recommended list. While several states reported that only one curriculum is on their list, two state-funded preschool programs (Arkansas and Minnesota Voluntary Pre-K/School Readiness Plus) reported 17 curricula on their list (see Table 8-2). Minnesota's quality rating and improvement system, Parent Aware, has an extensive list of approved curriculum. *The Creative Curriculum for Preschool* (Teaching Strategies) was the most frequently reported curriculum on the list, reported by 27 out of 30 programs (90%); this is followed by *HighScope Preschool Curriculum*, reported by 21 programs (70%). Half of programs reported including *InvestiGator Club* (Robert-Leslie Publishing) and *Opening the World of Learning* (OWL) (Savvas Learning Company). Eight programs reported that *Tools of the Mind* was on their list and ten programs reported that Montessori was on their list. Moreover, a few states have developed their own curricula (see Box 8-1).

States were also asked to report the percentages of programs implementing each of the comprehensive curricula on their list (Table 8-2). However, only

---

BOX 8-1
State-Developed Curricula: *STREAMin³*

A few states have now developed their own, readily available curricula through collaborative partnerships. For example, with funding from the Virginia Department of Education, researchers at the Center for Advanced Study of Teaching and Learning at the University of Virginia developed the *STREAMin³* comprehensive curriculum, which is available free or at low cost to birth-to-5 programs receiving public funds in Virginia (see https://streamin3.org). *STREAMin³* focuses on science, technology, reading, engineering, art, and math content, as well as core skills: relationships, self-regulation, thinking, communicating, and movement. Implementation of this program incorporates integrated experiences, intentional teaching, and interactions between teachers and children (known as the 3 Is). According to Amanda Williford (public listening session, March 27, 2023), educators requested a coherent comprehensive curriculum that would not require putting together several domain-specific curricula, which is a challenging task considering high rates of staff turnover. To meet the needs of family child care providers, the curriculum covers infants through preschoolers. Scope and sequence are articulated across this age span. Professional development, coaching, and assessment tools are provided. *STREAMin³* is research based and has been piloted widely, but a large-scale evaluation study was impeded by the COVID-19 pandemic.

SOURCE: Public Listening Session with Amanda Williford to the committee, March, 27, 2023.

TABLE 8-2 Percentage of State-Funded Preschool Programs Using Each Comprehensive Curriculum

	Arkansas	Georgia	Louisiana NSECD	Michigan	Mississippi	North Carolina	Rhode Island	Virginia
Bank Street College of Education	0	0	0	0	0	0	0	0
Big Day for PreK (Houghton-Mifflin)	8	1	8	0	0	0	0	28
Connect4Learning (Kaplan Early Learning Company)	0	0	0	14	0	0	0	0
Core Knowledge Curriculum Series (Preschool)	5	0	0	0	0	0	0	0
The Creative Curriculum for Preschool (Teaching Strategies)	21	34	40	47	0	94	65	34
Curiosity Corner	0	0	0	0	0	0	0	0
DLM Early Childhood Express (McGraw-Hill)	2	0	0	0	0	0	0	0
Frog Street DIG: Develop, Inspire, Grow	4	0	4	0	0	0	0	14
HighReach Learning Curriculum (Carson-Dellosa Publishing)	0	0	0	0	0	0	0	0
HighScope Preschool Curriculum	0	16	0	38	0	3	5	4
InvestiGator Club (Robert-Leslie Publishing)	2	3	0	0	0	0	0	0.1
Little Treasures (Macmillan/McGraw-Hill)	0	0	0	0	0	0	0	0
Montessori Curriculum	0	0	0	0.003	0	0	0	0
Opening the World of Learning (OWL) (Savvas Learning Company)	1	5	4	0	100	0	0	0.5

PreK On My Way (Scholastic)	3	0	0	0	0
Reggio Emilia	2	0	0	0	0
Tools of the Mind	0	0	0	1	1.2
We Can Early Learning Curriculum (Voyager Sopris Company)	0	6	0	0	0
Waldorf Curriculum	0	0	0	0	0
State-developed curriculum	45	0	0	0	30
Locally developed curriculum	0	5	0	0	0.1
Other curricula*	6	30	44	<1	0	2	18

*Other curricula include Georgia: *Alpha Skills Pre-K Curriculum* (2.10%), *Benchmark*, *Ready to Advance Early Learning Program* (5.86%), *Frog Street Pre-K* (4.76%), *Frog Street Excel* (10.95%), *Kaplan's Beyond Centers and Circle Time* (0.61%), *Learn Everyday* (0.77%), *Splash into Pre-K* (0.28%), and *WINGS*; *Wonder, Interests, Needs, Goals, and Skills* (1.11%); Louisiana NSECD: *Frog Street Pre-K*—Frog Street Press, Ages 3–4; Michigan: *Project Approach*; Virginia: KinderCare, STREAMin³, Blueprint, LaPetite Academy, Early Innovators Childtime, *Empowered Child Learn Every Day*, *Three Cheers for Pre-K*.

NOTE: NSECD = Nonpublic School Early Childhood Development.

eight programs (of 30) were able to report this information: Arkansas, Georgia, Louisiana Nonpublic School Early Childhood Development, Michigan Great Start Readiness Program, Mississippi, North Carolina, Rhode Island, and Virginia. *The Creative Curriculum* was the most commonly used curriculum in five of these states, and in North Carolina, it was used by 94% of programs. Mississippi reported that all programs used *OWL*, but this curriculum was used by only a small percentage of programs in other states. Arkansas (45%) and Rhode Island (30%) both reported substantial percentages of programs using state-developed curricula. Without data from more states, it is hard to know if these states provide a representative picture of curriculum use across states and programs within state-funded preschool. These eight states enrolled just 11% of all children in state-funded preschool in 2020–2021.

Beyond comprehensive curriculum, only 13 state-funded preschool programs in eight states (Arkansas, Delaware, Louisiana [all three programs], Minnesota Voluntary Pre-K and School Readiness Plus [VPK/SRP], Oklahoma, Pennsylvania [all four programs], South Carolina, and Tennessee) reported having a list of approved subject-specific curricula for preschool (see Table 8-3). Literacy and social-emotional development

TABLE 8-3 Subject-Specific Curricula Used in State-Funded Preschool

	Subject-Specific Curricula	Domains Covered
Arkansas	*Launchpad for Pre-Kindergarten* by Really Great Reading & *Heggerty Phonological Awareness for Pre-Kindergarten*	Literacy
Delaware	For a list, see https://www.delawarestars.udel.edu/wp-content/uploads/2021/10/ECE-Supplemental-Curricula-Examples-updated-Oct-29-2021.pdf	Healthy lifestyles, literacy, social-emotional development, science, math
Louisiana (all three programs)	*Blueprint for Early Literacy*—Children Literacy Initiative; *Eureka Math*—Great Minds	Literacy and math
Minnesota Voluntary Prekindergarten/School Readiness Program	For a list, see https://www.parentaware.org/wp-content/uploads/2022/04/PA-011-Aligned-Curricula-March-2022.pdf	Literacy and social-emotional learning
Oklahoma	Not reported	Not reported
Pennsylvania (all four programs)	For a list, see https://www.education.pa.gov/Early%20Learning/Early%20Learning%20Standards/Pages/default.aspx	Social-emotional development, language and literacy, science, approaches to learning through play
South Carolina (First Steps)	*Conscious Discipline*	Social-emotional
Tennessee	Tennessee Foundational Skills Literacy or another research-proven, sounds-first foundational skills model	Literacy

were the two most common domains covered by the approved subject-specific curricula. No information is available on actual use by programs of these curricula. New Jersey (all three programs) reported that districts could submit requests to the state to use supplemental, domain-specific curricula. This is a surprising finding given that some subject-specific, evidence-based curricula have been found to be highly related to positive outcomes for children.

IMPACT OF THE COVID-19 PANDEMIC ON SUPPORTS FOR CURRICULUM IMPLEMENTATION

In fall 2020, 28 state-funded preschool programs (45%) reported changes to state supports for curriculum implementation as a result of the COVID-19 pandemic (Friedman-Krauss et al., 2021). These changes tended to increase flexibility and move training and resources online. For example, one common change was to allow curricula to be implemented through online/virtual instruction, both synchronous and asynchronous. Several programs reported shifting coaching, training, and professional development online to a virtual format as well as additional training and guidance around implementing curricula through a virtual platform. In the District of Columbia, community-based organizations within the state-funded preschool program could request a waiver of the requirement to use a comprehensive curriculum consistently.

FIDELITY OF CURRICULUM IMPLEMENTATION

Fidelity of curriculum implementation is the extent to which teachers implement a curriculum as intended by the developers and is important for considering teacher professional development needs and evaluation of teacher and child outcomes (Pence et al., 2008). Existing research has shown that higher curriculum fidelity scores are associated with greater child gains (Hamre et al., 2010; Wasik et al., 2006), and low fidelity scores are associated with poor outcomes (Carroll et al., 2007; Clements et al., 2011; Durlak & DuPre, 2008; O'Donnell, 2008; Odom, 2009). The importance of fidelity is often associated with its influence on child outcomes when a specific curriculum is evaluated for effectiveness. One notable reason for the existence of fidelity checks is the observed discrepancy across the practices of teachers who use the same curriculum (Jenkins et al., 2019).

Fidelity is typically measured along one or more of the following three domains: "adherence (the extent to which curriculum was implemented as designed), dosage (the amount of time spent implementing key components of curriculum), and quality (the extent to which the curriculum was implemented using high-quality practices)" (McCormick et al., 2019, p. 4).

The most measured dimension of fidelity is adherence, also referred to as "the bottom-line measurement of implementation fidelity" (Carroll et al., 2007, p. 15). As Cordray and Pion highlighted in a review of existing research on fidelity, developing quality fidelity measurement is inherently complex, labor-intensive, and a long-term research endeavor—and the "majority of programs (interventions) in local organizations are not nearly as sophisticated" (Cordray & Pion, 2006, p. 121).

Fidelity of implementation is documented using varying methods, from self-reported checklists to full instruments. In research, self-reports and observational checklists are seen as dubious because of their subjectivity and unassessed reliability (Sarama et al., 2016). In practice, the typical way to ensure fidelity is through a combination of self-reports, coach observations, and use of checklists. This approach is the most prevalent in Head Start programs, for instance, where fidelity of implementation is ensured through coaching and using checklists, but much less so by using fidelity tools (Doran et al., 2022). This approach to fidelity is also reported in experimental studies, often without any information about internal consistency, reliability, or psychometric characteristics (e.g., DeBaryshe & Gorecki, 2007; Fischel et al., 2007; Lonigan et al., 2015). In contrast, more robust fidelity measures undergo multiple rounds of refinement, often with the support of curriculum developers and multiple rounds of classroom observations (e.g., Assel et al., 2007; Clements & Sarama, 2008; Nesbit & Farran, 2021).

States were asked to report about systems in place to ensure curricula were being implemented with fidelity during the 2017–2018 school year (Friedman-Krauss et al., 2019). Of the 61 state-funded preschool programs that year, 35 (57%) reported that there was no system in place to ensure fidelity of curriculum implementation, or it was determined locally. Given the importance of high-quality curricula implemented with fidelity for supporting children's learning and development in preschool, this high percentage of state-funded preschool programs not monitoring fidelity of curriculum implementation is concerning.

Nine programs reported that the state has a system for ensuring that curricula are implemented with fidelity. Six programs reported that the state required local programs to establish a system for ensuring that curricula are implemented with fidelity. Eleven other programs reported other systems for ensuring fidelity of curriculum implementation. Many of these reported using some combination of coaching, monitoring, and additional funding available to support fidelity of curriculum implementation.

For example, Alabama reported that ongoing monitoring, coaching, and training were used to ensure proper curriculum implementation. Specifically, monitors work with program administrators to ensure that First Class Voluntary Pre-Kindergarten grants are properly administered, provide appropriate leadership to teaching staff in concert with coaches to improve instruction, and support the development of leadership skills necessary for effective program management and improvement (Friedman-Krauss et al., 2019). In Iowa, Area Education Agencies provide training and support for curriculum adoption and implementation, and guidance for fidelity and funding is available to support curriculum implementation and training. Louisiana reported relying on a system of regular coaching at the local level and funding for training and professional development, in addition to state and regional training and technical assistance.

WHO ATTENDS PRESCHOOL PROGRAMS WITH CURRICULUM SUPPORTS?[6]

All children in state-funded preschool are in programs that provide at least one support for selecting curriculum. However, although only six programs do not provide at least one support for implementing curriculum (and therefore do not meet NIEER's Curriculum Supports benchmark), almost 27% of children in state-funded preschool are in these programs. Florida and Texas have two of the three largest state-funded preschool programs in terms of the number of children enrolled. Those two states alone enroll one-quarter of all U.S. children in state-funded preschool. Efforts to improve supports for curriculum implementation in Florida, Texas, and Colorado (as it moves toward universal preschool) would positively impact a large number of children.

The states that do not meet the Curriculum Supports benchmark (especially Florida and Texas) are also demographically diverse. In Florida, 20% of preschool-age children are Black/African American, and 31% are Latine/Hispanic. In Texas, 12% of preschool-age children are Black/African American, and 49% are Latine/Hispanic. In Colorado, 32% of preschool-age children are Latine/Hispanic. Alaska has a high percentage of preschool-age children who are American Indian/Alaska Native (18%). Colorado and Texas reported demographic information on children enrolled in their state-funded preschool programs as well. Sixty-one percent (61%) of children enrolled in the Texas Public School Prekindergarten were Latine/Hispanic, and 50% of children enrolled in the Colorado Preschool Program were Latine/Hispanic. Given the diversity of children in these programs that do not meet the Curriculum Supports benchmark, improving supports for curriculum implementation is needed to ensure equity of access to high-quality state-funded prekindergarten. Supports specifically focused on curriculum implementation for multilingual learners are essential as well.

---

[6]This section is drawn from a paper commissioned by the committee for this study (Friedman-Krauss, 2023).

IMPLICATIONS FOR ASSESSMENT

Assessment is a systematic information-gathering process. Early childhood experts recommend integrating assessment of child progress into preschool curricula, with the goal of informing instruction. Embedding assessment into curriculum materials creates opportunities for children to share their understanding and for teachers to monitor and adjust instructional activities to support children's development (Fine & Furtak, 2020; NRC, 2008). That is, as described throughout the earlier chapters, assessment enables teachers to understand where a child is developmentally, know what the next step is in a developmental progression, and then tailor their instruction to that level rather than use a one-size-fits-all approach to pedagogy (see Chapters 6 and 7 for assessments related to targeted populations). Teachers can then better rely upon the child's cultural and linguistic assets, providing enriching learning experiences, and establishing a safe and nurturing environment (see Chapter 5). In this way, individualization is consistent with the equity and antibias framing that is foundational to the committee's vision for preschool curricula.

Assessment systems may include observation, documentation of children's work or portfolios, checklists, rating scales, and norm-referenced tests (National Association for the Education of Young Children & National Association of Early Childhood Specialists in State Departments of Education, 2009). In 2003, NAEYC urged policy makers and early childhood stakeholders to develop and use comprehensive systems of curriculum, assessment, and program evaluation guided by sound early childhood practices, effective early learning standards, and program standards. Likewise, the National Research Council (2001, 2006, 2008) contends that a successful system of assessments must be coherent along three dimensions:

- *Horizontally coherent*—assessment systems, curriculum, instruction, and early learning standards target the same goals for learning and work together to support children's developing knowledge and skill across all domains.
- *Vertically coherent*—all levels of the system (classroom, center, school or program, and state) share an understanding of the purposes and uses of assessment tools.
- *Developmentally coherent*—the assessment system draws on what is known about how children's content knowledge, abilities, and understanding develop over time and what they need to progress at each stage of the process, which would also inform instruction.

Assessment data have the potential to enhance teaching and program operations to improve outcomes for children. Curriculum-based, formative assessment systems (such as the Work Sampling System, the High Scope

Child Observation Record Advantage, or Teaching Strategies GOLD) may involve prompts or opportunities for evidence that are embedded in classroom activities, as well as guidelines for teachers about how to document or collect the evidence (through observation and collection of examples) and how to use evidence to assess child skill level on specific indicators. However, some research suggests that teachers over- and underestimate children's skills using these measures (e.g., Vitiello & Williford, 2021), which can be associated with child characteristics like race and gender (Mashburn & Henry, 2004).

Assessment may also involve more traditional knowledge assessments administered by teachers and/or on a computer, in which skill level is determined by responses to test items. Early childhood experts (e.g., Clark, 2015; Datnow et al., 2007; NRC, 2008) recommend the use of curriculum-based assessments plus instructional practice data (e.g., Classroom Assessment Scoring System), developmental screening tools (Brigance and DIAL-4), and data provided by family members. The triangulation of multiple assessment data sources has the potential to provide deeper insight into children's development and shed light into necessary adjustments (Keeley, 2014). The data can provide information about what curricular aspects work, what needs improvement, and what could be done within and beyond the classroom to support better curriculum implementation (Gullo, 2013). Data can then be used to make programmatic decisions and monitor the consequences of those decisions—a process known as data-driven decision making (Abbott et al., 2017). When the assessment systems are embedded in daily program activities and used as a tool for continuous improvement and collaboration, the systems can enhance multilevel outcomes, from children to families to classrooms to larger systems (Yazejian & Bryant, 2013). And, as described in Box 8-2, data-driven instructional approaches, such as multitiered systems of support, can advance equity by helping teachers use data to ensure that every child receives needed instructional supports.

However, it remains largely unknown what educators know about assessment data and how to use the data. The research on early childhood teachers' assessment data use, confidence, and training is scant. And recent studies (e.g., DeMonsabert et al., 2022; Little et al., 2019) have found that although most early childhood teachers regularly collect and use multiple types of data to plan their instruction, they generally receive little and sporadic professional development on collecting and using assessment data. This can be particularly problematic given the increasing calls for teachers to use assessment to individualize instruction as a way to realize the potential of high-quality curriculum and support children from diverse backgrounds.

Teachers' training and confidence in their assessment skills seem to vary by setting: Head Start and public preschool teachers tend to receive more

BOX 8-2
Multitiered Systems of Support

Multitiered systems of support (MTSS)—an approach to data-driven instruction used in elementary classrooms, with potential applications in preschool classrooms—are designed to meet the needs of all learners. MTSS is a framework for providing high-quality instruction for all students, identifying students needing supplemental or more intensive supports, and providing additional or more intensive support for those who need it (Thurlow et al., 2020). Although it is used in elementary grades more commonly than in preschool, MTSS may offer useful evidence about data-driven instruction. While MTSS frameworks vary somewhat, they are often conceived as having three tiers of increasingly intense supports (Figure 8-2): Tier 1 offers universal supports available to all students; Tier 2 provides supplemental supports to those students who are lagging behind their peers; and Tier 3 offers individualized, intensive supports for those who need them (see Figure). MTSS usually offers comprehensive supports (academic and social-emotional), plus school-wide infrastructure for MTSS implementation (Batsche, 2014). Indeed, "MTSS" is sometimes considered an umbrella term that covers many different approaches and interventions, including curriculum design, teacher professional development, school culture change, and family and community engagement (Batsche, 2014; Thurlow et al., 2020). A common feature of

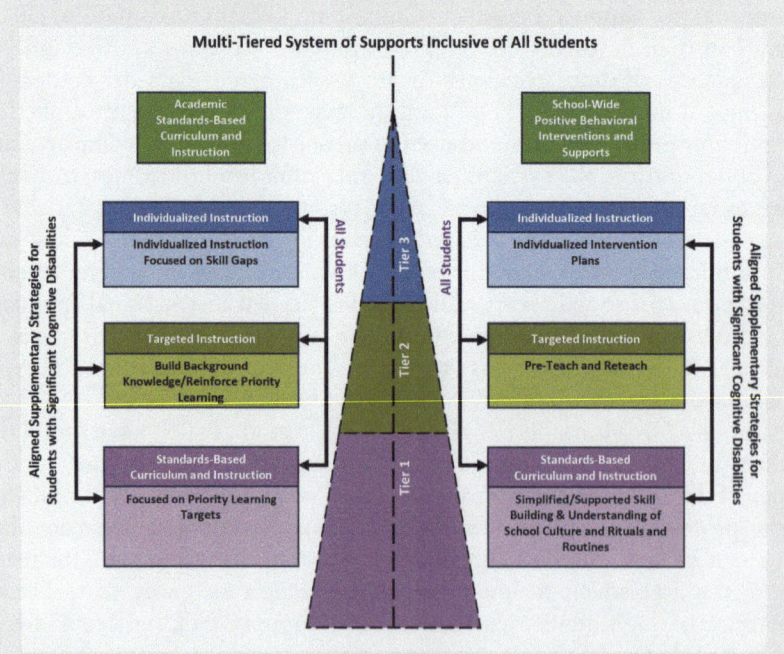

FIGURE 8-2 Multitiered system of supports inclusive of all students.

CURRICULUM DECISION MAKING AND SELECTION 351

> **BOX 8-2 Continued**
>
> the MTSS framework is that it offers schools a structure for organizing processes to provide a continuum of supports for children based on identification of a gap between expected and actual performance (Lane et al., 2016). Indeed, effective implementation of MTSS requires interweaving intervention/supports and assessment, because the assessments help identify who needs which supports and how children respond to the provision of those supports (Chafouleas & Iovino, 2021).
>
> MTSS may be especially beneficial for multilingual learners (Chapter 7) and children with disabilities (Chapter 6). MTSS can facilitate inclusion and integration of multilingual learners or children with disabilities because it provides districts and schools with options to offer a continuum of embedded services that are responsive to children's diverse abilities, rather than, for example, placing children with disabilities in separate, restrictive environments (Thurlow et al., 2020). Recent MTSS models, such as the MTSS for Reading in Early Elementary School (MTSS-R), include a focus on providing high-quality instruction to all students, including students with disabilities who are served in the general education classroom, by supporting the general education teacher and the collaboration between the general education teacher and special education and other staff (e.g., content specialists and aides). The implementation of MTSS-R seeks to promote better identification of students needing supplemental support and students with specific learning disabilities. The Institute of Educational Sciences is currently evaluating the impact of two MTSS-R strategies, which differ in how closely that curriculum is linked to supplemental support and in the use of alternative curricula for students with disabilities. States such as Massachusetts are encouraging school districts to draw on MTSS to create district curriculum accommodation plans that outline specific strategies for helping educators incorporate inclusive practices in curriculum implementation and assessments. This growing body of work will shed light on how MTSS can be best connected to curricula in order to support all children.
>
> SOURCES: Thurlow et al. (2020, p. 6); see also Batsche, 2014; Chafouleas & Iovino, 2021; Lane et al., 2016.

assessment training and be more confident in their assessment skills than teachers in private preschool settings (DeMonsabert et al., 2022). Reviewing existing research and surveying a sample of 1,258 early childhood practitioners across 13 states, DeMonsabert and colleagues (2022) identified five factors that support teachers' use of assessment data: (1) availability of supports to build teachers' capacity to use data; (2) availability of resources (e.g., time and funding) to assist teachers in implementing data-informed instructional practices; (3) individual teacher knowledge and beliefs about assessment data use; (4) policy requirements related to assessments; and (5) family interest in assessment data use for individualization. When these factors are not present (as is often the case), early childhood educators are less likely to use data effectively to tailor instruction and, in doing so, to advance equity (DeMonsabert et al., 2022). Also, a small body of literature indicates that the main use of assessment data is to monitor individual child outcomes or evaluate specific teaching practices, rather than to improve preschool programs as a whole (see Little et al., 2019). That is, it is unclear to what extent assessment data contribute to improving preschool programs and making them more equitable.

Family members can play an important role in integrated assessment and data-driven instruction. By involving parents and other family members in integrated assessment, teachers can engage parents as mutual partners on a meaningful level, which has various benefits in supporting children's learning (Keeley, 2014). Families play a key role in the delivery of a formative curriculum; thus, involving family members in assessments can provide teachers with useful information for supporting each child's learning and can help parents better support student motivation and learning. In addition, family members may have insights into children's strengths and areas of development and provide historical, contextual, and cultural information that can shed light on children's instructional progress. Connecting with families about child progress and development also creates opportunities to identify and reduce measurement biases that may occur because of a student's cultural or linguistic background. When assessment information is shared and discussed with learners, families, and other relevant stakeholders, learning objectives and the features of excellent performance become transparent (Clark, 2015). A key strand for future research entails developing an in-depth understanding of high-quality dialogue between teachers, students, and peers; when instruction and assessments are characterized by high-quality interactions, learning becomes more transparent and accessible as assessment data for use by those involved in a child's overall learning experience (Clark, 2015). Data use and related changes should address multiple levels (not solely the child level) and consider aspects of the broader systems within which children and families function (Yazejian & Bryant, 2013).

Educators need to be mindful and mitigate potential biases in preschool assessments. Because bias is inherent to all humans and reflected in our endeavors, assessment instruments and practices carry potential for biases (Espinosa, 2005; Sprig Learning, 2021). To mitigate bias in assessment, early childhood experts recommend using a mix of formal and informal formative assessments, as well as culturally, linguistically, and individually appropriate assessments (Epstein et al., 2004; Gillis et al., 2009; NAEYC, 2005), although such instruments remain scarce. In the process of administering assessments and interpreting assessment results, there is often room for error, preconceptions, and bias (Gillis et al., 2009; NAEYC, 2005). It is important for preschool stakeholders, especially teachers and program leaders, to critically examine the assessment processes and determine how the assessors' backgrounds—including their identities, cultural stereotypes, and life experiences—may affect assessment-related decisions (NAEYC, 2005; Sprig Learning, 2021). National organizations and experts (Espinosa, 2005; NAEYC, 2005) recommend paying special attention to how linguistic mismatches (i.e., assessing children in languages other than the language or languages spoken at home) may interfere with assessment administration and outcomes (see Chapter 6). Mitigating biases should be an ongoing process and may require strong partnerships with families and hiring or consulting with professionals who are familiar with the children's home culture and individual capacities (Espinosa, 2005).

CONCLUSION

The ways in which curricula are selected, adopted, and implemented, both across and within states, are varied. The diversity of program types—each governed by different policies, regulations, quality standards, and funding streams—create a complex early childhood system with great variability in the experiences children have access to and in their learning outcomes.

In the committee's review of available research, a number of conclusions emerged:

- The states that do not meet the Curriculum Supports benchmark are demographically diverse, with high percentages of Black, Latine, and Native American/Alaska Native populations of children. Given the diversity of children in programs that do not meet the Curriculum Supports benchmark, improving supports for curriculum implementation is needed to ensure equitable access to high-quality state-funded prekindergarten.
- States and localities vary in their structural and systems-level determinants of program quality and access, and most states give preschool programs significant flexibility in their curriculum choices.
- Standards are typically created by national organizations or state departments of education, while curricula are often selected by local boards of education, officials, administrators, and teachers. There is little evidence that families and practitioners have a significant impact on the development of early learning standards.
- Although states differ in their learning goals and curriculum content expectations, most states' standards recommend that curricula be research based, developmentally appropriate, comprehensive, and sequenced toward achieving specific learning goals. There are two widely adopted curricula used by states; however, the degree to which these curricula improve child outcomes is a topic for debate.
- In many cases, publishers/developers, administrators, and teachers determine how well a given curriculum aligns with the state's learning standards.

- Given the importance of high-quality curricula implemented at fidelity for supporting children's learning and development in preschool, the high percentage of state-funded preschool programs not monitoring fidelity of curriculum implementation is concerning.
- Early childhood experts recommend integrating assessment of child progress into preschool curricula, with the goal of informing instruction. When the assessment systems are embedded in daily program activities and used as a tool for continuous improvement and collaboration, the systems can contribute to enhancing multilevel outcomes, from children to families to classrooms to larger systems.
- Family members can play an important role in integrated assessment and data-driven instruction. By involving parents and other family members in integrated assessment, teachers can engage parents as mutual partners on a meaningful level, which has various benefits in supporting children's learning as they may have insights into children's strengths and areas of development and provide historical, contextual, and cultural information that can shed light on children's instructional progress.
- School district, state, and federal contextual factors and policies can support curriculum effectiveness and equity. Additional contextual features that support the implementation of curricula and, subsequently, student outcomes include
  - funding (Barnett & Jung, 2021; Iruka et al., 2020; Manship et al., 2016; McCormick et al., 2019),
  - strong and reliable administrative leadership (Manship et al., 2016; McCormick et al., 2019), and
  - buy-in and support from administration (Lieber et al., 2010; McCormick et al., 2019; Odom et al., 2010).

The variability in how curricula are selected and assessed in the U.S. preschool landscape has implications for the quality of education that children receive. It is important to ensure that all preschool programs have access to high-quality curricula and that assessment is used effectively to inform instruction for all children.

REFERENCES

Abbott, M., Beecher, C. C., Petersen, S., Greenwood, C. R., & Atwater, J. (2015). A team approach to data-driven decision-making literacy instruction in preschool classrooms. *Young Exceptional Children, 20*(3), 117–132. https://doi.org/10.1177/1096250615602297

Assel, M. A., Landry, S. H., Swank, P. R., & Gunnewig, S. (2007). An evaluation of curriculum, setting, and mentoring on the performance of children enrolled in pre-kindergarten. *Reading and Writing, 20*(5), 463–494. https://link.springer.com/content/pdf/10.1007/s11145-006-9039-5.pdf

Barnett, W. S., & Jung, K. (2021). Effects of New Jersey's Abbott preschool program on children's achievement, grade retention, and special education through tenth grade. *Early Childhood Research Quarterly, 56*(3), 248–259. https://doi.org/10.1016/j.ecresq.2021.04.001

Barnett, W. S., Friedman-Krauss, A. H., Weisenfeld, G. G., Horowitz, M., Kasmin, R., & Squires, J. H. (2017). *The state of preschool 2016: State preschool yearbook.* National Institute for Early Education Research. https://nieer.org/state-preschool-yearbooks/yearbook2016

Batsche, G. (2014). Multi-tiered system of supports for inclusive schools. In J. McLenskey, N. L. Waldron, F. Spooner, & B. Algozzine (Eds.), *Handbook of effective, inclusive schools: Research and practice* (pp. 183–196). Routledge.

Bogard, K., & Takanishi, R. (2005). PK-3: An aligned and coordinated approach to education for children 3 to 8 years old. *Social Policy Report, 19*(3). Society for Research in Child Development.

Brooks-Gunn, J. (2003). Do you believe in magic? What we can expect from early childhood intervention programs. *Social Policy Report, 17*(1). https://srcd.onlinelibrary.wiley.com/doi/pdf/10.1002/j.2379-3988.2003.tb00020.x

Carroll, C., Patterson, M., Wood, S., Booth, A., Rick, J., & Balain, S. (2007). A conceptual framework for implementation fidelity. *Implementation Science, 2*, 40–49. https://doi.org/10.1186/1748-5908-2-40

Chafouleas, S. M., & Iovino, E. A. (2021). Engaging a whole child, school, and community lens in positive education to advance equity in schools. *Frontiers in Psychology 12*, 758788. https://doi.org/10.3389/fpsyg.2021.758788

Clark, I. (2015). Formative assessment: Translating high-level curriculum principles into classroom practice. *Curriculum Journal, 26*(1), 91–114. https://doi.org/10.1080/09585176.2014.990911

Clements, D. H., & Sarama, J. (2008). Experimental evaluation of the effects of a research-based preschool mathematics curriculum. *American Educational Research Journal, 45*(2), 443–494. https://doi.org/10.3102/0002831207312908

Clements, D. H., Sarama, J., Spitler, M. E., Lange, A. A., & Wolfe, C. B. (2011). Mathematics learned by young children in an intervention based on learning trajectories: A large-scale cluster randomized trial. *Journal for Research in Mathematics Education, 42*(2), 127–166. https://doi.org/10.5951/jresematheduc.42.2.0127

Cordray, D. S., & Pion, G. M. (2006). Treatment strength and integrity: Models and methods. In R. R. Bootzin & P. E. McKnight (Eds.), *Strengthening research methodology: Psychological measurement and evaluation* (pp. 103–124). American Psychological Association. https://doi.org/10.1037/11384-006

Datnow, A., Park, V., & Wohlstetter, P. (2007). *Achieving with data: How high-performing school systems use data to improve instruction for elementary students.* Center on Educational Governance, Rossier School of Education, University of Southern California. http://www.newschools.org/wp/wp-content/uploads/AchievingWithData.pdf

Datta, A. R., Gebhardt, Z., & Zapata-Gietl, C. (2021a). *Center-based early care and education providers in 2012 and 2019: Counts and characteristics* (OPRE Report No. 2021-222). Office of Planning, Research and Evaluation, Administration for Children and Families, U.S. Department of Health and Human Services. https://www.acf.hhs.gov/sites/default/files/documents/opre/cb-counts-and-characteristics-chartbook_508_2.pdf

Datta, A. R., Gebhardt, Z., & Zapata-Gietl, C. (2021b). *Home-based early care and education providers in 2012 and 2019: Counts and characteristics* (OPRE Report No. 2021-85). Office of Planning, Research and Evaluation, Administration for Children and Families, U.S. Department of Health and Human Services. https://www.acf.hhs.gov/sites/default/files/documents/opre/NSECE-chartbook-homebased-may-2021.pdf

DeBaryshe, B. D., & Gorecki, D. M. (2007). An experimental validation of a preschool emergent literacy curriculum. *Early Education and Development, 18*(1), 93–110. https://eric.ed.gov/?id=EJ772200

DeBruin-Parecki, A., & Slutzky, C. (2016). *Exploring pre-K age 4 learning standards and their role in early childhood education: Research and policy implications* (ETS Research Report Series No. 16-14). Policy Information Center, Educational Testing Service. https://files.eric.ed.gov/fulltext/EJ1124783.pdf

Demanchick, S. P., Peabody, M. A., & Johnson, D. B. (2009). Primary project: Fifty years of facilitating school adjustment. In A. A. Drewes (Ed.), *Blending play therapy with cognitive behavioral therapy: Evidence-based and other effective treatments and techniques* (pp. 219–235). Wiley.

DeMonsabert, J., Brookes, S., Coffey, M. M., & Thornburg, K. (2022). Data use for continuous instructional improvement in early childhood education settings. *Early Childhood Education Journal, 50*(3), 493–502. https://doi.org/10.1007/s10643-021-01168-3

Doran, E., Reid, N., Bernstein, S., Nguyen, T., Dang, M., Li, A., Kopack Klein, A., Rakibullah, S., Scott, M., Cannon, J., Harrington, J., Larson, A., Tarullo, L., & Malone, L. (2022). *A portrait of Head Start classrooms and programs in Spring 2020: FACES 2019 descriptive data tables and study design* (OPRE Report No. 2022-15). Office of Planning, Research, and Evaluation, Administration for Children and Families, U.S. Department of Health and Human Services.

Durlak, J. A., & DuPre, E. P. (2008). Implementation matters: A review of research on the influence of implementation on program outcomes and the factors affecting implementation. *American Journal of Community Psychology, 41*(3), 327–350. https://doi.org/10.1007/s10464-008-9165-0

Epstein, A. S., Schweinhart, L. J., DeBruin-Parecki, A., & Robin, K. B. (2004). Preschool assessment: A guide to developing a balanced approach. *Preschool Policy Matters, 7*, 1–11. https://www.ilgateways.com/docman-docs/faculty-resources/ece-resources/2742-oa-3-nieer-preschool-policy-matters/file

Espinosa, L. M. (2005). Curriculum and assessment considerations for young children from culturally, linguistically, and economically diverse backgrounds. *Psychology in the Schools, 42*(8), 837–853. https://doi.org/10.1002/pits.20115

Fine, C. G. M., & Furtak, E. M. (2020). A framework for science classroom assessment task design for emergent bilingual learners. *Science Education, 104*(3), 393–420. https://doi.org/10.1002/sce.21565

Fischel, J. E., Bracken, S. S., Fuchs-Eisenberg, A., Spira, E. G., Katz, S., & Shaller, G. (2007). Evaluation of curricular approaches to enhance preschool early literacy skills. *Journal of Literacy Research, 39*, 71–501. https://doi.org/10.1080/10862960701675333

Forry, N., & Wessel, J. (2012). *Defining school readiness in Maryland: A multidimensional perspective* (Publication No. 2012-44). Maryland Research Capacity Brief Series, Child Trends. https://cms.childtrends.org/wp-content/uploads/2013/03/Child_Trends-2012_11_27_RB_Defining.pdf

Freeman, R., & Karlsson, M. (2012). Strategies for learning experiences in family child care: American and Swedish perspectives. *Childhood Education, 88*(2), 81–90. https://doi.org/10.1080/00094056.2012.662116

Friedman-Krauss, A. (2023). [The state of curricula in state-funded preschool]. Paper commissioned by the Committee on a New Vision for High Quality Pre-K Curriculum.

Friedman-Krauss, A. H., Barnett, W. S., Garver, K. A., Hodges, K. S., Weisenfeld, G. G. & DiCrecchio, N. (2019). *The state of preschool 2018: State preschool yearbook*. National Institute for Early Education Research. https://nieer.org/state-preschool-yearbooks/2018-2

Friedman-Krauss, A. H., Barnett, W. S., Garver, K. A., Hodges, K. S., Weisenfeld, G. G. & Gardiner, B. A. (2021). *The state of preschool 2020: State preschool yearbook*. National Institute for Early Education Research. https://nieer.org/state-preschool-yearbooks/yearbook2020

Friedman-Krauss, A. H., Barnett, W. S., Garver, K. A., Hodges, K. S., Weisenfeld, G., Gardiner, B. A., & Jost, T. M. (2022). *The state of preschool 2021: State preschool yearbook.* National Institute for Early Education Research. https://nieer.org/state-preschool-yearbooks-yearbook2021

Friedman-Krauss, A. H., Barnett, W. S., Hodges, K. S., Garver, K. A., Weisenfeld, G., Gardiner, B. A., & Jost, T. M. (2023). *The state of preschool 2022: State preschool yearbook.* National Institute for Early Education Research. https://nieer.org/the-state-of-preschool-yearbook-2022

Fuligni, A. S., Howes, C., Huang, Y., Hong, S. S., & Lara-Cinisomo, S. (2012). Activity settings and daily routines in preschool classrooms: Diverse experiences in early learning settings for low-income children. *Early Childhood Research Quarterly, 27*(2), 198–209. https://doi.org/10.1016/j.ecresq.2011.10.001

Garland, S. (2011). Pre-K-grade 3 continuum gets sharper focus. *Education Week, 30*(22), 7.

Gillis, M., West, T., & Coleman, M. R. (2009). *Early learning observation & rating scale: Teacher's guide.* National Center for Learning Disabilities. https://www.getreadytoread.org/images/content/downloads/ELORS_forms/teacherguideshort2010.pdf

Gullo, D. F. (2013). Improving instructional practices, policies, and student outcomes for early childhood language and literacy through data-driven decision making. *Early Childhood Education Journal, 41*(6), 413–421. https://doi.org/10.1007/s10643-013-0581-x

Hamre, B. K., Justice, L. M., Pianta, R. C., Kilday, C., Sweeney, B., Downer, J. T., & Leach, A. (2010). Implementation fidelity of MyTeachingPartner literacy and language activities: Association with preschoolers' language and literacy growth. *Early Childhood Research Quarterly, 25*(3), 329–347. https://doi.org/10.1016/j.ecresq.2009.07.002

Iruka, I. U., DeKraai, M., Walther, J. C., Sheridan, S. M., & Abdel-Monem, T. (2020). Examining how rural ecological contexts influence children's early learning opportunities. *Early Childhood Research Quarterly, 52*(Part B), 15–29. https://doi.org/10.1016/j.ecresq.2019.09.005

Jacobson, L. (2009). *On the cusp in California: How PreK-3rd strategies could improve education in the Golden State.* New America Foundation. https://www.fcd-us.org/wp-content/uploads/2016/04/On_The_Cusp_in_CA.pdf

Jenkins, J., Whitaker, A., Nguyen, T., & Yu, W. (2019). Distinctions without a difference? Preschool curricula and children's development. *Journal of Research on Educational Effectiveness, 12,* 514–549. https://doi.org/10.1080%2F19345747.2019.1631420

Jenkins, J. M., Duncan, G. J., Auger, A., Bitler, M., Domina, T., & Burchinal, M. (2018). Boosting school readiness: Should preschool teachers target skills or the whole child? *Economics of Education Review, 65,* 107–125. https://doi.org/10.1016/j.econedurev.2018.05.001

Keeley, P. (2014). Formative assessment probes: Seeds in a bag, promoting learning through assessment. *Science and Children, 52*(3), 34–36. https://eric.ed.gov/?id=EJ1045995

Lane, K. L., Oakes, W. P., Cantwell, E. D., & Royer, D. J. (2016). *Building and installing comprehensive, integrated, three-tiered (Ci3T) models of prevention: A practical guide to supporting school success.* KOI Education.

Lieber, J., Hanson, M. J., Butera, G., Palmer, S. B., Horn, E., & Czaja, C. (2010). Do preschool teachers sustain their use of a new curriculum? *NHSA Dialog, 13*(4), 248–252. https://doi.org/10.1080/15240754.2010.513778

Little, M. H., Cohen-Vogel, L., Sadler, J., & Merrill, B. (2019). Data-driven decision making in early education: Evidence from North Carolina's Pre-K program. *Education Policy Analysis Archives, 27*(18), 1–23. http://dx.doi.org/10.14507/epaa.27.4198

Lonigan, C. J., Phillips, B. M., Clancy, J. L., Landry, S. H., Swank, P. R., Assel, M., Taylor, H. B., Klein, A., Starkey, P., Domitrovich, C. E., Eisenberg, N., Villiers, J., Villiers, P., & Barnes, M. (2015). Impacts of a comprehensive school readiness curriculum for preschool children at risk for educational difficulties. *Child Development, 86*(6), 1773–1793. https://doi.org/10.1016%2Fj.jecp.2021.105321

Manship, K., Farber, J., Smith, C., & Drummond, K. (2016). *Case studies of schools implementing early elementary strategies: Preschool through third grade alignment and differentiated instruction*. Office of Planning, Evaluation and Policy Development, U.S. Department of Education. https://files.eric.ed.gov/fulltext/ED571886.pdf

Mashburn, A. J., & Henry, G. T. (2004). Assessing school readiness: Validity and bias in preschool and kindergarten teachers' ratings. *Educational Measurement: Issues and Practice, 23*(4), 16–30. https://doi.org/10.1111/j.1745-3992.2004.tb00165.x

McCormick, M., Weiland, C., Hsueh, J., Maier, M., Hagos, R., Snow, C., Leacock, N., & Schick, L. (2019). Promoting content-enriched alignment across the early grades: A study of policies and practices in the Boston Public Schools. *Early Childhood Research Quarterly, 52*, 57–73. https://files.eric.ed.gov/fulltext/ED600990.pdf

McMahon, K. A., & Whyte, K. (2020). What does math curriculum tell us about continuity for Pre-K-3? *Curriculum Journal, 31*(1), 48–76. https://doi.org/10.1002/curj.8

Missouri Department of Elementary and Secondary Education. (2021). *Alignment: Missouri early learning standards and the Head Start Early Learning Outcomes framework*. https://dese.mo.gov/media/pdf/alignment-missouri-early-learning-standards-and-head-start-early-learning-outcomes

Morris, S., & Smith, L. K. (2021). *Examples of mixed-delivery early care and education systems*. Bipartisan Policy Center. https://bipartisanpolicy.org/blog/examples-of-mixed-delivery-early-care-and-education-systems/

National Academies of Sciences, Engineering, and Medicine. (2023). *Closing the opportunity gap for young children*. The National Academies Press.

National Association for the Education of Young Children [NAEYC]. (2005). *Screening and assessment of young English-language learners: Supplement to the NAEYC position statement on early childhood curriculum, assessment, and program evaluation*. https://www.naeyc.org/sites/default/files/globally-shared/downloads/PDFs/resources/position-statements/ELL_Supplement_Shorter_Version.pdf

National Association for the Education of Young Children & National Association of Early Childhood Specialists in State Departments of Education. (2009). *Where we stand on curriculum, assessment, and program evaluation.*. www.naeyc.org/files/naeyc/file/positions/StandCurrAss.pdf

National Center for Education Statistics. (2017). *Digest of education statistics: Table 202.30. Number of children under 6 years old and not yet enrolled in kindergarten, percentage in center-based programs, average weekly hours in nonparental care, and percentage in various types of primary care arrangements, by selected child and family characteristics: 2016*. https://nces.ed.gov/programs/digest/d19/tables/dt19_202.30.asp

National Center on Early Childhood Quality Assurance (NCECQA). (2020a). *Licensing trends 2017 child care centers*. Office of Head Start, Office of Child Care, Health Resources and Services Administration, Administration for Children and Families, U.S. Department of Health and Human Services.

———. (2020b). *Program participation: Fact sheet*. Administration for Children and Families, U.S. Department of Health and Human Services. https://childcareta.acf.hhs.gov/sites/default/files/346_2010_qris_fact_sheet_program_participation_final_508compliant.pdf

National Research Council (NRC). (2001). *Eager to learn: Educating our preschoolers*. Committee on Early Childhood Pedagogy, National Academy Press. https://doi.org/10.17226/9745

———. (2006). *Systems for state science assessment*. National Academies Press. https://doi.org/10.17226/11312

———. (2008). *Early childhood assessment: Why, what, and how*. National Academies Press. https://doi.org/10.17226/12446

———. (2015). *Transforming the workforce for children birth through age 8: A unifying foundation*. National Academies Press. https://doi.org/10.17226/19401

National Survey of Early Care and Education Project Team (NSECEPT). (2015). *Measuring predictors of quality in early care and education settings in the National Survey of Early Care and Education* (OPRE Report No. 2015-93). Office of Planning, Research and Evaluation, Administration for Children and Families, U.S. Department of Health and Human Services. https://www.acf.hhs.gov/sites/default/files/documents/opre/measuring_predictors_of_quality_mpoq_in_the_nsece_final_092315_b508.pdf

———. (2016). *Characteristics of home-based early care and education providers: Initial findings from the National Survey of Early Care and Education* (OPRE Report No. 2016-13). Office of Planning, Research, and Evaluation, Administration for Children and Families, U.S. Department of Health and Human Services. https://www.acf.hhs.gov/sites/default/files/documents/opre/characteristics_of_home_based_early_care_and_education_toopre_032416.pdf

Nesbitt, K. T., & Farran, D. C. (2021). Effects of prekindergarten curricula: Tools of the Mind as a case study. *Monographs of the Society for Research in Child Development, 86*(1). https://doi.org/10.1111/mono.12425

O'Donnell, C. L. (2008). Defining, conceptualizing, and measuring fidelity of implementation and its relationship to outcomes in K–12 curriculum intervention research. *Review of Educational Research, 78*(1), 33–84. https://doi.org/10.3102/0034654307313793

Odom, S. L. (2009). The tie that binds: Evidence-based practice, implementation science, and outcomes for children. *Topics in Early Childhood Special Education, 29*(1), 53–61. https://doi.org/10.1177/0271121408329171

Odom, S. L., Fleming, K., Diamond, K. E., Lieber, J., Hanson, M. J., Butera, G., Horn, E., Palmer, S. B., & Marquis, J. (2010). Examining different forms of implementation and in early childhood curriculum research. *Early Childhood Research Quarterly, 25*(3), 314–328. https://doi.org/10.1016/j.ecresq.2010.03.001

Pence, K. L., Justice, L. M., & Wiggins, A. K. (2008). Preschool teachers' fidelity in implementing a comprehensive language-rich curriculum. *Language, Speech, and Hearing Services in Schools, 39*(3), 329–341. https://doi.org/10.1044/0161- 1461(2008/031)

Reynolds, A. J., & Temple, J. A. (2008). Cost-effective early childhood development programs from preschool to third grade. *Annual Review of Clinical Psychology, 4*(1), 109–139. https://doi.org/10.1146/annurev.clinpsy.3.022806.091411

Rice, C. (2008). *Developing an advocacy strategy for New Jersey's P-3 agenda inside and out.* Association for Children of New Jersey. https://www.fcd-us.org/wp-content/uploads/2016/04/InsideAndOut.pdf

Sarama, J., Clements, D. H., Wolfe, C. B., & Spitler, M. E. (2016). Professional development in early mathematics: Effects of an intervention based on learning trajectories on teachers' practices. *Nordic Studies in Mathematics Education, 21*(4), 29–55. https://ncm.gu.se/wp-content/uploads/2020/06/21_4_029056_sarama.pdf

Severns, M. (2012). *Starting early with English language learners: First lessons from Illinois.* New America Foundation. https://static.newamerica.org/attachments/2335-starting-early-with-english-language-learners/Starting_Early_With_English_Language_Learners.e8e593babc47492699c220dccbf6d443.pdf

Sprig Learning. (2021). *Dealing with implicit bias in early learning assessments.* https://www.spriglearning.com/dealing-with-implicit-bias-in-early-learning-assessments/

Stewart, S. (2020, April 1). *Curriculum is key.* National School Boards Association. https://www.nsba.org/ASBJ/2020/April/Curriculum-Is-Key

Stipek, D., Clements, D., Coburn, C., Franke, M., & Farran, D. (2017). PK-3: What does it mean for instruction? *Social Policy Report, 30*(2). https://files.eric.ed.gov/fulltext/ED581657.pdf

Thurlow, M. L., Ghere, G., Lazarus, S. S., & Liu, K. K. (2020). *MTSS for all: Including students with the most significant cognitive disabilities.* National Center on Educational Outcomes, TIES Center. https://nceo.umn.edu/docs/OnlinePubs/NCEOBriefMTSS.pdf

Vitiello, V. E., & Williford, A. P. (2021). Alignment of teacher ratings and child direct assessments in preschool: A closer look at teaching strategies GOLD. *Early Childhood Research Quarterly, 56,* 114–123. https://psycnet.apa.org/record/2021-58824-011

Wasik, B. A., Bond, M. A., & Hindman, A. (2006). The effects of a language and literacy intervention on Head Start children and teachers. *Journal of Educational Psychology, 98*(1), 63–74. http://dx.doi.org/10.1037/0022-0663.98.1.63

Whitaker, A. A., Jenkins, J. M., & Duer, J. K. (2022). Standards, curriculum, and assessment in early childhood education: Examining alignment across multiple state systems. *Early Childhood Research Quarterly, 58,* 59–74. https://doi.org/10.1016/j.ecresq.2021.07.008

Yazejian, N., & Bryant, D. (2013). Embedded, collaborative, comprehensive: One model of data utilization. *Early Education and Development, 24*(1), 68–70. https://doi.org/10.1080/10409289.2013.736128

9

Examining Variation in Curriculum Effects

Decision makers are rarely interested in evidence that applies only to the specific samples, conditions, and outcomes included in research studies. Rather, they are interested in applying study results to predict—or to generalize—findings to their own populations, settings, and outcomes of interest. Generalizing findings requires (1) study results that are internally valid and replicable; (2) curricula, study samples, contexts, and outcomes that are representative of conditions that are to be generalized over; and (3) knowledge about the extent to which findings may vary and why these findings vary (Cronbach, 1982; Shadish et al., 2002; Stuart et al., 2011; Tipton, 2012; Tipton & Olsen, 2018).

As described in Chapter 2, the evidence base on preschool curricula includes findings from many rigorous, internally valid evaluations, some of which have been replicated over multiple studies. Yet gaps remain in the types of curricula, study samples, contexts, and outcomes that are represented in the existing literature. These include questions about the effects of culturally responsive curricula; the effects of curricula in different settings including family child care or for-profit contexts; the effects on less commonly studied child outcomes, such as problem solving and curiosity, child positive racial identity, and multilingual learners' growth in home language; and the effects on other widely adopted instructional approaches to preschool, such as Montessori.

Emerging research on preschool curriculum also suggests variation in curriculum effectiveness. Given the diversity of early childhood conditions under which curricula are delivered, research about curriculum effectiveness should describe the specific contexts, settings, and populations under which the curriculum effect was observed. This is because study findings are often dependent on contexts and unstated theoretical assumptions under which the study was designed and carried out. For example, a curriculum may have a small average effect in improving students' early literacy skills, but the magnitude of the effect may be much larger (or smaller) in different preschool settings (e.g., Head Start versus child care center), with more experienced educators delivering the curriculum, and for students with different home language experiences. Effects may also vary by the type of study design (e.g., experimental versus quasi-experimental).

When curriculum effects vary substantially because of differences in student characteristics, in how the curriculum was delivered, in settings under which the curriculum is delivered, and in outcomes examined, findings observed under one specific set of circumstances will often not be observed under a different set of circumstances. This implies that different curriculum approaches may be more (or less) appropriate for addressing students' developmental and learning goals. In these cases, the program administrator's goal is not to select a preschool curriculum that is the most effective "on average," but to identify the curriculum that is most effective for their specific students and context. For example, program administrators in tribal communities may seek curriculum approaches that teach children academic and social-emotional skills in ways that are culturally responsive and well-aligned to the norms, mores, and goals of their community and families; educators who have children with disabilities in their classrooms may need curricula that address the unique learning needs of their specific students.

The evidence base for a new vision of preschool curriculum, therefore, must address the multiple and complex ways in which children, educators, and their environments interact with curriculum and its delivery. And yet, generating evidence to understand variation in curriculum effects remains elusive and challenging. This chapter focuses on research and methodological issues that arise in designing and implementing studies for evaluating variation in curriculum effectiveness. The committee first presents a framework for understanding why curriculum effects may vary across different studies and contexts (Steiner et al., 2019). The framework describes both programmatic and study-related factors that may be critical for determining the size of curriculum effects. Next, the chapter discusses challenges with identifying sources of effect variation within studies and across multiple studies. Finally, we present conclusions drawn from a review of the literature on curriculum effectiveness.

IDENTIFYING SOURCES OF EFFECT VARIATION

The overarching mission of many researchers of early childhood education is to identify curriculum, practices, and policies that improve student outcomes. When curriculum effects are replicated over multiple studies with diverse settings, populations, intervention deliveries, and contexts, researchers and decision makers have increased confidence that findings can likely be generalized to their specific population or context of interest. However, when study findings are fragile, hard to replicate, and not robust for different populations of interest, the external validity of these findings is questioned.

All scientific conclusions about curriculum effectiveness are based on study findings drawn from samples of participants with specific settings, treatment protocols, and materials. The challenge arises when, in interpreting these findings, researchers fail to specify for whom and what the curriculum effects are intended to represent, as well as any potential constraints on generality that may either amplify or dampen the size of curriculum effects. In the absence of such information, program administrators may assume that study conclusions apply broadly to any sample or context. But when study findings fail to replicate, the trustworthiness of the finding is questioned, and their value for evidence-based decision making is doubted.

Given the diversity in contexts and settings for how preschool curricula are implemented and delivered—and the potential variation in students' responses to different curricular approaches—a research agenda that supports a new vision of preschool curriculum must seek to understand the extent to which curriculum effects are robust across contexts, settings, and populations. And, in cases where effect variation is observed, the evidence base must identify *why* effects varied to understand the populations and conditions under which findings do—and do not—generalize over.

There are multiple reasons why curriculum effects may differ across studies and study conditions. Steiner et al. (2019) proposed a framework for describing key sources of effect variation across different populations, contexts, and studies. The framework demonstrates that the size of an intervention effect depends on programmatic considerations as well as study design characteristics. "Programmatic considerations" include variations in the curriculum or intervention, the condition against which it is being compared, and the outcomes for which curriculum effectiveness is being measured. It also includes differences in student and setting characteristics that may interact with the size of the curriculum effect. When curriculum effects fail to replicate because of programmatic differences across studies, researchers conclude that curriculum effects will likely not generalize to other student populations, contexts, settings, outcomes, and treatment deliveries (Rubin, 1981).

"Study design characteristics" include methodology decisions that may affect the size and precision of an effect. When results are compared from studies with different design characteristics, they may differ because researchers' choices in methodology yielded different conclusions about curriculum effects. For example, one study effect may be obtained from a randomized controlled trial, while another study effect is obtained from an observational study. Curriculum effects across the two studies may differ because the latter suffers from selection bias, raising concerns about the validity of the study findings. Study findings may also fail to replicate because one or both studies lack statistical power for producing precise estimates of the curriculum effect. Decision makers are often not interested in study findings that fail to replicate because of methodology choices. However, in cases where both programmatic and study design characteristics vary simultaneously, it may be impossible to disentangle why study findings failed to replicate. Do curriculum effects differ across studies and study conditions because effects are not generalizable or because of study design choices? It may be impossible to know. A researcher or decision maker may mistakenly interpret incongruent study findings to mean that a curriculum effect fails to generalize, when the true reason may be because one of the studies lacked statistical power to detect curriculum effects.

A central goal for a research agenda supporting a new vision for preschool curriculum is examining the extent to which curriculum effects are generalizable—and when they are not—to variations in student populations, contexts, settings, and outcomes. This report describes reasons related to both programmatic and study design to explain why curriculum effects may vary. Chapter 2 summarizes the empirical literature examining programmatic reasons for why curriculum effects vary—including differences in curriculum type, in the outcomes used for assessing effectiveness, in the students—and their backgrounds, knowledge, and experiences—participating in the curriculum, in the characteristics of teachers using the curriculum, in the preschool setting under which the curriculum is delivered, and in macro conditions that may interact with how the curriculum is delivered (e.g., funding for preschool, state licensure requirements for preschool teachers). These characteristics may amplify or dampen the size of the curriculum effect and may interact in complex ways that affect the effectiveness of a curriculum (Tefera et al., 2018). For example, a curriculum may be especially effective for students with disabilities in public preschool settings but less so for children without disabilities in private child care centers. Understanding the extent to which curriculum effects vary by programmatic features is critical for determining the generalizability of study findings.

The following section describes study design–related reasons that curriculum findings may differ across studies and study conditions. They include differences in the treatment–control contrast for evaluating the curriculum, the research design used for identifying and estimating the curriculum effect, and the size of the sample used to evaluate the effect. While these characteristics are usually investigated to assess the generalizability of study findings, they are related to the feasibility, logistics, and ethics of conducting a study. Therefore, they are of special consideration for researchers and funders of studies on preschool curriculum.

Contrast Condition for Evaluating Curriculum

Curriculum effects are determined by comparing the average effects for students who participated in the curriculum with effects for students who did not. As such, what activities children engage with in both the curriculum and the control condition can have substantial impact on the size and direction of the effect. In preschool curriculum studies, children in the control condition may participate in a wide variety of activities. For example, they may be learning from a curriculum that teachers used prior to the introduction of the new curriculum, they may be engaged in an online activity on a computer or tablet, or they may not be enrolled in a preschool program at all. Usually, the control condition includes the learning activities, experiences, and instruction that the child would have received had they not participated in the curriculum under investigation. Given that these circumstances can vary widely across preschool settings—and that curriculum effects are determined by comparing outcomes for students who participated and did not participate in the curriculum—understanding what activities occurred in the control condition is critical for interpreting curriculum effects.

In general, studies with strong treatment contrasts—with more distinct intervention and control group differences—will produce effects that are larger than those of studies with weak treatment contrasts. For example, Duncan & Magnuson (2013) noted that programs evaluated before 1980 produced substantially larger effects than those evaluated later. They argue that one explanation for the decline in effects is that the "counterfactual conditions for children in the control group studies have improved substantially" (Duncan & Magnuson, 2013, p. 114). In more recent samples, children in the control group were much more likely to attend center-based care programs and were likely to experience higher-quality home environments with more educated mothers (Duncan & Magnuson, 2013).

Reanalysis of data from the Head Start Impact Study also concluded that the overall average effect masked substantial variations in Head Start effects that were related to differences in the control conditions (Morris et al., 2018)—here, the authors found evidence of sustained impacts for Head Start when the control consisted of children who stayed home and did not attend center-based care. Finally, in the early 2000s, the Preschool Curriculum Evaluation Research (PCER; 2008) program supported a series of experimental evaluations examining the relative performance of curricular approaches. A recent meta-analysis of the PCER data examined the performance of different curricular approaches against alternative counterfactuals (Jenkins et al., 2018). The authors looked at the performance of content-specific curricula in reading and math versus what they described as whole-child-focused curricular approaches, such as *HighScope* and *The Creative Curriculum*, and locally developed curricula.[1] Overall, the authors concluded that content-specific curricula produced larger effects on targeted outcomes than did whole-child approaches, and that whole-child approaches did not yield student-level effects that were reliably different from locally developed curricula. However, the original PCER evaluation studies were conducted 20 years ago, and the curricula represented in the control condition have been revised since then.

Research Design for Identifying Effects

"Research design" describes the methodological approach used for determining curriculum effectiveness. Most research designs involve the comparison of outcomes for one curriculum condition versus those obtained for an alternative condition. Students, teachers, or centers may be randomly assigned to different curriculum conditions, or they may be asked to select their own conditions. When participants select their own curriculum conditions, researchers may use statistical adjustment procedures to compare outcomes for students and classrooms that are observationally similar. The goal here is to ensure that differences observed in outcomes are the result of exposure to different curriculum approaches and not because of other differences between groups.

Research design features are important if the choice in methodology contributes to the size of the curriculum effect. For example, in a preschool evaluation where the curriculum is not randomly assigned but is selected by center directors, researchers may be concerned that center directors will be more likely to choose the curriculum being assessed because children in their centers are at risk for low academic achievement. By comparing outcomes for students in centers that selected the curriculum with those in centers that did not, the curriculum may appear ineffective—or even have negative effects—because students enrolled in the intervention centers were at greater risk for low achievement than students in the comparison centers. Although the researcher may use statistical procedures to ensure that both groups of children appear observationally similar, children across the two groups may also differ in ways that are unobserved by the researcher. In these cases, it can be difficult to differentiate why children in the curriculum condition exhibited lower outcome scores than those in the control condition—was it because the curriculum was ineffective or because there were other unobserved differences between children in the two groups?

---

[1] Some of the curricula evaluated as part of the 2008 PCER studies have undergone revisions in the time since these evaluations were conducted. As such, the versions currently used in classrooms may differ from those evaluated as part of these studies.

The modern program evaluation literature prioritizes clear interpretations of intervention effects—or the internal validity of a study—as the sine qua non for high-quality rigorous evaluations of program or policy effects (Campbell & Stanley, 1963). This is in part because empirical evaluations of methods have shown that, compared with experimental approaches, non-experimental methods can yield badly biased—or incorrect—results about intervention effectiveness (Fraker & Maynard, 1987; Lalonde, 1986; Wong et al., 2018). One benefit of experimental approaches, therefore, is that they yield causally interpretable effects when assumptions for the research design are met. Moreover, when deviations from the planned research design do occur—that may introduce bias in the intervention effect—it can often be detected by the researcher. Deviations from the planned research design may include differential attrition across intervention conditions, the inclusion of additional interventions that occur simultaneously with introduction of the curriculum, or failure to comply with randomly assigned intervention conditions. For these reasons, most evidence registries (e.g., What Works Clearinghouse,[2] Blueprints for Healthy Development[3]) have minimum requirements for inclusion that are related to the quality and implementation of the research design.

To date, the committee is unaware of any studies that have compared the magnitude of effects for curriculum effectiveness by research design. In a broader meta-analysis of 84 studies of early care and education curriculum effects, the effect size differences between evaluations in which interventions were randomly and nonrandomly assigned were not statistically different (0.25 standard deviations for randomized controlled trials versus 0.19 standard deviations for nonexperiments; Duncan & Magnusson, 2013). However, to be included in the meta-analysis required both experimental and quasi-experimental designs with more than 10 participants in each condition and less than 50% attrition. Quasi-experimental effects were limited only to those that included repeated measures approaches (e.g., change models, difference-in-difference models), regression discontinuity, propensity score matching, and instrumental variable approaches.

Sample Size

Finally, studies with small samples produce less precise effect estimates. In these cases, it can be difficult to detect effect variation at all, much less identify sources of the effect variation. In addition to producing imprecise effect estimates, small sample studies may include participants and conditions that are not representative of populations ultimately intended to receive the intervention or curriculum. For example, intervention conditions

---

[2] https://ies.ed.gov/ncee/wwc
[3] https://www.blueprintsprograms.org/about

may be administered by the researcher or developer and delivered under controlled settings, making the study more akin to a laboratory trial than field research. Participants, aware of their involvement in a small novel intervention, may also respond differently than they would have had they been involved in a scaled-up version of the intervention with many participants. In Duncan & Magnuson's (2013) review of program impacts in early care and education, small sample studies tended to have larger impacts, but these studies were also more likely to have researcher-developed programs and to have been conducted prior to 1980. For all of these reasons, studies with small samples may be most informative when they can be synthesized with effect estimates from other study efforts.

WITHIN- AND BETWEEN-STUDY APPROACHES FOR EXAMINING SOURCES OF EFFECT VARIATION

In the research literature, the programmatic and study design features are sometimes described as "moderators" of intervention effects. Moderators may be examined by comparing curriculum effects for different subgroups of participants within the same study (within-study approaches) or by comparing effects across multiple studies with different participants, settings, and sometimes research methodologies (between-study approaches).

The within-study approach offers the benefit of comparing effects for different subgroups of participants within the same study, who usually have observations on the same measures and have likely undergone similar study procedures (Bloom & Michalopoulos, 2013). Thus, if differential effects are observed between groups of participants, the researcher may have more confidence that effect heterogeneity is due to differences between subgroups of students and not because of other extraneous, study-related characteristics. However, within-study comparisons of effects are limited because studies often do not have sufficient sample sizes for detecting differential effects for subgroups of participants and settings (Sabol et al., 2022; Spybrook et al., 2016; Tipton, 2021). And, in the absence of strong theory guiding moderator analyses, researchers may be prone to conducting multiple moderator tests and reporting only statistically significant results. The challenge here is that these effects may be significant by chance, resulting in misleading conclusions about moderator effects.

The between-study approach compares results across different studies with variations in populations, settings, intervention conditions, and outcomes. The studies included in the review often have been screened to meet criteria for yielding interpretable results, including a valid and well-implemented research design. For example, the What Works Clearinghouse applies methodological requirements to education evaluation studies for inclusion in its evidence registry. It prioritizes study results with strong internal validity, such as those evaluated by experimental or well-implemented quasi-experimental designs. When results from multiple studies with similar interventions and outcomes are available, the What Works Clearinghouse uses meta-analytic approaches for examining the overall average effect of the intervention, as well as evidence for effect heterogeneity.

Prioritizing strong internal validity in evaluation studies, however, can introduce biases into the evidence base for summarizing intervention effectiveness. Although experimental designs are viewed as the gold standard approach for yielding unbiased intervention effects, these approaches require intervention conditions that can be manipulated or randomly assigned to participants (Shadish et al., 2002). Promising curricular approaches that are not easily evaluated by random assignment (or quasi-experimental approaches) may be omitted from the evidence base. For example, a systems-based policy reform or a curriculum designed for a specific tribal community and that cannot be randomly assigned may be excluded from the evidence registry. Criteria for study findings to be included in an evidence base require consideration of both internal and external validity of studies—in terms of the representativeness of interventions, contexts, and populations of findings included (Imai et al., 2008).

The focus on internal validity may also obviate other concerns with study quality, including the construct validity of the intervention and conditions being compared. For example, the researcher's interpretation and understanding of intervention components may not be well aligned with the participants' experience and understanding of the curriculum or program, or the contexts for how the curriculum was delivered. Also, intervention effects can be determined only for constructs and outcome domains that can be reliably and validly measured, which may be challenging in preschool studies that often require direct assessments of young children. Outcome measures may not adequately represent all the domain areas that are critical for healthy development; they may also fail to fully capture the learning and growth of children from marginalized communities, especially those who have different home languages from those represented in the assessment.

Finally, intervention effects can be obtained only for samples and settings that are accessible to researchers. Study samples are recruited for various reasons (Tipton & Olsen, 2022; Tipton et al., 2020). They may be locationally convenient, logistically feasible, and/or financially reasonable, but they are rarely obtained using random—or even purposive—sampling from a well-defined population of units, treatments, outcomes, settings, and times. Children from marginalized communities, or belonging to low-incidence disability groups, may be underrepresented in study samples, potentially limiting the generalizability of study results. If different types of curricula are effective for underrepresented children, the results will not be reflected in the evidence base.

Study effects may be averaged in meta-analysis without clarifying what, whom, where, or when study effects represent (Schauer & Hedges, 2021).

In meta-analysis, with enough study effects, the researcher may examine whether variations in curricular approaches, participant characteristics, and settings—as well as study design characteristics—are related to the size and direction of intervention effects. These relationships can be modeled as factors related to scientific and study design conditions (and their interactions) in a series of meta-regressions of effects. The approach allows researchers to observe and test the robustness of effects across different programmatic and study design features, as well as to begin to formulate hypotheses about the conditions under which effects may or may not vary.

However, even in meta-analysis, it is often unclear how the researcher can best interpret these associations, and whether these interactions causally moderate or dampen the size of the intervention effect. Moreover, these approaches do not allow for all sources of variation to be tested simultaneously.

To consider challenges with identifying sources of variation across multiple but coordinated studies, the committee examined experimental results produced by the PCER program, which was funded by the Institute of Education Sciences (IES). The goal of this initiative was to provide rigorous evidence about the efficacy of available preschool curricula. The initiative funded 12 research teams from across the country to experimentally evaluate 14 preschool curricula using a common set of measures (one curriculum—*The Creative Curriculum*—was evaluated twice by two different research teams, such that there were 15 evaluation studies of curriculum). Starting in fall 2003, the study's sample included predominantly low-income children enrolled in Head Start programs, state prekindergarten programs, or private child care centers. Outcomes for students' skills (reading, phonological awareness, language development, mathematics knowledge, and behavior) were examined at the end of the preschool and kindergarten years. Researchers also examined classroom-level outcomes, including measures for classroom quality, teacher–child interaction, and instructional quality. Results were analyzed and reported separately for each outcome and study because each team had its own sampling plan and randomization schemes. The final PCER (2008) report concluded mixed results for both the student- and classroom-level outcomes. While 8 of the curricula had statistically significant impacts on classroom-level measures, 7 did not. And 2 curricula showed significant impacts on at least some of the student-level measures at the end of the preschool year, while 13 did not have any statistically significant effects. By the end of the kindergarten year, 3 curricula demonstrated effects on at least some positive student-level outcomes, while 11 had no impacts and 1 had negative impacts.

PCER was funded with the goal of providing decision makers with definitive evidence for choosing preschool curriculum. The initiative required that curricula be evaluated using random assignment and include samples of children and programs that were of interest for decision makers. The programs included Head Start, state prekindergarten, and private child care centers in urban, rural, and suburban locations. The initiative also included standardized measures for assessing outcomes at the student and classroom levels, as well as for reporting curriculum fidelity and contamination of intervention conditions, and for assessing participant response rates and attrition. Finally, the effort included independent evaluations of curriculum conducted by 12 research teams, with technical support for conducting studies from two contract research firms. Given the well-defined target population, standardized method for data collection, and experimental design, the PCER initiative represents the acme of field evaluation methods for informing evidence-based decision making. So why did the PCER effort not yield more conclusive evidence for guiding curriculum choice?

One issue was the lack of statistical power for individual studies to detect significant effects. Random assignment occurred at the classroom or program level—with group sample sizes ranging between 11 and 40 clusters per evaluation study (the median group-level sample size was 18 classrooms or programs). Research teams reported minimum detectable effect sizes that ranged from 0.34 to 0.69 across composite student outcome measures, suggesting that individual studies were mostly underpowered for detecting statistically significant effects unless the magnitude of the effects was at least larger than a third of a standard deviation (PCER, 2008). The lack of statistically significant findings was perhaps not surprising.

Variations in study design characteristics also challenged the interpretation of results. Across the 15 evaluation studies (of 14 curricula), there were substantial differences in the comparison conditions for assessing curriculum effects, preschool settings in which the evaluations occurred, location of sites, and training of teachers on curriculum materials. For example, the evaluation of *Project Construct* found no statistically significant effects on student-level outcomes. The evaluation of *DLM Early Childhood Express with Open Court Reading Pre-K*, however, concluded statistically significant effects for student-level outcomes in reading, phonological awareness, and language. Explaining *why* there are different effects across the two curricula is more challenging. One reason may be that *DLM Early Childhood Express with Open Court Reading* is a more effective curriculum than *Project Construct*. Another reason could be that the teacher-developed materials in the control condition for *Project Construct* were more effective than the materials used by teachers in the control condition for the *DLM Early Childhood Express* study. Curriculum effects may also vary by preschool setting—the *DLM* evaluation took place in public prekindergarten classrooms in Florida, and the *Project Construct* evaluation took place in private child care centers in Missouri.

To address some of the challenges with interpreting results from the PCER initiative, Jenkins et al. (2018) reanalyzed results from the 2008

PCER study through a meta-analysis. By combining effect estimates across the 15 curriculum studies, the research team was able to address some of the ambiguity in conclusions due to weak statistical power for the individual studies; they also explored one hypothesis about why effects may have varied across studies. To conduct their analyses, Jenkins et al. (2018) compared curriculum effects according to four different treatment–control contrasts in the PCER initiative: (1) literacy-focused curriculum versus *HighScope* and *The Creative Curriculum*, (2) literacy-focused versus locally (or teacher-) developed curriculum, (3) mathematics-focused versus *HighScope* and *The Creative Curriculum*, and (4) *The Creative Curriculum* versus locally developed curriculum. Overall, the authors concluded that, compared with *The Creative Curriculum* and *HighScope*, the literacy- and mathematics-focused curricula had stronger evidence of improving student-level outcomes; they also concluded that there was not much evidence that *The Creative Curriculum* and *HighScope* improved students' school-readiness skills more than teacher- or locally developed curriculum approaches.

However, as discussed previously, the curriculum studies varied in multiple ways besides the treatment contrast investigated by Jenkins et al. (2018). If the type of treatment–control contrasts covaried with other setting characteristics (including the type of preschool setting, the fidelity of curriculum implementation), it may be difficult to make definitive conclusions about why these effects differed. As such, while post hoc approaches such as meta-analysis allow the researcher to explore and disentangle various predictors of effect variation, these analyses cannot allow us to definitively point to the "cause" of why curriculum effects varied, nor is it possible to separate whether multiple sources of variation produce differential effects simultaneously. For example, it may be possible that the effectiveness of different types of curriculum approaches vary by the type of preschool program that it is delivered under and for different types of children enrolled in the program. To make such a conclusion would require prospective research designs that intentionally vary multiple systematic sources of effect variation.

REPRESENTING SOURCES OF EFFECT HETEROGENEITY FOR GENERALIZED FINDINGS

The goal to identify what works under what conditions and for whom is not a new initiative in education research or in the evaluation of pre-K curriculum. Given the diversity in settings, populations, and conditions under which pre-K curriculum can be delivered, there is an intense desire to understand the extent to which and why curriculum effects vary. To address these concerns, IES introduced the Standards for Excellence in Education Research (SEER) in 2019, encouraging researchers to begin identifying the conditions under which intervention effects are generated. SEER asked grant recipients to specify intervention components, document the treatment implementation and contrast, and take steps to facilitate the generalization of study findings. The reasoning here was that it is difficult to identify sources of effect heterogeneity—even as correlational relationships—when it is unclear what the effects themselves represent. In its 2022 review of IES's work, the National Academies of Sciences, Engineering, and Medicine recommended that the agency prioritize the funding of studies to understand the extent to which intervention effects vary and that it begin to identify sources of effect variation. The preschool evaluation literature also calls for researchers to characterize and understand the extent to which intervention effects vary (National Academies for Sciences, Engineering, and Medicine, 2022).

CONCLUSION

Evidence about curriculum effectiveness is a central issue for the consideration of quality. Despite broad-based agreement by researchers and funders that understanding sources of effect heterogeneity is important for evidence-based decision making, the evidence on curriculum effectiveness often falls short of achieving these goals. The prior section described challenges that researchers face in understanding sources of effect variation. Results from individual studies—even large-scale, multisite trials—are often underpowered for detecting and testing for treatment effect variation (Sabol et al., 2022). In cases where results from multiple studies are combined, such as in a meta-analysis, it may be difficult to interpret the synthesized findings because individual study results may represent different populations, contexts, settings, and outcomes that are not well understood by the meta-analyst and reader. Even when multiple curriculum evaluation studies are planned and conducted in coordinated ways—such as in the PCER study—it may be difficult for researchers to understand and disentangle why effects differed across studies, given the multiple sources of effect variation that occurred simultaneously.

Data and quantitative and qualitative methods are needed to describe the rich contextual experiences for how preschool curricula are implemented and delivered, as are new analytic methods for examining and describing variations in effects. Ideally, evidence generated using these methods would

- accurately and reliably represent children's skills and knowledge, regardless of their cultural background, language, and abilities;
- represent curriculum—and curriculum components—that are feasible and desirable for delivery in real-world settings and compatible with the goals and objectives of educators and program administrators who select the curriculum; and
- employ methods and study design features to identify programmatic factors that moderate curriculum effectiveness.

Because effectiveness is determined by comparing outcomes from children participating in the curriculum with outcomes obtained from an alternative condition, it is crucial that comparisons represent conditions that program administrators, educators, and parents are also likely to face. Moreover, high-quality teaching requires that educators are responsive to the dynamic and individual needs of children in their classrooms, so adaptations from curriculum materials are likely to occur. Study findings that are informed by an understanding of how the curriculum was delivered in real-world settings, and the extent to which deviations occurred from the intended protocols for the intervention and comparison conditions can provide valuable insights on effectiveness. The issue then is how researchers should carry out a research agenda that addresses the evolving needs of a diverse early childhood education landscape. The future research agenda described in Chapter 10 of this report highlights three areas of work needed to support such a research endeavor.

REFERENCES

Bloom, H. S., & Michalopoulos, C. (2013). When is the story in the subgroups? Strategies for interpreting and reporting intervention effects for subgroups. *Prevention Science: The Official Journal of the Society for Prevention Research, 14*(2), 179–188. https://doi.org/10.1007/s11121-010-0198-x

Campbell D. T., & Stanley, J. C. (1963). Experimental and quasi-experimental designs for research on teaching. In N. L. Gage (Ed.), *Handbook of research on teaching* (pp. 171–246). Rand McNally.

Cronbach, L. J. (1982). In praise of uncertainty. *New Directions for Program Evaluation, 1982*(15), 49–58. https://doi.org/10.1002/ev.1310

Duncan, G. J., & Magnuson, K. (2013). Investing in preschool programs. *Journal of Economic Perspectives, 27*(2), 109–132. https://doi.org/10.1257/jep.27.2.109

Fraker, T., & Maynard, R. (1987). The adequacy of comparison group designs for evaluations of employment-related programs. *Journal of Human Resources, 22*(2), 194–227. https://doi.org/10.2307/145902

Imai, K., King, G., & Stuart, E. A. (2008). Misunderstandings between experimentalists and observationalists about causal inference. *Journal of the Royal Statistical Society Series A: Statistics in Society, 171*(2), 481–502. https://doi.org/10.1111/j.1467-985x.2007.00527.x

Jenkins, J. M., Duncan, G. J., Auger, A., Bitler, M., Domina, T., & Burchinal, M. (2018). Boosting school readiness: Should preschool teachers target skills or the whole child? *Economics of Education Review, 65*, 107–125. https://doi.org/10.1016/j.econedurev.2018.05.001

LaLonde, R. (1986). Evaluating the econometric evaluations of training with experimental data. *American Economic Review, 76*(4), 604–620. http://www.jstor.org/stable/1806062

Morris, P. A., Connors, M., Friedman-Krauss, A., McCoy, D. C., Weiland, C., Feller, A., Page, L., Bloom, H., & Yoshikawa, H. (2018). New findings on impact variation from the Head Start Impact Study: Informing the scale-up of early childhood programs. *AERA Open, 4*(2). https://doi.org/10.1177/2332858418769287

National Academies of Sciences, Engineering, and Medicine. (2022). *The future of education research at IES: Advancing an equity-oriented science.* The National Academies Press. https://doi.org/10.17226/26428

Preschool Curriculum Evaluation Research Consortium (PCER). (2008). *Effects of preschool curriculum programs on school readiness* (NCER No. 2008-2009). National Center for Education Research, Institute of Education Sciences, U.S. Department of Education. https://ies.ed.gov/ncer/pubs/20082009/pdf/20082009_1.pdf

Rubin, D. B. (1981). Estimation in parallel randomized experiments. *Journal of Educational Statistics, 6*(4), 377–401. https://doi.org/10.3102/10769986006004377

Sabol, T. J., McCoy, D., Gonzalez, K., Miratrix, L., Hedges, L., Spybrook, J. K., & Weiland, C. (2022). Exploring treatment impact heterogeneity across sites: Challenges and opportunities for early childhood researchers. *Early Childhood Research Quarterly, 58*, 14–26. https://doi.org/10.1016/j.ecresq.2021.07.005

Schauer, J. M., & Hedges, L. V. (2021). Reconsidering statistical methods for assessing replication. *Psychological Methods, 26*(1), 127–139. https://doi.org/10.1037/met0000302

Shadish, W. R., Cook, T. D., & Campbell, D. T. (2002). *Experimental and quasi-experimental designs for generalized causal inference.* Houghton, Mifflin and Company.

Spybrook, J., Kelcey, B., & Dong, N. (2016). Power for detecting treatment by moderator effects in two- and three-Level cluster randomized trials. *Journal of Educational and Behavioral Statistics, 41*(6), 605–627. https://doi.org/10.3102/1076998616655442

Steiner, P. M., Wong, V. C., & Anglin, K. (2019). A causal replication framework for designing and assessing replication efforts. *Zeitschrift für Psychologie, 227*(4), 280–292. https://doi.org/10.1027/2151-2604/a000385

Stuart, E. A., Cole, S. R., Bradshaw, C. P., & Leaf, P. J. (2011). The use of propensity scores to assess the generalizability of results from randomized trials. *Journal of the Royal Statistical Society Series A: Statistics in Society, 174*(2), 369–386. https://doi.org/10.1111/j.1467-985X.2010.00673.x

Tefera, A. A., Powers, J. M., & Fischman, G. E. (2018). Intersectionality in education: A conceptual aspiration and research imperative. *Review of Research in Education, 42*(1), vii–xvii. https://doi.org/10.3102/0091732X18768504

Tipton, E. (2012). Improving generalizations from experiments using propensity score subclassification. *Journal of Educational and Behavioral Statistics, 38*(3), 239–266. https://doi.org/10.3102/1076998612441947

Tipton, E. (2021). Beyond generalization of the ATE: Designing randomized trials to understand treatment effect heterogeneity. *Journal of the Royal Statistical Society Series A: Statistics in Society, 184*(2), 504–521. https://doi.org/10.1111/rssa.12629

Tipton, E., & Olsen, R. B. (2018). A review of statistical methods for generalizing from evaluations of educational interventions. *Educational Researcher, 47*(8), 516–524. https://doi.org/10.3102/0013189X18781522

Tipton, E., & Olsen, R. B. (2022). *Enhancing the generalizability of impact studies in education* (NCEE No. 2022-003). U.S. Department of Education, Institute of Education Sciences, National Center for Education Evaluation and Regional Assistance. https://files.eric.ed.gov/fulltext/ED617445.pdf

Tipton, E., Spybrook, J., Fitzgerald, K. G., Wang, Q., & Davidson, C. (2020). Toward a system of evidence for all: Current practices and future opportunities in 37 randomized trials. *Educational Researcher, 50*(3), 145–156. https://doi.org/10.3102/0013189x20960686

Wong, V. C., Steiner, P. M., & Anglin, K. L. (2018). What can be learned from empirical evaluations of nonexperimental methods? *Evaluation Review, 42*(2), 147–175. https://doi.org/10.1177/0193841X18776870

10

Conclusions, Recommendations, and Research Needs

Early childhood is a period of great developmental change that sets the foundation for all later learning and development. High-quality preschool is a key context for these developmental changes. However, as characterized throughout the report, early childhood education in the United States has been fragmented, leading to highly varied educational experiences for children. The early education system has not adequately accounted for the diverse voices, experiences, strengths, needs, and lived realities of all children, their families, and the early education workforce. With decades of research in early education showing significant effects of curricula on teaching and learning, there is a need for high-quality curricula to be grounded in strong evidence. This committee was tasked with articulating a new vision for high-quality preschool curriculum with special attention to the needs of Black, Latine, and Indigenous children; multilingual learners; children with disabilities; and children experiencing poverty.

As a part of conceptualizing a new approach to high-quality and equitable experiences for all children, it is crucial to reimagine the preschool curriculum. Many public programs are using curricula that do not meet the needs of all children. There is compelling evidence that access to high-quality early learning experiences may be limited and inadequate based on factors such as a child's race, location, gender, home language, disability status, and socioeconomic status. It is crucial to recognize that these characteristics themselves are not the cause of differences in experiences. Rather, differences in experiences stem from broader structural factors (e.g., resource inequity, discriminatory policies, biased interactions) that perpetuate disparate outcomes.

Forming a vision for high-quality curriculum that supports equity is a highly creative, complex endeavor in which multiple demands must be met and multiple resources used. The committee had to consider program quality—which encompasses structural aspects such as teacher–child ratios, teacher education and certification, and teacher compensation, as well as process quality—such as use of evidence-based curricula, the linguistic richness of teacher–child interactions, and teachers' consistent emotional responsiveness to all children. These dimensions of quality are interconnected and influenced by other systemic factors, such as funding and policy actions. Underinvestment in expanding access to high-quality experiences creates a barrier that often leaves even eligible children underserved and affects families from marginalized communities disproportionality.

To achieve this new vision, the committee considered a rich tapestry of factors that undergird curriculum effectiveness. These factors include the written content of the curriculum itself, including the learning theories underlying curricular approaches and adaptations available; cultural and linguistic appropriateness; the learning environments in which the curriculum will be delivered; supports and resources for teachers, including professional learning experiences (including preservice education and ongoing professional development), workplace culture, and teacher wellness; and the systems and policies in place, including drivers that influence policy makers.

Most important and central to these factors and to the vision is the child. The committee emphasizes the importance of every child being able to access and experience early learning environments that promote joy, affirmation, and enriching learning opportunities; protect them from stress and adversity; and prepare them for success in school and life. The preschool curriculum is a critical tool for ensuring that children are in early learning environments that meet these expectations. To ensure that children have the opportunity to thrive, it is crucial to acknowledge and understand the detrimental effects of inequities and adversities on children's minds and lives. This report presents evidence and examples of researched and other promising curricula, instructional strategies, and pedagogy that recognize and affirm children's cultural and linguistic strengths, which play a critical role in promoting their social and academic potential. The committee's vision for high-quality preschool curricula is characterized in Box 10-1.

KEY CONCLUSIONS AND RECOMMENDATIONS

The committee's statement of task did not include evaluation or rating of existing curricula against the criteria outlined in the committee's vision. The committee's key conclusions and recommendations are directly aligned with specific questions outlined in the study's charge and fall across the following

> **BOX 10-1**
> **Vision for High-Quality Preschool Curricula**
>
> The committee's vision for high-quality preschool curricula aims to fulfill the promise of an education that fosters holistic and healthy development and learning for every child, regardless of place or socioeconomic status, and affirms children's full identities, including race, culture, home language, gender, and ability. It is grounded in an equity and justice-oriented perspective from inception to implementation and evaluation, and therefore is designed with an understanding of the diverse contexts of children's development, including adverse and traumatic conditions. Curricula aligned with the committee's vision would:
>
> - incorporate the perspectives, experiences, cultures, languages, strengths, and needs of a diverse range of children, families, and workforce settings;
> - include rich and meaningful content that centers child engagement and agency;
> - include well-designed learning experiences, intentional responsive teaching strategies, well-defined objectives and outcomes, embedded formative assessments, and differentiation based on understanding children's ability levels, cultural and linguistic backgrounds, interests, and dispositions;
> - have a scope and sequence that follow children's ways of thinking and learning with research-validated learning trajectories, are culturally and linguistically affirming, and include effective supports for children with disabilities; and
> - demonstrate effectiveness in yielding positive school and life outcomes for the children and families they are intended to reach.
>
> Importantly, the committee recognizes that attention is also needed for issues of implementation and continuous quality improvement within a broader system. Curriculum in and of itself will not solve the deep, intractable challenges faced in early education from inadequate funding, inadequate wages, uneven workforce preparation and supports, and growing issues with staff recruitment and retention, to larger social and economic inequities. However, curricula can play a critical role in ensuring that, in spite of these systemic challenges, children, through their interactions with teachers, other adults, and peers in the learning environment will experience safe, healthy, affirming, and enriching learning opportunities that promote lifelong success.

four categories: (1) guidance for the content design, development, selection, implementation, and formative and summative evaluation of high-quality, equity-driven curriculum; (2) supports and professional development needed for equitable and effective curriculum implementation; (3) funding mechanisms, state and federal policies, and innovations to support the selection and use of effective and equitable preschool curricula; and (4) creation of an evidence base to advance curriculum development and implementation.

For each of these categories, the committee briefly summarized the findings from the chapters that support the committee's key conclusions and recommendations. These recommendations are followed by a research agenda focused on addressing current gaps in understanding the components, criteria, and features of high-quality preschool curricula.

Given the interdependency of the recommendations and recognizing the iterative and ongoing nature of implementation, the committee's stance is to align with the principles of continuous improvement models (Figure 10-1), to enable refining and formulating effective implementation strategies. In addition, the committee acknowledges the potential challenges in implementing some recommendations simultaneously. A continuous improvement framework can help surface important outcomes for measures that are in development, which can then be incorporated into the curriculum. Moreover, the staging of implementation may differ based on the needs identified by programs and states.

Such models offer a well-established approach for programs and localities to coordinate and optimize the effectiveness of their improvement efforts by understanding their specific needs and circumstances, eliminating ineffective practices, prioritizing the needs of underserved populations, and strategically planning and implementing curricula that meet the needs of the children and communities they serve. Making progress will

FIGURE 10-1 A continuous improvement model for advancing implementation of the committee's recommendations.
SOURCE: Committee generated.

also necessitate robust ongoing evaluation of successful and unsuccessful strategies to inform the identification of future needs. This process can help create a multidimensional improvement framework encompassing the holistic development of the child, the specifics of the program setting, and the broader sociocultural context of the community to guide future iterations.

Equity-Driven Preschool Curricula: Guidance for Content Design, Development, Selection, and Implementation

The preschool years are a sensitive period for establishing robust foundational skills that can significantly impact developmental trajectories. Throughout their early years, children's diverse lived experiences and family contexts profoundly shape how and what they learn, and their environments serve as rich sources of learning. These experiences can also provide insights for identifying curricular needs across diverse settings.

Throughout the report, the committee has presented robust evidence that access to high-quality early learning experiences is essential for children's development, yielding important academic and lifelong outcomes. Curriculum has emerged as an important component with the potential to positively impact instructional quality; classroom processes; and early learning for children, including those from minoritized backgrounds. Chapter 2 presents the evidence on what is known about the effects of preschool curriculum, noting a tension between the curricula that are predominantly used in preschool programs and those that have shown positive impacts on children's learning in targeted outcome domains. Evidence suggests that systematically combining different evidence-based, domain-specific curricula or integrating domain-specific curricula into comprehensive curriculum to support all domains of children's learning may yield promising impacts on children's learning. These findings highlight the need for a vision for developing new and refining existing curricula (as articulated in Box 10-1).

In developing curriculum, it is important to consider the science of early childhood learning and development, in addition to neurobiological and sociobehavioral research; these studies provide nuanced understanding of the influences of early life experiences on early childhood development and brain development. Chapter 3 characterizes this research to illustrate how it can lead to the construction of psychologically safe spaces that promote positive learning outcomes and success in school and life. The chapter also emphasizes the significance of the preschool years as a highly sensitive period of opportunity for enhanced learning and development; the inherent benefits of learning; and the importance of nurturing, responsive, and supportive early caregiving environments.

For children facing limited access to stimulating environments and positive experiential inputs, the preschool years can be a time of heightened vulnerability and missed opportunities, potentially leading to disparate outcomes in later years.

Given the evidence presented throughout the report, it is clear that curriculum significantly affects teaching and learning. Curriculum can support teachers' acquisition of content knowledge and ability to implement new approaches that support children's learning. Developing high-quality curricula is an opportunity to help educators support the learning and development of all children and leverage the varied contexts and experiences that shape children's learning and development. High-quality early childhood curricula must be equitable; individually, culturally, and linguistically affirming; supportive; and interactive. The evidence presented in Chapter 4 provides a framework for the development of research-based and empirically validated curricula and points to the essential components and characteristics of equitable preschool curriculum based on the most robust available evidence of the efficacy of existing curricula, starting with the need to reject the false dichotomies that have plagued the field. The key characteristics of high-quality, equity-driven preschool curriculum (elaborated on in earlier chapters) include research- and evidence-based child outcomes; scope and sequence; a focus spanning developmental domains and content areas or coherently incorporated domain-specific curriculum; content and learning domains that are covered in depth; clearly defined and specific developmentally appropriate learning goals; well-designed learning experiences and interactions; an emphasis on responsive, intentional teaching; guidance for preparing developmentally appropriate, engaging learning environments, materials, and schedules; support for culturally relevant, responsive, and sustaining teaching and learning; support for multilingual learners and various language systems; individuation and effective supports for children with identified disabilities; supports for individualized instruction for every child; supports for family engagement; ongoing assessment tools and strategies aligned with goals and experiences; and professional development.

Creating curricula that attend to each child's needs and foster their strengths does not necessitate a fully differentiated approach. By definition, well-constructed curricula offer inherent benefits for a broad spectrum of learners. However, children with specific needs and strengths, such as multilingual learners (Chapter 7) and those with disabilities (Chapter 6), may require additional support and adaptations. The key lies in striking a balance between core elements that benefit all children and intentional design features created, and included from inception, to address the unique needs of diverse learners. Research, grounded in rigorous, asset-based, and community-rooted principles, can provide the knowledge and resources necessary to guide the development and revision of curricula and expand the availability of curricula that incorporate these features.

Conclusions

Based on these findings, the committee concluded:

Conclusion 1: To create psychologically safe spaces that promote positive learning outcomes and success in school and life, it is vital to support holistic, healthy development and enable children to realize their potential by leveraging their assets and building on their prior knowledge—which is a product of their cultural and linguistic experiences at home and in their communities.

Conclusion 2: Learning is shaped by the interaction between the biological processes involved in brain development and early life experiences, including those with adults, other children, and the broader environment. Such interactions are embedded within social, cultural, and linguistic contexts. Children learn in a multiplicity of ways, including child-initiated and teacher-guided play, exploration, observation, social engagement, intentional teaching in small and large groups, individual hands-on experiences, and other pedagogy that is responsive to their strengths and interests.

Conclusion 3: In the development and evaluation of preschool curricula, it is important to include efforts to identify and reject long-held biases, deficit framings, and/or stereotyped assumptions about children from racially, culturally, and linguistically minoritized communities, as well as children with disabilities and children experiencing poverty.

Conclusion 4: Evidence-based preschool curriculum that is well implemented has been shown to help promote equitable outcomes in mathematics, language, literacy, and social-emotional skills seen at kindergarten entry, particularly for children living in poverty and Black and Latine children. However, studies have generally not assessed curriculum effects on home language development for multilingual learners.

Conclusion 5: A preschool curriculum that provides guidance for content-specific teaching, rich and varied learning experiences, and supports for all aspects of children's development (including linguistic and cultural adaptations) will likely be most effective in improving child outcomes. Some localities have created such curricula with promising impacts, largely by systematically combining different evidence-based, domain-specific curricula or integrating domain-specific curricula into a comprehensive curriculum to support all domains of children's learning.

Conclusion 6: Early childhood leaders and practitioners typically use comprehensive preschool curricula that are intended to address all domains of children's learning and development and are required by their funding agencies. When compared with domain-specific curricula, the most widely used comprehensive curricula have shown significantly smaller gains in domain-targeted outcomes, such as mathematics, science, literacy, and social-emotional development at kindergarten entry. There has been little evidence of differential effectiveness for nontargeted domains. Much of this research has been conducted in Head Start and other public programs serving children from marginalized groups, including children from families with low income, multilingual learners, and Black and Latine children.

Conclusion 7: Nearly one-third of young children growing up in the United States are growing up with exposure to more than one language in the home and could be considered multilingual. Research has shown that the most effective language model for multilingual learners teaches them English systematically while actively supporting their home language development. Full proficiency in more than one language is associated with cognitive, cultural, social, and economic benefits. However, most states, school districts, and local programs have yet to develop a procedure for accurately identifying preschool multilingual learners, rarely provide dual language instruction, and have few bilingual early childhood educators qualified to support home language development or provide dual language instruction. Additional research, materials, professional development, and multilingual educators can support the realization of the new vision.

Conclusion 8: Although family child care settings enroll a small proportion of children overall, they enroll a larger proportion of children from racially and linguistically marginalized populations, children from rural communities, and children from families experiencing poverty. Mixed-age programs are also common in family child care settings. However, few commercially available preschool curricula are designed for family child care settings, and few offer guidance in adapting curriculum or sequencing content for mixed-age groups.

Recommendations

Based on these conclusions, the committee makes the following recommendations:

Recommendation 1: In the next 5 years, federal agencies, state and school district policy makers, foundations and funders, publishers, and teacher educators should support the revision of existing curricula and development of new curricula to align with the committee's vision. These curricula should be developed or revised by collaborative teams of researchers, curriculum developers, teacher educators, and practitioners—informed by the needs of children, families, and communities—following equity-based and rigorous, empirically driven, iterative design and evaluation processes as described in this report.

Recommendation 2: In the next 5 years, program leaders should transition to adopting and implementing evidence-validated curricula that, when integrated coherently, support the learning and development of the whole child. Essential features of evidence-based curricula include developmentally appropriate learning goals, a scope and sequence, coherent alignment with specific domains, and rich content.

Recommendation 3: In the next 5 years, researchers and curriculum developers should (1) develop and evaluate appropriate criteria and metrics for assessing racial, cultural, linguistic, and ability bias in curricula; (2) continually review curricula for these potential racial, cultural, linguistic, and ability biases; and (3) develop and provide adaptations and revisions so that the curricula are culturally and linguistically responsive and foster an anti-bias, anti-racist, multilingual, and inclusive approach in early childhood education.

Recommendation 4: From the outset, curriculum developers, in partnership with researchers and teacher educators, should develop curricula and supporting materials in Spanish, English, and other languages commonly spoken by children with a home language other than English. Whenever possible, curriculum developers should include adaptations for other language groups and those who speak dialects of English, such as African American English; they should also consider the unique approach warranted in Indigenous communities that are invested in language revitalization and maintenance.

Recommendation 5: In the next 5 years, funders should support the development of new, or revision of existing, child assessment measures aligned with the committee's vision. These assessment measures should be both formative and summative, should consider the role of bias (e.g., race, language, culture, disability status) in assessment, and should capture the full range of meaningful child outcomes and experiences (i.e., including positive social-emotional development, positive racial identity for children of color, and bilingualism/biliteracy for multilingual learners).

Empowering Educators: Supports and Professional Development for Equitable and Effective Curriculum Implementation

Educators play a central role in facilitating connections between children, families, and curricular content. Supporting the professional needs of this crucial workforce is critical to ensure high-quality, equitable learning experiences for all children. Chapter 5 highlights the need to provide educators with the professional development and supports required for cultivating warm and affirming relationships with children, to ensure inclusive and prosocial peer interactions, and to provide consistent and proactive management of the overall classroom environment—all of which are integral elements of curriculum reform. Evidence shows that positive relationships with teachers and supportive classroom management practices can help mitigate stressful encounters that children might have with their peers, which can diminish children's sense of safety and their capacity and motivation to learn—factors that can affect the implementation of even the best-designed curricula. Educators need time and support to develop skills and expertise across various content areas, to develop reciprocal and engaged partnerships between families and educators (as discussed throughout this report), and to deepen expertise in culturally responsive teaching and professional learning opportunities to recognize potential biases.

As noted earlier in this chapter and in Chapter 2, because of the fragmentation of the early learning landscape in the United States, the current early childhood education workforce has a wide variety of professional development and qualifications. Moreover, the committee notes that, in order to cultivate advancements in child learning, preschool curriculum must be able to be implemented with high fidelity by teachers with a wide range of preparation and skills. However, systemic underinvestment and inconsistent early education policies are a persistent barrier to fostering a workforce that is knowledgeable, skilled, and empowered to support the learning and development of young children. It is critical for teacher preparation programs to articulate and embed qualifications that would allow educators to develop the knowledge base to effectively educate young multilingual learners (see Chapter 7) and increase attention on supporting the individual development and learning of children with disabilities, helping them achieve the goals in their individualized education programs and helping teachers embrace inclusion with a sense of efficacy (see Chapter 6). Evidence highlights the need for educative curricula for the early childhood workforce, which will require effort on the part of curriculum developers to build in specific content and structures, including domain content; consider how children think and learn about that content; and develop pedagogical strategies to support children's thinking and learning. Using educative curriculum materials can foster change in the broader educational system and in professional development in particular (see Chapter 4).

The committee emphasizes that the well-being of educators extends beyond professional development and coaching to include psychosocial, economic, and job-related supports, as well as their ability to cope with high levels of stress, which can influence attention, classroom management, quality of instruction, and their own ability to manage implicit bias (see Chapter 5). Both systemic and personal approaches to support educator well-being are necessary, including efforts to align the complexity, skill level, and essential nature of educating young children with the wages and other rewards provided to this essential workforce.

Professional development and coaching focused on curricula need to embrace the larger context in which educators teach and children learn. Specific education and coaching on scaffolding of inclusive and prosocial peer interactions; eliminating biases that undermine the development of close, affirming relationships with all children; and reliance on warm, consistent, and proactive classroom management strategies are essential to the effective delivery of equitable curriculum. The committee recognizes that implementing curriculum changes that foster the learning and development of diverse populations will be an iterative process that requires sustained commitment; collaboration with teacher educators; buy-in from teachers; provision of supports and professional development to facilitate implementation; ongoing assessment of progress; and further research on, and development of, research- and evidence-based curricula. Employing a continuous improvement model (Figure 10-1) may increase feasibility for program providers by encouraging ongoing refinement and adaptation to meet the needs of the communities they serve.

Conclusions

Based on these findings, the committee concluded:

Conclusion 9: Providing educators of young children with psychosocial, economic, and professional development supports is critical; however, the availability of such supports varies greatly based on funding streams and governing systems.

Conclusion 10: Educators of young children are not only intentional teachers but also sources of nurturance and security for children. The effective realization of these roles depends greatly on teachers' attention to fostering reciprocal and responsive relationships, examining and checking their biases, and cultivating a positive emotional environment, all of which affect the quality of the broader learning environment on which the provision of effective and equitable curricula depends.

Conclusion 11: Preschool programs generally offer children warm and emotionally supportive environments; however, some populations of young children, such as Black children and children who are multilingual learners, may experience various individual and systemic inequities (e.g., biased perceptions of behavior, assumptions about the value of languages other than English, conflictual teacher–child relationships). On average, preschool programs fall short in offering children rich content and in advancing children's thinking. This is especially true in mathematics, early language, literacy, science, and support for emerging multilingualism.

Conclusion 12: Strong connections between families and preschool staff are essential for understanding when and how to adapt preschool curricula to address the strengths and needs of children, in order to create a meaningful link between home and school experiences. Unfortunately, research continues to show that minoritized families, especially Black families and to some extent families that speak a language other than English, are less likely to report close relationships with teachers; likewise, teachers report less close and trusting relationships with them. Thus, it is important that curricula include guidance for educators focused on effective approaches and strategies to foster inclusive and culturally responsive home–school partnerships in support of children's learning.

Recommendations

Based on these conclusions, the committee makes the following recommendations:

Recommendation 6: Curriculum developers should incorporate resources and structures that help teachers gain knowledge about effective teaching strategies and practices, including bolstering content knowledge and understanding how children's thinking and learning can be best supported.

Recommendation 7: Early childhood educators should collaborate with families to co-construct curricular components that are meaningful and relevant for all children in the classroom; authentically elevate the role of families in supporting their children's development; recognize the diversity in and value of family practices and integrate these practices when possible; honor their languages, cultures, beliefs, traditions, and talents; and invite these assets into the classroom.

Recommendation 8: Program leaders and policy makers should ensure that educators receive professional development, regular in-classroom coaching, and access to materials tied to the implementation of evidence-based curricula, including supports for delivering curricula in children's home language alongside English, or for monolingual English-speaking teachers, supporting multilingual learners through cross-linguistic connections and other research-informed practices that bridge languages.

Recommendation 9: Curriculum developers should provide scaffolded supports,[1] developed in partnership with researchers and teacher educators, that increase opportunities for effectively integrating children with disabilities in general education early childhood settings while effectively meeting their unique developmental needs and fostering healthy peer relationships.

Investing in Equity: Funding Mechanisms, Policy Strategies, and Innovations to Support Selection and Implementation of Effective Preschool Curricula

Underpinning the committee's vision (Box 10-1) is the imperative to increase capacity for implementing and sustaining equitable access to high-quality preschool curricula in high-quality programmatic settings. The early childhood system is greatly varied with a diversity of program types—each governed by policies, regulations, quality standards, and funding streams that can differ both across and within states. While program administrators and educators retain some flexibility in selecting curricula, families and educators often possess limited direct influence over standards development, potentially hindering responsiveness to diverse needs.

Successfully expanding access to positive early childhood experiences also requires a nuanced understanding of community needs. As emphasized throughout this report, both community engagement and the holistic needs of the child need to be central tenets when implementing policy and

___
[1] Scaffolding is the process through which instructional supports are added to facilitate mastery of tasks by building on existing knowledge. As tasks are mastered, these supports can be adjusted and eventually removed.

programmatic changes. While high-quality early childhood education programs and access to high-quality curricula are demonstrably linked to long-term benefits across various life domains, research also exposes inequities in access and outcomes. Children from marginalized communities—including children of color, multilingual learners, children with disabilities, and children from low-income households—consistently experience less access to high-quality learning opportunities compared with their middle-class, White peers, highlighting the early education system's shortcomings in realizing its full potential for all.

Improving supports for curriculum implementation can help ensure equitable access to high-quality preschool curricula (see Chapter 8). Fidelity of implementation remains a critical factor often overlooked in state-funded programs. Effective assessment practices, integrated into daily routines and used for continuous improvement and collaboration, can significantly enhance outcomes across all levels, from individual children to families, classrooms, and broader systems. Furthermore, families play a crucial role in bolstering both assessment and instruction. Integrated assessment strategies that involve parents, families, and caregivers can foster meaningful teacher–family partnerships. These partnerships provide valuable insights into children's strengths, historical context, and cultural background, ultimately informing effective instructional learning strategies that promote all children's learning and development.

A key challenge in moving the field forward toward the committee's new vision is utilizing existing policy levers that can help shift choice and use of curricula to those that are aligned with the evidence base (e.g., providing public funding to incentivize developing and using evidence-based curricula, shifting regulations to allow and eventually require use of evidence-based curricula in public preschool programs). Expanding access to high-quality preschool experiences is a multifaceted endeavor that will include establishing a robust infrastructure for continuous assessment, monitoring, and improvement, as well as funding research on curriculum development and optimal program practices; creating and enhancing workforce support and development; and promoting widespread adoption of high-quality, evidence-based curricula.

Conclusions

Based on these findings, the committee concluded

Conclusion 13: To expand access to high-quality early educational experiences, there is a significant need for infrastructure to support the development, implementation, and evaluation of curricula and to encourage adoption of new or revised curricula that align with the committee's vision. This includes collaboration between researchers and practitioners, data collection that captures characteristics of the populations being served and the curricula being used in the programs children attend, quality measures that capture the strengths and lived experiences of all children, and professional development and supports for practitioners.

Conclusion 14: *High turnover rates are prevalent in the field of early education. Providing educators with the financial security and benefits that promote their physical and mental health is necessary for supporting the implementation of high-quality, equitable curriculum and maintaining a diverse, well-qualified workforce that is large enough to meet the demand of families for high-quality educational experiences for young children. Ongoing data collection is critical to assessing and addressing the needs of educators, programs, and the families and communities they serve.*

Recommendations

Based on these conclusions, the committee makes the following recommendations:

Recommendation 10: The U.S. Department of Education, in partnership with the U.S. Department of Health and Human Services and state early childhood education agencies, should

- create a research-practice-partnership network of diverse researchers and early childhood programs that are willing to engage in research to study curricula and practices aligned with the committee's vision;
- create a data system for capturing details on curricula being used in programs, along with characteristics of the children being served, the quality of programs, and a comprehensive set of outcomes;
- align quality metrics, measures, and rating systems with the new vision of curricula and associated practices;
- incentivize the adoption and use of high-quality curricula that align with the new vision; and
- provide quality improvement supports and resources for addressing equity and inclusion gaps.

Recommendation 11: As curricula aligned with the committee's vision are adopted and implemented, state and local early care and education agencies and public education institutions should develop policies, provide technical assistance, and target funding to support ongoing professional development for educators that aligns with the vision, as well as strong curriculum implementation, with strategies and resources for addressing the high staffing turnover rates experienced across the country in early childhood programs.

Recommendation 12: As curricula aligned with the committee's vision are adopted and implemented, state and local early care and education agencies and public education institutions should identify opportunities to expand children's access to schools, communities, and programs that implement these curricula and associated practices.

Bridging the Knowledge Gap: Creating an Evidence Base to Advance Curriculum Development and Implementation

Building on findings discussed earlier in this chapter, the committee underscores the continued necessity of improving the evidence base for curriculum efficacy across diverse populations. Establishing an evidence base that demonstrates effectiveness in varied contexts is key to realizing the committee's vision. Critical questions remain unanswered. For example, more research is needed to explore the effectiveness of culturally and linguistically responsive curricula. Additionally, limited research exists on the impact of curricula within diverse early childhood settings, such as family child care, for-profit organizations, charter schools, and faith-based institutions, as well as on less commonly assessed child outcomes such as creativity, problem solving, positive racial identity development, inclusive social skills, and the language development of multilingual learners in both their home language and English.

Research on early care and education quality and on early childhood curriculum largely has developed in silos. As a result, little is known about the reciprocal relationship between the overall process and structural quality of the settings within which curriculum is delivered and features of curricula that support early learning for all children. Due to statistical power and sampling limitations, the evidence is also somewhat limited on whether specific curriculum show differential benefits by child characteristics, although some evidence suggests that some curricula have larger impacts for certain child subgroups compared with their peers. The committee's review of the literature found a need for evaluations of preschool quality and effectiveness that incorporate information about the curriculum used and its features with information about the broader learning environments in which the curriculum is being delivered and for which groups of children the curriculum is most effective. This is crucial, as equity must be considered in all phases of research and development (see Chapter 4).

CONCLUSIONS, RECOMMENDATIONS, AND RESEARCH NEEDS   393

Chapter 9 highlights the need for data, as well as qualitative and quantitative data collection methods, in order to describe the rich and complex landscape of how preschool curricula are implemented and delivered and to examine and understand variations in effects. Determining whether curricula are effective requires establishing valid comparisons of outcomes from children who are participating in the curriculum and those in alternative conditions (e.g., control groups). These comparisons must reflect real-world settings encountered by program administrators, educators, and parents. By accounting for these contextual nuances, research findings can provide more valuable insights into the true and generalizable effectiveness of a given curriculum.

Conclusions

Based on these findings, the committee concluded:

Conclusion 15: Additional research could help determine the contextual factors and child characteristics that affect the differential effectiveness of curriculum approaches and their implementation.

Conclusion 16: To date, most evaluation studies of curricula have not assessed important outcomes such as development of children's creativity, positive identity, curiosity, and emergent multilingualism. Moreover, limited evidence is available on the effects of curricula on child outcomes such as sense of belonging, agency, and group pride; evidence is also limited on how teachers' implicit and explicit biases affect curriculum implementation. Such evidence is needed to ensure that curricula meet the needs of the whole child.

Conclusion 17: Currently, preschool curricula give little attention to the inequitable impact of racism, English language learning status, and disability status. More research is needed to understand the role of preschool curricula in supporting children's intersectional identities, in order to promote justice through healthy child development, equitable outcomes, and school success.

Conclusion 18: Culturally relevant and sustaining curricula and teaching have been identified as supports for important aspects of development, such as positive identity and racial pride. Additional research is needed to guide the development and implementation of culturally and linguistically affirming, anti-bias curricula for preschool programs, as well as to evaluate existing curricula on these dimensions. This includes much-needed research on defining what specifically is included in culturally and linguistically affirming and anti-bias curricula, what is effective, and what should be measured as outcomes.

Conclusion 19: Curricula with scaffolded supports, targeted adaptations, and accommodation for children with disabilities are crucial for authentically, meaningfully, and effectively supporting the full inclusion of children with disabilities. Future research could inform the development and testing of curricula that are designed for inclusive settings to address identified instructional needs and support equitable access, experiences, and supports for young children identified with disabilities or developmental delays.

Recommendations

Based on these conclusions, the committee makes the following recommendations:

Recommendation 13: In the next 5 years, publishers should collect and provide rigorous and meaningful evidence of improved short- and long-term academic and developmental outcomes for all children, with particular attention to Black, Latine, Indigenous, Asian, and Pacific Islander children; multilingual learners; children with disabilities; and children living in poverty. They should also document the experiences of children in grades K–2 and determine whether there is coherence in the curricular vision across the transition from preschool to these early grades.

Recommendation 14: Researchers should continue to conduct rigorous evaluations of curriculum approaches, along with implementation research, to assess the extent to which curricula promote children's holistic and healthy development and learning, regardless of place or socioeconomic status, and affirm children's full identities, including race, culture, home language, gender, and ability.

Recommendation 15: To build the necessary evidence base over the next 5–10 years, relevant federal agencies, states, and philanthropies should invest in ongoing research aimed at developing implementation systems to support the transition to evidence-based curricula that are practical and accessible. These investments should

- ensure the representation of Black, Indigenous, Latine, Asian, and Pacific Islander children, multilingual learners, children with disabilities, and children living in poverty in study samples with explicit attention to their unique experiences;

- support implementation research that describes and identifies effective practices used by individual educators and programs for delivering and adapting curricula in ways that are culturally and linguistically responsive and relevant for children and families in their programs;
- support studies that compare different domain-specific combinations and outcomes beyond those traditionally used, in order to capture new understanding of what the term "whole child" encompasses in a diverse society (i.e., to capture culturally and linguistically affirming and anti-bias practices);
- expand measured child outcomes of interest to include multilingual development, sense of belonging, agency, group pride, curiosity, creativity, and problem solving, and expand teacher outcomes to include the reduction of implicit and explicit bias, effective teaching, and cultural and linguistic responsiveness; and
- launch a federal technical assistance center that is grounded in implementation science, is dedicated to supporting the development of new curricula and the adoption and implementation of evidence-based curricula, and includes supports for assessing fidelity.

RESEARCH AGENDA

A crucial component of reimagining preschool curricula is ensuring there is a solid evidence base supporting the new vision. The evidence on curriculum effectiveness must go beyond recognizing the "average effects" of the curriculum; it must also begin to identify the particular situations, conditions, and groups where a curriculum's impact may vary.

However, understanding variations in curriculum effectiveness requires new infrastructure supports, methods, and perspectives in how early childhood education researchers gather evidence. This section highlights the need for a comprehensive research agenda to gather evidence on this new vision for preschool curriculum. This includes (1) creating resources to better understand and document study conditions of curriculum effectiveness; (2) standardizing approaches for examining, reporting, and interpreting potential sources of curriculum effect heterogeneity; and (3) organizing large-scale studies that coordinate multiple teams of researchers to address questions of critical scientific and policy relevance.

Throughout this report, the committee has also identified topics or themes for additional research areas. Box 10-2 outlines these potential areas of inquiry that future researchers in early childhood education may undertake as they continue to develop, adapt, and evaluate curriculum approaches aligned with the new vision.

BOX 10-2
Themes for Additional Research

- **Equity:** More research is needed to ensure that research and development studies include adequately large samples of Black, Indigenous, and Latine children; multilingual learners; children with disabilities; and children living in poverty and incorporate knowledge from various cultures to ensure that effects can be determined for these groups.
- **Multilingual learners:** More research is needed to develop and evaluate non–English language and bilingual versions in multiple languages of curricula and resources for multilingual learners. This research also needs to be conducted in the context of different classroom language models.
- **Locally specific versus widely disseminated curricula:** More research is needed to address the tension between creating locally specific, culturally relevant curriculum that is adaptable but also can be widely disseminated. This includes research examining the specific features of widely used curricula and the adaptations needed for communities with diverse learners.
- **Curriculum standards:** More research is needed to help curriculum developers coherently incorporate preschool early learning standards to facilitate teacher implementation and positive student outcomes.
- **Systemic exclusion and bias:** More research is needed on the ways in which systemic exclusion and bias interferes with children's access to effective curricula.
- **Supports for successful curriculum implementation:** More research is needed on supports for successful implementation of preschool curricula, including integrated professional development and child assessment for data-driven instruction. Research incorporating families' and teachers' experiences with curriculum implementation is particularly needed.
  - Interventions for reducing biases: More research is needed on interventions for reducing biases among preschool-age children and their educators when evidence of racial, linguistic, or other types of prejudice exists. This research is particularly critical given the pervasiveness and enduring damage that racial discrimination causes.
  - Fidelity assessment: There is a need for both research-validated fidelity assessment tools that are curriculum specific and tools that can be used across different curricula to support successful curriculum implementation.
- **Collaboration among investigators:** More research is needed that prioritizes collaborations among investigators who study curriculum development and implementation and those addressing questions aimed at ensuring high-quality, equitable early education experiences for all children. Priority questions for such collaborative teams include the following:
  - Does the effectiveness with which specific curricula are delivered by teachers and received by children vary with specific features of the broader early care and education context, such as the baseline emotional climate and educators' behavior management strategies?
  - What is the threshold of quality below which effective curriculum delivery is seriously compromised?
  - What are the specific types and levels of educator professional development/education/skill needed for the successful implementation of particular curricula?

> **BOX 10-2 Continued**
>
> - **Family involvement in assessment:** More research is needed to understand how family members can be involved in assessment to provide insights into children's strengths and areas of development, as well as provide historical, contextual, cultural, and linguistic information. This research can help identify and reduce measurement biases that may occur because of cultural or linguistic experiences.
> - **Dialogue among teachers, students, and peers:** More research is needed to develop valid and reliable measures for constructs of interest for multilingual learners, children with disabilities, children from historically marginalized populations, and those living in poverty—at all levels, including child, classroom, and program.
> - **Expansion of outcome measurements:** More research is needed to develop valid and reliable outcome measures of constructs, such as engagement, agency, curiosity, creativity, positive identity, and enjoyment of school. These measures need to be developed with the goal of reducing overall burden of assessment for teachers, researchers, and children.

In this section, the committee proposes three recommendations for a future research agenda, with the overarching objective of reshaping the paradigm governing preschool curriculum. Each recommendation precedes a brief discussion on its content.

Research Agenda Recommendation 1: Develop resources to understand and document conditions in curriculum effectiveness studies.

Developing resources dedicated to describing and understanding the multifaceted conditions under which preschool curricula are most effective entails creating a comprehensive and nuanced understanding of the factors that influence curriculum effectiveness. To that end, interpreting results from curriculum evaluation studies necessitates a comprehensive understanding of the curriculum's structure, implementation method, the benchmark it was compared with, the metrics used for assessing effects, and the contextual elements that might influence the curriculum's impact. This understanding is crucial for the specific population the study aims to represent and the demographic the results intend to resonate with. Difficulties arise when the researcher is unaware of the context under which the curriculum's effects were produced or when these conditions are inadequately conveyed to the decision makers reviewing the findings. Three specific research supports, outlined below, are needed for describing and understanding contexts, conditions, and populations under which curriculum studies are conducted.

Adopt a Standardized Reporting Framework

An important first step toward understanding, documenting, and communicating the conditions producing these results is adopting a standardized framework. This framework needs to account for and report the curriculum condition and its components, the comparison against which it is being evaluated, and the relevant population and settings.

A unified framework for understanding curriculum effectiveness is essential for two primary reasons. First, when assessing "effective curriculum" evidence, educators and program administrators might be drawn toward results produced from a context similar to that of their students and community. They expect these findings to better apply to their demographic. Second, when combining multiple studies, as in a meta-analysis, researchers often investigate whether study features correlate with curriculum effect magnitude. However, inadequate reporting in individual studies often hinders such analyses. Hence, a standardized framework is indispensable for comparing and deciphering results from various studies and for harnessing the power of meta-analyses.

Promote Early Childhood Education Data Infrastructure

Researchers may face challenges in data collection or may employ metrics that challenge comparison with other studies. Therefore, early childhood data systems that chronicle children's development and influencing factors are vital. A 2018 survey revealed that only 20 states could link certain early childhood education program quality metrics or licensing data to child-level K–12 data (King et al., 2018). Integrated data systems grant a more comprehensive view of children's learning contexts and offer opportunities to monitor their development as they progress from preschool through the K–12 years, which enables investigation of long-term effects of preschool curricula.

Collaborate with Study Participants to Describe Study Conditions and Interpret Results

Study participants often possess insights not entirely captured by standard data collection methods. Hence, collaboration among researchers and participants is paramount. For instance, an effect attributed by researchers to a curriculum's vocabulary lessons might stem from teacher-initiated parental involvement in home reading sessions. As such, it is critical that researchers and community members engage as collaborators or research partners on studies, co-constructing the meaning and nature of the intervention and control conditions and the outcomes of interest for the community and its families, as well as identifying key contextual characteristics that may be important for mitigating the effects of the curriculum. Participants may have insights about the ways in which a curriculum—and the control condition it is being compared with—may or may not be relevant for the community. They may also have information about how educators and children engage with and interact with materials. Community participatory approaches and qualitative methods such as ethnographic observations, interviews, and focus groups may be useful for ensuring that the characteristics defined are of interest to both the researcher and stakeholders involved in the program.

Research Agenda Recommendation 2: Standardize approaches for examining, reporting, and interpreting potential sources of curriculum effect heterogeneity.

The second recommendation underscores the importance of standardizing research methodologies and approaches. By establishing uniformity in the evaluation of curriculum effects across diverse contexts and student populations, researchers can gain valuable insights into the extent of variability in curriculum effectiveness. Standardization not only enhances the reliability of research outcomes but also facilitates meaningful cross- and within-study comparisons, ultimately advancing the field's collective understanding.

In addition to providing more accurate descriptions of intervention conditions, populations, settings, and outcomes that are represented by specific study samples, early childhood education researchers need to employ consistent methods when analyzing and reporting sources of curriculum effect variation within individual studies. Commonly, the exploration of effect variation is done by observing moderator effects—indicating whether results vary statistically based on different subgroup characteristics. These analyses often involve separate examinations of subgroups, comparing their effects or undertaking analyses on the complete sample with interaction components allowing differences among groups.

One challenge for interpreting results from these analyses is that it requires adequate statistical power for detecting differences in effects across subgroups. Moreover, a review of evaluation studies funded by the Institute for Education Sciences found that many studies were underpowered for detecting moderator effects within studies, despite requirements in the Request for Applications that ask for researchers to specify hypotheses for exploring variations in effects. It is important to note that funding limitations may affect researchers' ability to have sufficient statistical power to detect moderator effects within studies, as large sample sizes needed for such disaggregation are often cost prohibitive for many research studies.

The committee's findings suggest that future curriculum evaluation studies need to be designed with adequate power to not detect only average effects, but also variation in effects across theoretically important subgroups and contexts.

In the committee's review of the pre-K curriculum literature for identifying moderator effects, the variation in how authors reported moderator effects was striking. In many papers, it was unclear how moderated effects were estimated, for which subgroups and populations the moderated effects were estimated, and the interpretation of results. Moderation effects were often presented as figures without accompanying tables for how differential effects were produced. Often, it was unclear how many and which moderation analyses were originally conducted. Given that the probability of detecting statistically significant moderator effects increases as the number of tests are increased, it is difficult to interpret the result of a significant moderator effect when the number of tests conducted is unknown. To facilitate the interpretation of results from moderation analyses, researchers need to adopt standardized approaches for planning and reporting their results.[2]

Research Agenda Recommendation 3: Adopt a collaborative science approach for addressing questions of critical scientific and policy relevance.

The committee's third research agenda recommendation promotes a collaborative scientific approach, advocating for interdisciplinary cooperation among researchers to address critical questions pertaining to preschool curriculum. This collaborative endeavor aims to ensure that research aligns with both scientific rigor and policy imperatives.

Knowledge about the contexts and conditions under which curricula are (or are not) effective can rarely be established with a single study. Repeated trials with systematic variations across studies are needed to build an evidence base on what works for whom and under what contexts. This implies that instead of generating evidence that is intended to be summarized as a single average effect, the goal is to generate evidence for multiple curriculum effects that are expected to vary according to systematic differences in population and contextual characteristics. Generating such

---

[2]In recent years, reporting guidelines, such as the SPIRIT (Standard Protocol Items: Recommendations for Interventional Trials) and CONSORT (Consolidated Standards of Reporting Trials) checklists, have been introduced to enhance transparency and reproducibility of findings from randomized controlled trials. These checklists provide resources for researchers to fully report their research activities, from the research questions and hypotheses for designing the study, to the methods used for estimating effects, to how results are reported.

evidence requires multiple teams of researchers working together in coordinated ways to produce multiple study effects. For such endeavors to be successful requires: (1) collaborative approaches for organizing and managing teams; (2) infrastructure supports to organize data collection efforts, resources, and tools for conducting research initiatives; and (3) statistical methods for planning and analyzing study results.

Collaborative Science

In recent years, team science has emerged as a strategy for researchers in multiple fields to collaborate to address complex challenges that could not be accomplished individually (e.g., Human Penguin project, Many Labs 2 project, Many Numbers project). The goal is to bring together collaborators with combined knowledge and expertise to address research questions of critical importance. This may include collaborators from different geographic spaces; they may also have expertise in different disciplines, fields, and professions, or represent different organizations, agencies, and perspectives. The structure of the collaborations can take many forms, involving pairs or small groups of collaborators working together on a multisite study or large networks of researchers working on the same topic.

Although coordinated teams are essential for addressing questions about variation in curriculum effects, these efforts may also increase the number of challenges that research teams must navigate, including open and efficient group communication and management, differences related to epistemological and methodological differences among team members, and challenges related to team members receiving appropriate recognition and compensation for their contributions. The Science of Team Science[3] is a new field of study focused on understanding and developing processes and tools that can promote positive outcomes for tools and mitigate the challenges that often arise. The Team Science Toolkit addresses multilevel influences for team success, including intra- and interpersonal relationships, processes for creating shared research protocols, data repositories, and analysis protocols, as well as infrastructures for supporting collaborative efforts, especially across multiple institutions.

Infrastructure Supports

Promoting effective team science approaches in preschool curriculum research requires investments that support the development, organization, and maintenance of such initiatives. Researchers and evaluators of

---

[3] See https://www.inscits.org/scits-a-team-science-resources

preschool curriculum need training and support in evidence-based practices for promoting effective team science. As research teams become more diverse, researchers must have the training, support, and time to communicate effectively with team members, to build trust among collaborators, and to ensure that everyone on the team is recognized for their work. Researchers also need training on new tools for managing large-scale data collection, and for processing and sharing data securely with collaborators. Given the logistical complexities for collecting data in preschool settings, repositories in which researchers can share resources, tools, and measures would reduce duplication of efforts and improve the transparency of results. For example, the Annenberg Institute's EdInstruments[4] is a repository for common measures used in education settings, and the Center for Open Science[5] includes repositories for researchers to upload and share preregistration plans, study protocols, and data.

Statistical Methods for Summarizing Effect

Results from collaborative efforts to evaluate curriculum effects may be synthesized through meta-analysis. Meta-analysis is a statistical technique for summarizing research results from multiple studies examining curriculum effectiveness. By combining findings from diverse studies, meta-analysis can provide a more encompassing and precise measure of the curriculum's impact (compared with looking at results from a single study). This synthesis process helps in spotting consistent trends, ensuring that educators and policy makers can draw more informed and generalizable conclusions.

However, while results from meta-analysis are often informative, they must be interpreted with caution because findings typically hinge on correlational data. For example, a correlation between curriculum dosage and specific student outcomes does not necessarily denote a causal relationship. Strong correlations, even if recurrent across multiple studies, can still be affected by external factors that were not addressed in the primary research. Moreover, the potential for publication bias, where studies with significant positive outcomes are favored over those with nonsignificant or negative outcomes, might skew the perceived effectiveness of a curriculum. The diversity in study quality and the variability in implementation and context among studies also need to be factored in, as insights from meta-analysis are tied directly to the quality of the individual studies included.

When researchers foresee the need for a meta-analysis, they can strategically design a series of studies to optimize the resultant combined findings. By orchestrating individual studies with a subsequent meta-analysis in view, they can ensure uniformity in study design, assessment tools, and

[4]See https://edinstruments.org/about
[5]See https://www.cos.io

reporting criteria. Such planning allows for systematic exploration of potential moderating effects. For instance, researchers might systematically introduce variations in curriculum delivery methods or contexts across different studies. When these intentionally designed studies are later merged in a meta-analysis, researchers are better positioned to discern how specific factors (such as classroom environment or teacher training) might amplify or diminish the curriculum's effectiveness.

By uniting the efforts of scholars from various disciplines and perspectives, as well as practitioners, families, and children, the research community can develop a more holistic understanding of curriculum effectiveness and its implications for equitable education. Collectively, these recommendations for a future research agenda contribute to the establishment of a transformative vision for preschool curriculum that centers on equity. The overarching goal is to guarantee that children of all backgrounds enjoy equal access to high-quality early learning experiences, fostering equitable educational outcomes.

CLOSING THOUGHTS

Early childhood education is not merely a stepping stone to kindergarten and further schooling; it is the bedrock upon which a child's intellectual, social, and emotional development is laid and holds transformative power. Nurturing young minds and fostering positive learning environments and experiences sets the stage for a lifetime of success. This calls for a continuous commitment to refining and improving early education practices, ensuring that every child, regardless of background or circumstance, has access to learning experiences that spark curiosity, ignite imagination, and cultivate a sense of belonging. Every child also needs access to rich content and playful educational experiences that build their foundational skills. Early education is not just about preparing for the future; it is about shaping the present, empowering young learners to become confident, resilient, and engaged individuals.

Decades of research underscore the transformative power of high-quality early childhood education. While every child deserves a joyful, engaging, and enriching preschool experience, many children are denied equitable access to a system that recognizes and nurtures their unique strengths and the strengths of their families and communities. Equity in early childhood calls for a tailored curriculum that adapts to individual children's strengths and needs, cultural backgrounds, and linguistic contexts. Achieving equitable outcomes requires moving beyond the traditional notion of equality and embracing a differentiated approach that celebrates the diversity of cultural and linguistic backgrounds, individual abilities and strengths, and community strengths that can empower every child to reach their full potential.

To achieve equitable access to high-quality early childhood educational experiences for all children, the complexities of evaluating curriculum efficacy must be confronted, particularly in areas such as cultural and linguistic relevance. Meeting this challenge will require continued commitment to refining research methodologies and expanding the knowledge base, especially in critical areas such as antibias and antiracist pedagogy. Only through this inquiry and adaptation can the promise of equitable and transformative early childhood education for all children be fulfilled.

REFERENCE

King, C., Perkins, V., Nugent, C., & Jordan, E. (2018). *2018 state of state early childhood data systems*. Early Childhood Data Collaborative. Child Trends. https://cms.childtrends.org/wp-content/uploads/2018/09/ECDC-50-state-survey-9.25.pdf

Appendix A

Existing Curricula Identified by the Committee's Commissioned Literature Review

The committee's commissioned systematic search of the curricula identified 172 preschool curricula.[1] This search identified only those curricula that are included or referenced in publications or other publicly available resources. Preschool curricula that are proprietary, locally developed, or not included in published sources may not be represented in this count. It is important to recognize that curricula that have been excluded from the literature or are locally developed by educators may include curricula that are designed to be responsive to family and community needs and values, and that this represents a potential gap in the knowledge base about curricula. The committee did not review or evaluate these curricula as part of this study.

Curriculum Name	Availability	Multidomain ($n = 88$)	Domain-Specific ($n = 84$)
ABC Jesus Loves Me!	Commercially available	Y	
Abeka Christian Preschool Curriculum (similar to *Abeka Homeschool Curriculum*)	Commercially available	Y	
Adventures in Learning	Commercially available	Y	
Al's Pals: Kids Making Healthy Choices	Commercially available		Y

(continued)

---

[1]The count of the existing curricula includes different versions of the same curricula (e.g., we count *The Creative Curriculum for Family Child Care* and *The Creative Curriculum® System* as two curricula), but we did not count editions as separate curricula.

Curriculum Name	Availability	Multidomain (n = 88)	Domain-Specific (n = 84)
All About Preschoolers Curriculum	Commercially available	Y	
AlphaSkills Pre-K Curriculum	Commercially available	Y	
AMAZEworks Early Childhood Curriculum	Commercially available		Y
Amplify Core Knowledge Language Arts PreK	Commercially available		Y
Ascend Curriculum	Commercially available	Y	
Benchmark Ready to Advance	Commercially available	Y	
Beyond Centers and Circle Time Curriculum Pre-K Theme Series	Commercially available	Y	
Big Day for Pre-K	Discontinued	Y	
Big Math for Little Kids	Discontinued?		Y
Blueprint for Early Learning	Commercially available	Y	
Booked on Math Curriculum	Commercially available		Y
Bright Beginnings	Commercially available	Y	
Building Blocks Pre-K Math	Commercially available		Y
Carol's Affordable Curriculum!—Jumping Kangaroo	Commercially available	Y	
Carolina Curriculum for Preschoolers With Special Needs	Commercially available	Y	
Carrie Flower Emotional Kit	Commercially available		Y
Children's School Success	Commercially available	Y	
Children's School Success Curriculum—Plus	Commercially available	Y	
Circle of Education EduPod Pre-Kindergarten	Commercially available		Y
CIRCLE Pre-K Curriculum	Public, freely available for Texas public teachers	Y	

Curriculum Name	Availability	Multidomain ($n = 88$)	Domain-Specific ($n = 84$)
Connect4Learning Preschool	Commercially available	Y	
Conscious Discipline	Commercially available		Y
Core Knowledge Preschool Curriculum	Commercially available	Y	
Cozy Corner	Commercially available	Y	
Cultivating Oral Language and Literacy Talent in Students (COLLTS)	Commercially available		Y
Curiosity Corner	Commercially available	Y	
Curriculum on the Management and Promotion of Appropriate Social Skills	Commercially available		Y
Developing Talkers: Supplemental Academic Language Curriculum	Commercially available		Y
Develop. Inspire. Grow.	Commercially available	Y	
DLM Early Childhood Express	Commercially available	Y	
DLM Early Childhood Express Math	Commercially available	Y	
Doors to Discovery	Commercially available		Y
Drawing Children Into Reading	Commercially available		Y
Drawn2Learn Educational Series	Commercially available		Y
Early Childhood Hands-On Science	Commercially available	Y	
Early Engineering curriculum	Commercially available		Y
Early Innovators Curriculum	Proprietary	Y	
Early Learning Success	Commercially available	Y	
Early Literacy and Learning Model	Commercially available		Y

(*continued*)

Curriculum Name	Availability	Multidomain ($n = 88$)	Domain-Specific ($n = 84$)
Early Math with Gracie and Friends	Commercially available		Y
Earobics Foundations (online)	Commercially available		Y
Emerging Language and Literacy Curriculum	Commercially available		Y
Estrellita PreK	Commercially available		Y
Eureka Math	Commercially available		Y
Every Child Ready	Commercially available	Y	
Everyday Mathematics	Commercially available		Y
Excel Pre-K	Commercially available	Y	
FLEX Learning Program	Proprietary	Y	
Fireflies	Commercially available	Y	
Focus on PreK	Public, freely available for Boston Public Schools	Y	
Food Resource Equity and Sustainability for Health Preschool Curriculum	Commercially available		Y
Frog Street PreK–Threes	Commercially available	Y	
Fun Friends	Commercially available		Y
Fundations Pre-K	Commercially available		Y
Funnydaffer—Early Childhood Curriculum (online)	Commercially available	Y	
Funshine Digital (online only)	Commercially available	Y	
Galileo Pre-K Curriculum (online)	Commercially available	Y	
Gee Whiz Education (online)	Commercially available	Y	

Curriculum Name	Availability	Multidomain ($n = 88$)	Domain-Specific ($n = 84$)
Get Set for School (aka Writing Without Tears or Learning Without Tears)	Commercially available	Y	
GrapeSEED	Commercially available		Y
Growing and Learning with Young Native Children	Commercially available	Y	
Hands on Science Outreach Curriculum	Commercially available		Y
Head Start Research-Based, Developmentally Informed	Commercially available	Y	
Heggerty Phonemic Awareness Pre-Kindergarten l	Commercially available		Y
High Reach Learning Curriculum	Commercially available	Y	
HighScope Preschool Curriculum	Commercially available	Y	
I Can Problem Solve (formerly called Interpersonal Cognitive Problem Solving)	Commercially available		Y
IMPACT Social Studies	Commercially available		Y
Innovation by Design Curriculum for Preschool (online)	Commercially available	Y	
Inspire Science	Commercially available		Y
Journey on the Learning Care System	Proprietary	Y	
Kids R Kids	Proprietary	Y	
Kindness Curriculum (adapted)	Commercially available		Y
Knowledge Universe Early Foundations Prekindergarten	Proprietary	Y	
Knowledge Universe Early Foundations Preschool	Proprietary	Y	
Learning Experience Academic Program Curriculum	Proprietary	Y	
Language for Learning	Commercially available		Y

(*continued*)

Curriculum Name	Availability	Multidomain ($n = 88$)	Domain-Specific ($n = 84$)
Language-Focused Curriculum	Commercially available		Y
LEAP Into School! Language Enrichment Activities for Preschool	Commercially available		Y
Learn Every Day: The Preschool Curriculum	Commercially available	Y	
Learning A–Z	Commercially available		Y
Learning Connections	Commercially available	Y	
Let's Know!	Commercially available		Y
Let's Begin with the Letter People	Rebranded as Frog Street curricula		Y
Lexia Reading	Commercially available		Y
Life Essentials: Ready, Set, Go	Proprietary	Y	
Life Smart	Proprietary	Y	
Links to Early Learning	Proprietary	Y	
Links to Learning	Proprietary	Y	
Links to Literacy	Commercially available		Y
Literacy by Design	Commercially available		Y
Literacy Express Preschool Curriculum	Commercially available		Y
Little Treasures	Discontinued	Y	
Math Expressions—Pre-K–6 Common Core Math Curriculum	Commercially available		Y
Math Shelf	Commercially available		Y
McGraw-Hill My Math	Commercially available		Y
Merrel's Strong Start Pre-K Curriculum	Commercially available		Y
Mother Goose Time Preschool Curriculum	Commercially available	Y	
MTT Science	Commercially available		Y

Curriculum Name	Availability	Multidomain ($n = 88$)	Domain-Specific ($n = 84$)
Multisensory Center-Based Curriculum	Commercially available	Y	
Music Studio Marketplace: Music Reading/Literacy	Commercially available		Y
MyTeachingPartner	Commercially available	Y	
Nemours Reading BrightStart!	Commercially available		Y
Number Worlds	Commercially available		Y
Numbers Plus Preschool Mathematics	Commercially available		Y
Opening the World of Learning	Commercially available		Y
Passports: Experiences for Pre-K	Commercially available	Y	
PBS KIDS Transmedia Math Curriculum Supplement	Commercially available		Y
Peaceful Kids Conflict Resolution Program	Commercially available		Y
Peacemakers	Commercially available		Y
Phonemic Awareness	Commercially available		Y
Phonological Curriculum	Commercially available		Y
Pinnacle Curriculum (faith-based and secular)	Commercially available	Y	
Positive Action Curriculum and Program	Commercially available		Y
Pre-K Mathematics	Commercially available		Y
PreK For ME	Commercially available	Y	
PreK On My Way	Commercially available	Y	
Preschool Promoting Alternative Thinking Strategies	Commercially available		Y
PreschoolPalace.org	Proprietary	Y	

(*continued*)

Curriculum Name	Availability	Multidomain ($n = 88$)	Domain-Specific ($n = 84$)
Primrose Schools Balanced Learning Approach—Pre-kindergarten	Proprietary	Y	
Primrose Schools Balanced Learning Approach—Preschool	Proprietary	Y	
Problem Solvers	Public, freely available		Y
Quaver Pre-K 1st Edition (online)	Commercially available	Y	
Read It Again–PreK!	Public, freely available		Y
Read It Once Again	Commercially available		Y
Read Naturally	Commercially available		Y
Read, Play and Learn!	Commercially available		Y
Readiness Through Integrative Science and Engineering	Commercially available		Y
Reading Recovery	Commercially available		Y
Ready to Advance (*Listos y Adelante*)	Commercially available	Y	
Ready, Set, Leap!	Commercially available	Y	
Red Light Purple Light	Commercially available		Y
Redleaf Family Child Care Curriculum Complete Set	Commercially available	Y	
Responsive Early Childhood Curriculum plus explicitly social-emotional classroom activities	Commercially available	Y	
ScienceStart!	Commercially available		Y
Second Step Early Learning Program or *Second Step Social-Emotional Learning*	Commercially available		Y
Self-Determination Program	Commercially available		Y
Starfall Pre-K Curriculum	Commercially available	Y	

Curriculum Name	Availability	Multidomain ($n = 88$)	Domain-Specific ($n = 84$)
Stepping Stones Pre-K	Commercially available	Y	
STREAMin³	Commercially available	Y	
Structured Outdoor Play Curriculum: The Buddy Game	Commercially available	Y	
TELL Language and Literacy Curriculum	Commercially available?		Y
The Child Unique Montessori School	Proprietary	Y	
The Creative Curriculum for Family Child Care	Commercially available	Y	
The Creative Curriculum System for Preschool	Commercially available	Y	
The Empowered Child	Proprietary	Y	
The Incredible Years	Commercially available		Y
The InvestiGator Club Prekindergarten Learning System	Commercially available	Y	
The InvestiGator Club Just for Threes Learning System	Commercially available	Y	
The Lindamood Phoneme Sequencing Program	Commercially available?		Y
The Peace Education Foundation Socio-Emotional Development Program	Commercially available		Y
The Story Friends Curriculum	Commercially available		Y
Three Cheers for Pre-K	Commercially available	Y	
Together, We Inspire Smart Eating	Commercially available		Y
Tools of the Mind	Commercially available	Y	
TPS STEAM Early Years Foundation Program	Commercially available		Y
Tutor Time LifeSmart	Commercially available	Y	

(continued)

Curriculum Name	Availability	Multidomain ($n = 88$)	Domain-Specific ($n = 84$)
Vocabulary, Oral Language and Academic Readiness	Commercially available		Y
Waterford Upstart (formerly known as *Waterford Early Reading Program*)	Commercially available		Y
We Can Early Learning Curriculum	Commercially available	Y	
Wee Engineering	Commercially available		Y
Weekday Early Education Learn Curriculum (faith-based)	Commercially available	Y	
Where Bright Futures Begin	Discontinued	Y	
WINGS: The Ideal Curriculum for Children in Preschool	Commercially available	Y	
World at Their Fingertips	Proprietary	Y	
World of Wonders	Commercially available	Y	
World of Words	Commercially available		Y
Zoo-phonics	Commercially available		Y

Appendix B

Committee Member and Staff Biosketches

COMMITTEE BIOSKETCHES

SUE BREDEKAMP (*Co-Chair*), is an early childhood education specialist on curriculum, teaching, and professional development. She consults for national and state organizations, institutions of higher education, departments of education, and Head Start. As director of professional development at the National Association for the Education of Young Children (NAEYC), Bredekamp developed and directed the accreditation system for early learning programs and led the association's work on curriculum and assessment, early literacy, and teacher preparation. She edited NAEYC's 1987, 1997, and 2009 editions of *Developmentally Appropriate Practice in Early Childhood Programs Serving Children from Birth Through Age Eight*. Bredekamp is author of a teacher education textbook, *Effective Practices in Early Childhood Education: Building a Foundation* (4th ed.). She received the Visionary Leadership Award from the McCormick Center for Early Childhood Leadership; the Center on Enhancing Early Learning Outcomes named her one of 11 pioneers in early childhood education. Bredekamp was a member of the National Research Council's Committee on Early Childhood Mathematics, which produced the report *Mathematics in Early Childhood: Paths Toward Excellence and Equity*. She holds a Ph.D. in curriculum and instruction and an M.A. in early childhood education from the University of Maryland.

LINDA M. ESPINOSA (*Co-Chair*), is professor emeritus of early childhood education at the University of Missouri-Columbia. She has served as codirector of the National Institute for Early Education Research at Rutgers University and as vice president at Bright Horizons Family Solutions. Most recently, Espinosa was co-principal investigator for the Getting on Track for Early School Success: Effective Teaching in Preschool Classrooms project at the University of Chicago; she was also co-principal investigator for the Center for Early Care and Education Research—Dual Language Learners at Frank Porter Graham Child Development Institute at the University of North Carolina. Her recent research and policy work has focused on effective curriculum and assessment practices for young children from low-income families who are dual language learners. Espinosa's latest book, *Getting It RIGHT for Young Children from Diverse Backgrounds* (2015), focuses on quality education for dual language learners. She co-authored the *California Early Learning Foundations*, English Language Learners chapter; *California Preschool Curriculum Frameworks* English Language Development Chapter; and *Desired Results Developmental Profile, 2010*, English Language Development Assessment Measures. Additionally, Espinosa served as lead consultant for the Los Angeles Unified School District's transitional kindergarten program development team and is a member of the Council for Professional Development Governing Board. She was a contributing author of the National Academies of Sciences, Engineering, and Medicine report *Promoting the Educational Success of Children Learning English* (2017).

DEANA M. AROUND HIM is senior research scientist at Child Trends and adjunct faculty member at the Johns Hopkins School of Nursing. She also serves on the Tribal Early Childhood Research Center's leadership team. Around Him's research aims to improve the well-being of American Indian and Alaska Native children, youth, and families through community-based and -engaged approaches that meet their cultural and contextual needs. She has worked with centers that focus on strengthening tribal research capacity and policies, and she strives to conduct research and evaluation that respects tribal sovereignty, builds on cultural strengths, and produces outcomes that inform policy and programs. Around Him serves on the editorial board for *Maternal and Child Health Journal* and as co-chair for the Native Research Network's board of directors. Her training focused on the social determinants and life-course approaches to health, culturally responsive evaluation, research ethics, and maternal and child health. She earned her B.A. in community health from Brown University, M.S. with a concentration in maternal and child health from the Harvard School of Public Health, and Dr.P.H. from the Johns Hopkins Bloomberg School of Public Health.

GARNETT SAUNDERS BOOKER III is an early childhood teacher with District of Columbia Public Schools. Previously, he served as lead teacher at the University of Delaware Early Learning Center and taught in a Head

Start program and charter school. Booker's research on developmental play practices in early childhood resulted in creating a rough-and-tumble play space for young children at the Early Learning Center. He has also presented on practices that support developmental play in early childhood education and the developmental importance of Makers Space in early childhood programs. Booker received the Strattner Gregory Child Advocacy Award and the Rita Fillos Award from the University of Delaware. He holds a master's degree in human development and family studies.

DOUGLAS H. CLEMENTS is Kenney Endowed Chair in Early Childhood Learning, professor, and executive director of the Marsico Institute of Early Learning and Literacy at University of Denver's Morgridge College of Education. Previously, he worked as a kindergarten teacher for 5 years and a preschool teacher for 1 year, and he has since conducted research and published widely in the areas of (1) the learning and teaching of early mathematics; (2) computer applications in mathematics education; (3) creating, using, and evaluating a research-based curriculum and taking successful curricula to scale using technologies and learning trajectories; and (4) development and evaluation of innovative assessments of mathematics achievement, as well as mathematics teaching. Prior to his appointment at the University of Denver, Clements was a State University of New York (SUNY) distinguished professor at the University of Buffalo. He was a member of President Bush's National Math Advisory Panel and served on the National Research Council Committee on Early Childhood Mathematics. Clements received his Ph.D. in elementary education from SUNY at Buffalo.

LILLIAN DURÁN is professor in the Department of Special Education and Clinical Sciences at the University of Oregon. Her research is focused on improving instructional and assessment practices with multilingual children. Durán is currently involved in multiple efforts developing Spanish language and literacy assessments from preschool to 6th grade. She is also project director on several Office of Special Education Programs training grants focused on preparing master's and doctoral students to serve traditionally marginalized populations with disabilities with a focus on equity and improving educational outcomes. Durán frequently delivers presentations nationally on the topic of recommended practices in language and literacy practices with multilingual learners, and she has served on multiple equity and diversity councils including for the National Association for the Education of Young Children and for the Division for Early Childhood. Prior to her work in higher education, she worked for 9 years as an early childhood special education teacher. Durán holds a B.A. in elementary education from Antioch College and an M.A. in education and human development from The George Washington University.

IHEOMA U. IRUKA is research professor in public policy and founding director of the Equity Research Action Coalition at the Frank Porter Graham Child Development Institute at The University of North Carolina at Chapel Hill. She is leading projects and initiatives focused on ensuring that racially minoritized children and children from low-income households are thriving through the intersection of racial equity and culturally grounded research, program, and policy. Iruka's areas of expertise include family engagement and support, early care and education programs and systems, and quality improvement systems. She takes part in numerous national and local boards and committees, such as the National Advisory Committee for the U.S. Census Bureau and the Board of Educational Affairs for the American Psychological Association. Iruka is scientific advisor for the National Research Conference in Early Childhood and serves with the Brady Education Foundation. She was a member of the National Academies of Sciences, Engineering, and Medicine committees on Supporting Parents of Young Children and Applying Neurobiological and Socio-Behavioral Sciences from Prenatal through Early Childhood Development: A Health Equity Approach.

SUSAN C. LEVINE is Rebecca Anne Boylan Distinguished Service Professor of Education and Society in the Department of Psychology at the University of Chicago and inaugural faculty director of the UChicago Science of Learning Center. Her research focuses on the development of early spatial and numerical thinking, particularly on the kinds of adult–child interactions that foster learning in these domains. Levine studies how particular kinds of mathematical activities and conversations contribute to children's math learning, and how math-relevant learning opportunities can be increased through interventions, both at home and at school. She also studies the role of math attitudes in mathematical performance and interests with a particular focus on the intergenerational effects of adult math anxiety on math learning and math attitudes. Levine received her Ph.D. in psychology from the Massachusetts Institute of Technology.

JOAN L. LUBY is Samuel and Mae S. Ludwig Professor of Psychiatry (Child) at the Washington University School of Medicine, where she founded and leads the Early Emotional Development Program. She specializes in infant/preschool psychiatry, and for more than 30 years, her program of research has focused on early childhood affective psychopathology and emotional development. Luby has conducted some of the first large-scale empirical studies of preschool-onset depression and provided data on the validity, clinical characteristics, longitudinal course, and brain developmental outcomes of early-onset depression. With colleague Deanna Barch, she conducted a 17-year longitudinal study that investigates behavior and brain development using five waves of brain scanning, with a sample enriched for depressive symptoms arising at age 3 years. These findings have informed the impact of key psychosocial factors, including maternal support and early-life adversity, on brain and behavioral development. Luby's studies have established the powerful role of early childhood caregiver support and psychosocial adversity on neurodevelopment, and she has developed and tested a novel early parent–child intervention for depression that focuses on enhancing emotion development, showing powerful effects and neural change. She has published more than 200 papers and has been awarded numerous honors, including the Brain and Behavior Foundation Ruane Award and the American Psychiatric Association Ittelson Award.

CAMILLE MABEN served as executive director of First 5 California for the last decade. In that role, she staffed the California Children and Families Commission and directed the work of the agency and its staff. Through her leadership, First 5 California implemented several evidence-based and results-driven programs that focused on quality. Maben also served as division director of the Child Development Division at the California Department of Education, where she provided leadership and oversight to more than 700 early care and education contractors with a $1.7 billion budget. In her earlier work, she was appointed by the governor to serve as chief of staff for the Office of the Secretary of Education, where she coordinated and developed the governor's education policy agenda. Maben also served as senior advisor to the superintendent of public instruction for former state superintendent Delaine Eastin and has worked as a consultant to the Assembly Education Committee. Her early career was spent serving young children with nationally recognized Bev Bos at the Roseville Community Pre-School. Maben has served on numerous boards and committees, including 30 years as a Rocklin Unified School District board member.

DEBORAH A. PHILLIPS is professor emerita of psychology, and associated faculty of public policy at Georgetown University. She was the first executive director of the Board on Children, Youth, and Families of the National Research Council and the Institute of Medicine, and served as study director for *From Neurons to Neighborhoods: The Science of Early Child Development*. Phillips has also served as president of the Foundation for Child Development, director of child care information services at the National Association for the Education of Young Children, and congressional science fellow on the staff of Congressman George Miller. She has served on the National Board for Education Sciences (U.S. Department of Education), the National Scientific Council on the Developing Child at Harvard University, and the Research Advisory Board of the Committee on Economic Development. Phillips' research on the developmental impacts of early education—child care, pre-K programs, and Head Start—has been funded by the National Institutes of Health, the U.S. Child Care Bureau, and numerous national foundations, and has been recognized at White House conferences and in the State of the Union address. She is a fellow of the American Psychological Association and the American Psychological Society. Phillips received the 2022 Nicholas Hobbs Award from the American Psychological Association, the 2022 President's Distinguished Scholar-Teacher Award from Georgetown University, and the 2011 Distinguished Contributions to Education in Child Development Award from the Society for Research in Child Development. She completed her undergraduate degree in psychology from Stanford University and her Ph.D. in developmental psychology from Yale University.

CHRISTINA J. WEILAND is associate professor at the University of Michigan's School of Education and (by courtesy) Ford School of Public Policy, where she also codirects the Education Policy Initiative. Her research focuses on the effects of policies and interventions for children aged 0–8 years, particularly those from families with low incomes. Weiland's work is also characterized by strong partnerships with practitioners, particularly the Boston Public Schools Department of Early Childhood. Her work has been recognized by awards from multiple professional associations (i.e., Society for Research in Child Development, American Educational Research Association, Association for Education Finance and Policy) and supported by funding from the Institute of Education Sciences and multiple foundations. Weiland holds a Ph.D. from Harvard University in quantitative policy analysis in education.

VIVIAN C. WONG is associate professor in research, statistics, and evaluation in the School of Education and Human Development at the University of Virginia. Her research focuses on research designs for evaluating interventions in early childhood and K–12 systems. Wong has examined the effectiveness of state prekindergarten programs in five states, as well as the impact of half- versus full-day prekindergarten on students' achievement. As a methodologist, her expertise is in improving the design, implementation, and analysis of randomized experiments, regression-discontinuity, interrupted time series, and matching designs in field settings. Her most recent work emphasizes new methods for designing and analyzing systematic replication studies, especially for generalization purposes. Currently, Wong is principal investigator or co-principal investigator of multiple grants, funded by the Institute of Education Sciences (IES) and National Science Foundation, focused on systematic replication studies. Her work has appeared in the *Journal of Educational and Behavioral Statistics*, *Journal of Policy Analysis and Management*, and *Psychological Methods*. She is associate editor of *AERA Open*. Wong received her Ph.D. in 2011 from

Northwestern University and was awarded the Outstanding IES Predoctoral Fellow Award.

STAFF BIOSKETCHES

REBEKAH HUTTON (*Study Director*) is senior program officer with the National Academies of Sciences, Engineering, and Medicine. In addition to the present study, she is also currently study director of the Committee on the Impact of Active Shooter Drills on Student Health and Wellbeing. Previously, she was study director of the committees on Exploring the Opportunity Gap for Young Children from Birth to Age 8; Addressing the Underrepresentation of Women of Color in Tech; and Summertime Experiences and Child and Adolescent Education, Health, and Safety. Prior to working at the National Academies, Hutton was an education management and information technology consultant working on projects in the United States, as well as in Haiti, Equatorial Guinea, and Djibouti. She has also worked as program manager and researcher at the National Center on Performance Incentives at Vanderbilt University and as an English language lecturer in Tourcoing, France. During her time with the Board on Children, Youth, and Families, Hutton has also worked on projects focused on fostering the educational success of children and youth learning English; reducing child poverty; and promoting the mental, emotional, and behavioral health of children and youth. She received her M.Ed. from Vanderbilt University in international education policy and management.

TARA NAZARI is senior program assistant with the Board on Children, Youth, and Families. In addition to the present study, she supports the Committee on the Impact of Active Shooter Drills on Student Health and Wellbeing. Before joining the National Academies of Sciences, Engineering, and Medicine, Nazari worked as research assistant at the University of Maryland, assisting in the development of family and community-based interventions. She holds a B.S. in family science from the University of Maryland, College Park, and plans to pursue a master's in public health in the near future.

AMY STEPHENS is associate board director for the Board on Science Education of the National Academies of Sciences, Engineering, and Medicine. She is adjunct professor for the Southern New Hampshire University Psychology Department, teaching graduate-level online courses in cognitive psychology and statistics. Stephens has an extensive background in behavioral and functional neuroimaging techniques and has examined a variety of populations spanning childhood through adulthood. She was study director for the workshop on Graduate Training in the Social and

Behavioral Sciences and for the recently released consensus reports *Science and Engineering in Preschool Through Elementary Grades* (2022); *English Learners in STEM Subjects: Transforming Classrooms, Schools, and Lives* (2018); *Changing Expectations for the K–12 Workforce: Policies, Preservice Education, Professional Development, and the Workplace* (2020); and *Cultivating Interest and Competencies in Computing: Authentic Experiences and Design Factors* (2021). Stephens holds a Ph.D. in cognitive neuroscience from Johns Hopkins University and was a postdoctoral research fellow at the Center for Talented Youth and the John Hopkins School of Education.

ELIZABETH "LIBBY" TILTON is research associate with the Board on Children, Youth, and Families of the National Academies of Sciences, Engineering, and Medicine. In addition to the present study, she supports the Committee on Understanding Breastfeeding Promotion, Initiation and Support Across the United States. Tilton has a background in management—with specialties in training, logistics, and relationship management—and data analytics. She has a B.S. in human resources management from Salisbury University, a M.A. in industrial/organizational psychology, and is currently pursuing a Ph.D. in business psychology at The Chicago School, conducting research on narcissism and Machiavellianism in the context of leadership.

MEREDITH YOUNG is program officer with the Board on Children, Youth, and Families of the National Academies of Sciences, Engineering, and Medicine. She currently serves as study director for the project Understanding Breastfeeding Promotion, Initiation and Support Across the United States. In her time at the National Academies, Young has supported projects evaluating dietary reference intakes, federal feeding guidelines, obesity prevention and treatment initiatives, preschool curriculum, and the racial and economic opportunity gap in child outcomes. She has supported evaluation and strategic planning efforts at the National Academies, and she serves as a volunteer staff reader for other divisions. Young received a B.S. in human nutrition, foods, and exercise with a concentration in dietetics from the Virginia Polytechnic Institute and State University and an M.N.S.P. in nutrition science and policy from Tufts University.

Appendix C

Disclosure of Unavoidable Conflict of Interest

The conflict-of-interest policy of the National Academies of Sciences, Engineering, and Medicine (www.nationalacademies.org/coi) prohibits the appointment of an individual to a committee like the one that authored this consensus study report if the individual has a conflict of interest that is relevant to the task to be performed. An exception to this prohibition is permitted only if the National Academies determine that the conflict is unavoidable and the conflict is promptly and publicly disclosed.

When the committee that authored this report was established, a conflict-of-interest determination was made for each committee member, given the individual's circumstances and the task being undertaken by the committee. A determination that an individual has a conflict of interest is not an assessment of that individual's actual behavior or character or ability to act objectively despite the conflicting interest.

Douglas Clements has a conflict of interest in relation to his service on the Committee on A New Vision for High Quality Pre-K Curriculum because he is coauthor of two pre-K curricula—*Connect4Learning®*, published and sold by Kaplan Early Learning Company, and *Building Blocks™ PreK*, published and sold by McGraw-Hill.

The National Academies concluded that in order for the committee to accomplish the tasks for which it was established, its membership must include at least one person who has current experience in the creation, implementation, and evaluation of pre-K curricula. As described in his biographical summary, Clements is one of the foremost leaders in childhood education and curriculum development, including the development of the *Connect4Learning®*, a research-based and classroom-tested interdisciplinary prekindergarten curriculum, and *Building Blocks™ PreK*, a prekindergarten mathematics curriculum. He also has experience conducting efficacy studies for the U.S. Department of Education Institute of Education Sciences and other sponsors on the effectiveness of early childhood intervention programs. Through this work, Clements evaluates learning trajectories and preschool curriculum to identify features that make them more effective.

The National Academies determined that the experience and expertise of this individual was needed for the committee to accomplish the task for which it was established. The National Academies could not find another available individual with the equivalent experience and expertise who did not have a conflict of interest. Therefore, the National Academies concluded that the conflict was unavoidable and publicly disclosed it through the National Academies Current Projects System (https://nationalacademies.org/pa).